THE OXFORD ENGLISH LITERARY HISTORY

Volume 2. 1350–1547

THE OXFORD ENGLISH LITERARY HISTORY

General Editor: Jonathan Bate

1. to 1350: *The Literary Cultures of Early England*
   by Katherine O'Brien O'Keeffe and Linda Georgianna
2. 1350–1547: *Reform and Cultural Revolution*
   by James Simpson*
3. 1533–1603: *The Elizabethans*
   by Jonathan Bate
4. 1603–1660: *Literary Cultures of the Early Seventeenth Century*
   by Katharine Eisaman Maus
5. 1645–1714: *The Later Seventeenth Century*
   by Margaret Ezell
6. 1709–1784: *The Eighteenth Century*
   by John Mullan
7. 1785–1832: *The Romantic Period*
   by Fiona Robertson
8. 1830–1880: *The Victorians*
   by Philip Davis*
9. 1875–1914: *From 'Victorian' to 'Edwardian'*
   by Joseph Bristow
10. 1910–1940: *Modern Letters*
    by Chris Baldick
11. 1930–1970: *Literature among the Wars*
    by Rick Rylance
12. 1960–2000: *The Last of England*
    by Randall Stevenson
13. 1948–2000: *The Internationalization of English Literature*
    by Bruce King

* already published

This series was conceived and commissioned by Kim Walwyn (1956–2002), to whose memory it is dedicated.

THE OXFORD ENGLISH
LITERARY HISTORY

Volume 2. 1350–1547

Reform and Cultural Revolution

JAMES SIMPSON

OXFORD
UNIVERSITY PRESS

OXFORD
UNIVERSITY PRESS

Great Clarendon Street, Oxford OX2 6DP

Oxford University Press is a department of the University of Oxford.
It furthers the University's objective of excellence in research, scholarship,
and education by publishing worldwide in

Oxford New York

Auckland Bangkok Bogotá Buenos Aires Cape Town Chennai
Dar es Salaam Delhi Hong Kong Istanbul Karachi Kolkata
Kuala Lumpur Madrid Melbourne Mexico City Mumbai Nairobi
São Paulo Shanghai Taipei Tokyo Toronto

Oxford is a registered trade mark of Oxford University Press
in the UK and in certain other countries

Published in the United States
by Oxford University Press Inc., New York

First published 2002

British Library Cataloguing in Publication Data

Data available

Library of Congress Cataloging in Publication Data

The Oxford English literary history.
p. cm.
Includes bibliographical references (p.) and indexes.
Contents: —v. 2. 1350–1547 : reform and cultural revolution / James Simpson
1. English literature—History and criticism.
PR85 .096 2002 820.9–dc21 2002025038

ISBN 0–19–818261–9

10 9 8 7 6 5 4 3 2 1

Typeset in Adobe Sabon
by Regent Typesetting, London
Printed in Great Britain
on acid-free paper by
Biddles Ltd.
Guildford and King's Lynn

This book is dedicated to the memory of my brother
Robert Lyndon Simpson

Multas per gentes et multa per aequora vectus . . .

Acknowledgements

In the exhilarating work of writing this book I have incurred many debts, which I acknowledge here with gratitude. Jonathan Bate has been a constant presence; among his many contributions, I signal in particular his wisdom in allowing the problematic of each period to inform the shape of different volumes. I also thank him for his very acute reading of the entire typescript. In tandem with Sophie Goldsworthy of OUP, Jon has ensured that the writing of these volumes has been a cooperative and collaborative experience. Many friends have been at the ready to help: David Benson, Julia Boffey, Rachel Boulton, Chris Cannon, Tony Edwards, Penny Granger, and Ad Putter each commented on at least one chapter. Chris Clark and David Wallace proved invaluable interlocutors. My colleagues in Girton College Cambridge and the Faculty of English, University of Cambridge have been unfailingly supportive and generous, particularly Juliet Dusinberre, Anne Fernihough, and Jill Mann. Hundreds of scholarly debts are registered in the notes, although notes alone cannot register my indebtedness to the literary critical and historical work of Douglas Gray, Derek Pearsall, and Tony Spearing, and to the bibliographical work of Tony Edwards. C. S. Lewis's volume in the earlier Oxford History of English Literature, although not mentioned in the notes, has been a model of what literary history might achieve.

The Arts and Humanities Research Board awarded me one term's leave to complete the project.

Trial chapters have been published as articles: Chapter 1 in *New Medieval Literatures*, 1 (1997), 213–35; Chapter 2 in *New Medieval Literatures*, 4 (2000), 213–42; Chapter 3 in *Speculum*, 73 (1998), 397–423; Chapter 4 in *Journal of Medieval and Early Modern Studies*, 29 (1999), 325–55; and Chapter 7 in *The Yearbook of Langland Studies*, 14 (2000), 1–25. I am grateful to the editors of these journals for permission to republish this work.

Finally, I offer very warm thanks to the indefatigable Frances

Whistler of OUP, and to the equally tireless Rowena Anketell for her copy-editing.

General Editor's Preface

The Oxford English Literary History is the twenty-first-century successor to the Oxford History of English Literature, which appeared in fifteen volumes between 1945 and 1997. As in the previous series, each volume offers an individual scholar's vision of a discrete period of literary history.[1] Each has a distinctive emphasis and structure, determined by its author's considered view of the principal contours of the period. But all the volumes are written in the belief that literary history is a discipline necessary for the revelation of the power of imaginative writing to serve as a means of human understanding, past, present, and future.

Our primary aim is to explore the diverse purposes of literary activity and the varied mental worlds of writers and readers in the past. Particular attention is given to the institutions in which literary acts take place (educated communities, publishing networks, and so forth), the forms in which literary works are presented (traditions, genres, structural conventions), and the relationship between literature and broader historical continuities and transformations. Literary history is distinct from political history, but a historical understanding of literature cannot be divorced from cultural and intellectual revolutions or the effects of social change and the upheaval of war.

We do not seek to offer a comprehensive survey of the works of all 'major', let alone 'minor', writers of the last thousand years. All literary histories are inevitably incomplete—as was seen from the rediscovery in the late twentieth century of many long-forgotten women writers of earlier eras. Every literary history has to select: in so doing, it reconfigures the 'canon'. We cast our nets very widely and make claims for many works not previously regarded as canonical, but we are fully conscious of our partiality. Detailed case studies are preferred to summary listings.

[1] Since volume 1, to 1350, covers many centuries, it is co-written by two scholars.

A further aim is to undertake a critical investigation of the very notion of a national literary heritage. The word 'literature' is often taken to refer to poems, plays, and novels, but historically a much wider range of writing may properly be considered as 'literary' or as belonging within the realm of what used to be called 'letters'. The boundaries of the literary in general and of *English* literary history in particular have changed through the centuries. Each volume maps those boundaries in the terms of its own period.

For the sake of consistency and feasibility, however, two broad definitions of 'English Literary History' have been applied. First, save in the polyglot culture of the earliest era, we have confined ourselves to the English language—a body of important work written in Latin between the fourteenth and the seventeenth centuries has been excluded. And secondly, we have concentrated on works that come from, or bear upon, England. Most of the writing of other English speaking countries, notably the United States of America, is excluded. We are not offering a world history of writing in the English language. Those Americans who lived and worked in England are, however, included.

So too with Scottish, Irish, Welsh writers, and those from countries that were once part of the British Empire: where their work was produced or significantly disseminated in England, they are included. Indeed, such figures are of special importance in many volumes, exactly because their non-English origins often placed them in an ambivalent relationship with England. Throughout the series, particular attention is paid to encounters between English and other traditions. But we have also recognized that Scottish, Welsh, Irish, African, Asian, Australasian, Canadian, and Caribbean literatures all have their own histories, which we have not sought to colonize.

It would be possible to argue endlessly about periodization. The arrangement of the Oxford English Literary History is both traditional and innovative. For instance, the period around the beginning of the nineteenth century has long been thought of as the 'Romantic' one; however we may wish to modify the nomenclature, people will go on reading and studying the Lake Poets and the 'Shelley circle' in relation to each other, so it would have been factitious to introduce a volume division at, say, 1810. On the other hand, it is still too soon for there to be broad agreement on the literary-historical shape of the twentieth century: to propose a single break at, say, 1945 would be to fall in with the false assumption that literature moves strictly in tandem with events. Each volume argues the case for its own period as a period, but at the same time beginning and ending dates are treated flexibly, and in many cases—especially with respect to the twentieth century—there is deliberate and considerable overlap between the temporal boundaries of adjacent volumes.

The voices of the last millennium are so various and vital that English literary history is always in the process of being rewritten. We seek both to chart and to contribute to that rewriting, for the benefit not just of students and scholars but of all serious readers.

Jonathan Bate

Contents

List of Figures

Abbreviations

BJRL	*Bulletin of the John Rylands Library*
DNB	*Dictionary of National Biography*
EETS	Early English Text Society
EHR	*English Historical Review*
ELH	*English Literary History*
ES	Extra Series
JMEMS	*Journal of Medieval and Early Modern Studies*
JWCI	*Journal of the Warburg and Courtauld Institutes*
LSE	*Leeds Studies in English*
L&P Henry VIII	*Letters and Papers, Foreign and Domestic, of the Reign of Henry VIII* . . . calendared by J. S. Brewer et al., 21 vols in 33 (Longman, Green, Longman and Roberts, 1862–1910)
MED	*Middle English Dictionary*, ed. H. Kurath, S. M. Kuhn, and R. E. Lewis (University of Michigan Press, 1954–2001)
MLR	*Modern Language Review*
MS	*Mediaeval Studies*
MLN	*Modern Language Notes*
MLQ	*Modern Language Quarterly*
N&Q	*Notes and Queries*
NLH	*New Literary History*
PBA	*Proceedings of the British Academy*
PMLA	*Publications of the Modern Language Association of America*
PQ	*Philological Quarterly*
REED	Records of Early English Drama
RES	*Review of English Studies*
RSTC	*A Short-Title Catalogue of Books Printed in England, Scotland and Ireland and of English Books Printed Abroad 1475–1640*, ed. A. W. Pollard and G. R. Redgrave, 2nd edn. rev.

	W. A. Jackson et al., 3 vols (Bibliographical Society, 1976–91)
SR	*Statutes of the Realm,* ed. T. E. Tolmins et al., 11 vols. (Dawsons, 1810–1828; repr. 1963)
SAC	*Studies in the Age of Chaucer*
SN	*Studia Neophilologica*
SP	*Studies in Philology*
SS	Supplementary Series
YES	*Yearbook of English Studies*
YLS	*Yearbook of Langland Studies*

A Note on References and the Presentation of Texts

Brief biographical information on selected authors will be found at the end of the volume, together with bibliographies covering their major works and some of the most notable modern scholarship concerning them. In addition, there are suggestions for more general reading relevant to the literary history of the period. The bibliographies are intended as starting points for further study, not comprehensive listings of the kind found in the *Cambridge Bibliography of English Literature* and other sources (the majority of which are now published in electronic form). Whenever possible, the Author Bibliographies include recommended modern editions. An asterisk indicates the edition that has been used in the main body of the book.

Quotations in the text from works written in the period are usually followed by a reference in parenthesis. Where possible, these references are given in a form that does not depend on access to a particular edition (e.g. book and line number), but for works without convenient sub-division, the citation is of the page number of the edition asterisked in the relevant Author Bibliography or in the Works Cited. Where further clarification is needed, the reference appears in a footnote. All references are keyed to the list of Works Cited at the end of the book.

In the presentation of original texts, all letter forms have been modernized.

Introduction

Despite its size, this book has a very simple, central, and consistent theme: that the institutional simplifications and centralizations of the sixteenth century provoked correlative simplifications and narrowings in literature. If literary history and criticism is, as I believe it should be, ancillary to the complex history of freedoms, then this is a narrative of diminishing liberties.

The fundamental observation that drives the argument of each chapter is as follows: in the first half of the sixteenth century, a culture that simplified and centralized jurisdiction aggressively displaced a culture of jurisdictional heterogeneity. Many revolutionary moments in European history have effected a displacement of this kind, and the characteristics of such repudiation can be generalized. Sudden concentrations of cultural and political power both permit and necessitate an aggressive physical and ideological demolition of the 'old' order. Accordingly, such concentrations provoke cultural practices that stress the values of unity and novelty above all. The fact of a sudden historical break itself presupposes a large concentration of power. Thus the stress on unity: whereas the old order will be redescribed as subject to a bedevilling complication of lines of authority, the new order will highlight a simple chain of command. A sudden, politically driven break in history will prize novelty because a new dispensation must legitimate itself, and must, therefore, redescribe the repudiated order as 'old' and depleted. These values of unity and novelty will inform all cultural practices, and especially architecture, historiography, jurisprudence, theology, philology, politics, painting, and literature.

In the shift from 'medieval' to the 'early modern', until at least the middle of the sixteenth century in England, histories of each of these fields could be written within the following contrasts, with the medieval description preceding the early modern: unresolved generic juxtaposition versus attempted generic coherence; complicated accretion versus cleanness of line; development and addition versus conversion; a recognition of historical totality versus a return to originary purity that involves a rejection of large slices of intervening history; consensus versus the intelligence of central command.

Blanket terms that roughly cover these opposed sets of practices are 'reform' and 'revolution' respectively. 'Revolution' is unproblematic, designating as it does the moment of sudden break by which imagined return to an originary moment is made. 'Reform' as a description of medieval cultural practice might seem problematic, precisely because the revolutionary moment claims all power of reform unto itself, committed as it is to describing the old order as immobile. The very term 'Reformation' makes that claim. To describe the 'medieval' as the culture of 'reform' might seem especially surprising, given the very deep-set scholarly commitments, from the sixteenth century forwards, to the notion of a culturally static Middle Ages. I choose the word, nevertheless, partly to emphasize the ways in which many medieval works do lean into the future with a reformist impulse, but more out of necessity. A cultural field characterized by a diverse and highly segmented set of jurisdictions will, of necessity, be a field in which different jurisdictions speak to, check, and reform others. That will, in part, be their very function.

This, then, is a history committed to redescribing the passage from 'medieval' to what is variously called the 'Renaissance', the 'early modern' period, or the 'Reformation'. The chronological bounds have been chosen not primarily for the significance of their beginning and end, but rather for what they traverse. Certainly the beginning and end have their significance: 1350 roughly marked, as we will see in the volume as a whole, a newly articulate vernacularity with which the cultural revolution of the 1530s had to contend. And the death of Henry VIII in 1547 marked the beginning of a vertiginously volatile period of cultural change with its own, separate demands. I cannot help but trespass occasionally into the 1550s and beyond, since the reformist practice of 'medieval' literatures did not in each case end in 1485, or 1534, or 1547: the shift from a reformist to a revolutionary practice differed from field to field, and in some cases (especially the drama) I take the story outside my set bounds. In other cases the shift to a revolutionary practice was not itself a Tudor phenomenon: thus

Lollard theology, which flourished between 1380 and 1420, fits my account of revolutionary practice fairly neatly.

The principal strategy of the chronological choice remains, though, the concern to question the standard periodic assumptions within which one might have expected this book to have been written. Literary history by both medievalists and early modernists has tended, that is, to accept a little too uncritically the standard periodization of a Middle Ages that ends at, say, the accession of Henry VII in 1485. The chronological choice of this volume is made in the conviction that we stand to learn a great deal more about both the terms 'medieval' and 'early modern' by recognizing the historical interests that have defined the terms themselves to date. Periodic boundaries are not, so this book argues, great natural crevasses within whose non-negotiable terms we are obliged to think. As the terms within which we think historically, we should also recognize that they are themselves historically produced. As such, they are in this book susceptible of historical reflection: each chapter briefly summarizes the scholarly history of a given area, by way of revealing the ways in which strictly defined periodic thinking has organized and constrained memory. Precisely because periodic terms are historically contingent, I ask the reader to supply quotation marks whenever they are used, marks that I do not myself always supply for fear of labouring a point.

Given the instability of the basic terms of their subject, literary historians may be forgiven for labouring many other points, too: the contingency of each one of the three final terms in the title of this series, 'Oxford English Literary History', begs many questions. I will not labour their answers here, and trust instead that the reader will find answers in the practice of the book at large. Some brief, explicit address is nevertheless required, especially for the last three, and I do so in reverse order.

Work on this book has convinced me of the profoundly contingent nature of historical writing. Initial choices do commit us to certain perspectives at the expense of others. The present volume generates its discussion, as has been said, from within the problematic of medieval versus early modern, highlighting the qualities of 'reformist' versus 'revolutionary' cultural practice. That choice precludes or sidelines many others that could have been made. One could write a literary history determined by, for example, codicological, or metrical, or geographical perspectives. Certainly the larger theme of sixteenth-century centralization pursued in the book keeps such perspectives within view. The momentous shift from manuscript to print beginning, in England, in the 1470s itself contributed to a centralization of literature and of the language itself. Whereas, as we shall see, the fourteenth and fifteenth century witnessed a flourishing of literary forms in a wide variety of dialects across the whole of England, the introduction of printing contributed powerfully to the narrowing of metrical and linguistic possibility for English writing. England's earliest printers, for example, showed almost no interest in the rich tradition of alliterative verse that flourished in the west of England from the middle of the fourteenth century. Print culture's centralization of literature and the language of literature could easily form the principal theme of a literary history; in the present volume it is an undercurrent.

There are also, no doubt, perspectives that could not have been chosen simply because the present moment unconsciously determines our vision and interests. The conscious, initial choices are not, by definition, determined, since they *are* choices, and the choice is made on the basis of what seems most important. A correlative of the contingency is, however, the need to argue: precisely because one's terms are not pre-given, they need to be justified. This 'history' does not, then, take for granted what literary history must be; instead, precisely by virtue of its contingency of perspective, it also argues. It is not, certainly, a mere survey.

The concept of 'literature' is itself contingent, and needs some justification. Put very baldly, at least five plausible definitions of material to be included or excluded as 'literary' present themselves to me: (i) *formal* (works that conform to certain metrical and rhetorical norms); (ii) *functional* (works designed especially as entertainment); (iii) *positivist* (those works that were regarded by writers and readers within the period as forming a poetic tradition); (iv) *relation to historical 'truth'* (i.e., on a scale of historically 'true', verisimilar, and fabulous, works that fall into the last two categories); and (v) '*discursive*', by which I have in mind works that deliberately unsettle discursive norms, within whatever discourses they might be operating. Any single one of these frames would, in isolation, impoverish what seems to me the fit matter of this book. For the most part, I use flexible combinations of all these definitions, though the last (i.e. 'discursive') seems to me the most powerful; I will not often be discussing works that do not unsettle discursive norms. To illuminate the ways in which works might unsettle such norms will obviously require reference to those norms, but I will not feel bound to consider works that seem to me to fall squarely within the discursive practice of, for example, historiography, theology, medicine, moral instruction, and so on.

A literary history implies, then, exclusions of work in many other discourses. This point is worth emphasizing, since it underlines the need for a certain modesty in the literary historian: 'literary' discourse is a small part of the history of writing in this, as in any other period.[1] Neither is the history of writing itself the history of culture, since the cultural practice of many English people in this period was not a literate practice. Certainly the centuries of this history saw a widening of literacy;[2] they equally saw the introduction of print technology in the 1470s, which allowed for immeasurably wider dissemination of material.[3] Latin literacy was always high amongst the clergy of Anglo-Saxon and later medieval England. By 1400, however, as much as 30 per cent of the population was able to read and often write in English; basic literacy in English was taken for granted amongst both men and women of the gentry and aristocracy. Legal and commercial pressures, combined with the increasing need for literacy in the business of saving one's soul, created an environment in which schooling was widely available to the laity.[4] As many as eighty-five towns and villages boasted grammar schools between 1450 and 1499; the figure rose to one hundred and twenty-four in the following three decades. Many of these schools had been founded in the fourteenth and fifteenth centuries, and of these many had been

[1] For a very clear account of the concentrations of written discourse across all areas of book production (e.g. canon law, civil law, common law, medicine and science, school texts, theology), see the individual chapters of Hellinga and Trapp (eds.).

[2] See Parkes, and Trapp, 'Literacy'.

[3] For the introduction of printing, see Hellinga, 'Printing'. For the larger European picture, see Eisenstein. For MS production from 1375, see the essays in Griffiths and Pearsall (eds.). For the rates of survival of literary manuscripts, see Edwards and Pearsall.

[4] See Doane and Amsler for further references.

endowed to provide free schooling.[5] All that having been said, access to and interest in 'literature' was far from a mass phenomenon, except with regard to drama.

'English' involves more exclusions than one would wish. There is no sustained discussion here of Latin or Anglo-Norman writing within the period; Continental sources; or of the literatures of Wales, Scotland, or Ireland. The lack of sustained reflection on other languages being used within England is justified by the powerful move to use English for literary writing after about 1350.[6] Continental sources: I hope it will be obvious how much literary writing was engaged with Continental and, ultimately, Middle Eastern sources within the terms of this history. English writers were closely in touch with Latin, French, Italian, German, Dutch, and, later in the period, Greek and Hebrew materials, with differing concentrations at different times. At the same time, I have often been conscious of resisting the temptation, for reasons of economy, to enter into detailed discussion of the English text's relation to its source. The decision not to deal with Cornish, Welsh, Scottish, and Irish materials in any consistent way is partly a matter of limited expertise (I am unable to read Celtic languages), and partly a matter of respecting the integrity of literary systems. I do include sustained discussion of Scots material that is of signal importance to English literature, either by way of response or contribution. My choices there are, however, determined more by the inability to resist temptation than by any coherent principle of selection.

This is a long book. Two hundred years is a long time. Many chapters are divided between a central, sustained discussion of an especially revealing contrast between a 'reformist' and 'revolutionary' work, and further short sequences that offer coverage of sorts by brief discussion of many other texts. Readers whose time is short may wish to read only the sustained discussion. Readers whose time is shorter may wish to read only single chapters, which have been written as extractable units.

[5] Lander, p. 155.

[6] For Anglo-Norman writing in the period, see Crane, 'Anglo-Norman Cultures', and further references; for Latin writing up to 1422 at least, see Rigg.

1

The Melancholy of John Leland and the Beginnings of English Literary History

'The Renaissance invented the Middle Ages in order to define itself; the Enlightenment perpetuated them in order to admire itself; and the Romantics revived them in order to escape from themselves.'[1] Brian Stock's wonderfully pithy epigram must of course simplify, but one source of its potency is its implicit point that many cultural movements in the West, since the fourteenth century, generate themselves by contrast or identification with 'the Middle Ages'. In this chapter I focus on the founding moment of the very concept of 'the medieval' in English history. I do so in the conviction that cultural history remains disablingly locked into large periodic descriptions whose usefulness we might outlive. In such large periodic categorizations, the 'medieval' continues to figure all that is other to modernity; in response to this otherness, the function of scholarship is to define and reaffirm the 'medieval'.[2] This schema governs the vision of *both* those who, in a variety of disciplines, accept the self-valuations of sixteenth-century humanists and reformers alike to be instituting

[1] Stock, p. 543. See W. K. Ferguson for wide-ranging confirmation.

[2] The relevant German term is *Geistesgeschichte*. The term designates a concept of the past as neatly divided up into clearly defined periods, in which the synchronic relations between all aspects of a given culture at a given time are regarded as more significant, united as they are by a common 'spirit', than diachronic relations. For a critique of the Hegelian model, see Gombrich. For a critique of the 'relentlessly synchronic' practice of New Historicism, see Patterson, 'Historical Criticism and the Development of Chaucer Studies'.

a new, enlightened age, *and* those who oppose the claims of the enlightened new age by contrasting it with superior, 'medieval' values. Both historical projects accept and perpetuate a rigid account of what constitutes an 'age'.[3] This book as a whole seeks to reconfigure the relation between the medieval and the early modern as that distinction might work in literary history. It begins, accordingly, with the beginnings of British literary history itself, beginnings whose difficulties belie the simplicity of any strict division between the medieval and the early modern. For in the bibliographical work of John Leland and John Bale, we observe, so I will argue, a heroic yet doomed attempt to seal off the 'medieval' past.

I

In 1533, near the opening of a revolutionary decade, Henry VIII thought to investigate the literary stocks of his realm. The year before, Henry had restrained the payment of annual taxes to Rome, and in the following years, up to 1539, there followed a series of measures designed to nationalize the property of English religious houses and the faith of the English people. Although no official records survive, we are told by the seventeenth-century antiquarian Anthony Wood that John Leland (?1503–52) was commissioned 'to make a search after England's antiquities, and to peruse the libraries of all cathedrals, abbies, priories, colleges', and also 'all places wherein records, writings and secrets of antiquity were reposed'.[4]

However seriously Leland undertook his commission (and we shall see that it destroyed him), the directive to Leland clearly played

[3] Amongst English Renaissance (or early modern) studies in a variety of disciplines, definition of 'humanist' practice is consistently generated by distinction from 'medieval' attitudes, notably the medieval inability to think with historical perspective. A sample confirms my point: for poetry, see Greene, *Light in Troy,* ch. 2; for political thought, see A. Ferguson, *Articulate Citizen*, p. 33 (and *passim*); for English historiography, see Levine, ch. 1. For the Romantic revival of the Middle Ages, with its rejection of classicism, its revaluation of national traditions, and its attendant conservative nostalgia for the medieval period, see W. K. Ferguson, pp. 114–63. For 20th-cent. academic versions of a hermetically sealed Middle Ages, embodying superior, non-individualist values, see the critique of D. W. Robertson by Patterson in 'Historical Criticism and Development of Chaucer', pp. 26–39. See also Fradenburg.

[4] Wood, 1, col. 198.

a very insignificant part in the larger pattern of Henry's expropriation of the monasteries. By contemporaries Henry was, of course, praised for his love of learning. In sending Leland out 'to serche and peruse the Libraries of hys realme . . . before their utter destruccyon', Henry, we are told, exercised 'a stodye of thynges memorable, and a regardynge of noble Antiquitie, whyche bothe are to be commended hyghly'.[5] A large supply of letters written to Thomas Cromwell throughout the decade attests, however, to less scholarly interests that the King may have had in monastic holdings. These letters were written by commissioners whose responsibility it was to suppress the monasteries—to evict the religious, to take inventories of the property, and in many cases to destroy the buildings. Very often these letters use a language of indignation against 'superstition' and 'idolatry', but their consistent theme is the material value of the expropriated goods, the profits to be derived from the King's commission to 'pull down to the ground all the walls of the churches, steeples, cloisters, fraters, dorters, chapter houses, with all the other houses, saving them that be necessary for a farmer.'[6]

There is no mention of books in these letters to Cromwell, just as there is no mention of monastic libraries in the instructions to the Court of Augmentations, created to administer expropriated monastic property.[7] This is perhaps unsurprising, since the monastic dissolution, both started and completed in the years 1536–9, was the largest transfer of land in England since the Norman Conquest; presumably books were of little consequence and value amid such enormous transfers of property and wealth.

Certainly massive numbers of books were lost or destroyed: John Bale's lament in 1549 about the mistreatment of books from monastic holdings squares with the estimations of recent scholars concerning the magnitude of the loss; Bale complains that many of the new owners of the monasteries

> reserved of those lybrarye bokes, some to serve theyr iakes, some to scoure theyr candel styckes, and some to rubbe their bootes. Some they solde to the grossers and the sope sellers, and some they sent over the see to the

[5] Bale, *Laboryouse journey*, C1^{v} (*RSTC* 15445).

[6] Cited from a letter from the commissioner in Lincolnshire, written in Aug. 1538 to Thomas Cromwell. In *Letters to Cromwell*, ed. Cook, p. 181.

[7] See Fritze.

bokebynders, not in small nombre, to the wonderynge of the foreyn nacyons.[8]

If the fate of books was of little significance in royal policy in the last twenty or so years of Henry's reign, what clearly was of consequence was the refashioning of the past. In the official culture of England throughout the period 1534 (the Act of Supremacy) to 1547 (the death of Henry VIII), the 'past' receded rapidly, as it recedes in any revolutionary period. Take for example the Act exonerating England from 'exaccions payde to the see of Rome' near the beginning of this period of radical change, in January 1534. Article 13 clarifies the intention of the Act, by saying it should not be thought that the King or his subjects 'intende[d] . . . to declyne or vary from the congregacion of Christes Churche in any thynges concernyng the veray articles of the Catholike feith of Christendome'. Instead, the measures taken are designed only to 'represse vice and for good conservacion of this Realme in pease unytie and tranquyllitie . . . insewing moche the olde auncient customes of this Realme in that behalf'.[9]

This parallels the aims of conservative literary satire: the Act is, apparently, in no way revolutionary; on the contrary, precisely in order to preserve the 'auncient customes of the Realme', it is necessary to 'suppresse vice'. Contrast that posture with the kind of thing we find at the end of the reign, even when Henry wished to restrain the force of the revolution he had initiated. An Act of 1545, for example, suppressed a huge network of communal institutions, 'Chantries, Hospitalles, Fraternityes, Brotherheddes, Guyldes'. In this statute, it was precisely the 'auncient customes of this Realme' that were suppressed, or, in the case of 'Fraternityes and Brotherheddes', customs that date from the middle of the fourteenth century. Just after the end of Henry's reign in 1547 these institutions had themselves become representative of 'superstition and Errors', 'by devising and phantasinge vayne opynions of Purgatorye and Masses satisfactorye to be done for them which be departed'.[10]

8 Bale, *Laboryouse journey*, B1^r^. See also C. E. Wright, 'Dispersal in the Sixteenth Century'.

9 *SR*, 25 Henry VIII, ch. 21, art. 13 (3. 469).

10 *SR*, 1 Edward VI, ch. 14, art. 1 (4.1. 24). (The Edwardian statute restates and embellishes Henry's statute of 1545: *SR*, 37 Henry VIII, ch. 4.)

It is precisely as the newly unified Church and State of the 1540s repels the recent past that English literary history begins. For the first stocktaking of British writing derives from these events. I have in mind the work of two scholars, John Leland and John Bale, both of whom produced large scholarly lists and accounts of British authors. Leland's work *De viris illustribus* did not appear in his lifetime, for reasons we shall look to in a moment (it was published for the first time in 1709 as *Commentarii de scriptoribus britannicis*).[11] Bale's *Scriptorum illustrium maioris britanniae catalogus* was published in two volumes (1557, 1559).[12] This great work was constructed principally on the basis of three other books: it is heavily dependent on Leland's *De viris illustribus* (available to Bale in manuscript); on Bale's earlier *Illustrium maioris britannie scriptorum . . . summarium* (1548) for the sections both books have in common;[13] and on Bale's own working notes, his *Index britanniae scriptorum*, a scholarly list of authors and works first published in 1902. Certainly attempts to catalogue writers within a given tradition had been made prior to Bale and Leland: in the fourteenth century, for example, a certain Henry of Kirkstede (b. *c.*1314) had compiled a *Catalogus scriptorum ecclesiae*, itself a source for Bale's *Catalogus*,[14] and Bale himself had been engaged on a compilation of Carmelite authors before his Protestant conversion.[15] The works of Leland and Bale that concern us here are, however, the first attempts to shape a British, or even an English, tradition as an identifiable national tradition of letters.

To my mind Bale and Leland together participate within, and in some ways establish, powerful frames for the writing of English literary history. I highlight two related aspects of their enterprise. In the first place, they paint a chiaroscuro picture of ages, in which they see themselves as writing on the boundary of one, positive, epoch, about another, negative period ending in the immediate past. Both writers seek to highlight the brilliance of their own age, and to contrast that with the darkness of the past. In their anxiety to do so, however, they

11 For Leland's oeuvre and biography, see Carley, 'John Leland'.

12 For Bale's oeuvre and life, see Happé, and McCusker.

13 (*RSTC* 1295). Many of Bale's errors in the *Summarium* have been corrected in the *Catalogus*, after, presumably, a more careful reading of Leland.

14 See Rouse.

15 See Beal, vol. 1, pt. 1, item 18, p. 58.

reveal that ages are no natural passage from one set of cultural practices to another. On the contrary, the very concept of an age is itself the product of history. In particular, they reveal that only new concentrations of political power enable such powerful redrawings of the periodic map. Secondly, they claim to speak with the voice of a coherent modernity, in which a reformed religion sits easily and naturally with humanist learning. In fact, however, they speak for radically different cultural enterprises. Together they expose the dividedness of mid-sixteenth-century English historiography. Bale the millenarian Protestant constantly differs from Leland the civic humanist, even as he would speak with Leland as the joint voice of a coherent new age.

II

Let us begin with a small text presented by John Leland to Henry VIII on New Year's Day 1546: Leland's 'New Year's Gift'. For this little work effectively declares the melancholy impossibility of the massive projects upon which both Bale and Leland were engaged.

Like many scholars, Leland clearly had difficulty in reducing his notes to publishable form. His problem was, however, especially pronounced because he had so many notes, so large a topic, and so many approaches to it. His topic is nothing less than 'Britain'; and the aspects of Britain in which he is especially interested are its historiography, geography, 'literary' history, and local history. This ambitious enterprise is articulated for us in the 'Gift'. Presumably anxious about his lack of scholarly production, in this little work Leland confidently advertises the riches forthcoming from his pen. He promises Henry that he will publish in four books the names, lives, and work of the great writers of Britain (the *De viris illustribus*). The book will be modelled on the catalogues of ecclesiastical writers by, say, St Jerome, but, says Leland, 'I have more exspacyated in thys campe, than they ded, as in a thynge that desyred to be sumwhat at large, and to have ornature' ($C7^{v}$). His second projected work follows from the first: in travelling all over England and Wales in the previous six years in search of books, Leland asserts that there is almost neyther cape nor baye, hauen, creke or pere, ryver or confluence of ryvers, breches, washes, lakes, meres, fenny waters, mountaynes, valleys, mores, hethes, forestes, woodes, cyties, burges, castels, pryncypall manor places, monasteryes, and colleges, but I haue seane them, and noted in so doynge a whole world of thynges verye memorable. ($D4^r$)

On the basis of notes made in these journeys, Leland promises a description of Britain that he intends to call the *Liber de topographia britanniae primae*,[16] from which he plans to commission a 'quadrate table of sylver', upon which the 'worlde and impery of Englande' shall be engraved for Henry's pleasure and instruction. As if this were insufficient labour, Leland goes on to say that he has 'mater at plenty' prepared for the purpose of writing a history to be entitled *De antiquitate Britannica*, or *Civilis historia*. The number of volumes will match the administrative divisions in England and Wales—'so I esteme that thys volume wyl enclude a fyfty bokes'; each volume will recount the local history of the shire to which it is devoted. Leland also promises four books on the islands around Britain under Henry's subjection, and finally, 'as an ornament and a ryght comely garlande', a book to be called *De nobilitate britannica*, which will outline the noble families of Britain, 'so that all noble men shal clerely perceyve theyr lyneal parentele' ($E3^r$).

Now the project is clearly impossible in the obvious, practical sense of being overambitious for one life's work, and Leland was in any case about 43 in 1546. More revealingly, the project's insuperable challenge derives from its very conception. Only now in English history does it become possible to take up a vantage point that pretends to encompass the whole of Britain, and that pretends to map the totality of Britain with an interlocking set of cultural maps: the geography of *prima Britannia* is overlaid not only by its national and its local history, but also with a 'literary' map of British writers. One critical problem here is that of scale. As 'Britain' becomes entirely visible as a subject, that is, it both shrinks and, by the same token, immeasurably expands. For on the one hand Leland promises to reduce the whole country to the dimensions of an engraved silver tablet, designed for the King's pleasurable and proprietorial inspection. On the other, it is precisely because the whole country now

16 A work distinct from Leland's *Itinerary*.

opens up for the King's inspection that it seems to expand and to recede into elusive and ungraspable detail, both geographical and historical.

The obsessive listing of geographical features cited above ('. . . breches, washes, lakes, meres, fenny waters . . .') itself suggests the ways in which the country multiplies into infinite recess precisely as it promises to open itself up to the monarch's view. The same is true of the historical detail. Leland, wanting 'to wade further in thys matter', argues that in uncovering the geographical detail, so too does he uncover historical detail: 'almost no man can wele gesse at the shaddow of the auncyent names of hauens, ryuers, promontories, hilles, woodes, cities' and so on ($D7^{v}$). As the scholar seeks to see with the proprietorial eye of his royal master, he would seem to feel his vision both empowered and overwhelmed: he can see everything, but by the same token everything expands in detail until it evokes nothing but the shadow of what has disappeared. It is especially poignant, in the light of the impossibilities of scale in Leland's enterprise, that the 'New Year's Gift' to Henry turns out not to be a book (a standard gift of author to patron at New Year in this period), but rather a booklet promising books. As Bale says later, addressing Edward VI, about this little text: 'For fyrste it was geven of the Author, to youre most noble father of famouse memory *insteade of* a lowly newe yeares gyft' ($A3^{r}$; my emphasis).

A problem of scale, however, is not the only self-defeating aspect of Leland's project. More pressingly self-defeating, or rather self-destroying, is the relationship between antiquary and patron. Henry is, of course, Leland's patron. Leland envisions such an ambitious cultural mapping for the greater glory of Henry Tudor, but ultimately that same Henry also stands behind the massive destruction of the years 1536–40. As Margaret Aston has said, Henry is the first 'iconoclast monarch to grace, or disgrace, the English throne', and it is the very process of iconoclasm that energizes the antiquarian enterprise.[17] Leland's *raison d'être* for constructing a British past is in part, then, the destruction of that past on the orders of Leland's own patron. Leland is himself, accordingly, an agent of destruction, and the very object of his attention as antiquary, the past seen as some-

17 Aston, 'English Ruins', p. 255.

thing distant and sharply *different*, is itself a product of his moment. His own act of recording the past is a part of the process that destroys, or, if you will, creates, 'the past'.

That Leland himself saw the matter in this light we can have no certainty. In the 'New Year's Gift' of 1546 we hear nothing of that, and how should we, given that Leland is writing a begging letter of sorts to his royal patron? There, instead of criticism of Henry's wholesale destruction of libraries, we rather find praise of the King's learning. Leland's 'costly enterprise', is, he says to Henry, 'roted vpon your infynyte goodnesse and lyberalyte' (C1^{r}), and he goes on to declare that the fourth volume of his projected *De viris illustribus* will begin at, and therefore include, 'the name of your majeste, whose glorie in learnynge is to the worlde so clerely knowne'. Leland lists other British kings who had some reputation for learning, but goes on to set Henry above them: 'conferred with your grace, they seme as small lyghtes (yf I maye frely saye my judgmente, your hygh modestie not offended) in respect of the daye starre' (D1^{r}). Bale rightly says that Leland was so learned that he might 'well call him self *Antiquarius*' (B5^{r}), since Leland now examines the past as something distant and fragmentary: he surveys the newly created monastic ruins 'tanquam tabulata naufragii' ('as the debris of a shipwreck'), to use John Aubrey's evocative phrase.[18] The peculiarity of this situation, however, is that Leland's own patron has provoked the sense of fragmentation by providing the ruins. Leland is an exemplary case of what modern scholars have dubbed a humanist 'historical solitude'; by the same token, he is an ideal case from which to historicize that solitude.[19]

The text of Leland's 'Gift' did not survive in its original form; only Bale's re-presentation of it preserves it for us, now retitled by Bale *The Laboryouse journey and serche of Johan Leylande for Englandes antiquitees*, printed in 1549, three years after its composition. Henry is now dead, and Leland insane, soon to die in 1552; the text is now addressed officially to Edward VI, a child of 9, but

[18] Ibid. 251.

[19] The phrase 'historical solitude' is taken from Greene, *Light in Troy* (title of ch. 2). Greene uses the phrase to designate the sense of historical rupture characteristic of humanist thought, and to distinguish this humanist trait from the ahistorical habits of mind of writers before Dante (p. 17).

evidently aimed at a wider readership, whom Bale wishes to enlist as supporters of a campaign for textual preservation. Leland's text is now surrounded and invaded by Bale's additions: a dedicatory letter to Edward, and a preface 'to the Reader' precede Leland's text, while a conclusion encouraging book preservation and a list of British authors follow it. Bale also slices Leland's text up and interweaves his own comments, thus enlarging and transforming Leland's 'Gift'. Despite the fact that Leland still lives at the time the text is published, Bale speaks as if Leland were incapable of doing so himself. Leland was indeed incapable, since, as Bale says, by this time he had fallen 'in such a frenesy at thys present, that lytle hope I have of hys recover, wherby he myghte fynyshe such thynges as he began' ($B3^{v}$).

I need not dwell on the pathos of this text, except to say that we only hear of Leland's impossibly ambitious projects within the frame of his failure. Leland is given space by Bale to announce his plans, but no sooner does he do so than Bale's voice, in this newly constructed text, intervenes. Leland promises Henry the engraved silver tablet of Britain's geography; Bale interrupts: whether Leland produced this gift, Bale cannot tell, for in the following year (1547), 'both the king deceaced, and Lelande also by a most pytiefull occasion fell besides his wittes, and is not yet fully amended' (D6r). 'Leland' (Bale's text clearly demarcates both voices) goes on to promise Henry a written map of Britain, by which a painter might reproduce a visual map. 'Bale' shepherds the text: 'Yf this worke were not yet fully accomplished (as the matter is now in doubte) by reason of his troublous dysease, great pytie it were but his labours shoulde come to some learned mannes hande'...($D7^{r}$) On 'Leland' goes, laboriously: 'Yea, and to wade further in thys matter, where as now almost no man can wele gesse at the shaddow of the auncyent names'($D7^{v}$).

Many explanations for Leland's madness have been offered, none of which will ever satisfy, precisely because madness, by definition, defies definition. I myself prefer a version of the seventeenth-century antiquarian Anthony Wood's explanation. Leland was 'undertaking so immense a task, that the very thoughts of completing it did, as 'tis said, distract him. At the time of the dissolution of the monasteries, he saw with very great pity what havoc was made of ancient monuments of learning' (col. 198). From what has been said already, however, it will be clear that sheer immensity is not the only challenge Leland faced. In the first place, the immensity is itself the product of a point of view so central and so totalizing that it feels free to claim the whole of British history for itself. The entire past becomes visible as 'history' precisely because Leland is committed to the construction of a wholly new age. More damagingly, the project of historical recuperation that Leland sets himself must of necessity produce a divided consciousness, since Leland, in a 'highly schizophrenic' situation, is himself an agent of the destruction of the very past he seeks to recuperate.[20]

Leland was not the only English person of the last two decades of Henry VIII's reign to experience a deeply divided consciousness. Certainly in his case the division was intolerable, but the destruction of the monasteries, and especially of their libraries, could not fail to produce division in the minds of people who both cared about England's past, and who were at the same time committed, for whatever reason, to the new ideological order. John Bale (1495–1563) is himself a striking example of such division. He presents himself in Leland's text as the scholarly shepherd, and, implicitly, as the scholarly executor for the mentally lamed Leland; Bale is the voice of sanity stepping in to carry on where poor Leland had failed. In fact, however, the position of the scholarly executor turns out to be just as divided, if not more so, than that of his now insane scholarly forebear. Bale, of course, was an enthusiastic Protestant, writing in 1549 under a Protestant regime. But so far from being triumphalist, Bale's tone in the *Laboryouse journey* is urgent and fraught, caught as he is between delight and horror at the destruction of monastic culture. He applauds the destruction of the buildings, but deplores the attendant loss of books. The characteristic posture of Bale's prose in the *Journey* is lamentation:

> Yet this would I have wyshed (and I scarsely utter it wythout teares) that the profytable corne had not so unadvysedly and ungodly peryshed wyth the unprofytable chaffe . . . I meane the . . . Lyvelye memoryalles of our nacyon, wyth those laysy lubbers and popyshe bellygoddes. ($A7^v$)

In the new context for Bale's publication of Leland, with Henry dead, and the king a child of 9, Bale can, unlike Leland, publicly

[20] See Carley, 'John Leland's *Cygnea Cantio*', for the phrase 'highly schizophrenic' (p. 233).

lament the destruction of libraries. Also unlike Leland, Bale wholeheartedly and consistently praises the destruction of the monasteries themselves. But he is torn by the destruction and/or dispersal of monastic literary culture: 'oure posteryte maye wele curse thys wycked facte of our age, thys unreasonable spoyle of Englandes moste noble Antiquytees' (B2^{r}). Bale and Leland together produce a threnody, Bale lamenting Leland's own fragmentation in the larger context of libraries being fragmented.

Bale's position is so divided, in fact, that his metaphors for praising the wickedness of the popish past (i.e. darkness) and the virtue of the Protestant present (i.e. light) become confused. Leland uses the standard metaphors, by saying to Henry that he intends to bring forth books 'out of deadly darkenesse to lyuelye lyght' (B8^{r}). Or later in the 'Gift', he promises to open the window 'that the lyght shal be seane . . . by the space of a whole thousand yeares stopped up' (D7^{v}). Bale recycles and politicizes the imagery: he cites St Paul in declaring that the ruler does not act in vain, but, as in Henry's case, 'destroyed monasteries, convents and colleges for their wyckednesses sake', and at the same time resolved to bring forth monuments of learning 'from darkenesse to a lyvely light' (B8^{v}). The simplicity of this scheme breaks down, however, as Bale pursues his theme. What upsets Bale almost more than papish superstition is Protestant destruction of books; he addresses the 'noble and learned' readership in his preface, exhorting them to tread underfoot the example of the destroyers, 'and brynge you into the lyghte, that they kept longe in the darknes, or els in these dayes seketh utterly to destroye' (B2^{v}). The imagery of darkness threatens imperceptibly to spill into a description of the Protestant present; here and elsewhere all that has been ostensibly suppressed in the superstitious monastic past resurfaces in Bale's denunciation of that Protestant present.

The most powerful passage of this kind cites Erasmus, after having denounced the 'slouthfull neglygence of thys wycked age, whych is muche geven to the destruccyon of thynges memorable':

> Wyth muche payne I absteyne from wepynge (sayth he in a certen Epystle) so oft as I in readynge the Cataloges of olde writers, do beholde what profyghtes . . . we have lost. My grefe is also augmented, so oft tymes as I call to remembraunce, what yll stuffe we have in stede of their good writynges. We fynde for true hystoryes, most fryvolouse fables and lyes, that we

mygthe the sonner by the devyls suggestion, fall into most depe errours, and so be lost, for not belevynge the truthe. ii Thessa.ii. (D4[r])

This passage reveals the profoundly divided sensibility of the revolutionary thinker, undoing the new order of which he is a champion. For Bale believes that he is allowing in light where there has been darkness for 'a whole thousand yeares'. He is concerned here and elsewhere in his intensely polemical oeuvre to draw the distinctions between his own moment and the immediate past as sharply as he possibly can. Triumphalism, however, here undoes itself: sensitive to the claims of the monastic past as he is, Bale implicitly allows for the possibility that the revolutionary period is the period of darkness, the period of 'fryuolouse fables and lyes', of the 'deuyls suggestion', and of 'depe errours'. The remarkable inversion of the symbolic system of Protestant propaganda implicit in this passage is strikingly reinforced by the biblical passage to which Bale directs us. The verse from the Second Epistle to the Thessalonians threatens damnation to those who are persuaded by the devil's blandishments (2 Thess. 2–10). Antichrist in this passage turns out not to be the Catholic Church so much as its challenger.

If Bale is implicitly undoing his new world here, this is surely an implication of which either he is unconscious, or at least from which he wishes to distance himself: it is possibly significant that he puts this passage into the mouth of Erasmus, but nevertheless blurs the line of demarcation between his own voice and that of his source. Unconscious or not, the passage is symptomatic of the divided consciousness we observed in Leland: it suggests that the intellectual journey upon which Bale is embarked was, however energetically Bale set about it, itself spiritually laborious, toiling him as it did in the doubts of moral and ideological inversion.

III

Leland and Bale both reveal, then, a division of consciousness with regard to the past: as the new age is announced triumphally, so too does triumphalism undo itself. And if this is true of the relation with the past, division is also visible as the new age formulates its own unity. For the attempt of the *Laboryouse journey* to present the two voices of Bale and Leland as occupying one historical position fails. Bale would have it that he is completing Leland's work, both in the *Journey*, and in the importation of much of Leland's bibliographical work wholesale, though usually acknowledged, into the *Catalogus*. More than once in the *Laboryouse journey* does Bale pray that Leland's labours 'shoulde come to some learned mannes hande, that he mighte laudably finish it to the commen use'(D7^{r}), surely a reference to Bale himself. And so Bale would also have it, correlatively, that his project is indistinguishable from Leland's, since both are, to use Leland's words, seeking to 'open this wyndow, that the lyght shal be seane, so long, that is to say, by the space of a whole thousand yeares stopped up' (D7^{v}). They are both, in their own self-presentation, recovering the true Britain, 'painting' the country, in Leland's paradoxical formulation, 'with hys natyue colours' (E4^{r}). But when we compare the historiographical positions of Leland and Bale respectively, we observe that their concept of the past bifurcates at the very moment Bale would unite it. Comparison of the two distinct sets of interests is unavoidable, precisely because Bale is so anxious to come in on top of Leland's voice, constantly differing from him even as he pretends merely to seal and complete Leland's project. Both Leland and Bale present themselves as writing from the positive side of an epochal division, but the more Bale interrupts, the less convincing becomes their joint claim to speak for one new age, against one past age.

Leland is a civic and literary humanist, committed to the recovery of classical ideals in the service of the state. Bale is a radical Protestant. It may be that what primarily concerns both writers is simply the preservation of monuments of the past, but the way in which they formulate their concern with the past is sharply different. Formally, Leland also accepted the new religion, and it would surely have been impolitic for him not to have done so. He writes, however, without much characteristically Protestant flavour, and is primarily concerned with secular history in the service of royal power.[21] Bale, by contrast, wishes to shape a Protestant historiography, in which English history conforms to and fulfils scriptural revelation.

[21] Leland did write one treatise defending the prerogatives of the English monarch over the Pope: *Antiphilarchia*, Cambridge, University Library, MS Ee.v.14.

Consider, for example, Leland's introductory remarks, summarizing his commission from Henry. Certainly the rhetoric is Protestant, but these are the reported words of Henry's commission, not Leland's. He says that he has been commissioned to search out libraries in order that the writers of Britain should come to light, and that Scripture might be properly taught, with 'all manner of superstycyon, and crafty coloured doctryne of a rowte of Romayne Byshoppes, totally expelled oute of thys your most catholyque realme' (C1^{r}). Bale capitalizes on these remarks to recast the enterprise as the recovery of a specifically Protestant literary tradition. He declares that, although the majority of writers were 'wholly given to serve Antichristes affectes in the parelouse ages of the Churche',

> Yet were there som amonge them, whiche refusynge that office, sought the onlye glorye of their Lorde God. In the middest of al darkenesse, have some men by all ages, had the livynge sprete of Goddes chyldren, what though they have in some thynges erred. Gal.iiii. Never yet were the spelunkes [caves] of Abdias wythoute the true Prophetes of God. (C1^{v})

As we shall see when we turn to the actual practice of Leland and Bale respectively as literary historians, Leland's sympathy towards *all* British writers of fame is undiscriminating as to ideology. Even in the 'Gift', when he praises the accomplishments of British theologians as expositors of Scripture, he is unembarrassed about saying that 'both after the auncyent forme, and sens the scholastycall trade they have reygned as in a certayne excellencye'. In Bale's intervention immediately following, scholastic theologians become 'the infynyte rable of the barbarouse and brawlyng sentencyoners' (D3^{r}).

What does concern Leland as a humanist is the style of writing designed to promote royal interests. Describing historical works that he has found and intends to publish, Leland says that he also intends to rewrite them, since English writers who were otherwise learned did not take pains to produce their histories in a 'floryshynge style'. Leland's interest in these works is evidently not of the purely philological kind said to be characteristic of humanism. On the contrary, the main purpose of preserving these texts is to press them into royal service, for which they must be 'delycately clothed in purpure' (C5^{r}). Bale immediately chimes in to reject this last proposal of Leland: it is unnecessary to rewrite historical works in a 'more eloquent stile', since, he argues, authority accrues to them by appearing in their native simplicity. He defends this lack of concern for rhetoric by appealing to the style of the Scriptures: 'God hath chosen (S. Paule saith) the folyshe and weake thynges of the worlde, to confounde the wyse and myghtye' (C4^{r}). Leland's enterprise is in part the creation of a timeless literary pantheon that serves royal interests, while Bale seeks to serve the interests of the English Church by constructing its authentic documents. The interests of both coincide at the point of asserting royal prerogatives enthusiastically, but rhetoric is essential for one and irrelevant to the other.

We can observe, then, two very distinct traditions, each rather anxious to claim identity with the other in the *Laboryouse journey*. Leland represents a humanist tradition that seeks to enlarge national glory by gathering all that is 'British'. He is especially concerned to bring to light what he calls 'hystoryographers', mostly monastic writers of secular history who, he says to Henry, 'with grete dylygence, and no lesse faythe, wolde to God wyth lyke eloquence, prescribed the actes of your moste noble predecessours' (D3^{r}). Bale, on the other hand, is especially concerned to delineate a Protestant literary tradition that extends back across the historical divide on which Bale thinks he is writing, since, as he says, 'in all ages have there bene some godly writers in Englande, which have both smelled out, and also by theyr writynges detected the blasphemouse fraudes of thys Antichrist' (C6^{r}).[22] But both traditions offer support to each other: Leland makes appropriate gestures about the Papacy, if always in terms of papal incursion of English royal jurisdiction, and never in millenarian language, while Bale's text rests limpet-like on Leland's, claiming merely to complete when in fact he capitalizes on Leland's text to further quite distinct interests. If Bale, however unwittingly, allows for the possibility that now, in the new age, 'fables' have replaced 'true histories', then one such fable may be that the period ended by the Protestant Reformation consists of one single, consistent cultural block. This is an idea no less fabulous than the notion that post-Reformation England constitutes another, new cultural block, consistent in its self-definition and practice. Even as Bale would assert such a claim, he reveals its fragility.

[22] My comparison of Bale and Leland is consonant with Ross.

IV

What is the actual practice of these two scholars in their construction of a 'British' 'literary' heritage? John Bale's *Catalogus* (printed 1557–9) contains bio-bibliographical entries under the following names: Richard Hampole, John Wyclif, 'Robert' Langelande, John Mandeville, Richard Maidstone, John Trevisa, John Gower, Geoffrey Chaucer, Thomas Hoccleve, William Thorpe, Walter Hilton, John Lydgate, Reginald Pecock, John Hardyng, Juliana Barnes, William Caxton, John Tiptoft, Thomas Malory, Stephen Hawes, John Colet, John Skelton, Thomas More, William Tyndale, Thomas Elyot, John Leland, Thomas Cranmer, and John Bale (for example, among a total of 1,400 entries).[23] Each entry contains a small biography, an account of the main positions taken, if the writer is polemical, and a list of known works produced, followed by such information as Bale has about the author's death. On the face of it, this is unquestionably the beginning of English literary history both as a whole, and, by the same token, for the period 1350–1550.

Of course that statement needs immediate qualification. The whole scope of Bale's work as bibliographer is set in an immeasurably wider historical field than 1350–1550. He ranges from the furthest reaches of Celtic history to his own age, and he includes what are now regarded as 'literary' authors only because they fall within his own discursive frames. The historical period of greatest textual activity in the vernacular, from 1350, holds no categorical claim on Bale's attention.[24] Neither does the discursive concept of the 'literary' or 'poetic'. In his 'New Year's Gift' Leland advertises the discursive groupings of the works he has gathered under two principal headings of theology and history ($D2^r$–$D3^r$). He nowhere mentions poetic texts in the work, and although he does of course list poets in the *De viris illustribus*, his interest in 'literature' is much less consistent than we might expect. Of the distinctively 'literary' writers just listed from Bale's compilation, only Gower and Chaucer had appeared in Leland. In any case, the list cited from Bale contains only

[23] Bale divides his authors up into groups of 100 (*centuriae*); of the writers listed here all appear in the sixth, seventh, and eighth *centuriae*, except 'Hampole' (Richard Rolle), who is placed in the fifth *centuria*.

[24] Although Rolle is the first author whom Bale notes as writing in the vernacular.

a handful of 'literary' writers, and even these appear in Bale normally for their polemical positions on religious questions rather than for their contribution to a 'literary' tradition. It is not until Thomas Warton's brilliant *History of English Poetry* (1774–81) that England produces a history of specifically 'literary' discourse, aiming to cover the period from the Conquest to the end of the seventeenth century. So if Bale and Leland do constitute the beginnings of English literary studies, this is an accident of history, insofar as 'literature' is not a discursive category to which either writer directs his bibliographical energy.

In retrospect, however, the bio-bibliographical industry of Leland and Bale *does* constitute the beginnings of the study of English literature from 1350. Let me turn to these large bibliographical projects, by way of setting the same phenomena into relief that we observed in the *Laboryouse journey*. We observe, that is, a strictly maintained period division, by which both writers generate commentary by the degree to which authors conform to, or differ from, the darkness of their age. We also observe, between Leland and Bale, a largely different formulation of what constitutes tradition, even as both scholars would lay the foundations for a new and ostensibly coherent epoch.

The notion of tradition of necessity contains principles of both identity and change. For Leland and Bale the identity that qualifies all writers for inclusion in their catalogues is 'Britishness'. This category was itself highly charged, since England was now making very strong claims to Ireland, Wales, and Scotland. Wales had been made a principality by Edward I in 1282, but only in 1536 was Wales formally unified within the administrative structure of 'Britain'. Henry VIII sealed the twelfth-century Norman invasion of Ireland by proclaiming himself king of Ireland in 1541. And Henry also sought, though failed, to annex Scotland after the death of James V in 1542. Bale made good this failure culturally, by including Scottish authors in his *Catalogus*. Furthermore, the notion of 'Britain' had to be redefined in radical ways after the Act of Supremacy, which accentuated a newly defined 'British' identity against Continental Europe. Already in 1530 Henry had claimed imperial status for himself.

The category of 'Britishness', then, defined the aggressively shaped identity within which Bale and Leland worked. What of difference?

Both see themselves as writing on one, positive, side of a massive historical divide, looking back to the relatively recent past as if to a distant epoch. What, however, constitutes that divide, and therefore difference, is, for either writer, quite distinct. For Leland writers can be differentiated historically by their respective rhetorical expertise. Thus, for example, he praises Richard Rolle (d. 1349) with faint admiration:

For the massive barbarity [*ingens barbaries*] of that time occupied the whole of Europe; and with the Roman Empire gradually declining, the purity of the Latin language, being corrupted by the uncultivated, also declined. Hampole, however, distinguished himself as much as he possibly could, despite the infelicity of his age.[25]

Leland is writing about a Latin style only two hundred years earlier than his own. He writes as if Rolle were still within what used to be known as the 'Dark Ages', with the decline of Latin being correlative with the decline of the Roman Empire itself. This is purely humanist in its alignment of rhetoric and imperial power, but also typical of sixteenth-century humanism in England in its exaggeration of historical difference.

Even when Leland's admiration for the effort to imitate classical models is rather more fulsome, he still frames discussion of the late fourteenth century as an age wholly different from his own. Thus when he comments on Gower, the discussion of Gower's Latin interestingly blurs with the remarks on Gower's vernacular writings. Leland remarks that Gower's imitations of Ovid were 'more studied than felicitous':

And neither should this appear surprising, especially in that semi-barbarous period [*semi barbaro seculo*]: for hardly in this our own flourishing age [*hac nostra tam florenti aetate*] should anyone be found who could well express the overflowing felicity of Ovid's verse. Let us then bear with whatever is infelicitous in Gower, and set him forth as the first 'polisher' of the native tongue. For before his time, the English language lay uncultivated and almost entirely unformed. There was no one who could write any work elegantly in the vernacular worthy of a reader. (2. 414)

[25] Leland, *Commentarii*, 2. 348. Translations of Leland's Latin are mine.

From here Leland goes on to say that Gower's works are still read by the learned, 'in hoc florentissimo tempore' ('in this most flourishing period').

As we have seen, Leland is writing in a context of enormous political change, involving radical breaks with the past. In that context, he generates discussion of texts from the perspective of strictly contrasted periodization. He claims absolute temporal breaks that form self-enclosed ages, or cultural blocks. His way of describing Gower's period (i.e. the late fourteenth century), as 'semi-barbarous', or Rolle's as plainly or even massively 'barbarous', as distinct from his own 'flourishing' or 'cultivated' age, is only a hair's breadth away from the standard terminology of modern cultural history, of a Middle Age and a Renaissance. The image of 'flowering' is consistent, indeed, with the metaphor of rebirth embedded in the term 'renaissance'.[26] One feature of this strictly maintained periodic perspective is to generate positive or negative comment by the standard of what defines the new age boundaries. In this case the standard is the 'humanist' standard of rhetorical excellence, and so Gower is singled out as a partial exception to the general rule of rhetorical incivility.

This characteristic of periodic thinking is much more pronounced

[26] For the development of the ideas of 'Renaissance' and 'Middle Age', see esp. W. Ferguson. The roughest outlines of the story, according to Ferguson, are as follows: Italian writers of the last half of the 14th cent. began to declare reawakenings in the fields of literature and painting especially, without using the word *rinascita* (though using many semantic cognates), and without labelling the whole period as one of revival (pp. 1–28); Northern European Protestant historians, under the influence of Erasmus especially, developed a periodic conception, by labelling the millennium preceding the beginning of the sixteenth century a period of darkness and obscurity (pp. 29–55). At the same time, 16th-cent. Italian writers, especially Vasari, began to use the word *rinascita* to describe the revival of arts in Italy from Giotto forwards (pp. 60–5). It is not, however, until the 19th cent., in the introduction to vol. 7 of Jules Michelet's *Histoire de France*, that the term 'Renaissance' is used to describe 'a period in general European history' (pp. 174–7). The correlative notion of a 'Middle Age' is necessarily generated at each of these decisive moments. Terms like *media aetas*, *media tempora*, can readily be found in 16th cent. Protestant polemic, but it is not until the last quarter of the 17th cent. that the German pedagogue Christoph Keller used a tripartite conception of European history (antiquity, the middle age, modern times) as the basic principle of historiographical organization (pp. 73–7). See also Huizinga, 'Problem of the Renaissance', and Panofsky, ch. 1, for a more specific discussion of the development of the idea of a 'renaissance' in Italian painting and literature from the 14th to the 16th cents.

in Bale. For one thing, his periodic schema is itself explicit. Interwoven with his *Catalogus* is another work by Bale, his *Acta Romanorum Pontificum*; in this work he narrates the history of the Papacy, particularly in relation to England, through the lens of apocalyptic history, in which the popes play the role of Antichrist. So Bale's history of 'letters', for want of a better term, is conditioned by the explicit apocalyptic and polemical frame within which it is set. It is this historical frame that generates the focus and sympathies of Bale's discussion. Like Leland, he seeks out forerunners of the new age, but his forerunners are religious prophets, not expert rhetoricians. Take, for example, his enthusiastic account of another fourteenth-century poet, William Langland, not mentioned by Leland. Bale frankly admits a certain ignorance about the poet, calling him 'Robertus Langelande', but goes on to say this:

> This, however, appears quite clear, that he was one among the first disciples of John Wyclif, and that, in fervour of spirit, under attractive colours and allegories, he published a pious work in English, which he called *The Vision of Piers Plowman* . . . In this erudite work, on account of various and happy similitudes, he prophetically foresaw many things, which we have seen come to pass in our own days. (*Catalogus*, p. 474; my translation)

This entry is typical of Bale's historiographical perspective: what is especially worth attention and preservation from the past is prophetic of the present, the prophetic that by definition stands above the darkness and limitations of vision that surrounded it. The same accent, more pronounced, is found in Bale's account of Wyclif as one standing alone among a host of enemies,

> . . . as in the dark heart of errors and in the obscurities of the devilish locusts and hypocrites, as a great-hearted fighter for Christ he stood for his truth . . . Alone and first, after the liberation of Satan did he stand forth, and carried the light of truth in that murky age [*in calignoso illo seculo*]. (p. 450)

The broad lines of focus are identical to those of Leland: Bale too, sees the late fourteenth century as from a position of light, looking back from the enlightened sixteenth century as into the distance and into the dark, in which he descries single outstanding figures who resist the obscurity and barbarity of their age. The standards, however, by which Bale measures the greatness of the past are wholly different from those of Leland. The description of Wyclif here is, for example, explicitly millenarian in its historical placing and praise; past greatness is defined by the degree to which the past prophesied the coming of the new religious age, freed from the papal Antichrist. His reference to the 'liberation of Satan' refers to a standard Protestant millenarian idea, that Antichrist was let loose on the world around the year 1000, a date that John Foxe, writing in 1563, shifts to 1324.[27] The period of greatest interest for literary writing in Middle English is, then, included within the period of greatest darkness for Christian history.

Bale's construction of the past is both like and unlike Leland's. Both write as from the side of a great historical victory over the forces of darkness, and both attempt to perceive the heroic forerunners of that victory back in the benighted past. The criteria, however, by which their praise and blame of the past are generated differ sharply. Leland looks out especially for rhetorical excellence and the renovation of letters and of secular historiography, while Bale trains his eye rather to locate the proto-Protestant prophet. Beyond their commitment to a British tradition newly brought into focus by the Tudor monarchy, they really have very little ideological ground in common.

Of disagreement with Leland, however, we find very little in Bale's bibliographical work. Bale is certainly aware of differences between his own historical interests and Leland's. In his unpublished epitome of Leland's *De viris illustribus*, he privately expresses anxiety about Leland's inclusiveness: 'One thing, perhaps, will cause displeasure, and it certainly does not please me, that many things are here treated without discrimination of doctrine and a searching of spirits, and wicked things admitted as holy.'[28] In the public production of the *Catalogus*, however, there appears no trace of criticism of Leland. Occasionally Bale will gesture to the difference of tone employed by the two, as when he says, about the poet William Herebert, that 'hereafter I will use the more gentle words of Leland' (p. 404), but on the whole Bale writes in such a way as to suggest no conflict or difference of interest between them. As with the mini-project of re-

[27] For Bale's computations, see Fairfield. For Foxe's elaborate scheme, see Foxe, 4. 724–6.

[28] Cambridge, Trinity College MS R. 7. 15, fo. 2v (my trans.).

publishing Leland's 'Gift' as the *Laboryouse journey*, so too with the immeasurably larger project of absorbing Leland's bibliographical work into the *Catalogus*: both recyclings of Leland's material present themselves as working in tandem with Leland, merely completing what Leland had failed to publish.

Bale is scrupulous to cite Leland, and accusations of plagiarism are ill-founded. In fact Bale cites Leland frequently, and the effect of those citations is to suggest a complete harmony of interest between the two writers. Bale will, even, easily adopt Leland's rhetorical posture at times. When the writer under discussion is regarded as a Lollard, for example, Bale is prepared to praise that writer's contribution to the renovation of the English language. Thus Thomas Hoccleve, whom Bale, in spectacular error, regarded as a closet Wycliffite, is also described as 'a not unworthy beautifier of the paternal language' (p. 537), or John Trevisa is described as one who translated the whole Bible into English, and who was among the first who 'polished the vernacular, and who tried to raise it from barbarity' (p. 518). So far from suggesting difference, for Bale the 'moderns' form a unified block, whether they are primarily civic humanists or Protestant in their practice. The extraordinary eighth *centuria* of the 1557 volume, which constitutes Bale's hall of modern fame, reveals the same feature, since Protestant writers like Frith, Tyndale, Rastell, Ridley, Latimer, Cranmer, and Bale himself, for example, are equally praised beside writers who can fairly be described as civic humanists, such as Richard Pace, Christopher St Germain, Thomas Elyot, and John Leland, who is himself tucked fascinatingly between entries for Henry VIII and Edward VI. The praise for modernity finds its culmination in the eulogy for Henry VIII, who also receives an entry in this *centuria*. Henry 'crushed idolatry, blasphemies, and sects; he restored letters, reintroduced the Gospel, promoted piety, and renovated the faith' (p. 670). Modernity is presented, that is, as a unified block, legitimated and animated by the person of the King.

The scholarly projects of Leland and Bale both labour under profoundly divided impulses. Both seek to preserve a past that their present *must*, in some ways, destroy. Because the present needs to legitimate itself by sharp distinction from the past, it must erect crystal-clear epochal boundaries to distinguish the dark, superstitious past from 'this perfection which we now see'. This act at once petrifies the past, by literally ruining it, in the case of the monasteries, *and* provokes the desire to preserve the 'monuments' of the past. Leland, as we have seen, is himself an agent of the destruction, however much an awareness of the present as both destructive and constructive is more explicit in Bale. While their heroic bibliographical work would present, under Bale's guidance, the united face of a new and triumphalist age, both writers cannot help but reveal difference between and within themselves. By the same token, they reveal the historical sources of the very different traditions to which they each belong, undoing the notion of a sealed, past age even as they would affirm it.

Both writers, working from within a strictly applied periodic understanding, try to locate prophets in the past, figures who foresaw or in some way presaged the perfection of the present. Their prophets are of a very different kind: Leland looks for the examples of a secular historiography to press into royal service, who might possess the attendant rhetorical excellence that royal service demands; Bale, on the contrary, works within a millenarian conception of history, and the prophets he identifies foresee a new English, Protestant Church. However much their conceptions of history differ, neither draws much attention to potentially radical differences; on the contrary, Bale presents his work as merely completing or deploying Leland's. Just as secular, classically inclined humanist is set effortlessly beside reformist theologian in Bale's hall of fame, so too does Bale efface any sense of potential discrepancy between himself and Leland. Even as this apparently coherent ideological enterprise is constructed, its incoherence becomes visible. Bale and Leland together, as they are deployed in Bale's *Catalogus*, reveal the histories behind at least two very different traditions of English writing, one secular in orientation, and classically inspired, the other biblical and millenarian. And in so doing, Bale's *Catalogus* unconsciously undoes the claims of his own, 'new' age to present a wholly coherent, new front.

What draws both camps, civic humanist and Protestant, together is their mutual interest in the jurisdiction of the English Church, and, so, their mutual interest in underwriting the supremacy of the Tudor monarchy within a British history. What turns out to be distinctive about the 'new age' in which Bale and Leland write is not the presence of wholly new humanist or ecclesiological ideas, but rather the political supremacy of an English monarch who can so thoroughly nationalize and centralize English institutions. 'British' historiography itself, as practised by Leland and Bale, only becomes possible under such a political dispensation: a perspective that claims access to the whole of Britain's history and geography—every last fenny water, in Leland's case—is only possible from a vantage point whose totalizing pretension was impossible in any earlier period of English history. As we see in Leland's case, this totalizing perspective, and this divided consciousness, at once energizing and overwhelming, cannot help but produce melancholy of a kind.

V

Leland and Bale's divisions of history expose the obviously historical motives behind strict periodic divisions. In some ways their work provides analogies for the current practice of English cultural history, itself conducted within strictly demarcated periodic divisions between what we would call a 'Middle Age' on the one hand, and an age of 'Reformation' and 'Renaissance' on the other. In other ways their work, or at least the enormous pressure and significance of their historical moment, remains *causative*: writers throughout the centuries since the mid-sixteenth century have continued to perceive the boundaries between the 'Middle Ages' and the 'Renaissance' and/or 'Reformation' (in England) in ways *determined* by the pressures of Henry VIII's cultural revolution.[29]

The present in which any historian writes affords certain historically contingent vantage points, drawing the mind to certain kinds of knowledge at the expense, no doubt, of others. The vantage point of Bale and Leland is at the same time full of promise and damagingly limited. For the cultural revolution through which they lived provoked in them an extraordinary energy for scholarship of a high

[29] I do not, of course, mean to ignore the continuing influence of a wider European context of Protestant and humanist polemic that claims the arrival of a new age. But these intellectual traditions are empowered by political circumstances, and in England the significant political circumstance is the Henrician revolution. For the wider context, see W. K. Ferguson.

order within the resources available to them. At the same time, however, the revolution of the 1530s radically limited their perspective on the past, as revolutions tend to. I end this chapter by justifying, in turn, the chronological boundaries of this book, and its fundamental discursive division into secular and religious matter.

The history of Middle English literary studies as a scholarly discipline has hardly begun.[30] The contrast with Old English Studies is striking,[31] and the slow development and self-consciousness of Middle English studies may in part be attributable to the polemical orientation of the sixteenth and seventeenth centuries, when scholars eagerly pursued study of the pre-Conquest period for evidence of a native British Church prior to the Tudor Reformation, while the best the post-Conquest period could produce was occasional prophets in a time of greatest institutional darkness, when 'Satan was loosed'. The theory that Satan was loosed in the period 1360 to 1533 has of course rather waned since the sixteenth century, but it seems to me that Middle English and Renaissance or early modern studies still operate within disablingly strict periodic divisions, according to which the 'medieval period' continues to figure all that is other to modernity.[32]

In this book I avoid treating any of the following as self-evident periodic categories: the 'Middle Ages', the 'Renaissance', the 'early modern period', the 'Reformation'. Rather than treating historical periods as self-enclosed, self-explanatory, and petrified in their oppositions one to the other, I consider each of these categories as historically determined. Thus the temporal limits of this book extend across one of the most entrenched divisions of cultural history, of the 'Reformation' and 'Renaissance' of the 1530s. The book does, in its course, reinstate periodic divisions, according to which 'medieval'

[30] Some studies on distinct areas have made an excellent beginning. See esp. A. Johnston; Ruggiers (ed.); Edwards, 'Some Observations'; and Patterson, 'Historical Criticism and Development of Chaucer'. See also D. Matthews, and C. Brewer.

[31] For the beginnings of Old English studies, see C. E. Wright, 'Dispersal of the Monastic Libraries and Beginnings'.

[32] For a powerful critique of the treatment by early modernists of the 'medieval', see Aers, 'Whisper'. See also Patterson, 'On the Margin'. Of course strict periodization is not confined to medieval or Renaissance studies: the Hegelian model of *Geistesgeschichte*, with its roots in Vico and Herder, and its offspring in Foucault, remains the dominant form of cultural history.

literature is characteristically 'reformist', as distinct from the revolutionary qualities of much Tudor writing. The characteristics of a 'reformist' versus a 'revolutionary' literary culture will, indeed, be the central theme of the entire book.

Neither do I treat 'Reformation' and 'Renaissance' as in any way coherent categories. On the contrary, I detect readily visible and profound differences between secular and religious traditions of writing across the two centuries 1350–1550. Traditions of civic humanism and religious reform are readily detectable in English writing in the period from 1350; some of these are continuous with developments post-1530, while others are blocked or narrowed by the political and cultural pressures of the early sixteenth century. I am not attempting to recite the forward march of humanism and Protestantism; on the contrary, one of the central and consistent themes of the book that follows is that the discursive forms of both humanist and Christian reformist writing are significantly more liberal in the earlier part of the period than the later: both sixteenth-century classically inspired civic humanism and Protestantism were, on the whole, much more absolutist, much more consistently in favour of royal supremacy, than anything we find earlier in the period. Both cultural strands in the sixteenth century testified to the centralizing of power, both of Tudor kings and of the Protestant God, and both traditions were governed by the magnetic field of that single and supreme power. The force of that magnetism was all the greater in England precisely because central secular and religious institutions were unified. This book contributes to the history of liberties. The story it tells is, however, by no means one of progressive acquisition of discursive space in opposition to central power, but rather the reverse.

2

The Energies of John Lydgate

In 1549 the Duke of Somerset, then Lord Protector during the minority of Edward VI, destroyed buildings in different parts of London in order to produce materials for the construction of his own palace, Somerset House. He chose a site on the Strand, and pulled down both a parish church and the inns of the bishops of Chester and Worcester, making 'levell ground'.[1] The destroyed buildings produced insufficient materials, whereupon the Duke attempted to pull down the parish church of St Margaret in Westminster. The demolition gang, however, fled when the parishioners arrived to protect their church, armed with 'bows and arrows, staves and clubs'.[2] The priory church of St John, outside the walls, proved more vulnerable, and, in the words of the sixteenth-century antiquary John Stow,

> the Church for the most part, to wit the body and side Iles with the great bell tower (a most curious peece of workemanshippe, graven guilt, and inameled to the great beautifying of the Cittie, and passing all other that I have seene), was undermined and blowne up with gunpowder, the stone thereof was imployed in building of the Lord Protectors house at the Strand.[3]

The other building destroyed by Somerset was, again according to Stow, 'one great cloyster on the north side' of St Paul's:

[1] Stow, 2. 93. For Stow's conservative interests in writing the survey, see H. Baron.

[2] Cited from the account of the attempted demolition by Heylyn, pp. 72–3. Heylyn's account of the demolition largely corresponds with Stow's. Heylyn, who was a Laudian apologist, 'was the first writer who has attempted to estimate the losses as well as the gains of the religious convulsion of the sixteenth century' (*DNB* 9. 774). Even Somerset's supporters were shocked by the demolition; see Brigden, *London*, pp. 473–4.

[3] Stow, 2. 84–5.

About this cloyster, was artificially and richly painted the dance of Machabray, or dance of death, commonly called the dance of Pauls: the like whereof was painted about S. Innocents cloyster at Paris in France: the meters or poesie of this dance were translated out of French into English by Iohn Lidgate, Monke of Bury, the picture of death leading all estates, at the dispence of Ienken Carpenter, in the raigne of Henry the sixt.[4]

There was also an elaborately decorated chapel in the cloister. Stow again: 'In the yeare 1549, on the tenth of Aprill, the sayd Chappell, by commaundement of the Duke of Sommerset, was begun to bee pulled downe, with the whole cloystrie, the daunce of death, the Tombes and Monuments: so that nothing thereof was left but the bare plot of ground.'[5] More than a thousand cartloads of bones had earlier in the same year been taken from the burial site and dumped in unhallowed ground outside the city.[6]

The Duke of Somerset's home-making plans conform to one pattern of change deep-set into cultural history, whereby the new order generates powerful hostilities to the *ancien régime*, at the same time as it draws on the materials of the old order to construct the new. There are, of course, many models for historical transition, but they all, in my view, fall into two basic categories: one kind of historical transition aims to destroy and efface the immediate past, while another recognizes historicity. I call the first the revolutionary model, and the second the reformist model. The revolutionary model obsessively advertises its own novelty, and operates within strictly defined and contrasted periodic schemata. The second, instead, highlights continuities across historical rupture. Each deals differently with artefacts and buildings of the past: the revolutionary model works by iconoclasm and demolition, while the reformist model operates by accretive *bricolage*. Each has a different sense of history's heroes: for the revolutionary model, heroes are wholly uncharacteristic of the repudiated past, standing out as freakish beacons in the general darkness surrounding them. The reformist model, on the other hand, recognizes that heroes emerge from within the dynamic of history. In rhetorical terms, the characteristic trope of the revolutionary model is antithesis, while the reformist model deploys *translatio* (i.e. metaphor), or simile. Thus some instances of the reformist model use

[4] Ibid. I. 327. [5] Ibid. 328. [6] Ibid. 293.

typological metaphor to account for historical change, by recognizing the historical reality of the old order, as they simultaneously posit the force of change, reform, and futurity within that order.[7] Other instances of the reformist model deploy similistic exemplarism, by drawing freely from the whole past (not just 'enlightened' segments of it) for models by which the present might measure and govern itself. The reformist model recognizes that the old order *is*, either by identity or likeness, the future, and so reformists posit continuities between the past and its future.

There can be no doubt but that the Duke's practice, conducted within a triumphalist Protestant regime, conforms to the revolutionary model of historical transition. The very act of unearthing the dead, and dumping a thousand cartloads of their bones on unhallowed ground, itself marked a sharp break with the system by which the community of the living negotiated for the community of the dead. As we saw in Chapter 1, chantries, along with a range of other popular religious and social institutions, were abolished by Henry VIII in 1545, in an Act that was restated and embellished in Edwardian form in 1547: 'Chantries, Hospitalles, Fraternityes and Brotherheddes' are to be suppressed, since they have come to represent 'superstition and Errors', 'by devising and phantasinge vayne opynions of Purgatorye and Masses satisfactorye to be done for them which be departed'.[8] The aggressively hostile royal invasion of popular institutions and custom was matched by the territorial invasion and destruction of a variety of institutional buildings.

The Duke's freedom to reshape history was made possible, of course, by a new, if unstable, concentration of political power: only the parishioners of St Margaret's in Westminster had the resources to resist him, by force, whereas the Dean and Chapter of St Paul's had no power to complain, because a recent Act had reduced them to the status of the King's tenants.[9] No one could defend the priory of St

[7] By 'typological metaphor', I refer to the interpretative practice of seeing metaphorical correspondences between Old Testament events (e.g. the sacrifice of Isaac) and Christ.

[8] *SR*, 1 Edward VI, ch. 14, art. 1 (4/1. 24). (The Edwardian statute restates and embellishes Henry's statute of 1545: *SR*, 37 Henry VIII, ch. 4 (3. 988–93).)

[9] Heylyn (p. 73) makes the point about the Dean and Chapter's change of status; Heylyn's reference is to the Act of Supremacy of 1534, *SR*, 26 Henry VIII, chs. 1–3 (3. 492–9).

John, since the order to which it had belonged had been suppressed, and its property taken into the King's hands, in 1541.[10] The massive institutional *simplification* of English society that occurred in the 1530s made both possible and necessary a powerfully aggressive ideological and physical attack on the human and material institutions of the recent past.

In this chapter I take the occasion of Somerset's destruction of the cloister containing Lydgate's *Dance Machabré* for two distinct sets of reflections. In the first place, we might look to this moment as in some ways exemplary of the treatment of Lydgate's poetry more generally, from the 1530s to the present day. With one exception, I do not of course suggest that scholars have wished to destroy Lydgate's corpus, even though our knowledge of much of this work is conditioned by the manner of its survival from destruction: the same John Stow who recorded London's past was, for example, also responsible for annotating, collecting, copying, and publishing much of Lydgate's poetry.[11] While most scholars stop well short of the one extreme, later instance of wishing Lydgate's corpus destroyed, scholarship has, nevertheless, continued to work within powerfully periodic conceptions of cultural change, according to which the end point of scholarly attention is to reaffirm and reify 'the medieval'. For reasons we will look to in a moment, Lydgate is a critical figure in the economy by which Middle English literature is placed and received as 'medieval' in cultural history. Precisely because of this, to historicize Lydgate is equally to open up a new perspective on the entire history of Middle English writing, a perspective from which the remainder of this book will be written.

In the second set of reflections, I turn to the *Dance Machabré* itself, and beyond it to Lydgate's oeuvre more generally. For there we find a body of poetry pretty consistently concerned with historical

[10] *SR*, 32 Henry VIII, ch. 24 (3. 778–81).

[11] For a succinct summary and a further contribution to the evidence of Stow's concern with Lydgate, see Edwards and Miller. For Stow as a literary antiquary and editor, with especial regard to Chaucer, see Hudson, 'John Stow', pp. 55–6 and 57 for references to Stow and Lydgate. Stow's house was subject to an official raid in 1569 in search of papistical books; in addition to forbidden literature, Stow was found to possess 'a great store of folishe fabulous bokes of olde prynte as of Sir Degory, Triamour', along with 'old phantasticall popishe bokes prynted in the olde tyme, with many such also written in olde Englisshe on parchement'. Cited from Stow, vol. 1, pp. xvi–xvii.

mapping, and consistently working within a variety of reformist textual practices. Whereas the iconoclastic regime of the mid-sixteenth century caricatured the later medieval centuries as monolithic, the institutional and cultural reality was in fact much more heterogeneous. Precisely because power was decentralized and dispersed across a series of institutions in the fourteenth and fifteenth centuries, any single perspective that claimed the past for itself was impossible. The fundamental condition of a reformist cultural practice is the complexity of adjacent, competing institutions, each of which produces its own accounts of the past. This was precisely the institutional environment within which Lydgate worked. More than any other Middle English poet, Lydgate is a thoroughly public writer, the map of whose writing equally maps many of the institutional discourses of non-university, literate fifteenth-century England. The massive concentration of political and religious power in the first half of the sixteenth century activated the aggressive historical imagination of sixteenth-century antiquaries and propagandists. Correlatively, the much more decentred discursive and institutional world of fourteenth- and fifteenth-century writers produced, by contrast, a reformist imagination.

I

In Chapter 1, I argued that the 1530s and 1540s witnessed the beginning of Middle English 'literary' studies, in the heroic bibliographical work of John Leland and John Bale. For the first time in English historiography did it become possible to view Britain from a single perspective, and equally to separate off, and therefore construct, the recent past with crystal clarity.[12] Leland the civic humanist and Bale the radical Protestant shared very little but their hostility to the superstitious and barbarous past and their championing of the brilliant, new present. They had almost entirely different interests in the present, but they joined forces to present the ostensibly coherent face of a wholly new modernity. One aspect of their chiaroscuro representation of historical periods was their desire to isolate forerunners

[12] For the decentred production of historiography in the 14th cent., see John Taylor.

of the brilliant future back in the benighted past. These forerunners were represented as freakish exceptions to the rule of incivility or superstition by which they had been surrounded. On the whole, Bale's heroes were entirely different from Leland's, since Bale wanted to create a specifically Protestant cultural tradition, while Leland trained his eye to elucidate a sequence of largely historiographical figures who could be pressed into royal service. When, however, the figure was insignificant for the purposes of religious polemic, Bale was unusually generous; his treatment of Lydgate in his *Catalogus* (published 1557–9) exemplifies this generosity, while at the same time erecting some of the frames for Lydgate's reception up to the present day.

Lydgate did not appear in Leland's *De viris illustribus*, but Bale praises him as the premier poet of his time. He creates for Lydgate a (wholly spurious) humanist's progress, including study periods in Padua and Paris, and a post as tutor to noble children; Lydgate, he says, sought to fill for the English the role that Dante and Alain Chartier had already played for their peoples. He recognizes both Lydgate's metrical variety and wide learning, and says that 'after Chaucer he was certainly the greatest "*illustrator*" of the English language'. The greatest wonder for Bale is whence Lydgate managed to gain so much eloquence and erudition in 'so primitive an age' ('in aetate tam rudi').[13] Certainly the praise of Lydgate has not survived, but two aspects of Bale's placing of him have: first, Lydgate cannot be spoken of without reference to Chaucer, and secondly, he writes in a culturally impoverished age. It is also significant that Bale underplayed Lydgate's monastic profession, stressing instead his humanistic achievement as 'artium omnium scientissimus' ('deeply learned in all branches of knowledge').

Bale's work, demonstrably the product of long labours, was published in the late 1550s, at the end of twenty of the most active years for Lydgate publication (an activity not to be repeated until the years between 1882 and 1935).[14] England's (and Scotland's) earliest

[13] Bale, *Scriptorum . . . catalogus*, p. 586.

[14] These years mark a massive publication of Lydgate material, mostly by the EETS, mostly by German scholars in the ES. It is thanks to the EETS's catholic policy that we are in a position to measure Lydgate's real stature, since the following works by Lydgate were published in these years: *Temple of Glas*; *Reason and Sensuality*; *Troy Book*; *Minor Poems* (2 pts.); *Siege of Thebes*; *Fall of Princes*; *The Two Nightin-*

printers had produced a huge amount of Lydgatian material, both secular and religious, from Caxton in the late 1470s until Pynson in the 1520s.[15] From the 1530s to the 1550s the Lydgate industry continued to flourish, with the publication of the following works: *The payne and sorowe of euyll maryage* (1530);[16] *The Life of Our Lady* (1531);[17] *The Complaint of a Lover's Life* (?1531);[18] *The Life of Saint Alban* (at the instigation of the monks of St Alban's in 1534);[19] *The Serpent of Division* (1535 and 1559);[20] *Stans Puer* (before 1540);[21] *The Churl and the Bird* (?1550);[22] the huge *Fall of Princes* (twice in 1554);[23] and the *Troy Book* (1555).[24]

In the pattern of this voluminous printing activity, we can already see one aspect of the closing down of Lydgate's fortunes, since there were no independent religious works printed after 1534, which was also, not coincidentally, the date of the Act of Supremacy. In the ambience of this publication, we can also observe a further pressure

gale Poems; *Serpent of Division*; *Secrees of Old Philosophres*; *Pilgrimage of the Life of Man*. In addition, the following works were published by German presses: *SS. Albon and Amphabal*, ed. Horstmann; *Isopes Fabules*, ed. Sauerstein; *The Complaint of the Black Knight*, ed. Krausser; *Fabula Duorum Mercatorum*, ed. Zupitza; *Lydgate's Horse, Goose and Sheep*, ed. Degenhart, and the *Dietary*, ed. Förster, 'Kleinere Mittelenglische Texte'. The full history of the foundational German contribution to Middle English studies has yet to be written.

[15] *The Chorle and the Birde*: Caxton, ?1477 (*RSTC* 17008); Pynson, 1493 (*RSTC* 17010); and de Worde, ?1497 (*RSTC* 17011), 1510 (*RSTC* 17012); *Stans Puer*: Caxton, 1477 (*RSTC* 17030); and de Worde, 1510 (*RSTC* 17030.5), 1520 (*RSTC* 17030.7); *Horse and Goose*: Caxton, ?1477, twice (*RSTC* 17018 and 17019); and de Worde, 1495 (*RSTC* 17020), 1499 (*RSTC* 17021), 1500 (*RSTC* 17022); *Temple of Glas:* Caxton, 1497 (*RSTC* 17032); de Worde, 1495 (*RSTC* 17032a), 1500 (*RSTC* 17033), 1506 (*RSTC* 17033.7); Pynson, 1503 (*RSTC* 17033.3); and Berthelet, ?1529 (*RSTC* 17034); *Pilgrimage of the Soule*: Caxton, 1483 (*RSTC* 6473); *Life of Our Lady*: Caxton, 1484, twice (*RSTC* 17023, 17024); *Fall of Princes*: Pynson, 1494 (*RSTC* 3175), 1527 (*RSTC* 3176); *Siege of Thebes*: de Worde, 1497 (*RSTC* 17031); *Virtues of the Mass*: de Worde, 1500 (*RSTC* 17037.5), 1520 (*RSTC* 17038); *Complaint of the Black Knight*: Chepman and Myllar, 1508 (*RSTC* 17014.3); *Secreta Secretorum*: Pynson, 1511 (*RSTC* 17017); *Troy Book*: Pynson, 1513 (*RSTC* 5579); *Testament*: Pynson, 1520 (*RSTC* 17035); see further Blake, 'John Lydgate'.

[16] de Worde (*RSTC* 19119).

[17] Redman (*RSTC* 17025).

[18] de Worde (*RSTC* 17014.7).

[19] Herford (*RSTC* 256).

[20] Redman (*RSTC* 17027.5); Rogers (*RSTC* 17028).

[21] Redman (*RSTC* 17030.9).

[22] Mychel (*RSTC* 17013).

[23] Tottel (*RSTC* 3177); Wayland, twice (*RSTC* 3177.5, 3178).

[24] Marsh (*RSTC* 5580).

on Lydgate's standing. Even before the death of Henry VIII Chaucer had been isolated as the official Tudor representative. An Act of 1542, for example, banned Tyndale's Bible, along with 'all other bookes and wrytinges in the English tongue . . . contrarye to that doctrine [established] sithens the yere of our Lorde 1540'; all these 'shalbe . . . clerlie and utterly abolished, extinguished and forbidden to be kepte or used'. As the Act proceeds, its extraordinary ambition becomes clear, attempting as it does to restructure the entire discursive history of English writing. The following, for example, are excepted from the ban: the King's 'proclamations, injunctions, translations of the Pater Noster, Ave Maria, and Crede, psalters, primers, prayers, statutes and lawes of the Realme, Cronicles, Canterburye tales, Chaucers bokes, Gowers bokes and stories of mennes lieves': all are excepted unless, the Act takes care to point out, the King should change his mind.[25] Lydgate, who had routinely been placed in a triumvirate of founding English authors with Chaucer and Gower throughout the fifteenth century,[26] was here omitted from a much more restricted version of the pre-Reformation official literary canon. This official version of the literary past was endorsed by the increasingly anti-papal version of Chaucer presented by Thynne's edition of Chaucer, first published in 1532, without the spurious and virulently anti-papal *Ploughman's Tale*. In the 1542 reprint the *Ploughman's Tale* is added, though remaining outside the *Tales*. By the time of the ?1550 reprint, it had been incorporated within the *Tales*, just before the *Parson's Tale*.[27]

Chaucer had, then, been rendered thoroughly Protestant by 1550,[28] and by 1570 his Protestantism was a confirmed fact, as presented in Foxe's enduringly influential *Acts and Monuments* (second

[25] *SR*, 34 Henry VIII, ch. 1. 1 (3. 895). I have punctuated the text.

[26] For Lydgate's position in this triumvirate, see D. Brewer (ed.), *Chaucer: The Critical Heritage*, esp. 1. 68 (Ashby); 81 (Dunbar); 82 (Hawes, where Lydgate is preferred as a model to Chaucer); and 85 (Skelton). See also Stephen Hawes, *Comfort of Lovers*, ll. 15–28 (p. 93).

[27] For the history of Thynne's inclusion of the *Ploughman's Tale* in the *Canterbury Tales*, see Hudson, 'John Stow', p. 59.

[28] Publishers were quick to attribute proto-Protestant works to Chaucer in separate editions: see *Jack uplande complyled by the famous G. Chaucer* (J. Nicholson, 1536), *RSTC* 5098; *The Ploughman's Tale* (T. Godfray, 1535), *RSTC* 5099.5; and *The Plouumans tale compylled by syr G. Chaucher [sic] knyght* (W. Hyll, 1548), *RSTC* 5100.

edition): here Chaucer and Gower were revealingly taken out of historical sequence, and placed on the very boundary of the Reformation, adjacent to Luther. Chaucer, according to Foxe, 'saw into religion as much as even we do now, and uttereth in his works no less, and seemeth to be a right Wicklevian'.[29] By this time even Lydgate's secular works needed to be smuggled through under the aegis of Chaucer: in Stow's 1561 edition of Chaucer, for example, Lydgate's *Destruction of Thebes* appeared tacked on to the end of the *Canterbury Tales*.[30] The other main channel for the survival of Lydgate's reputation as a secular poet was in versions of the *Mirror for Magistrates*, where the model provided by Lydgate in the *Fall of Princes* was taken over and adapted to more contemporary figures. Wayland's *Fall of Princes* edition of 1554, for example (replete with royal insignia on the title-page), was designed to have the *Mirror* added as Part II, before that part of the edition was suppressed.[31]

So much publication of Lydgate material between the late 1470s and the 1550s clearly implies that the closing down of his reputation was less a matter of changing tastes and more a matter of political injunction and cultural imperative. If we refer for a moment back to our point of departure, the *Dance Machabré*, there is no doubt of its forcefulness in the sixteenth century. Not only was it printed at the end of Tottel's edition of 1554, but Sir Thomas More also refers to the psychological power of 'The Dance of death pictured on Pawles'.[32] Apart from the minimally religious *Dance*, however, Lydgate's religious verse disappeared altogether from the presses after 1534, and the secular verse now struggled against a stark periodization of pre- and post-Reformation English culture. Already in Robert Braham's preface to the 1555 edition of the *Troy Book*, Pynson's 1513 edition is described as having been printed 'in the tayle . . . of the dercke and unlearned times'.[33]

[29] Foxe, 4. 248–50.The interpolation does not appear in the 1st edn. (1563). Foxe also printed *Jack Upland* as definite proof of Chaucer's Protestant convictions. For this, and the ongoing reception of Chaucer as Protestant, see Georgianna.

[30] *RSTC* 5075. The text I call the *Destruction of Thebes* is customarily called the *Siege of Thebes*; I argue for the change of title in Simpson, '"Dysemol daies"', p. 15 n. 1.

[31] See W. A. Jackson, and, further, Edwards, 'Influence of Lydgate's *Fall of Princes*'.

[32] Cited from *The Dance of Death*, ed. Warren, p. xxiv.

[33] Braham's preface is reproduced in Lydgate, *Troy Book*, ed. Bergen, 4. 60–5.

One central aspect of this starkly contrastive periodization was the official cultivation of Chaucer as the primary poet, and almost the *sole* poet, of pre-Reformation England. In Sir Brian Tuke's preface to Thynne's 1532 edition of Chaucer, Chaucer is presented as an unnaturally gifted figure in the context of his barbarous period:

> It is moche to be marveyled howe in his tyme whan doutlesse all good letters were layde a slepe thoughout the worlde . . . [that] suche an excellent poete in our tonge shulde as it were (*nature repugnyng*) sprynge and aryse.[34]

Braham's preface of 1555, to which I have just referred, repeats the same ideas, and can praise Lydgate only as a reflex of Chaucer. Lydgate is 'the verye perfect disciple and imitator of the great Chaucer, the onelye glorye and beauty of [our tunge]' (p. 63). Braham effectively eclipses his ostensible subject Lydgate with Chaucer, as the only object worthy of his attention:

> . . . as it hapned the same Chaucer [lost] the prayse of that tyme wherin he wrote beyng then when in dede al good letters were almost aslepe, so farre was the grossenesse and barbarousenesse of that age from the vnderstandinge of so devyne a writer. (p. 63)

Not only, by this account, did no other writers manage to write as Chaucer (a point to be reformulated many times in the twentieth century), but even Chaucer's own readers are pictured as incapable of understanding him (another point with a long future ahead of it).

Co-ordinates of the kind established by Tuke, Braham, and Bale define the area within which discussion of Lydgate is conducted, from the revival of interest in medieval studies in the late eighteenth century until and including our own time. The logic of strict periodization (medieval versus Renaissance) determines the need for an exception to prove the rule. This unnatural exception is invariably Chaucer, who is consistently dragooned as a forerunner of the forces of whatever new ideological order takes control of the field of literary studies. Lydgate is doomed to imitate Chaucer, but equally doomed to fail in the attempt.

The logic of periodization has, if anything, grown stronger, and if

[34] Cited from Blodgett, p. 35; my emphasis.

Chaucer is unnaturally exceptional, Lydgate, as his closest competitor, becomes representative of the medieval, or, in the words of William Webbe's essay of 1586, 'superstitious and odde matters then . . . requesite in so good a wytte'.[35] With the renewal of Middle English studies in the late eighteenth century, the damning logic of periodization is most obvious in the Jacobin Ritson's ferocious anticlerical attack on Lydgate, published in 1802, as a 'voluminous, prosaick, and drivelling monk'; he wrote 'stupid and fatiguing productions'; he 'disgraces the name and patronage of his master Chaucer', and his works should be consigned to 'base and servile uses'.[36] The periodic placing of Lydgate was also, however, characteristic of much more sympathetic late eighteenth-century critics, such as Thomas Gray and Thomas Warton.[37] Warton's actual discussion of Lydgate's works is well informed and fresh; by way of introduction, however, he recycles clichés that are already 250 years old: after the spring of Chaucer, he says, we expect summer, but 'winter returns with redoubled horrors . . . Most of the poets that immediately succeeded Chaucer, seem rather relapsing into barbarism, than availing themselves of those striking ornaments which his judgment [*sic*] and imagination had disclosed'.[38]

The clichés are now 450 years old, but criticism still repeats them, caught as it is in the disabling logic of periodization. One reason for this may be sloth; Lydgate did, after all, write about 145,000 lines. Cultural history as a history of sloth and inertia is certainly possible —it is much easier to dismiss Lydgate as unreadable than to come to grips with such a vast oeuvre. Another reason, however, is the place Lydgate consistently occupies in narratives of the movement from medieval to Renaissance. By the logic of the medieval and Renaissance divide, Lydgate above all is invested with an extraordinarily powerful periodic representativeness: not only is Lydgate himself

[35] Webbe, *Discourse of English Poetrie* (1586), 1. 242.

[36] For Ritson's admiration for the French Revolution, and his adoption of the Republican calendar, see the entry in *DNB*.

[37] Thomas Gray's discussion of Lydgate ('Some Remarks on the Poems of Lydgate', (*c.*1760) is in fact almost wholly a discussion of the *Fall of Princes*, and is extremely warm in praise of Lydgate. While Lydgate lacks the 'certain terrible greatness' of Chaucer, 'yet is there frequently a stiller kind of majesty both in his thought and expression, which makes one of his principal beauties'. Cited from Thomas Gray, *Works*, ed. Mitford, 5. 308–9.

[38] Warton, 2. 51.

dull-witted, but his dull wits become the flagship for a dull and very medieval fifteenth century.

The Duke of Somerset's demolition of a 'superstitious' monument neatly coincides with one aspect of Johan Huizinga's account of the Burgundian fifteenth century (first published in 1919). Huizinga, the most influential cultural historian of the later Middle Ages in the twentieth century, described the whole period as one of autumnal 'waning', where the vegetative metaphor often gives way to a narrative of putrefaction. The dance of death lies near the heart of Huizinga's periodic description: 'Towards 1400 the conception of death in art and literature took a spectral and fantastic shape. A new and vivid shudder was added to the great primitive horror of death.'[39] The churchyard of the Holy Innocents in Paris, the model for Lydgate's version, represents the heart of this horror: 'There', says Huizinga, 'the medieval soul, fond of a religious shudder, could take its fill of the horrible.'[40] This cult of the bizarre and morbid encapsulates Huizinga's account of a pathological, manic-depressive age.

Twentieth-century critics of Lydgate are, of course, more measured in their account of fifteenth-century culture than Huizinga.[41] As with Huizinga, however (and as with sixteenth-century scholars), they continue to work within very strictly defined periodic boundaries. And, in the logic of the study of Middle English writing, Lydgate is invariably invested with a powerful, medieval representativeness, beside the great exception of Chaucer. In what remains of this section, I turn to three powerful critics to see this logic in action. Twentieth-century discussion of the fifteenth century, and of Lydgate in particular, worked within a strictly periodic, or *geistesgeschichtlich* conception, whereby fifteenth-century literature was useful precisely by way of manifesting the 'medieval' norm. The massive scale of work devoted to Chaucer in that century did nothing whatsoever to render the medieval–early modern divide more supple. On the contrary, Chaucer served as the prophet of the new

[39] Huizinga, *Waning of the Middle Ages*, pp. 139–40. For an extended critique of Huizinga's view and his followers, see Page, ch. 5. See also Huizinga's own penetrating critique of the 'Renaissance' as a historiographical concept: 'Problem of the Renaissance' (1st pub. 1920).

[40] Huizinga, *Waning of the Middle Ages*, p. 143.

[41] Pearsall critiques Huizinga's view in his article ('Signs of Life').

age, however that age was figured.The truth of this can be gauged from the ways in which later twentieth-century criticism of Chaucer, or of fifteenth-century poetry, was concerned on the one hand to claim Chaucer's unique status and, with equal passion, to clear a massive space around Chaucer by claiming that none of his fifteenth-century followers understood his poetic enterprise. As is characteristic of strictly periodic thinking, the discussion of other, 'medieval' writers, and especially of Lydgate, was generated by saying that they were *not* like Chaucer, and that in their unlikeness they conform to their age. Where Chaucer is a 'Renaissance' poet, his fifteenth-century imitators are irredeemably 'medieval'.

Twentieth-century Anglo-American reception of Lydgate characteristically set him up against a prescient Chaucer, by way of dismissing him as an unthinking, 'medieval' reactionary. The most powerful of these works is Derek Pearsall's *John Lydgate* (1970), a seductively written book whose great value easily survives its consistently periodic convictions.[42] Those convictions are, however, in no way incidental to the book's entire argument. The theme is announced early on:

> The coherence of his [Lydgate's] work as a whole is to be found, not in terms of its relation to his inner self or to any concept of the self-realizing individual consciousness, but in terms of its relation to the total structure of the medieval world, that is, the world of universally received values, traditions, attitudes, as well as, or more significantly than, the world of 'real life' (pp. 5–6).

The implied point of studying Lydgate becomes, then, discovery of the medieval world, a point explicated in the book's peroration, where Lydgate is said to be a 'type of the Middle Ages', 'impregnably medieval', an ideal 'introduction to medieval literature, presenting its themes and methods in their basic form, without the complications of experiment, ambiguity, or even, sometimes, of individual thought' (pp. 298–9). This might suggest that 'medieval' literature is capable of initiative, but Pearsall consistently implies not only that

[42] Further references to this book will be made by page number in the body of the text. Pearsall's views are consistently maintained across twenty or more years; see Pearsall, 'Chaucer and Lydgate', and 'Lydgate as Innovator' ('My argument has always been that Lydgate's importance and his claim on our attention is his representative and noninnovatory medievalness', p. 5).

Lydgate is 'impregnably medieval', but also that the word 'medieval' is itself shorthand for a culture almost incapable of 'experiment, ambiguity, or even . . . individual thought'. Thus it is stated that Lydgate is 'prolific, prolix and dull' (shades of Ritson), but that these features are valuable precisely insofar as Lydgate is 'perfectly representative of the Middle Ages. In him we can see, at great length, and in slow motion, the medieval mind at its characteristic work' (p. 14). If Huizinga's late medieval type is frenetically active, Pearsall's is a plodding dullard. Again, in the *Troy Book*, what is described as Lydgate's ahistorical treatment of the story is characteristic of both the 'Middle Ages' and of Lydgate at the same time: Lydgate's moralizing additions 'are in a sense the body of the work, for it is through them that Lydgate makes sense in his own terms of a historical narrative which for the Middle Ages could make sense in no others' (p. 129). Lydgate, for Pearsall, *is* the Middle Ages.

The only signs of life in Lydgate are derived from Chaucer, whom Pearsall presents as 'not a very representative medieval poet' (p. 6). Lydgate is described as being enormously in Chaucer's debt (p. 49), and, at the same time, as incapable of imitating him; the attempt to follow Chaucer is, for the whole of the fifteenth century, 'to imitate the inimitable' (p. 68). Of course Pearsall discusses the many non-Chaucerian sources for Lydgate's poetry, but if Lydgate has any conscious idea of his place in a tradition, this is restricted, in Pearsall's narrative, to his attempt to imitate the inimitable Chaucer.

The second, equally powerful, equally impressive book that nevertheless generated its narrative out of an almost identical periodic logic is A. C. Spearing's *Medieval to Renaissance in English Poetry* (1985).[43] The introduction lays the cards very clearly on the table: admittedly generalizing, Spearing has it that 'medieval culture tends to take a somewhat low view of man, seeing the human condition as one of separation from its true source of value in God' (p. 2). He then reaffirms two standard views of the Renaissance: that it manifests a consciousness of poetry as 'a vocation, an autonomous sphere of human activity', and that it expresses 'a new sense of the historical distance and difference inherent in classical texts . . . together with a sense of the possibility of overcoming that distance and difference by

[43] Further references to this work will be made by page number in the body of the text.

creative imitation' (p. 6). After a chapter explicating the Renaissance qualities of Chaucer, Spearing turns to his fifteenth-century successors, first and notably Lydgate, about whom it is instantly said that the very existence of his long works is an indication of the way in which Lydgate 'is quite un-Chaucerian' (p. 66). This un-Chaucerian quality is not, however, the result of conscious choice by Lydgate; on the contrary, the following discussion of the *Siege of Thebes* underlines the difference as the product of failed imitative ambition. As with Pearsall, Spearing's Lydgate can only imitate Chaucer, but is forever doomed in the attempt: 'the more Lydgate imitates Chaucer, the less, in one sense, he can be like him' (p. 70).

This is clearly a no-win situation for Lydgate. The comparison of Lydgate's *Thebes* and the *Knight's Tale* insists on the hopelessness of Lydgate's predicament. Thus it is argued, for example, that the *Knight's Tale* can, with qualification, be thought of as a 'chivalric romance', while '*The Siege of Thebes*, despite the generally retrogressive, "medieval" nature of Lydgate's talent, cannot' (p. 84). This is because Lydgate, as a monk, is opposed to the 'very substance of romance'. Here, if we accepted Spearing's argument, we glimpse the possibility that Chaucer is, apparently, the more medieval of the two poets. Just as Lydgate is about to gain on Chaucer, however, the possibilities of this moment are quickly turned against him. His hostility to human aggressiveness provokes his frequent resort to 'Christian moralization of his narrative', which soon becomes 'un-Chaucerian', and then, almost as quickly, becomes exemplary of Lydgate's inability to 're-imagine a classical pagan culture in its own terms': 'It was precisely this achievement of the historical imagination, so surprising in an English poet of the fourteenth century, that Lydgate, like most of Chaucer's followers, was least able to grasp and develop' (p. 86).[44] The argument of these few pages, then, reaffirms the inexplicable singularity of Renaissance Chaucer contrasted with his irreducibly 'medieval' followers.

If the economy of this critical system needs one exception, it is equally true that it can tolerate *only* one. All challengers to the excep-

[44] Spearing's surprise that Chaucer was able to stand outside history has a long tradition behind it, going back as far, at least, as Tuke's (1532) 'nature repugnyng' remark cited above, and including Foxe's (1570) astonishing placement of Chaucer after Colet and before Luther, cited above.

tion, and Lydgate is the most powerful challenger, need to be rigorously excluded; for this reason, perhaps, Chaucer's fifteenth-century followers are figured as Oedipally incapable of matching the father figure: there 'seems to have been a widespread anxiety among his poetic descendants about the impossibility of the task they were undertaking' (p. 107). This last theme is elaborated in my third example, Seth Lerer's *Chaucer and his Readers* (1993), where 'Lydgate and the members of the Chaucer cult of the first decades of the fifteenth century' are again pictured as both mesmerized and incapacitated by Chaucer. Their

'myths of performance' . . . and the creation of the narrative personae who enact them, are a far cry from the sophistications of the *Troilus* narrator . . . Theirs is the voice of dullness and ineptitude, a voice conditioned by the literary system of a father Chaucer and his children and, moreover, by a patronage system of childish kings and ambitious magnates.[45]

Lerer's study is generated by the principle that we can only understand a poet historically, by recognizing the historical nature of our own predispositions. A study of Chaucer's *Nachleben* would seem ideally directed to that aim, but Lerer's study suffers from a paradox. Fifteenth-century Chaucerians have no serious role to play in our understanding of Chaucer, since they serve, in Lerer's reading, only as examples of childishly inadequate readings of Chaucer. The implication of Lerer's reading is that twentieth-century readers knew what Chaucer was really like, and that fifteenth-century readers had failed to grasp that. The fifteenth century effectively becomes, in this reading, a mini-Middle Ages, across whose darkness we look to the true model Chaucer. The result of this supposedly historicist reading is to leave Chaucer untroubled as history's big exception. Spearing and Lerer both argue that Chaucer's followers were overawed by Chaucer; it might equally be possible to argue that it is twentieth-century critics who were oversensitive to Chaucer, as they, like Foxe, tirelessly sought to place him outside history.[46]

Each of these studies of Lydgate, then, worked, explicitly or

[45] Lerer, *Chaucer and his Readers*, p. 23. Lerer's image of the medievals as children, or at least as exhibiting 'simpler' forms of life, has a long ancestry: see e.g. Warton, 1. A2r; Burckhardt, p. 143; Huizinga, *Waning of the Middle Ages*, p. 9.

[46] Lerer's subsequent book, *Courtly Letters*, completes the diptych of an obtuse 15th cent. that cannot grasp Chaucer, against a knowing 16th cent. that can.

implicitly, within clearly demarcated periodic divisions, according to which the medieval period was described in negative terms; Chaucer stood out as the astonishing exception, and Chaucer provided the standard by which to reaffirm the 'impregnably' medieval qualities of his followers. Chaucer's fifteenth-century followers were represented as massively dependent on, yet strangely ignorant of, the 'true' Chaucer; the more they tried to imitate him (and it is only Chaucer whom they attempted to imitate), the less they could be like him.

II

Now it is of course possible that these and very many lesser scholars are right. Prima facie, however, their case looks implausible to me, for the following reasons: it is in the first place premissed on the notion of a historical freak. Secondly, it presupposes that scholarship does itself have access to the true Chaucer, unlike Chaucer's 'dull' fifteenth-century imitators. Thirdly, it insists on Lydgate's total dependence on Chaucer when almost none of Lydgate's works is directly imitative of Chaucer: those poems that do relate to Chaucer's do so with more powerful strategies in mind than slavish imitation.[47] Finally, it paradoxically insists on Lydgate as retrogressive and reactionary even at the moment he is translating works, by Boccaccio, for example, that are hailed as examples of proto-humanism.

If, as I am suggesting, the motor of this consensus is the need to

[47] This is a huge topic in itself. The argument that Lydgate is primarily concerned to 'fortify . . . preliminary structures thrown up by Chaucer' is most succinctly put by Pearsall, 'Chaucer and Lydgate', p. 51; 'It could also be argued that Lydgate's career, poem by poem, is a determined effort to emulate and surpass Chaucer in each of the major poetic genres that Chaucer had attempted' (p. 47). See also Watson, 'On Outdoing Chaucer', which, while it warns against taking 15th-cent. professions of dullness at their face value, seems almost to collapse into precisely that position in its conclusion on Lydgate (pp. 100–1). One way to broach this problem is to reveal the intelligence of Lydgate's response to Chaucer; another is to measure the breadth and width of Lydgate's engagement with Continental and biblical poetry, which extends well beyond Chaucerian bounds. For an example of the first approach, see Simpson, '"Dysemol daies"'; of the second approach, see Ch. 3, below. For a persuasive argument that we should not take 15th-cent. professions of dullness at their word, see D. Lawton, 'Dullness and the Fifteenth Century'.

reaffirm the strictness of division between medieval and Renaissance or early modern, then the best way of testing it is to scrutinize that division. One way of doing this would be a diachronic investigation, designed to render more supple and historical the notion of humanism itself. Most Anglo-American critics have strenuously denied that Lydgate has anything of humanism. Late nineteenth- and earlier twentieth-century German scholarship, to which, incidentally, we owe most of our editions of Lydgate,[48] had, by contrast, argued that many works by Lydgate are indeed exemplary of proto-humanism.[49] Both positions, however, imply that sixteenth-century humanism was itself without a history in the centuries preceding the sixteenth.[50] This debate seems sterile to me, since it is perfectly clear that the traditions of secular, politically directed writing in which Lydgate worked had long histories behind them. *Reason and Sensuality* (?pre-1420)[51], the *Troy Book* (1412–20), and the *Destruction of Thebes* (1422–3), for example, each have graded cultural horizons,

[48] Late 19th-cent. German philology, much more advanced than its English counterpart, produced many of our key editions of Lydgate's works. For an account of scholarship, both editions and studies, from 1818 to 1951, see the list of scholarship, both editions and studies, by Schirmer, *John Lydgate*, app. 2. Between 1873 and the mid-1930s, this scholarship is predominantly German. For more complete bibliographical accounts of Lydgate, see Renoir and Benson; and Edwards, 'Lydgate Scholarship'.

[49] See esp. the powerful article by Brie; Brie's argument applies only to the *Fall of Princes*, and rigorously excludes the *Troy Book* and the *Destruction of Thebes* from the account of humanism, since, according to Brie, in these works 'die Antike rein vom mittelalterlich-ritterlichen Standpunkt aus gesehen ist' (p. 268). Brie's views are repeated in modified form in the excellent study by Schirmer, *John Lydgate*, p. 207. See also the arguments about the *Destruction of Thebes*, in Renoir, *Poetry*, ch. 8. The arguments of both Schirmer and Renoir are repudiated by Pearsall, 'Lydgate as Innovator', pp. 10–13.

[50] This is the view of the two standard works on 'early' English humanism; see Schirmer, *Der englische Frühhumanismus*; and Weiss. What these scholars mean by early 'humanism' in England is the scholarly and rhetorical practice initiated by Italian scholars who sought patronage in England throughout the 15th cent., and by the English scholars who studied in Italy in the 15th and early 16th cents. The epigraph to Weiss's study is a citation from Leland's 'Instauratio bonarum litterarum'; both Weiss and Schirmer follow closely, in their account of humanism, in the tracks first established by Leland and Bale.

[51] Some doubt about the attribution to Lydgate should be registered: Stow is the first person to attribute this work to Lydgate, in BL MS Additional 29729, a collection of Lydgate material copied by Stow in 1558 from a 15th-cent. MS. *Reason and Sensuality* is one of Stow's additions to the collection.

in which classical Rome and the humanism of the twelfth and thirteenth centuries figure prominently. The discursive space of these works and their sources are entirely secular; ethical values, in which prudence is at the centre, are given a wholly political definition; and the clerical, yet secular voice of these works offers that prudence, appropriately couched in persuasive rhetoric: rhetorical power and historical knowledge, that is, consciously minister to political need. By any broad definition of humanism, these works are not so much proto-humanist, as humanist.[52] Certainly in the *Fall of Princes* (1431–9), Lydgate comes into contact with newer versions of Italian humanism, but if that strand of his output looks forward to things to come, his *romans antiques* written up to 1423 Anglicize a long tradition of Latin and French humanist enterprise.

In what is left of this chapter, however, I do not propose to pursue that diachronic investigation. Instead, I return to the cloister of St Paul's for a synchronic look at Lydgate's oeuvre, by way of offering a perspective for the remainder of this book. Whereas Section 1 concentrated rather on destruction, here I focus instead on the reformist construction of that cloister. In particular, I will underline the jurisdictional complexity of the institutions within which Lydgate worked. All Lydgate's oeuvre manifests this discursive variety, both within and especially between works. So far from being monolithic, 'Lydgatian', or 'impregnably medieval', the corpus is riven by distinct, often exclusive, generic and discursive commitments. My larger argument is that this decentred discursive field disallows any single appropriation of the past. On the contrary, the pasts mapped by Lydgate form a heterogeneous set of traditions, and nourish a heterogeneous, competing set of institutions.

In his *History of English Poetry* (1774–81), Thomas Warton, one of Lydgate's best critics, described the *Fall of Princes* as a kind of drama: 'The work . . . is not merely a narrative of men eminent for their rank and misfortunes. The plan is perfectly dramatic, and partly suggested by the pageants of the times.'[53] Lydgate did indeed write 'pageants', or mummings, just as he wrote in detail and with great interest about the dramatic performances of the ancient theatre in

[52] For a broader definition of 'humanism' and the scholarly background to the term, see Simpson, *Sciences and the Self*, pp. 15–19.

[53] Warton, 2. 63.

the *Troy Book*.[54] Many of his poems, too, were effectively dramatic scripts, designed to accompany visual effects, either dramatic, painted, or carved.

The *Dance Machabré* is one such text, in which Death, as leader of the dance, addresses a representative of each order of society in turn. These typical figures respond, with varying degrees of non-enthusiasm, to Death's polite but teasing invitation. The whole text, apart from the '*Verba translatoris*' and '*auctoris*' that head and end it, is made up of dramatic encounters between Death and his dancing partners. The text gains its pungent and amusing effect not from any ghoulish horror, as Derek Pearsall has rightly argued, but rather from a sustained and unsettling, if amusing, social comedy.[55] The script works from the scenes of enjoyment and embarrassment found at any dance, and transforms each in its new context. Death mocks the Cardinal's timidity to join in: 'Ye ben abasshed hit semeth and yn drede | Sire Cardynal' (ll. 89–90); the Empress would rather not dance with this ugly but forward suitor: 'Lat se your hand my lady Empresse, | Have ye no disdeyn with me for to daunce' (ll. 65–6); the aristocratic King hesitates to join in so popular a dance: 'I haue not lerned here-a-forne to daunce | No daunce in sothe of fotynge so savage' (ll. 113–14); John Rikelle, 'some tyme tregetowre [conjurour] | Of noble harry kynge of Ingelonde' (ll. 516–17) cannot escape by tricks from this invitation: 'For dethe shortli nowther on see ne londe | Is not deceyved be noon illusiouns' (ll. 519–20). An enormous range of social types is addressed, in a descending hierarchical order: Pope, Emperor, Cardinal, Empress, King, Patriarch,

[54] Lydgate's mummings (Bishopswood, Eltham, Hertford, London, Windsor, Mercers, and Goldsmiths) are all edited in Lydgate: *The Minor Poems*, pt. 2, nos. 40–6 respectively. In an extended addition to his source for the *Troy Book*, Lydgate adds a detailed account of a classical theatrical performance (2. 842–926). There may be a close relationship between the mummings and the description, since, as Glynne Wickham argues, Lydgate is in fact describing the theatrical practice of his own day; see Wickham, *Early English Stages*, 1. 192–5. Lydgate certainly accentuates the tragic power of the theatre to show how kings can be overthrown, and also stresses the proximity of the tragic theatre to the palace of Priam (2. 943), both of which are relevant to the enterprise of the *Troy Book* itself. For an argument that Lydgate contributed to the composition of the N-Town Cycle of plays, see Gibson, 'Bury St Edmunds, Lydgate, and the N-Town Cycle'.

[55] See Pearsall, 'Signs of Life', and, for the more technical inventiveness of Lydgate's translation of this text, J. H. M. Taylor.

Constable, Archbishop, Baron, Lady 'of great estate', Bishop, Squire, Mayor, and right down the social scale to Parson, Labourer, Friar, Infant, and Hermit.

The lower we go, the more moving become the encounters: the Labourer, for example, in a life of 'grete trauaile', has 'wisshed after dethe ful ofte | Al-be that I wolde have fled hym nowe' (ll. 553–4); or the Infant's inarticulate cry is pitiful: 'A a a a worde I can not speke | I am so yonge I was bore yisterdai' (ll. 585–6). Generally, however, the figures of this poem are not powerless; on the contrary, its overall effect is derived precisely from the levelling of death, as each type articulates the sources of its own power in the face of death, before whom no resistance is possible. The shorthand image of society in this poem is one of a complex set of self-enclosed and overlapping jurisdictions, and in each case Death targets with an unerring eye the sources of comfort, ease, and power enjoyed by different occupational types. Jurisdictional fragility is most obvious in the case of legal figures, where legal terminology sparkles as Death's own powers of arrest extinguish it. Thus the Sergeant accuses Death of legal impropriety: 'How dare this dethe sette on me areste?' (l. 369); the Bailiff is bidden to come to a 'newe assise | Extorcions and wronges to redresse' (ll. 267–8). This neutralization of jurisdictional power is certainly most obvious in the legal figures, but almost each type is confronted by the evanescence of his or her claims to particular powers, jurisdictions, and authorities. Death underlines the vulnerability of military conquest, for example, telling the Prince that neither Charlemagne nor Arthur could resist death with 'ther platis ther armour or ther maile | Ther strong corage ther sheeldes defensable' (ll. 134–5). Likewise, Death's invitation to the Mayor plays on the notion of the freedom of the city, beyond feudal powers:

> Come forth sir Mayr which had governaunce
> Bi pollicie to rewle this cite
> Thouh your power were notable in substaunce
> To flee my daunce ye have no liberte
> Estate is noon nor worldly dygnyte
> That may escape out of my dangeris [jurisdictions]
> To fynde rescew exaumple ye may se
> Nouthir bi richesse nor force of officeres.
>
> (ll. 257–64)

In this short poem, then (672 lines in octave stanzas), Lydgate draws on two resonant metaphors of societal bonding (the dance and the procession) to undo society. The society pictured can only be undone, however, by a force as powerful as death, precisely because it is structured by so complex a set of adjacent, interdependent, and competing jurisdictions. The highest powers are international (Pope, Emperor, Cardinal, for example), but it is by no means the case that the intranational set of institutions, beginning with the King, derives authority in any simple, line-management style from the monarch. On the contrary, feudal, civic, and religious powers, themselves heavily subdivided, form a complex vertical and horizontal pattern of jurisdictions, which extend beyond the king. The only point where all vectors meet is, of course, Death itself. By the time Paul's churchyard is demolished in 1549, the structure of English society looks very different: the international roles of Pope, Emperor, and Cardinal have either been assumed by the King or abolished, while Abbot, Abbesse, Carthusian, Monk, and Friar Minor have all disappeared from the institutional structure of England. Short of Death, all vectors in 1549 meet at the point of the King, and there are fewer vectors in any case.

The society that produced a version of this poem on the walls of the Pardon churchyard was itself no less complex in tissue than the society the poem represents. For aristocrats, both male and female, for urban, mercantile communities, and for religious communities, both monastic and parochial, Lydgate produced texts that jointly form a heterogeneous collage of differently figured histories.[56]

Let us take our bearings into that career from 1426, when, most probably, Lydgate translated the *Dance Machabré* from a French text he found on the walls of Holy Innocents churchyard in Paris.[57] He was in Paris as an official poet for the English occupation of northern France, a fragile and doomed enterprise initially agreed in the Treaty of Troyes (May 1420). Lydgate's own king was the 4-year-

[56] For the best documented account of Lydgate's life, see Pearsall, *John Lydgate (1371–1449): Bio-Bibliography*.

[57] For the history of the Holy Innocents fresco, see Clark, ch. 3. In ch. 1 Clark considers scattered British examples; he does not mention the 'Dance of Pauls' hanging used in All Saints', Bristol, which was annually hung in the church from 1449 to 1450; see *Pre-Reformation Records of All Saints', Bristol*: Pt. I, ed. Burgess, index under 'Dance of Pauls'.

old Henry VI (Henry V had died in 1422), and the kingdom of England was divided in an uneasy balance between Henry V's two brothers, John Duke of Bedford (Regent in France) and Humphrey Duke of Gloucester (Protector in England while Bedford was in France). The fragility of the situation is evident in the most explicitly apologetic piece of Lydgate's career, *The Title and Pedigree of Henry VI*, translated from a French original under Richard Beauchamp, Earl of Warwick's patronage in 1426. Warwick was acting regent in France, while the Duke of Bedford was back in England trying to keep his brother and uncle (Cardinal Beaufort) from civil war.[58] In the period leading up to the occupation of Paris, Lydgate had prepared England's military rulers for the catastrophic fiasco that France turned out to be, by writing the histories of two fallen cities, Troy and Thebes. Both narratives trace a history of chivalric and bureaucratic disaster that stands urgently in need of prudential wisdom devoted to purely secular ends. The *Troy Book* had been commissioned by Henry V in 1412, and was completed by 1420. The dating of Lydgate's *Destruction of Thebes* is currently a matter of dispute, but in my view it was written *after* the death of Henry V, in 1423, precisely by way of warning of the dangers of civil war between Henry V's surviving brothers.[59]

The fact that these texts were written in English itself marked the arrival of English vernacular literary culture. Chaucer and Gower had chosen, very deliberately, to write in English, as distinct from French (a more obvious choice for secular literature), in the last three decades of the fourteenth century. They did so without, for the most part, obvious aristocratic patronage. At the same time, however, English gradually gained administrative credibility: in 1362 parliament acknowledged the right to use English instead of French and Latin, and from 1386 records of parliamentary debate were written in English. Only with the Lancastrian kings Henry IV (1399–1413) and Henry V, however, did English become a language for royal communication: the future Henry IV issued his challenge to the throne in English, and Henry V used English for official proclama-

[58] For an extendable account of the unsteadiness of this apparently triumphalist attempt to eulogize Henry VI as king of both France and England, see Patterson, 'Making Identities', pp. 92–3.

[59] For the date, see Simpson, '"Dysemol daies"', p. 16, n. 2.

tions for the first time in 1416, a year, significantly, after his victory against the French at Agincourt.[60] In precisely these years English literary manuscripts become deluxe objects, as we can see, for example, in Figures 2, 3, 4, and 5.[61]

In addition to these accounts of military disaster, Lydgate had also written other, amatory works for an aristocratic patronage, probably prior to the Parisian sojourn. Some of these are smaller complaints, written in the voice of a complaining lover, whether man or woman;[62] others, like the *Temple of Glas* (?1420), are more extended accounts of the trials of arranged aristocratic marriage, while another, the brilliant *Reason and Sensuality* (?pre-1420), is a philosophically informed, Ovidian elegy, which playfully explores the propensity of aristocratic love to revisit and repeat the catastrophes of history. This work was described by C. S. Lewis as 'one of the most beautiful and important pieces' produced between Chaucer and Spenser, but it has been wholly ignored since.[63] And after the Parisian period, Lydgate continued to write for aristocratic patrons: the massive *Fall of Princes* (1431–9) was written under the patronage of Humphrey Duke of Gloucester, appropriately since Humphrey's own spectacular and brutally sudden fall in 1447 fits neatly into the pattern of the work he had commissioned.

The relatively small and incidental *Dance*, then, was produced at the height of English power in France, after Lydgate had been deeply engaged with the Lancastrian regime, and just as deeply critical of the English military project for the previous fourteen years. The work, a kind of literary spoil from the great capital Paris, was produced under the aegis of powerful aristocratic patronage. In England itself the work was received, however, by a different set of institutions. Lydgate wrote many works for the London bourgeoisie, particularly after the Parisian period, from the late 1420s.

[60] For the idea of a Lancastrian 'language policy', see Fisher, 'Language Policy'.

[61] For the increased production and survival of literary MSS from the early 15th cent., see Edwards and Pearsall.

[62] Thus e.g. *Complaint of the Black Knight*, *The Flour of Courtesy*, *A Gentlewoman's Lament*, *A Lover's New Year's Gift*, in Lydgate, *Minor Poems*, pt. 2, nos. 3, 4, 5, and 7 respectively. To Lydgate is also attributed the *Complaint for My Lady of Gloucester and Holland* (ibid., no. 27), a remarkably powerful, beautiful, and frankly dangerous lament written on behalf of the Duke of Gloucester's abandoned wife Jacqueline of Hainault.

[63] Lewis, p. 277.

These include a royal entry for Henry VI, commissioned by the Lord Mayor on behalf of the City of London (1432),[64] and a series of mummings, or dramatic pieces, written for the Sheriffs of London, the London Mercers, and the Goldsmiths.[65] For the Goldsmiths he also produced a life of St George, to accompany 'the devyse of a steyned halle', for 'thonour of theyre brotherhoode and theyre feest of Saint George'; likewise, 'at the request of a werthy cityseyn of London', he wrote a lively dialogue of marital dispute, *Bycorne and Chychevache*.[66] For this society Lydgate may also have written his *Fabula Duorum Mercatorum*; the sophisticated animal fable *Debate of the Horse, Goose and Sheep* and the *Isopes Fabules*; and the courtesy book *Stans Puer*.[67]

It was this London society that deployed Lydgate's *Dance Machabré*. In 1430 the Town Clerk of London, John Carpenter, obtained a licence from the King to found a chantry for one chaplain in the chapel of the Virgin Mary on the north side of St Paul's.[68] Carpenter was the author of the *Liber Albus*, which records the customs and institutions of the City of London. According to Stow, as we have seen, he paid for Lydgate's poem to be painted, along with the fresco, on the cloister. Carpenter's enrichment was one of a number of largely civic benefactions of the area from the early fifteenth century. The cloister had first been renovated by one Thomas More, Dean of St Paul's in the reign of Henry V; a library had been built by one Walter Sherrington in the reign of Henry VI, 'well furnished with faire written bookes in Vellem'; at the north door of St Paul's the same benefactor had founded a chapel, just as there was a chapel on the north side of St Paul's, founded in 1400 in memory of Adam Berie, Alderman and Mayor of London in 1364. Along with the cloister and its chapel, all these benefactions were destroyed in the reign of Edward: of the library books, writes Stow, 'few of them now do remaine there'; the chapel on the north door was 'pulled downe'; and the chapel on the north side of the Cathedral was suppressed.[69] We often tend to forget that the period attacked by Tudor iconoclasts as 'superstitious' is not so much the 'Middle Ages' as a more

[64] *Minor Poems*, pt. 2, no. 32.
[65] Ibid., nos. 40, 45, and 46 respectively.
[66] Ibid., no. 11.
[67] Ibid., nos. 21, 23, 24, and 55 respectively.
[68] See T. Brewer, p. 29.
[69] Stow, I. 328.

specific period. Apart from its ecclesiastical and intellectual targets, the Tudor cultural revolution has in its destructive sights a culture of civic benefaction in England, dating especially from the mid-fourteenth century.

To call the *Dance Machabré* 'Lydgate's' is, then, itself a kind of shorthand. 'Lydgate' is more a point across which this poem traverses, in its path from Paris to London, from aristocratic to civic patronage, from French to English, from wall to text to wall. Lydgate's treatment of this work is in every sense a 'translation', or 'carrying across', since the work is, in this cultural ambience, wholly in transit. His translation of a work for the London bourgeoisie was, further, entirely in keeping with a much larger movement justifying translation of Latin and Continental vernacular material into English that had been gathering force from the last half of the fourteenth century.[70]

There was, of course, one further, grounding source of institutional authority Lydgate possessed, which derived from his clerical status as monk. The translation of the *Dance* may be made possible by aristocratic patronage, and its reception by civic society, but its voice, and its London architectural placing, were clerical. Before the *Dance*, Lydgate had already produced works in specifically clerical discourses for both aristocratic and clerical patrons. For the Dean of the Chapel Royal, for example, he had written an adaptation of Psalm 102, *Benedic anima mea* (1414–17), and for Henry V, the extraordinary and ambitious *Life of Our Lady*. In the Parisian period he also translated the *Pilgrimage of the Life of Man* for Thomas Montacute, Earl of Salisbury (1426); and after the Parisian period, he translated ambitious lives of both St Edmund (1433–4) and St Alban (1439), each designed to underwrite local monastic foundation in the vernacular. The patrons of these works were the abbots of Bury St Edmund's (Lydgate's own house) and St Albans respectively. He also wrote many Marian lyrics, often designed to accompany pictures, some of which were for royal patrons, such as the *Valentine to Her that Excelleth All*, written to Henry VI and his mother Queen Katherine (?1429). Again for a female patron (Anne, Countess of March) and readership, he wrote the *Legende of St Margaret*

[70] For which see Wogan-Browne et al. (eds).

(1429–30), the patron saint of childbirth;[71] the *Invocation to St Anne* (for Anne, Countess of Stafford), and the *Virtues of the Mass* for Alice, Countess of Suffolk. He also produced religious texts for non-aristocratic textual communities: the *Procession of Corpus Christi*, for example, seems to be a précis of a dramatic procession;[72] or the *Legend of St Austin at Compton* relates a conversion miracle to be told 'in many shire and many Cite'.[73]

The *Dance*'s address to a clearly demarcated variety of institutional representatives was, then, entirely in keeping with much of Lydgate's religious and secular verse, which in large measure answered to commissions from particular institutions and is itself designed to serve, implicitly and often explicitly, distinct institutional and historical interests. In some of this verse Lydgate shaped an extraordinarily mannered, Latinate style (the 'aureate' style) for religious subjects, probably in response to the plain English of Lollards, used for translation of theological material and regarded as highly dangerous by the official Church.[74]

Not only was the *Dance* produced by the very kind of society it represents, but it is also structured, in its pattern of different voices, by a set of protocols characteristic of such a society. The poem proper is bracketed off by two distinct areas of verse, the *verba translatoris* and the *verba auctoris*; likewise, it is bounded at its end by the voice of 'Machabre', an academic doctor, and, finally, 'lenvoye de translatoure'. The opening words of the translator are those of an apparently anonymous moralist who addresses his audience indifferently as to class, as 'yee folkes harde herted as a stone'. He also relates his source (an 'exaumple whiche that at Parise | I founde depicte ones on a walle', ll. 19–20); who prompted him to translate it (some French clerics); the style of translation ('pleyne'); his intention (that the proud may amend their lives); and, not least, the way in which it should be read ('emprenteth in yowre memorialle')—the work is designed to be visually memorable and emotionally power-

[71] For Lydgate's relations with women readers, see Boffey, 'Lydgate's Lyrics'. Given the breadth of Lydgate's address to women readers, incidentally, it is perhaps significant that he adds four women (The Lady of Great Estate, the Abbess, the Gentlewoman Amerous, and the Empress) to his French source of the *Danse*.

[72] *Minor Poems*, pt. 1, no. 11.

[73] Ibid., no. 38 (l. 405).

[74] For which, see Ch. 7, below.

ful. This translator's voice is clearly demarcated from, and precedes, that of the *auctor*, who then entirely subsumes the voice of the translator. In one version of this poem a marginal gloss gives over one of the stanzas spoken by the *auctor* to a higher source of authority, 'Angelus'.[75] In his turn, the voice of Death, presented dramatically addressing each estate, now subsumes that of both translator and *auctor* altogether, since the dialogue is purely dramatic. Only at the end do the voices of *auctor* and translator reappear, the *auctor* in the guise of 'Machabre the Doctore', with Lydgate, who here names himself, appearing in humble form as a patronized poet addressing 'lordes and maistres' and asking for 'godeli supporte'.

The poem is itself, then, highly segmented formally, both by way of getting itself into a position of authority (Death's voice), and in Death's own highly articulated form of address to respective orders of society. Authority is by no means a given here, just as, correlatively, 'Lydgate' is by no means a given. Authority is, instead, parcelled out, and negotiated within each of these segments: Death, of course, only pretends to negotiate with his polite invitations, but this position of absolute power can only be approached by a graded series of disclaimers, in which both *translator* and *auctor* disclaim authority over the matter precisely by way of standing in for that authority. The translator found it on a wall (l. 20), while the *auctor* (or Angelus) declares God's authorship: 'Of oon matier god hath forged al' (l. 56). The act of representing this divine power generates a critical change of status for both translator and *auctor*, since by the end of the poem it is the academic voice of the 'Machabre the Doctoure' that articulates the final admonition. This powerful and authoritative voice delivers its warning, after which 'Lydgate' takes over as the humble petitioner for aristocratic support, who addresses 'my lordes and maistres al in fere', and prays 'loweli' for their correction and 'godeli supporte'. After this sure-footed and complex shifting of discursive position, Lydgate ends by excusing his rhetorical incivility: 'have me excused my name is Jon Lidgate' (l. 670). An author is named, but, as is characteristic of manuscript culture, authorship is by no means a sovereign category. This lack of authorial propriety can be

[75] There are fifteen MSS in all, which fall into two main groups, within which there is also variation. See *Dance of Death*, ed. Warren, pp. xxiv–xxxi; updated by Seymour, 'Some Lydgate Manuscripts', pp. 22–4.

seen in the shape of manuscript books, which do not, on the whole, gather authors into collections.[76] Only in print culture does an author assume apparent command over his oeuvre, as in the first collected 'Works' of Chaucer in 1532 (Fig. 1).

There are, then, voices of high authority articulated in this poem, but they are mediated by a graded series of voices who impersonate them. We have already seen how this poem is, in its external history, entirely 'in transit', moving across geographical, institutional, and discursive spaces. That the 'translator' should farewell it in an envoy, or 'send-off', is wholly in keeping with its mobile nature. Mobility is, however, not only external to the poem: within its very segmented structure (a structure entirely characteristic of Lydgate's oeuvre), authority is dispersed between God, Death, the Angelus, the poem's patrons, its translator and its *auctor*. The energy of the whole text derives from the way in which authority is translated, represented, and renegotiated between these different sites.

III

In summary, Lydgate's *Dance Machabré* is a perfectly representative artefact of a 'reformist' culture, no less representative if a good deal simpler than a huge array of possible examples from Lydgate's oeuvre, or from fourteenth- and fifteenth-century writing more generally. The fundamental condition of that reformism is a sufficiently wide and complex dispersal of jurisdictional power as to disallow any cultural monopoly. The fundamental textual characteristics of that reformism are as follows: (i) an accretive reception of historical artefacts, which recycles those artefacts without disguising the historicity either of the artefacts or of their reception; (ii) a complex parcelling out and impersonation of authority; and (iii) clearly segmented stylistic and/or structural forms. Each of these points deserves some elaboration, in which I permit myself to generalize from Lydgate's example.

I begin with the first characteristic: because the decentred institutional conditions of fourteenth- and fifteenth-century England

[76] For which see Edwards, 'Fifteenth-Century English Verse Author Collections'.

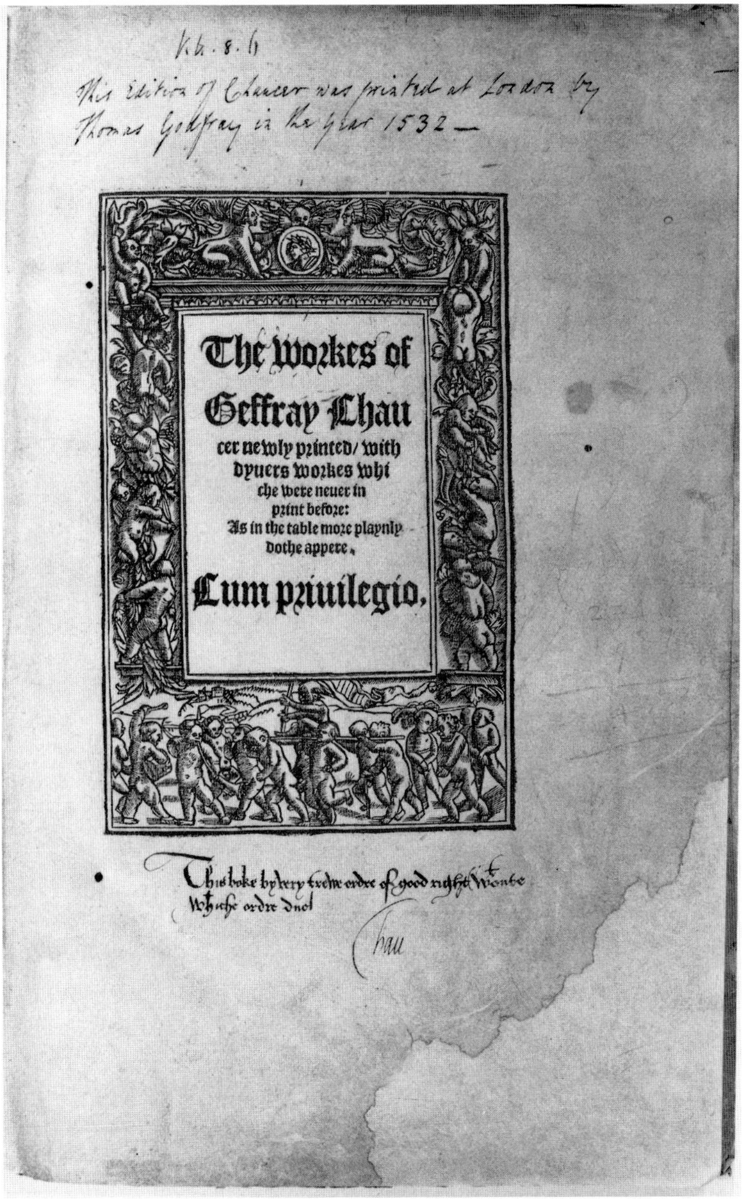

Fig. 1. *The Workes of Geffray Chaucer*, ed. William Thynne, title-page (1532).

disallow cultural monopolies, artists build on to artefacts from the past accretively rather than beginning afresh. Textual practice in such a society is not at all embarrassed about locating the presence of the writer receiving an old text, and about marking the bits that he or she adds to the source text. Writers in such a textual culture often represent themselves as readers, whose rereading of old texts produces a rewriting. This rewriting reveals a complex layering of textuality, where texts from different sources are juxtaposed to form a composite yet heterogeneous whole; this is even true of apparently autobiographical works (Langland's *Piers Plowman*, or Lydgate's *Testament*, for example), where the self can only be expressed through a complex textual collage. One might oppose this accretive translatorial practice to sixteenth-century conceptions of translation, which claimed to be stripping away historical accretion and promising access to an originary, true text.

My second characteristic: recent scholarship in both literary and editorial theory has theorized the often visible distinction between different kinds of writerly and readerly activity in the one text;[77] this has dislodged the deep-set expectations of readers trained in romantic habits of reading, whereby the sovereign author is the unmediated and sole source of a text. In this book I capitalize on these theoretical perceptions for literary history more generally, by contrasting reformist and revolutionary translation practice. Most English writing, secular or religious, of the period 1350–1550 is translation. Transposition of texts from one language to another in this period is the central act whereby 'English' literature is formed by dynamic interaction with Continental literatures; it is also the central and powerfully contested act whereby new classes of reader within England gain access to previously inaccessible materials. Whereas, however, both medieval and Renaissance scholarship regards imitative, direct translation of an originary source as truly historical, as distinct from the ahistorical habits of 'medieval' translation, I will be arguing that reformist translation is the more truly historical textual practice. Such translation, that is, does not posit any historical rupture in the reception of texts, and so is unembarrassed about explicitly locating the presence and interests of the writing reader in the present. This

[77] See esp. Minnis, *Medieval Theory of Authorship*, and Machan, *Textual Criticism*.

perspective, furthermore, opens up the very notion of translation, since reformist textual practice explicitly recognizes its historical passage, or 'carrying across', from, say, Troy, Rome, or Jerusalem to England or Scotland, or from Latin, French, or Italian to English. That such translation practice dresses up its classical or biblical actors in medieval dress is an index of explicit readaptation rather than of historical distance being collapsed.

Fourteenth- and fifteenth-century writers often represent themselves as the last point in a complex gradation of authorities. Authority derives both from textual and institutional sources, but precisely because the patterning of this parcelling out is complex, it is often also divided. Texts from this period do not at all speak with one voice, be it the one voice of the source or the one voice of the patron. On the contrary, there are often conflicting sources, and sometimes, explicitly or implicitly, more than one patron. Authority accrues to authors not by identification, but rather by representation: authors impersonate the authority of their source texts and patrons, just as Lydgate successively impersonates his *auctor*, God, Death, and the academic doctor in the *Dance Machabré*. Authors have, furthermore, the right to speak within their texts by virtue of their own status as *litteratus*, be they secular authors (like Chaucer) or religious (like Lydgate). Lydgate, indeed, himself speaks in the role of a secular clerisy in his *romans antiques*, whose persuasive ends are almost wholly secular. Precisely because writers must impersonate different authorities, they cannot be restricted to maintaining the discursive posture of their profession, or, for that matter, their gender. Neither are they beholden to imply a single authoritative voice, all deviations from which are 'ironic'.

Because writers must impersonate a variety of authoritative voices, the word 'propagandistic' is inappropriately applied to writing of this period. That word implies a simplistic ventriloquism of centralized power, leaving writers no choice but total identification or total resistance. While Lydgate was demonstrably an official poet, and an official poet for kings whose power rested on the shaky foundations of a *coup d'état*, he was not by any means a propagandistic poet: his *romans antiques* are consistently anti-imperialistic; his Ovidian *Reason and Sensuality* points to the ineluctible stupidity of aristocrats, who reproduce catastrophe; his *Fall of Princes* serves as a powerful reminder to aristocrats that their reputation is ultimately in the hands of random Fortune and of poets whose power will outlive that of their masters; and the satiric *Churl and the Bird* quietly implies that the Churl stands in for obtuse aristocratic patronage. In all these works, Lydgate implies in a variety of ways the intimate relation of poetry to politics.[78] Lydgate was in no way a marginal poet, and his official roles as poet were indeed something new in late medieval English literary writing; that did not, however, prevent him from contesting aristocratic practice. The complex and divided discursive field in which he worked inevitably produced such contestation.

The third feature of a reformist textual practice is its formal segmentation. Unresolved stylistic and discursive juxtaposition is the principal formal quality of a reformist culture. Critics have observed this 'inorganic', partitioned formal quality of Chaucerian verse in particular, but have wrongly theorized its sources in theology.[79] Its sources are rather in the complex institutional demarcations of fourteenth- and fifteenth-century society. The oeuvre of single authors is riven by generic affiliations that are not merely distinct but also at odds in their semiotic, historical, and ethical premisses. This is true not only of the secular–religious divide (the basic division), but also of divisions within secular and religious writing. It is for this reason that this book is not organized within the category of the 'author', since, as we have seen in the case of Lydgate, authors do not present themselves or practise as sovereign entities, or, in the case of multi-authored and anonymous works like the drama, for example, do not present themselves at all. While I respect the authorial enterprise within given works, and across given oeuvres, the really telling comparisons in this diachronic history are between works within the same broad discursive tradition, across the period 1350–1550. The book is not even organized within narrowly generic categories, because writers before and including, say, Skelton (d. 1529) simply do not observe the generic decorum of neoclassical writing. A clearly maintained generic decorum implies an easily visible social hierarchy. When lines of institutional power are multiform and overlapping, so too do texts manifest multiform and juxtaposed generic

[78] The best preliminary article on this large subject is Ebin, 'Lydgate's Views'.

[79] Jordan. For an argument that Jordan misapplies the particular theological context he adduces, see Simpson, '*Ut Pictura Poesis*'.

affiliations. Only the broader modal, adjectival categories of this book are sufficiently capacious to incorporate the generic heterogeneity of texts like *Troilus and Criseyde* or *Piers Plowman*.[80]

Earlier in this chapter I took various critics to task for investing Lydgate with a powerful periodic representativeness. I am conscious that I have done precisely that myself. The Lydgate of this chapter has, however, become 'Lydgate', a name which marks the point at which an extraordinarily wide range of literary forms, from a variety of languages, *auctores*, and patrons, translates into a form consumable by a wide range of readers and institutions. The critics I have singled out would not take issue with my account of the diversity of Lydgate's production; it is thanks to Derek Pearsall, indeed, that we are in a position to see that very diversity. By insisting on Lydate's 'medievalness', however, these critics seem to me to have accepted a sixteenth-century logic of periodization, which highlights Chaucer by darkening the practice of his 'followers'. They thereby attribute a solidity and a stolidity to whatever is 'medieval' (i.e. non-Chaucerian). There is nothing 'Lydgatian' or 'solid' about Lydgate's heterogeneous oeuvre, which is riven in genre, style, and semiotic practice. And neither is it stolid: each work is highly mobile, traversing different discursive jurisdictions with agility. It is no more or less representative than Chaucer's oeuvre, not to speak of the work of any number of named or anonymous writers in the fourteenth and fifteenth centuries.

The primary aim of this chapter and the last has been to elucidate the cultural features of 'revolutionary' and 'reformist' cultures respectively. A secondary aim has been to offer instances of exemplary authorial careers within those contrasted environments. The following eight chapters turn to the actual writing of the centuries 1350–1547, suitably divided, and in each case observe the collision between a culture of reform and its revolutionary counterpart.

[80] For the notion of 'mode', see A. Fowler: 'modal terms never imply a complete external form. Modes have always an incomplete repertoire, a selection only of the corresponding kind's features, and one from which overall external structure is absent' (p. 107).

3

The Tragic

In this chapter I survey a range of narratives of war that trace the fall of a king and his city or empire. The argument that shapes the material is, simply, that the fourteenth- and fifteenth-century examples of such narrative marked out their opposition to militarist, imperial pretensions in a variety of ways. Translation of Virgilian epic in the early sixteenth century, by contrast, revived ideals of imperial conquest.

I

In his *Anglica Historia*, first published in 1534,[1] Polydore Vergil (*c.*1470–1555), the Italian scholar resident in England from 1502 until the death of Henry VIII, recounts a polite scholarly encounter between himself and Gavin Douglas. In the last year of his life the bishop and poet Douglas (*c.*1475–1522) was in exile in London, abandoned by both friend and enemy in Scotland, and under threat from Wolsey in England.[2] Vergil recounts Douglas's attempt to intervene in Vergil's history of England, with regard to the matter of Scottish origins. Having retailed the standard version, according to which the Picts and Scots do not invade that land until after the Roman withdrawal, Vergil pauses to recount a visit by Gavin Douglas, with whom he 'fell into friendship'. Douglas, he goes on,

> vehemently requiered mee that in relation of the Scottishe affaires I showlde in no wise follow the president of a certaine contriman of his,

[1] For the details of composition and publication, see Hay, *Polydore Vergil*, ch. 4.

[2] For Douglas's biography, see Bawcutt, ch. 1.

promisinge within few dayse to sende mee of those matters not to be contemned, which in dede hee perfourmed, in which there was a verie ancient originall of that people.[3]

Vergil himself is very sceptical about myths of origin in the overall narrative of his *Historia*. He has no hesitation in defining the cultural pressures that produce and promote so evident a tissue of fabrications as Geoffrey of Monmouth's *Historia regum Britanniae* (1136), since

in the olde time . . . manie nations weare so bowlde as to derive the beginninge of theire stocke from the Goddes (as especiallie the Romaines did), to thentent the originall of there people and citties mighte bee the more princelie and prosperous. (vol. 1, bk. 1, p. 31)

The narrative that Douglas wanted Vergil to insert had it that Gathelus, an Athenian prince, having fled to Egypt, married the Pharaoh's daughter, one Scota, with whom, in search of new territory, he settled in Portugal, after fleeing from the plagues that had struck Egypt. Three hundred years later, his offspring, before the birth of Christ, came into Albion. Vergil delicately destroys this implausible story, by pointing out to Douglas, 'even as frindlie as trewlie', that none of the Roman historians of Britain mentions the Scots; Douglas, whom one suspects of trying his luck, graciously accepts Vergil's arguments, and there ends a small story about a fake story.

Behind this learned and ostensibly urbane encounter, however, lay a violent history of Anglo-Scottish relations from at least the end of the thirteenth century. From that time a succession of English kings had deployed an alternative, 'Brutish' myth of origins, derived from Geoffrey of Monmouth's *Historia regum Britanniae*, to justify their overlordship of and incursions into Scotland. Edward I, Edward III, Henry IV, and Henry VI all used, or were encouraged to use, stories of Scottish obeisance to British kings,[4] and especially to Arthur,

[3] Polydore Vergil, *English History*, ed. Ellis, vol. 1, bk 3, pp. 105–6. Ellis's edn. (of bks 1–8 and 23–5) is of a 16th-cent. trans. (as far as 1485) into English of the 1546 edn. of Polydore Vergil's Latin work.

[4] For Edward I, see R. S. Loomis, 'Edward I: Arthurian Enthusiast'; for Edward III and Henry VI, see Gransden, 2. 68 and 276 respectively. For Henry IV, see Stones. See also Gransden, 2. 76, for the prose *Brut*'s assertion of English overlordship of Scotland on the grounds of Brutus's conquest of the whole island.

to bolster their claims to Scotland. Neither was imperialist deployment of British materials restricted to Anglo-Scottish relations: the memory of Arthur's successful Continental campaigns is very much alive in the immensely popular *Brut*'s description of Edward II's Continental failures (vol. 1, ch. 220, p. 262). 'History' derived from Geoffrey of Monmouth was also used in Anglo-papal relations, as late as the Act of Appeals of 1533, which opened with reference to British myths about both Constantine and Arthur: 'by diverse sundry old authentic histories and chronicles it is manifestly declared and expressed that this realm of England is an empire'.[5] British material seems to have receded in propagandistic importance in the early Tudor period,[6] but its powerful reflorescence in Elizabethan poetry was underwritten by the tone of Leland's own, freshly composed epitaph (1544) for Arthur the imperialist, which praises him for having subjugated the Saxons, the Picts, the Scots, the French, and the Germans.[7]

Douglas's failed intervention in Polydore Vergil's narrative, then, cannot be innocent of the ways in which myths of origin are deployed for imperialist purposes. Neither is the improbable story of Gathelus and Scota so innocent, since, when we examine it, we observe a deep structural parallel to both the *Aeneid* and the Brutus myth: all three stories present a hero expelled from the East, moving as an exile through foreign territory, before finally settling a new-found, Western land. The stories are myths of origins, to be sure, but set in parallel, it is obvious that the two later narratives do not only look backwards. They also look aggressively sideways to each other and to the *Aeneid*, just as the *Aeneid* looks to Homer; each, that is, frames its narrative in such a way as to displace alternative foundation myths.[8] As has long been recognized, Geoffrey's *Historia regum Britanniae* begins with Virgilian parallels, providing a prophesied and genealogical descent for the British that can compete with its classical forebear, and thus also provide the British, or more

[5] Cited from Scarisbrick, *Henry VIII*, pp. 272–3. For comparable French propaganda deploying Trojan origins, see Beaune.

[6] For which see Anglo, '*British History*' and Carlson, 'King Arthur and Court Poems'. For a revisionist view, see D. Starkey, 'King Henry and King Arthur'.

[7] Leland, *Assertio inclytissimi Arthuri*, p. 134. This work was written in response to Polydore Vergil's history.

[8] This point is well made by Singerman, pp. 272–6. See also Waswo, p. 272.

accurately the Normans, with a founding myth of comparable stature to that of the *Aeneid*.[9] So too with the Gathelus myth: it must compete with, and outdo, the myth of Brutus, just as it must displace the myth of Aeneas by providing a genealogical link with the past. In the late eighteenth and nineteenth centuries, nationalist cultural movements produced the Northern European Romantic resuscitation of the 'medieval'; such movements displaced classical cultural models by an appeal to genealogical sources of cultural inspiration.[10] So too, we can see, do Brutus and Gathelus provide a 'middle age', a narrative that fills in, with genealogy and territorial possession, the vast gap between the fall of a past empire and the rise of a new nation. Geoffrey of Monmouth is in every way a 'medievalist'.

Implausible as the Gathelus myth might be, then, it was nevertheless clearly freighted with real enough burdens: it was designed to displace both territorial domination by the English, and, at some further reach, cultural domination by Roman models. That Douglas should raise the issue so 'vehementlie' is certainly understandable within the context of Anglo-Scottish military relations: the conversation takes place, after all, only eight years after the battle of Flodden (1513), the disastrous battle in which the Scottish King James IV and much of his nobility were killed. Douglas's passion on this question is, however, all the more interesting for the fact that, in another discursive field, it is none other than Douglas himself who introduced Virgil's *Aeneid* to a new readership, as an analogical model, an exemplar of aristocratic and imperial action that makes no genealogical claim whatsoever. His remarkable translation of Virgil's text was accomplished in an astonishingly short time—sixteen months by Douglas's own account—and finished on 22 July 1513, six or so weeks before Flodden.[11] In that year Douglas gave up writing poetry altogether. Contrary to his promise in the work's Conclusion to dedicate himself to contemplative writing, he engaged, unsuccessfully, in politics, particularly by way of supporting the activities of his nephew, the Earl of Angus, who had married the Dowager Queen Margaret, sister to Henry VIII.[12]

[9] See esp. the powerful article by Ingledew.

[10] See W. K. Ferguson, pp. 114–19.

[11] Gavin Douglas, *Virgil's 'Aeneid', translated into Scottish Verse*, ed. Coldwell, vol. 4, p. 194.

[12] Bawcutt, pp. 20–1.

In its self-presentation, Douglas's *Eneados* is an exemplary 'Renaissance' text. Douglas has no doubt but that Virgil's own 'principall entent' was to eulogize the Romans, and especially the 'clan Iulyan', given that the Emperor Augustus 'was of that hows and blud'.[13] It is, however, his very awareness of the genealogical import of Virgil's text for the Romans that determines Douglas's own presentation of the *Aeneid* as an analogical model for the Scots: through Aeneas Virgil 'blasons' 'All wirschip, manhed and nobilite', with every endowment of 'a gentill wycht, | Ane prince, ane conquerour or a valyeand knycht' (9, Prologue, 330–2).[14] No less than Aeneas as a man, Virgil, 'Thys maist renownyt prynce of poetry' (9, Prologue, 75), is himself exemplary as a poet. Writing for an emperor, Virgil provides the model for 'The ryall style, clepyt heroycall, | Full of wirschip and nobilnes our all . . . Observand bewte, sentens and gravyte' (9, Prologue, 21–6). Douglas's awareness of the profundity of 'sentence', no less than the rhetorical beauty and *gravitas* of Virgil's text, compels him to fidelity of translation, for all his disclaimers about rhetorical inadequacy. Just as Octavian 'but [without] rebellioun, al quhar [everywhere] obeit was he' (9, Prologue, 62), so too must the authority of Virgil be unswervingly obeyed in the attempt to follow his 'sentence': Douglas is fixed as to a stake—'Rycht so am I to Virgillis text ybund' (1, Prologue, 297–9). And bound he was: he produced a remarkably faithful and full translation of the entire text,[15] where the integrity of the classical work was preserved by Douglas's fidelity to a philological model of translation.[16]

In the person of Douglas, then, we seem to have a figure who is at the same time 'medieval' and of the 'Renaissance', though in the wrong order: he produces an exemplary text, the first translation of the *Aeneid* into English (or 'Inglys'), which makes no genealogical claim. Instead, his translation of the *Aeneid* is seriously and success-

[13] Douglas's own note to 1. v. 102.

[14] 'A noble man, a prince, a conqueror or a courageous knight'.

[15] Of course there are anachronisms in Douglas's translations, and it is also true that his decision to render Virgil's work into couplets produces a much-expanded text. For both of these aspects of his translation, see Bawcutt, pp. 128–30 and p. 137 respectively.

[16] For Douglas's posture as a translator, poised between possibilities of either a textually faithful, disinterested translation or one fitted to the needs of the receiving audience, see Ghosh, '"Fift Queill"'.

fully committed to the philological goal of faithful reproduction of poetic 'sentence' and rhetorical gravity. *Later*, in his encounter with Polydore Vergil, we find him promoting a very 'medieval' text, a text that is generated by a notion of genealogical authority above all: because the ancestors of the Scots occupied the territory of Scotland before Brutus arrived, their offspring in sixteenth-century Scotland owe no obeisance to the king of England. Both of these narratives are thoroughly political, in different ways: the Gathelus story lays claim to territorial possession by reference to genealogical descent from a particular past, while the *Aeneid* translation lays claim to cultural power simply by reference to *its own existence* as a cultural artefact. Making no genealogical gesture to links with an ancestral past whatsoever, the translation of Virgil presents itself simply as a philological achievement: by virtue of Douglas's linguistic capacity, vernacular readers of Scots, as opposed to English, have been given access to the best, most princely of all models, regardless of ties of blood.[17] The 'medieval' narrative generates its power by 'carrying on' a single tradition, while the 'Renaissance' text claims its authority by virtue of 'being like' a different tradition.

We have, then, two traditions: the genealogical and the analogical, represented respectively by the Gathelus/Brutus narratives, and the *Aeneid* translation. Both are produced by, and themselves sustain, particular social and political formations. The first, 'medieval' tradition is presupposed by a social structure dependent on genealogy for the possession of land and, therefore, of power. Social and literary historians detect a shift, around the year 1000, beginning in the north and west of France, from a system whereby land was dispersed 'horizontally' across a family, between women and men, to a system whereby land was preserved intact by being transmitted 'vertically' from father to oldest son, by primogeniture. Howard Bloch puts the matter in this way:

> Chivalry itself, transformed from a relatively open class into a closed and patroclinous caste, was no longer merely an indication of economic status but a hereditary sign of superiority. Henceforth, nobility represented a

[17] Douglas expresses his linguistic nationalism in the Prologue to Book 1, where he declares his translation to be 'kepand na sudron [southern English] bot our awyn langage' (1. Prologue, 111).

quality of birth, and a man was powerful because his ancestors, sometime around the year 1000, were already in command.[18]

This system of distributing land was at the heart of feudal society, according to which land belonged to a lineage, rather than to an individual. It also implies the explosive energies of such a society, since all those excluded from land by the system of primogeniture had to find it elsewhere, either by marriage or war, or both. The importance of lineage in this system also stood behind the mythic historiography of England's 'Brutish' origins, since, according to that historiography, possession of land was synonymous with lineage and power. However much Geoffrey of Monmouth's *Historia regum Britanniae* (1136) recounts the transmission of land from one race to another (Britons to Saxons), the text is written for the Norman conquerors of England, conquerors who themselves claimed Trojan ancestry.[19] Norman imperial claims are underwritten by their ancestral link to the imperialist Arthur, just as the Tudor cultivation of Arthur evokes ancestral connections, through Henry VII's Welsh lineage.

If the historical imagination of the 'Brutish' tradition is coherent with a particular social structure, the same is true of the textual practice represented by Douglas's *Aeneid* translation. This text, as I have said, makes no genealogical claim whatsoever; instead, it offers access to a model of nobility, both poetic and monarchical, by 'being like', or imitating its classical exemplar, 'the trewe Patterne of Eloquence'.[20] Of course the aristocratic, feudal structure of both English and Scottish society did not disappear in the early sixteenth century, but the central political problem of both British and French monarchs in this period is their relation with a powerful feudal aristocracy. Civil war among competing and overlapping aristocratic families characterizes the fifteenth century in Scotland, and in England from at least the end of the reign of Richard II until the reign of Henry VII, whose assumption of royal power in 1485 almost entirely lacked ancestral legitimation.[21] The development of a more central-

[18] Bloch, p. 68. See also Bartlett, pp. 49–50.

[19] For the Trojan descent of the Normans, see Ingledew, p. 687.

[20] The cited phrase is from Roger Ascham, *The Schoolmaster*, bk. 2, p. 283. For the importance of rhetorical imitation in the period post-1500, see Greene, *Light in Troy*.

[21] For Scotland, see Nicholson, *Scotland*. For England, see Keen, and Lander. For

ized monarchy in the sixteenth century is correlative with the decline of feudal power, and the rise of a non-noble literate class, who claim 'nobility of soul' through the capacity to understand and to imitate cultural models. Literate bureaucrats and poets had claimed nobility of soul against aristocratic privileges throughout the medieval period, but the political conditions of the early sixteenth century, and particularly in England, give a dramatic impetus to the idea.[22] In this social environment, literacy and the capacity to imitate classical models become the hallmarks of a newly defined nobility, according to which nobility is produced by analogy rather than genealogy. This point is complicated by the fact that Douglas is himself an aristocrat; whatever his own political position, however, his textual practice is unquestionably one of imitating a noble exemplar, just as he presents the *Aeneid* as a moral, philosophical, and rhetorical exemplar for his readers, especially in the Prologues to Books 1 and 11.

The story I have so far told sits easily with the main lines of established cultural history: we have a 'medieval' and a 'Renaissance' tradition. The medieval tradition does not suddenly stop and give way to the other: popular traditions of genealogical historiography continue to compete with humanist exemplarism throughout the Tudor period. But the textual practices I have described can be easily situated within the standard schemata of cultural and literary history: a massively appropriative and mythical historiography designed to promote a sense of continuity and identity is contrasted with a philological project that preserves the integrity of the classical text. The lack of genealogical link with the classical text allows for the recognition of historical difference.

The 'medieval' textual practices I have described here are indeed characteristic of hugely popular traditions of mythic historiographical writing in the fourteenth and fifteenth centuries in England. Geoffrey of Monmouth's Latin *Historia* survives in no fewer than 217 manuscripts, many of which were copied in those centuries.[23]

the problem as seen from a Tudor perspective, see Elton, *England under the Tudors*, ch. 1.

[22] For the earlier tradition, see Minnis, 'From Medieval to Renaissance?'; for the influence of the idea in the Tudor period, see Skinner, 'Sir Thomas More's *Utopia*', pp. 135–47.

[23] See Crick.

And for a more popular audience,[24] the prose *Brut* was an uncritical reproduction and continuation of an Anglo-Norman translation of Geoffrey's Latin text; it survives in an equally impressive 221 manuscripts. The original French text of this work, begun at the end of the thirteenth century, was translated into English sometime between 1350 and 1380, and was brought up to date throughout the fifteenth century.[25] There are 166 surviving manuscripts of this work in English, which 'makes it the most popular secular work of the fifteenth century in England'.[26] There can, therefore, be no denying the massive popularity of this tradition: it would seem to have been the principal lens through which English readers perceived British history. Even Polydore Vergil, who distrusted the Geoffrey of Monmouth material and the Gathelus story in equal measure, conceded a place in his own history of England to Geoffrey's narrative, 'albeit not altogether without indignation' (vol. 1, bk. 1, p. 33).

As I have said, Geoffrey of Monmouth's history of the Britons sets itself as a competitor to Virgil's *Aeneid* by providing an alternative myth of invasion and territorial possession, constructed, in part, to suit the needs of the Norman conquerors of Britain. As in Virgil, Geoffrey's conqueror is produced by the diaspora of Trojan heroes in search of land after the destruction of Troy. If all the Trojan writing produced in the 'medieval' period were assimilable to this largely imperialist model, and presented as one 'Troy Book',[27] then the rest of this chapter would be redundant. In fact, however, the distinctively *literary* tradition of Troy narratives in the fourteenth and fifteenth century in England is not at all assimilable within the frame of Geoffrey's *Historia*. On the contrary, this powerful body of writing stands in the starkest contrast to the Geoffrey of Monmouth tradition (hereafter the 'Galfridian' tradition) in every way. The literary tradition can fairly be described as anti-Galfridian and anti-Virgilian at the same time: anti-Galfridian because it makes no serious play with the genealogical potential of the Troy narrative, being relent-

[24] For the audiences of Geoffrey and the vernacular *Brut*, see Riddy, 'Reading for England'.

[25] For the vernacular *Brut*, in both French and English, see Taylor, *English Historical Literature*, ch. 6.

[26] For the MSS of the Middle English *Brut*, see Matheson, p. 254.

[27] Thus Ingledew. The very title of this otherwise excellent article suggests that there is, effectively, only one 'Troy Book'. The same is true of Waswo.

lessly exemplarist; and anti-Virgilian because it entertains no hopes for the divinely sanctioned foundation of empire. In this tradition the victors of the Trojan war are destroyed no less completely than the Trojans themselves. The tradition is intensely historical, but history holds no promise of transition from catastrophe to empire; history is instead the story of societies imploding under the pressure of poor decisions and the cumulative weight of events. The gods, let alone a Christian god, have no serious role to play; no territory is won, and humans with the best intentions are drawn into a vortex of historical forces that destroys them and their cities.

The bulk of this chapter (Sections II–III) will substantiate these claims about Troy narratives, by way of a comparison between Douglas's *Aeneid* and the alliterative *Destruction of Troy*. In section IV, I consider the literary presentation of Thebes, Camelot, and Macedonia, where we see the same story of history treacherously unfolding towards catastrophe. Finally, in Section V, I return to Surrey's translation of the *Aeneid*, by way of detecting there, too, an anti-imperialist statement. The main point I want to make is that literary narratives of kings and civilizations in the fourteenth and fifteenth centuries are tragedies. They are 'sad stories of the death of kings', and are in no way imperialist or propagandistic, not even covertly, not even when they try to be.

II

There are two significant pre-sixteenth-century literary retellings of the story of the Trojan war, both of which are extraordinarily ambitious works.[28] They are as follows: Lydgate's *Troy Book* (1412–20), 30,117 lines in rhymed five-stress couplets; and the alliterative *Destruction of Troy*, 14,044 lines of unrhymed alliterative verse, which makes it the longest alliterative work produced in the period. There are, too, less powerful versions of the Trojan narrative: the anonymous Laud *Troy Book* (of uncertain date, but likely to have been written after 1343, and before the first quarter of the fifteenth

[28] One should also mention Caxton's translation of Raoul Le Fèvre's Troy narrative, *The Recuyell of the Historyes of Troye*, produced between 1468 and 1471. Book 3 of this work is ultimately a translation of Guido.

century), 18,664 lines in four-stress couplets;[29] Caxton's *History of Troy*, published from Bruges in 1473–4 as the first printed book in English; and Caxton's *Eneados* (printed 1490), a wonderfully anarchic, if finally chaotic presentation of the Aeneas story whose Virgilian pretensions are almost completely derailed by different and incompatible versions of the Dido story.

The author of the *Destruction of Troy* was a certain Master John Clerk of Whalley in Lancashire, the site of a Cistercian abbey.[30] It makes reference to *Troilus and Criseyde*, and must also therefore post-date 1385; it must also, I think, pre-date 1400, since a passage in the *Siege of Jerusalem* (also pre-1400) seems evidently drawn from the *Destruction*.[31] The single surviving manuscript was copied between 1538 and 1546, by Thomas Chetham, of Nuthurst, Lancashire.[32] Lydgate's version seems to have been far more popular and was more widely dispersed: it survives in twenty manuscripts, and two printed editions (1513 and 1555),[33] whereas the Laud *Troy Book* and the *Destruction of Troy* survive only in single manuscripts. In the discussion that follows I refer mainly to the alliterative *Destruction of Troy*, with occasional reference to Lydgate's poem. My argument applies equally well to either work, but the alliterative work is more in need of retrieval from critical neglect, though only by a very small margin.[34] I discuss Chaucer's *Troilus and Criseyde*

[29] The date remains unsettled. Wülfing rebuts the argument of Kempe for a date pre-*Troilus and Criseyde*, but remarks that the 1343 date looks plausible as a *terminus a quo*.

[30] Spotted from the initial letters of the chapter headings (forming an acrostic of the author's title, name, and place), by Turville-Petre, 'Author of the *Destruction of Troy*'.

[31] For the relationship between the *Siege of Jerusalem* and the *Destruction*, see *Morte Arthure: A Critical Edition*, ed. Hamel, pp. 54–5. For the allusion to *Troilus and Criseyde* in the *Destruction*, see both C. D. Benson, 'Chaucerian Allusion', and Sundwall.

[32] For which see Luttrell.

[33] For a list of MSS of Lydgate's *Troy Book*, see Renoir and Benson, p. 2168.

[34] The one exception to general critical neglect of both poems, and the Laud *Troy Book*, is C. D. Benson's excellent book, *History of Troy*. Lydgate's Troy narrative is more usually dismissed as a typical example of the 'medieval' incapacity to recreate historical reality, the incapacity not to appropriate classical narrative for Christian apologetic purposes. See e.g. Pearsall, *John Lydgate*, p. 129. The same is true of criticism on the alliterative *Destruction*; see e.g. Barron, pp. 112–17. I also disagree with Barron's classification of the work as 'romance', and his discussion of it under the heading 'The Matter of Rome'.

(*c.*1385) in Chapter 4, since it is not, despite being set in Troy under siege, a narrative of the war itself.

All these works, despite their distinctive stamp, are primarily translations of one source, Guido delle Colonne's *Historia destructionis Troiae* (1287),[35] written by a Sicilian judge, and itself a translation, into Latin prose, of the French *Roman de Troie* of Benoît de Sainte-Maure (*c.*1160),[36] written in octosyllabic couplets. Benoît's text, in its turn, took its impulse from, though massively expanded, two versions of the Trojan war that both claimed, falsely, to be eyewitness accounts, whereas both were probably composed in the first century AD, in Greek. The Latin versions of these two texts were of later date: that of the Cretan Dictys and the 'Trojan' Dares date from the fourth and sixth centuries respectively.[37]

The narrative of Virgil's *Aeneid* needs no recapitulation. A brief synopsis of the less well-known Guido-narrative may be helpful. The Argonauts, en route to Colchis, having sought temporary haven in Laomedon's Troy, are repudiated. Having won, with Medea's help, the Golden Fleece, Jason later returns to Troy with Hercules to avenge the unintended insult of Laomedon. Jason destroys the city, and takes the Trojan Princess Hesione captive. Priam, Laomedon's son, rebuilds the city, and plans his revenge in counsel sessions whose deliberations are reported in detail, in which the voices arguing against revenge are defeated, especially by Paris' account of his dream of the Judgement of Paris. Paris goes to Greece and abducts Helen; the Greek army gathers, but before attempting a landing, sends ambassadors to sue for peace. Their arrogantly stated request is denied by the Trojans. A sequence of fierce battles follows, in the first of which Hector chivalrously refuses to capitalize on his strong position to destroy the Greeks; after more battles, Antenor is exchanged for Briseid ('Cryseyde' in Lydgate's version); and after yet more battles, Hector, warned by Andromache not to fight that day, is treacherously killed by Achilles. Palamedes, critical of Agamem-

[35] For which see the convenient English trans., *Guido delle Colonne: Historia destructionis troiae*, trans. Meek. For Guido's own career, see Chiàntera.

[36] The best recent discussion of this work is Nolan, *Chaucer*, pp. 14–47, 63–70, 96–117. The subject of this admirable book, and especially its discussion of counsel sessions (e.g. pp. 63–70), is of more general relevance to this entire chapter.

[37] For which see *Chronicles of Dictys of Crete and Dares the Phrygian*, trans. Frazer.

non's leadership, is elected commander of the Greeks. On the anniversary of Hector's death, Achilles falls in love with Polyxena, a daughter of Priam. After unsuccessfully trying to persuade the Greeks to end the war, having been promised Polyxena should he succeed, Achilles angrily withdraws from the fight. Palamedes is killed and Agamemnon re-elected commander. The tide of battle turns in favour of the Trojans, led now by Troilus. Finally roused to fury, Achilles kills Troilus by underhand means, and drags his body around the walls of Troy. Penthesilea, having arrived to help the Trojans, is finally killed by Pyrrhus, the son of Achilles called to avenge his father, who had been assassinated by Hecuba. Aeneas and Antenor plot successfully to betray Troy, outmanoeuvring Priam in counsel sessions. The wooden horse is introduced into the city, which is then destroyed. Bad weather prevents the Greeks returning, because, according to Calchas, Achilles' death remains unavenged; he declares that Polyxena must be sacrificed by way of recompense, since she was the cause of Achilles' death. Having been betrayed by Antenor, she is found and murdered by Pyrrhus. Hecuba, now crazed, is stoned to death. (At this point in the narrative the Laud *Troy Book* ends; Lydgate and the alliterative poem follow to the end of Guido's text.) Before the victorious Greeks return home, Ajax is murdered, apparently by Ulysses; a storm destroys much of the Greek fleet; 200 more ships are destroyed by a false sign deliberately set up by King Nauplus, whose treachery has been provoked by a false story. Disaster awaits the rest of the Greeks on their arrival home: Agamemnon is murdered; Pyrrhus, having abandoned Andromache and ravished the wife of Orestes, is murdered by Orestes, and his kingdom of Thessaly is taken over by Laomedon, the son of Andromache and Hector; Ulysses is murdered by Telegonus, his son by Circe.

This, then, is the story of Troy that dominates the imagination of literary readers and, possibly, listeners,[38] throughout the fourteenth and fifteenth centuries in England. Of course the story does not suddenly cease to exert its power at the beginning of the sixteenth century, when Douglas's Virgilian Troy narrative appears (Lydgate's

[38] Both the *Destruction* and the Laud *Troy Book* address their audience as listeners. This posture is plausible for the Laud version; whether listeners really could take in the 14,044 lines of the *Destruction* must be an open question.

Troy Book, was, for example printed in 1513 and 1555, just as Shakespeare's *Troilus and Cressida* (1601–2) is a product of the Guido-tradition). Reflection on the quality of this story, and comparison with Douglas's *Aeneid*, will, however, suggest some of the reasons why this fundamentally anti-Virgilian version of Troy managed to displace the *Aeneid* for so long.[39]

III

When Aeneas arrives in Carthage, he happens upon the magnificent temple of Juno, in the process of being constructed by Dido on the site where a huge horse's head was found, taken to be a sign of the city's future military strength and economic prosperity. On entering the temple he admires the workmanship, when, Douglas writes,

> . . . as he wondrit for ioy,
> He saw perordour all the sege of Troy, [in order]
> The famus batellis, wlgat throu the warld or this, [published · before]
> Of Kyng Pryam and athir Attrides. [both]
>
> (I. vii. 67–70)

The very existence of the images comforts Aeneas, but the images themselves, and in particular the vision of Troilus being dragged behind his empty cart, head in the dust, or of Hector's corpse, trawled around Troy by Achilles, provoke feelings of pathos, 'Murnand sair and wepand tendyrly, | The flude of terys halyng [pouring] our [over] hys face' (I. vii. 84–5). Finally, Aeneas recognizes himself in the picture, and, just before Dido enters, he sees Penthesilea, still fighting, a woman who 'stowtly recontir durst with men' (I. vii. 134).

With this little scene Virgil achieves one simple effect, and another, much more complex. The vision allows Virgil simply to recapitulate the siege of Troy, through intense, ecphrastic focus on moments of high pathos and Trojan defeat. The more complex effect consists in the historical freighting of this scene. As Aeneas goes forward in his journey, so too does he go backward; he arrives in Carthage only to

[39] For the tradition of the *Aeneid* in England from the12th-cent., see Baswell.

be met by images of what he is escaping. This recursion naturally involves pain for Aeneas, but the real pathos of this scene, when considered from a distance, concerns Dido rather than Aeneas.[40] For however much what Aeneas sees here is 'fenyeit ymagery' (1. vii. 83), or 'nyce figuris' (1. viii. 2) what turns out to be evanescent in the larger scene is rather the solid temple in process of construction; the queen who builds it; and the city of which it is the sacral centre. Even the temple's votive goddess Juno will be defeated. Carthage, the future great competitor and enemy of Rome, is already heading for destruction, despite appearances: as Aeneas wonders at images of Trojan defeat, we are conscious rather of impending defeat for Dido, to be destroyed precisely by her generosity to the exiled and nearly destitute Aeneas.

Dido enters, magnificently, 'Like to the goddes Dian with hir rowt [body of retainers]' (1. viii. 8), at the very moment that Aeneas beholds the mural of Penthesilea fighting; Dido's entry prevents Aeneas moving on to witness Penthesilea's death. The huntress Penthesilea, whose moon-shaped shield evokes Diana, is drawn to her death by her sympathy for apparently defeated Trojan exiles.[41] Likewise the scene marks out Dido as a victim of her sympathy for Trojans. So Aeneas' recursion turns out to be a case of *reculer pour mieux sauter*, however much cruelty, for women especially, that may involve; apparent defeat and destitution turn out only to mark Aeneas as already victorious.

We have no choice but to see this scene as from a distance. Aeneas is himself invisible, enveloped by Venus in a cloud, as the decisive, though unseen, presence in Carthage. Just as Dido cannot see the force that will govern her fate, so too Aeneas cannot, except fleetingly, see the gods who shape his. Already Neptune has calmed the storm, in the same way that 'sum man of gret autorite' can suddenly calm the inflamed populace simply by appearing (1. iii. 92–100), and soon after, before Aeneas arrives in Carthage, a serene Juppiter is to calm the enraged Venus:

[40] For the theme of recursion in Virgil's *Aeneid* with respect to 12th-cent. Old French works, see Patterson, 'Virgil and the Historical Consciousness'.

[41] The references to Diana associated with female victims also look forward to Camilla in Bk. 11. Camilla also bears the arms of Diana (11. 652).

Smylyng sum deil, the fader of goddis and men [a little]
With that ilk sweit vissage, as we ken, [same · know]
That mesys tempestis and makis the hevennys cleir, [calms]
First kissit his child, syne said on this maneir: [then]
'Away sik dreid, Cytherea, be nocht efferd, [such]
For thi lynage onchangit remanys the werd. [fate]
As thou desyris, the cite salt thou se, [shall]
And of Lavyne the promyst wallis hie. [high]
Eik thou salt rays abuf the sterrit sky [raise]
The manfull Eneas and hym deify.
My sentence is nocht alterit as thou traistis.' [believe]

(1. v. 47–57)

Already, then, before Aeneas sees himself in the mural of Juno's temple, he is central and irreplaceable to the picture of the *Aeneid*, his future assured.

This pattern of returning to the past by way of gaining energy for the future is fundamental to the whole poem, and is especially pronounced in Books 2–3. In these books Dido's presence becomes the magnet and generator of history, drawing Aeneas to recount the past fall of Troy in such a way as to underline, for us, the future fall of Dido in the future rise of Rome. No less than Laocoon, helplessly toiled as a sacrifice to history (2. iv), Dido is marked as history's victim by Aeneas' retrospective account of Troy's collapse and his journeys so far. Late into the night in Carthage, he recounts to the capitvated Dido his last moments with Creusa, whose ghost, Aeneas reports, had exhorted him to leave her behind without remorse, assured in the knowledge that 'the hie governour of the hevin abufe' has destined him to settle in Italy and to marry the daughter of a king (2. xii). Aeneas' vain attempt to embrace Creusa, when 'thrys, al waist [in vain], my handis togeddir clappit', is simply the prelude to his discovering a huge band of followers ready to go into exile with him: vainly embracing the past propels Aeneas forwards to the Italian land and marriage for which he will leave Dido, Dido who is listening to these very prophecies. The same is true of Book 3, where Aeneas recounts the prophecy of Apollo himself, on Delos. The god promises a maternal return for the future, since Aeneas will, he foretells, return to the land whence the Trojans first came: 'To seik your ald moder mak you bane [prepare yourself]' (3. ii. 58). Having mistakenly settled on Crete, the Trojan gods appear to Aeneas in a vision in order to repeat the same prophecy about returning to the source of Troy, only this time they specify Italy:

> Thar beyn our propir setis and our herbry; [are · place of
> Tharof com Dardane and his brothir Iasyus, settlement]
> And from that ilk prince, Schir Dardanus, [same · Sir]
> Is the discens of our genealogy. [descent]
>
> (3. iii. 36–9)

The providential history that champions Aeneas engineers forward movement by temporary recursion, in such a way that the entire pattern of history is painfully immanent in the narrative's every moment. Nowhere is this more prominent, as one would expect, than in Book 6, where Aeneas' encounter with the victims of the past such as Dido, or the mutilated Deiphobus, is a prelude to his encounter with the shade of Anchises. Of course historical recursion means that Aeneas can never escape violence: as the Cumaean Sybill prophesies, he will find *before* him, in Italy, 'Batalis, horribil batalis', and rivers of blood, new versions of the rivers of Troy, along with 'ane othir Achil, born als [also] of a goddes' (6. ii. 15–23). But pious recursion to paternal roots guarantees success, and the possibility of return to the upper world, a return that is propelled by Anchises' prophecy of the Roman empire and its leaders following from the genealogy of Aeneas. The pattern of virtuous return, and of escape from the darkness of history, is sketched by the Sybill before they descend. Douglas's translation of these famous lines runs as follows:

> Of goddis blude, Anchises son Troiane,
> It is richt facil and eith gait, I the tell, [easy · easy path]
> Forto descend and pass on down to hell;
> The blak yettis of Pluto and that dirk way [gates]
> Standis eveir oppin and patent nycht and day:
> Bot tharfra to return agane on hycht, [on high]
> That is difficil wark, thar lawbour lyis. [lies]
> Ful few thar bene, quhom heich above the skyis [whom]
> Thar ardent vertu hass rasit and uphyeit. [raised]
>
> (6. ii. 100–9)

This, then, is the characteristic movement of the *Aeneid*, whereby the forward movement of history is generated by a backwards movement of divinely sanctioned, providential return to beginnings. Of course there are serious complications to this scheme, not simply coterminous with its terrible process of victimization. Or, to put it another way, Aeneas himself may in part become a victim, possessed as he finally is, like Hercules the mythical saviour of Pallanteum, of a terrible violence on seeing the belt of Pallas on Turnus (12. xiv). Douglas clearly wants to minimize these complications, since, with however much diffidence, he translates a thirteenth book, originally composed in Latin by the fifteenth-century Italian humanist Maffeo Vegio. This is crudely imperialistic material, which invents not only the marriage of Aeneas and Lavinia, but also, by way of ending, the deification of Aeneas.[42]

If this is the providential pattern of empire in the *Eneados*, how does it compare with the making of history in the 'Guido-tradition', as exemplified by the alliterative *Destruction of Troy*? Douglas himself says in the Prologue to Book 2 that although the 'dedly tragedy | Twiching of Troy the subversioun and fall' is known everywhere, it will be told differently now, following Virgil, 'than ever was tofor hard in our tong'. Perhaps Douglas has in mind the anti-Virgilian account of Guido delle Colonne, an author whom Douglas dismisses in a note as 'your pevach [peevish] and corrupt Gwido'.[43]

In the *Aeneid* history is set by Destiny; read by the gods; and disseminated to oracles and Muses, who inspire the human poet. In the *Destruction* history is made by aristocrats in committees, and recorded by bureaucrats in diaries. The title of the Cretan Dictys' work is *Ephemeris belli trojani* (*The Diary of the Trojan War*). This narrative posture, of a simple day-by-day recording of events as witnessed, determines every aspect of the ideology of the *Destruction*. In

[42] There has been some controversy in Douglas studies as to whether or not his translation is 'political', with Bawcutt, pp. 124–5, taking issue with Coldwell (Douglas, *Virgil's 'Aeneid'*, ed. Coldwell, vol. 1, pp. 19–38). Coldwell argues that Douglas presents the *Aeneid* as a statement of monarchical supremacy; Bawcutt replies that Douglas did not especially emphasize the political aspects of the work in his translation. My own position is much nearer to Coldwell's, simply because the *Aeneid* is inherently an intensely political work. Certainly the *Aeneid* was promoted as an appropriate text for the education of rulers in the Tudor period in England. See e.g. Elyot, *Booke Named the Governour* (1531), 1. 10, and Nicholas Grimald's eulogy of the *Aeneid* in *Tottel's Miscellany (1557–1587)*, ed. Rollins, vol. 1, no. 137, p. 99. More generally, see Cattaneo, pp. 252–3.

[43] Note to 1. v. 28.

the first place, nothing imperceptible by the uninspired human observer is allowed into the story. The poem is resolutely secular and human in its purview: the gods play almost no part, and their action is represented only through the generally mistaken or deliberately manipulative account of human interpreters. The poet immediately distances himself from Homer, who tells 'how goddes foght in the filde, folke as thai were' (l. 45),[44] just as he distances himself from Homer's prejudiced account of the war. Precisely because the truth about the war is open to human manipulation, the Guido-tradition is aware of the ways in which Homer has skewed events to favour the Greeks;[45] as eyewitnesses from different sides, the combined accounts of Dictys and Dares are a guarantee of truth. And so far from pretending to inspiration, these texts underline their transmission through different languages and authors. Unlike Douglas, who proudly presents his *Aeneid* as wine freshly drawn from the grape, not poured 'fra tun to tun' (5, Prologue, 53), the poet of the *Destruction*, like all writers in the Guido-tradition, places his own work in a long line of textual transmission and linguistic change (Prologue, 27–98).

The posture of the diarist also determines the representation of history in the *Destruction*. In the *Aeneid*, as we have seen, the whole of history is often painfully immanent in each moment of the narrative; the *Destruction* could not be more different in its representation of history unfolding. In this text history is, as I have said, initiated by the volition of aristocrats, and takes its course from the contingent and entropic force of events spiralling out of individual human control. Counsel sessions and diplomatic receptions are therefore of vital significance, pregnant as they are with different possible futures; there are few counsel sessions in the *Aeneid*, where advice comes more often than not from heaven. In the *Destruction*, two counsel sessions are especially important for the Trojans, the second a grim commentary on the first. In the first (Book 6), the Trojans decide how best to reply to the earlier destruction of Troy by the Greeks, and the abduction of Hesione, Priam's sister. Priam's firm resolve to exact vengeance on the Greeks opens the book; the elaborate process of

[44] John Clerk, *The Gest Hystoriale*, ed. Panton and Donaldson. All citations are from this edn. A new edn. of this work is urgently required.

[45] See also *Destruction*, ll. 10312–61.

discussion, first with a full parliament, and then with a small council of Priam and his inner circle, serves merely to confirm the vengeful royal will. The parliament consents readily to the plan for war; the inner council takes a while longer to arrive at the same decision. Here the first to reply to the weeping Priam's call for vengeance is Hector, who recognizes the need to avoid shame by answering insults from anyone of equal status to themselves: 'Hit were shortly a shame and a shire greme [source of pure anger]' (l. 2218), since the pain of insult is, he says, directly proportional to the status of the person offended. This candid acceptance of a shame ethos is, however, tempered in Hector's speech by a call to prudence:

> Let oure gate be so governet, [way of proceeding ·
> that no grem folow, anger]
> Ne no torfer betyde, ne no tene after. [disaster · grief]
> Over lokes all lures to the last ende, [losses]
> What wull falle of the first furthe to the middis;
> Sue forthe to the secund, serche it with in,
> And loke to the last end, what lure may happyn.
> (ll. 2239–44)

The terms of the debate are replayed, in increasingly emphatic versions of the two poles of the argument: a call to avenge a wounded aristocratic pride on the one hand, against a philosophical call to temperate and prudential action on the other. Of course the impetuous and militarist voices win, persuaded in part by Paris' account of his dream that he patently misinterprets to satisfy his own desire. The militarists are also persuaded by Troilus' dismissal of the clerical voice of Helenus, who has prophesied disaster. Priests are always afraid of war, and in any case, the future is literally unpredictable; why heed 'a mad priste, | That never colde of no [knew anything about] knighthode, but in a kirke chyde?' (ll. 2526–52).

And so the Trojans freely determine to go to war and self-destruction. The second counsel session (Book 28) occurs when most speakers in the first council are dead: Hector, Deiphobus, Troilus, and Paris have all been killed in battle. Antenor and Aeneas, who have decided to betray Troy, dominate it. In this context of considerably diminished options, the arguments are replayed as a corrupt parody of the first council. Debate now only masks the treacherous plan of Priam secretly to assassinate Antenor and Aeneas, and of the traitors to betray Troy. Now the peace argument is conducted by the traitors, simply for the purpose of destroying the city. The space for rational, prudential argument conducted on its own terms has now given way to the sinister manipulation of aristocratic lords capable of waging civil war against their king. Antenor and Aeneas both forestall Priam's plot to assassinate them by appearing surrounded by 'frendes' and 'affynité', 'as plentuus of pepull as Priam hymselvyn' (l. 11388). They outmanoeuvre Priam in swaying the popular decision, and so seal the destruction of the city, which then happens very quickly in the following book. The city falls, then, not primarily through military weakness: the crucial events happen not on the battlefield but in the council chamber or parliament. Civil implosion is a much more significant factor than military action in the overall destruction of the city. And civil implosion also overtakes the Greeks, who fall victim to assassination by apparent allies on their return home. Books 30–6, which recount the return of the victorious Greeks, turn out to be by far the most savage and internecine of the whole work.

In the *Destruction*, then, history is held in the balance by purely human passions and decisions. Nothing assures kings of their legitimacy or of their power: Agamemnon is, for example, successfully challenged as leader of the Greeks, just as Priam is matched and beaten by his powerful lords. Whereas Virgil's text resonates with providential history at every point, the *Destruction* sounds an ominous note for kings. Whereas Virgil's text begins *in medias res* in such a way as to propel the narrative into a future determined by a past, the *Destruction* proceeds by a 'natural', almost journalistic order, where anything can happen tomorrow.[46] Royal power depends on nothing but itself and especially its management of bureaucratic procedure. History turns, that is, on the entirely contingent decisions of counsel sessions, and on the practice of diplomatic missions; the record of history is the record of bureaucratic failure. The background against which argument, diplomacy, and war take place is flat, without any of the historical depth of Virgil's narrative.

History also turns, of course, on the fortunes of war, which the

[46] For the theory of ordering narrative, see Simpson, *Sciences and the Self*, pp. 75–81.

Destruction recounts in elaborate detail. Even here, however, the narratorial voice is concerned to judge the efficacy of military action rather than to glorify chivalry. The clearest example of this is in Hector's meeting with Ajax in Book 15. The day's fighting has gone decisively in the Trojans' favour, when Hector meets the Greek Ajax, his cousin through Ajax's mother, Hesione, Hector's aunt, abducted in the first destruction of the city. Once Hector recognizes him, he chivalrously sets aside the hostility of war out of a generous and familial gesture, inviting Ajax to 'Turne unto Troy and talke with his cosyns, | His honerable Em [uncle], and other of his fryndes' (ll. 7095–6). Ajax declines, but successfully requests that Hector stop the relentless Trojan advance for that day. Hector's consent is met with trenchant criticism from the narrator, set off in the manuscript by a separate rubric. Hector is savagely criticized for his chivalric gesture, since he could have entirely destroyed the Greeks that day: a man, says the narrator, must never fail to seize the opportunities of fortune, which never reappear (ll. 7056–7124).

The only way heroes can be magnified in the *Destruction* is through their tombs, and indeed the work becomes a kind of necropolis of magnificent, technologically advanced tombs for fallen heroes. The first and most spectacular of these, emblematic of all the rest, is Hector's, which is a splendid and elaborate construction that manages to preserve the corpse of Hector intact and lifelike by virtue of balsamic liquids that flow constantly, driven by ingenious devices (ll. 8726–8825). The poet's description of the tomb places so much emphasis on the very ingeniousness of the craftsmen who constructed it that heroism is displaced by admiration for macabre engineering. There is nothing here of the divine technology of the *Aeneid*, such as the Vulcanic shield of Aeneas that glorifies the hero and his imperial line (Book 8), or the Venereal medicine that cures the wounded Aeneas in Book 12. In the trenchantly secular *Destruction* the fame of heroes, such as it is, remains wholly dependent on human authors and human technologies. There is, certainly, no stellification of dead heroes (Fig. 2).

Hector's tomb occasions Achilles' first sight of Polyxena. By way of concluding this comparison of Douglas's *Eneados* and the *Destruction*, I turn to the critical question of their respective treatments of women as victims, and in particular of Polyxena. In both texts

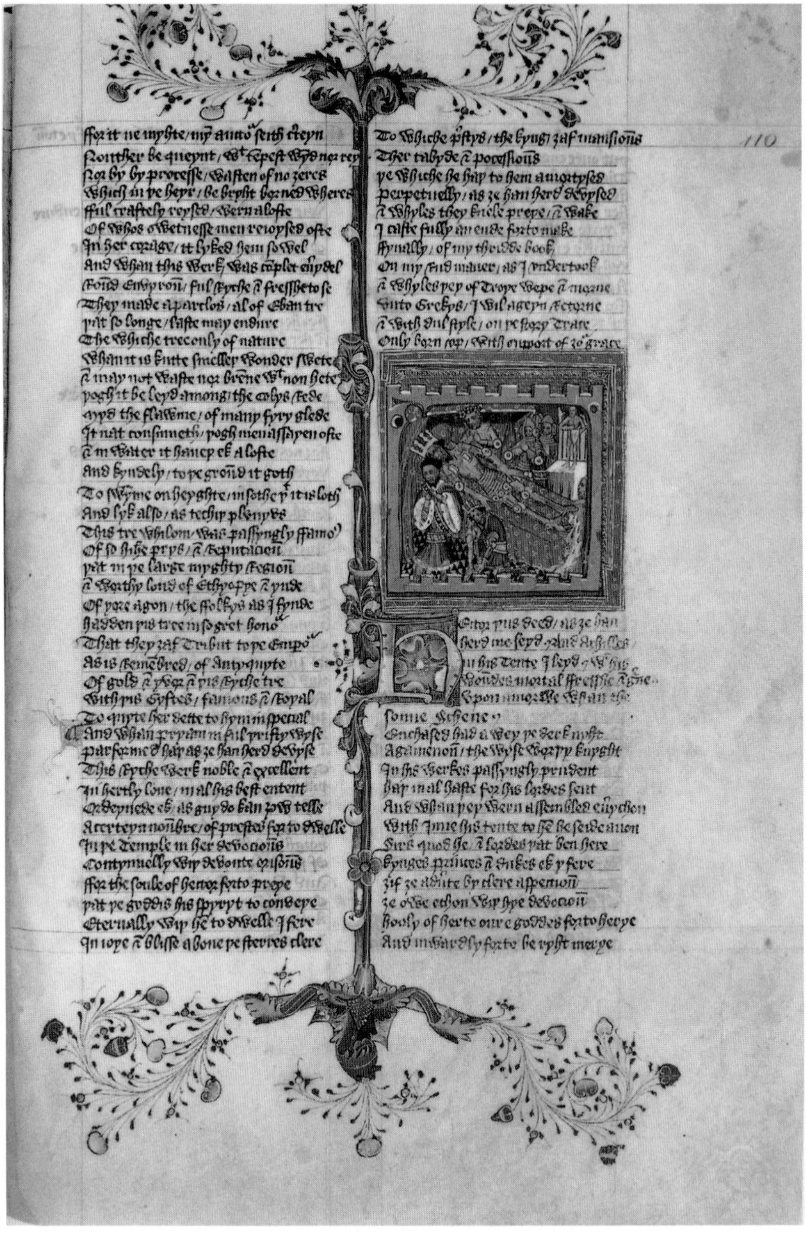

Fig. 2. The death of Hector. Lydgate, *Troy Book*. Oxford, Bodleian Library, MS Digby 232, fo. 110r (*c*.1420–35).

women fall victim to the machine of empire and war: in the *Aeneid* the obvious instances are Creusa, Dido, and Camilla. Given the peculiarly Virgilian representation of history, always looking back as it goes forward, there is no shortage of sympathy for these victims. The forward march of the imperial project nevertheless demands female victims: each of these women stands metonymically for the territories that the proto-imperial hero must leave, traverse, and possess respectively. Douglas, even more than Virgil, can fairly be said to highlight and champion Aeneas's imperial mission in this respect.

A need to victimize women seems to drive Douglas's own poetic mission to translate the *Aeneid* in the first place. For in the Prologue Douglas positions his translation with respect to earlier, vernacular Virgilian enterprises that have come to grief on their representation of Dido. The first target of his acrimony is Caxton's *Eneados* (1490), which presents wholly different and incompatible versions of the Dido story. Douglas indignantly, though rightly, points out that Caxton's treatment of Dido occupies half the book:

> I red his wark with harmys at my hart, [pain]
> That syk a buke but sentens or engyne [such · without
> Suld be intitillit eftir the poet dyvyne. meaning or skill]
>
> (1, Prologue, 146–8)

Caxton is not Douglas's only historical obstacle, however. Chaucer's presentation of Dido in the *Legend of Good Women* is another. Despite his reverence for Chaucer, Douglas effectively lays charges against Chaucer for having 'gretly the prynce of poetis grevit' in the finally Ovidian account of Dido in the *Legend*. For, he says, in that work Chaucer at the same time claims to follow Virgil, and yet calls Aeneas a traitor. Douglas stands incredulous at the charge of treachery against Aeneas, since 'Virgill dyd diligens | But [without] spot of cryme, reproch or ony offens | Eneas for to loif [praise] and magnify' (1, Prologue, 419–21), and he goes on to excuse Aeneas before excusing Chaucer's weakness, 'For he was evir, God wait [knows], all womanis frend' (1, Prologue, 449). In this Douglas shows himself the 'Renaissance' author for whom the text is what an author wrote, rather than what a reader makes of it.[47] His

[47] I say this with the qualification that Douglas did incorporate material from the explanatory apparatus of the Latin editions he was using into the body of his text

incapacity, or refusal, to register sympathy for Dido is reaffirmed in his own words in the Prologue to Book 4. There Douglas follows a long attack on 'the furyus flambe of sensualite' with a long apostrophe to both Dido and a personified Lust, with whom Dido is nearly identified. Douglas begins by declaring his own tears for Dido, and those of St Augustine (d. 430), a reference to Book 1. xiii of the *Confessions*; he goes on, however, to attack her as exemplary of uncontrolled passion, 'In hir faynt lust sa mait [mad], within schort quhile [while], | That honeste [virtue] baith [both] and gude fame war adew [neglected]' (4, Prologue, 254–5). Aeneas and his imperial mission remain unmentioned here, and Dido has become an ethically reduced exemplum, detached from the historical process that destroys her. Chaucer might be excused, but Dido certainly is not.[48]

I concede that the situation in the *Destruction* is not, on the face of it, entirely different. When Bresaid must leave Troilus (Book 19), the author of the *Destruction* refers us, surely, to *Troilus and Criseyde* for a more detailed account of their grief at parting: 'Whoso wilnes [desires] to wit of thaire wo fir [further], | Turne hym to Troilus, and talke there ynoghe' (ll. 8053–4).[49] He follows this, however, with an admonition to the male reader, translated directly from Guido, to distrust women, who are 'unstable and not stidfast, styrond [variable] of wille' (ll. 8055–67). The admonition would suggest that the author of the *Destruction* has failed to respond to Chaucer's realization of the historical 'process' that betrays Criseyde. The larger narrative of the *Destruction*, however, is unflinchingly conscious of a hideous, male-driven historical process that demands female sacrifice. There are many examples of this, but none more revealing or more painful than the destruction of Polyxena, whose downfall begins at the tomb of Hector.

On the anniversary of Hector's death, a strange and fatal meeting occurs between Achilles and Polyxena. In a period of truce and free passage among enemies, Achilles the slayer of Hector has gone to

(Bawcutt, pp. 110–24). This material is concerned with the meaning of individual words and phrases, rather than interpretation on a larger scale. He will also, rarely, insert remarks into the body of his translation that serve to distance him from the pagan practices represented in the *Aeneid*. See Bawcutt, p. 132.

48 See also Desmond, ch. 5.

49 This reference to Chaucer's poem also occurs at the equivalent point in Lydgate's *Troy Book*; see C. D. Benson, 'Chaucerian Allusion', and Sundwall.

observe Hector's ingenious tomb, where he observes the strange sight of intact Hector sitting preserved and lifelike. The wounded figure here, however, is not Hector, but Achilles himself, as he is pierced by the sight of Hector's grieving and dishevelled sister Polyxena:

> The faire heris of that fre flammet of gold, [noble one · flamed]
> All aboven on hir brest and hir bright swire, [neck]
> That sho halit with hond, hade it in sonder, [pulled]
> And puld it with pyn, pité to behold. [grief]
>
> (ll. 9135–8)

Achilles' response to this sight is identical with that of Troilus on first seeing Criseyde in the temple: he is struck by Cupid's arrow, returns to his tent, and laments. In the first sequence of his passion, it would seem that love and war are inimical, since Achilles refuses to fight any more, having made an agreement with Hecuba that, should he marry Polyxena, the siege will be lifted. Very quickly, however, we are reminded that love of this kind is precisely what initiated the war and what propels it. At a council of the Greeks Achilles makes an impassioned speech about the folly of fighting a war, and of leaving home, for the sake of one woman (ll. 9323–62). Achilles' own speech is itself driven, however, by his desire for one woman, a desire excited by her grief for one of Achilles' own victims. Achilles' love, and his speech promoting peace, turn out to be reflexes of the war machine. This conclusion becomes inevitable once Achilles is stung into action: just as his love for Polyxena is traceable to his underhand killing of Hector, so too does it provoke him to kill Troilus in just as underhand a way.

Achilles' love for Polyxena, that is, serves merely as a kind of stopper, obstructing his rage only to have it explode all the more powerfully on the battlefield (Book 26). Polyxena's position in all this is wholly passive, and remains so until after the destruction of the city. Her fate, however, is intimately bound with that of Achilles, since she is sacrificed on his tomb by Pyrrhus, Achilles' son, come to fight to avenge his father's death. The Greeks are prevented from leaving Troy by bad winds; Calchas instructs them to sacrifice Polyxena, by way of atoning for the assassination of Achilles. Antenor seeks her out in hiding, and hands her over to Pyrrhus, who murders her with a 'pale sword' immediately after she delivers this speech, rendered from indirect speech in the source:

Me is lever . . . in my lond degh, [preferable · die]
Then be exild for evermore, erdond in sorow; [greiving]
In othir provyns and pertis povert to suffer, [parts]
In thronge and in thraldom threpe with the werld. [crowds · struggle]
Therfore welcum, iwis, is my wale deth. [desired]
My maydynhed I merk to myghtifull goddis: [dedicate]
Accepte hit as sacrifise, and my saule to. [soul]
This holly with hert here I beseke.

(ll. 12131–8)

However much in the background she is for most of the poem, Polyxena turns out to be central to the narrative, since her grief at Hector's death initiates a terrible and determinant pattern of violence and recrimination. This momentum of violence can only finally be resolved by her sacrifice, which ends the Trojan war by allowing the Greeks to return, to their own disasters.

The Polyxena–Achilles plot is interwoven with the Criseyde–Troilus story, as told in Chaucer's *Troilus and Criseyde*, in a variety of ways: the men fall in love in the same way; Calchas, Criseyde's father, encourages the Greeks to keep fighting, despite Achilles' pleas to stop; Achilles' first victim in his renewed attack is Troilus; and Calchas and Antenor (for whom Criseyde is swapped) seal Polyxena's death at the hands of Pyrrhus. The Polyxena narrative serves, however, to put into much sharper and more brutal relief the forces that drive war, and the extremely limited options they leave for women. War, in the *Destruction*, is produced not only by bureaucratic failure, but more profoundly by the traffic in women. Medea, Hesione, Helen, Breseid, Polyxena, Cassandra, and Andromache are all the victims of brutal and improper appropriation by men. However much Guido might be explicitly anti-feminist at points (the author of the *Destruction* much less so),[50] the narrative as a whole takes the lid off static anti-feminist exemplarism. The poem cannot help doing this: however much the speeches of Achilles in favour of

[50] For examples of Guido's anti-feminism, see Bks 2. 294 (Medea), 7. 104 (Helen), 19. 159 (Briseida), 32. 126 (Clytemnestra). The author of the *Destruction* either deleted or toned these passages down; see C. D. Benson, *History of Troy*, p. 47.

stopping the war are themselves driven by his desire for Polyxena, they nevertheless unmask the gross stupidity and gratuitous destruction of the whole enterprise (ll. 9323–62; 9743–84). Women in this narrative have very little room for movement; the fact that some of them adapt to circumstances, as Helen does (ll. 3279–3392), serves to delineate the larger contours that are repeated in the micro-world of Chaucer's *Troilus and Criseyde*, a text in which a satisfied Troilus offers Pandarus 'my faire suster Polixene, | Cassandre, Eleyne, or any of the frape [crowd]' (3. 409–10).[51]

As I said earlier, the Guido-tradition, in each of its two post-*Troilus* English manifestations, is anti-Galfridian, and anti-Virgilian. For the most part, the opposition to both Geoffrey and Virgil amounts to the same thing, since the Guido-tradition does not produce narratives of migration and territorial possession. Unlike both the *Aeneid* and the *Historia regum Britanniae*, that is, this version of the fall of Troy never really moves from a site of civic destruction. The story opens with a sequence in which Laomedon's Troy is razed; this event is simply expanded in greater detail in the destruction of Priam's Troy. The destruction of cities is equally the theme of the Greek return, repeated in a series of smaller-scale disasters across the whole of Greece. The geography of this tradition is entirely coherent, but the narrative moves wholly within the destructive circuit of the Aegean, never out into new territory. The problem posed by this narrative, that is, is how monarchical and chivalric societies can preserve what territory they already hold, especially when the shame culture of those societies propels them forward into self-destruction. The problem is lodged in especially acute form, since the societies of this narrative are not in any way underwritten by divine sanction, just as their historical purview is generally limited by the bounds of a very fallible human reason. The only prophetic voices, notably that of Cassandra, are consistently silenced. Fortune is pervasive, history extremely treacherous.

These narratives are especially pertinent to English and French

[51] My discussion of the Achilles–Polyxena relationship is parallel to that of Patterson, *Chaucer and the Subject of History*, pp. 119–22. My own understanding of the whole of what I call the 'Guido-tradition' squares with Patterson's larger discussion of the tradition stemming from Benoît's *Roman de Troie* (ibid. 114–26). For a much more extended discussion of *Troilus and Criseyde*, see Ch. 4, below.

aristocratic readers in the later medieval period. This Troy story is not a colonial narrative of war between technologically disparate powers. This is instead a narrative of war between technologically equal belligerents; it powerfully describes, thereby, the nature and pattern of Anglo-French conflict throughout this period. The heights of English victories over France under Edward III (1328–77) and Henry V (1414–22) were each followed by periods of internal depletion and civil war. Medieval English kings, as I argue at greater length in Chapter 6, tended to incur civil war by not pursuing war against France. The option of foreign war was, however, not without its own terrible dangers, since the enemy was certainly a technological equal. The Guido Troy-narrative tells the story of foreign war between equals leading to civil war; this is precisely what happened in England in the reign of Henry VI: the unsustainable victories of Henry V between 1415 and 1420 led to civil war in England, after the final loss of all French territories in 1453.

Both Lydgate and the author of the *Destruction* are well aware of the *Aeneid*. The *Destruction*-author mentions Virgil with approval in his prologue, a point at which Lydgate, following Guido, is more sceptical.[52] The *Destruction* also mentions the *Aeneid* at the moment Aeneas leaves Troy in exile:

> Now what worthe of that wye, and his [became · man]
> wale godis, [excellent]
> Fro he Tuscan had takyn, tellis hit not here. [after]
> Of his wondurfull werkes who wilnes to know, [desires]
> Go loke at the lede, that his lyfe wroght. [man · composed]
> Virgell, full verely, thos vertus can tell, [truly]
> In a boke that buerne of that bold made, [man · courageous man]
> That Enyodos, with noble men, is to nome cald. [entitled]
>
> (ll. 12908–14)

This, much more flattering than the equivalent, non-committal reference in Guido, sounds friendly enough. It comes, however, after a long sequence of wholly treacherous actions by Aeneas, who has betrayed not only Troy, but also his co-conspirator Antenor (Book 30).

52 For Guido's non-committal references to Virgil, see 5. 69, 12. 237, 32. 251. Elsewhere (Prol., 32, 35. 228), he says that Virgil's account is vitiated by his reliance on fables.

Aeneas leaves because he is banished as a traitor. At the equivalent moment in Lydgate, Lydgate links the Guido-tradition of Aeneas as traitor to Troy with the Ovidian tradition of Aeneas as traitor to Dido: 'But for al that, how he was unkynde, | Rede Eneydos, and ther ye shal it fynde' (5. 1451–2).[53] In these texts, then, there can be no doubt: their own unremitting hostility towards Aeneas is merely the most obvious sign of the profound ideological rupture between them and the *Aeneid*. Lydgate closes his *Troy Book* by wishing imperial fame on 'that noble myghti conquerour', Henry V, 'So that his name may be magnified | Here in this lyf up to the sterres clere, | And afterward, above the nynthe spere, | Whan he is ded, for to han a place' (5. 3600–3). After the previous five books, this can only sound hollow, more like a superficial courtly gesture after the powerful and minatory story that precedes it.

As for hostility to the Galfridian tradition, there is very little explicit comment on that in these texts. Both the *Destruction*-poet and Lydgate make passing reference to the Troy story as depicting the deeds of ancestors. The alliterative poet opens by placing the Tory story in a category of 'aunters . . . olde of aunsetris nobill' (l. 5), but never afterwards refers to the Trojan ancestry of the Britons. Lydgate makes the same, superficial gesture (Prologue, 167), though he does take it further later in Book 1. After recounting the way in which the small quarrel between Jason and Laomedon grew into a catastrophe, he leaves his source to describe the foundation of Western European nations from the Trojan diaspora (1.811–919). He does mention Brutus here,

> After whom, yif I schal nat feyne,
> Whilom this lond called was Breteyne;
> For he of geauntys thorugh his manhood wan [giants]
> This noble yle, and it first began.
>
> (1. 833–6)[54]

Nothing else is made of this material. The closing reference to Henry V being born 'by discent of lyne | As rightful eyr' to the kingdoms of

[53] Other references to Virgil by Lydgate in the *Troy Book* are as follows: 2. 341–56, 2. 7125–63, both prompted by Guido.

[54] The Laud *Troy Book* does offer an account of Arthur's conquests (ll. 5931–54), but only by way of demonstrating how fickle Fortune is.

both France and England is much more specific in its genealogical reference (Envoy, 5–6);[55] even this encouragement to territorial possession, however, could not be more thoroughly qualified by the text that precedes it. Genealogy guarantees very little indeed in the Guido-tradition, either within the Graeco-Trojan society represented, or between the texts of that pan-European tradition and their readers.

In the fifteenth century the main literary tradition of Troy, then, as distinct from the chronicle tradition of the *Brut* material, had no sympathy for ancestral or imperialistic pretensions. Instead, this tradition represented the failures of militarist societies, and those failures are produced from the very territorial and matrimonial dynamics by which such societies are driven. Before looking more briefly to other 'tragic' narratives of the fall of civilizations in this period, I conclude this section by trying to answer the question of why such texts appealed to royal and aristocratic, or gentry readers. That they did have such appeal would seem clear from the manuscript evidence. Lydgate's *Troy Book* was written at the request of Henry V, and many of the fifteenth-century manuscripts of that work are deluxe books, lavishly produced with illuminations for aristocratic readers.[56] The 1513 print, by Richard Pynson, was, according to Pynson, printed at the command of Henry VIII.[57] The patron of the *Destruction*'s author is, unfortunately, unknown, despite the fact that the scribe promises to declare the name of 'the knight that causet it to be made',[58] just where a gap in the manuscript occurs. But the patron of the scribe, Thomas Chetham, was probably the Earl of Derby, for some of whose manors Chetham was bailiff. Thorlac Turville-Petre conjectures that the author's patron was a member of the Stanley family, later the Earls of Derby.[59]

Very simply, I suggest that the Guido-tradition both represented and was produced by a division of power between aristocrats and

[55] For the specific force of this reference to post-Conquest 'rights' to France, see Patterson, 'Making Identities'.

[56] For a description of almost all the MSS, see Lydgate, *Troy Book*, ed. Bergen, pt. 4, pp. 1–54. For the high quality of *Troy Book* MSS, see also L. Lawton.

[57] Lydgate, *Troy Book*, ed. Bergen, pt. 4, p. 58.

[58] Clerk, *Gest Hystoriale*, ed. Panton and Donaldson, p. lxx.

[59] Turville-Petre, 'Author of the *Destruction*', p. 268. See Putter, *Introduction to the 'Gawain'-Poet*, pp. 28–37, for the plausibility of this suggestion.

the learned, whom I shall call 'clerics'; this recognized division of power allowed clerics a permissible voice that is trenchantly opposed to aristocratic military, marital, and bureaucratic practice.[60] The clerical voice of the narrator holds up to aristocratic readers the spectacle of their own downfall, cast down by their own readiness to mount the wheel of Fortune, as represented in Figure 3, an illumination accompanying Lydgate's *Troy Book*. The catastrophes of the *Destruction*, as I have shown, are generated by the failure of bureaucratic procedure. Counsel sessions are badly conducted, and diplomatic missions poorly executed, contrary to the ostensible wishes of executive power. The narrative cries out for prudential, clerical voices to guide aristocratic behaviour. There are relatively few 'clerical' voices heard from within the work, and unless they flatter militarist impulses, as in the case of Calchas, they are dismissed by knightly swagger. This is the fate of Helenus' intervention in the first Trojan counsel session, just as the philosopher Protheus fails as he warns Priam to listen 'with a loue ere, | And wirke after wit, that worship may folow' (ll. 2650–1). His failure gives way to the impassioned but useless prophecy of Cassandra, and, finally, to the rueful voice of the poet himself, who reflects that if the council had been swayed by Hector, Helenus, Protheus, and Cassandra, Troy would still be standing (ll. 2711–24).

The absence of effective clerical voices from within Trojan and Greek societies is, however, made good by the presence of the prudential poet in the work itself. If these societies of the past failed for want of philosophical reflection, the work presents itself as saying, then *contemporary* readers might be able to avoid the same mistakes by attending to this very work, and to the clerical voice of its author and translator. This voice, it should be stressed, does not, on the whole, promote specifically Christian morality. Both Lydgate and the *Destruction*-author translate the long sequence from Guido about the uselessness of idol-worship (Lydgate, *Troy Book*, 2. 5391–5940; *Destruction*, 4295–4458), but the point of this is not so much Christian apologetics as to underline the vacuity of relying on divine voices for guidance. The voice of the narrator is either one of lament for fallen Troy, which is especially pronounced in the Laud *Troy*

[60] For the 12th-cent. debate between *miles* and *clericus*, see Putter, '*Sir Gawain and the Green Knight*', pp. 197–201, and further references there.

Fig. 3. The Wheel of Fortune. Lydgate, *Troy Book*. Manchester, John Rylands Library, MS English 1, fo. 28v (*c.*1420–35).

Book,[61] or that of prudential and practical wisdom. It proposes more effective political action, rather than any Christian counsel to turn aside from a deceptive world.[62] We have already seen this in the criticism of Hector's chivalrous but tactically stupid mercy to Ajax; the same voice is, for example, also marked off from the narrative by way of concluding the fall of Laomedon's Troy, where the narrator warns against the few angry words that may ignite a huge and destructive fire:

> Lo, how fortune is felle and of fer caste, [fierce · far-sighted]
> That drawes in a dede hate in a derke wille,
> And of a litill hath likyng a low for to kyndull, [fire]
> That hepis into harme in a hond while. [grows · short]
>
> (ll. 1447–50)

The presence of this clerical voice, then, marks a division of discursive power in the work itself. This is not so much the narrative of great kings and warriors; it is that narrative as commented on and arranged by a distinct, clerical voice, capable of intervening in and shaping it for persuasive ends. No such division of power exists in the *Aeneid*, since the poet there takes his voice from the same divine sources that moved history in the first place. Aeneas' own voice, as the narrator of Books 2–3, is almost indistinguishable from that of Virgil. Douglas does try to intervene in the narrative, but the decorum of his philological project strictly delimits his voice to the Prologues, while the area of the text itself remains inviolate.

The shaping, distinct presence of the narrator in works of the Guido-tradition had two important effects.The first is rhetorical. These texts come in segments; the decorum of their transmission allows a translator to intervene at will. So far from being representative of a collapse from the sublime style to a petrified mannerism,[63]

[61] See, for e.g., ll. 9891–9992, not in Guido.

[62] I disagree with Barron, pp. 114–15, on this point. It is true that Lydgate makes a final call for withdrawal from the world, *Troy Book*, 5. 3546–86. This, however, very much in the pattern of the epilogue to *Troilus and Criseyde*, is the only such call in a huge poem.

[63] The terms I use here are drawn from Auerbach's great essay 'Camilla, or the Rebirth of the Sublime', where he compares the Old French *Enéas* (1150–60) with the *Aeneid*. The terms of his dismissal of the Old French poem are duplicated in discussions of Lydgate's treatment of *romans antiques*; see e.g. Pearsall, *John Lydgate*, p. 129: 'Endless digression, description, astronomical periphrasis, apostrophe . . .

this rhetorical procedure is designed to provoke a certain alienation of the reader from the action. The reader of Virgil is indeed spell-bound by a sublime style; the reader of the *Destruction* is detached from, and asked to analyse, the processes of history.

The second effect concerns the anachronism of these texts. It is curious that anachronism, which presents classical warriors as medieval knights, should for so long have been taken as the key sign that the 'medieval' period had no historical sense.[64] Curious, because a rigorous commitment to the integrity of the past has never, in my view, been characteristic of literary discourse in any period: literary texts, certainly successful ones, project themselves into their own modernity. And in any case, anachronism is a very superficial marker of historicity: a sense of historical process is surely a more significant index of 'a sense of history', and the Guido-texts have this in bulk. The charge of anachronism is, however, especially irrelevant with the texts of the Guido-tradition, since their whole purpose is to show 'the very age and body of the time his form and pressure'. Lydgate, in fact, does make serious efforts to create a sense of historical propriety, particularly with his description of the theatre in ancient Troy (2. 860–926), and, unlike the popular Laud *Troy Book*, neither Lydgate nor the *Destruction*-author put inappropriate, Christian expressions into the mouths of their characters. But historical propriety cannot afford to go too far, since these texts are meant to be persuasive: they are addressed to a warrior class of a feudal, or 'bastard-feudal', society.[65] The fiercely competitive, aristocratic power blocks in both Trojan and Greek society are characteristic of the readership for whom these texts were designed.

The fact that a text of the *Destruction*'s quality should be produced

philosophical reflection, moral exhortation—these are what Lydgate adds to the translation, but they are in a sense the body of the work, for it is through them that Lydgate makes sense in his own terms of a historical narrative which for the Middle Ages could make sense in no others.'

[64] A classic statement of this ubiquitous idea may be found in Auerbach, 'Weary Prince', pp. 320–1: 'Although two past cultures—the antique and the Judeo-Christian—were of great importance within the frame of medieval civilization . . . there was yet such a lack of historical consciousness and perspective that the events and characters of those distant epochs were simply transferred to the present forms and conditions of life.' For its application to Middle English literature, except Chaucer, see e.g. Spearing, *Medieval to Renaissance*, chs. 1–3.

[65] For an extremely clear picture of such a society, see S. Walker.

in a non-metropolitan dialect is itself indicative of the relatively decentred literary and aristocratic culture of the fourteenth and fifteenth centuries. But if political power is decentred, so too is discursive power, since, as I have argued, works in the Guido-tradition are projected from a secular clerical position, which can be fiercely oppositional to aristocratic practice. By contrast, the *Aeneid* translations of the first half of the sixteenth century by Douglas and Surrey were written by aristocrats whose family fortunes were extremely vulnerable to the power of monarchs.[66] Both Douglas and Surrey exemplify Castiglione's ideal of the cultivated courtier, but the discursive identification of *miles* and *clericus* this implies offers no distinct, clerical perspective from which to observe and analyse aristocratic society.[67] In the fifteenth century the 'tragic' is the preserve of clerics, who certainly address the interests of secular warriors, but who speak from a distinct and partly oppositional discursive position.

IV

Troy is not the only fallen *polis* of English vernacular literature of the fourteenth and fifteenth centuries. Thebes is 'brittened and brent to brondez and askez',[68] just as the empires of both Arthur and Alexander collapse with the death of those heroes. In this section I offer a brief conspectus of the main narratives of these fallen kingdoms. I argue that the model of the anti-imperialistic Guido-tradition, as projected from a clerical yet secular (i.e. learned though not specifically Christian) perspective, is also apparent in each of these stories. It even governs Arthurian texts that are reflexes of the Galfridian tradition. What is spectacularly highlighted by the *literary*, as distinct from the chronicle, representation of Arthur is his collapse, and the delusory ambitions of empire that propel him to failure. The texts discussed are as follows: Lydgate's *Destruction of*

[66] For the family fortunes of Douglas, see Bawcutt, ch. 1; for the dreadful family history of Surrey, see the popular but reliable biography by Chapman.

[67] Surrey owned and annotated a copy of Castiglione's *Il Cortegiano*; see Cattaneo, p. 43 n. 76.

[68] 'Destroyed and burnt to charred wood and ashes'.

Thebes (traditionally dated 1422); the alliterative *Morte Arthure* (*c.*1400); Malory's 'The Tale of Noble King Arthur That Was Emperor Himself Through Dignity of His Hands', and his 'Most Piteous Tale of the Morte Arthure Saunz Guerdon' (completed by 1469, published by Caxton 1485); and *The Wars of Alexander* (between 1350 and 1450).

(*a*) Lydgate's *Destruction of Thebes*

Lydgate's *Destruction of Thebes*, traditionally known as the *Siege of Thebes*,[69] tells the story of Thebes from its foundation by Amphion until its destruction by Theseus, in 4,716 lines of five-stress couplets. After narrating the story of Oedipus, this narrative, which is ultimately dependent on the twelfth-century *Roman de Thebes*,[70] tells the story of the fraternal strife between Polynices and Etiocles; the main action of the story concerns the Argive mission, under Adrastus, to enforce a proper exchange of power in Thebes. This mission ends with the destruction of the entire Argive force, as well as of the two warring brothers, before the city itself is destroyed by Theseus, 'That noght was left but the soyle al bare' (l. 4561).

If the Guido-tradition of Troy marks the difference between prudential, clerical voices on the one hand and impetuous, knightly voices on the other, this division is even more heavily accentuated in Lydgate's Theban narrative. Here the aged figures, and especially the pagan priest Amphiorax, all counsel prudential restraint before undertaking a war, however just the cause. Amphiorax attempts to dissuade the Argive parliament from declaring war, by predicting

> Her dysemol daies and her fatal houres, [their]
> Her auenturys and her sharpe shoures,
> The froward soort and the unhappy stoundys, [ominous
> The compleyntes of her dedly woundys, fate · times]
> The wooful wrath and the contrariouste [malevolence]
> Of felle Mars in his cruelte. [malign]
>
> (ll. 2893–98)

[69] I argue that the title should be the *Destruction of Thebes* in Simpson, '"Dysemol daies"'.

[70] The immediate source of Lydgate's Theban poem is a prose redaction of the *Roman de Thèbes*; see Renoir, 'Immediate Source of Lydgate's *Siege of Thebes*'.

This speech is met with the derision of the entire parliament, but especially that of 'sowdeours [soldiers], | And of lordes regnyng in her flours' (ll. 2935–6).

This pattern of encounter, where philosophic wisdom about the critical importance of foresight is disastrously ignored and dismissed by the impetuous and chivalric young, repeatedly generates the catastrophes recounted in Lydgate's narrative. The clerical–chivalric opposition also governs the narratorial position from which the tale is told, since Lydgate the monk ambitiously tells his story as a Canterbury tale, replying to the Knight. He pictures himself as having joined the return journey of Chaucer's Canterbury pilgrims to London; whereas Chaucer's Knight had halted the tragic stories of the Monk on the outward journey, here, on the way back to London, the clerical Lydgate takes up the challenge of tragedy. And he does so by addressing the Knight's own Theban narrative: Lydgate's story ends precisely where the Knight's begins, with the destruction of Thebes by Theseus. So in this extended version of the *Canterbury Tales*, events that happen *earlier* than those of the *Knight's Tale* are recounted *after* it. One effect of this is simply to provide an unsettling reminder that the events of the *Knight's Tale* are but a reflex of the larger destructive, fratricidal patterns that dominate and destroy Thebes. Just as the *Troy Book* reduplicates the story of *Troilus and Criseyde*, by painting it back onto the larger historical canvas from which Chaucer's narrative has been scaled down, so too does Lydgate's Theban narrative set Chaucer's Theban tale into a larger historical perspective.

Another effect of this relationship with Chaucer's Knight is to stress the *contemporary* relationship between knights and clerics. Lydgate highlights his own status as clerical narrator addressing knights, offering them a text which is itself prudential, and which seeks to persuade where the clerical figures within his narrative had failed. Lydgate's reflection on the fall of ancient cities is not at all proposed as an antiquarian exercise. The pagan setting is on the contrary strategic: it permits a wholly secular vision of politics and war, and it does so in order to persuade English knights against imperial mission, and against the dangers of civil war. Whatever the date of this text, and my own view is that it post-dates the death of Henry V, it offers an extremely powerful admonition against lightly taking on war, whether civil or against France, whatever the perceived justice of the cause.[71] And if it was written before the death of Henry V, then it was almost freakishly prophetic of the threat of civil war between Henry's brothers after his death. Lydgate's anachronism within the pagan setting has persuasive intent, since he is heading back to his contemporary London, often called 'Troynovant', as he narrates.

(*b*) The alliterative *Morte Arthure*

From the late fifteenth century in England many humanists were sceptical of, or downright hostile to, Arthurian material. Thus Roger Ascham (1515–68) in his *Schoolmaster* (published 1570) dismissed it as 'bold bawdrye', 'good stuffe, for wise men to laughe at' (bk. 1, p. 231). Such writers instead favoured imitation of classical materials alone.[72] It may be, however, that earlier English 'humanists' were equally sceptical of the Arthurian myth. We find no extended engagement with Arthurian material in Chaucer, Gower, or Lydgate.[73] This is a mysterious but surely significant absence. I myself ascribe it to the clear distance those writers set between themselves and an ancestral, militarist, aristocratic ethos. However that may be, the powerful Arthurian tragic writing of the period was either written in a non-metropolitan dialect, or produced by gentry society. I am thinking of two works in particular: the alliterative *Morte Arthure*, probably composed around 1400, in a Lincolnshire dialect, but copied between 1420 and 1440 by Robert Thornton, a member of the minor Yorkshire gentry;[74] and the material in Malory's *Works* relating directly to the rise and fall of Arthur's kingdom. Sir Thomas Malory can now be fairly certainly identified with the Warwickshire

[71] The text is dated by its editors to 1421, on the basis of what they see as a celebratory reference to the treaty of Troyes (ll. 4690–3). The reference to the treaty is certainly there, but in my view the poem is anything but celebratory. If it is written before the death of Henry V, it is a remarkably accurate prediction of the situation after his death. For my argument about the date, see Simpson, '"Dysemol daies"'.

[72] For some examples of humanist fastidiousness about Arthurian materials, see Carlson, 'King Arthur and Court Poems'. The change, in the 12th cent., from the classicizing *romans antiques* to the Arthurian romances of Chrétien de Troyes, may represent another classical–Arthurian divide.

[73] For the very few references in these poets to Arthurian material, see the references collected in Dean, pp. 130–9.

[74] For information on Robert Thornton, see J. J. Thompson, pp. 2–5.

knight of that name whose thoroughly inglorious career fighting on both sides in the civil wars of the fifteenth century ended (not to speak of previous imprisonments) in prison, where he wrote his Arthurian works, and where he died in 1471.[75] But even if these works did emanate from landed society, they nevertheless structured their received Arthurian material in such a way as to underline the treacherousness of foreign or civil war.

The alliterative *Morte Arthure* (4,346 lines) is a spectacular text, both rhetorically and structurally. As in all the vernacular works more or less derived from Geoffrey of Monmouth's account of Arthur in the *Historia regum Britanniae*, Arthur is presented as a charismatic figure, larger than life and central to the action at almost every point. His presence is dramatically and strategically realized for the reader through the power of his highly coloured courtly and military rhetoric: every action in the poem is generated by a speech of Arthur, and only when 'spekes he no more' (l. 4327) can the poem end. Arthur's oratory and action is served by the poet's own peculiarly mannered alliterative practice, alliterating on the same letter across up to ten consecutive lines (e.g. ll. 2483–92, a speech of Arthur). Structurally, too, the work is spectacular, since the poet deals very decisively with his received material to create an almost geometrical pattern of rapid rise and very sudden, almost breakneck crash. The poem begins with a businesslike summary of Arthur's conquests, as related in detail in the 'literary' chronicle sources, especially Wace's *Roman de Brut* (1155) and Lawman's *Brut* (?early thirteenth century), both sources used by the alliterative *Morte*-poet. The two parts of the main narrative then follow: Arthur's relentless and almost successful campaign across France, from eastern France south across the Alps into Italy, and down almost to Rome to be crowned emperor (ll. 64–3217); and his fall, initiated by his dream of Fortune, and effected by Mordred's treachery in Britain (ll. 3218–4346).

Up to Arthur's dream of Fortune, the poem is not at all characterized by the features of the *roman antique*, as exemplified in the Troy narratives, or in Lydgate's *Thebes*. Here there is no critique of war, and no persuasive and prudential clerical voice. On the contrary, the

[75] For Malory's biography, see P. J. C. Field, esp. pp. 124–5, for the width of Malory's sympathies.

poem fairly bristles with militarist confidence and conviction. Arthur's initial reply to the envoys from Rome, who claim tribute from Arthur, carefully calibrates courtesy and menace (ll. 133–55). This menace becomes a decision in the counsel session then called by Arthur (ll. 231–406), where no clerical voice resists the consistently warlike speeches of Arthur's magnates, and where the poet omits Gawain's speech in praise of peace from his sources (e.g. Lawman's *Brut*, ll. 12451–8). Just as this text is about 'elders of alde tym and of theire awke [brave] dedys' (l. 13), so too does Arthur claim ancestral rights to Roman tribute, by title of conquest. His ancestors Belinus and Brennius, he says, were Roman emperors; 'as awlde men telles',

> Thei coverde the Capitoile and keste doun the walles, [threw]
> Hyngede of theire heddys-men by hundrethes at ones. [hanged · leaders]
> Seyn Constantyne our kynsmane conquerid it aftyre.
>
> (ll. 280–2)

Recourse to title in this text, then, serves only to disclose an anterior possession by violence and superior might: Arthur's reply to the Emperor effectively amounts to a challenge on these terms, inspired as he is by the comparable power of his ancestors. The poet himself does nothing to mute or question this challenge. On the contrary, the confrontation between Arthur and the Roman Emperor escalates into a strangely magnified account of western aggression towards Rome and beyond, since the Roman allies turn out to be entirely drawn from both Africa and Asia (ll. 570–609). If the Brutus myth traces a movement from the East to the nations of the West, then this poem is a case of the empire striking back at its source with a militant orientalism.

There is, to be sure, a wonderful inset digression (ll. 2513–2716) in Arthur's aggressive eastwards push, where Gawain meets the significantly named Priamus, a knight whose ancestry is metonymic for the East: he numbers among his ancestors not only Alexander, but also Hector of Troy, Joshua, and Judas Maccabeus. The two knights do battle with each other, but the violence turns out to be constructive, and allows the momentary imagination of alternative relations between West and East: Gawain and Priamus are healed of their wounds by waters offered by Priamus from the rivers of Paradise. The western aggressor, that is, is restored by eastern sources, and the exchange ends on friendly terms. These alternative relations nevertheless insist on the superiority of the West, even if the West recognizes the sources of its energy in the East. Priamus comes over to the Arthurian side, and he does so in such a way as to reaffirm the brutal realities of war: the sequence is followed by some of the most violent descriptions of battle in the poem (e.g. ll. 2760–83); Priamus then deserts his lord, and is followed by his men, who complain that they have not been paid for the last four years (l. 2928).[76] Arthur's relentless eastward and southern movement continues, from the Siege of Metz, across the Alps into Lombardy and Tuscany:

> Towrres he turnes and turmentez the pople;
> Wroghte wedewes full wlonke, wrotherayle synges,
> Ofte wery and wepe and wryngen theire handes,
> And all wastys with werre there he awaye rydez—
> Thaire welthes and theire wonnynges wandrethe he wroghte.
>
> (ll. 3153–7)[77]

Through to the Italian campaign, then, this text would hardly seem to conform to the deeply pessimistic Guido-tradition: Arthur is a triumphalist hero, and he is very definitely 'our' hero; for the narrator, the readers of his text form a collective whole with the British warriors in it. Arthur's apparently irresistible advance, so far from being questioned by the poet, is set into vibrant, almost lurid relief by the poet's mannered rhetoric. If there are historical resonances in this representation, they would seem to be designed to evoke the Continental victories of that Arthurian enthusiast, Edward III.[78] But just as the poet draws on textual sources from different periods of English history, from the twelfth to the fourteenth century,[79] so too does he, in my view, compress different historical phases of the French war into the historical memory of his one poem. For from this point on,

[76] This sequence is discussed by Patterson, 'Romance of History'.

[77] 'He overturns towers and torments the people; he made proud widows to sing of misery, often to curse and weep and to wring their hands. Wherever he rides he wastes with war, and reduced their wealth and their dwellings to a sorry state.'

[78] For the evidence, see W. Matthews, pp. 184–7. This does not invalidate a later date for the poem, for which see L. D. Benson. For Edward III's own Arthurian enthusiasms, see R. S. Loomis, 'Chivalric and Dramatic Imitations'.

[79] For the many sources, both Latin and vernacular, of this poem, see *Morte Arthure*, ed. Hamel, pp. 34–53.

Arthur plunges into abject failure and civil war, reminiscent of the period 1369 forwards; by 1372–3 most of the gains of 1360 had been lost again, and were not regained before the end of Richard II's reign.[80] Arthur's changed fortunes are signalled decisively by his long account of his dream of Fortune, where he sees the Nine Worthies on Fortune's wheel, and experiences her blandishments himself, before being violently swept downwards. The philosopher's interpretation of the dream is unequivocal, determining the steep slope of decline for the rest of the poem: Arthur's power is finished, and he must prepare for his end. The clerical voice that has been silent for so long in this text now glorifies Arthur as one of the Nine Worthies, including Priamus' doomed ancestors Alexander, Hector, Joshua, and Judas Maccabeus, in the very act of writing him out of history as a violent invader:

> Chalange nowe when thow will, thow chevys no more.
> Thow has schedde myche blode, and schalkes distroyede,
> Sakeles, in cirquytrie, in sere kynges landis.
> Schryfe the of thy schame and schape for thyn ende.
>
> (ll. 3397–400)[81]

The disposition of the clerical voice of this text, then, is different from that found in the Guido-tradition. There the reader is made aware of significant errors throughout the text, whose cumulative effect is to produce military disaster; in the *Morte*, on the contrary, the force of the clerical voice is withheld for one powerful and decisive intervention. This effect is less subtle, but the oppositional philosophical perspective is, however, just as forceful. Brutus material is, here, finally disallowed a propagandistic use of the kind made by English kings. Instead the work brings to the fore the dynastic fragilities inherent in Geoffrey's text; as Lee Patterson has said, the Galfridian material 'never lost its capacity to call into question the very purpose for which it was designed.'[82]

80 For the military history of these years, see Keen, pp. 251–90.

81 'You may complain now as much as you like, you will achieve no more. You have shed much blood, and destroyed innocent men in pride, in the lands of many kings. Confess yourself of your sin, and prepare for your end.'

82 Patterson, 'Romance of History', p. 203.

(*c*) Malory

Malory's *Works* can only really be understood in the context of romance, and I shall have more to say about them in Chapter 6. For the moment I restrict myself simply to observing that Malory's own deployment of Arthurian material is, like the alliterative *Morte*, and like the Trojan narratives considered above, profoundly pessimistic about the possibility of sustaining political power in a treacherous world. Whereas, however, the alliterative poem focuses especially on the dangers of pursuing foreign war, Malory's text more consistently underlines the instabilities within chivalric society that lead to civil war. For Malory, victory in Continental wars turns out to be irrelevant.

Just as the alliterative *Morte*-author exploits earlier British versions of the reign of Arthur to reflect his own historical experience, so too does Malory exploit the alliterative *Morte*, which was his principal source for his one imperial book, 'The Tale of the Noble King Arthur That Was Emperor Himself Through Dignity of His Hands'. This very title, however, would suggest telling differences between this work and the alliterative *Morte*: in the alliterative poem, Arthur does *not* become emperor, since at the critical juncture he fails. In Malory's version, however, Arthur is crowned in Rome, returns victorious to Britain and to Guinevere, and 'there was never a solempner metyng in one cite togedyrs, for all maner of rychesse they brought with hem at the full'.[83] This ending is an index of the many ways in which Malory's work is a simplification and sentimentalization of the alliterative work. Here Arthur chooses trusty regents, and not the perfidious Mordred, while he is away; the battle scenes are abbreviated and sanitized; Arthur's shortened speeches lose their ferocity; Priamus is converted and christened; Arthur has no dream of Fortune, but moves effortlessly and in good conscience to his coronation in Rome, and 'there was none that playned on his parte, ryche nothir poore' (I. 245). These changes in narrative disposition, which have the effect of domesticating the triumphalist militarism of the earlier text, are correlative with the change from verse to prose. If the highly charged verse brings a militant Arthur

[83] *Works of Sir Thomas Malory*, ed. Vinaver, rev. Field, I. 246. All citations are from this edn.

dramatically present to the reader, Malory's early prose, with its much looser rhythm and flatly paratactic syntax, distances the action. The many traces of alliteration in the prose serve only to highlight the way in which the aural richness of the verse has been diluted. Of course this is partly to do with the different audiences of these texts: the *Morte*-author presents himself as reciting to a listening audience, whether or not he really did so, whereas Malory writes for a private reader. But the very different formal practices also, as I say, work in tandem with the altogether gentler presentation of Arthur as conqueror.

There is, then, nothing explicitly anti-imperialist in this section of Malory's works, just as there is no call whatsoever for an oppositional clerical voice. That having been said, Arthur as victorious emperor turns out to be an irrelevance in the larger scheme of Malory's work, since Malory is much more nearly concerned with civil war. It has been persuasively suggested that the presentation of Arthur in this book is designed to recall the victories of Henry V in France between 1415 and 1420;[84] if that is true, then the historical memory of Malory's whole book reveals those Continental victories to have been a delusive distraction from the internal threats to fifteenth-century English society. As he transformed the earlier, alliterative text, Malory was himself writing as an imprisoned participant in the civil war in England that followed the collapse of any claim to France by the middle of the fifteenth century. Malory's changes to his source are, I think, conscious preparations for the later collapse of Arthurian society from within. This is evident in both his additions and omissions from the alliterative text. The most significant addition is, perhaps, the much higher profile that Lancelot has in Malory's version. In the alliterative poem Cador makes a bold attack when it might have been best to retire (Alliterative *Morte*, 1637–1945); he does so precisely that he should not be shamed by Lancelot, 'that with the king lengez' (Alliterative *Morte*, 1720). In Malory's version, by contrast, Lancelot heads the escort, and fights so well that 'was he honoured dayes of his lyff, for never ere or that day was he proved so well' (1. 216). When Cador reports to Arthur in the alliterative text, Arthur expresses anger at Cador's impetuosity,

[84] See ibid. 3. 1367–8, for a summary of the evidence.

to which he replies with a speech of fierce loyalty to Arthur (Alliterative *Morte*, 1928–37). Arthur, controlling the situation with a mixture of anger and tenderness, accepts the defence. In Malory's equivalent scene, Arthur expresses a muffled displeasure of the same kind, but is rebuffed by his knights' affirmation that individual pride counts for more than strategic prudence and the monarch's interest: '"Not so," sayde sir Lancelot, "the shame sholde ever have bene oures." "That is trouthe," seyde sir Clegis and sir Bors, "for knightes ons shamed recoverys hit never"' (1. 217–18). Here the scene ends.

Malory also omits material from the alliterative text, only to use it later. This is most obviously true of the entire sequence narrating Arthur's fall (*Morte*, 3218–4346). Malory clearly knows that he will use a different version of Arthur's death, drawn principally from his main source, the thirteenth-century French Vulgate cycle's prose *Mort Artu*.[85] In any case he cannot have Arthur's death come at the end of his narrative of Continental war, because he intends to insert many romances between that narrative and the collapse of Arthur and his empire. The effect of these intervening romances (i.e. Lancelot, Gareth, Tristram, the Holy Grail, Lancelot and Guinevere), before the deferred fall, profoundly modifies the significance of that fall.[86] In the alliterative text civil dissension is certainly a factor in Arthur's collapse, but the fall itself occurs principally because Arthur is wholly focused on his imperial mission. In Malory's overall structure, the intervening romances are decisive, since they generate irresolvable civil tensions between warring aristocratic groups over which the king has no power. Lancelot is, I concede, the king of France; recognizing defeat, his distribution of lands constitutes a remarkably detailed map of south-western France in the fifteenth century, including areas fought over by the English in 1453.[87] Lancelot's leave-taking is certainly nostalgic for those Continental claims, but equally a recognition of their futility. In any case, Lancelot's leave-taking is represented as much more an act of civil fragmentation, provoked ultimately by Lancelot's adulterous relationship

[85] For Malory's massive indebtedness to French prose sources, see ibid., notes to vol. 3.

[86] I discuss the relation of Malory's romances to his tragic narratives in Ch. 6, below.

[87] *Works of Sir Thomas Malory*, ed. Vinaver, rev. Field, 3. 1205. This passage is not in Malory's source; see ibid. 1640–2.

with the queen, and immediately by Gawain's relentless pursuit of Lancelot for having accidentally murdered his brother. From the perspective of the end of Malory's book, the apparent triumphalism of Arthur's imperial conquest turns out to look like a distraction, a non-stick victory whose simplicities are revealed by the infinitely more dangerous business of managing magnates. Malory himself has difficulty in managing magnates, since his own focus is so consistently on Lancelot rather than Arthur here. This sympathy is manifest in an echo that now resurfaces from the alliterative text, concerning the wheel of Fortune. In the *Morte* Arthur's dream of Fortune's wheel decisively marks the beginning of his fall; here Malory transfers it to Lancelot, who regrets that he must leave the 'most nobelyst Crysten realme':

> But fortune ys so varyaunte, and the wheele so mutable, that there ys no constaunte abydynge. And that may be preved by many olde cronycles, as of noble Ector of Troy and Alysaunder, the myghty conquerroure, and many mo other: whan they were moste in her royalté, they alyght passynge lowe. And so faryth hit by me. (3. 1201)

(*d*) *The Wars of Alexander*

Alexander clearly stands behind stories of tragic fall in this period. I conclude this section with a few words about one of the many Alexander narratives produced in both England and Scotland in this period,[88] the remarkable alliterative poem *The Wars of Alexander* (5,803 lines). This work survives in two manuscripts, neither of which is a complete text, but one nearly so, and, like the alliterative *Morte*, seems to have moved northwards in transcription, in this case from what was possibly a north-western original, to County Durham, the dialect area of both manuscripts.[89] It is not possible to date the work more securely than between 1350 and 1450.[90] The

[88] For other English Alexander texts, see *Alexander*, *The Letters of Alexander to Dindimus, King of the Brahmins*; *Prose Life of Alexander*. For a conspectus of medieval British Alexander material, see Bunt.

[89] For the northwards 'retreat' of alliterative texts throughout the 15th and into the 16th cents., in both composition and transcription, see Pearsall, 'Alliterative Revival', p. 38.

[90] See *Wars of Alexander*, ed. Duggan and Turville-Petre, pp. xlii–xliii for authorship and date.

work is a translation of one recension of a late twelfth-/early thirteenth-century Latin work, the *Historia de preliis Alexandri Magni*, and so, like all the non-Virgilian texts discussed in this chapter, is a vernacular version of a Continental text originally composed, sometimes from earlier materials, in either the twelfth or thirteenth centuries.

The narrative of the poem is divided between Alexander's conquests, culminating in his victory over Darius (Passus 1–15), and his further, extraordinary journeys to the East and beyond, where his insatiable curiosity propels him into both outer space and sea's depths in a metallic and glass submarine (Passus 16–27), before his final return to Babylon, where the alliterative text breaks off, and death by poisoning. Of course there is a pleasing fascination with the marvellous in this second section, but it is much more than that. Alexander the imperialist becomes Alexander the anthropologist; in both guises he is very much a philosopher himself, but the experience of the anthropologist threatens to undo the achievement of the imperialist. In Passus 18, for example, Alexander crosses the Ganges to know more of the manner of life of the Brahmins. The Brahmin Dindimus replies, by letter, that teaching wisdom to Alexander is useless, since 'thi tent [purpose] is all on terrandry and tourment of armes' (l. 4380). He nevertheless goes on to describe the utopian life of the Brahmins, based as it is on need alone (Passus 19), and to condemn the violent laws and related polytheism of the Greeks (Passus 20). Alexander's reply to this is a pure instance of Western orientalism, since he fiercely redescribes the Brahmins' simple life as a bestial existence that lacks the technological and material resources for anything more complex. The West, by contrast, is faced with moral choice precisely because it has the materials and technology to provoke choice: 'Mekill [great] variaunce of vertus environis oure saules' (l. 4759). Alexander ends the encounter by declaring that if he did invade, he would equip them with arms, and teach them to be knights (l. 4833). The rather desperate rejection of the Brahmin is followed by a second potential image of Alexander that faces him on the other side of the known world: he encounters a wild man, wholly governed by appetite, whom he captures and burns (ll. 4866–89).

Alexander's repression of these mirror or inverted images of himself does nothing, however, to repress the anti-imperialist theme that runs even throughout the first, imperial section of the poem. Philosophers, not kings, are triumphant in this work. Alexander is even born of a runaway king-cum-philosopher (Nectanabus); 'clerkes' produce kings, just as the king's own messages, always in the form of clerically composed letters, express the transience of earthly possession. This is true of Alexander's first letter to Darius, which paints a majestic picture of Fortune's wheel (ll. 1972–87), and expresses agnosticism with regard to divine favour, since gods have 'no dole [pity] ne no daliance of dedly bernes' (l. 2003); the only thing for which he can hope is earthly fame. And this same philosophical reflection on the treacherousness of power is echoed in Darius' own letter of defeat, in which he acknowledges his own fragility (ll. 3380–3448). Speeches of this kind, in which enemy kings confide their shared comprehension of imperial delusion, stand at the heart of this brilliant alliterative work.[91]

V

Many histories could have been written from the material referred to in this chapter. One could, for example, have written the history of prosodic change, especially since the demands of the tragic, in need of a sonorous and resonant line that can sustain large-scale continuous narrative, do provoke important metrical innovations. From the four-stress couplets of the popular Laud *Troy Book*, which presents itself as romance, poets concerned to create a tragic effect adopt the fuller metrical possibilities of either the four-stress alliterative line or the five-stress rhyming couplets of Lydgate's *Troy Book*. In the last two cases the metrical capacities of the longer line, more fit for tragic matter than the four-stress couplet, are correlative with more complex thematic ambitions, as in, for example, the *Destruction of Troy*

[91] I should alert the reader to the deliberate omission of an alliterative poem, *Siege of Jerusalem*, ed. Kölbing and Day, from this discussion. One might have thought that it naturally belongs here, since it, too, treats the fall of a city. It resists my case for the generally anti-imperialistic and anti-propagandistic quality of 'fall' narratives of this period (it was probably composed in the 1390s). Finally, however, I think it confirms my case, by being the exception to the rule. It is a thoroughly objectionable work of fervid anti-Semitism, unlike almost anything else in the later medieval period in that respect.

and the *Troy Book*. The same prosodic bifurcation, between a form fit for a more popular and a more sophisticated audience, is strikingly visible later in the period, in the contrast, say, of Caxton's prose and Douglas's five-stress couplet in his *Eneados* for the translation of Latin hexameters. Douglas's metrical choice is conservative, drawing as it does on Chaucer's own innovation for thematically ambitious ancient matter, in the *Legend of Good Women*. In contrast to that metrical conservatism, the great metrical innovation for tragic material is Surrey's introduction into English, from Italian models of Virgilian translation into *verso sciolto* (literally 'loose verse'), of blank verse.[92]

Given that every text discussed here is a translation, one could equally have written the history of translation practice in the period. The very fact of so many Continental works being translated from Latin and French into the English vernacular marks a new confidence and sophistication in English as a medium for large-scale literary narrative. One could also distinguish a range of possible kinds of translation. Whereas, for example, the *Destruction* is an extremely faithful translation of its source, with only occasional embellishments by the poet, as is, on the whole, the *Wars of Alexander*, other translations, while firmly in the trace of the source text, feel much freer to expand and embellish, notably Lydgate in his *Troy Book*. The closest translations are unquestionably the *Aeneid* translations; this proximity represents a different notion of translation, whereby the translator is, in Douglas's words, 'attachit ontill a staik' (1, Prologue, 297). The absolute, 'princely' authority of Virgil's text also banishes the translator from his translation, and into his prologues. The fourteenth- and fifteenth-century translations present themselves as acts of textual transmission, with, for example, frequent references to the source from within the narrative. The Virgil translations, by contrast, seek as far as possible to pass in silence the fact of an accretive textual tradition. Douglas goes so far actively to repudiate such a practice. The text is nothing but itself, not what readers have made of it.

The material of this chapter could also contribute to the history of the book, and in particular to contrasts between a culture of the

[92] For the Italian models, see Cattaneo, pp. 323–8.

manuscript and the printed book. The different, roughly contemporary versions of the same Troy narrative in different dialects between 1385 and 1412 bespeak the decentred quality of book production in a manuscript culture. By the same token, the small numbers of manuscripts, and their great expense, bespeak the low circulation of these narratives, among aristocratic and gentry readers and audiences. Print culture offers a contrast on both fronts: it is centred in London, and actively contributes to the establishment of a single dialectal norm (that used in London) for literate culture, and to the development of prose, designed for private readers. That greater centralization is balanced, however, by a much wider dissemination. The fact that a history of Troy was Caxton's first choice for a book printed in English clearly suggests that there was a much wider audience waiting for these grand founding narratives of Western Europe than could be catered for by expensive manuscripts. Caxton's sense of the market was borne out by the experience of printers who followed his lead: as we have seen, Lydgate's *Troy Book* was printed in both 1513 and 1555.

In this chapter I have, however, addressed the 'politics' of these texts, by way of understanding their representation of, and relation to, political power. One effect of this approach is to redress the balance whereby translated texts have traditionally been considered wholly from a strictly philological perspective. Romantic presuppositions about the ultimate identity of authors and their texts continue to obstruct discussion of translations. This is immediately apparent in the scholarship of almost all the works discussed above, which, exiguous as it is in many cases, is almost wholly taken up with matters of how a translator manages the metrical, syntactical, and rhetorical challenges of translating into his own language.[93] Criticism of Malory's *Works* and the alliterative *Morte* is the exception, since both manifest a high degree of 'translatorial' initiative. This kind of criticism is especially pronounced with the *Aeneid* translations, where scholars have tended to dismiss 'medieval' understanding of

[93] I hasten to add that I am not critical of this often invaluable work; I merely point out the perspective that dominates it (along with studies of source, author, date and provenance). Some examples: for the *Destruction*, Turville-Petre, *Alliterative Revival*, *passim*; D. Lawton, '*Destruction of Troy*'. For Douglas, see Kratzmann, ch. 6; for Surrey, Cattaneo, ch. 3.

classical texts as distorted by ethical and theological prejudices; for these scholars the great achievement of both Douglas and especially of Surrey is to have produced a purely philological translation, unencumbered by readerly prejudice, and, correlatively, making no appeal to such prejudice. This approach does have the value of highlighting the extraordinary linguistic achievement of both Surrey and Douglas; on the other hand, it seriously impoverishes our understanding of these works, since it assumes that there is such a thing as pure literature, undisturbed by and undisturbing of the discourses that inevitably surround 'literature' in the moment of its translation.

Some conclusions: the fourteenth and fifteenth centuries produced a powerful body of vernacular historical writing concerned with the fall of kings and empires. The presuppositions of this body of writing can be distinguished from those of two other traditions: (i) the popular historiographical tradition of imperial foundation and expansion, as expressed by the prose *Brut*, for example, and as deployed by English kings for propagandistic purposes; and (ii) the inifinitely more sophisticated narrative of imperial foundation embodied in Douglas's *Eneados*. Unlike either of these traditions, the fall literature, most powerfully expressed in works of what I have called the Guido-tradition, is resolutely anti-imperialistic in a variety of ways. These narratives all powerfully express a sense of a historical sequence generated by poor decisions, and unfolding towards a catastrophe beyond the power of any king to control. The philosophical, prudential voices within the narrative are silenced, with disastrous consequence; an alternative philosophical voice, in opposition to unthinking chivalric aggression, is offered by the prudential practice of these narratives themselves. All this is is especially true of the *romans antiques* discussed above (i.e. the Troy, Thebes, and Alexander narratives), which present themselves as wholly exemplary, but the model also holds even for literary narratives of ancestral fall in the Galfridian tradition.

It may be that some of the oppositional force of the earlier Troy tradition survives one way or another in the Virgilian translations of Douglas and Surrey. Douglas's own prologues veer rather nervously around the inviolate text of Virgil, moving as they do from panegyric of Virgil's poetry (1, 9), and his theology (6), to utter dismissal of the divine pantheon of Virgil's 'mawmetis [idols]' (10). The most extraordinary of these prologues, however, is that to Book 8, written in alliterative meter, in which a satirical Conscience figure who appears to Douglas in a dream dismisses the *Aeneid* translation as 'bot brybry [nothing but wretchedness]', after a long and powerful satirical description of the world as upside-down. Douglas, in his turn, wakes to dismiss this figure, and, along with him, a large tradition of vernacular satirical writing, as 'faynt fantasy'.[94]

Surrey, too, manifests, perhaps unknowingly, doubts about Aeneas's relentless forward movement of empire. If anyone should have read the Guido-tradition, it was Surrey (b. 1517), whose own short life and appalling family history are exemplary of the fragility of aristocratic power: Surrey was beheaded at the age of 29.[95] Perhaps he had read in that tradition, since from his imprisonment in Windsor in 1537, he remembers his boyhood, 'in greater feast then Priams sonnes of Troye', spent with the now dead prince at Windsor.[96] This prison-poem in no way looks forward to the new empire that will rise from the ashes of Troy. The *Aeneid* translation was undertaken after 1538, and possibly before 1540; it has heavy debts to Douglas's translation, then circulating in manuscript,[97] and also draws on two Italian translations, one of Book 2 and the other of Book 4. Perhaps Surrey's choice of book for translation was determined by his Italian models; in the light of his own biography, it remains at least fitting, however, that he should have chosen the two books that most fully express the themes of the Guido-tradition, the falls of Troy (2) and Dido (4).[98]

[94] For a development of this idea, see Canitz.
[95] See Chapman.
[96] Cited from Howard, *Poems*, ed. Jones, no. 27, l. 4, p. 25.
[97] For the early circulation of the *Eneados*, see J. A. W. Bennett.
[98] In addition to Cattaneo, see Henry Howard, '*Aeneid*', ed. Ridley.

4

The Elegiac

The literatures of love and war are intimately related, not least because an immensely influential Ovidian tradition pits them against each other. In Ovid's *Amores*, gracile Elegy, the presiding spirit of Ovid's poetry of unfulfilled desire, confronts ponderous Tragedy (3. 1), only to dismiss her with insouciance: the pleasures and pains of erotic pursuit displace the ostensibly serious matters of tragic verse. In this chapter I highlight the powerful continuities of this Ovidian tradition across the period 1350–1550, continuities that have been obscured by the readiness of scholars to accept the claims of the Renaissance itself a little too readily. I call the matter 'elegiac' by way of locating it in an Ovidian tradition of love poetry in which the unfulfilled lover turns away from public affairs.

Scholars of sixteenth-century English lyric writing accentuate its novelty by aligning it with the lyric postures of Petrarch; here I argue that Ovid, not Petrarch, is the key figure in what is taken to be a characteristically 'Renaissance' elegiac tradition. And if that is true, then this elegiac poetry is not so much a Renaissance as an Ovidian tradition, which extends in English writing from Chaucer right through to Surrey and well beyond. A significant continuity, then, is one accent of the chapter. Another is change: writing of the kind considered in this chapter also has its 'reformist' and 'revolutionary' forms. Cupid concentrates power in punishing ways; some love poetry of the period, and especially from the late fourteenth century, works to reform that centralized and exacting power. Other love poems, particularly the sixteenth-century examples, remain subject to the young tyrant.

The premiss of the chapter is that literary form testifies to historical possibility. The very compartmentalized structure of the sonnet as practised by Wyatt and Surrey itself bears witness to an inquisitive and threatening discursive environment. The stylistic homogeneity of that body of lyric writing is symptomatic of the single power in whose sway those poems are held. The form of late fourteenth-century elegy, by contrast, is characteristically heterogeneous in both style and structure. Formal disjunction implies a decentring of discursive power: these texts traverse competing discursive jurisdictions, out of the tyranny of Cupid and back into a reformed politics.

I

Thomas Wyatt, who was born in 1503, died of natural causes in October 1542. In 1536, and again in 1541, he had come very close to dying of a sharp-bladed unnatural cause. In 1536 he was implicated in the series of executions surrounding the fall of Anne Boleyn, and in 1541 his enemies attacked him after the execution in 1540 of Wyatt's most powerful protector, Thomas Cromwell. He was arrested for treason and imprisoned in the Tower; before his trial the Privy Council ordered that all his household goods as would be 'mete for the Kinges Maiestes use' should be sent to London, and that Wyatt's family and servants be evicted from the house, once the servants had been given some wages and a 'good lesson to use themselfes honestly'.[1] Wyatt escaped death on this occasion not by his detailed and powerful defence, which he may never have delivered,[2] but rather by the intervention of Queen Catherine Howard, soon to be beheaded herself; he also confessed to all the charges, 'yelding himself only to His Majesties marcy'.[3]

Henry Howard, Earl of Surrey, who was himself destined for decapitation in 1547, wrote this sonnet in praise of Wyatt:

> Dyvers thy death doo dyverslye bemone,
> Some that in presence of that livelye hedd
> Lurked, whose brestes envye with hate had sowne,

[1] Cited from Wyatt, *Life and Letters*, ed. Muir, p. 177.
[2] Ibid. 187–209. [3] Ibid. 210.

Yeld Cesars teres uppon Pompeius hedd.
Some that watched with murdrers knyfe
With egre thurst to drynke thy guyltless blood,
Whose practyse brake by happye end of lyfe,
Weape envyous teares to here thy fame so good.
But I that knowe what harbourd in that hedd,
What vertues rare were tempred in that brest,
Honour the place that such a jewell bredd,
And kysse the ground where as thy corse doth rest
  With vaporde eyes; from whence such streames avayle
  As Pyramus did on Thisbes brest bewayle.[4]

This is a suicidal poem, not only because the reference to Caesar implicates the King among those falsely mourning Wyatt, but more powerfully because the last line expresses a powerful, even erotic desire for suicide.[5] The very structure of the sonnet generates suicidal aggression, since it aims both to excite tears and to incriminate by tears: apparent distinctions between diverse ways of grieving for Wyatt collapse, as both groups of 'some' in the first two quatrains turn out to be identical. The only true tears are those of Surrey himself, whose act of publishing a statement of communal grief for Wyatt recoils into a repudiation and exposure of communal grief. This sonnet was published along with two other elegies for Wyatt probably not long after October 1542. It was the first poem of Surrey to be printed.[6] Jealously guarding his exclusive passion for Wyatt as alone authentic, however, Surrey arouses a public only to embarrass and antagonize it. The opening gesture of communal activity is displaced by a trenchant fencing off of private, if now inaccessible spaces.

The ferocity of Surrey's publicly displayed privacy is an index of a fragile and dangerous social world, where professions of authenticity are immediately and plausibly subject to alternative, suspicious readings. Surrey himself does this here, just as, of course, he invites the very same reading of his own 'sincerity'. The reference to Caesar's

[4] Henry Howard, '. . . *Poems*, ed. Jones , no. 29'.

[5] Surrey's poetics have been described as 'suicidal' by Crewe, ch. 2. Surrey's elegy for Wyatt, 'The great Macedon' (published along with 'Dyvers thy death'), is much more directly hostile to Henry VIII, by interpreting Wyatt's *Penitential Psalms* as a direct attack on the 'false concupiscence' of rulers (Henry Howard, *Poems*, ed. Jones, no. 31).

[6] *Tottel's Miscellany*, 2. 154.

feigned grief, for example, refers to Wyatt's own sonnet on this very theme, 'Caesar, when that the traitor of Egypt', since that sonnet argues that 'every passion | The mynde hideth by colour contrary | With fayned visage' (ll. 9–11).[7] I do not suggest that Surrey is insincere here, but the suicidal extremity of his grief may itself protect Surrey from charges of insincerity, since his own family had most to gain by, and were delighted by, the execution of Wyatt's patron Cromwell; Piramus, too, regards himself as responsible for what he takes to be Thisbe's death.[8] Just as the extremity protects Surrey, though, it also exposes him by correctly presaging his own death.

By the standards of a critical tradition begun by the likes of Surrey himself, this is very much a poem of the 'Renaissance', and participates in a 'renaissance' tradition of praise. The tradition of epideictic poetry is well exemplified by other tributes to Wyatt. The antiquary John Leland (?1503–52), for example, wrote an elegy for his friend Wyatt and dedicated it to Surrey in 1542, as one of the few things Leland published before his madness in 1547. In it he recounts Wyatt's apotheosis; asserts that Wyatt was in England the poetic equal of Dante and Petrarch in Italy; declares that Wyatt was a phoenix, whose death has produced another, in Surrey; and, among other things, has it that the English language was uncultivated and its verse unworthy of note ('sine nomine') before Wyatt polished it. If Wyatt was a phoenix, he is implicitly the first.[9] Leland's elegy exemplifies what we might call militant humanism, quite unembarrassed about eliding poetic with imperial honours (e.g. apotheosis).

Surrey's elegy, however, is much more profoundly exemplary of what are taken to be 'Renaissance' predicaments, insofar as it is on the one hand the product of a mobile, divided, and self-fashioning voice, and, on the other, its voice is acutely conscious of history as needing, if unlikely to achieve, resurrection.

Both these predicaments shape Surrey's sonnet; substantiation of

[7] Wyatt, *Collected Poems*, ed. Muir and Thomson, no. 3.

[8] For the Howards' delight at Cromwell's arrest, see Casady, pp. 79–80.

[9] John Leland, *Naeniae in mortem Thomae Viati equitis incomparabilis* (1542), *RSTC* 15446. See Wyatt, *Life and Letters*, ed. Muir, pp. 262–9 for a translation of the entire text. See also P. Thomson (ed.), *Wyatt: The Critical Heritage*, pp. 24–7. For another account of Wyatt (and Surrey) that stresses their signal importance as 'the first reformers of our English meetre and stile', see Puttenham, p. 60. For Leland's epideictic poetry more generally, see Carley, 'John Leland in Paris'.

this point reveals not only that these two determinative features of 'Renaissance' practice are interrelated, but also that they are produced by courtly environments of a threatening kind. A tradition normally derived from Petrarch sees historical thinking as ideally governed by the need to recover what has been lost from the classical past.[10] Such a view was produced by Italian humanists in the fourteenth century, so the standard account runs, and underwrote the humanist enterprise of resurrecting ancient societies 'in their own terms'. One scholar has more recently pointed out that such a view of the past must of necessity be elegiac, since it implies a 'historical solitude', an intervening period of loss, which isolates and impoverishes the historical consciousness, and from which the past must be recuperated.[11] In this sonnet Surrey certainly represents himself as isolated and impoverished, even if the past he needs to resurrect has been foreshortened in time, since it is the immediate, rather than the classical, past that escapes him. The classical past, in fact, is itself metaphorically revived only to constitute the time of loss, since the false are weeping, now, 'Cesars teres uppon Pompeius hedd'. The English poetic past is also evoked only to be neutralized as a larger source of tradition. Chaucer's famous lines 'And kis the steppes where as thow seest pace | Virgile, Ovide, Omer, Lucan and Stace' (*Troilus and Criseyde*, 5. 1791–2), with its own echoes of Statius (*Thebaid*, 12. 816–17), here give way to the concept of tradition possible only as an act of commemorating irredeemable loss: 'And kysse the ground where as thy coorse doth rest'.

If a 'sense of the past' is one cardinal feature of 'Renaissance' self-presentation, the other is a flexible, divided, and therefore 'fashionable' self. In scholarship, we might conveniently derive this tradition from Burckhardt's 'Discovery of the Individual' in the Italian Renaissance, but the concept still flourishes, lately readapted to suit the history of subjectivity.[12] In contrast to the 'radical stasis of the medieval

[10] For an exemplary and lucid account of this position, see Panofsky, ch. 1.

[11] Greene, *Light in Troy*, ch. 1.

[12] The seminal work is Burckhardt, pt. 2, 'The Development of the Individual'. The more recent history of the concept derives from a seminal article by Greene, 'Flexibility of Self'. Greenblatt's influential *Renaissance Self-Fashioning* is indebted to, and develops, Greene's article. For a critique of the simplistic way in which this view is almost always underwritten by a conviction that medieval subjectivity was both stable and conceivable only within larger collectivities, see Aers, 'Whisper'.

personality', the 'Renaissance' self, or subject,[13] is endowed with a confusing yet potentially limitless multiplicity. This psychic potential, of which Petrarch is again taken to be the originary exemplar, demands the intervention of a 'fashioning' hand.

As we have already seen, Surrey's sonnet unquestionably reveals the self-fashioning subject, since the courtiers who weep for Wyatt are revealed as actors in a theatrics of grief with its own complex and deceptive code. More dangerously and profoundly divided from himself here, however, is Surrey himself. The whole enterprise of this sonnet distinguishes the duplicitous multiplicity of masks used by Wyatt's enemies from Surrey's own singular and integrated experience of grief. This integrity can only be expressed, however, by marking its impossibility, in the absence of Wyatt. A Piramus without Thisbe lies marked for suicide precisely because Piramus' identity is so intimately bound up with that of his lover. Surrey's grief is so extreme that he even distorts the Ovidian narrative, in which Thisbe weeps over the nearly dead Piramus (*Metamorphosis*, 4. 55–166), to suggest that it is he, Surrey, who expires. The enterprise of the sonnet might be to expose false 'diversity': the evocation of Chaucerian pluralism in the opening line gives way, after all, to a very un-Chaucerian affirmation of the one, singular authentic response. This integrity turns out, however, to be itself an example of 'diversity', since not only does the sonnet present a double address ('*thy* guyltless blood'; '*that* hedd'), but its voice irreducibly differs from 'itself', complaining the impossibility of its integrity. The poem may well expose false diversity, but its own voice never escapes 'diversity' of a radical kind.

Surrey's poem, then, not only manifests these two cardinal qualities of the 'Renaissance' predicament (a sense of historical rupture, and a divided self); it also reveals that these two postures are intimately related: the intensity of historical loss threatens the integrity of self; history and selfhood are here in symbiotic relationship. Although early modern or 'Renaissance' scholars do not make the connection between historical rupture and fracturing of self that I make here,[14] discussion of Surrey's little poem confirms the standard

13 Greene, 'Flexibility of Self', p. 246.

14 Greene, *Light in Troy*, brushes against the perception: 'Quite possibly because

recitation of cultural history, by scholars of both pre- and post-1500 British writing, whereby 'Renaissance' poetry manifests these two defining features of modernity: historical solitude and the consciousness of self as open to construction. Surrey's poem therefore exemplifies the larger point that the 'Renaissance' produces elegy.

In this chapter I argue instead that elegy produces the Renaissance, or important aspects of it, at any rate. And if that holds true, then what are traditionally labelled as the defining features of 'Renaissance' poetry are characteristic of a powerful and various tradition of courtly and Ovidian elegiac writing in English and Scots from Chaucer's *Book of the Duchess* (*c.*1369) right through to Wyatt and Surrey. This tradition consistently alerts readers to the ways in which a self fragmented by its thraldom to power disrupts any sense of historical continuity. What distinguishes the possibilities for the recuperation of both self and history in this tradition is, I think, the discursive freedom available to a given writer: the tighter the discursive constraints, the smaller the possibilities of restoring a sense of historical contour and continuity. The emphatically 'Renaissance' qualities of historical rupture and division of self are especially pronounced, therefore, in writers who operated from the threatened margins of a fragile and dangerous discursive environment. The sixteenth-century consciousness of the past in elegiac poetry, 'thirl[ed] [pierced] with the poynt of remembraunce' as it often is, distinguishes itself only by virtue of the extreme menace surrounding and producing it.[15]

The period investigated by this book offers an extremely rich variety of elegiac poetry; I choose to centre discussion on the decades 1370–90 and 1530–50, since both these historical sequences mark the high points of monarchical centralism in the period 1350–1550, or at least, in the earlier decades, *claims* to central power.[16] Both equally produce elegiac love poetry of a high order. All Ovidian love

the discovery of history came the more readily to him [Petrarch] because he was by birth a dislocated individual' (p. 100).

[15] Citation from Chaucer, *Anelida and Arcite*, l. 211. I have not had space to discuss this penetrating example of Chaucerian elegy here; see Patterson, *Chaucer*, ch. 1.

[16] For Richard II's claims to absolute power, see Saul. For the reality of Henrician centralization and concentration of power, see Elton, *Tudor Revolution*.

poetry is sensitive to the ways in which elegy draws on, yet seeks to neutralize, history; this double move characterizes both the elegiac writing produced in the 1370s and 1380s, and that of the 1530s and 1540s. What distinguishes these two bodies of writing, however, is the greater discursive freedom enjoyed in the earlier decades, a freedom that allows re-entry into the current of social and historical life.

II

Chaucer's 'Complaint Unto Pity', of uncertain date but almost certainly post 1372, generates extraordinary power by virtue of its self-cancelling. The work of 119 lines divides into two sections: a narrative (ll. 1–56), in which the narrator recounts his impulse to complain to Pity, only to find her dead, 'and buried in an herte'; and the recitation of a formal complaint, the text that the narrator had prepared to read to Pity, whom he now finds dead. He recites the now useless document to us (ll. 57–119). This whole poem swallows itself, since it can only enact its impotence. The complaint, which the narrator holds 'writen in my hond', presents fictionally as having been written *before* his discovery of Pity's death, and is therefore itself now useless. Not only is it useless, but the mourners at the graveside (Beauty, Jolyte, Assured Maner, Honeste, and Wisdom, for example) are agreed as to the time at which the narrator will be executed. Accordingly, the narrator dares not show the text of his 'bille' to his enemies, though he does reveal it to his readers. Once we read it, however, we realize that whatever narrative openings it may have allowed have *already* been cancelled in the formulation of the legal document in the first place. It sets up an opposition between Pity and the tyrant Cruelty; without Pity, 'ther is no more to seyne' (l. 77); 'ye sleen hem that ben in your obeisaunce' (l. 84). Even as they are made, however, these pleas collapse into a recognition that Pity herself embodies the Queen of the Furies (l. 92), indistinguishable from her tyrannical enemy Cruelty. The very formulation of the means to legal redress insists on the impossibility of redress, and the impotence of the plaintiff's voice in a tyrannical environment: 'What nedeth to shewe parcel of my peyne?' (l. 106). The document ends with an affirmation of what the impulse of its composition had originally denied (i.e. Pity's death):

> Sith ye be ded—allas that hyt is soo—
> Thus for your deth I may wel wepe and pleyne
> With herte sore and ful of besy peyne.
>
> (ll. 117–19)

Narrative falters in this situation, since all the resources of narrative are defeated. The sequence of time is itself destroyed, since everything must always remain already as it is. The poem gestures towards narrative sequence along the lines of '*first* I found Pity dead, and *then* I read out the bill I had written before I knew of her death'; but the Complaint reveals that Pity's death underwrites the entire text as its premiss. The temporal stasis is underlined by the identity of the last line with the second; and, furthermore, the second stanza deliberately confuses the tenses. Most of this text reads in a simple past tense, as if it were a narrative that happened once in the past; the second stanza, however, quietly reveals that all this has happened before, many times: 'And when that I, be lengthe of certeyne yeres, | Had evere in oon a tyme [i.e. continually] sought to speke, | To Pitee ran I al bespreynt with teres' (ll. 8–10). The legal forms of the work also establish the idea of a 'process', both legal and literary, only to highlight the case's completion, and to reaffirm the plaintiff as the already sentenced criminal. Even the finality of death, both Pity's and the narrator's, turns out to be subject to the rule of desire-driven repetition: 'Ever setteth Desir myn herte on fire' (l. 101).

This text, then, rests marooned in the self-division of its voice. The voice has no option but self-destructively to seek its coherence in communion with another whom it knows to be hostile and inaccessible. It also unmoors from ethical stabilities, since his enemies include Honeste and Wisdom. And this self-division corrodes, as it must, any sense of historical sequence: the desire for union in time so tyrannically dominates as to dissolve time altogether. An acute consciousness of the necessity and uselessness of the document itself replaces any sense of historical sequence, as the voice impotently writes itself out of society and history.

Chaucer's 'Complaint' has no known source; all its features are, however, ultimately Ovidian. The act of writing a document that the author knows to be useless already evokes the Ovidian tradition of the *Heroides*, the series of letters written by often dying heroines, just as it provokes a very Ovidian awareness of the act of writing itself.[17] The most instrumental and bureaucratic of forms, such as petitionary letters and formal bills, are used precisely in order to underline their impotence as diplomatic instruments; this impotence provokes an intense consciousness of the act of writing in and for itself, as the only possible expression of a divided self. The use of legal forms for amatory purposes also draws on broadly Ovidian tactics, since Ovid's amatory works all represent a collapse of properly distinct discursive realms into the one field ruled by the tyrannical figure of Cupid: the legal, medical, pedagogic, political, and military, for example, all cede to the amatory.[18] Deploying the forms of public affairs and civic responsibility itself implies a turning away from that world, from which the Ovidian narrator is an exploitative recusant.

Refusal of the world of public affairs, however, turns out in Ovid's amatory poems merely to replicate the relentless pressures of that public world in private 'affairs': the narrator of the *Amores*, for example, consistently expresses the unrelenting pressures of a tyrannical Cupid. Love might seem to offer privacy and retreat, but that asylum turns out to be every bit as political as the world outside it, since it stands under the remorseless jurisdiction of the tyrannical boy-prince Cupid.

In this political environment the subject is at once driven and impoverished by his allegiance to an unrelenting power, to the point that all solidarities, including solidarities within the self, become evanescent, vitiated as they are by deception and its consequent distrust.[19] Precisely because the subject is under threat of demolition, it dominates and divides self-consciousness to the point of fragmenting narrative and uncoupling historical sequence.[20] The forms, both

[17] References to the act of writing, and its uselessness, are frequent in the *Heroides*; see e.g. 3. 1–4; 3. 98; 4. 7–16; 7. 3–6; 10. 139–52; and 11. 1–6.

[18] For this aspect of Ovid's amatory poetry, see Solodow.

[19] For Ovid's distrust of even the most intimate communication with his lover, see e.g. *Amores*, 2. 5. 51–62.

[20] In all his amatory poetry, Ovid refers exploitatively to historical narratives, only to dimiss their properly historical value. The essence of the position is expressed in

metrical and structural, of Ovid's amatory poems in the voice of a despairing lover (*Amores*, *Heroides*), are fragmented with respect to history, produced as they are from a massive asymmetry between self and its world: defeated but rampant desire exploits history, but has no interest in historical sequence or meaning.[21] At the same time, these texts, and especially the *Heroides*, express the pathos, the 'historical solitude', of history's victims. In this summary account of Ovid's amatory postures, I readily concede that I have omitted what is funny in them, but I do so because the reception of an Ovidian tradition by English vernacular poets tends to reaccentuate the darker underside of Ovid's brilliantly surfaced and sophisticated works. The potential violence of Ovidian love, for these poets, hovers always close to the surface.

The 'Complaint Unto Pity' may be an especially streamlined and poignant example of Chaucer's Ovidianism, but it is exceptional only insofar as it offers no escape from the demands of ineluctable power. I use it to introduce a continuity and a contrast in the elegiac poetry across the period of this history. Late fourteenth- as much as sixteenth-century elegiac writing up to 1547 works from this Ovidian problematic. Whereas, however, the late fourteenth-century examples work to establish extraordinary discursive freedoms beyond Cupid's sway, the sixteenth-century examples remain locked in the young tyrant's power. In this section I compare the Ovidianism of the *Confessio Amantis* (first released in 1390, 33,446 lines of four-stress couplets, divided into eight books), and Chaucer's *Troilus and Criseyde* (8,238 lines in rhyme-royal stanzas,[22] divided into five books.

Both these poems signal the extraordinary confidence of writers to commit themselves to English for literary matter of high ambition.

Amores, 3. 12. 15–16: 'cum Thebae, cum Troia foret, cum Caesaris acta, | ingenium movit sola Corinna meum'.

21 The fragmented sequence of the *Amores* e.g. has no very precise relation to historical order. Ovid himself makes play of the metrical relation of elegiac couplets to the proper metre of what he calls tragic poetry: Cupid steals a foot of the hexameter to produce a five-foot line, and a hobbling metre, unable to sustain the long march of historical narrative (*Amores*, 1. 1–4); the very metre of Ovid's elegiac poetry is therefore dependent on, yet recusant to, a tragic, historical mode.

22 'Rhyme-royal': a seven-line stanza, in which each line has five stresses, with the rhyme scheme ababbcc.

Whereas Gower had written in both French (*Mirour de l'homme*, 1376–8) and Latin (*Vox clamantis*, before 1386), the more daring *Confessio* translated and adapted a very wide range of classical Latin and medieval French matter into English. In *Troilus and Criseyde* Chaucer translated, yet significantly expanded, Boccaccio's Italian *Filostrato* (late 1330s). Chaucer had made his decisive encounter with Italian poetry in two diplomatic trips to Italy, in 1372–3 and 1378; there he saw, in the writing of Dante, Petrarch, and Boccaccio, the extraordinary reach of which vernacular poetry was capable. The *House of Fame* (1374–80) was the first Chaucerian work to register the shock of the Italian new, but only in *Troilus and Criseyde* does Chaucer signal his arrival in the first league of Continental making: as noted above, he sends the poem, which he addresses as 'litel myn tragedye', to 'kis the steppes where as thow seest pace | Virgile, Ovide, Omer, Lucan and Stace' (5. 1791–2). Both the *Confessio* and *Troilus* survive in large numbers (fifty-one and sixteen respectively) of often splendid manuscripts, and they were both clearly current later, long after their initial release: Caxton printed both poems in 1483. The printer Berthelette printed the *Confessio* in 1532 and 1554. *Troilus* was printed by Wynkyn de Worde in 1513 and in the first collected works of Chaucer, Thynne's edition of 1532.

The mid-1380s were dangerous times for members of Richard II's household and affinity. In the 'Wonderful' Parliament of 1386 the Lords and Commons successfully resisted the King's claims for a massive fiscal subsidy, and went a good deal further by having the King's chief ministers dismissed, and his chancellor impeached. A commission of fourteen lords was set up to govern the country, while Richard himself, at the age of 20, was still officially not of an age to rule. Richard responded by withdrawing from London, and framing a set of questions to judges, the answers to which condemned his principal opponents as traitors, and therefore worthy of death. The five main lords opposed to the King themselves responded with an 'Appeal for Treason' against Richard's most powerful supporters. The upshot of this was a brief civil war in late 1387, in which the Lords Appellant defeated the King's army; marched to London and confined the King; and forced him to summon parliament. This parliament, the so-called 'Merciless' Parliament, met in February 1388, and convicted eight of the King's closest supporters of treason, all of whom were executed, with many more being expelled from court.

One of the smaller fry also executed in the purge of 1388 was Thomas Usk, a London bureaucrat who, in the treacherous world of London City politics of the earlier 1380s, had turned informant against his anti-establishment master John of Northampton. He had joined the establishment party of Nicholas Brembre, Lord Mayor of London from 1383, and close ally of Richard II.[23] Usk's betrayal turned out to be fatal, since the faction he joined was the especial target of the Appellants. After the execution of Brembre in February 1388, Usk was drawn, hanged, and beheaded the following month. His head was displayed on the portal of Newgate.

Usk was also an author of wide learning and real accomplishment; he composed his elegiac *Testament of Love* between 1384 and 1386, after he had been released from prison on earlier charges of having supported John of Northampton. The work itself is a complex but barely disguised plea for preferment, which seems to have been successful in itself, as Usk was appointed under-sheriff of Middlesex in October 1387, just six months before his execution. In the *Testament* Usk presents himself as a faithful lover, by way of repairing his reputation for political infidelity. He also presents himself as a philosophical lover, deploying Boethian ideas about the evanescence of worldly fame precisely in order to reinstate his own worldly 'fame'. The overall strategy of the work owes a good deal to Chaucer's *Troilus and Criseyde*, since Usk aligns himself with the faithful Troilus,[24] and appeals to Chaucer as 'the noble philosophical poete in Englissh' for a discourse on the question of free will and God's foreknowledge, a poignant reference in the light of Usk's own imminent fall.[25] The praise of Chaucer is significant as the first, contemporary index of the immediate fame of Chaucer's *Troilus*, which must have been finished around 1385. It also points to Chaucer as himself another king's man, who withdrew from politics in this dangerous period, and who also wrote two elegiac works in the mid-

[23] Strohm, 'Politics and Poetics'.

[24] Compare e.g. Usk's protestation that, as a 'lover' he has not 'played raket, "nettil in, docke out,"' (*Testament of Love*, ed. Skeat, l. 166), with *Troilus and Criseyde*, 4. 460–1.

[25] Usk, *Testament of Love*, ed. Skeat, p. 123; cf. *Troilus and Criseyde*, 4. 96–1084.

1380s centrally concerned with fidelity and betrayal (*Troilus and Criseyde* and the *Legend of Good Women*). And beyond Chaucer, Usk's use of love elegy to discuss politics under cover points to the other great elegiac poem that must have been begun in the mid- to late 1380s, John Gower's *Confessio Amantis*. As with the 1530s, Ovidian elegy dominated as the literary mode of the 1380s, a mode by which poets turn aside from, yet comment on, the public world. Depending on the discursive resources available to them, writers also regained a historical consciousness by this mode. I leave discussion of the lesser figure Usk until the end of this chapter.

The prologue of Gower's *Confessio* speaks from a philosophical position of rationalism to attack the division of the contemporary political world. In Book 1, however, the narrator himself falls prey to this very division in succumbing to the power of Cupid, and so abandons the matter of politics and history. These shifts in narratorial position invoke the opening of Ovid's *Amores*, where the narrator recounts that he was about to write powerful and historical matter, when Cupid laughed and stole a metrical foot, to produce elegiac couplets. The poet complains at this improper invasion of discursive fields rightly belonging to other deities, when Cupid shoots him and commands that Ovid's own pain be matter for his poetry. This leaves the poet both cut off from the public world, emptied of matter, and equally under a new and unremitting 'political' regime: 'uror, et in vacuo pectore regnat Amor' ('I burn, and Love reigns in the abandoned heart', *Amores* 1. 1. 26). Being a subject to Cupid determines the 'subject' of Ovid's poetry, just as, in Gower's poem, the subject status of Amans, the narrator's name under the dispensation of Cupid, also produces the material of the entire poem. Venus, who appears after Cupid, demands that Amans confess himself to her priest Genius, by way of confirming that he serves without hypocrisy. Amans' Ovidian confession to Genius, which occupies the rest of this long poem, is generated in response to this demand for evidence of truthful service in love.[26] If the confession should reconfirm Amans' integrity as a faithful subject to Cupid, however, the rest of the poem can only confirm the impossibility of psychic

[26] For the Ovidian quality of Amans' confession, see Simpson, *Sciences and the Self*, pp. 143–4.

integrity under the tyrannical regime of Cupid. Amans can only speak from, and deepen, the fissures of a self already divided.

This psychic division occasionally surfaces explicitly, as in Amans' account of the psychomachia within the person of which he is a part; here the two principal parts of the soul, will and reason, gather psychological forces around themselves in the manner of courtiers gathering adherents (3. 1120–92). Of course there is a certain comedy in Amans' position, since he seems innocent of many of a lover's 'sins', often wishing, in fact, that he *could* have been guilty. Comedy also derives from the bathetic incongruence of scale between Amans' own little problem and that of the exemplary stories he is offered. Or so it seems initially; as the *Confessio* progresses, the destructive self-division of Amans tends to converge with the same destructive forces represented in the stories themselves. Furthermore, his self-division gradually shifts into a corrosive self-hatred and despair, to which he confesses in Book 4. He confesses 'in Tristesce al amidde | And fulfild of Desesperance' (4. 3498–9):

> And I, as who seith, am despeired
> To winne love of thilke swete,
> Withoute whom, I you behiete, [promise]
> Min herte, that is so bestad,
> Riht inly nevere mai be glad.
> For be my trouthe I schal noght lie,
> Of pure sorwe, which I drye [suffer]
> For that sche seith sche wol me noght,
> With drecchinge of myn oghne thoght [tormenting]
> In such a wanhope I am falle, [despair]
> That I can unethes calle, [hardly]
> As forto speke of eny grace,
> Mi ladi merci to purchace.
>
> (4. 3468–80)

Even as Amans lays claim to integrity here, he denies it, since alienation from the larger self to which he ideally belongs premisses his utterance. Just as he is barred access to 'himself', so too does he remain isolated within such society as he represents around him. Dominated by desire, he either obsessively distrusts everyone who has dealings with his lady, or else has no interest whatsoever in people who have no bearing on the fulfilment or thwarting of his desire (e.g. 2. 17–78).

Consistent with the themes of this chapter, Amans' isolation from 'himself' equally implies an alienation from history and historical meaning. In a thoroughly Ovidian manner, Genius, like the *praeceptor amoris* of the *Ars Amatoria*, frequently adduces stories from large-scale historical sequences, especially from the histories of Troy and Alexander, by way of encouraging the lover's enterprise. Almost by definition, these stories are emptied of their historical sense, partly because the sequence of which they form a part has been fragmented and randomly dispersed across the poem, and partly because Amans could not be less interested in historical meaning in the first place. There are no fewer than sixteen narratives drawn from the Benoît–Guido corpus of Troy and its bloody aftermath (discussed in Chapter 3), which are especially relevant to Gower's London, itself often, if tendentiously, called 'Troynovant'.[27] These stories do not, however, add up to a coherent narrative, because the order of their presentation has no relation to their original sequence, and also because they are deployed in such a way as to evacuate their political significance. Amans himself, for example, adduces the example of Achilles leaving aside his arms in order to win the love of Polyxena (4. 1693–1710), by way of arguing, against Genius, that a lover need not be a soldier. Amans would make a poor soldier, and so this is very Ovidian in both its comedy, and in the terrible resonances of the Achilles and Polyxena story that are evoked only to be ignored.[28]

So Amans exemplifies the self-divided narrator: 'Thus am I with myself oppressed' (3. 49), and this self-division at once marks his division from the political and historical world. His incapacity to think historically (or at least in narrative sequence) is underscored in Book 6, where Amans explicates his reading practice. Asked to confess to the sin of 'love delicacy', Amans confesses himself 'guilty', since he thinks endlessly about his lady. If he hears of her being spoken about, or if he hears her singing, then he is 'fro miself so ledd, | As thogh I were in paradis' (ll. 870–1):

[27] For a list of Troy stories in the *Confessio*, see ibid. 221, note 29. Gower himself calls London 'New Troy' at *Confessio Amantis*, first recension, Prol. 37. For the controversy raised by this appelation in the 1380s, see Patterson, *Chaucer*, p. 161.

[28] For the tragic narrative of Achilles and Polyxena, see Ch. 3, above.

And ek in other wise also
Fulofte time it falleth so,
Min Ere with a good pitaunce [morsel]
Is fedd of redinge of romance
Of Ydoine and of Amadas,
That whilom weren in mi cas, [once]
And eke of othre many a score,
That loveden longe er I was bore.
For whan I of here loves rede,
Min Ere with the tale I fede;
And with the lust of here histoire [pleasure · their]
Somtime I drawe into memoire
Hou sorwe mai noght evere laste,
And so comth hope in ate laste,
Whan I non other fode knowe.
And that endureth bot a throwe. [short while]
(6. 875–90)

This is very much a case of reading for the pleasure, or 'lust', of the text; but Amans' pleasure deludes, since the therapeutic comfort it ministers lasts only a short while, before, presumably, the process repeats itself. One of the reasons why the comfort of these texts evanesces is because, in Amans' reading, their historical difference and contours are flattened: each lover, past or present, is 'in my case', reduced to a simulacrum of Amans himself. He might draw these stories 'into memoir', but Amans' memory, governed by sexual desire alone, has no depth. His shallowness of reception applies not only to these stories, but also to each of the eighty-odd narratives offered him in the *Confessio*. The whole work is effectively a representation of reading remembered, since Genius acts in the service of desire to reproduce stories from the thesaurus of images which he controls.[29] And Amans 'reads', or remembers, each of these stories recast as a romance or potential romance, as a narrative of lovers that 'were in mi cas'. The narrative of Paris and Helen, for example, along with the exempla of Achilles and Polyxena, and Troilus and Criseyde, are used to make the point that men should not initiate love affairs in temples (5. 7195–7609). Genius concludes by saying that

[29] The word *thesaurus* ('treasure-chest') is the very word used by psychological theorists in the Aristotelian tradition, to describe the imagination. For Aquinas's usage, see Simpson, *Sciences and the Self*, p. 259 n. 34.

Amans can seek love where he will, but should beware of doing so in holy places, as if the disastrous narratives of Paris, Achilles, and Troilus would all have been romances had they not initiated their loves in temples. He evokes tragedy only to ignore it.

All that has been said about Amans applies equally to the representation of Troilus as a lover in *Troilus and Criseyde*. Gower offers a comically reduced six-line epitome of Chaucer's poem in the *Confessio*:

> And Troilus upon Criseide
> Also his ferste love leide
> In holi place, and hou it ferde,
> As who seith, al the world it herde;
> Forsake he was for Diomede,
> Such was of love his last mede.
>
> (5. 7597–602)

Despite this joke, Gower's poem comes very much in the wake of *Troilus*, using it as both model and serious target. For Chaucer, too, generates the narrative of his own poem of a lover by deflecting the world of tragic, 'historical' narrative of the kind discussed in Chapter 3: early in Book 1, the narrator directs anyone interested to read the story of 'how this town com to destruccion' in Homer, Dares, or Dictys; for him to tell the story of the city's destruction would be 'a long digression' from his matter (1. 141–7). This spectacularly inverts the generic commitments of the historical 'tragic' tradition, which locates narratives of amorous passion within the larger canvas of civic destruction. Here civic destruction is posited as itself the digression from the story of one lover.

This Ovidian asymmetry is sustained, insofar as it can be, by the narrator in imitation of Troilus' and Pandarus' own turning away from the world of public action. For Pandarus, the world of public affairs serves as the material of fiction, as when, for example, he pretends that plotters are active against Criseyde in order to possess her goods (2. 1415–21), merely as a way of engineering a meeting between Criseyde and Troilus. Or in Book 3 Troilus uses the alibi for being out at night, in fact seducing Criseyde, of waking all night in the temple of Apollo, 'to sen the holy laurer quake, | Ere that Apollo spak out of the tree, | To telle hym next whan the Grekes sholde flee' (3. 542–4). Troilus deploys the Aeneas-like action of seeking prophetic voice for the common good as an excuse for turning aside from the world of public action.

And just as Troilus and Pandarus turn their backs on the public world, so too does the force of Troilus' desire neutralize the significance of the consistently threatening historical exempla that crowd the margins of this narrative. Promoting himself as a good counsellor for lovers despite his own unsuccessful record as lover, Pandarus cites the instance of Phoebus' skill in medicine, even though he could not heal himself. Pandarus says that he found this example in a letter that the shepherdess Oenone wrote to Paris: 'yee say the letter that she wrote, I gesse?' (1. 656), he asks Troilus.[30] This letter derives from Ovid's *Heroides* (5); when we do read it, we see that Pandarus has completely ignored the terrible force of the whole letter in which Oenone attacks Paris for having abandoned her for Helen; predicts the future betrayal of Paris's new lover; and cites Cassandra to prophesy the fall of Troy. What interests Pandarus in the letter is what amatory tips it may accidentally offer. In Book 2 Helen does appear with her future lover, Deiphobus, whose mangled face Aeneas will encounter in the underworld (*Aeneid*, 6. 494–7), but here their appearance is engineered by Pandarus by way of getting Criseyde into Troilus' room. Issues of betrayal and death are alluded to only in order to be deflected. Or again, in Book 2 Pandarus finds Criseyde reading a book with her women companions. 'Is it of love?' Pandarus asks (2. 97), to which Criseyde replies that it was in fact the narrative of the siege of Thebes, and that they had just got to point where Amphiorax, the one figure who forsees the destruction of the Argive force, is swallowed into hell (*Thebaid*, 7). This hair-raising narrative of a prudential figure dying in spectacular horror is evoked only to be displaced by the rather edgy social comedy of Pandarus' amatory manipulations.

This list could be extended: almost every name incidental to the main narrative, such as Oreste and Antigone, carries with it terrible connotations of the fall of Troy or Thebes, just as Troilus' own name bears Troy within it, proleptically alluding to, but deferring, an

[30] Phoebus does not actually appear in *Heroides*, 5; the letter does contain Oenone's point that she knows the art of healing, but cannot heal herself (ll. 149–50).

inevitable destruction.[31] In each such case, however, Chaucer manages, by an Ovidian tactic, to 'plant' the suggestion only for it to be contained and temporarily neutralized within a social comedy. Troilus himself tells Pandarus to 'Lat be thyne olde ensaumples' (1. 760); the narrator, avowedly serving the servants of love (1. 15), ostensibly follows Troilus' command to ignore the force of historical example. Like the narrator of the *Confessio* in Book 1, he encourages his readers to accept the ahistorical, and de-historicizing, law of Love, who can

> The fredom of youre hertes to him thralle;
> For evere it was, and evere it shall byfalle,
> That Love is he that alle thyng may bynde,
> For may no man fordon the lawe of kynde. [violate]
>
> (1. 235–8)

So just as one lover's elegy generates the large-scale absorption and neutralization of historical narrative in the *Confessio*, so too does Troilus' divided self generate and justify the 'tragedy' of *Troilus and Criseyde* (5. 1786). As with Gower's English poem, a grieving lover stands at the heart of *Troilus*, divided around the pleasure and the torture of his subjection. Troilus utters the first Petrarchan lament in English, in which he articulates the unresolvable bewilderment of delicious pain (1. 400–20). Insofar as this is true, both English poems owe profound debts to Ovid's *Amores*, a work also generated from the same subjection; that also manifests an exploitative recusancy from the world of public affairs; and that also deploys only to ignore memory of history's disasters. These English works, like the *Amores*, are driven by the iterative force of desire, which seeks refuge from the relentlessness of history by fragmenting it.

In itself, this signals a poor starting place for narrative; to generate narrative, both texts have recourse to another Ovidian voice, that of the *praeceptor amoris* (teacher of love), the voice who both encourages love with practical stratagems, in the *Ars amatoria*, and who apparently teaches how to stop loving, in the *Remedia amoris*. In Gower's poem Genius fulfils the same role as Pandarus in Chaucer's,

[31] For the texture of classical allusion in *Troilus and Criseyde*, see Fyler, and Wetherbee, *Chaucer and the Poets*.

since both act as teachers in the art of love, just as both offer remedies against the inevitable delusions of love. Through these voices both poets recognize the limitations of elegy, limitations that are at once emotional and political.

Both Pandarus and Genius draw on Ovid for examples; both use proverbs by way of instructing the lover; and both devise stratagems. Pandarus himself describes his own activity as 'engyn' (3. 274), and well he might, since the principal sense of the word is something like 'skilful contrivance'. The first three books of *Troilus and Criseyde* are full of Pandarus' constructions in the service of Troilus; indeed the narrator likens his activity to that of an architect, who sends 'his hertes line out fro withinne | Aldirfirst his purpos for to wynne' (1. 1068–9).[32] The word 'engin', however, also has a psychological sense, meaning 'imagination' (Latin *ingenium*); the technologies that Pandarus engineers, his 'engines', are produced by his 'engin', or imagination. This psychological sense predominates in Gower's Genius figure, who represents the imagination of the narrator, an imagination in the service of Amans, just as Pandarus' *engin* serves a desiring Troilus.[33]

Pandarus and Genius themselves both act like architect-poets, shaping their matter according to a plan. In both cases, however, the planning exposes convergences between the worlds of the lover and the brutal historical world on which he has turned his back. The planning in both cases reveals that whether we regard the amatory narratives as a digression from the historical or vice-versa, both tell the same story. In these elegies what had looked like the place of private asylum turns out to replicate the brutality of the public world from which it had seemed to escape.

The last thing that Chaucer says about *Troilus and Criseyde* before he sends it off into the world is that it is designed as an exemplum against men who betray women: 'Beth war of men, and herkneth what I seye!' (5. 1785). On the face of it, this looks implausible at the end of Book 5, the main narrative of which has been Criseyde's cruel betrayal of Troilus, especially her letter gratuitously

[32] Lines drawn from a treatise on poetics: Geoffrey of Vinsauf's *Poetria Nova*, pp. 16–17.

[33] See further Simpson, *Sciences and the Self*, ch. 6. For the larger history of the concept of Genius, see Nitzsche.

accusing Troilus of infidelity (5. 1611–17). On reflection, however, the warning against treacherous men persuades: Criseyde has been swapped for Antenor, who will betray Troy; she herself has been betrayed by the Trojan parliament in Book 4, which breaks Hector's promise to Criseyde that she can live with full rights in Troy, despite her father's betrayal of the city; and she has also been betrayed, by his own account, by Pandarus himself (3. 274–80), who invents plots against her, and invents stories of her infidelity by way of engineering her love for Troilus. Of course the gravity of Pandarus' 'betrayal' is modified by the ways in which Criseyde seems to catch up with him, and at moments cautiously allows herself to be drawn to Troilus. Chaucer does, nevertheless, frame the beginning of Pandarus' activity on Troilus' behalf with a sinister reference to Philomela: Pandarus slumbers to the song of the swallow Procne,

> Til she so neigh hym made hire cheterynge
> How Tereus gan forth hire suster take,
> That with the noyse of hire he gan awake.
>
> (2. 68–70)

Troilus, too, after Pandarus' first success in arranging a meeting, promises to reward him, as I mentioned in Chapter 3, with 'my faire suster Polixene, | Cassandre, Eleyne, or any of the frape' (3. 409–10). Many points of the poem, and especially the consummation scene of Book 3, provisionally resist a reading that elides the private and public worlds of Troy, but the poem as a whole cannot help exposing that its micro-world has replicated the macro-world of which it is a part; what looked like a digression from a war provoked by the capture of women turns out to converge with the same story.

It is not simply that history breaks into the small, enclosed spaces provisionally engineered by Pandarus, though that is also true. Those small spaces have also, from one perspective, themselves been the scene of betrayal. When Troilus surveys the Greek camp from the walls of Troy in Book 5, we recognize that this poem, which began as elegy, does indeed turn out to be a 'litel . . . tragedy' (5. 1786), since it offers no escape from the jurisdiction of a punishing Cupid, who rules the private and public worlds of this poem. Or, to put it another way, the poem exposes an elision between Cupid's punishing regime and that of the larger historical world. This conclusion becomes inescapable in the courtship of Diomede, where the connections between the 'lover' Diomede and the terrible history of Thebes bear in relentlessly upon Cassandra and Troilus (5. 1443–1526).[34]

In the *Confessio* the story of Amans, too, for all his bathetic helplessness, converges with the world from which he has turned. This is especially true of the relation between Books 6 and 7. In Book 6, which treats Gluttony, Amans confesses to an all-consuming, even self-destroying psychological obsession, to the exclusion of all solidarities; dominated 'with fantasie and with desir', he goes to bed and feeds himself with fragmented erotic images of his lady:

> Bot yit is noght mi feste al plein,
> Bot al of woldes and of wisshes, [desires]
> Therof have I my fulle disshes,
> Bot as of fielinge and of tast,
> Yit mihte I nevere have o repast.
> And thus , as I have seid aforn,
> I licke hony on the thorn,
> And as who seith, upon the bridel
> I chiewe, so that al is ydel
> As in effect the fode I have.
>
> (6. 922–31)

By the end of Book 6, Amans is understandably 'fed up' with this repetitively sterile psychological round, and, having heard earlier of Aristotle's instruction of Alexander, asks for a digest of that cursus, for, as he says, 'min herte sore longeth' to understand it (6. 2408–19). Genius, too, 'longeth sore' for a change of subject, something drawn from 'the scoles of Philosophie'. In Book 7, which immediately follows, Genius produces stories from the treasury of the imagination, as he has done throughout the *Confessio*, but here the imagination is governed by rational desire, and not by sexual desire alone. Most of the matter of this book is devoted specifically to the discipline of politics, and is drawn from an encyclopaedic work by Dante's teacher Brunetto Latini, written (1262–6) while in exile from the republican city of Florence.[35] Whereas Gower's contemporary John Trevisa translated large-scale encyclopaedic and political prose

[34] See further Patterson, *Chaucer*, chs. 1–2.

[35] For further discussion, see Ch. 5, below.

works, the *De proprietatibus rerum* and Giles of Rome's *De regimine principum*, into English in the 1390s, Gower built that kind of material into a literary structure.

The story of Lucretia is the longest narrative he tells. It exposes the political motives and consequences of cupidinous rapacity. The story is told from Ovid, *Fasti*, 2. 685–852, and relates both the treacherous betrayal of the Gabines by Aruns (son of Tarquin) and his subsequent rape of Lucrece. The description of his desire for Lucrece closely parallels that of Amans. As Aruns goes to bed, his rapacity having been aroused by Lucrece's fidelity, he replicates her image in imaginative reconstruction: 'he pourtrieth hire ymage' in elaborate detail (7. 4868–4903), in precisely the way Amans had earlier 'fed on' his lady in imaginative reflection. Aruns is subject both to his will and imagination in his determination to rape Lucrece, whereby the sexual and military activities of 'this tirannysshe knyght' (7. 4889) become indistinguishable. The world of elegy has been brought into direct contact and identity with the political world that it replicates. There can be no escape from politics, since the psyche itself constitutes a 'political' arena.

Aruns is subject to Cupid, and subjects his imagination to desire, in precisely the way Amans is and does. This might suggest that the lover cannot escape tyranny, since both the private and the public worlds of this poem turn out to be governed by tyrants. In the *Confessio* Gower certainly hints at the possibility of elegy and tragedy coalescing into one extended nightmare, but that is not at all the position of the poem as a whole. On the contrary, Gower affirms the possibility of psychic reintegration, whereby the imagination, personified by Genius, operates as a mediator between abstract reason and sensual desire. The very possibility of the Lucrece story, told as an exemplum against tyranny in sexual and political practice, and ending with the exile of kings, itself testifies to the possibility of an imaginative remembrance of stories that is not driven by concupiscent desire; an alternative, fully ethical, and political exercise of the imagination is possible. The poem as a whole is a fable of the psyche, in which the relations of the soul mirror the ideal practice of Gowerian politics, whereby the abstract principle of law, the king, has commerce with the body politic by the mediation of counsellors, or parliament, capable of imaginative apprehension. The poem does register the capacity to escape from Cupid's jurisdiction, and to return to the political discourse of the Prologue.

That return to the public world is, however, profoundly reformist. In this poem sexual desire, and by association the body politic, is by no means simply repressed by abstract, monarchical reason. On the contrary, Gower recognizes the jurisdiction of the body as a fundamental aspect of the political order; that recognition is only possible by an act of imaginative remembrance and apprehension, achieved by the regenerative, 'genial' principle of Genius himself. Equally, such remembrance turns out to be a remembrance of poetic tradition, since poetry, as distinct from pure philosophy, is the sole medium capable of preserving and remembering the exemplary particularities of sensual pain and pleasure through narrative. For this reason Amans, now a reintegrated John Gower, can mount a moving, revisionary conspectus of many of the stories with which he has 'fed' himself earlier in the poem, and which he now observes from a position of sympathetic detachment (8. 2440–2744).[36]

The *Confessio*, then, like Chaucer's *Parlement of Foules*, reinstates sexuality at the heart of the political, and in so doing represents an Ovidian modification of the Neoplatonic and imperialist Latin traditions to which these poems address themselves.[37] These elegies are capable of a return to the political and historical world, of transgressing the jurisdiction of the apparently irresistible power of a tyrannical Cupid. That return can only be made, however, by an implicit and, in Gower's case, occasionally explicit critique of political absolutism. The politics of these poems are generated in a real sense from the body's interaction with reason. They oppose the absolutism of an abstract and transcendent reason deriving from inspired intuition of universal order. Mediation that incorporates the whole body politic, by parliament and/or counsel, stands at the heart of these works.

If the *Confessio* finally coheres, *Troilus and Criseyde* disintegrates in the most productive, challenging way. In Gower's poem the

[36] This places Gower in an aesthetic and political tradition critiqued by Eagleton, although he does not extend back beyond the 18th cent.

[37] For a full account of the poetic Neoplatonism of the 12th cent., see Wetherbee, *Platonism and Poetry*; for a larger argument about the way in which this Neoplatonic tradition is received and critiqued by 14th-cent. English poets, see Simpson, *Sciences and the Self*, esp. ch. 9.

sensual will, imagination, and reason all finally share one flexible position; *Troilus and Criseyde* ends rather with courageous discursive fragmentation. Pandarus can supply no imaginative contrivance to console the grieving lover Troilus, and can have no further mediatory role in the poem after Book 4. So too with the institution of political mediation, the Trojan parliament, which in Book 4 expresses nothing but short-sighted pragmatism in its preparedness 'wommen for to selle' (4. 182). We are finally left with extreme differences between Troilus' Boethian and Stoic detachment from, or even derision of, worldly suffering on the one hand (5. 1807–27), and Criseyde's radical pragmatism on the other, committed as she is to survival in a world whose opacity she fully recognizes (5. 1054–77). The poem itself commits its readers to a certain pragmatism, since the real traitor in this poem so full of traitors is Fortune herself, the 'traitor commune' who erupts into the carefully enclosed but fragile world of Troilus and Criseyde at the beginning of Book 4. Fortune's action is so powerful and decisive in this situation of war as to exert extreme pressure on individual fidelities and allegiances. Both Troilus and Criseyde respond to the news of parliament's decision to exchange Criseyde by declaring their own deaths (4. 323–9; 4. 778–91 respectively); from that vantage point Criseyde's individual betrayal in Book 5 bites as the unpalatable and inevitable coda to a philosophical plot of Fortune's ruthless power that is already complete by the end of Book 4.

Troilus and Criseyde, like Chaucer's *House of Fame*, confronts the problems of establishing a poetic tradition by sustained rereading and rewriting of the narrative of a woman.[38] Just as Dido complains that she will be shamed in the poetic tradition that will commemorate her (ll. 345–60), so too does Criseyde:

> Allas, of me, unto the worldes ende,
> Shal neyther ben ywriten nor ysonge
> No good word, for thise bokes wol me shende.
>
> (5. 1058–60)

Almost as soon as she has uttered this prophecy, the narrator confirms it, by saying that 'her name, allas, is publysshed so wide', that any further attack on her would be otiose (5. 1093–9). This pos-

[38] See further Summit, *Lost Property*.

ture of simple reticence, however, is displaced by much more serious obstacles to 'blaming' Criseyde, since what 'Criseyde' *is* now becomes problematic. Criseyde's prophecy of a bad name follows the short sequence in which, we are told, she weighs up the advantages of having Diomede as a lover, and decides to stay with the Greeks (5. 1023–9). The narrator's access to Criseyde at this point fragments. Suddenly she can no longer be simply 'Criseyde', but a distanced personage in books, not one, but many: 'after this the storie telleth us'; 'I fynde ek in stories elleswhere'; 'But trewely, the storie telleth us'; 'Take every man now to his bokes heede'. All these lines gather around Criseyde's prophecy of a bad literary fame (5. 1037–89), insisting in their own way that the book we thought we were reading has itself fragmented into a whole library of potentially conflicting authorities.

'There is non auctour telleth it, I wene', the narrator says about a detail of Criseyde's relation with Diomede (5. 1088). The comment might apply to the whole of Criseyde's story in Book 5, since, in a profound sense, there can indeed be no way of telling it. Criseyde takes major decisions in this poem out of a shrewd appraisal of the conditions in which she finds herself. However painful it finally turns out to be, Troilus can afford to fall in love in Book 1 with whomsoever he will; and there is no extended narrative of his falling in love, since it happens in a single, visionary moment (1. 272). The narrative of Criseyde 'falling in love', by contrast, is rather the narrative of her deciding whether or not to take a lover. Precisely because she cannot afford to fall in love 'casually', to use Chaucer's term, her emotional life is represented as a matter of circumstance, decision, and, therefore, of process. The representational consequences of this are evident in Book 2, by stark contrast with the representational template by which Troilus' emotional life is represented in Book 1. In Book 2 the long sequence in which we are virtually alone with Criseyde (2. 687–931), as she moves from practical considerations of her position to hearing Antigone's beautiful lyric about the bliss and ease of love, and then to her powerful dream of painless violence, is an astonishing poetic achievement of sustained intimacy, the first of its kind in English poetry.[39] The very persuasiveness of that

[39] See further D. R. Howard.

representation of psychological 'process', however, is the premiss of Criseyde being unrepresentable in Book 5. For in Book 5 her repetition of almost the same process, under an equally pressing male advance, produces a discontinuity of self that threatens to compromise sympathy, and certainly disables the resources of narrative. Chaucer's very openness to the circumstantial conditions of Criseyde produces an extraordinary enlargement of stylistic protocols;[40] equally, however, this very openness finally produces an unfinishable poem. It is surely significant that there should be so many attempts to end it, from Book 4 forwards, just as the *Legend of Good Women* is yet another attempt to close it down, as an outraged male readership attempts to silence it with narratives of women as 'relics'.

Elegy produces a particular sense of the past: the self-divided complainant of elegy is, by virtue of being divided from himself, equally and painfully cut off from a remembered but irrecuperable history. In *Troilus and Criseyde* the narrator himself finally remains cut off from a remembered history, since his story becomes unrepresentable. The narrator's incapacity to represent history derives not, however, from his subjection to the power of Love; on the contrary, his extraordinary discursive freedom to represent the fate of one of history's potential victims, Criseyde, finally disables the resources of his great, unresolved poem. One of the most beautiful manuscripts of the poem movingly represents Chaucer performing the text, while in the background Criseyde enters her new world, as she is swapped for Antenor outside the gates of Troy (Fig. 4).

III

In the 1370s and 1380s, then, some substantial Ovidian elegies allowed for ways of recovering history and reforming the practice of politics. Elegy that seems to turn its back on the world represented in tragic, historical narratives can finally address that world both by way of questioning its assumptions and reforming its brutalities. This in itself would be the occasion to turn to the matter of Chapter 5, policy and satire; to do that immediately, however, would be to

[40] See the still powerful study of Muscatine, ch. 5.

Fig. 4. Chaucer performing before a court; in the background, Criseyde is swapped for Antenor. Corpus Christi College Cambridge, MS 61, frontispiece (early fifteenth century).

lose the opportunity to observe the operations of elegy in poetry of the 1530s and 1540s, another period of English literary history characterized at the same time by elegiac poetry, extremely dangerous politics, and potentially tyrannical kings. By contrast with the poetry of the 1380s, what we observe in the last two decades of the reign of Henry VIII are Ovidian postures wholly locked out of any possibility of re-entering the current of history. In this poetry the poetic persona remains both threatened and mesmerized by an absolute power, unable to escape the historical dislocations and emotional circularities that such a position necessarily entails.

If the 1380s were dangerous times for anyone of political consequence associated with the court, the same applies to the 1530s. Henry's divorce initiated massive discursive changes in England: this is most obviously true of the break with Rome, but the consequences of that break filtered down to restructure English society in a multitude of ways. Obviously such radical breaks with the past create crises of allegiance for some consciences, but crises of conscience aside, the discursive environment became plain dangerous for *everyone* engaged in politics. In this revolutionary period monarchical power both advanced forwards into familial and institutional structures, and at the same time withdrew into a heightened privacy. Power withdrew into the 'privy chamber', which at once concentrated yet veiled the King's governance.[41] The advance of monarchical power can be seen in a variety of ways. New structures of surveillance were, for example, established,[42] where life or death could often hang on the interpretation of single remarks or gestures.[43] At a more popular level, as I argued in Chapter 1, monarchical power restructured and distanced the past: the liturgical year was restructured with the abolition of many feast days; or, for example, the structure by which the community of the living communicated with the dead was nationalized and minimized, with the abolition of purgatory, of fraternities, and of chantries.[44]

[41] See D. Starkey, 'Intimacy and Innovation'.

[42] See e.g. the letters sent to Cromwell by his spies from all over the kingdom, in Elton, *Policy and the Police*.

[43] Both Wyatt and Surrey were in the position of having to defend their lives against charges of having spoken improperly. For Wyatt, see *Life and Letters*, ed. Muir, pp. 196–8, and P. Thomson, *Sir Thomas Wyatt*, ch. 1. For Surrey, see Cattaneo, ch. 1.

[44] For which see Duffy, pt. 2.

These movements of central power were effected and backed up by punitive legislation. In 1542, for example, an Act was passed to purge the kingdom of false doctrine. The Act banned Tyndale's Bible, and along with that 'all other bookes and wrytinges in the English tongue, teaching or comprysing any matiers of Cristen religion, articles of the faithe or holy scripture . . . contrarye to that doctrine [decreed] sithens the yere of our Lorde 1540'. All these 'shalbe . . . clerlie and utterlie abolished, extinguished and forbidden to be kepte or used'.[45] This might sound like a matter of religious books alone, but as the Act proceeds, its extraordinary scope emerges, designed as it was to restructure nothing less than the entire shape of English discursive history. Bibles in English not translated by Tyndale were excepted, as long as all annotations and preambles were either cut out or blotted as to be unreadable; furthermore, all of the King's 'proclamations, injunctions, translations of the Pater Noster, Ave Maria, and Crede, psalters, primers, prayers, statutes and lawes of the Realme, Cronicles, Canterburye tales, Chaucers bokes, Gowers bokes and stories of mennes lieves, shall not be comprehended in this act', unless, the Act continues, the King should change his mind.[46] These exceptions made the import of the Act only more draconian, since they excluded, by implication, any other literature printed before 1540 apart from the King's official publications, histories, and the works of Chaucer and Gower.[47]

In Acts of this kind, the antiquity of a text effectively ceased to legitimate anything. Discursive history was to begin anew from 1540, because the King said it would. Books that were allowed from before that date were permissible, again, simply because the King willed that they be so, and the King's will could, the Act takes care to point out, change. Neither a projected future nor any sort of past legitimated texts: on the contrary, discursive legitimation was wholly a matter of the King's arbitrary desire. Of course this Act was promulgated towards the end of Henry's reign, but the implicit supremacy of the King's will over any and all forms of discursive practice can be found in royal proclamations much earlier in the

[45] *SR*, 34 Henry VIII, ch. 1. 1 (3. 895). I have punctuated the text.

[46] Ibid.

[47] For the prints of Chaucer and Gower to which this Act refers, see respectively Blodgett, and Machan, 'Thomas Berthelette'.

mid-1530s.[48] Scholars detect the first flowerings of English 'Renaissance' literature in this discursive environment, in the poetry of Wyatt especially. In this section I look to the elegiac secular writing of Wyatt and Surrey by way of suggesting that the discursive features hailed as characteristic of 'Renaissance' poetic practice are in fact the product of the peculiarly repressive discursive conditions of the Henrician court. So far from being the product of a liberating rediscovery of the past, this body of elegiac writing insists on the helpless historical and social isolation of the poetic self.

Royal policy in the 1530s and 1540s attempted to create something of a historical vacuum, whereby all that preceded had to be read under the title of Henry's own imprimatur. When we turn from Tudor royal policy to recent criticism of Wyatt and Surrey's poetry, we also find a historical vacuum. One authoritative critic who so treats them makes the point explicitly: 'Both [Wyatt and Surrey] must have been aware of themselves as attempting something new, as filling a vacuum. (This is the way they were perceived during the remainder of the century and for that matter today).'[49] The vacuum behind them, so the standard account runs, is both historical and psychological: Wyatt and Surrey were on the one hand the avatars of a wholly new sense of the unstable, Petrarchan self, and were also conscious of writing across a 'cultural rupture'.[50] Petrarch, in this almost ubiquitous account, towers as 'one of western Europe's seminal figures', introducing a quite new discourse of divided, unstable psychological life;[51] 'Petrarchism was in fairly precise ways the distinctive genre of the English Renaissance, its literary life bracketing the era. . . . So the historical record almost compels us to discuss Petrarchism in terms of the period concept.'[52] On the very rare occasions when these accounts do mention Ovid, it is very much in passing, and he is in any case distinguished from Petrarch as the poet of 'real sexual consummation'.[53] From the discussion of

48 For Henrician censorship more generally, see Loades, and Ch. 7, below.

49 Greene, *Light in Troy*, p. 245.

50 Ibid.

51 Waller, 73. See also Greene, 'Flexibility of Self'.

52 Kerrigan and Braden, p. 158.

53 Waller makes no sustained reference to Ovid in his discussion of Petrarchanism; the very distorted account of Ovid as the poet of 'sexual consummation' is cited from Kerrigan and Braden, p. 175. For Petrarch's own indebtedness to Ovid, see Hardie.

Chaucer and Gower's Ovidian postures in Sections I and II of this chapter, I hope it will be incontrovertibly clear just how distorted is this account of Petrarch's influence. The anxiety to shore up the periodic distinctiveness of the 'Renaissance' leads these critics, in my view, to peculiar omissions of Ovid in their account of just how 'seminal' Petrarch was in the matter of representing the psyche as threatened, divided, and mobile. The deletion of Ovid from these literary histories is equally a deletion of a long history of Ovidian poetry in English behind Wyatt and Surrey, not to speak of a massive European tradition of elegiac writing from at least the twelfth century.[54]

The accounts of 'Renaissance' scholars are, I am arguing, seriously lacking in historical depth. Curiously, however, the importance attached to Petrarch in these accounts relates centrally to Petrarch's 'truly historical' consciousness. As someone who feels himself irredeemably cut off from a classical past, Petrarch is often hailed as the first European capable of a truly historical understanding. Translators of Petrarch, notably Wyatt and Surrey in English, are also, by association, understood to mark crucial stages on the way to a 'humanist' historical consciousness.[55]

Petrarchan elegy and the peculiar, pathetic cast of Petrarchan historical consciousness are, as we have seen, deeply connected: historical consciousness and consciousness of self always stand in symbiotic relationship. If the self is divided, then it is, by the same token, cut off from historical continuities, and vice versa. Let me now turn to some examples of Wyatt and Surrey's elegiac poetry, by way of arguing that Petrarch provides a perfect model for early Tudor elegiac writers *unable* to regain a historical consciousness, locked as

[54] For the vast tradition of the European love lyric before the 16th cent., see Dronke.

[55] See esp. Greene, *Light in Troy*, ch. 12, where Petrarch is accorded the status of an honorary classical poet, insofar as Wyatt's imitations of Petrarch are presented as exemplary of Wyatt's rediscovery of a classical antiquity and his genuinely historical consciousness. Wyatt's poetry simply will not bear this freighting; see e.g. Helen Cooper, 'Wyatt and Chaucer': 'Wyatt is generally no more—if no less—dependent on sources and influences than any other significant English writer before the eighteenth-century invention of originality' (p. 105). Writers unconcerned to shore up the specifically 'Renaissance' distinctiveness of Wyatt give a much truer picture of continuities of tradition between Chaucer and Wyatt. See e.g. J. Stevens, ch. 8, and P. Thomson, *Sir Thomas Wyatt*, ch. 5.

they are into the spiralling and relentless erosions of a marooned self. Unlike the elegiac poetry of the 1380s, this body of writing cannot move beyond the jurisdiction of an absolute power, often figured as Cupid; it is therefore unable to regain and reform the public, political, historical world that elegy always implies. Such poetry, I suggest, stands in significant relation to its revolutionary cultural context, in which not only must Wyatt and Surrey frequently disown their own incriminating pasts, but also in which royal policy has arbitrarily interred a national past. Close imitation of models in which power inheres in this context turns out not to be exemplary of a truly historical consciousness so much as of the reverse.

Comparison of the long elegiac poems of the 1380s with the very short lyrics of the 1540s is unusual but justifiable in various ways. The modal, rather than strictly generic, category of my chapter allows this comparison, but so too do the reading and writing habits of Henrician courtiers themselves. In the so-called 'Devonshire' Manuscript, for example, we find, among the many Tudor love lyrics, some of which were composed in the Tower, amatory excerpts from longer poems, and especially from *Troilus*, by Hoccleve and Chaucer.[56] For Ricardian as for Henrician readers, courtly elegy was made up of a continuous spectrum of verse from the very short form to the very long.[57]

In *Troilus and Criseyde* Troilus retreats to his 'chambre . . . allone' as soon as he is wounded by the sight of Criseyde, there to sing alone the first Petrarchan song in English (1. 400–20). Like Petrarch, Petrarchan imitators also retreated into the small rooms, or *stanze*, of poetry, and elevated what had been minor forms in so doing. Whereas both Chaucer and Gower referred to their 'balades, roundels, and virelayes' as a marginal, almost throwaway, aspect of their oeuvre,[58] in the sixteenth century small, retracted forms became the prime vehicle of elegiac expression. Petrarch's introduction of

[56] For the best history of this fascinating MS, see Southall; for the 'medieval' contents of the MS, see Seaton.

[57] For accounts of the rhetorical coherence of lyric writing, from the very short, free-standing lyric to the lyric embedded in longer forms, see Robbins, 'Middle English Court Love Lyric', and 'Structure of Longer Middle English Court Poems'.

[58] Citation from *Legend of Good Women*, F.423. See also *Confessio Amantis*, 1. 2727.

the sonnet, first translated in English in that form by Wyatt, was certainly a peculiarly apt form for the expression of an unresolved and divided voice, capable as it is of various smaller 'rooms', or stanzas, which set contesting positions of the same voice against each other. But the novelty of the sonnet, and particularly of the sonnet sequence of later Elizabethan poetry, should not be allowed to occlude the fact that earlier forms like the roundel and ballade were also exploited for the expression of a voice locked into a cycle of divided positions. Neither should it be allowed to disguise the Ovidian background to these retracted forms, whose absence of full narrative context sharpens the poignancy of emotional biography. Later Elizabethan sonnet sequences, no less than, say, Charles d'Orléans's wonderful sequence of short forms in English verse (1415–40) were attempts in the vernacular to imitate the model of Ovid's *Amores*.

Wyatt and Surrey did not write sequences of sonnets, and Wyatt continued to compose in earlier forms such as the roundel and ballade, as well as other short forms like the *strambotto*, a single eight-line stanza imitated from the late fifteenth-century Italian poet Serafino.[59] Short elegy is, as one would expect, the locus par excellence of formal inventiveness. Whatever the short form, however, it was consistently exploited by Surrey, and especially by Wyatt, for nearly the same ends of expressing a voice isolated in time and trapped into its own undoing.

The neutralization of voice in Wyatt's poetry appears forcibly in his exploitation of lines that are formally highlighted, such as first lines or refrains: 'Behold, Love!'; 'Was I never, yet, of your love greeved'; 'Farewell, Love, and all thy lawes for ever'; 'Though I my self be bridilled of my mynde'; 'Patience'; 'What no, perdy, ye may be sure!'; 'My lute be still, for I have done'; 'In eternum'; 'It is impossible': each of these lines, taken from poems in the Egerton manuscript,[60] is set into formal relief only in order for its claim to be denied. The effect of this self-directed irony in each case paralyses the voice as agent, caught as it is in stasis between the undecidable poles of two opposed claims. This effect contributes to the poems' own

[59] P. Thomson, *Sir Thomas Wyatt*, p. 211.

[60] Wyatt, *Collected Poems*, ed. Muir and Thomson, nos. 1, 9, 13, 27, 39, 45, 46, 71, 77, respectively.

uncertain status with regard to time, since the affirmations of cause and effect that each lyric makes are inevitably incapacitated: Wyatt's distinctive 'But since . . .' promises yet never achieves logical advance.

The resources of narrative are repeatedly paralysed within poems, and from poem to poem, until the very categories of change and stability in time themselves become indistinguishably blurred:

Eache man me telleth I chaunge moost my devise. [must]
And on my faith me thinck it goode reason
To change [purpose] like after the season,
Ffor in every cas to kepe still oon gyse
Ys mytt for theim that would be taken wyse, [fit]
And I ame not of suche maner condition,
But treted after a dyvers fassion,
And therupon my diver[s]nes doeth rise.
But you that blame this dyver[s]nes moost,
Chaunge you no more, but still after oon rate
Trete ye me well, and kepe ye in the same state;
And while with me doeth dwell this weried goost,
My word nor I shall not be variable,
But alwaies oon, your owne boeth ferme and stable.[61]

Unravelling this remarkably dense lyric can only lead to a voice alienated both from itself and from us. The opening affirmations suggest a hearty acceptance of the common view that one should change one's badge of allegiance, or 'devise' to suit one's own interests in changing circumstances. As the logic of the poem progresses, however, it becomes clear that the voice has no trust whatsoever in this common approbation of changeful self-interest; on the contrary, this voice is different from that of 'each man' precisely by virtue of his faithful adherence. Faithful adherence, however, demands change, in the ability to learn how to 'convert my will in others lust'.[62] Two kinds of wisdom are being abjured by this voice, then: the worldly wise 'wisdom' that encourages self-interested change, and the higher, Stoic wisdom that encourages stability of self. The stability of this

[61] Ibid., no. 10. The emendations are prompted by Muir's notes.
[62] Citation from Henry Howard, *Poems*, ed. Jones, no. 13, l. 17.

voice is wholly dependent on changeful others, to the point that stability and change become interchangeable, just as the last line undoes its apparent meaning, since he is, in one sense, *already* 'ferme and stable' in his faithful mutability. In this state where stability in time can only be defined by repetitive and exhausting diversity, then, 'my word and I' must remain fractured. The plain style of this poem, and possibly its metrical irregularity, are themselves expressive of a plainness that cannot be direct.

Tottel was the first printer of this poem, just as he was the first to print most of Surrey's shorter verse, whereas the lyric poetry of both gentlemen poets had earlier circulated only in manuscript.[63] Tottel, whose *Miscellany* was first published in 1557, divided the Wyatt collection into amatory poems and others, mostly satires. For the amatory poems he invented titles of this kind, for example: 'The louer lamentes the deth of his loue' (no. 102). In itself this was a perfectly reasonable procedure, and one that is followed by modern editors, but it did have the effect of diminishing, in two ways, the discursive resonance of these elegiac poems. In the first place, it is probable that some of these lyrics were not love elegies at all: Tottel's heading 'The louer lamentes the deth of his loue', for example, introduces a sonnet ('The pillar perished is . . . ') considered by critics to refer to the execution of Wyatt's patron, Thomas Cromwell, in 1540; it certainly translates a sonnet by Petrarch lamenting the loss of his patron. In the second place, these poems, even when they are clearly expressions of unrequited love, had a significant relation to the political. As with all Ovidian elegy, the intensity of desire is expressed by strategic use and deflection of political and historical matter: the elegiac lover is always at the same time the courtly lover, and he formulates the experience of love in exactly the terms of courtly manoeuvre. The social condition of the lover always parallels, and is often indistinguishable from, that of the isolated, threatened, and unrequited suitor for courtly recognition.

Wyatt and Surrey both formulate the experience of unrequited

[63] For the MS evidence of Wyatt's verse, see Wyatt, *Collected Poems*, ed. Muir and Thomson, pp. xi–xix. The vast majority of Wyatt's verse survives from four MSS, all of which seem to have been either for private use or for circulation among an intimate group. The same seems to be true of the surviving manuscripts of Surrey's work; see Henry Howard, *Poems*, ed. Padelford, pp. 259–60. See also Marotti.

love in the terms of courtly operation. Surrey's 'When ragyng love with extreme payne', for example, was entitled innocuously enough by Tottel 'The louer comforteth himself with the worthinesse of his loue' (no. 16). In the text itself, however, the lover's comfort is of a particularly uneasy kind: in his 'extreme payne', 'at the poynte of death', the voice calls to mind the Trojan war, and takes comfort in the fact that his love is worthier than Helen's, for whom so much blood was shed. So, the argument of the poem runs, 'I never will repent, | But paynes contented still endure' (ll. 25–6). This logic of self-justification is put under critical pressure, however, by the atrocity of the war remembered only to be dismissed: the narrator recalls not only the ten years' war, in which many 'a bloudy dede was done', but also the fleet becalmed, 'Till Agamemnons daughters bloode | Appeasde the goddes that them withstode' (ll. 11–12).[64] By the time we arrive at the lover's self-justification, the horrors of war have been confronted only to be ignored. The poem's logic claims to justify the lover, while in fact its justification serves only to underline the massive and disabling asymmetry that pertains between the lover and his world.

Wyatt's oeuvre is even more sharply characterized than Surrey's by Ovidian resonances between the political and the amatory. Many of the poems draw on the language and forms of political redress only to expose their incapacities. Take, for example, the roundel 'Behold, Love!':

> Behold, Love, thy power how she despiseth!
> My great payne how litle she regardeth!
> The holy oth, wheof she taketh no cure [oath · consideration]
> Broken she hath: and yet she bideth sure,
> Right at her ease: and litle she dredeth.
> Wepened thou art: and she vnarmed sitteth:
> To the disdaynfull, her liff she ledeth:
> To me spitefull, without cause, or mesure.
> Behold, Love!
>
> I am in hold: if pitie the meveth,
> Goo bend thy bowe: that stony hertes breketh:
> And, with some stroke, revenge the displeasure

[64] Citations are from Howard, *Poems*, ed. Jones, no. 1.

Of thee and him, that sorrowe doeth endure,
And, as his lorde, the lowly entreath.
    Behold, Love![65]

This lyric invokes jurisdictional boundaries only to efface them. The complainant addresses Love as one who can punish the apostasy of his lover, but the very insouciance of the apostate undoes the form of the request, since it becomes clear that the lover represents, rather than resists, Love. By the time 'Behold, Love!' has been repeated three times, Love is no longer a vocative, but an object. Initially we observe the lover addressing his lord, Love, whereas the last command is to us: it is we who are to behold the single and absolute power of Love, embodied in the cruelty of the lover. This adjustment of the refrain's meaning neutralizes the apparent enterprise of the whole piece: as the roundel circles in on itself, we understand that the solidarities and jurisdictions implicit in the opening address collapse. An environment of unrelievable, unmeasurable threat replaces the civil order; here the psyche can be conscious of nothing but its own vulnerability before a hostile and impersonal power. The civil order implicit in the first line, indeed, turns out itself to be drained of any real powers of civic redress, since the voice of the poem is in the first place that of an informer prompting a lord to strike in vengeance. The whole poem implies a speaker already so deeply 'in hold' that he can do nothing but recapitulate his own subservience.

This lyric of Wyatt, then, which is wholly characteristic of his oeuvre, works very much within the same traditions we observed in Chaucer's 'Complaint Unto Pity'. What distinguishes the sixteenth-century from the fourteenth-century elegiac work, however, is the complete incapacity of the later period to voice anything but the paralysis at the heart of elegy. Nowhere in Wyatt's elegiac poetry do we find, in structural, stylistic, or conceptual categories, any movement out of that disabling pain into the more complex stylistic and emotional jurisdictions of Chaucer or Gower's wider elegiac output. Nowhere, that is, does Wyatt's elegiac poetry move from the threatened margin at whose centre looms an absolute, faceless, and unremitting power. Whether or not that power is impersonated by Wyatt's 'lover' or his political enemies is indifferent, since in both

[65] Citations are from Wyatt, *Collected Poems*, ed. Muir and Thomson, no. 1.

cases the operations of power are identical: 'I love an othre and thus I hate my self ' expresses in a 'love' poem the same experience of enthralled fragility we find in the poem lamenting the loss of Cromwell: 'And I my self my self alwayes to hate'.[66]

The discursive conditions implied by Wyatt's elegiac poems possess the simplicity of absolutism. The oeuvre is singular, entirely coherent in the restrictiveness of each poem's conceptual positioning and style, a style whose plainness disowns craft only to reveal an inescapably crafty world. Why elegy should be represented in such singularity in this period, while the earlier tradition is characteristically variegated both formally and discursively, is a very large question. It can only be answered, indeed, in the context of a large survey of the kind conducted by this book, where the discursive narrowing in the sixteenth century is confirmed from many perspectives. For the moment I conclude by observing that the astonishing burst of Ovidianism in the late fourteenth century has the discursive freedom to reactivate and reform the political world from an elegiac base. Of course there are many other shorter courtly poems from the fourteenth and fifteenth centuries that also express love's hopelessness and cruelty.[67] Sixteenth-century elegiac poets up to the 1550s speak, however, consistently in the mode of Echo, as anorexic voices repetitively unable to generate civic solidarities from within the experience of Cupid's tyranny. They speak like Echo, or, by the same token, like Dido on the point of suicide, having no comfort 'But in the wynde to wast [their] wordes', unable to challenge or reform the political world by which they are crushed.[68] Contrary to the standard view of cultural history that these are the poets who reactivate a sense of history, historical and civic consciousness are the victims of these poignant and often beautiful poems.

66 Ibid., nos. 26 and 236 respectively.

67 For a collection of which, see *Secular Lyrics of the XIVth and XVth Centuries*, ed. Robbins. For the MS preservation of these works, see Boffey, *Manuscripts of English Courtly Love Lyrics*.

68 Citation from Wyatt, *Collected Poems*, ed. Muir and Thomson, no. 53.

IV

The central contrast of the chapter having been made, the picture should be nuanced by retracing our steps to Chaucer's pre-*Troilus and Criseyde* career. Each of those poems incorporates and is generated by lyric complaint.[69] Each is driven by an Ovidian deflection, even neutralization, of history, just as it reveals the conditions in which history and politics can be reactivated and reformed by the elegiac experience. The profoundly Ovidian quality of Chaucer's poetic career is also incomplete without reference to *Troilus and Criseyde*'s sequel, the lurid and powerful *Legend of Good Women* (first composed 1386–8).

The *Legend* clearly marks a turning point in Chaucer's poetic career. It presents itself as a penance for *Troilus and Criseyde*, and in it Alceste, by way of defending Chaucer, lists all the works he has composed that have sustained the interests of Cupid. She names the following works, whose dates are all probabilities as given here: *The Book of the Duchess* (1369), *The House of Fame* (1374–80), *The Parlement of Foules* (*c.*1378–84), and the *Knight's Tale* (written, before the composition of many of the *Canterbury Tales*, *c.*1385–6), along with many 'balades, roundels, and virelayes'. She might also have included the powerful and intense *Anelida and Arcite* (*c.*1378–85). Chaucer styles himself as a new Ovid in the Prologue to the *Legend*, under attack from an imperious and imperial moral and literary arbiter, just as Ovid suffered exile by Augustus. In so doing he exploits the occasion to signal his profound engagement with Ovid up to this decisive point in his poetic career.[70] For each of these works I sketch the Ovidian dialectic of history and the self.[71] In each, that is, we find an elegiac and Ovidian sympathy with the demands of the grieving and/or loving self, provisionally set above the relentless demands of 'history'. At the same time, Chaucer just as consistently underscores the ways in which the retreat to a private world can easily replicate the brutality and violence of the historical world. The compulsiveness of love can flatten history and dissolve

[69] For which see Davenport.

[70] The mid- to late 1380s were also a decisive and dangerous point in Chaucer's career as a bureaucrat, for which see Strohm, 'Politics and Poetics'.

[71] Ovid stages a debate between *Elegia* and *Tragoedia* in *Amores*, 3. 1.

solidarities. These poems nevertheless trace a return to the realm of historical consciousness and social solidarity, a realm ideally reformed by the experience of suffering.

(*a*) *The Book of the Duchess*

The Book of the Duchess, 1,334 lines of four-stress couplets, is Chaucer's earliest datable poem. Heavily indebted to works by the French poet Machaut (*c.*1300–1377),[72] it also clearly marks its fundamental allegiance to Ovid. The melancholic voice of a lover, who needs, by an Ovidian conceit, a 'physician' to cure him, narrates. Unable to sleep, he reads, and finally sleeps. In his dream, he comes across a socially superior reflex of himself, a grieving and plangent knight, dressed in black and alone in a forest. The knight, apparently locked into a cycle of deepening and self-destructive grief, denies that anyone could cure him, 'Noght al the remedyes of Ovyde, | Ne Orpheus, god of melodye', nor any doctors (ll. 567–72). With these lines Chaucer signals the challenge of the poem, to act as a *remedium amoris*, offering therapy to a grieving lover from a failed lover. In the represented action of the poem, the dreamer operates like a homeopathic doctor, provoking pain in order to diminish it: by pretending ignorance of the Black Knight's real loss he provokes the mourner to express and thereby confront the source of his grief.[73] This represented therapy is itself very subtle, partly because it disguises subtlety, but the poem itself is more so, again by its use of an Ovidian text.

In order to while away the sleepless night, the dreamer reads the story of Ceys and Alcione, a narrative drawn from the *Metamorphoses* (11. 410–750). In the abbreviated version recounted to us by the dreamer, Alcione, anxious for her absent husband on a sea-voyage, is visited in a dream by the zombie Morpheus, who, as a messenger of Juno, has been sent to impersonate Ceys and to announce his death by drowning. Morpheus consoles so poorly that Alcione promptly dies within three days. On the face of it, this failed

[72] See *Chaucer's Dream Poetry*, ed. and trans. Windeatt, pp. 3–40; 58–72; 139–48.

[73] Pandarus practises the same therapeutic strategy in *Troilus and Criseyde*, 1. 561–4, and 4. 428–32.

consolation presents an inauspicious model from which to launch a consolation for the Black Knight, especially because the dreamer, who can hardly sleep, seems just as insensitive a consoler as Morpheus, who can hardly wake up. In fact, however, Chaucer draws on this Ovidian resource so as both to console and to disguise consolation. The similarities between the dreamer and Morpheus serve to disguise consolation, by marking out both as equally ham-fisted. The model also, however, generates restorative dissimilarities: the Black Knight manages his own consolation, as he articulates the source of his grief; and the consolation is of a purely secular kind, achieved by the resources of human artifice rather than any divine intervention whatsoever, be it Christian or pagan. By reconstructing the image of his dead wife, the knight 'resurrects' her as an icon (ll. 805–1041), which, as a humanly constructed artefact, both recognizes and resists temporality. Once the knight has both constructed this verbal simulacrum of his wife and recognized that she is dead, the poem can come to an end, the 'he(a)rt-huntyng' done for the time, and the Emperour Octavyen, whose own 'hert-huntynge' frames the dialogue, can return to his castle.

Chaucer wrote this poem for John of Gaunt, son of Edward III. By virtue of his marriage with Blanche, Duchess of Lancaster, whose death this poem memorializes, Gaunt was the greatest landowner in England. The castle to which 'Octavyen' returns encodes references to Gaunt's palaces and names, just as it encodes Gaunt as Augustus, and, by implication, Chaucer as Ovid, writing for an Augustan court. The work was, no doubt, a commission, of a kind with the elaborate tomb ordered by Gaunt to commemorate his wife, who died of plague in 1369.[74] The poem's light-footed tact certainly suggests the practice of a court poet writing on command to a very powerful patron. Unlike the *Legend of Good Women*, however, this poem is shaped rather by Ovidian than Cupidian perspectives: the Ovidian resources of the work, drawn from both the amatory works and the *Metamorphoses*, allow Chaucer a space both to speak and to

[74] For the relations between the poem and the tomb for Blanche, see Hardman, '*Book of the Duchess*'. Consolation is a convenient occasion for a young poet to impress a patron; see e.g. the model consolation offered as a rhetorical exercise by Thomas Wilson, in the first rhetorical treatise in English, *The Arte of Rhetorique, for the use of all suche as are Studious of Eloquence, sette forth in English* (1553), *RSTC* 25799, I. iv^{v}. Wilson's consolation is explicitly Christian, unlike Chaucer's.

disguise his voice, just as it allows him to negotiate between the demands of history and the self. The chamber in which the narrator finds himself in his dream is glazed with the story of Troy, and adorned with murals of the *Romance of the Rose* (ll. 321–34). These two textual models represent the extremes of violent tragedy and egoistic elegy, between which jurisdictions the commemoration of Blanche in the *Book of the Duchess* negotiates with such tact.

(*b*) *The House of Fame*

Chaucer's earliest datable dream-poem is the work of a youngish poet ambitious to fashion a persona that will both serve and yet impress in courtly circles. His next work, *The House of Fame* (2,158 lines of four-stress couplets, divided into three books), which has no stated patron nor obvious occasion, expresses ambitions rather to enter the society of European literature. If, drawing on Ovid, Chaucer commemorates a single woman within an ongoing history in the earlier poem, in the later poem he takes up an Ovidian vantage point to disrupt and reshape the very notion of what constitutes history itself. This work has been hailed as the first evidence of Chaucer's 'Renaissance' capacities, since it so obviously situates itself in a tradition of vastly ambitious, especially Dantean, vernacular enterprise; makes the first invocation in English poetry; and lays claim to poetic fame.[75] It certainly registers the powerful influence of Italian vernacular poetry newly revitalized by the extraordinary achievement of Dante, Boccaccio, and Petrarch. I agree about the remarkable ambition of this poem, but I would, from the argument of this chapter as a whole, argue instead that Chaucer's commitment to Ovid provokes him to challenge these ostensibly 'Renaissance' ideals. Once again, commemoration, this time of a whole poetic tradition, is shaped within the terms of Ovidian elegy, but the very rigour of the Ovidian commitment brings Chaucer into direct conflict with 'Renaissance' ideals of fame, including, even, Ovid's own fame. This reformulation disallows the 'Renaissance' practice of stellifying authors by way of apotheosis, forever abstracting them from the 'news' for which they are responsible.

[75] Spearing, *Medieval to Renaissance*, pp. 22–30.

The text blazoned on this poem is not ostensibly by Ovid, but rather by Virgil. The dreamer dreams that he finds himself in Venus' temple, and, after being struck by the image of Venus, reads the text of the *Aeneid* engraved onto a brazen tablet along the walls of the temple: 'I wol now synge, yif I kan, | The armes and also the man' (ll. 143–4). The un-Virgilian qualification, 'yif I kan', here turns out to be strategic since the narrator, a poet called 'Geoffrey', cannot, in fact, read Virgil's poem, not even in its vernacular rendering. The story of Aeneas is epitomized in spare style until Geoffrey arrives in Dido's Carthage, at which point Virgil's narrative is arrested, both by complaint and narratorial exclamation. The forward movement of the Virgilian narrative is disrupted both by Dido's laments for the bad fame that will attach to her hereafter, and by the narrator's own sympathetic reading of her position. This reading is so sympathetic, indeed, that it derails the Virgilian narrative altogether.

The engraved text is rewritten as it is reread, to the point that its eternal stabilities give way to an entirely new text: 'In such wordes gan to pleyne | Dydo of hir grete peyne, | As me mette redely— | Non other auctor alegge I' (ll. 311–14). Of course another *auctor* and text stand behind this disruption, and Chaucer confronts the reader with the jagged incoherences of the narrative by reference to its contradictory classical sources; of all the words spoken by Dido as she died, 'Who to knowe hit hath purpos, | Rede Virgile in Eneados | Or the Epistle of Ovyde' (ll. 378–9). In a nice touch Dido herself cites Virgil so as to subject his authority to scrutiny. In lamenting the loss of her name, she recalls Virgil's lines about the mobility and maliciousness of Fame (*Aeneid*, 4. 174–88): 'O wikke Fame—for ther nys | Nothing so swift, lo, as she is!' (ll. 349–50).[76] Virgil's own work, articulated as if by an inspired voice, can afford to describe fame without incurring the danger of having been itself produced by Fame's mendacity. Chaucer, by contrast, has the Virgilian figure of Dido cite Virgil for precisely this reason: Dido not only evokes the oppositional Ovidian account of Dido (*Heroides*, 7), but she also thereby exposes the Virgilian narrative as open to question. The inspired status of the Virgilian voice looks only like another of Fame's ruses to disseminate 'truth'.

[76] *Aeneid*, 4. 174 is the source marginally cited by two of the three MSS of the poem, Oxford, Bodleian Library, MS Fairfax 16, and MS Bodley 638.

Dido's elegy has extraordinary consequences, by way of reorienting Chaucer's attitude towards all 'history'. For if the Ovidian reading of Dido unveils inspiration and immutable 'Fame' as themselves human productions, then Chaucer's own poem cannot itself escape the implications of that exposure. Two of the poem's own invocations (ll. 523–8; 1091–1109) derive from Dante's *Commedia*, just as the Eagle who swoops to elevate him through the heavens echoes *Purgatorio*, 9. 19–33. Both invocation and astral voyage underline the extraordinary claims Dante makes for his vernacular poem, but Chaucer invokes these gestures only to disclaim them: fat Geoffrey declines the Eagle's offer of a journey to the immutable region of the stars, and prefers instead to visit the House of Fame.[77] Here he witnesses a pantheon of classical and medieval poets responsible for the primary divisions of historical matter: the writers of Israelite, Theban, Trojan, and Roman history. Almost the only exception to these 'tragic' poets is Ovid, 'Venus clerk', quietly placed beside Virgil, who sustains 'the fame of Pius Eneas' (l. 1485). The logic of the poem, however, propelled by Dido's elegiac complaint against Aeneas, insists on the disruptive power of Ovidian matter; so far from wanting to claim fame for himself, Chaucer rehearses these ostensibly 'Renaissance' gestures only to disown them. Geoffrey wants 'tydynges' for his poetry, not petrified classical exemplars for imitation.

Whereas Petrarch attempted to write a modern, Virgilian '*alta tragedía*' in the form of his imperialistic *Africa*,[78] Chaucer leaves Virgil and even Ovid behind here, asking to go to the House of Rumour, where 'rumour' means both 'noise' and 'gossip'. In this improvised and mobile structure, itself derived from *Metamorphoses*, 12. 39–63, truth and falsehood struggle to escape into the world against each other, until they agree to go coupled, 'fals and soth compouned' (l. 2108). Chaucer's adoption of this form of history might seem like an irresponsible choice given the alternative classical and vernacular models, both Virgilian and Dantean, so forcefully present in the work. *The House of Fame* as a whole reveals, however, that all human 'fame' has historical, labile sources. Setting aside sacred

[77] For the logic of this preference, see Simpson, 'Dante's "Astripetam Aquilam"'.

[78] Citation from Dante, *Inferno*, 20. 113 (referring to the *Aeneid*); Petrarch's *Africa* was begun in 1338. See Petrarch, '*Africa*', trans. Bergin and Wilson.

texts, since the Bible is significantly absent from the House of Fame, no human poet escapes this condition, least of all Chaucer. Insofar as he can be, Ovid is himself left behind in the House of Fame, but the movement beyond Ovid is initiated by Dido's Ovidian elegy. A commitment to Ovidian elegy recasts the entire European tradition in this poem, just as it produces a renewed understanding of what 'history' means. Sympathy for history's victims, who are usually women, by a poet who is not himself Cupid's victim serves to reformulate the very notion of history and remembrance. Chaucer admits the point that Ovid's Elegy makes in the *Amores*, as she argues with Tragedy: 'prima tuae movi felicia semina mentis' ('It was I who first provoked the fertile seeds of your enterprise', 3. 1. 59): passionate, private experience generates history in the first place.

(*c*) *The Parlement of Foules*

We have no evidence that Chaucer knew Petrarch's Virgilian imitation *Africa* (begun in 1338), which was written in commemoration of Petrarch's hero Scipio Africanus the Elder (235–183 BC), destroyer of Carthage. Chaucer certainly understood, however, Scipio's enormous prestige, since Ovidian deflection of all that Scipio stands for drives Chaucer's next Ovidian poem, the brilliant, densely allusive, and wonderfully polished *Parlement of Foules* (one hundred rhyme-royal stanzas, minus one line). The closing portion of Cicero's *De re publica* (54–51 BC), which recounted the dream of Scipio (the *Somnium Scipionis*), was the only portion of that work to survive, preserved in the late antique commentary on it by Macrobius (fl. late fourth, early fifth century). The commentary not only explicated the Platonic model of the ideal philosopher-king; it also offered the seminal discussion for the kind of inspired dream it was that allowed Scipio the Younger to visit the heavens, as a foretaste of the rewards of the statesman who serves 'commune profit'. The work thus comes freighted with the tightest connection between imperial conquest and divine sanction: forging the imperial history of the city comes with the endorsement of the Reason of the universe itself.

Chaucer's narrator reads and epitomizes '"Tullyus of the Drem of Scipioun"' (ll. 29–84), by way of distinguishing his own very different enterprise and his own kind of dream.

The narrator's reading ends and the dream begins in this way:

> The day gan faylen, and the derke nyght,
> That reveth bestes from here besyness, [takes · their
> Berafte me my bok for lak of lyght, activity]
> And to my bed I gan me forto dresse,
> Fulfyld of thought and busy hevynesse;
> For bothe I hadde thyng which that I nolde, [did not wish]
> And ek I ne hadd that thyng that I wolde.
>
> (ll. 85–91)

This stanza provisionally aligns Chaucer with both Aeneas and Dante: *Inferno* 2 begins with an evocation of these Virgilian lines (e.g. *Aeneid*, 3. 147 and 8. 26), where, as in the Virgilian source, the hero prepares to undergo a divinely sanctioned journey inspired by vision. These poetic references set in parallel a poetic tradition of imperial enterprise with the philosophical tradition of the *Somnium Scipionis*, but in so doing the stanza also marks the dreamer's elegiac dissatisfaction with that inheritance. The whole text had begun with an elaborate periphrasis of Love, 'the dredful joye alwey that slit so yerne' (l. 3). Love is acknowledged as the presiding deity of this text; this being so, Chaucer is not accommodated by the entire poetico-philosophic tradition within which the poem has so far moved. He reads with desire, just as Geoffrey rereads the *Aeneid* in the *House of Fame*, but the *Somnium Scipionis* has nothing more penetrating to say about erotic desire than that those who follow it shall 'whirle about th'erthe alwey in peyne' (l. 80). The narrator sleeps and dreams, having been left unsatisfied by the book and the tradition it so powerfully represents.

As in the *House of Fame*, Chaucer's rereading of a text produces a rewriting, this time in the dream, where the dreamer himself is guided by Africanus up to, but not through, the gates of the goddess Nature's realm. The gates of this space cite the inscription over Dante's hell (*Inferno*, 3. 1–9) only to divide its absolutism; whereas Dante's lines promise an eternal and hopeless hell, shaped by 'il primo amore', for those who enter the gate, Chaucer's gate promises both the paradise and hell of human love for those who pass into Nature's realm. The realm of Nature rewrites the political narrative of Scipio's dream by transfiguring it: Nature operates like a monarch presiding over a parliament, where all birds, on St Valentine's Day, are arranged hierarchically to 'take hire dom and yeve hire audyence' (l. 308) in choosing their mate. The poem's very structure therefore bears an Ovidian mark, since the terms of the public world are deflected but deployed in order to describe the operations of erotic love.

The procedures of the parliament reveal, however, that the 'real' politics of 'commune profit' are indeed served by the generative exercise of erotic love, as exemplified by the lower birds. At the same time, Nature's garden contains victims stranded by erotic passion, cut off from time and society: the temple of Venus occupies one section of the garden, whose sultry atmosphere is fanned by sighs, 'Which sikes were engendred with desyr' (l. 248), and the walls of which are adorned with a series of images of mainly Ovidian lover-victims. The poem never resolves this double possibility of a sexuality either regenerative or imprisoning, as it cannot, since both possibilities are 'natural'. The goddess Natura in Alan of Lille's *De planctu Naturae* (*c.*1160–70) is the model for Chaucer's goddess.[79] Whereas, however, Alan's Natura is a spokesperson for the Reason that governs the natural universe, Chaucer's Nature makes a critical qualification when it comes to determining which eagle the female eagle should take: 'If I *were* Resoun, thanne wolde I | Conseyle yow the royal tercel take' (ll. 632–3, my emphasis). With this single subjunctive, Chaucer opens up a significant difference between himself and his Neoplatonic poetic and philosophical frames: passionate love may not be rational, but it *is* natural. Equally, however, Chaucer opens up a massive difference between his poetry and the classical and late antique imperialist texts to which he alludes via the *Somnium Scipionis*: unlike these texts, Chaucer the Ovidian recognizes the centrality of sexual love in any account of the political.[80]

Each work of Chaucer leading up to *Troilus and Criseyde* is, then, propelled by Ovidian elegy, of the narrator and/or of figures within the poems. In each poem we are presented with a lover abandoned

[79] For which see Economou.

[80] Hans Baron argues that Cicero's commitment to civic action, expressed throughout his work but especially in the *Somnium Scipionis*, was recovered only fully by Florentine civic humanists from the late 14th cent.; Chaucer's creative and critical use of the *Somnium* in the *Parlement* reveals the same interest in the work.

by, or at least resistant to, the processes of the public world of history and politics. Each poem expresses an Ovidian sympathy for that rejection of public concerns, but equally recognizes the necessity for return to the historical world. That return, however, has the power profoundly to recast the very notion of what constitutes the 'historical', as in the *House of Fame*, or to institute sexuality at the heart of any account of the 'political', as in the *Parlement*. In these poems the complaints of self-divided lovers, addressing an irretrievable source of comfort, do not, finally, prohibit the texts themselves from returning to a modified version of the historical and political.

Given these discursive possibilities, these poems also have the power to resurrect the continuities of historical tradition. Whereas a 'Renaissance' account of history is characteristically produced by an ineluctable sense of rupture, and is locked into the pathos of intense historical solitude, these elegiac poems have the discursive resources to retrieve a sense of historical contour and change. The *House of Fame* is about this very problem, but the *Parlement* also addresses it centrally. The narrator of that poem declares early on that just as new corn comes from old fields, so too does 'new science' come from 'olde bokes' (ll. 22–5). This renewed fertility of old books can only be accounted for by the fact of their being read in new circumstances. The present does not wholly appropriate old books, but rather interacts with them in a dialectical relationship.[81] The historical memory of the *Parlement* is astonishingly long and shaded, going back as it does via Dante (d. 1321) and Alan of Lille (d. 1202) to Macrobius (fourth century) and then Cicero (d. 43 BC), and behind them to the pre-Virgilian hero Scipio (late 3rd century BC). Chaucer himself is aware of these historical perspectives, but his awareness can in no way be described as characteristic of the 'Renaissance', since he does not posit any rupture, or middle age. Instead, his understanding of torn old books fully registers its own historicity, by virtue of its own reception through a continuing tradition of change, opposition, and renewal. Old books themselves are presented as welcoming this process; the narrator wonders why he dreams of Africanus, the figure about whom he has just read,

[81] This Gadamerian account was first argued by Ferster, *Chaucer on Interpretation*.

But thus seyde he: 'Thow hast the so wel born
In lokynge of myn olde bok totorn,
Of which Macrobye roughte nat a lite,
That somdel of thy labour wolde I quyte.'

(ll. 109–12)

In this poem, at least, Chaucer is not a Renaissance poet, because no medieval period disrupts his access to the past. On the contrary, the poem exposes the ahistorical denial of historicity in 'Renaissance' thinking, with its removal of the 'middle age' from the process. Renaissance fame is premissed on historical suppression.

(*d*) *The Legend of Good Women*

If *Troilus and Criseyde* opens astonishing discursive freedoms, its successor, *The Legend of Good Women*, works by contrast within extremely tight ideological and stylistic limits. The poem was produced in the later half of the 1380s, a period of extreme tension, as we have seen, between Richard II and his aristocratic competitors. In the 'Record and Process' of Richard's own renunciation of the throne in 1399, we find Richard being charged with oppressive activity of exactly the kind represented in the poem.[82] Of course the 'Record and Process' was a highly charged piece of political propaganda, and I refer to it here not by way of suggesting, or denying, that these really were the discursive conditions within which Chaucer worked in between 1386 and 1388, and after 1394, from which date the Prologue seems to have been revised.[83] Whatever the truth of the document, the one thing it certainly does is to describe tyranny in terms of a wilful appropriation of discursive power. Richard is consistently accused of exercising an arbitrary will, 'pro sue libito voluntatis', and in each case this exercise of arbitrary will is an instance of specifically discursive infringement. He is accused of wilfully

[82] The Latin text is in *Rotuli Parliamentorum*, 3. 415–53, and there is an English trans. in *Chronicles of the Revolution*, ed. Given-Wilson, pp. 168–89.

[83] For the dating of the *Legend* and its two prologues, see *Riverside Chaucer*, ed. Benson, p. 1060. For the treacherous discursive conditions of the mid-1380s see Strohm, 'Textual Environment'. The discursive conditions of the 1390s were no less fragile and dangerous; see Saul.

distorting the process and altering the records of parliament;[84] when challenged on the dispensation of arbitrary justice, Richard had fiercely replied that the laws were 'in his mouth', or 'in his breast', and that he did, by his own wilful judgement, whatever pleased him ('secundum sue arbitrium voluntatis . . . quicquid desideriis eius occurrerit' (para. 16)); he so terrified his counsellors that they dared not speak the truth in giving counsel (para. 23). The document ends by recording a sermon by Archbishop Arundel, in which the King's childish will is personified: 'Cum igitur puer regnat, Voluntas sola regnat, Ratio exul'.[85]

The narrator of *The Legend of Good Women*, 2,723 lines of five-stress couplets, opens by encouraging his readers to give credence to books, since without them 'Yloren were of remembraunce the keye' (F.26). The text as a whole, however, refuses easy access to remembrance's key, since it is governed by the profoundly ahistorical and tyrannical figure of male desire, personified by Cupid. In the Prologue of this dream-poem, Chaucer represents his waking self as up on May Day to watch the daisy unfold,

> For to ben at the resurrectioun
> Of this flour, whan that yt shulde unclose
> Agayn the sonne, that roos as red as rose,
> That in the brest was of the best, that day,
> That Agenores doghtre ladde away.
>
> (F.110–14)

This elaborate periphrasis is on the face of it astrological, and might be translated thus: 'in order to be at the rising of this flower, when it should open towards the sun, that was on that day in the centre of the zodiacal sign of Taurus'. Why, however, should Chaucer refer to Taurus in this cryptic way? The mythical decoding of the periphrasis of the last three lines would read in this way: 'the sun, which was in the breast of the bull, the form that Jupiter took on when he raped Europa'. The ostensibly utopian scene of May Day is, then, cryptically framed within a scene of tyrannical violence by the king of the

84 Para. 8 in *Chronicles of the Revolution*, ed. Given-Wilson. (Latin text from *Rotuli Parliamentorum*, 3. 418).

85 'When a child rules, Wilfulness alone is king, and Reason an exile'. See *Chronicles of the Revolution*, ed. Given-Wilson, p. 186 (*Rotuli Parliamentorum*, 3. 423).

Gods, a violence that initiates the founding of Thebes, and the figuring of 'Europe' itself as the product of *raptus* from an Asian shore (*Metamorphoses*, 2. 846–3. 131). This is clearly a large weight for so small a flower to bear, but the rest of the narrative operates within an absolutist environment that necessitates the secret encoding of male violence and the repression of historical narrative.

Once asleep, Chaucer dreams of the daisy and the sun again, though transfigured as Alceste, the archetypically faithful wife, and Cupid, the God of Love. Alceste is decorated with daisy-shaped arrangements of pearls, the Latin word for which is also the French word for daisy (*margarita/marguerite*), while Cupid is crowned with a sun. Just as the daisy of the Prologue can be 'resurrected' only with regard to the sun, so too is Alceste activated only in response to the sun-god Cupid. Cupid confronts Chaucer with charges of heresy, for having translated the *Romance of the Rose* and having written 'of Criseyde . . . That maketh men to women lasse triste' (F.332–3). Cupid is very definitely a reader here, but he wants only stories of faithful women, of which Alceste is the exemplar. Alceste is activated by Cupid's charges; although she warns Cupid against acting like 'tirauntz of Lumbardye' (F.374), she herself participates in a tyrannical process, since she deflects Cupid's anger only by refusing Chaucer a chance to reply to the charges, and instead shuts him up with a warning that 'Love ne wol nat countrepleted be | In ryght ne wrong; and lerne that at me!' (F.476–7). Justice, writing, and reading can only be practised within the circuit of Cupid's gratified desire.

Chaucer receives his commission, or 'penaunce', out of this trial of authorship, to write a 'legende' of good women, 'whil that thou livest, yer by yere' (G.471). This is an act of commemoration, by way of declaring the 'renown' of Alceste, but remembrance is both produced and tightly constrained by the demands of Cupid. Alceste signifies all faithful women: beside other Ovidian heroines, she 'passeth al'; and her flower, the daisy, with which Alceste is conceptually identified, 'passeth our alder pris in figurynge' (F.298). But if Alceste does figure all womanhood, and does evoke a eulogistic remembrance of womanhood, this can only be in order to reflect Cupid's glory through feminine suffering. When, for example, Cupid first catches Chaucer observing the daisy, he claims sole possession: 'Yt is my relyke, digne and delytable' (F.321). Alceste is only 'delytable' to

Cupid insofar as she suffers for men. Her power to act as a 'relyke' in the religious sense of reflecting Cupid's numinous power, that is, derives only from her capacity to be a relic of men, abandoned in order to be martyred. All the other women in the *Legend*, like their counterparts in Ovid's *Heroides*, are abandoned by men; Alceste has gone one better by abandoning herself, as it were, for her husband, since she offers to die if Admetus can be resurrected.

If Alceste does signify and surpass all faithful women in such a way as to gratify Cupid's desire, Cupid's own relationship with the treacherous men of the legends is suppressed, as it must be, given his power as patron. The narrative of Dido's disastrous love for Aeneas, for example, makes reference to the role of 'Cupido, that is the god of love', ensnaring Dido as he impersonates Ascanius (ll. 1140–44). This reference to the *Aeneid* (1. 643–722) quietly lets the cat out of the bag that it was Cupid himself who was in the first place instrumental in the suffering of the very women whose patience he wants Chaucer to magnify. The attempt to put the cat straight back in the bag only heightens the effect: 'but, as of that scripture, | Be as be may, I take of it no cure' (l. 1144–5).[86]

Commemoration, or 'resurrection', in the *Legend*, then, is both provoked and denied by the tyrannical power of male desire. Cupid governs the field of memory in this work, and in so doing he flattens the historical contours of each story, since each legend must, effectively, tell the same story of feminine readiness to suffer. Chaucer promises to write back into history, since he disowns an interest in the contemporary courtly dispute manufactured between adherents of the flower or the leaf;[87] he says that he will write instead 'Of olde storye, er swich stryf was begonne' (F.196). The anterior 'strife' of treachery, rape, and murder in these stories outscales courtly quibbles about flowers and leaves altogether, but the full extent and meaning of that violence, by both men and women, is disallowed. Critics have often complained that the legends are repetitive, and therefore an artistic failure. Such comments fail to recognize that the repetitiveness derives from the circularity of Chaucer's patron Cupid, who, like Tarquin in the legend of Lucrece, compulsively

86 I have argued this more extensively in Simpson, 'Ethics and Interpretation'.

87 For the courtly amusement of the competition between adherents of Flower and Leaf, see J. Stevens, pp. 180–2.

repeats the same round of obsessive desire, 'Th'ymage of hire recordynge alwey newe' (l. 1760). For readers prepared to decode the suppressed allusiveness of the work, it becomes a powerful representation of de-historicized art, rather than an example of such historical flattening. In the tyrannical discursive environment governed by Cupid, 'remembrance's key' is extremely difficult to find, visible only in the traces of its suppression. If *Troilus and Criseyde* represents an extreme of finally unmaneageable discursive freedom from an elegiac base, *The Legend of Good Women* represents the reclamation of elegy's field of memory by a figure of tyrannical male desire. After it, Chaucer moves beyond the nexus of elegy and tragedy, and heads for Canterbury.

V

Thus far I have been discussing the 'politics' of love poetry. There are, of course, many other ways of understanding elegiac practice in the period of this book. Some of the best scholarship on this lyric poetry has, for example, persuasively argued that such poetry is better regarded as a social practice rather than an expression of personal feeling, let alone as an attempt to write great poetry. This kind of writing, so it is argued, functioned as courtly entertainment and display; it was the textual adjunct to courtly diversions of the kind referred to in many of the texts: St Valentine's Day, the competition between adherents of the Flower and the Leaf, May Day, and so on.[88] One early fifteenth-century poem, *The Floure and the Leaf*, indeed, is a representation of precisely such a courtly entertainment. There is much evidence to support this contention. Certainly in literary works themselves the exercise of courtly manner, especially in amorous dalliance, was highly esteemed. The courtiers of the provincial court in the late fourteenth-century romance *Sir Gawain and the Green Knight*, for example, are especially delighted at Gawain's arrival, so it is said, because they will see 'sleghtez of thewes | And the teccheles termes of talkyng noble [dextrous social demeanour and faultless terms of noble speech]' (ll. 916–17); a few lines further on

[88] See ibid., pt. 2, ch. 9, and Olson.

this noble speech is delimited to 'luf talkyng' (l. 926). In any courtly context social manner is a synecdoche for the whole civil order, since skill in dalliance, a critical test of social manner, is a necessary attribute of the aspiring courtier. Thus the Squire in Chaucer's General Prologue to the *Canterbury Tales* is admired for his courtly accomplishments, among which are skill in riding, jousting, dancing, writing, drawing, and table manners, in addition to which 'He koude songes make and wel endite' (l. 95).

Many of the attested authors of elegiac poetry were indeed associated closely with the royal court, either as courtiers or as bureaucrats. The most socially elevated names are Henry Howard, Earl of Surrey; Charles d'Orléans, an extraordinarily accomplished lyric poet, and prisoner in England for twenty-five years from 1415;[89] and James I of Scotland, equally an English prisoner, whose authorship of the *Kingis Quair* (1424) is probable.[90] Poems are also attributed to William de la Pole, Earl (later Duke) of Suffolk, keeper of Charles d'Orléans from 1432 to 1436.[91] Below the level of aristocrats, Wyatt was by no means the only example of courtly making by a high-level diplomat and courtier; Richard II's household knight Sir John Clanvowe seems certainly to have written a delightful elegiac poem, *The Book of Cupid* (*c.*1387–91), just as the soldier, diplomat, and courtier Sir Richard Roos (*c.*1410–82) turned a crisp translation (856 lines) of Alain Chartier's *La Belle Dame Sans Mercy*. Lower down the social scale, aside from the diplomat and bureaucrat Geoffrey Chaucer, we should include lesser bureaucrats like Thomas Usk (d. 1388), Thomas Hoccleve (d. 1426),[92] and Steven Hawes (b. *c.*1475).[93] The dominant literary mode for almost all these figures was elegy: almost all of them wrote, most exclusively, elegiac poems, whether as self-contained lyrics, lyrics set into a sequence, or lyrics set into a larger narrative frame. Across the entire period of this history, then, we can see the traces of what one recent scholar has called

[89] For a brief biography, and further references, see Charles d'Orléans, *Fortunes Stabilnes*, ed. Arn, pp. 12–27.

[90] For a brief biography and further references, see James I of Scotland, *Kingis Quair*, ed. Norton-Smith, pp. xxi–xxv.

[91] Texts preserved in Oxford, Bodleian Library, MS Fairfax 16; for a selection of them, see *Secular Lyrics of the XIVth and XVth Centuries*, ed. Robbins, pp. 185–90.

[92] See J. A. Burrow, *Thomas Hoccleve*.

[93] See Edwards, *Stephen Hawes*.

a 'Court of Cupid', poetry written by, and in the first instance possibly for, a courtly, and/or bureaucratic circle.[94] Those at the lower end of the courtly spectrum, professional bureaucrats if not professional literary authors, clearly had instrumental purposes in writing, by way of improving their position in court. Many at the higher end of the spectrum also wrote: this is the one genre in which we find many noble authors. They may also have had instrumental purposes in writing elegiac verse; if so, however, those purposes were served by private, manuscript circulation.

Listing court poets in descending order of social rank as I have just done may give the impression that courtly making of this kind filtered down the social scale from above; this is misleading, since it was rather the case, in England at any rate, that courtly composition probably ascended the social scale, beginning with non-noble bureaucrats, and imitated thereafter by nobly born courtiers. Certainly the vernacular makers who give the most powerful impetus to this tradition in England (i.e. Chaucer and Gower) were not themselves nobly born, and rather transmitted a larger Continental tradition whereby non-noble figures claimed nobility of soul by virtue of the finesse of their sentiments.[95] If this means that non-noble figures could practise a 'courtly' style of loving, the entire tradition nevertheless retains the marks of its bureaucratic origins.

The literary system of elegiac writing in this period was, indeed, informed by bureaucratic practice. This is true of the content of the poems, representing as they often do scenes of bureaucratic procedure, with lovers writing bills, seeking access to the source of power, and presenting petitionary documents. Lydgate's *Temple of Glass* is a good example, and *The Assembly of Ladies* (*c.*1470–80) a better: it is written from the perspective of a woman suitor in a sentimental court, and gives the most intimate and amusing account of the elaborate passage to the seat of power. Bureaucratic protocols also shape the form of these works, couched as they often are in bureaucratic formulas, as letters patent from Cupid, commissions, petitions, and so forth. Charles d'Orléans's sequence begins with a royal letter patent:

[94] Green, ch. 4.
[95] See Minnis, 'From Medieval to Renaissance?'.

The god Cupide and Venus the goddes
Whiche power han on all worldly gladnes:
We hertly gretyng sende of oure humbles
To lovers alle.[96]

Hoccleve's *Letter of Cupid* (1402) ends with the protocols of the same bureaucratic form:

Wryten in the ayer the lusty moneth of May,
In oure paleys where many a milion
Of louers trwe han habitacion,
The yere of grace ioyful and iocunde
A thousande and foure houndred and secounde.[97]

Bureaucratic style also informs the petitionary status of narrators. To write about one's most intimate and vulnerable emotions in bureaucratic form may be one paradox of this tradition, but another is that whereby very powerful men position themselves as a hopeless suitor for power. The first of these paradoxes is Ovidian: the lover deploys bureaucratic form precisely in order to mark his turning away from the field of civic action. The second may have a deep psychological sense, particularly as some of these powerful men were in prison when they wrote, actively conducting an epistolary campaign to have themselves released. The poetry remains positioned in the person of power's suitor, who exercises his bureaucratic skills by way of gaining access to emotional plenitude.

The very production of writing itself in this tradition is often represented within a bureaucratic model, as documentary production by professional writers on behalf of patrons. In his teasingly hide-and-seek way, Charles d'Orléans can pose as a kind of scribe, producing love lyrics on a bespoke, or commissioned basis for friends, who, 'he or she', would

Pray me that y wolde suche labour take
Of ther complayntis as they to me tolde,
In a roundell or balade them to make.

(ll. 4652–4)

[96] *Fortunes Stabilnes*, ed. Arn, ll. 1–4, p. 137.

[97] See Hoccleve, *Works: The Minor Poems*, ed. Furnivall and Gollancz, rev. Mitchell and Doyle, p. 91, ll. 472–6. For discussion, see Flemming.

Whether or not he was really bidden to translate it, Richard Roos's *La Belle Dame sans Mercy* opens with an account of the work's production, whereby Roos says that he is commanded to translate the book, 'Which mayster Aleyn made of remembraunce, | Cheef secretarie with the king of Fraunce' (ll. 11–12): one bureaucratic context in France is absorbed into another in England.

The monk Lydgate was almost certainly commissioned to write love complaints. The scribe of Lydgate's 'Ballade, of Her that hath all Virtues', heads the text in Cambridge, Trinity College MS R.3.20, as a commissioned document: 'Loo here begynnethe a balade whiche that Lydegate wrote at the request of a squyer that serued in loves court.'[98] Of course the title may be invented, but given Lydgate's status as monk, it is clear that his love complaints 'The Complaint of the Black Knight', the 'Floure of Curtesy', 'A Gentlewoman's Lament', 'A Lover's New Year's Gift', and so on, were written on command, as a bureaucrat writes for, and in the voice of, both male and female patrons. In the 'Complaint of the Black Knight',[99] much indebted to the *Book of the Duchess*, the narrator explicitly compares himself to a professional scribe; in disclaiming capacity to set down the 'wofull compleynt' made by the aristocratic sufferer, he writes

> . . . euen-like as doth a skryuener,
> That can no more what that he shal write,
> But as his master beside dothe endyte.
>
> (ll. 194–6)

The plangent aristocrat, however, is just as powerless as his professional scribe, since he describes himself as being without legal redress in the court of his lady's affections:

> Atturney non ne may admytted ben
> To excuse Trouthe, ne a worde to speke;
> To Feyth or Othe the Iuge list not sen,
> Ther ys no geyn but he wil be wreke. [avenged]
>
> (ll. 281–4)

However much, then, the humble bureaucratic scrivener takes care to exaggerate his servile status as mere copyist, his aristocratic

[98] Lydgate, *The Minor Poems*, pt. 2, p. 379.
[99] Ibid., no. 3, pp. 382–410.

patron is no less disempowered in legal procedure. To call this literature 'courtly' is appropriate only so long as we remember that the court is centrally a bureaucratic office, a place where favour is sought and official business transacted. The literary texts mimic the textual system of government offices in content, style, and even in their mode of production.

What follows to conclude this chapter is a sequence of three brief discussions of elegiac writing from across the period. The first looks to the elegiac production of two lowish-level bureaucrats, Thomas Usk and Stephen Hawes, in real difficulty, deploying elegy by way of manoeuvring in court circles, and not as form of entertainment. The second moves a long way up the social scale, to the royal authors James I of Scotland and Charles d'Orléans, both of whom composed from or about prison. The final section looks to an astonishing poem that extends well beyond its elegiac base to critique the entire tradition, Henryson's *Testament of Cresseid*, written probably in the 1470s. When we look to these texts, we shall see that the historical distinction I have made in this chapter as a whole, between the discursive freedom of fourteenth-century elegy against the powerful limitations of sixteenth-century material, needs qualification. Limitation and freedom are also a matter of the circumstances of individual writers.

(*a*) Thomas Usk's *Testament of Love* and Stephen Hawes's *Comfort of Lovers*

This coupling may seem odd: Usk (d. 1388) wrote his work in 1385, whereas Hawes (d. 1511) apparently wrote the *Comfort* very soon after the accession of Henry VIII in 1509; Usk wrote in prose, Hawes in verse. They do, however, share a great deal, since both were fairly minor figures in broadly court circles, and both deployed elegy, saturated with their own personal difficulties, to appeal to the 'love', for which we should read 'beneficence', of a powerful woman. Both exploited the fidelity of the elegiac complainant as a code for the political fidelity of the trustworthy bureaucrat.

In Chaucer's *Franklin's Tale* the squire Aurelius, in love with a lord's wife, 'no thyng dorste he seye, | Save in his songes somwhat wolde he wreye [conceal] | His wo, as in a general compleynyng'. In this dangerous situation, he deploys an elegiac mode to make many 'Songes, compleintes, roundels, virelayes' (5. 943–8). He exploits, that is, a publicly acceptable form of entertainment to express his private passion and interest. The *Comfort of Lovers* (938 lines in rhyme-royal stanzas), surely one of the most peculiar poems written in the period of this history, was published in 1510, the year after Henry's accession and not long before Hawes's death. Hawes seems to be rather in the position of Aurelius, since the poem expresses anxieties about declaring the exact nature of the passion that animates it both in its represented action and in its very oblique posture towards readers. Hawes' earlier and longer poem *The Pastime of Pleasure* (published in 1509) traces a journey through pedagogic and chivalric sources of instruction, through love, and finally to Eternity. It may have biographical content, but as a whole it serves as a courtesy book, balancing both humanistic and chivalric accomplishment, for the courtier aspiring to the pattern of the Burgundian court.[100] In the *Comfort of Lovers*, by contrast, enigmatic references to fraught intrigues of court life entirely overbear any general application, and any 'general compleynyng' the poem might pretend to make. The poem opens with complaint about an unspecified grief, when the narrator sleeps and dreams of a lady to whom he dare not reveal the name of his lover. The lady confirms that Hawes has written 'unto the high pleasure of the reed and the whyte' (l. 193), and should therefore have no fear for the future; they pass into a tower, where Hawes must confront the chivalric challenge posed him by three mirrors, of his past life, his future life, and of prophecy inspired by the Holy Spirit respectively. In meeting these challenges, the narrator meets Pucell, the heroine of his earlier *Pastime*, and he himself becomes the protagonist of that work, Amour. He falteringly declares his love, at which point Pucell refuses him, insisting that she is promised to 'a myghty lorde' (l. 861).

Hawes was a groom of the King's Privy Chamber from 1503; the last payment in which he is listed as a poet is dated 1506.[101] The *Comfort of Lovers* must refer to Hawes's circumstances as a court poet to Henry VII, and, presumably, to his loss of position even

[100] For the decisive influence of Burgundian models on the courts of Edward IV and Henry VII, see Kipling, *Triumph of Honour*.

[101] Edwards, *Stephen Hawes*, p. 2.

before the accession of the new king in 1509. The poem fairly brims with the expression of intense threat and insecurity: the narrator seems to have acted as a spy, and yet now to be implicated in the treachery of those for whose surveillance he was responsible. 'For fere of deth where I loued best | I dyde dysprayse to knowe theyr cruelte | Somwhat to wysdome accordynge to behest' (ll. 170–2), he confesses to the first lady he meets; in the mirror of his future he sees 'preuy malyce his messengers had sent | With subtyll engynes to lye in wayte' (ll. 404–5). Whereas the experience of love in many elegiac poems is figured in the metaphor of courtly intrigue, in this poem love is posed rather as the solution to 'real' courtly menace. The Pucell is clearly of very high social status, and it has been plausibly argued that she represents Mary Tudor, Henry VIII's sister.[102] Elegy here can in no way be described as a turning away from political life; on the contrary, it is inescapably a manoeuvre in the dangerous world of court intrigue.

Appeal to the love of a royally born 'mistress' by a minor court official need not be read literally; as we shall see with Usk, this appeal is a code for political fidelity, and it appeals not for love, but rather for protection and patronage. Whatever the precise biographical truth of this disquieting poem, its imagination of extreme threat is of wider cultural significance. In particular, it imagines time and tradition in surreally distorted ways, as pointing wholly to Hawes himself. This is not only true of his deployment of the poet's own past text as a stage onto which he can step in his new-made work. That is not at all unusual; what is extremely odd, however, is that Hawes should be at once so massively dependent on legitimating traditions, both genealogical and literary, and so spectacularly opportunistic with them. On the one hand, he declares his homage to the triumvirate of Gower, Chaucer, and Lydgate, by way of generating his own humble enterprise (ll. 22–8), while on the other he inverts the humility topos by drawing comfort from the fact that the 'bokes made in antyquyte' by these same three poets predicted 'the felicyte | Of my lady and me' (ll. 285–6). Literary tradition exists to legitimate Hawes; in important ways it is *about* Hawes. So too does chivalric tradition point

[102] Fox, p. 59. I think Fox misreads the conventions in suggesting that Hawes was appealing to Mary as a potential lover.

unequivocally to the line of Hawes: the sword on the third mirror can only be drawn by 'one persone chosen by god in dede | Of this ladyes kynred . . . his mater for to spede' (ll. 507–8). Needless to say, Hawes draws it. Connections between past and future hang dangerously by a thread in this poem, and Hawes reacts to this threat with an understandable but surreal account of historical legitimation: he represents himself as simultaneously on the extreme margin and at the epicentre of great affairs. If poets under Henry VIII, drawing on Italian models, register the fragility of historical tradition, so too does Hawes, writing by Burgundian models, under Henry VII.

Ricardian writers, too, draw on the resources of elegy to express personal and political frustrations. Sir John Clanvowe's 290-line *Book of Cupid*, often known by the less authentic title of *The Cuckoo and the Nightingale* (written between 1386 and 1391), moves in a sophisticated and elegantly self-deprecatory mode to expose the lover's incapacity to sustain the absolute power of Cupid.[103] Usk's *Testament of Love*, by contrast, is not at all elegant in its three long books of prose, and not at all offered as entertainment. Whereas Clanvowe was one of Richard II's household knights, and faithful to him throughout the Appellants' crisis of 1388, Usk wrote from much lower down the scale, and attempted to extricate himself from the bad fame he had incurred by political treachery earlier in the 1380s. Both works nevertheless reveal the ways in which elegy is the best way to tackle questions of political fidelity under conditions where directness is impossible.

The *Testament of Love* defies easy paraphrase, but the work is fundamentally indebted to the *Consolation of Philosophy* of Boethius (480–524), the late antique Roman bureaucrat unjustly imprisoned and executed. Book 1 recounts the appearance of Love to the imprisoned complainant Usk; Love provokes Usk to articulate the source of his grief, which is principally the absence of his lady 'Margaret'; in Book 2 Love takes Usk through the Boethian arguments against the gifts of Fortune, such as wealth, honours, and especially fame. In the third book the argument turns rather to specifically Christian reflection on the nature of divine grace. Usk clearly enlists Boethius to suggest that he, too, is an unjustly accused

103 Patterson, 'Court Politics and the Invention of Literature'.

bureaucrat. Whereas, however, Boethius moves consistently within philosophical discourse, Usk draws on both amatory and theological models.

The overall argumentative strategy of the work is obscure: on the one hand Usk writes in prose, 'a chalky purtreyture', in 'rude wordes and boystous [unrefined]' in order that the readers may the more clearly understand his meaning (p. 1),[104] while on the other he often declares that he is unable to declare his true meaning to his lady. The man who can declare his 'prevy mone' to his friend is much relieved, but 'mokel [much] more is he joyed, that with herte of hardinesse dare complayne to his lady what cares that he suffreth' (p. 133). Almost every argumentative gambit of the work leaves a shadow of what cannot be said, and succumbs to the pressure of the unsayable. The very Boethian posture of disclaiming interest in worldly fame, for example, is clearly deployed in such a way as to regain his worldly reputation; or the calls to theological grace in the third book implicitly evoke the secular grace for which he longs from his probably royal 'lady'.[105] The initial letters of each chapter of the entire work, indeed, spell out an acrostic begging for such grace: 'Margarete of virtw, have merci on thin Usk'.[106] Above all, the topos of the lover Margaret, the pearl from whose perfection he bids grace, remains deeply and mysteriously coded, evoking yet refusing to explicate the source of political protection and beneficence to which he appeals. In Boethius' work, the feminized figure of Philosophy provides the entire solace, or, to use Boethius' word, sufficiency, that the complainant Boethius needs; in the *Testament*, by contrast, Love can do no more than encourage Usk to seek solace beyond the bounds of the book. The work is, as Usk himself says, not 'sufficiently maked'; there 'be many privy thinges wimpled and folde' in it (p. 144). He prays at the end that every reader might know through what 'intencion of herte' it was made (p. 145), but this hermeneutic clarity is itself posed as a matter of grace, precisely because Usk himself is not in a position to petition directly. In practice understanding this fascinating but opaque work depends principally on connecting the frank

[104] Quotations from Usk are taken from *Testament of Love*, ed. Skeat, 6.

[105] For queens as political intercessors in Ricardian England, see Strohm, 'Queens as Intercessors'.

[106] For the acrostic, see *Testament of Love*, ed. Skeat, pp. xix–xx.

confessions of Usk's treacherous act of informing against his former master (pp. 26–30, 84) with the pleas for beneficence. Clanvowe and Usk both, from their different positions, draw on Chaucer to figure themselves as faithful lovers, as 'lovers clerk[s]' (p. 47); for Usk, and probably for Clanvowe, these elegiac professions of fidelity encode political messages: aspiration for Usk, and disillusionment for Clanvowe.

(*b*) Charles d'Orléans's English Lyrics and James I of Scotland's *Kingis Quair*

Charles Duc d'Orléans (1394–1465), nephew to Charles VI of France, was captured at Agincourt in 1415; he spent the next twenty-five years a prisoner in England. James I, King of Scotland (1394–1437), was captured in 1407 and remained a prisoner in England until 1424. Both royal prisoners are now generally accepted as the authors of poems in English, Charles of a long sequence of brilliant lyrics, for the most part translations of his own compositions in French, in a variety of forms. This makes him the first non-native English- or Scots-speaking author to compose a large-scale literary work in English. To James is attributed the accomplished *Kingis Quair* (1,379 lines in rhyme-royal stanzas). Charles seems certainly to have composed in prison, before his release; although the *Kingis Quair* narrates James's imprisonment, it seems to have been composed immediately after his release from prison and marriage to Joan Beaufort in 1424, and before his return to Scotland, where he was assassinated in 1437.

These two bodies of elegiac writing represent two very different developments of elegiac possibilities. For Charles literal imprisonment is consistently evoked yet not made explicit by the imprisoning environment of sentiment, the 'Prison of Grevous Displesaunce' (l. 1012), in which he is trapped.[107] For one extended sequence he seems to gain acquittance from his punishing master Cupid, but that period, too, gives way to further subjection. The circularity of each lyric, whether ballade or roundel, each shaped by repetitive refrains,

[107] Spearing, 'Prison, Writing, Absence'. All quotations from Charles's English lyrics are from *Fortunes Stabilnes*, ed. Arn.

also marks the sequence as a whole, in which there is, finally, no discursive or emotional advance. The one moment where a discursive shift out of the jurisdiction of Cupid is promised, when his first lover dies, gives way to a sequence in which he offers emotional nourishment to other lovers. This second sequence itself, however, capitulates to Venus, as the narrator falls in love again, from which point his voice again becomes the complaining 'I', forever emotionally imprisoned. The *Kingis Quair*, by contrast, recounts a time in which the narrator was literally in 'strayte ward and in strong prisoune' (l. 169). In response to falling in love with a woman whom he sees from his prison window, the narrator falls asleep and dreams. In his dream he escapes the narrowly confined space of his prison, and traverses the heavens in a wholly optimistic journey that promises him psychological release. His astral voyage is equally a traversing of discursive jurisdictions: although the narrator promises to Venus to 'lyve under your law' (l. 356), he is directed by Venus to the royal court of Minerva. The goddess of reason accepts his suit, on condition that he promise to love chastely and faithfully, and sends him on to the one remaining goddess whose approbation is necessary for success, Fortune. The dream ends with James climbing onto Fortune's wheel, and the poem ends soon after with celebration that he has indeed had good fortune. This poem opens with an account of the King reading Boethius' *Consolation*, and is more generally saturated with references to the works of Chaucer in particular. Whereas, however, Chaucer's elegiac works expose the violent and treacherous relations between the realms of Cupid and Reason, the *Kingis Quair* sees its way through to a wholly integrated discursive world, in which the jurisdiction of Cupid slots neatly into the larger patterns of Reason and Fortune. Although Boethius dismisses Fortune and earthly love as a source of true happiness, James's poem trusts Fortune and elevates erotic love as a constructive principle of the universe.

Despite the fact that Charles's lyrics have almost none of the philosophical reference and confidence of the *Kingis Quair*, they explore with much greater intensity the extremely confined and narcissistic space of imprisoned loving. Charles is in every way caught in a bureaucratic maze, from which writing offers the only escape and yet deepens the problem. It is true that once he decides to withdraw from

Cupid's service, then Cupid himself becomes a more constitutional and tractable monarch, calling a parliament to ratify the lover's acquittance (ll. 2886–2909). This proves, however, to be a temporary release, and the narrator ultimately reverts to his initial posture, as a divided self, reduced endlessly to write and to read the text of his own subjection. Erotic pleasure, forever deferred, is refigured as the heart's self-destroying act of pleasurable and insatiable reading, in 'the Romaunce of Plesaunt Pancer':

> In this book whiche he redde is write and bounde
> As alle dedis of my lady dere,
> Which doth myn hert in laughtir oft abound
> When he hit rett or tellith the matere, [reads]
> Which gretly is to prayse, withouten were, [doubt]
> For y my silf delite it here, mafay,
> Which, if thei herde, so wolde eche straungere;
> Thus is my slepe yfalle into decay.
>
> (ll. 420–27)

Certainly much of this collection is designed as, and indeed represents itself as, courtly diversion; at its most penetrating it nonetheless articulates the exhausting nullity of the imprisoned and isolated subject: 'Me thynkith right as a sypher [zero] now I serue, | That nombre makith and is him silf noon' (ll. 2042–3).

(*c*) Robert Henryson's *Testament of Cresseid*

Elegy almost always begins from, and often ends in, the position of the suitor for grace, however desperate and however marginal might the suitor's position be. Henryson's astonishing *Testament of Cresseid* (617 lines of largely rhyme-royal stanzas), by contrast, traces the brutal movement of absolute exclusion from courtly society. This Scots poem demands attention at this point as by far the most powerful response to *Troilus and Criseyde*. Other elegies, as we have seen, move from the discourse of the amorous suitor to adjacent discourses, whether they be philosophical or political. The *Testament*, precisely by virtue of the sudden brutality of its geographical move from court to leper-house, severely tests the capacities of any discourse to meet Cresseid's condition. Henryson seems to have been both a notary and a schoolmaster in Dunfermline, and to have written around 1475.[108] Whereas many post-Chaucerian elegiac texts pillage *Troilus and Criseyde*, only Henryson confronts the deepest challenge of that text, the representation of Criseyde, head-on. The results are extremely dark and very powerful. Henryson calls his poem a 'tragedie', and so it is, but only by virtue of its penetrating account of the massive deficiencies of the enclosed world of amorous elegy.

Cresseid has now been abandoned by Diomeid, and has become a prostitute in the Greek camp. Having accused Venus and Cupid of betrayal, she falls in an 'extasie' and stands witness to the glittering procession of the planets assembled for parliament; the elaborate process of law concludes with sentence of venereal disease being passed on Cresseid, by melancholic and leaden Saturn:

> I change thy mirth into melancholy,
> Quhilk is the mother of all pensiuenes; [which]
> Thy moisture and thy heit in cald and dry;
> Thyne insolence, thy play and wantones,
> To greit diseis; thy pomp and thy riches
> In mortall neid; and greit penuritie
> Thow suffer sall, and as ane beggar die.[109] [shall]

Cresseid must pass to the 'spitaill house [leper hospital]' at the town's end. Her beautiful but self-exculpatory complaint (ll. 407–69) is met with contempt by the lepers—'Go leir [learn] to clap thy clapper to and fro' (l. 479). Troylus, riding by, is deeply distressed by the faint recognition he has of Cresseid through her now disfigured face, and gives her alms. When told that her benefactor was Troylus, Cresseid falls in a swoon, only to articulate a searching self-accusation, and to compose her testament. Troylus engraves the epitaph on her tombstone, and the poet ends by refusing to speak more of Cresseid: 'Sen sho is deid I speik of hir no moir' (l. 616).

Like many purely elegiac poems, the *Testament of Cresseid* represents a suitor enmeshed in bureaucratic and legal forms. The action of the poem is framed by Cresseid's accusation against the gods on

[108] Henryson, *Poems*, ed. Fox, pp. xiii–xxv. For the best literary study, see Douglas Gray, *Robert Henryson*.

[109] ll. 316–22. All citations from Henryson, *Poems*, ed. Fox, pp. 111–36.

one side, and her self-accusation on the other; and her fate is decided by the elaborately punctilious process of the astral court, as precise legal form is preserved in a trial leading to Cresseid's damnation for blasphemy. This prosecution conducted by the parliament of the gods, however, seems entirely to usurp the discursive power of any other form of redress. The metaphor of the planets conducting their business by legal process may give pictorial form to the 'law' of Nature, but it does so only to underline Nature's complete lack of justice. Nature's law is only a 'law' in the sense of its inexorable predictability and immutability in this poem, not in the sense of its conformity with a calibrated application of justice. Cresseid is punished with a hideous venereal disease, which entirely outscales her 'fault', and provisionally beggars the power of any human discourse. Certainly her plangent inset complaint, with its nine-line stanzas and rhetorically beautiful recollections of a Boethian *ubi sunt?* tradition,[110] serves only to highlight the failure of that lyric tradition to meet this situation. The only intelligible, human sound worth making is, by the estimation of the old leper lady, the noise of the clapper soliciting alms. From this collapse of intelligence, the poem must edge back to some kind of fit human judgement. Judgement comes not, however, from the poet: 'Sen scho is deid I speik of hir no moir' is his final disclaimer. The judicial sentence of the planets, and especially of rhetorician Mercury with his 'pregnant sentence', has so thoroughly pre-empted poetic 'sentence' that the human poet stays his voice.[111] Troylus' own text, too, written in golden letters on Cresseid's tomb, implicitly recognizes the gratuitousness of judgement: the epitaph simply states the plain truth that Cresseid, 'Sumtyme countit the flour of womanheid, | Vnder this stane, lait lipper, lyis deid' (ll. 607–8). The only human 'sentence' on Cresseid, and so the only really intelligible comment on her situation, is made by Cresseid herself. Crucially, it is not a judgement, but an accusation:

> Thocht sum be trew, I wait richt few ar they; [know]
> Quha findis treuth, lat him his lady ruse; [fidelity · praise]
> Nane but my self as now I will accuse.
>
> (ll. 572–4)

[110] The *ubi sunt?* ('where are they?') tradition, frequently found in medieval poetry, cites past examples of power and beauty only in order to underline their transitory nature.

[111] See Mann, 'Planetary Gods', p. 101.

The narrators of many elegiac poems appear to write themselves out of history; only does Henryson, in this poem of extremity, follow the lover into oblivion and recognize the reality of the 'blasphemer' Cresseid. Whereas Criseyde disintegrates in Chaucer's poem into a whole library of conflicting books, Henryson recognizes her just as Troylus does, since the image of the person, whole and continuous, is

> Sa deip imprentit in the fantasy
> That it deludes the wittis outwardly,
> And sa appeiris in forme and lyke estait
> Within the mynd as it was figurait.
>
> (ll. 508–11)

5

The Political

Elegy, as we have seen, points to the realm of the political, and so in this chapter I turn directly to political writing. One key text, Thomas More's *Utopia*, proposed a solution to the problem of politics that is in fact consonant with the practices of cultural revolution that took place in England within twenty years of its publication. A politics that claims legitimacy from abstract reason alone, without constraint by the whole body politic, will inevitably institute a political order in which historical and institutional differences between subjects are minimized in the face of their identity before abstract power. And as power becomes increasingly abstract, so too, of course, do subjects themselves. Despite More's elaborate attempts to disguise the centrality of power in the commonwealth of Utopia, the system is premissed, as we shall see, on a draconian repression of the body politic in the name of a centralized reason.

By contrast, the fifteenth century provides a series of 'literary' works that consistently constrain royal power in a way that would be unpublishable (not unthinkable) in the reign of Henry VIII. From these texts I generate a model of the Aristotelian political imagination that contrasts very sharply with the Platonic ideals of the sixteenth century. The political imagination of the fourteenth and fifteenth centuries negotiates the needs of both the body and the head of the whole body politic, whereas the sixteenth-century models generate their politics wholly from the top down, in repression of the larger body.

I

Thomas More (1478–1535) hailed the coronation day of Henry VIII in 1509 as a clean break with the past. He begins his *Carmen gratulatorium* by encouraging England to mark the day with a pure white stone, whose purity marks the 'limit of servitude' and the 'beginning of liberty'.[1] The young king will restore the nobility to its ancient rights, abolish the merchant's fear of excessive taxation, and reinstate the pristine force of laws. Henry's munificent enlightenment comes as no surprise, since his natural wit has been cultivated by a liberal education in both poetry and philosophy (ll. 116–19). There are certainly dark touches in More's panegyric: Henry is praised for having instantly arrested and imprisoned anyone who threatened the universal joy at his coronation (ll. 96–7), but the poem brushes these yesterday's men aside in its unbridled optimism for a future in which justice will be restored and Henry's royal wife will abundantly produce male offspring.

More's *Utopia*, whose original title is *De optimo republicae statu deque nova insula Utopia* (*Concerning the Best State of a Republic and the New Island of Utopia*, 1516) also promises a brilliant new future, underwritten by the cultivation and exercise of reason. The angelic messenger Raphael Hythlodaeus has arrived back from a voyage to the New World with news of a 'new island [*de nova insula*]', whose inhabitants believe that the divine maker of the universe has 'sett furthe the marvelous and gorgious frame of the worlde for man to beholde; whome onlye he [i.e. God] hathe made of wytte and capacytye to consydre and understand the excellencye of so greate a woorke'.[2] While the Utopians do have a history going back to the conquest of the island by King Utopus 1,760 years before Hythlodaeus' visit, it is 'wytte and capacytye to . . . understand' the rational order, rather than history, that informs every aspect of their social organization. They keep chronicles, but there can be very little real change to record, since Utopus devised the entire system: 'kyng

[1] Thomas More, *Latin Poems*, ed. Miller et al., pp. 100–13. Further references to this edition will appear in the text.

[2] All English citations of *Utopia* are taken from the 1551 trans. of Ralph Robinson, for which see the *Utopia of Sir Thomas More*, ed. Lupton, 2. 6, p. 218. Further references to this edn. will be given in the text. The authoritative edn. of the Latin version, with modern translation, is *Utopia*, ed. Surtz and Hexter.

Utopus himself, even at the first begenning, appointed and drew furth the platte fourme of the city into this fasion and figure that it hath nowe' (2. 2, pp. 131–2). Population might grow, and Utopia might become involved in external wars (the two most powerful sources of change in sixteenth-century England), but these destabilizing forces are managed so as to minimize their power to change anything. Utopia has achieved the end of history, and so would promise, if we accept the argument that More indeed believed this state to be the best, to end English history.[3]

Can More slice across history quite so cleanly? One of the key models for *Utopia* is Tacitus' *Germania* (AD 98), which also adopts an ethnographic approach to a people on the far edge of the 'civilized' world in such a way as to challenge the 'civilized' readers of its polemical ethnography.[4] Like More, Tacitus felt himself to be writing in a period of political collapse, and if the *Germania* is one response to the corrupting opacity of political life, his *Annals* (AD 115–20) is another, in which Tacitus records the horrendous aristocratic violence of post-Augustan imperial Rome, up to the death of Nero. More's own career up to and including *Utopia* exhibits the same set of responses to aristocratic violence. His brilliant *Richard III* (composed in both English and Latin in 1513) is a very model of Tacitean annalistic narrative, syntactically terse and ethically open-eyed as it is about the horrific and violent manipulations of the last pre-Tudor king. However much *Utopia* may claim to escape the predations of history and take us into the sunny world of sweet reason, however, it cannot escape that history. The figure of Cardinal Morton, for example, links the two works: in Book 1 of *Utopia* he exemplifies the pragmatic politician who nevertheless listens seriously to Hythlodaeus' rational arguments; *Richard III* breaks off, infuriatingly, at the point where the same Morton is planting the seeds of a *coup d'état* against Richard. Of course *Richard III* is itself a work of Tudor apologetics, and Morton's sedition is itself an act of breaking with the dark and vicious past. Nonetheless, Morton's avuncular reasonableness in *Utopia* is premissed on his sowing the seeds of violence in *Richard III*.

[3] For the argument that More meant Utopia to be taken as the best form of government, see Hexter, and Skinner, 'More's *Utopia*'.

[4] *Utopia*, ed. Surtz and Hexter, p. clxii.

The violence of power is not only to be found outside *Utopia*: Book I of that work represents a series of counsel sessions, each of which moves progressively further away from 'reality'. Hythlodaeus first recounts the remembered dinner party at Cardinal Morton's, then the imagined war council of the King of France, from which he moves to the imagined taxation strategies of 'some king'. If this progessive shifting of fictional mode is a preparation for the wholly ideational Utopia, it is also an escape route from the claustrophobic theatre of self-interested and violent political manoeuvre. Even at the end of that route, however, just before Hythlodaeus prepares to discourse on the island that has put an end to history, history resurfaces in the most disconcerting form. Hythlodaeus, having ignored the fact that Cardinal Morton *was* prepared to try out a version of his scheme, concludes his account of these counsel sessions by arguing that it would be a waste of time to advise kings, since plain speaking grounded in ethical conviction has no purchase on royal policy. More concedes that pure philosophy uninformed by rhetorical skill would indeed be counter-productive; a counsellor must be like an actor, knowing when and how to deliver his part, and being prepared to play within the limits of the dramatic genre in hand: Hythlodaeus' plain speaking would, he says, be like a philosopher suddenly declaiming the speech of Seneca, from the pseudo-Senecan tragedy *Octavia*, in a comedy by Plautus.[5] The intellectual openings of this argument close off very suddenly, since it implies that the philosopher is obliged to play in base comedies, and to abandon the part of Seneca altogether.

But does Seneca inspire a Tudor intellectual to persuade kings anyway? In fact the reference to Seneca is chilling, since *Octavia* is a play bathed in blood, in which Nero, who has murdered his mother and will murder his concubine, arranges for the murder of his wife. Seneca's part is nostalgically to remember the Golden Age as the age of ideal justice perceptible by the philosopher, just before his royal pupil Nero enters to order the heads of two 'friends'. At the heart of More's crucial argument for participation in government stands the example of the Stoic Seneca, whose suicide is the only viable response to his pupil's violence. If *Utopia* promises entry into a Platonic world

[5] *Utopia*, ed. Lupton, p. 98.

of fully formed, ahistorical ideas, it cannot help exposing an awareness of Seneca and Tacitus, who write out of the chaos of imperial history. Even as *Utopia* attempts to escape from the violence of history, it betrays a prescient and accurate awareness that violence lies in the future.

II

Twentieth-century historians of the sixteenth century, no less than More himself, stressed the sharpness of the break between medieval and early modern political thought and practice. Despite their differences, the abiding theme of both intellectual and institutional historians of the Tudor period last century was the triumphant and wholly progressive break with the medieval past effected by both sixteenth-century intellectuals (the 'humanists') and bureaucrats. Geoffrey Elton, the most influential institutional historian of the twentieth century, championed what he himself called the 'revolution' in Tudor bureaucracy. His great book *The Tudor Revolution in Government* (1959) traced the sudden break with the medieval practice of personal government and the establishment of a national bureaucracy: 'the duality of state and church was destroyed by the victory of the state, the crown triumphed over its rivals, parliamentary statute triumphed over the law of Christendom, and a self-contained national unit came to be . . . the consciously desired goal'.[6]

Elton dealt with the embarrassment of what he calls 'Tudor temper and bluster' by brushing it aside: it is 'one of the paradoxes of sixteenth-century history that a dynasty, which saw the personal power of the monarch at its height and the importance of court life greater than ever, could also transcend the purely personal view of royal duty and treat England and the nation as the true basis of the state'. Absolutist pretentions (what Elton called 'the personal impetus') were a temporary mirage, merely a good and transient sign of national strength below: 'England was not able to do without the visible embodiment of her nationhood until she had first passed through a condition where that visible embodiment was more

[6] Elton, *Tudor Revolution*, p. 3.

obvious than the national foundation beneath.'[7] Elton dealt with this paradox by making Henry VIII's brilliant bureaucrat Thomas Cromwell, and not Henry, the undisputed hero of his history. Cromwell brought into being 'a nation at last fully conscious of its nationhood'; while the 'apparent emphasis lay on the monarchy, the real stress was already on its [England's] national character', a 'national character' given voice by Cromwell.[8]

Influential intellectual historians writing in the wake of Elton equally posited a sharp break between medieval and 'humanist' political thought. Arthur Ferguson's book *The Articulate Citizen and the English Renaissance* (1965) begins by arguing that the 1530s (the decade of Cromwell) were 'unusually conducive to thoughtful discussion', given the combination of great administrative changes and the existence of a group of 'humanists', men who 'saw the national community in the clear . . . light shed from the freshly interpreted store of classical example. With equal clarity they saw that it was their duty, as Elyot put it, "to profit thereby to my natural country".'[9] In Ferguson's account, the 'humanists' formed a coherent, idealistic, and progressive fraternity who disinterestedly devoted themselves to the good of the commonwealth, and who were in a position to do so effectively because they understood 'reality'. In this they were unlike their hopelessly beleaguered medieval predecessors, to whom Ferguson devoted five chapters. Because the 'inveterate character of traditional habits of thought' in late medieval England rendered thinkers incapable of perceiving anything more than the 'all-embracing purpose of God' as the moving force in society, they conceived of social ills in purely ethical and individual, rather than institutional, terms. Acceptance of the 'limitations established for all time by the will of God' prevented medieval thinkers 'from recognizing the necessity for some clearly defined sovereign authority from which the active policy essential to the modern state . . . must in the final analysis emanate'.[10]

Nowhere did Ferguson confront the complicity of humanist thought with the absolutist pretentions of Henry VIII, since for

[7] Elton, *Tudor Revolution*, p. 4.
[8] Ibid.
[9] A. B. Ferguson, *Articulate Citizen*, pp. xiii and 169 respectively.
[10] Ibid. 32–3.

Ferguson humanists are 'civic humanists' (with republican affiliations), a category he draws from Hans Baron who defined it as a strictly 'Renaissance' phenomenon.[11] Although intellectual historians since Ferguson have dated 'civic humanism' well before Baron's watermark of 1400 in Florence, and although they have looked much harder at the complicity of many humanists with despotic regimes,[12] Ferguson's book has remained largely unchallenged as an account of the medieval to Renaissance contrast for political literature and thought across the fourteenth to the sixteenth centuries in England.

Accounts of the kind produced by Ferguson have gone unchallenged by both early modern and medievalist scholars, principally because the fifteenth century has appeared to be such a historical vacuum for the story of 'the nation'. Early modern scholars rightly share with Thomas More a desire to start afresh after the political history of the fifteenth century. More than any other century of English political history, the fifteenth manifested a terrible and violent instability at the centre. The century began with the *coup d'état* of Henry IV against Richard II in 1399, and was to witness a further five violent seizures of the crown: in 1460 by Edward IV; in 1470 by Henry VI (briefly reclaiming his crown); in 1471 by Edward IV (again); in 1483 by Richard III; and in 1485 by Henry VII. The only 'brilliant' reign of the century, that of Henry V between 1413 and 1422, turned out to destroy the foundations for lasting peace throughout the rest of the century, mainly by the impossibly ambitious and finally ruinous project of laying claim to the throne of France, and partly by the accident of leaving an 8-month-old child as king of both England and France in 1422. Henry VI's infancy was just one of the late fourteenth- and early fifteenth-century examples of the weakness of a system heavily dependent on the person of the king: Richard II never escaped the vulnerability of becoming king at the age of 11; Henry IV was forced temporarily to retire through ill health; Henry VI, the grandson of an insane French king, suffered bouts of insanity; and Edward V was almost certainly murdered as a child-king.

[11] See the extraordinarily influential article by H. Baron.

[12] For both these points, see Skinner, *Foundations of Modern Political Thought*, vol. 1, chs. 2 and 5 respectively. For the complicity, see also Hankins.

Civil war is the leitmotif of fifteenth-century political history, and, unlike the civil war of the seventeenth century, the internal wars of the fifteenth arouse no philosophical passions for one side or another whatsoever. These are philosophically neutral wars, fought for power, and in such a way as to reduce legal procedure to a weapon of power. The fifteenth century breaks the thread of institutional history, and as long as early modernist historians were looking for the story of the 'nation', then the revolution of the 1530s was the ideal place to start weaving a new story.[13]

Neither, for the most part, were twentieth-century medievalist historians any more positive about the institutional and intellectual quality of political life at the centre of fifteenth-century politics. Such historians were in flight from the historiographical legacy of William Stubbs, who had laid the grounds for the discipline of modern academic history with his monumental, three-volume work *The Constitutional History of England* (finished in 1878). As we have seen, twentieth-century institutional historians saw the centralized Tudor bureaucracy, established in blessed rejection of 'medieval' practice, as the source of political liberties. Stubbs, by contrast, had seen things very much the other way around. Like More, he too saw Tacitus' *Germania* as a foundation model of political liberty and probity; German traditions of common law imported by Saxon conquerors in the fifth century, untouched by Roman law, 'suggest the probability that the polity developed by the German races on British soil is the purest product of their primitive instinct'.[14] These German traditions of liberties generated Stubbs's narrative of the 'national character', a category so strong as to survive the Norman Conquest. Right up to Magna Charta, the very high point of the Constitution, 'the continuity of national purpose never fails: even the greatest struggle of all, the long labour that extends from the Reformation to the Revolution, leaves the organization, the origin of which we have been tracing, unbroken in its conscious identity, stronger in the strength in which it has preserved, and grown mightier through trial'.[15] For Stubbs, himself writing at the end of a

[13] See also Ch. 7, below, for the parallel historiography of the Reformation.

[14] Stubbs, I. 11. For the importance of Tacitus' *Germania* for Stubbs, see Burrow, pt. II.

[15] Stubbs, I. 682.

century of romantic nationalism, the great forces shaping national institutions were driven from the Germanic traditions of English medieval history, and had to survive *attack* from the 'trial' of Reformation to Revolution.

Stubbs's *Bildungsroman*, in which England was at the same time conscious of her destiny as the champion of liberty and instinctively training herself for it, was rejected by twentieth-century medieval historians less for its racist undertones than for its political *naïveté*. K. B. McFarlane in particular developed an alternative, anti-Stubbsian account of late medieval politics. The historiography of the eighteenth century, another period in which politics appeared to be a matter of power rather than philosophical conviction, provided his model. What determined political practice for McFarlane were the concrete relations of sets of individuals in the search for power; these factional groupings so dominated in McFarlane's account as to eclipse both institutional and intellectual history. McFarlane's own historiography, first articulated in the late 1930s, and that of his many followers, remained 'resolutely unconceptual'.[16] However much late twentieth-century historians of the fifteenth century produced a flourish of studies, most of this work concentrated on local political networks and cultural consolidation;[17] none of it, with one exception, challenged the view of modern scholars of the sixteenth century that the fourteenth and fifteenth centuries were largely a wasteland for political ideas concerning the public good.[18]

In this chapter I revise this consensus insofar as it determines our understanding of English vernacular political writing. My point of departure is the early fifteenth century, years that Stubbs himself found so puzzling as to defeat his triumphalist narrative. Stubbs's Germanist fantasies of 'national character' are frankly repulsive from the experience of the twentieth century. In volume 3 of the *Constitutional History* (from Richard II until 1485) however, Stubbs abandons that theme altogether, as the internecine complexity of his subject defeats his search for 'constitutional' features. There are no

[16] The citation is taken from Carpenter, 'Political and Constitutional History'. This article is indispensable for an overview of post-Stubbsian English medieval historiography.

[17] See e.g. Carpenter, *Locality and Polity*. For both the political instability and the cultural consolidation in the latter half of the century, see Lander.

[18] The exception is the excellent book by Watts.

great figures, no disputes in which a constitutionalist can side, just a lot more detail to deal with, and most of it rather grubby. Stubbs's abandonment of his earlier narrative is not explicit, but all the more revealing for that. He approaches the fifteenth century warily, quietly dropping the idea of a *conscious* constitutionalism that had been so important a part of his narrative right up to and including the thirteenth century: the historian, he says at the end of volume 2, stands in danger of 'substituting his own formulated conclusions for the programme of the leaders, and of giving them credit for a far more definite scheme and more conscious political sagacity than they would ever have claimed for themselves'. It looks as if the development of political institutions was 'guided by some great creative genius', yet it is 'scarcely ever possible to distinguish the creative genius'.[19] As his narrative undoes itself, so too does he dismiss the fifteenth century as a time when the history of liberty gave way to 'the ruder expedients of arms, the more stormy and spontaneous forces of personal, political, and religious passion'.[20] The great, shaping energy flowing from earlier centuries seems in Stubbs's account to have dissipated itself in the fifteenth century. At the same time, almost despite himself, he grudgingly concedes that the reign of Henry IV was indeed an age of 'constitutional experiment', more by accident than design, or more by the stand-off of competing forces than by the conscious programme of any heroic figure.[21]

The point of stand-off at which Stubbs's narrative fails, the reign of Henry IV (1399–1413), is my own point of entry into the political writing of these centuries, precisely because a point of stand-off is most likely to produce a broadening of the base of discursive participation. I begin with works of 'policy', to which the substance of this chapter is devoted. Works at the margins of policy, recommending either complete withdrawal from or ethical critique of the political arena, will be considered separately.

[19] Stubbs, 2. 538.
[20] Ibid. 3. 2.
[21] See e.g. ibid. 245–54.

III

Chaucer's last poem was possibly his 'Complaint to his Purse' (1399–1400), a small petitionary poem (twenty-six lines) to Henry IV in which Chaucer unquestionably rejected his earlier allegiance to Richard II. Despite the fact that Chaucer had been a 'king's man' in his professional life as diplomat and bureaucrat throughout the stormy and treacherous reign of Richard II, he sends off this amusing little poem to his empty purse to 'the conquerour of Brutes Albyon, | Which that by lyne and free eleccion | Been verray kyng', begging him to 'have mynde upon my supplicacion'.[22] This way of addressing the new king Henry is very precisely formulated, since the terms Chaucer uses (conquest, election, and lineage) stand in close relation to the mostly shaky claims on which the usurper Henry claimed his legitimacy.[23] The plea was apparently successful, since in February 1400 Henry not only backdated continuation of Chaucer's annuity from Richard II, but also added an annuity of forty marks a year.

This little text serves as the model for a great deal of political writing in the late fourteenth, and especially in the fifteenth, century. In the first place, it comes at the beginning of a reign, when the discursive environment may be a little freer, and when it may serve a writer's purpose to advertise his service. Works of either satire and/or policy are frequent in the opening stages of a reign: the Prologue to the B version of *Piers Plowman* (*c.*1377) is written soon after the coronation of Richard II; *Richard the Redeless* (*c.*1400) pretends to offer correctives to Richard II, but the poem's real target must in fact be the newly crowned Henry IV, since it is clear that Richard has already been deposed; Thomas Hoccleve's *Regement of Princes* is written in 1412 to Prince Henry, when it had become clear that he was soon to assume power; and later in the century George Ashby's *Active Policy of a Prince* (1463) is addressed to the exiled Prince Edward, son of Henry VI, while Sir John Fortescue's work *The Governance of England* may orginally have been written for the same ill-fated and exiled Prince Edward, and was thereafter altered as a presentation to Edward IV in 1471.[24]

22 'The Complaint of Chaucer to his Purse', in *Riverside Chaucer*, ed. Benson, p. 656.

23 See Strohm, 'Saving Appearances'.

24 For the topos of addressing royal children, see Patterson, '"What Man Artow?"'.

In the second place, texts of this kind do not evoke profound philosophical divisions on the nature of the political order. Chaucer may be citing the terms of Henry's legitimacy, but the terms themselves are not specific to Henry as opposed to Richard; on the contrary, they are used precisely because they are intended to persuade all readers by appealing to universally accepted grounds of royal legitimacy. Political works throughout the fifteenth century may be supporting one king or another, but the principles of rule, unlike the principles of ecclesiastical dominion, are not themselves in dispute. The fact that works can be rededicated to opposing patrons with only minor change itself implies the stability of political discourse.

Thirdly, and this is more specific to Lancastrian than Ricardian kingship, there is a direct and personal relationship between poet and ruler. None of Chaucer's previous works, with the exception of the *Book of the Duchess* (1369), is dedicated so explicitly to a patron, let alone a royal patron. The *Book of the Duchess* is itself written for John of Gaunt, Duke of Lancaster, and so effectively begins a tradition of Lancastrian patronage that runs deeply throughout that dynasty. Lancastrian kings demonstrably patronized vernacular poetry and poets (Lydgate and Hoccleve are the most high-profile examples) in ways for which there is no evidence in Ricardian writing 1377–99. The only Ricardian vernacular work addressed to Richard II is Gower's *Confessio Amantis* (1390), but the account of Richard's patronage there is at best casual. Richard and the poet happen to bump into each other while boating on the Thames, when Richard suggests that Gower 'english' something (Prologue 24–92*); this dedication scene was in any case deleted, and by 1392–3 Gower rededicated the *Confessio* to Henry Bolingbroke, the future Henry IV and the first Lancastrian king, for whom Gower was writing again in 1400. It would seem that even before they were kings, the Lancastrians recognized the value of poets. John Duke of Bedford even had images of Lancastrian vernacular poets worked into his magnificent devotional book, the Bedford Hours (1414).[25]

Everything I have said so far would seem to confirm what we might expect of fifteenth-century political poetry from the views of

[25] See S. Wright.

the intellectual and institutional historians cited above: this is self-serving poetry that aspires to a personal relationship with the king through the articulation of universally accepted truisms. It is, it might be said, the poetry of the king's household, rather than a discourse addressed to and for the nation. The king holds the purse strings, and the poet speaks for the king's payment. That is true, but it is precisely the 'household' quality of this little poem that may point to the power of fourteenth- and fifteenth-century political poetry to constrain the king.

Aristotelian-derived political theory placed politics (the governance of states) as the supreme practical science above, yet dependent on, the lower practical sciences of ethics (governance of the self) and economics (governance of a household).[26] For this reason works on household management and courtesy books are part of a larger, 'political' field.[27] Chaucer's little poem to his purse is divided between the jurisdiction of the household and the state: he complains to his mistress purse, 'quene of comfort and of good companye' to be 'hevy again, or elles moot I dye'. He makes this complaint only 'to yow, my purse, and to noon other wight'. After three stanzas the poem ends, however, and there follows, marked off in the manuscript, a different address, 'Lenvoy de Chaucer', which is an apostrophe to the 'conquerour of Brutes Albion'. The address of the poem is double, at first only within the realm of the household to his metaphorical 'queen', but secondarily, and principally of course, to the real king. The poet's dependence on the king is bodily, but the dependence is not at all unidirectional: in the specifically political envoy, Chaucer offers Henry precise, technical words of political discourse that confirm him as 'verray king'. Chaucer's household is certainly dependent on money from the king, since money, gendered as female, is his 'saveour as doun in this world here'; but the king is equally dependent on Chaucer's words. Henry is especially dependent precisely because his claims to the crown are fundamentally illegitimate. Poetry of this kind is traditionally called begging or petitionary poetry, but that implies a relationship of pure dependency, whereas

[26] For this scheme, and futher references, see Simpson, *Sciences and the Self*, 217–29.

[27] For the richly represented genre of courtesy books in later medieval England, see Nicholls, app. A and B.

this petition implicitly invites a contract between Chaucer's household and the king's state.[28] Political words and household money are proposed for exchange here.

(*a*) Hoccleve's *Regement of Princes*

I concede that Chaucer's poem itself is hardly the basis for a full-blown politics of royal constraint. I want now to make that case with regard to the *Regement of Princes* (1412), a poem written by another member, like Chaucer, of the king's household, Thomas Hoccleve. This poem survives in forty-five manuscripts, making it one of the most widely copied vernacular poems of the fourteenth and fifteenth centuries. Many mansucripts were owned by fifteenth-century aristocratic or gentry readers.[29] In it we find the same features of political address: the poem is divided between the jurisdiction of the household and the state, and it certainly marks the dependency of the first on the second. In much more powerful ways, however, it also marks the dependency of the king on the whole body of his subjects.

Thomas Hoccleve (1367–1426) was a clerk of some standing in the Office of the Privy Seal, an office that, while still officially a part of the king's household, had in fact long since established itself as an arm of a national bureaucracy.[30] The 'household' status is important for Hoccleve's poetry, since his earliest datable works (*The Epistle of Cupid*, *c.*1402, and three petitionary poems, including the amusing *Male Regle* of 1405) draw on the protocols of bureaucratic style to express relationships that are yet wholly personal. The *Male Regle* (448 lines in eight-line stanzas), indeed, petitions the king's sub-treasurer to pay him his wages in such a way as to equate the impersonal category of cash with the terms of personal bodily health. Hoccleve represents himself as the broken body, the very 'mirrour ... of riot and excesse', and the poem is ostensibly addressed to the god Health, petitioning him for mercy after having led a dissolute life, which is related in delightful detail. In fact, of course, the poem is really aimed at the sub-treasurer, who is mentioned only in pass-

[28] For a conspectus of such poetry, see the excellent article by J. A. Burrow, 'Poet as Petitioner'.

[29] See Perkins.

[30] Brown, 'Privy Seal Clerks'. For Hoccleve's life records, see J. A. Burrow, *Thomas Hoccleve*.

ing, as Hoccleve discreetly, or not so discreetly, requisitions Health to drop in on the sub-treasurer, and to let him have 'a tokne or tweye | To paie me that due is for this yeer' (ll. 419–20). The terms of bodily health are here confounded with those of financial health, since, as Hoccleve says, 'my body and purs been at ones seeke' (l. 409).

This little poem not only declares Hoccleve's own bodily fragility, but also implies traces of national weakness. In 1404–5, in a period of national financial crisis, the King's Council suspended payments of annual salaries. Hoccleve is forced to speak primarily because the state is weak. Hoccleve specifically denies that he is asking for payment for that year, about which he will not 'speke a word' out of fear, since he is 'so sore agast' (l. 424). However much the primary weakness is Hoccleve's, then, that is itself a product of the King's weakness, and in asking for payment Hoccleve promises not to speak about the scandal of cancelling payment. The declaration of dependence also declares the grounds of a pact, whereby the poet's words will be properly governed. The declaration cannot be made, however, without acknowledging the King's own indigence.

In the *Regement of Princes* these interdependent relationships of state and household are writ very large indeed. Like Chaucer's 'Complaint', the poem is formally divided between the private and the public. In a short opening complaint (ll. 1–112), Hoccleve complains of his mental depression at the thought of his future poverty in old age. He then goes out of the city for a walk after a sleepless night and meets an indigent but philosophically informed old man, with whom he conducts a dialogue (ll. 113–2016). The aged philosopher gradually gets Hoccleve to articulate the source of his anxiety; having failed to persuade Hoccleve to accept the irregularity of his payment and his future poverty in patience, the old man finally urges him to write something for Prince Henry. There follows the *Regement* proper, addressed directly to the young prince (ll. 2017–5463). Even in the very disposition of the poem, the needs of Hoccleve's household (2,016 lines) are nearly balanced with the needs of the kingdom (3,446 lines). As in the case of the beautiful illumination where Hoccleve gives the *Regement* to the prince, both subject and ruler are represented in the same scale (Fig. 5).[31]

[31] British Library, MS Arundel 38, fo. 37^{r}.

Fig. 5. Hoccleve presents his *Regement of Princes* to the future Henry V. London, British Library, MS Arundel 38, fo. 37r (*c.*1420).

On the face of it, however, the dependence is wholly on Hoccleve's side. The opening complaint is encapsulated by the striking image of Thought (mental depression and anxiety) vampirically sucking the 'fresschest of my blod' (l. 90). Financial anxiety and an anaemic, sleepless body produce only a desire for solitude and death; and even at the end of the work, after Hoccleve has been persuaded to break his morbid silence, the text is sent off in embarrassed poverty before its royal addressee: who gave it the impertinence, Hoccleve asks, to show itself before the plenitude of the prince in its rhetorically impoverished state, 'nakid . . . of eloquence' and in its 'kirtil bare also' (ll. 5440–5)? In the dialogue Hoccleve looks to the future and sees nothing but poverty: he is not paid regularly now, and when he is 'out of court' in old age without any influence whatsoever, he won't be paid at all: 'my purs . . . may be a ferthyng shethe' (l. 837). He has a wife to maintain, and his health is already almost broken by the back-breaking, eye-destroying, solitary labour of writing, of staring 'upon the sheepes skyn' (l. 1014). Even the words he writes for extra payment are worth nothing. When he is cheated out of payment for the scribal work he does on the side for powerful lords, he dares not complain; on the contrary, he treats the extortioner politely, 'lest he reporte amis, and make us shent' (l. 1515). The words of the powerful have 'credit' in all senses, whereas the words of the poor man are worth nothing.

If Hoccleve seems wholly dependent on the future king, Henry, by contrast, is presented as the source of plenitude and good health. He is young, and in a position to profit from the kind of advice traditionally given in works of the *Secreta Secretorum* kind. This extraordinarily popular genre, derived from Arabic sources, implies that the king's own bodily and moral health are the fountainhead of good governance.[32] Aristotle, so runs the fiction of the genre, was too old to be present to advise his young pupil Alexander how best to conquer, and so wrote a secret document of which the cardinal points are conservation of the king's own health through diet and medicine; ethical probity, including skilful exercise of largesse; and knowledge

[32] Over 500 MSS of the *Secreta* survive from across Europe; for the extraordinary (and enduring) popularity of the genre in England see *Secretum Secretorum*, ed. Manzalaoui. For a survey of this material that reveals its hermeneutic complexity, see Ferster, *Fictions of Advice*; and see also Green, pp. 140–9.

of physiognomy. Governance and diet go together, both implied by the word 'regiment', and preserved in modern French *régime*. Hoccleve, then, implicitly poses as the aged Aristotle, instructing Alexander-cum-Henry in the virtues of fidelity, justice, pity, patience, chastity, and liberality.

In addition to these apparently platitudinous generalities, however, Hoccleve also offers his young king-to-be much more historically pertinent material. The Lancastrian regime had survived its very unstable early years, but there remained much ideological work to be done in repairing what may be called the crisis of legitimation. Hoccleve offers to perform this labour in a variety of ways. Dynastic rupture is played down: Richard II was cast down by 'Fortune' (l. 23) and Henry IV is hardly mentioned. The ideal models are the figures on either side of the rupture by one remove: Henry V for the future, while Henry Duke of Lancaster and John of Gaunt, the Prince's great-grandfather and grandfather respectively, are the great political exemplars of the recent past.[33] Most spectacularly, Hoccleve advertises himself as an apologist for royal policy in its draconian persecution of heresy. Whereas John of Gaunt had in fact been rather sympathetic to Wycliffe, Lancastrian kings immediately turned on Lollards as a convenient enemy.[34] Near the very beginning of the Dialogue, Hoccleve refers to the burning of the Lollard John Badby in 1410, a burning halted by Prince Henry to offer the victim a last chance to repent. Badby refuses, and was 'brent . . . unto asshen drie' (l. 287). Later in the *Regement* proper, Hoccleve will cite the example of the brazen bull, an instrument of torture in which the victim is placed while a fire is lit under the bull, and the victim's cries of torment are accordingly bestialized and magnified through the mouth of the bellowing bull. The king in the exemplum accepts the gift, but decides to victimize its ingenious but malign inventor as a trial run (ll. 3004–3338). The example of Badby is proferred as an instance of Henry's mercy, but Hoccleve is in fact making a brazen bull of his own poem, with which to bestialize and magnify the torment of the Lollard, in the service of Lancastrian orthodoxy.

[33] For the detail of these references, see Simpson, 'Nobody's Man', p. 174.

[34] For further discussion of Lollardy, see esp. Ch. 7, below. For the orchestrated and self-serving nature of the persecution, see Strohm, *England's Empty Throne*, ch. 2.

Hoccleve is unquestionably offering the service of his words, then, in return for some portion of the future king's largesse. He generates his plea to Henry by representing his own diminished body, but that body can be replenished only at the expense of other, heterodox bodies. Insofar as that is true, Hoccleve's dependency would seem to go so far as to champion the king's unlimited and newly instituted power over the bodies of his subjects: the statute introducing burning for heretics was first ratified in 1401.

Human bodies are, however, characteristically unmanageable and full of surprises. Let me now turn to the ways in which the young prince is taught that his *régime* is dependent on his respecting the irrepressible bodies of his orthodox subjects. A king should not talk too much: 'it is fair and honurable, | A kyng from mochil speeche him refreyne'. He should instead, advises Hoccleve, be sparing in his speech, since 'mochil clap wole his estate desteyne [damage]' (ll. 2416–22). What is fit for a king, however, may be suicidal for his subjects. If Henry can afford to be silent, Hoccleve cannot. 'Clap', meaning 'idle and unprofitable speech', is often deployed by Hoccleve to dismiss yet articulate unpalatable truths: he apologizes to the old man in the Prologue, for example, for having done nothing but 'jangle and clappe' (l. 1035). The 'clap' of the whole Prologue is presented as a therapeutic and wholly private encounter, which takes place outside the city, not at all designed for public consumption. In fact the Prologue appears in all the manuscripts together with the *Regement* proper, and serves to express the subject's absolute necessity to speak up for himself. The old man asks Hoccleve if he has any 'friend' who will stand up for him and his exploited fellow clerks in the royal court: 'yis, fadir, yis. Ther is oon clept Nemo' ['yes, father, there is one called "Nobody"'] (l. 1487). The clerks dare not complain of the injustice done them, 'lest our conpleynte oureselven overthrowe' (l. 1526). The private, therapeutic, accidental Prologue may appear evanescent beside the formally constructed, rhetorically shaped text of the *Regement* proper, but the private conditions of the Prologue allow Hoccleve to complain of the injustice being practised in the King's bureaucracy: clerks are irregularly paid by the King, and cheated by lords for extra work. As a result they foresee an indigent and miserable old age. The 'clap' of the Prologue allows Hoccleve to complain without complaining. In so doing he not only reveals how the impersonal text of royal advice is itself produced out of the injustice of the King's bureaucracy; he also reveals how the virtues pertinent to a king and those relevant to his subjects diverge. A king can afford to be silent, whereas his subjects must speak up. Edward III, Hoccleve reports, used to dress up in 'simple array' and go out among the people to hear what they said about him (ll. 2556–62); the rhetorically 'simple array' of the Prologue saves Prince Henry the trouble of masquerade.

Trouble at the office may hardly seem like the stuff of a national polity, but the structure of the text cannot help but magnify the significance of Hoccleve's household economics for the whole kingdom. If Henry promises to pay an annuity and then withdraws it, he creates thereby a 'privy silence'. Aggrieved silence is a theme to which Hoccleve returns at the end of the poem, when he warns Henry that civil peace in itself is no guarantee of a healthy body politic, since below that peaceful surface may lie 'irous thoughtes'. The old man cautions the depressed Hoccleve against fretting 'thought', since its 'violence is ful outrageous', and 'unwise is he that besy thoght ne dredeth'. The implications of this ostensibly private and therapeutic advice for the larger body politic are immediately obvious, since it was, according to the old man, precisely 'thought' that provoked the heresy and sedition of Badby (ll. 267–87).[35] Hoccleve's self-destructive 'thought' generates this whole text, and is not by any means wholly acommodated at its end.

The *Regement* connects the honouring of written contracts of salary payment with Prince Henry's fulfilment of his coronation oaths. The poem contains extremely forthright demands that Henry pay his civil servants what he promised he would. Unpaid service demands vengeance by God, along with murder and disinheritance (ll. 4173–9); should Henry not pay, he proves to be 'a brekere of a covenaunt' (l. 4802). These pressing demands to honour written agreements recapitulate the very first section of the *Regement* proper, dealing with the king's coronation oaths. Should a king break those oaths, then he loses both credit and credence: merchants will not lend to him (l. 2381), and no one will bother to engage him in contract, since 'Litel enchesoun [reason] hath he forto speke, | To whos wordes

[35] A point made by Hasler, p. 171.

is geven no credence' (l. 2221). Faith is the very condition of discourse: 'Feith causith eek of men the communynge' (l. 2209), and the king's faith is most visibly and durably on show in written documents, whether they be coronation oaths or the king's own 'lettre and seel'. Hoccleve gives the king a writing lesson for his written promises, since 'writinge wil endure' (l. 2371); he also teaches the king about reading: all readers of all the king's promises need faith in the king's readiness to bind himself to those promises. One of the written works that will endure, indeed, is Hoccleve's *Regement* itself.[36]

So far from being wholly diminished in this text, then, Hoccleve's psychic and economic straits are made to resonate throughout the whole public sphere. Hoccleve seeks to win payment from the future king, but the Prince is also taught how he might win 'the peples voice' (l. 2885) by attending to the needs of the body politic. This balance of payment and words was in fact precisely true of the relations between king and parliament in the reign of Henry IV. Throughout his reign, Henry was chronically short of money. The proportion of royal income derived from taxation, and therefore requiring consent of parliament, had climbed by the early fifteenth century to more than 80 per cent; it is no accident that in exactly these years the Commons of parliament 'enjoyed a greater influence over the business of central government than at any time before the seventeenth century'.[37] In the many parliaments of Henry's reign, the function of the Commons was both to grant taxes and to represent the grievances of the realm. This double function itself implies a relation between the giving of money and the king's receipt of words. The power of the Commons in the early fifteenth century is also perceptible in their demand, made in 1401, 1404, and 1406 that the King bind members of his Council, the body of advisers in permanent service to the King, to do their duty in an open oath taken in Parliament, and that the King himself should promise to take their advice.[38] In their anxiety to repudiate Stubbs, twentieth-century historians hastened to deny that this represented any form of 'premature constitutionalism',[39] but it

[36] For the hermeneutic themes of Hoccleve's *Regement*, I am indebted to the fine study of Perkins. See also D. Lawton, 'Dullness and the Fifteenth Century'.

[37] Gillingham, p. 73.

[38] A. L. Brown, 'Parliament', pp. 136–7.

[39] Ibid. 134.

seems to me that such historians were themselves caught in Stubbsian categories in making this claim. Certainly the Commons were not promoting abstract ideals of parliamentary control; they were capitalizing on the weakness of the King to raise the binding power of their own speech. Negotiation that broadens the base of consent usually emerges out of political stand-off rather than from ideals alone.

At the very least, then, Hoccleve enters into a compact with the future king: if he is properly paid, his future words will serve the king's interests.[40] The poem itself, however, is projected from a state of disequilibrium between the needs of king and subject, whereby the bodily presence of the articulate subject, along with the needs of the larger body politic, loom unpredictably large.

In the late twentieth-century resurgence of Hoccleve scholarship, scholars argued that Hoccleve was in every way a king's man, self-serving by serving the Prince.[41] The most subtle of these accounts had it that despite the desire to be sycophantic, Hoccleve was unable to disguise the ideological vacuum at the centre of a usurping regime. The textual unconscious of this poem, so it was argued, returned to expose the emptiness of the Lancastrian claim.[42] Certainly the production of extremely fine early copies of the poem and its circulation among those close to Henry V would imply high-level endorsement of the text.[43] Neither self-serving nor high-level acceptance of the text, however, need damage my case that the *Regement* constrains the king by its representation of the unruly, potentially unregimented body politic. Ideologically weakened kings may be good news for financially straitened literate subjects, since such kings stand in especial need of articulate support. Not only that, but Henry IV had himself been obliged to stake his claim against, among other things, the bad and wholly arbitrary governance of Richard II. As we have seen in Chapter 4, the 'Record and Process' by which Richard was deposed accused Richard of abusing due political process by appointing his favourites as counsellors, by browbeating them when their advice was unpalatable, and by altering the records of Parlia-

[40] As indeed they would seem to have done; see Ch. 7, below, for discussion of the *Remonstrance against Oldcastle*.

[41] Powerfully argued by Pearsall, 'Hoccleve's *Regement of Princes*'.

[42] Strohm, *England's Empty Throne*, ch. 7.

[43] For which see Pearsall, 'Hoccleve's *Regement of Princes*', and Perkins.

ment. When challenged on his dispensation of arbitrary justice, the document reports that Richard replied fiercely that the laws were 'in his mouth', or 'in his breast', and that he did, by his own wilful judgement, whatever pleased him ('secundum sue arbitrium voluntatis . . . quicquid desideriis eius occurrerit').[44] As Quentin Skinner has argued, the best strategy for oppositional voices is to adopt positions that one's opponents *must* concede;[45] issues of sincerity or even of self-serving do not impinge on the fact that a given position is the one that neither side can afford to ignore. Such a strategy necessarily implies, indeed, that a self-serving position will have to enlist larger notions of the political good. While Hoccleve's is not precisely an 'oppositional' voice, he does capitalize on Lancastrian vulnerability, and his self-serving does evoke the needs of the body politic more widely. The target audience's acceptance of the text demonstrates the success of the strategy.

The argument that Hoccleve was a straightforward royal apologist also fails to take into account his extreme tentativeness about discursive exchange. No such traces appear in, for example, the wholly laudatory *Gesta Henrici Quinti* (1416–17), written in Latin and presenting Henry in theocratic terms. Hoccleve's very strategy of moving from complaint, to dialogue, and only then to royal address itself implies a discursive caution of a kind not to be found in the straightforward accounts of royal commission in, say, Lydgate's contemporary *Troy Book*.

Furthermore, the ostensibly platitudinous ethical advice turns out more often than not to be advice about accepting advice. In the *Regement*, Alexander, about to destroy a city, sees his old schoolteacher approach, and swears *not* to do anything he asks. The philosopher accordingly asks that Alexander *should* destroy the city, to which advice a chastened Alexander binds himself (ll. 2301–31). Unlike the open-eared Edward III, King Lysimachus crucified his honest counsellor (ll. 2556–83); a 'fool sage' successfully persuades a king not to exercise misplaced mercy (l. 3145); the defamed King Pirus laugh-

[44] *Rotuli Parliamentorum*, ed. J. Strachey, 3. 415–53. For an English trans. see *Chronicles of the Revolution* ed. Given Wilson: 'Record and Process', pp. 168–89 (at para. 16).

[45] A point most powerfully argued by Skinner, 'Principles and Practice of Opposition'.

ingly accepts the dangerous excuse of his detractors that they would have said much worse if the wine had not run out (ll. 3389–3402); Julius Caesar patiently accepts a charge of low birth (ll. 3513–28). The most subtle of these reading lessons is the example of King Antigone, who, hidden behind a curtain, overheard his subjects complaining about him. The King suddenly drew the curtain aside, saying 'gooth hens, lest the kyng yow heere, | For the curtyn hath herde al your mateere' (ll. 3536–42). For a wholly subservient text, these high-profile examples of caution would be massively excessive to demand; to describe them as the return of the textual unconscious is to imply an implausibly weak level of consciousness. Royal ethics, this poem implies, are largely coincident with subtle hermeneutics. Once read as a subtle act of communication itself, the ethical advice so often derided as naïve can be redescribed as a sustained performance of royal instruction. Hoccleve offers Henry a mirror of princes in which Henry is taught to read the reflection of his subjects' bodies.

(*b*) Early Lancastrian Policy Texts

The politics of the *Regement* emerge from the *lack* of congruence between different jurisdictions: the household and the state each unsuccessfully compete for domination over the other, and out of this stand-off emerges a potential contract between household and king. This is not 'constitutionalism' in the sense of applying pre-formed ideas to the practice of politics, but a political practice does emerge that constrains both household and state. The same is true of near-contemporary texts written out of parliamentary concerns, to which I now turn.

Richard the Redeless (856 alliterative lines in the surviving text, divided into four passus) speaks for another jurisdiction, the 'House' of Commons. The poem's ostensible address is to Richard II, and it proposes to remedy Richard's lack of good counsel, or 'rede'. The real target must, however, be Henry IV, since the poem brims with barely concealed reference to Richard's deposition, including clear references to the widely publicized deposition document that convicted Richard, the 'Record and Process'.[46] That *Richard* makes

[46] For references in the poem to the 'Record and Process', see Passus I. 98–

reference to this document might suggest that the poem is itself an example of Lancastrian apologetics, but this would be difficult to sustain. In the first place, the indirection of addressing the deposed Richard allows for a very free criticism of kings, and therefore, implicitly and necessarily, of Henry. This poem, too, registers the dangers of speaking: a personified Reason encourages courageous and plain speaking (2. 69–76), but more significantly the poet both savagely attacks royal abuse of parliamentary procedure, and also lampoons parliamentarians for their silence in the face of Richard's tyranny. With reference to the 'Shrewsbury' Parliament of 1398, he describes the way Richard packed the Parliament with his placemen, and goes on to mock the silence of these sycophants in the face of Richard's unprecedented call for taxation revenues:

> Somme slombrid and slepte and said but a lite;
> And somme mafflid with the mouth and nyst [mumbled · did not know]
> what they ment;
> And somme had hire and helde therwith evere, [payment]
> And wolde no forther affoot for fer of her maistris. [fear]
>
> (4. 62–5)

Henry's attack on Richard's abuse of parliament may have been a necessary expedient in the business of deposing a legitimate king, but after the deposition there is no particular advantage for him in stressing such points. *Richard* is not an example of simplistic Lancastrian apologetics; more plausibly, it capitalizes on the discourse of parliamentary privilege that Henry was obliged to use to justify his usurpation, and exploits it to press parliament's claims for a say in the control of taxation and the king's household expenditure. Qualified opposition works by adopting a position that its opponent cannot dismiss.

Hoccleve and the *Richard*-poet speak from different, and possibly opposed, interests. Hoccleve speaks for himself, out of the royal household, and makes no reference to parliament. He accordingly names himself as a payable household poet, and speaks in a metropolitan mode. The author of *Richard the Redeless* speaks for

106. The 'Record and Process' was entered in the Rolls of Parliament and circulated to certain monastic houses for entry in their chronicles. See *Chronicles of the Revolution*, ed. Given-Wilson, p. 168.

parliament, which consistently sought to limit expenditure on the royal household throughout the period 1376 (the 'Good' Parliament) to the end of the reign of Henry VI. The author, while he clearly knows parliamentary procedure from the inside, remains anonymous; he sets himself in Bristol, and writes in a non-metropolitan mode, the south-western alliterative style.[47] However much their interests may be distinct, both claim a redistribution of discursive power.

This parliamentary voice is also adopted by the slightly later *Mum and the Sothsegger* (?1409), possibly written by the same poet.[48]The poem (1,751 alliterative lines, though missing something from the beginning and end) begins by instructing the king on how he might govern his household in such a way as to avoid rebellion against taxation. The most important officer would be a truth-teller, but none such are to be found, since 'he may lose his life and laugh here no more, | Or [be] y-putte into prisone or y-pyned [tortured] to deeth | Or y-brent [burnt] or y-shent [destroyed] or sum sorowe have' (ll. 167–9). Before the narrator can elaborate on his ideal of a truth-teller, he is silenced for his *naïveté* by Mum, who articulates the powerful arguments in favour of keeping silent. The narrator searches authoritative institutions for advice about who is right, but finds no answers. Old books merely repeat the 'homely usage of the old date, | How that good governance gracieusely endith' (ll. 312–13). The universities offer no more enlightenment, since their disciplinary categories do not deal with the ethics of political practice. The friars, canons, parish priests, and cathedral churches are all dumb on the matter of truth-telling, along with the secular institutions consulted by the narrator. The vision of a wounded and suffering truth-teller forces him to recognize the strength of Mum's arguments, as he falls in grief in a swoon. The authoritative figure he meets in this dream encourages him to finish his book, at which point he wakes and opens a bag, 'where many a pryve poyse [poem] is preyntid withynne' (l. 1344). The poem ends with an account of the

[47] For the distinction between a formal and an informal corpus of alliterative poetry, see D. Lawton, 'Middle English Alliterative Poetry'.

[48] For the history of the relations between these two texts, see *Piers Plowman Tradition*, ed. Barr, pp. 15–16. *Mum and the Sothsegger* is also edited in the same volume.

satirical documents that pour forth from this bag: quires, volumes, rolls, pamphlets, scrolls, writs, schedules, all summarized and 'fulle to the margyn' with complaint (l. 1346).

Despite its apparent call for free speech, this poem in fact promotes complaint within specific jurisdictions, and especially within parliament. The very structure of its narrative implies yet despairs of the sheer complexity of discursive authority in England. A diverse range of institutions that should be responsible for speaking the truth fails to do so, and this failure legitimates the existence of the poem itself as the channel through which an extraordinary plurality of voices can be heard at its end. The open bag of the poem's close is not, however, an invitation for anyone to protest. One of the complaints he takes out is, indeed, an attack on idle tale-telling 'atte nale [over ale]' (l. 1390) and on the spreading of rumour against lords; such rumours 'been so light of fote, thay lepen by the skyes' (l. 1402). This criticism replicates complaints made by Henry IV in a letter of 1402 to the Bishop of Exeter, where he says that malicious complaints about his governance are made 'in taverns'.[49] Not only does the *Mum* narrator want to constrain such 'rumour', but he chooses this moment to produce the absolutist example of the Great Khan, who was so successful a ruler for having ordered all his lords to kill their heirs. No sooner has he made these absolutist moves, however, than he excepts parliament from discursive restrictions: 'I carpe [speak] not of knightz that cometh for the shires, | That the king clepith [calls] to cunseil with other' (ll. 1460–1).

This privileging of parliament echoes the most authoritative voice in the poem, that of the aged dream-guide, who encourages the voicing of complaint precisely because members of parliament have failed to express the nation's grievances. Sedition would have been avoided if the knights of the shires had spoken up 'in parliament', the 'place that is proprid to parle [speak] for the royaulme' (l. 1132). None of the political works of the early Lancastrian reign promoted free speech; they each instead promoted the specific privileges of given jurisdictions, and they each conceived of complaint to the king

[49] For this reference, and other legislation against spreading malicious rumour against 'the great men of the realm', see Simpson, 'Constraints of Satire', pp. 17, 20. See also *Piers Plowman Tradition*, ed. Barr, p. 352 for proclamations and a parliamentary petition by the Prince of Wales against rumour in 1405 and 1406.

contractually. Questions of payment, either of salaries or of taxation, were never far from questions of discursive practice. As one of a set of short and pithy parliamentary texts dated to these early Lancastrian years said, the Commons are the source of England's political health, but only when Lords are short of cash do they get to know what the Commons think:

To wete if parlement be wys, [know · wise]
The comoun profit wel it preves. [proves]
A kingdom in comouns lys,
Alle profytes, and alle myscheves.
Lordes wet nevere what comouns greves [know]
Til here rentis bigynne to ses.[50] [cease]

The reign of Henry IV was indeed, then, a moment in which a variety of institutional jurisdictions made powerful claims for a contract with the king. It *may* be the case that claims to represent an alternative voice merely offered the appearance of alterity, while they really served the interests of the status quo. This sobering perception drove a wide range of New Historicist study, and it received its most lucid and seminal statement in an essay by Stephen Greenblatt on, significantly, Shakespeare's *Henry IV* and *Henry V*. Subversiveness, by Greenblatt's account of the action of these plays, 'is at the same time contained by the power it would appear to threaten. Indeed, the subversiveness is the very product of that power and furthers its ends.'[51] Not only does *Henry IV*, Part 2 represent this mirage effect of subversiveness, but it has that very effect itself on its audience; Shakespeare reveals that the 'founding of the modern state' as represented in this play leaves the audience 'compelled to pay homage to a system of beliefs whose fraudulence somehow only confirms their power, authenticity and truth'.[52] From the perspective of this chapter so far, it may appear not only that Shakespeare was engaged in the management of a particularly uncomfortable period of English history, but also that Greenblatt himself accepted the impossibility of alterity

[50] In Oxford, Bodleian Library MS Digby 102; see *Twenty Six Political and Other Poems*, ed. Kail, no. 3, ll. 97–102, p. 12. A new edn. of these crisp and intelligent poems is needed.

[51] Greenblatt, 'Invisible Bullets', p. 24.

[52] Ibid. 42.

rather too easily. The very narrowness of his model, by which 'Power' is opposed to, yet ultimately productive of, 'subversiveness', may itself have ignored the historical possibility of a complex set of jurisdictions competing for discursive participation. The simplicity of the opposition implies an oversimple account of 'Power'.

(*c*) Before and After the Early Lancastrian 'Experiment'

The Regement of Princes is in one sense an anti-theoretical poem. Its politics are produced from the interaction of mind and body, and never escape an awareness of the body's unpredictable and irrepressible demands. It is indebted to a powerful Aristotelian tradition that has a built-in scepticism about political theory. The presuppositions of this tradition are as follows: that the ideal form of a given entity is an *embodied* form; that the political order is a natural and desirable phenomenon, produced, intelligible, and controlled by human powers; and that the political order is either self-sufficient or at the very least a desirable good in and for itself. This tradition fed into late medieval English vernacular poetry from the political writings of both French and Italian scholastic theologians and Italian republican intellectuals. It is represented in English vernacular works both before and after Hoccleve's *Regement*.

While Hoccleve himself was wholly within this tradition, his approach to it was not philosophical. He was, however, very familiar with a recent vernacular text that had exposed the abstract structure of such thinking, insofar as it can become abstract. Hoccleve certainly praises Chaucer in the *Regement* (ll. 1961–74; 4978–5012),[53] but he also describes Gower as 'my maister' (l. 1975), and he was responsible for copying at least one manuscript of Gower's *Confessio Amantis*.[54] Gower is in fact much more obviously the major presence behind the *Regement* than is Chaucer, since both Gower and Hoccleve draw on the same sources and exploit some of the same exempla, creating in effect a largely non-Chaucerian tradition of explicitly political address in the vernacular for the rest of the

[53] Hoccleve was also responsible for what is possibly the first portrait of Chaucer (designed to accompany ll. 4978–5012 in each MS), one beautiful copy of which survives in British Library, Harley MS 4866, fo. 88.

[54] For which see Doyle and Parkes.

fifteenth century.[55] As we have seen in Chapter 4, the amatory narratives of the *Confessio* tend inevitably to resuscitate the political discourse that the Prologue had dismissed. Both because the psyche itself turns out to be a political arena, ruled by the tyrant prince Cupid, and because the predatory brutalities of sexual desire have explicitly political consequences, political reflection often resurfaces in this text. Book 7 in particular presents itself as the advice of Aristotle to Alexander. That master-pupil relationship evokes the pseudo-Aristotelian tradition of the *Secreta Secretorum* mentioned above, but the divisions of Book 7 are also demonstrably shaped within more genuinely Aristotelian traditions. The cursus of Genius's instruction is arranged according to a threefold division of the sciences, into the theoretical sciences (theology, physics and mathematics, the last of which itself contains arithmetic, music, geometry, and astronomy); rhetoric; and the practical sciences of ethics, economics, and 'policie', this last being Gower's translation of Latin *politica*.

Gower's division of the sciences is fundamentally Aristotelian, and informs the whole of his poem. It is derived directly, though with modification, from the Florentine Brunetto Latini's *Li Livres dou Tresor* (written in exile in France in 1262–6). Brunetto's republican *Livres* had earlier in the fourteenth century been drawn on by London city officials, who adapted it to English political structures.[56] Gower, too, adapts the republican text to monarchical conditions, but preserves Brunetto's strictly secular definition and privileging of politics. Politics, by Brunetto's Aristotelian account, is the art that offers beatitude among things 'made by nature', and is accordingly the queen of the natural sciences:

The art, therefore, that teaches how to govern a city is the principal, sovereign, and mistress of all the sciences, since many honourable sciences are contained within the field of politics, as for example rhetoric, military

[55] The closest Chaucer comes to this kind of writing is his own tale in the *Canterbury Tales*, the *Tale of Melibee*, a narrative of both household and communal 'politics'. The gendered psychology of the tale, whereby the irascible husband Melibee represents the will, his wounded daughter Sophie abstract reason, and his wife Prudence the imagination, is parallel to the 'political' psychology of Gower's *Confessio Amantis*. For an illuminating discussion of this tale and its cultural background, see Wallace, *Chaucerian Polity*, ch. 8.

[56] For which see Reynolds, pp. 197–8.

science, and the governance of households. Politics is noble, furthermore, because it gives direction to all the sciences under it, of which it is the complement, for its end is the complement of all the other practical arts. The good of this science is, accordingly, the good of humans, since it constrains them to act well.[57]

This passage is itself a translation of Aristotle's *Nicomachean Ethics* (1094[b]) and serves to illuminate the extraordinarily high status Gower gives to politics not only in Book 7, but in the whole of the *Confessio*. He gives apparent primacy to theology, but he passes over that very quickly (7. 73–134), and moves to the implications of the other theoretical sciences, and especially astronomy, for the human body. By far the most thoroughgoing treatment is given to politics (7. 1711–5438), with the implication that only through politics can the unpredictable motions of the body, moved naturally both from within and without, be stabilized. This perception is also implied in the relation of Book 7 to the rest of the poem, since the other seven books treat ethics and economics: politics, the discourse of Book 7, contains and directs the unstable movements of amatory desire.

For Gower, in the *Confessio* at least, politics is the highest science, the science that promises 'beatitude' on earth. So far from sustaining any theocratic notion of kingship, both Gower and Hoccleve authorize lay authority in the vernacular. Both cite, for example, the instance of King Lycurgus who, having himself established good laws, leaves his kingdom with the intention of never returning, on condition that his subjects obey the law until he returns. Part of his strategy is to tell his subjects that the laws were made by the gods: 'It was the god and nothing I' (*Confessio*, 7. 2971). There are differences between the tellings (*Confessio*, 7. 2917–3028; *Regement*, 2950–89), but both champion the purely secular engineering of governance.[58] Theocratic pretentions are themselves the product of wholly secular strategy.

This Aristotelian privileging of politics also determines and justifies the poetic mode of the *Confessio*. Aristotle argues that the practical sciences are not susceptible of demonstrative clarity, but that they are approximate sciences that call forth the practical

[57] Brunetto Latini, *Li Livres dou Tresor*, ed. Carmody, 2. 2, pp. 176–8. My trans.

[58] For a powerful account of this reclamation of lay authority, see L. Scanlon, chs. 9 and 10.

reason, the reason that adjusts itself to particular and material circumstances.[59] A Middle English translation, made in the 1380s by John Trevisa, of the influential Aristotelian-derived *De regimine principum* (*c.*1285) by Giles of Rome, says that the manner of the practical sciences is 'by liknes rude and boystous'.[60] Unlike mathematics, the practical sciences do not admit of certainty, since they deal with singulars; accordingly, their rhetorical mode should be exemplary and persuasive. Giles himself does not in fact take his own advice, but Gower does. The whole mode of the *Confessio* is by narrative example, since narrative is capable of replicating the exemplary particularities of sensual pain and pleasure. As I argued in Chapter 4, Gower's Genius functions as the imagination, who negotiates between the abstract rule of reason and the irrepressible force of sensual desire, personified by Amans. The politics that emerges from this interaction is one in which the abstraction of law is informed by, and informs, corporal need. This information requires imaginative apprehension, and so Gower's politics equally imply a poetics.[61]

Precisely because politics in this tradition is a product of the sensual and the particular, it can never achieve autonomy and stability. Gower's own politics are, like Hoccleve's, centred on constraint of royal power; just as abstract reason must recognize the jurisdiction of the body, so too must the king recognize the proper jurisdiction of the body politic. He does that through the mediation of imaginative counsel, which deploys its prudential knowledge of narrative and its understanding of reason to guide the king. In the same way that for Aristotle the intellect rules the appetites 'with a constitutional and a royal rule',[62] so too does the body politic ideally recognize the representativeness of the king, while demanding representation at the

[59] For a profound and historically wide-ranging account of this literary-legal tradition, see Trimpi, ch. 10.

[60] Oxford, Bodleian Library, MS Digby 233, fo. 1va. Edited as *Governance of Kings and Princes*, ed. Fowler et al. For Trevisa's writing of this text, see David C. Fowler. See also Hanna, 'Sir Thomas Berkeley', pp. 897–8.

[61] Fuller accounts of the points in this and the previous paragraph can be found in Simpson, *Sciences and the Self*, chs. 7 and 8.

[62] Aristotle, *Politics*, ed. and trans. Everson, 1254^{b}, p. 6. The Latin translation of the *Politics* at this point uses precisely the terminology of 'constitutionalism' used by scholastic political thinkers: 'intellectus autem [dominatur] appetui politico et regali [principatu]'. See Aristotle, *Politica*, ed. Michaud-Quantin, p. 9.

same time. If that is the ideal, however, the pressure of narrative in the *Confessio* also pulls in the reverse direction. The voice of Diogenes, the philosopher who refuses to serve kings, sounds powerfully in the *Confessio* (3. 1201–1311, and 7. 2217–2320), and well it might: if the political showpiece of the text is Aristotle's teaching of Alexander in Book 7, the rest of the narrative has many stories of Alexander's violence and imperialist rapacity, practised both before and *after* his education.[63] Rationally conceived Aristotelian politics have a necessarily labile relationship with the body, and so must fail to become wholly autonomous theory. The unbounded promise of reason to escape the disasters of history must always be held in check by a counter-awareness of the tenacity of both history and the body.[64] The Aristotelian tradition of intellectual commitment to the active life, implicitly or explicitly expressed by all 'Aristotle to Alexander' texts, cannot repress the argument for sceptical resignation.[65]

Before Hoccleve, then, Gower had produced a more fully theorized account of a secularized and Aristotelian limited monarchy. Before Gower himself, another vernacular English poem expresses the same 'bodily' politics, and also registers the intransigencies of households within the larger body politic. The alliterative *Wynnere and Wastoure* (unfinished at 503 lines, written in 1352 for the court of Edward III), brilliantly exposes the heterogeneous interests of nobles, merchants, and the king in a wonderfully candid account of national economic policy. Winner the retentive merchant and Waster the spending noble defend their respective economic practices before the king, each attacking the other on ethical grounds. The king's own judgement expresses no ethical judgement whatsoever; on the

[63] The Alexander stories (all of them negative) can be found as follows: 3. 1201–1311 (in which he is rebuked by Diogenes); 3. 2363–2437; 3. 2438–80; 5. 1571–90; 6. 2273–2366; Bk 7.

[64] For the philosophical scepticism of the *Confessio*, see esp. Dimmick, 'Patterns of Ethics', ch. 5.

[65] Space precludes a full-scale revision of H. Baron's argument that intellectual commitment to the active life of politics is found only from the early 15th-cent. in Florence, with the championing of Cicero. Each of the English 'policy' texts discussed in this chapter implies a commitment to the active life of political engagement. For the Italian context, see Skinner's rebuttal of Baron, in Skinner, *Foundations of Modern Political Thought*, vol. 1, chs. 3 and 4. For the range of views on intellectual participation in government and their classical derivation, see Skinner, 'More's *Utopia*', pp. 125–35.

contrary, he orders Winner to go to Rome and gain as much money as he can, while Waster is to go to Cheapside and encourage a Falstaffian consumption. Discursive relations are very clear in this poem: the king is interested in the economic health of the whole commonwealth, and cares nothing for ethics; individuals may convincingly defend their economic activity in ethical terms, but seen from the perspective of national policy ethics are irrelevant. What counts instead is the fruitful interaction of competing sectors of the economy. Consumption and production go hand in hand: 'Whoso wele [profit] schal wyn a wastour moste he fynde, | For if it greves one gome [man] it gladdes another' (ll. 390–1). This poem, along with the *Libelle of Englyshe Polyce* of 1436, gives the lie to the idea that 'economic nationalism' is restricted to the sixteenth century.[66]

After Hoccleve, the Aristotelian vernacular tradition continues, but its exponents suffer from extreme old age and political vissicitude of a kind with which the tradition was largely unable to deal. In 1449, at the age of 78 and having lived through the reigns of five monarchs, Lydgate died, apparently dropping dead in the act of writing his *Secrees of Old Philosoffres*. The text is remarkably diffuse, and simply stops at line 1491, a line appropriately about the power of death to consume everything, even Lydgate. The text is continued by a Lydgate disciple, Benedict Burgh (*c.*1413–83), who gives Henry VI the tip, among other things, that spots around the eyes are a very bad sign in a counsellor (ll. 2605–11). Just before 1450, the year of the Duke of York's first challenge to the visibly failing Henry VI, the loss of Normandy, and the rebellion of Jack Cade, spots around the eyes were the least of Henry's problems.

The topos of Aristotle's old age in the *Secreta Secretorum* is literalized in the tradition of the *Secreta* in these years. Another version was translated in 1450 for Henry VI by the octogenarian copyist and bookseller John Shirley (1366–1456), 'in the last dayes of his grete age, so as his ignorant feblesse wolde souffise',[67] and in 1463 George Ashby, aged almost 80, wrote his own work of policy, *The Active Policy of a Prince* (918 lines in rhyme-royal stanzas), and the *Dicta et Opiniones . . . Philosophorum* (1,263 lines in rhyme-royal stanzas,

[66] See McGovern. McGovern readily acknowledges the antecedents of the theory of 'Economic Nationalism' in scholastic Aristotelian theory.

[67] *Secreta Secretorum*, ed. Manzalaoui, p. 229.

possibly part of the same work as the *Active Policy*) for the young Prince Edward, son of Henry VI.[68] Ashby had formerly been a clerk in the Signet Office, and no text could more eloquently express the treacherousness of civil service in the last half of the fifteenth century, since it is written for a royal patron in exile, soon to be killed in battle. The opening invocation of poetic lineage, to 'maisters Gower, Chaucer and Lydgate', cannot disguise Ashby's overwhelming sense of threatened royal lineages: he tells young Edward that he may read 'the ruine of high estates and translacion' in old chronicles, before acknowledging that everyday recent experience will give him 'daily probacion' of the same story, since 'Ther hath be in late daies right grete change | Of high estates and grete division' (ll. 169–70). Ashby may have written the poem in prison, since his moving *Prisoner's Reflections* (350 lines in rhyme-royal stanzas) was also written in 1463, as Ashby was broke and imprisoned in the Fleet prison. The *Reflections* are effectively addressed to no one, or at best 'to folk troubelyd and vexed grevously' (l. 310). Saturated with Hocclevian echoes, the poem expresses precisely the misery of aged indigence that Hoccleve had feared. Like Hoccleve in the *Regement*, Ashby encourages Prince Edward to pay the wages of his men in the *Active Policy* (l. 296); in particular he should pay 'suche as be makers. | These may exalt your name and werkes' (ll. 613–14). In neither of his works, however, can Ashby capitalize on the contract implicit in poems of this kind, since in the one his audience seems to be the new regime of Edward IV, to whom he can only beg forgiveness for any 'errour or fayned opinion' (*Reflections*, 325), and in the *Active Policy* his patron is in exile.

From the evidence of the texts written mid-century, one could be forgiven for thinking that the Aristotelian tradition is effectively moribund. That would, however, be a serious error, since it continues to find powerful and articulate voices right up to Thomas Starkey's *Dialogue between Pole and Lupset* (1529–32). Even in the turmoil and dislocations of civil war, however, this tradition finds its most theoretical and coherent vernacular expression in the writing of Sir John Fortescue (*c.*1395–*c.*1477). Fortescue, who had been

[68] Ashby, *Poems*, ed. Bateson. New editions are needed. For recent revision of the dating and coherence of Ashby's works, see two articles by Scattergood, 'Date and Composition of George Ashby's Poems', and 'George Ashby's *Prisoner's Reflections*'.

appointed Chief Justice of the King's Bench in 1442, accompanied Henry VI and Queen Margaret to exile in Scotland in 1461, where he wrote a series of pro-Lancastrian tracts. In 1463 he followed the royal party to a further seven years' exile in northern France. After the total defeat of Lancastrian hopes in the battle of Tewkesbury (1471), he repudiated his earlier Lancastrian works, and became a member of Edward IV's council. Clearly this was a voice that, once it had recanted, Edward could not afford to be without. One of the works possibly written in exile for Prince Edward, but later revised and presented to Edward IV in 1471, is *The Governance of England*.

In the conditions of extreme political instability in which he found himself, we might expect Fortescue to advocate a much more draconian royalist policy against opposition of any sort. Ashby had done something of this kind in the *Active Policy*, for example, when he advised the young prince to put down 'al maner rebellyon' (l. 388), to crush any pretenders to the throne (ll. 415–21) and to set up a spy network (ll. 618–24). Fortescue, however, remained resolutely within the traditions of limited monarchy that he had inherited from scholastic thinkers, especially Thomas Aquinas (*c.*1225–74). He certainly recognized the instability of his time, and accordingly advocated that the king should be more powerful than any of his subjects, and that he should massively enlarge his sources of stable and permanent income, so as to avoid financial vulnerability (chs. 9, 10, and 19). All considerations of the king's exercise of power are, however, governed by the fundamental principle Fortescue inherited from the thirteenth-century Aristotelians he cites, a principle enunciated immediately in chapter 1. There are two kinds of kingdom, he says, one in which lordship is exercised regally, and the other in which it is exercised both politically and regally. The two are distinguished as follows; the regal king

mey rule his peple bi suche lawes as he makyth hymself. And thefore he may sett uponn thaim tayles [taxes] and other imposicions, such as he wol hym self, without thair assent. The seconde kyng [ruling 'politically' and 'regally'] may not rule his peple bi other lawes than such as thai assenten unto. And therfore he mey sett upon thaim non imposicions without thair owne assent.[69]

[69] Fortescue, *Governance of England*, ed. Plummer, chapter 1, p. 109. (A

From here he cites his sources (Aquinas and Giles of Rome)[70] and remarks on God's anger with the Israelites when they changed from both political and regal rule as narrated in Judges, and chose kings for themselves who ruled only regally.

The Old Testament example is strategic, since Fortescue is basically a secularist in the matter of governance.[71] At the beginning of an earlier, Latin treatise, *De laudibus legum Anglie*, written in exile for Prince Edward, son of Henry VI, he represents himself calling the young prince away, significantly, from chivalric exercise to instruct him in matters of state. When the Prince declares his interest in divine law alone, Fortescue replies by humanizing divine law: all law is divine, since it was God who prompted humans to devise positive law. Once he has the Prince focused on the significance of human law, Fortescue presses the point to declare that human happiness on this earth derives from the exercise of secular justice.[72] The king's sovereignty in a political order derives from the people, a point buttressed by both the historical myth of the Trojans settling and choosing a king, and the organic metaphor of the body. The heart pre-exists the head, and the head is joined to the heart by the sinews; accordingly, 'the king who is head of the body politic is unable to change the laws of that body, or to deprive that same people of their own substance uninvited or against their wills' (ch. 13).

In Aristotelian-inspired politics the abstract rule of reason is produced by, and is answerable to, the 'body' from which it derives its sovereignty. For Gower, Hoccleve, and the author of *Richard*

modernized version is available in *On the Laws and Governance of England*, ed. Lockwood.

[70] For confirmation that these ideas were indeed to be found in the sources Fortescue cites, see Wilks, pp. 200–29.

[71] Fortescue is also credited with translating into English some works by the French bureaucrat Alain Chartier. For the evidence, see both *Fifteenth Century English Translations of Alain Chartier's 'Le Traité de l'Esperance' and 'Le Quadrilogue Invectif'*, ed. Blayney, and *Familiar Dialogue of the Friend and the Fellow*, ed. Blayney. These texts, all originally written in lament for the civil wars that weakened France earlier in the 15th cent., were very appropriate for English conditions later in the century. If Fortescue did translate these texts, they contradict his own works, since the Chartier texts foresee a theological solution to political problems.

[72] *De laudibus legum Anglie*, trans. as *In Praise of the Laws of England*, in *On the Laws and Governance of England*, ed. Lockwood, introd. and ch. 4. The text was written in 1468–71. Further chapter references will appear in the text.

the Redeless the body registers its pressure through amatory desire, financial anxiety, or the Commons in parliament respectively. Fortescue was a judge, and for him the real constraint on the king's action derived from his obligation to be constrained by English law, a broader category than any of the constraints just mentioned. Unlike the civil law operative in France, English law is devised historically by the community of the realm in statute, and put into action in the jury system (chs. 17–22). Even the jury system itself is, for Fortescue, premissed upon natural and material categories, since it depends on the natural fertility of England, a fertility that creates the conditions of a wealth that is distributed through common law. Only a certain prosperity can ensure the ready availability of twelve honest men who are not open to bribery. The alternative is the inquisitorial system of civil law, whose use of torture to pull bodies apart appals Fortescue (ch. 22).

When Plummer first edited the *Governance* in 1885, in the wake of Stubbs's *Constitutional History*, he called it the 'earliest constitutional treatise written in the English language'.[73] Already by 1936 scepticism towards Stubbs had set in, when S. B. Chrimes dismissed the constitutional interpretation so far as to describe Fortescue as the forerunner of Hobbes rather than of, say, Locke.[74] By Chrimes's account, because Fortescue could not conceive of the law without the king, or vice versa, and because the people could in no way remove the king without dissolution of the body politic, then the king's power was effectively absolute.[75] Certainly the political system envisaged by Fortescue is led by the royal will; the king is representative of his kingdom, but in order to represent the body politic, his will must be unconstrained by any special interest.[76] For this reason counsel becomes the most important act in the political process, and it is by no means casual that Fortescue should devote a chapter to the very specific details of a properly run council (ch. 15). But the king can be constrained: the scholastic tradition within which he is working clearly envisages the possibility of the people legitimately overthrowing a tyrannical king.[77] It would surely have been impolitic for

[73] Fortescue, *Governance of England*, ed. Plummer, p. 86.
[74] Chrimes, pp. 319–24.
[75] A view maintained by Gillespie.
[76] For an extremely clear account of this theory of kingship, see Watts, ch. 1.
[77] For which see Wilks, pp. 187–8, 221, and 223–25.

Fortescue to make this point either to Prince Edward, whose father Henry VI had just been overthrown, or to Edward IV, who had also been temporarily overthrown in 1470. But sovereignty derives from the people in this system, and they can exercise that sovereignty in extreme emergencies.

None of what we have seen in this chapter so far is 'parliamentary democracy': different authors posit different arenas in which counsel could be contractually proferred to the king, and they figured the mode of constraining the king differently, not necessarily through parliament. But all the works we have considered so far in Section III did aim to limit the power of the king, and they did so by asserting a division of sovereignty between the body and its head, a jurisdictional multiplicity that characterized the society over which kings in the fourteenth and fifteenth centuries ruled. In my view the politics of these works express what might fairly be called a constitutional particularism: constitutional because the king is held to pre-existing contracts, but particularist because the institution that claims a contract with the king does not represent, or necessarily even claim to represent, 'the people'. Fortescue is not at all the 'first' writer of a vernacular constitutional text; instead he is the most direct spokesperson for the Aristotelian political tradition of thirteenth-century scholasticism, a tradition with many vernacular reflexes in fourteenth- and fifteenth-century England.

(*d*) *Utopia*

Thirteenth- and fourteenth-century Italian and French institutions, both political and academic, jointly stand behind the English vernacular Aristotelianism we have so far considered. While thinkers like Brunetto Latini (*c.*1220–94) were exiles from republican Florence, scholastic theologians like Aquinas (1225–74), himself Italian, wrote within the institutional context of the University of Paris. Political theory in the fifteenth century continued to derive from Italy, but the tenor of that theory reflected the new Italian political reality of increasingly despotic forms of government taking root throughout the century.[78] Like any government, these despotisms required apologists

[78] Skinner, *Foundations of Modern Political Thought*, vol. 1, ch. 5; and Hankins, pp. 128–30.

and rhetorically expert spokesmen. Whereas republican writers had developed notions of republican liberties in an address to the whole body of the citizens, humanist theorists of the fifteenth and early sixteenth centuries were directly employed by and addressed princes; such theorists stressed security rather than liberty. There is a world of difference between, for example, Brunetto's *Livres dou Tresor* (1260–5) and Machiavelli's *Il Principe* (1513). The main educational consequence of this development was a revaluation of rhetoric at the expense of logic, with a correlative mockery of scholasticism.[79]

English kings and princes had employed Italian or Italian-trained writers of this kind throughout the fifteenth century, just as English scholars sought their education in Italy. Duke Humphrey of Gloucester (d. 1447), for example, employed Tito Livio Frulovisi to write a eulogistic history of Henry V,[80] and commissioned a translation into Latin of Plato's *Republic* by Pier Candido Decembrio. Later in the century Henry VII employed Bernard André, Pietro Carmeliano, and Polydore Vergil to produce official letters, occasional poetry, and histories.[81] A succession of English scholars, including Sir John Tiptoft, went to Italy from the 1450s, and especially to the school of Guarino at Ferrara.[82] The larger environment that determined the need for scholars trained especially in humanistic letter-writing (*ars dictaminis*) was the growing complexity of secular bureaucracies; this need equally provoked the establishment of many schools in fifteenth- and early sixteenth-century England, of which Henry VI's foundation at Eton in 1440 and John Colet's at St Paul's in 1509 were only the most celebrated.[83] A further

[79] For which see Grafton and Jardine, introd. and ch. 1. The argument of the book, which squares with my broader argument in the present volume, is succinctly stated on pp. xiii–xiv: 'The older system [i.e. scholasticism] had fitted perfectly the needs of the Europe of the high middle ages, with its communes, its church offices open to the low-born of high talents and its vigorous debates on power and authority in state and church. The new system [i.e. 'humanist' education] . . . fitted the needs of the new Europe that was taking shape, with its closed governing élites, hereditary offices and strenuous efforts to close off debate on vital political and social questions'.

[80] Written 1437. See Titus Livius Frulovisi, *Vita Henrici Quinti*, ed. Hearne.

[81] See the excellent study by Carlson, *English Humanist Books*.

[82] The classic study of this group is Weiss. For Tiptoft, and his translation (1460) of Buonaccorso da Montemagno's *De vera nobilitate*, see Tiptoft, 'Of True Nobility'.

[83] See Hay, 'England and the Humanities', pp. 305–67, and further references.

consequence of this development was a much closer relation between patron and writer, since a purely lay clerisy had no independent base in the institution of the Church. Although no writer in the period of this history made a living solely from literary writing, many writers emerged from bureaucratic service; such writers have always been closely dependent on courtly favour, but it may be significant that literary fictions of dependency are much more fraught in the Tudor period, in the work of Hawes or Skelton, for example. As recent scholars have argued, the period 1475–1525 saw the initial emergence of the professional writer in England.[84]

With the exception of Lydgate, all the English writers of political works so far mentioned in this chapter were themselves secular bureaucrats or lawyers. As we have seen, however, they wrote out of particular jurisdictions, and inherited discursive materials, that promoted the constraint of royal prerogative. What of the secular bureaucrats in sixteenth-century England? What discursive materials did they use, and what form of politics did they promote? My prime example is Thomas More's *Utopia* (1516), which, while written in Latin, was published in English in 1551. The Latin text was published near the beginning of the reign of Henry VIII; the English text was produced in the short Edwardian period of censorship relaxation, sixteen years after More had been executed for treason in 1535.[85] The dates of *Utopia*'s publication might suggest that the text can only be published in relatively liberal conditions; as we shall see, however, *Utopia* itself promoted the most draconian repression of discursive liberty; Henrician policy and action, including the execution of More himself, provided a revealing confirmation of the polity of Utopia.

If in reality political theory must derive from specific institutional and educational environments, in *Utopia* it derives from nowhere. At the end of Book 2, Hythlodaeus exposes what Marxist theorists would call 'ideology', the presentation of the interests of a specific group as both natural and in the public interest. He declares that contemporary 'common wealthes' are nothing but 'a certein conspiracy of riche men, procuringe theire owne commodoties under the name and title of the common wealth' (2. 9, p. 303). More himself

[84] Carlson, *English Humanist Books*, ch. 1.

[85] For the relaxation of censorship in 1547, see Ch. 7, below.

sedulously avoids the possibility that the polity of Utopia could be thought to represent any interest group whatsoever. The existence of the island is discussed in a period of *otium*, or relaxation, by disinterested intellectuals, and the work fictionally presents itself as passing among an international group of enlightened philosophical spirits, who communicate in the lingua franca of Latin. News of the island comes from the New World, a world with only the barest contacts with More's own, and with no lines of lineage back into the European past. Monsters on the other side of the world, 'because they be no news' (p. 33), are dismissed by More as he interrogates the philosopher-traveller Hythlodaeus: what More wants is news of political structures, not the monsters of classical or medieval travel narrative, let alone the monsters of England's own recent political past. In the dialogue of counsel in Book 1, indeed, Hythlodaeus implies the neutral strangeness and novelty of the Utopian system by arguing that it would be absolutely irrelevant and obnoxious to any actual European political system. The negative prefixes to Utopian proper names (translated as Nowhere Island, River Without Water, Prince No-People, and so on) not only imply More's scepticism about the possibility of such a polity even as he promotes it; they also preserve the island intact from any trace of actual history.

One aspect of the apparently unideological disinterestedness of the island is its difficulty of access. Geographically the island is entirely self-enclosed, since King Utopus had himself ordered a channel to be dug separating Utopia from the neighbouring land mass. It is dangerous even to try to regain entry to the island, since the channel is full of treacherous reefs that only the local pilots can navigate. The entirely self-sufficient Utopians do not proselytize, and they have not commissioned Hythlodaeus to promote their interests; on the contrary, Hythlodaeus denies the utility of his information, and wants only to be off. His readiness to be away, indeed, renders verification of the details of Utopia impossible. While More goes to considerable pains in his authenticating devices for his conversations with Hythlodaeus, the man himself has now disappeared, and the whereabouts of the island are uncertain. Peter Giles's prefatory letter remarks that Hythlodaeus did mention briefly in passing where the island was, but neither More nor Giles hear the crucial geographical details: by an unlucky chance a servant talked to More at that moment, and one of the crewmen coughed, from a cold he had caught on board ship (pp. xcviii–xcix). The very authenticating device of the sailor's cough equally prohibits authentication. Like the island itself, news about it is very precise, self-enclosed, and untouchable. It has all the clarity of a Platonic idea, complete at its own point of origin.

If the news of Utopia is complete and untouchable at its point of origin, so too is the Utopian commonwealth without significant historical development, either in the past or the future. In the past the conquest of the island by King Utopus 1,760 years before Hythlodaeus' visit was a complete victory over the previous inhabitants. No trace of this previous civilization exists except some words, since the conquering king 'brought the rude and wild people to that excellent perfection, in all good fassions, humanitie, and civile gentilnes, wherein they now go beyond al the people of the world' (2. 1, p. 118). This initial perfection promises to last for ever; in his conclusion, Hythlodaeus declares that the Utopians have 'laid such foundations of their common wealth, as shall continew and last, not only wealthely, but also . . . shall endure for ever' (2. 9, p. 307). The only changes are literally superficial: Utopus laid the ground plan of the city 'even at the first begenning', in the 'fasion and figure that it hath nowe' (2. 2, pp. 131–2); the chronicles can only record some development in the civility of domestic architecture.

The wholly rational, disinterested polity of Utopia, then, has escaped the predations of history, and seems, superficially at any rate, a remarkably generous and tolerant society. The Utopians practise an economy of communism, whereby all commodities are shared according to need; they share the burdens of physical labour; and they willingly cultivate the mind by attending public lectures after work. Above all, they practise religious tolerance. Very soon after his conquest King Utopus issued a decree 'that it shoulde be lawfull for every man to favoure and followe what religion he would' (2. 9, p. 271). Europeans bring two things to Utopia: Greek learning and Christianity. Both are readily appreciated, but the second introduces fanaticism: the Utopians quickly exile the Utopian convert to Christianity who becomes a Christian bigot (2. 9, p. 270). Varieties of religious persuasion are permitted, and even heretics from the broad terms of orthodoxy established by Utopus are allowed to defend their positions within certain confines (2. 9, pp. 272–7). Written in 1516, precisely on the verge of a period of unprecedented European religious persecution in which More was himself an active participant, *Utopia* imagines a society in which religious freedom is the right of all citizens.

This toleration, however, masks draconian demands of obedience to the state. Closer inspection of religious tolerance itself reveals that religious division is precisely the condition of Utopus' conquest and power. Before his conquest, Utopus hears that the inhabitants of the island are in a state of 'continuall dissention and stryfe among themselfes for their religions', and immediately recognizes that this is 'the only occasion of hys conquest over them all' (2. 9, p. 271). Utopus sanctions religious variety partly because he thinks it will further the interests of religion, but mainly because it contributes to his own control. Certainly tolerance is not in itself a value upheld at every turn in the Utopian polity, since tolerance allowed in one area simply exposes the higher loyalty demanded of citizens by the state. The most striking example of this are the fierce restrictions on political discussion described in the section dealing with the magistracy. The counsellors of each city's 'prince' are elected yearly, but changed only rarely. They meet each three days with the prince, where they 'dyspatche and ende' any controversy among the 'commoners', which disputes are in any case 'very fewe'. This remarkably efficient political process has a powerful constraint, however: it is a capital offence for anyone to 'have annye counsultatyon for the common wealthe owte of the cownsell, or the place of the common electyon' (2. 3, p. 137). The reason given for this ferocity is that such a system avoids tyrannical and private exercise of power by the leaders; there is no mention of the desires of any private individual or group of individuals to consult.

Neither could there be, since privacy is itself in exile in Utopia. In his conclusion Hythlodaeus claims that Europeans may talk about the common good, but that each person seeks only his private wealth. In Utopia, 'where nothing is pryvate, the common affayres be earnestly loked upon' (2. 9, p. 299). The fundamental assumption of the Utopian polity, indeed, is that private interests are necessarily pathological, and that decisions are to be based not merely on community, but rather on identity of interest. Apart from the absence of private property, the most obvious sign of the abolition of privacy is the identity of urban spaces and constant surveillance of all citizens. Cities may be larger or smaller, but they all observe an identical plan; the fifty-four cities each 'agreyng all together in one tonge, in lyke maners, institucions, and lawes' (2. 1, p. 119); private houses are identical and interchanged; doors have no locks and give admittance to anyone; meals are taken in common, overseen by the magistrate and with the young set among the old, so that 'nothyng can be so secretly spoken or done at the table' that will not be perceived; travel requires permission. All Utopia is, in Hythlodaeus' words, 'one famelie or housholde' (2. 6, p. 170), but this is to say that there are no households. Politics, for writers in the Aristotelian tradition, consists in the contracts made from the conflicting interests of different jurisdictions. Utopia has so nationalized the family, however, as effectively to abolish it, since there are no distinct private jurisdictions. Utopians have so identified with the abstract reason of the state that they have become identical. It is said that they enjoy the Greek satirist Lucian (second century AD), but this is implausible, since appreciation of irony necessarily involves the ability to adopt different positions.[86]

The only properly named Utopian is the king Utopus; the other inhabitants of the island are referred to in the third-person plural pronoun. Utopus' own name, however, itself threatens to become a common name 'No place'; I conclude this discussion of *Utopia* by pausing on the presence and curious absence of the king. More reported a daydream in a letter to Erasmus written in 1516 that 'I have been marked out by my Utopians to be their king forever.'[87] More dreamed of power just a year before he formally entered the service of Henry VIII,[88] but his humanist's dream of power very appropriately emerges from Utopia itself, since that society has so thoroughly absorbed the disinterested abstraction of Reason that the king himself is invisible yet omnipresent.

On the face of it, More's dream misunderstands the constitution of Utopia, since there is, apparently, no king on the island. Every thirty families elect an official representative (a 'Syphograunt'), each ten

[86] More himself translated Lucian in 1505–6; see More, *Translations of Lucian*, ed. Thompson.

[87] More, *Selected Letters*, ed. Rogers, letter 11, pp. 83–5, at 85.

[88] Hexter, p. 135.

of whom in turn elect another (a 'Tranibor'). This second tier of officials serves as the permanent council of the 'princeps'. The office of 'princeps', however, does not represent the whole island. Instead, in each of the fifty-four cities the 'people' of each quarter nominate a 'princeps', from among which four names the Syphograunts of each city elect the prince (of the city) for life. There is only one national assembly, which takes place annually with three representatives from each city, the manner of whose election is unspecified (2. 1, p. 119). The structure of city government is quite carefully constructed, while the national government is vague and almost non-existent. There is apparently no place for More's fantasy of personal kingship, since there is no king. Certainly the Latin text does not style Utopus as a king, although the English translation does.

Or is there a king? Constitutions of the kind described by More are usually characteristic of federations of states with heterogeneous traditions (e.g. Switzerland). The laws, language, customs, and architecture of each Utopian city are, however, identical, and imply a moment of massive centralization *prior to the existence* of the political process. The political process does not deal with difference, that is, since it is premissed on the abolition of difference. So while Utopia is superfically a 'representative democracy with free elections',[89] this democracy is itself premissed on, and designed to disguise, its opposite. More himself cannot confront this contradiction, since while he makes it plain that King Utopus established the whole constitution, he does not describe the process by which King Utopus abolished himself. In a profound sense, however, Utopus did not abolish himself, since the signs of centralization are everywhere apparent. The Utopians do not have proper names, since propriety is a crime in Utopia. King Utopus, however, does have a proper name. More tries to dissolve the propriety of 'Utopus' by making it a common name (No place) that shades into an adverb (Nowhere), but he cannot do away with the all-powerful and enduringly powerful king. King Utopus is Nowhere and Everywhere at the same time, a proper and a common noun. More's fantasy of being king of all Utopia is in fact a very accurate account of the Utopian constitution, since the commonality of Utopia is necessarily premissed on its opposite,

[89] *Utopia*, ed. Surtz and Hexter, p. 398.

an opposite visible in the trace of the single proper name. It also produces its opposite, since the slaves of the Utopians must necessarily become the 'private' property of the corporation of Utopians. King Utopus is the mirror image of Hythlodaeus' all-consuming sheep in Book 1: just as the brutish and bodily animal consumes all of contemporary England, the purely abstract Utopus/reason consumes all Utopia.

While More poses, then, as the wholly non-ideological, disinterested spokesman for a purely rational polity, the work exposes a desire for massive centralization, and for the abolition of jurisdictions not answerable directly to the state. Such an argument seems to ignore the playful, Lucianic quality of *Utopia*, but if *Utopia* is, as many critics have argued, a game, then it seems to me a peculiarly dangerous game, whereby the player successively exposes and conceals a dream of absolute power. The centralizing impetus of *Utopia* derives in part from More's primary sources; it is also precisely predictive of Henrician polity in the 1530s. Plato's *Republic* is More's primary model and rival: in the prefatory verses fictionally written by Hythlodaeus' nephew, More has it that *Utopia* is a 'rival, perhaps even a victor over Plato's city'.[90] Plato's *Republic* also promotes the abolition of private and separate jurisdictions, just as Henrician policy itself did in the 1530s.

That abolition is a large topic, but suffice it here to list four consecutive chapters of a Henrician statute of 1536. Chapter 25 deals with the punishment of sturdy beggars, including the proviso that any idler who, after having been publicly whipped for idleness once is caught again, shall be whipped again and 'have the upper part of the gristell of his right eare clene cutt of',[91] a sign recommended by Hythlodaeus for thieves, but considered by Morton suitable also for vagrants (1. 25, pp. 68, 72). Chapter 26 of the statute is very Utopian in spirit, designed as it is to abolish differences of law and language between England and Wales by incorporating Wales wholly within the jurisdiction of England; chapter 27 establishes the Court of Augmentations in order to administer the nationalized properties of the monasteries; and chapter 28 dissolves the smaller abbeys.[92] More's

[90] Ibid. 21.
[91] *SR*, 27 Henry VIII, ch. 25.10 (3. 560).
[92] Ibid., chs. 26–8 (3. 563–78).

Utopia, with its many strategic similarities to sixteenth-century Britain, expresses the Platonic desire for the identification of kings and 'rationalizing' philosophers. In so doing it not only predicts the rationalization of the 1530s, but also exposes the humanist ideology of disinterestedness: texts of this kind speak in the joint interests of centralizing kings and the bureaucrats who serve them. In Utopia, indeed, the prince is himself elected from among the caste of scholars, a small but very significant detail of the electoral system that More only mentions in a later section (2. 4, p. 148). Of course in Henrician England there are dangers for such bureaucrats. *Utopia* itself would have justified More's execution in Utopia, since it discusses policy outside the Council; in this sense More also accurately predicted his own execution.

It is certainly the case that the new economic conditions of the sixteenth century, and especially the massive rise in both population and prices, exerted new bureaucratic pressures; from the evidence of the literary, intellectual, and legislative history here, however, there is no call to describe this period as the expression of 'constitutional' consciousness. For Elton the Tudor monarchy was 'powerful only as long as it did not go outside the limits laid down by a nation'.[93] This effaces the ways in which the 'nation' was in many ways a product of Tudor legislation that had itself dissolved many limits on state power, limits that are clearly visible in the articulate regiminal works of the fifteenth century.

(*e*) Policy in the 1530s

Utopia was by far the most radical 'policy' text published in the reign of Henry VIII. What of the 1530s, the decade that in Ferguson's formulation was 'unusually conducive to thoughtful discussion'? In this section I deal briefly with three representative vernacular examples, Sir Thomas Elyot's *The Boke Named the Governour* (1531); Richard Morison's *Remedy for Sedition* (1536); and Thomas Starkey's *Dialogue between Pole and Lupset* (composed between 1529 and 1532).

Elyot's *Boke Named the Governour* need not detain us very long,

[93] Elton, *Tudor Revolution*, p. 4.

since it is rather an educational than a political treatise. Elyot's own political persuasions, or at least what are presented as such, are very clearly stated at the beginning of the work: without order chaos ensues, and order proceeds from a single fountainhead. Just as the intellect is the highest part of the soul, so too should those of higher understanding rule over those of lower, 'where they may se and also be sene' (bk. 1, ch. 1). In particular, a monarchy is necessary for the preservation of order; aristocracy and democracy lead easily to disorder, terror, and cruelty (1. 2). The immediate consequence of this is that a king requires 'magistrates'; these should be chosen (how is not said) from among those already 'superiour in condition' and wealthy (1. 3), and they should advise the king (Elyot has nothing to say about parliament). The rest of Book 1 offers a programme of liberal education for the aristocratic magistracy, whose most interesting feature is the extended comparison of dancing and prudence (1. 19–25). The remaining two books expatiate on the cardinal virtues, which the governors must practise. Elyot's reading is very wide and delightfully eclectic, but the text abjures specific institutional questions altogether, and stays on the much safer ground of aristocratic education in the humanities, liberally seasoned with suitably distant classical example.

Richard Morison's *Remedy for Sedition* (1536) is much more of the moment, written as Henrician apologetics for Henry's brutal repression of the northern-centred Pilgrimage of Grace of 1536, the most concerted rebellion against Henry's religious reforms.[94] The text is a rather simple call to obedience to the king's laws; its most interesting aspect is the deployment of characteristically humanist positions and learning in the name of obedience. Unlike Elyot, Morison was not nobly born, and like Starkey he had been educated in Padua.[95] Accordingly, he defines nobility more broadly than Elyot, and appeals directly to the King for confirmation of the 'nobility of soul' argument: the King has always declared, he says, that 'true nobilite is never, but where virtue is' (B.i^{v}). Henry is himself a master of the sciences (F.iv^{r-v}), and he should promote the education of his people, since lack of education, and not poverty, provoked the

94 *RSTC* 18113.5.
95 See *DNB*.

rebellion in the first place. This may sound appropriately enlightened, but the rest of the treatise rigorously excludes almost everyone from the benefits of education. Only the sons of nobles and the better part of gentlemen should be educated; 'it is no part of peoples play to discusse actes made in the parlyment' (B.iv), since 'Lordes must be lordes, comunes must be comunes' (B.iv).Tenants must be of the same religion as their lords, and the 'kinges grace shall never have true subiectes, that do not beleve as his grace doth' (D.iii), and neither should Englishmen call themselves Northerners and Southerners, since they are all Englishmen (E.i). The most striking exhibition of humanist learning in the name of popular repression comes in the citation of Chaucer. Morison knows his poetry, and cites both Dante and Chaucer to the effect that the vulgar are inconstant; the stanza-long Chaucerian citation is from the *Clerk's Tale*, lines 995–1001. While the Clerk expresses these sentiments in support of Griselda oppressed by the tyrannical Walter, Morison's use, and alteration, of Chaucer would put him on the side of Walter. Morison addresses the insurgents thus:

> O sterne people uniuste and untrewe
> Ay undiscrete, and chaungynge as a fane [weathervane]
> Delytynge ever in rumours that be newe:
> For lyke the mone ever waxe ye and wane
> Your reason halteth, your iugement is lame
> Youre doom is false, youre constance evyll preveth; [judgement]
> A full great foole is he that on yow leveth. [believes]
>
> (B.i^{r})[96]

The argument that true nobility consists in the cultivation of virtue rather than in birth or wealth had been used by many non-noble, and some noble, European writers throughout the thirteenth to the fifteenth centuries.[97] Morison's deployment of the topos looks more like a pitch for his own promotion than the basis of any broadening of popular education or engagement in politics.

[96] For the 'official' versus the 'unofficial' versions of Chaucer in Henrician England, see Watkins, and Lerer, *Courtly Letters*, esp. ch. 5.

[97] For a conspectus of examples and further references, see Simpson, *Sciences and the Self*, p. 295. For 16th-cent. reception of the idea, see Skinner, 'More's *Utopia*', pp. 135–47.

Both Elyot's and Morison's works were immediately published, whereas the final text of policy I consider, Thomas Starkey's *Dialogue between Pole and Lupset*, remained unpublished until the nineteenth century. Whereas Elyot steered cautiously clear of anything like a specific programme of reform, and while Morison's pamphlet devised reform in the service of specific royal needs at a moment of crisis, Starkey's text, by contrast, brims with very radical and considered proposals for far-reaching reform. The nature of these proposals demonstrates both that the Aristotelian tradition I have described above was still a perfectly serious option in the sixteenth century, and that political, vernacular Aristotelianism is very conscious of its differences from the Platonic models adopted by, say, More.

Starkey (*c.*1495–1538) spent thirteen years in Italy after finishing his Oxford MA. While in the later 1530s he, too, acted as a mouthpiece for Cromwell, the republican ideals of both Venice and Padua find powerful expression in the *Dialogue* (1529–32), mainly through the voice of his patron Reginald Pole.[98] The whole text became thoroughly unpublishable from early in the 1530s, not only because Pole refused to acknowledge Henry's supremacy in the Church, but also, more profoundly, because many of Starkey's proposals would have become treasonous by 1534. Although the unfinished state of the manuscript itself does not divide the work into chapters, I follow the divisions of one editor, which seem to me to divide the work by its proper conceptual parts.[99]

In chapter 1 Lupset persuades Pole of the superiority of the active life; while he agrees with Pole that many philosophers have shunned the life of active engagement because they have had such bad kings, Henry is a good king, ready to be instructed by his counsellors. Pole is persuaded by Lupset's arguments, after which the dialogue turns to the theoretical basis for the political order. Pole argues that the worldly prosperity of a single man offers a model of the ideal for the commonwealth, to which Lupset counters with Christian arguments about the superiority of poverty. Pole's reply to this argument is

[98] For biography, and further references, see Thomas Starkey, *Dialogue between Pole and Lupset*, ed. Mayer, pp. vii–xii.

[99] *Dialogue between Reginald Pole and Thomas Lupset*, ed. Burton. I will cite by chapter and page number in the body of the text.

decisive for the rest of the dialogue: while some argue that the soul is the whole man, others, 'more agreeing to the common reason of man', affirm that man is rather 'a certain nature which riseth of the union and conjunction of the body and soul togidder' (ch. 2, p. 52). This anthropology, or conception of human make-up, drives Pole's thoroughly Aristotelian politics, since he remains committed to an embodied conception of the political order, whereby the 'soul' finds its fullest expression in the body. The body he interprets as 'the multitude of people', and the soul is 'civil order and politic law adminstered by officers and rulers' (ch. 2, p. 55). Pole explicitly registers the anti-Platonic force of this argument. Whereas in *Utopia* the body is a necessary evil whose needs must be satisfied before the life of the mind can be attended to, for Pole the pressures of the body are themselves what rightly inform the life of the mind. While Plato, he says, might agree with Christ that the soul only is 'the very man, whereof the body is but a prison', Aristotle's whole man is, by contrast, body and soul together; accordingly, 'felicity in the highest degree is not without worldly prosperity' (ch. 2, p. 54).

The most radical of the proposals Pole makes is for an elected monarchy. He argues that the primary problem from which England has suffered has been the tyrannical wilfulness of unelected kings: a country cannot be well governed 'where all is ruled by the will of one not chosen by election but cometh to it by natural succession; for seldon it is that they which by succession come to kingdoms and realms are worthy of such high authority' (ch. 4, p. 99). It is true that Pole later withdraws this point on a practical objection that such a system would cause dissension, but the principle remains intact; indeed, he returns to it when the discussion considers how best to institute the ideal commonwealth. After the death of Henry VIII, there should be a parliamentary election for his successor, who 'should not rule and govern all at his own pleasure and liberty, but ever be subject to the order of his laws' (ch. 5, p. 154). Pole favours a 'mixed state', for when any one part of the state has complete power, 'the rest shall suffer the tyranny thereof and be put to great misery' (ch. 6, p. 165). In Pole's view this process is now at its height, and requires the institution of a variety of checks, including a powerful connection between the king's council and parliament.

Starkey's unpublished dialogue is a fitting place to end the argument of this chapter concerning the shape of 'policy' across the period of this history. Starkey speaks for the Aristotelian tradition of 'bodily' politics that we have seen in various forms throughout the fourteenth and fifteenth centuries, of which the main characteristic is constraint of the king. Starkey's is a much more thoroughgoing example of the tradition, and his system of institutional checks on royal authority is more complete than anything previously proposed, even by Fortescue, for whom parliament counted little. For Starkey, the concentration of power in the hands of the king is a process that culminates in the reign of Henry VIII; the literary evidence of this chapter would concur with that analysis. The republican influence on English monarchical thought did not cease in the mid-sixteenth century, but it did become unpublishable. A paradox may lie behind this narrowing of intellectual space: once the printing press had given much greater access to books, then that very liberty of access produced a restriction of published thought. It is perhaps significant that early printers did not exploit texts in the broadly Aristotelian political tradition, despite their evident popularity in manuscript right through the fifteenth century: Hoccleve, for example, was not printed at all. Fortescue was not printed in English until 1567.

IV

If we were to imagine the realm of politics spatially, then to write policy is to find a way into that space. Almost all the works we have so far considered were produced by way of securing preferment or payment, and of necessity they commit themselves to the active life. Other varieties of broadly 'political' writing are instead written either on the boundary of the political space, or else altogether on the outside, in complete and conscious rejection of the active life. The writing produced from both these positions is expressive less of political thought than of social experience: life within the physically and psychologically narrow conditions of court life both repels and attracts. In this section I deal briefly with examples of each of these two positions, before ending with a discussion of political fable literature.

(*a*) Withdrawal

Stoicism promoted engagement in the active life, but Stoics also knew that 'the slipper top of | Of court's estates' was a dangerous game; every political career ends in failure, then as now, and the Stoic needs to cultivate the resources to deal with that failure, in time. Wyatt's own lyric on the subject, translated from the Stoic Seneca's *Thyestes*, contrasts the measured life of cultivated withdrawal with the lurid and sudden end of the courtier, whom 'death grip'th right hard by the crop | That is much known of other, and of himself, alas, | Doth die unknown, dazed, and with a dreadful face'.[100] Certainly in the sixteenth century there are new models for contemplative withdrawal, but the need for models of withdrawal is constant throughout the period of this history. In the sixteenth century, for example, before writing *Utopia* and before joining the king's service, More had translated and published a text from Medicean Florence, the *Life of Pico* (*c*.1510), which, in contrast to the earlier writings of republican Florence, eulogized the life of retirement and withdrawal for the modern scholar. Offered a position in a king's court, Pico replies that he 'neither desired worship ne worldly richess but rather set them at nought that he might the more quietly give him self to studie and the service of god'.[101] Later in the reign Thomas Wyatt had offered a timely gift to Queen Katherine (of Aragon) in New Year 1527, Plutarch's *Quyete of Mynde*, in which he offers Stoic advice on the preservation of mental tranquillity whatever one's circumstances.[102]

Fifteenth-century texts also advocate a life of scholarly retirement. Thus Lydgate in his *Fall of Princes* (1431–8) points out to his patron Humphrey Duke of Gloucester that poets need peace. They also need payment, however, and Lydgate accordingly proceeds to ask the prince for some bounty (3. 3823–71). If in that fantasy poetic retirement might be on good terms with the world, the overall force of this huge text is rather designed to prepare governors for brutal falls. The

[100] 'Stand whoso list upon the slipper top', in Wyatt, *Complete Poems*, ed. Rebholz, no. 49, p. 94.

[101] More, *Life of Pico*, ed. Edwards, p. 66.

[102] The text was printed by Pynson in ?1528; see the facsimile edn., Wyatt (trans.), *Plutarch's Quyete of Mynde*.

sheer density, variety, and rapidity of noble descents in this work finally beggars any ethical account of why kings fall; they just do, whatever their ethical status. Lydgate himself does not offer the philosophical resources to deal with that inevitable fall, but fifteenth-century English readers had translations of Boethius' Latin *Consolation of Philosophy* at hand, made in prose by Chaucer (before 1387) and in verse by John Walton (*c.*1410).[103] Boethius' work is the ideal text for both nobles and bureaucrats whose luck has run out. Boethius (d. 524) wrote the *Consolation* in prison; his opening laments about the injustice by which he was sentenced to death on false charges of corruption in the imperial bureaucracy quickly give way to his acceptance of Philosophy's Stoic counsel. All gifts of Fortune are transitory, and do not provide self-sufficiency, which can only be found in the stability of the eternal soul. The philosopher should contribute to the commonwealth, but calm, even impassive resignation is the only appropriate response to the predictably unpredictable changes of worldly fortune.

Boethius' work of resigned and philosophical detachment on the one hand, and 'Aristotelian' works of political engagement on the other are not exclusive. The old man in Hoccleve's *Regement* plays the role of Philosophy to the lamenting bureaucrat Hoccleve, who rejects the Boethian advice. Unlike the old man, Hoccleve's fortunes are not entirely depleted, and so he commits himself to the active life.[104] The rejection of Boethius is not, however, uncompromising: Stoic detachment is the threshold across which any intelligent participation in politics must first pass, and to which it will later return. Walton's verse translation accompanies Hoccleve's text in three manuscripts, setting Boethius (withdrawal) and Aristotle (engagement) together. The same pattern is found in the patronage of Walton's text: the Berkeley family not only patronized Walton's Boethius, but also, probably, Trevisa's translation of Giles of Rome's *De regimine principum*.[105] Engagement in politics is a virtue, and necessary in any case; all the same, one wants the psychological escape route planned in advance.

[103] Walton (trans.), *Boethius: De Consolatione Philosophiae*, ed. Science.
[104] Simpson, 'Nobody's Man'.
[105] Hanna, 'Sir Thomas Berkeley'.

(*b*) Curial Satire

The texts we have just considered advocate complete rejection of politics, or rather prepare their readers for rejection *by* politics. This penultimate subsection considers works fictionally presented on the edge of court, poised either for re-entry or rejection. These works manifest the divided consciousness characteristic of enclosed and attractive, yet threatening communities. Whereas, as we saw in Chapter 4, scholars of the early modern period have claimed that mobile, performative, divided selves are specific to post-medieval texts, my examples are drawn from across the span of this history. The theatrical and divided self is not specific to the Renaissance; it is specific to certain kinds of community.

A range of late fourteenth-century poets practise a broad satire designed to address and criticize each order of society ('Estates Satire'). In English the Prologues to Chaucer's 'General Prologue' to the *Canterbury Tales* (*c.*1390), Gower's *Confessio Amantis* (1390), and Langland's *Piers Plowman* (B version, *c.*1377) each adopt a narratorial position that is engaged yet non-partisan. The voice both surveys and implicitly addresses the whole nation, conceived as a set of occupations or estates.[106] Gower does the same thing in Latin in his *Vox Clamantis* (pre-1386). This inclusive mode is not, however, practised in the fifteenth century, mainly, presumably, for reasons of censorship on anticlerical material.[107] In the sixteenth century satire of broadly this kind reappears in what might be called 'fool' satire: Alexander Barclay's generously inclusive *Ship of Fools* (produced for Pynson's press in 1509) welcomes fools of all varieties without discrimination. The same is true of Erasmus's *Encomium Moriae* (1511), which turns the favourite humanist mode of panegyric against humanists, courtiers, and a broad range of ecclesiastical types. An English translation by Sir Thomas Chaloner was published as *The Praise of Folie* in 1549, once censorship had been relaxed, but by which time the broad range of estates satirized by Erasmus in 1511 no longer existed in England.[108]

106 For Estates Satire, see Mann, *Chaucer and Medieval Estates Satire*; for the narratorial perspective, see Middleton, 'Idea of Public Poetry'.

107 For which see Ch. 7.

108 Erasmus, *The Praise of Folie, by Sir Thomas Chaloner*, ed. Miller.

As distinct from Estates Satire, varieties of court, or 'curial', satire are much more consistently practised throughout the period of this history. Book 1 of *Utopia* is itself a reflex of the genre, but the most concentrated compendium of anti-curial topoi is the pithy little *Curial* of Alain Chartier, translated and published by Caxton in 1484, in the middle of Richard III's short reign. The work is a letter written in prose by a courtier to his brother, dissuading the brother from following him into the indignities and dangers of court from the peace of private life, yet never once suggesting that he will himself abandon the court. The critique of court is not at all political; it is, rather a critique of a particular mode of life in which the courtier is robbed of any of the decencies of private existence. One eats and sleeps badly, is never alone, and is forever subject to the attack of competitors for the king's favour. Words are weapon and defence: the courtier says he is surrounded night and day, 'for I have nede to beholde on what foot that every man cometh to me, and to note and marke the paas and peryl of every worde that departeth from my mouth'.[109]

The fact that Caxton could print this for a large market suggests that the words of curial satire are not themselves very dangerous. The same is true of Skelton's early *Bouge of Court* (?1498), since that was also published (by Wynkyn de Worde in 1499), and may draw on the conventions of court drama.[110] In it the narrator, a court poet, is certainly trying to enter court life, as indeed Skelton (?1460–1529) was for most of his career, with varying success under two monarchs.[111] For all that, the poem (539 lines in rhyme-royal stanzas) is unsettling 'entertainment', representing as it does the suicide of the poet-courtier. Wanting to begin, the poet is unable to start the work, for fear of being like the fool who 'clymmeth hyer than he may fotynge have' (l. 27); he falls asleep and dreams that he boards a ship owned by Dame 'Saunce Pere', with whose merchandise the ship is loaded. Accosted and threated by Danger, the narrator declares that his name is Drede. Encouraged by Desire, Drede stays on board, but the rest of the poem consists of Drede's encounters with his 'companions' on board, a series of extremely menacing court types.

[109] Caxton (trans.), *The Curial, Made by Maystere Alain Charretier*, ed. Furnivall, p. 11.

[110] See Winser.

[111] See G. Walker, *John Skelton*.

The whole sequence concludes with Drede's attempted suicide as he jumps overboard, at which point he wakes to write the little poem we have just read. During the dream sequence the craft of writing is exposed as vulnerable and enfeebled beside the real exercise of craft practised by the courtiers. On the face of it, the writing of the poem at the end might mark a moment of authorial courage and decisiveness after the authorial diffidence of the dream sequence, where writing is hidden. The moment of authorial courage at the end, however, resolves back into its reverse, as we are returned to the hesitancy of the poem's opening. The poet as critic of the court is himself overtaken by the persona of Drede, so much so that a secondary sense of 'drede' emerges: beyond 'fear', the word can mean 'doubt, uncertainty'.[112] Drede is drawn by the desire of the 'bouche', or 'pouch', of court, but this desire diminishes the authority of his own *bouche* or mouth. This is less an example of court satire than a representation of money speaking, and thereby failing to gain any solid ground from which to launch court satire. The poetic incapacity represented *in* the poem is very nearly balanced by the incapacities *of* the poem; this very incapacity, luridly focused in the attempted authorial suicide, is the source of the poem's power.

Skelton's *Bouge of Court* may be 'entertainment', but its unresolved excesses, both of courtly viciousness and authorial fragility, resist easy categorization. The same is not true of Skelton's rival for court favour, Alexander Barclay, in his *Eclogues* (*c.*1514), where assertions about the danger of speaking unsuccessfully attempt to distract attention from flattery. Barclay pitches his court satire from the perspective of eclogue: shepherds debate the pros and cons of court life. This unlikely scenario (translated from the Latin *De Curialium Miseriis* of Aeneas Sylvius Piccolomini, later Pope Pius II), is more believable, however, than the attacks on court life, since those attacks are outweighed by eulogies of past and potential patrons, which include John Morton, John Alcock, Henry VII, Henry VIII, and the Duke of Norfolk. Barclay wants nothing more than to be accepted in court.[113] The same is true of Dunbar in his court satires for James IV of Scotland, which amusingly express the

[112] *MED*, sense 4 (a).
[113] For Barclay's career, see Fox, ch. 3.

courtier-poet's total exhaustion and yet display his extraordinarily energetic power of verbal invention, particularly in the exercise of invective.[114]

If Barclay's pastoral pose fails to match the preciosity of Virgilian political allusion, Sir Thomas Wyatt's Horatian pose allows for a much tauter balance between the power of court and that of country propriety. Wyatt drew on Seneca to express the appalling brutalities of courtly punishment in both 'Stand Whoso list' and 'Who list his wealth and ease retain', the second of which almost certainly evokes the unforgettable trauma of witnessing the execution of Anne Boleyn in May 1536.[115] His satires adopt instead a Horatian posture of country detachment from the alienating lubricities of court life.[116]

'Mine own John Poyntz' (103 lines in *terza rima*),[117] imitated from a satire (1532) by the exiled Florentine Luigi Alamanni, was probably written soon after Wyatt's own temporary exile from court in 1536, having narrowly escaped execution. Horace's praise of propriety informs the linguistic, topographical, and ethical stance of the poem. Linguistically, Wyatt disowns the courtier's rhetorical practice of both antithesis (calling black white to please the king, ll. 19–57), and paradiastole, the figure whereby one uses the mean virtue to describe the extreme vice (or vice versa), 'As', for example, 'drunkeness good fellowship to call' (ll. 58–75). Instead Wyatt praises linguistic propriety, and so deploys homely proverbial and alliterative techniques. Geographically, he is 'at home', 'in Kent and Christendom', hunting and hawking, or, in bad weather, reading. These rhetorical and geographical affinities, which are at once claims of ethical propriety, stand poised against the incursions on privacy implied or expressed by the same text. In 1536 'Christendom' means something very different for Wyatt in Kent than it did for Chaucer, to whom Wyatt alludes; indeed, Wyatt himself expresses a disgust for the practices of France, Spain, Flanders, and Rome. This very much implies his presence in the king's England, just as the 'clog', an impediment attached to the foot, does also (l. 86). Wyatt may praise Cato, who committed suicide rather than accept the rule of Caesar

114 See, e.g. Dunbar, *Selected Poems*, ed. Bawcutt, nos. 55–7.
115 Wyatt, *Collected Poems*, ed. Rebholz, no. 123, p. 154.
116 See C. Burrow.
117 Cited from *The Complete Poems*, ed. R. A. Rebholz (Penguin, 1978), no. 149.

(l. 38), but this very reference is altered from Alamanni's 'Brutus'. Wyatt's very expression of propriety consists mostly of negative statements, speaking about court even as he abjures it. Wyatt may declare that he is unable to 'cloak the truth' (l. 20), but he is himself 'wrapped within my cloak' (l. 5): his affirmation of propriety is at the same time directed towards court, to whose service Wyatt soon returned, possibly as an assassin.[118] The potential collapse of anti-curial propriety into curial impropriety is dramatized in Wyatt's third satire (1538), where the narrative voice persuasively insists on the fact that there is no alternative to survival in court. The narrator's voice is of course ironic, but the irony undoes itself.[119]

The variety of Tudor curial satire may imply that the intensely self-conscious and self-doubting posture of such writing may be characteristic of the early modern period. Certainly the increasing dependence of writers on Tudor courtly patronage elicits such writing, and certainly the unrelievably nightmarish experience of court expressed in, say, Skelton's *Bouge of Court* or Hawes's *Comfort of Lovers* (1509),[120] is unmatched by earlier examples. For all that, the rhetorical and psychological theatricality of curial satire have very long traditions.[121] Such writing is not so much a periodic as a sociological phenomenon, the product of small, highly articulate, and highly competitive social groupings.

One early fifteenth-century example must suffice, which, while not exactly curial satire, expresses exactly the alienating and destabilizing experience of court life found in all curial satire. After proferring the *Regement of Princes* in 1412, Hoccleve seems to have been taken on as a spokesman for official policy, exemplified by his strident *Remonstrance against Oldcastle* (1415).[122] Probably just before this, in 1414, Hoccleve seems to have suffered a nervous breakdown of sorts, the isolating social effects of which he complains in his moving *Complaint* and *Dialogue* of 1419–20 (1,239 lines in rhyme-royal stanzas).[123] Like the *Regement*, these compan-

[118] For the circumstantial evidence that Wyatt's assignation was to assassinate Cardinal Pole, see Brigden, '"The shadow that yow know"'.

[119] D. Starkey, 'Court'.

[120] See Ch. 4, above, for discussion.

[121] For the development of such writing in the episcopal courts, see Jaeger.

[122] For which see Ch. 7, below.

[123] For the precise dating, see J. A. Burrow, *Thomas Hoccleve*, pp. 16–29.

ion texts are designed to reintegrate Hoccleve with both powerful patrons, in this case Humphrey Duke of Gloucester, and a broader readership.

Negotiated reintegration through this poem is much more difficult, however, since the position from which Hoccleve starts is not penury, but the imputation of madness. Whereas curial satirists often imply their own authenticity by addressing a friend, Hoccleve's problem is that his friends themselves distrust him. When he goes into 'Westmynster Hall', his place of work as a clerk, he sees the expression of his former friends 'abaten and apalle' (l. 74); if he avoids 'the prees [the throng]' of the court, then his 'friends' consider him 'fallen in ageyn' (l. 182). This no-win situation is most powerfully expressed in Hoccleve's account of his private self-reflection. Fleeing his friends, he retreats to his room and to his mirror, to see if his face 'any othir were it than it oghte' (l. 159), and to amend it for public consumption. Paradoxically, the place of greatest privacy turns out to offer no asylum, invaded as it is by the public gaze. The first solution to this experience of eroding self-confidence is Boethian withdrawal, an insulated self-sufficiency in which he cares not for the 'peples ymaginacioun' (l. 380). While ostensibly accepting this authoritative Stoic escape route, Hoccleve in fact rejects it, since in the Dialogue that follows he actively pursues the alternative possibility of persuading his readership, in the person of a friend who drops by, that he is sane. The friend's acceptance of Hoccleve's sanity implies that the Boethian solution is in fact a recipe for further madness, since the way to real cure lies in 'communyge', or dialogue. Boethian resignation, the text implies, is the very last thing Hoccleve needs. The friend, who initially tries to dissuade Hoccleve from publishing his Complaint, is now persuaded that publication will be productive. His change of mind turns on Hoccleve's argument that no one can fully judge 'how it standith with anothir wight [person]' (l. 478). The premiss of publication, then, is recognition of authorial privacy and integrity.[124] A qualification for successful operation under the intense and invasive scrutiny of court is the cultivation of a private and integral self.

[124] Simpson, 'Madness and Texts'.

(c) Political Animals

Aristotle's perception that humans are political animals informs most of the policy writing that we have observed in this chapter. A small but extremely pointed tradition of animal fable makes rather different mileage out of the same connection, by exposing the bestiality of power.[125] Animals are never far away from political satire: the Prologue to Langland's *Piers Plowman* suddenly takes the indirection of animal fable as soon as specific matters of royal control are broached; *Richard the Redeless* narrates recent political history in animal terms; Wyatt's second satire is a version of the Town Mouse and Country Mouse. The specific tradition of animal fable tends to despair of political reform and therefore of the poet's power to promote that reform. That despair finds voice especially in a long sequence of talking bird poems.

Robert Henryson's *Fables* (2,975 lines in rhyme-royal stanzas) are by far the most powerful example of the genre.[126] Henryson (*fl.* 1460–80) was a schoolmaster and also, possibly, a notary public in Dunfermline, Scotland; his Aesopian fables take up the legal situations of this standard school text to reshape the tradition in astonishingly powerful ways. While some of these narratives (e.g. 'The Two Mice') gain their comedy from the imitative pleasure gained from watching animals act like humans, most of the fables are instead dark, often Swiftian reflections on the fact that humans are like animals. While the 'Lion and the Mouse' holds out the possibility of the lion-king recognizing his dependency on the mice-commons, for the most part these fables work on either side of the failure of policy: on the one hand the brutal dog-eat-dog world of the law of nature neutralizes any power that positive, human law might have, and so on the other no discourse but that of impotent despair or prayer merits consideration.

A key feature of fable is the necessity to maintain territorial and linguistic propriety: in Henryson's fables animals suffer immediately they step outside their own boundaries. By the same token, these stories also underline the consequences of rejecting apparent impro-

[125] For a brief conspectus of animal fable in English, see Simpson, 'Beast Epic and Fable'.

[126] Henryson, *Poems*, ed. Fox, pp. 3–110; see also D. Gray, *Robert Henryson*.

priety too easily. The cock in the 'Cock and the Jasp' carefully rejects the jasp as improper to his own low station, and is reprimanded for it. The narrator's rebuke to the cock implicitly also rebukes his human readers who disregard animal stories from the dunghill of literature as irrelevant to human concerns. The difficulties and dangers of maintaining propriety are the constant theme of political bird poems across the period of this history. Chaucer's *Manciple's Tale* (362 lines in five-stress rhyming couplets) plays a critical function in the winding down of the *Canterbury Tales* (1390–1400); Chaucer marks the withdrawal of his own voice from the public realm with the story of Apollo's bird, who is punished for speaking the truth in terms rhetorically fit for base and scandalous actions. The narrative ends with the recommendation of silence, except in speaking about God; from the perspective of this tale, the following *Parson's Tale* is not so much salutary as safe. The brutal silencing of the truth-telling satirist marks the larger silencing of poetry, as Apollo in fury breaks his own 'mynstralcie, | Both harpe, and lute' (ll. 267–8).

The connections between lyric and satire are also at issue in Lydgate's brilliant little *Churl and the Bird* (386 lines in rhyme-royal stanzas), in which the lyrical bird refuses to sing once it has been imprisoned by the churl. The churl releases the bird only on condition that it will offer him wisdom once released. One piece of wisdom the bird offers is not to desire the impossible, but the churl weeps in anguish when the bird goes on to tell him that he contained a precious jewel that the churl could have had if he had not released him. Only now does the bird reveal that he is empty, and that the churl is all the more fool for having wished for the impossible. The model of poet–patron relations in this complex poem is of poetic shrewdness and patronal stupidity, in the face of which poetic shrewdness is articulate but helpless. The deeper thrust of the poem is that noble patrons must not dismiss a narrative about churls as improper to their own interests. Henryson's beautiful 'Preaching of the Swallow' expresses despair at the ineffectiveness of the prudential voice, warning the Commons more than the king, while Skelton's *Speke Parrott* (520 lines in varying metres, written 1519–22) also deploys the speaking bird to create an extraordinarily mobile satiric voice, which is at once gossipy, polyglot, malicious, and dismissible as the ravings of a chatterbox.

The larger contrast of this chapter is between an Aristotelian-derived tradition of the political imagination, characteristic of the fourteenth and fifteenth centuries, with its sixteenth-century Platonic counterpart. The contrast within texts of withdrawal, curial satire, and animal fable across the period is smaller, since these texts tend to express the irreducible continuities of political involvement. Aristotelian political 'theory', as we have seen, necessarily stands in labile relation with the unpredictable body politic. Such instability produces romance, the form in which the dictates of abstract reason are most fully sublimated and absorbed by the body. It is to that form that the next chapter turns.

6

The Comic

In Book 2 of Lydgate's *Troy Book* (1412–20) Hector is asked by his father Priam to confirm Priam's vengeful decision to visit war upon the Greeks. Hector's reply is an accomplished rhetorical performance, in which he confirms only to rebut his father's bellicosity. He articulates two ethical constructs, which may be called the chivalric and the prudential, beginning with what he takes to be the less persuasive option in this situation, the chivalric. On the face of it, this system seems more powerful, since it is underwritten by the natural order of the universe. Nature herself demands that every man desires recompense for wrongs done him, but as one ascends the chain of 'nature', so this law presses all the harder:

> Namly to swiche that with nobilite [especially · such]
> Kynd hath endewed, and set in highe degre; [Nature · endowed]
> For to swiche, gret repref is and schame, [reproof]
> When any wrong be do unto her name;
> For eche trespas mote consydered be, [must]
> Iustly mesurid after the qualite
> Of hym that is offendid, and also,
> After the persone by whom the wrong is do.
>
> (2. 2193–2200)

To those born 'of gentyl blood' a wrong done is incomparably more injurious than to a 'wreche', and so, Hector concludes, the Trojans should seek vengeance in order to augment their reputation for knighthood; Hector himself declares that he longs to 'schede the Grekys blod'. This is a powerful statement of chivalric ethics, in which all the essential aspects of such a system are stated: action, which takes the form of physical violence, is predicated on the preservation of name above all, and name is itself predicated on birth. The more nobly born one is, the greater the demand to avenge 'iniuries compassed of malys'; not to do so is to incur the worst of all chivalric conditions, shame. This is a remarkably simple ethical system, with very few categories: birth, shame, and violence, where the only category that admits of gradation is birth.

Hector, however, is an expert rhetorician. His defence of a chivalric response turns out merely to be a way of capturing the good will of his audience, before he proceeds to dismiss that very reponse:

> But first I rede, wysely in your mynde [advise]
> To cast aforn and leve nat behynde, [consider]
> Or ye begynne, discretly to adverte [before]
> And prudently consyderen in your herte
> Al, only nat the gynnyng but the ende,
> And the myddes, what weie thei wil wende.
>
> (2.2229–34)

The key word here is 'prudently': prudence is the central virtue of the so-called cardinal virtues (prudence, temperance, justice, and courage), a classical ethical system known throughout the medieval period through, among many other sources, compendia of Cicero's *De Officiis*.[1] Like the chivalric system, this ethical construct is concerned with action in the world, but unlike the chivalric it is concerned with survival. All other considerations are secondary to the primary goal of completing a sequence of actions materially better off than when one started, with one's probity intact. Hector argues very forcefully here that the Trojans will be worse off for this war, and they need only consider the strategic situation to recognize that. Even if the Trojans can count on the support of all Asia, the Greeks hold the balance of power with Europe and Africa behind them. If Troy initiates a war, Hector argues, the Trojans will be put 'alle to destruccioun' for one woman, who might in any case die very soon. So, he recommends, the Trojans should act 'by dissymulacioun', by which he means that they should pretend that no injury has been done, and thereby avoid the need to activate the entropic forces of war. Having articulated the chivalric position by speaking like a knight, that is, Hector looks to the future and speaks as a secular

[1] For the reception of this tradition in Middle English poetry, see Burnley.

cleric. The first ethical system is restricted to a particular class, whereas the second can be practised by anyone with the wit to perceive possible futures. This *miles–clerus* (knight–scholar) opposition runs deep through the *Troy Book* and, indeed, throughout Lydgate's other tragic narratives.[2]

In this chapter I use the distinction between a chivalric and a prudential ethics to distinguish two opposed literary versions of the comic in the period of this history. On the one hand, a chivalric ethics presides over, and is questioned by, romance, while on the other a prudential ethics informs much Chaucerian comedy. By the word 'comic' I invoke the classical and medieval sense of a story with a happy ending, the sense by which Dante's *Commedia*, not a notably amusing work, is 'comic'. And by treating the comic as the fourth of a series of chapters on largely secular writing, I equally complete a sequence of literary types derived from classical sources though preserved in medieval rhetorical tradition: the tragic, the elegiac, the satiric, and the comic.[3] This set of literary types can be, as it is in the case of Gower's *Confessio Amantis*, a system: the elegiac evokes, exploits, yet refuses to confront the implications of tragic narrative that represents the fall of cities; political writing does confront the implications of the tragic, yet does so from a theoretical perspective, while only the comic is capable of invoking yet absorbing the destructive violence of both tragedy and elegy. In both its chivalric and prudential forms, the comic not only bears a political freighting, but bears it well. Before turning to that question, however, some ground-clearing is necessary.

I

By including romance in my discussion of the comic, I immediately collide with a tradition of literary history. Whereas romance represents the actions of aristocratic figures, a classical tradition has it that

[2] See Ch. 3, above, and Simpson, '"Dysemol daies"'. For the tradition of the soldier–cleric opposition more generally, see Putter, '*Sir Gawain and the Green Knight*', pp. 197–201.

[3] For a medieval rhetorical treatise that defines literary types as the tragic, the satiric, the elegiac, and the comic, see Matthew of Vendôme, *Ars versificatoria*, ed. Faral, p. 153.

comedy is restricted to the non-aristocratic. In the *Troy Book* itself, Lydgate himself transmits this tradition in his account of the theatre built in the New Troy. There both comedies and tragedies were performed, of which the 'final difference' is this: comedy begins in difficulty, and 'afterward endeth in gladnes; | And it the dedis only doth expres | Of swich as ben in povert plounged lowe' (2. 849–51). Tragedy, by contrast, moves from prosperity 'and endith ever in adversite', representing the conquest of 'riche kynges and of lordes grete' (2. 852–59).[4] While Chaucerian comedy largely fits this stricture, romance does not, since more often than not it represents aristocratic society. This collision need not detain us for long, since it has not been a source of confusion in literary history; discussion of classical theatrical comedy and medieval romance have been conducted independently of each other. Besides, even if romance does represent aristocratic figures, these are very often subject, as we shall see, to the shame of poverty.

By excluding chivalric stories that do not have a happy ending (like Lydgate's *Troy Book*, or the alliterative *Morte Arthure*) from my discussion of romance, I also collide with a much more powerful tradition of literary history, which *has* been a source of deep confusion. The neoclassicizing movements that have shaped the frames within which we understand Middle English literature have seriously blurred our vision by describing *all* chivalric writing as 'romance'. This is true both of sixteenth-century humanists in their rejection of the chivalric, and of eighteenth-century scholars in their wary but fascinated submission to the seductions of medieval 'romance'.

A tradition begun in the sixteenth century has it that only in the Renaissance do we find a cultivated and courtly aristocracy, who rejected the chivalric brutalities of their medieval forebears. Sixteenth-century attacks on chivalric practice and literature are easy to find. In *Utopia* (1516) Thomas More derides every aspect of a chivalric culture in his city-state republic: hunting is described as beastly; conspicuous display is mocked; the claims of family are subjected to the demands of the state; and above all, the art of war is an impersonal, disagreeable, and entirely prudential matter, in which deception and

[4] For classical and medieval traditions of both comedy and tragedy, see Kelly, who stresses the relative rarity of the definition of tragedy given here and in Chaucer's *Monk's Tale*; see *Riverside Chaucer*, ed. Benson (7. 1971–82).

mercenaries should be used as far as possible. In his attack on chivalric culture, More implicitly heralds what he presents as a new kind of statesman, who is more scholar than soldier. That same theme is championed in Elyot's *Boke Named the Governour* (1531), where, even if Elyot remains wedded to an aristocratic ideology, his programme of education for the aristocracy is largely bookish, and the books are resolutely classical and non-chivalric. By 1545, in Ascham's *Toxophilis*, this division between a learned and courtly nobility versus its ignorant, chivalric counterpart is cast in strictly periodic and literary terms. 'In our fathers tyme', he says, 'nothing was red, but bokes of fayned chevalrie, wherin a man by redinge, shuld be led to none other ende, but only to manslaughter and baudrye.' By this account no other books were read in the dark and recent past, and they all taught nothing but violence and licentiousness. Ascham goes further in collapsing possible distinctions within chivalric literature by collapsing institutional divisions within pre-Henrician society: 'These bokes . . . were made the moste parte in Abbayes, and Monasteries, a very lickely and fit fruite of such an ydle and blynde kinde of lyvinge.'[5] By a synecdochic logic, Ascham equates romances with chivalric education, which equals the total literary output of the medieval period, which itself equals papistry.

The absurd severity of Ascham's Protestant and humanistic prejudices has not of course gone unchallenged, but his transformation of the *miles–clerus* opposition into a periodic division has been remarkably durable, in cultural histories of both courtliness and of chivalry. Renaissance scholars tend to accept the soldier–scholar distinction as a periodic distinction without demur.[6] Even in cultural histories that do trace the medieval origins of courtliness, we find the same story narrated of a shift from the 'medieval knight's individualistic ethos' towards the sixteenth-century model of the 'docile and diplomatically adroit servant of princes'.[7] Correlatively, the cultural

[5] Cited from Parins (ed.), p. 56. For Ascham's elaboration of this argument in the *Schoolmaster* (1563–70), where Ascham aims specifically at Malory's *Works*, see ibid. 56–7. Other humanist attacks on chivalric ignorance can be found in e.g. Richard Pace, *De fructu qui ex doctrina percipitur*, pp. 23–5; Thomas Starkey, *A Dialogue between Pole and Lupset*, ed. Mayer, p. 126: these works were written in 1517 and 1529–32 respectively.

[6] See e.g. Dowling, ch. 6.

[7] This citation is from Scaglione, p. 287.

history of knighthood by medievalists has until recently been dominated by Johan Huizinga's *Autumn of the Middle Ages* (first published in 1919, immediately after the war that seemed to mark a full stop to chivalry). Huizinga argued that late medieval knighthood in all its forms (military, theatrical, and literary) was an obsolete cultural form whose spectacular displays were both a symptom of, and designed to disguise, its political vacuity and helplessness before the realities of late medieval warfare. Despite the fact that Huizinga's critics have for the most part underestimated the richness of his argument, for our purposes we need only observe that for Huizinga chivalric culture in all its forms was a coherent cultural block, and characteristic of a dying period.[8] From the perspective of scholars of both the early modern and the medieval 'periods', then, a bellicose, extravagant and fundamentally blind chivalry was characteristic of the Middle Ages, while its prudential, courtly critique had to wait for the Renaissance.

Largely anti-chivalric movements in cultural history, then, gave the soldier–scholar distinction a periodic valence, with the effect of understanding all 'medieval' chivalric writing to express the same ethos. Pro-chivalric movements have equally, however, produced their own, correlative confusions, particularly by identifying all that is chivalric with 'romance', which in turn stands for the Middle Ages. Sixteenth-century humanists mark the beginning of a period of imitative neoclassicism by rejecting both chivalry and romance. Eighteenth-century scholars heralded the end of that neoclassicism by a return to the same pairing. They did so, however, by identifying romance, chivalry, and the Middle Ages in precisely the way sixteenth-century humanists had; the key difference is that whereas the sixteenth-century scholars had rejected this cultural block, late

[8] Huizinga, *Autumn of the Middle Ages*, ch. 3. The fullest application of Huizinga's position to English writing is that of A. B. Ferguson, *Indian Summer of English Chivalry*. Huizinga's strongest critics have been military historians, who have demonstrated that chivalry was not militarily obsolete in the 15th cent. See e.g. M. Vale. In my view Huizinga's critics have not appreciated the richness of his argument for cultural history. Huizinga argues that the cultural display of chivalry is not at all useless; on the contrary, it is doing hard cultural work. Huizinga's own background was in anthropology, and he may be called an early exponent of 'New Historicism', insofar as he is prepared to see the cultural significance of apparently otiose display. For the poverty of his English reception, see Aston, 'Huizinga's Harvest'.

eighteenth-century readers were prepared, at a safe distance, to submit themelves to its fascinations. Sixteenth- and seventeenth-century interest in the vernacular Middle Ages had been driven by ecclesiological and institutional passions, and so turned to the pre-Conquest period and to institutional texts in particular.[9] In the last half of the eighteenth century, impelled by an interest in the nation and its specific social history, scholars began taking an active interest in specifically 'literary' texts, and especially romance.[10] Precisely because romances were evidently, to eighteenth-century readers, the product of naïve minds, so too were they rich avenues for unimpeded access to the social history of the Middle Ages: these 'works of fancy' are 'the most authentic historical documents with respect to the manners and customs of the time in which they were composed'.[11]

For these scholars chivalry and romance were intimately related, if not identifiable. Thus Richard Hurd's *Letters on Chivalry and Romance* (1762) admirably reads romance as a code for the sociological realities of the 'feudal constitution'; this interpretation is underwritten, however, by his persuasion that the social institution of chivalry produced only one literary fruit, romance:

> The ages, we call barbarous, present us with many a subject of curious speculation. What, for instance, is more remarkable than the Gothic CHIVALRY? or than the spirit of ROMANCE, which took its rise from that singular institution? (p. 79)

This same view is shared by Thomas Warton in the second edition of his *Observations on the Fairy Queen of Spenser* (1762; 1st edn. 1754); chivalry, he says,

> taught gallantry and civility to a savage and ignorant people . . . its magnificent festivals, thronged with noble dames and courteous knights, produced the first efforts of wit and fancy.[12]

Not only by these accounts is romance the immediate product and servant of chivalry, but both, in their purest, pre-Spenserian form, are characteristic of the Middle Ages.

[9] See Ch. 1, above, for Anglo-Saxon studies.

[10] See esp. W. K. Ferguson, ch. 5.

[11] Cited from the extraordinarily rich book by Arthur Johnston, p. 26. See also Ganim.

[12] Cited from Arthur Johnston, p. 106.

In his great *History of English Poetry* (1774–81), Warton, good eighteenth-century rationalist that he tries to be, champions sixteenth-century humanism as exemplary of 'a restless disposition in the human mind to rouse from its lethargic state, and break the bonds of barbarism'. In England this 'mighty deliverance' occurred only at the end of the fifteenth century, when the 'mouldering gothic fabrics of false religion and false philosophy fell together'.[13] While Warton celebrates this deliverance, however, he does so in the very terms of romance, since his story of the 'mighty deliverance' is a mini-plot from romance. Warton also bewails the imaginative consequences of this deliverance. Already in the introduction he expresses relief that the twelfth-century restoration of classically informed 'polite letters' failed, since

> imagination would have suffered, and too early a check would have been given to the beautiful extravagancies of romantic fabling. In a word, truth and reason would have chased before their time those spectres of illusive fancy, so pleasing to the imagination, which delight to hover in the gloom of ignorance and superstition, and which form so considerable a part of the poetry of the succeeding centuries.[14]

Romance, then, stood at the beginning of non-Chaucerian Middle English literary studies, and romance stood synecdochally for all that produced it: chivalry in the first place, but behind chivalry, 'superstition', by which Warton meant the Catholic Middle Ages. The most important editions of non-Chaucerian Middle English texts from the start of specifically Middle English studies in the late eighteenth century were romances.[15] These were produced in a spirit of intrigued yet fascinated condescension, yet they gave rise to an astonishing nineteenth-century medieval revival, which embraced both chivalry and romance with deadly earnest.[16] This generally reactionary movement was as much social and architectural as literary, but in keeping with its eighteenth-century sources, it identified romance

13 Warton, 2. 408.

14 Ibid. K.4.r.

15 See Edwards, 'Some Observations' and Arthur Johnston. For the social presuppositions of this editorial work, and especially that of Sir Frederic Madden, see Matthews, *Making of Middle English*. For the societies that promoted pre-20th-cent. editorial work, see Steeves.

16 For 19th-cent. medievalism, see Girouard, and Chandler.

literature with chivalric society, and regarded both as essentially medieval. Its periodic convictions were, indeed, productive of its remarkable energy, since the movement took off in alarmed historical flight from the French Revolution, and thought it found a safe historical haven in the Middle Ages for a patriarchal society.

Sixteenth-century *anti*-chivalric humanism and the medieval revival begun by *pro*-chivalric eighteenth-century antiquarians have both contributed to a blurring of our understanding of romance. Sixteenth-century neoclassicism established the durable notion that cultivated, anti-chivalric courtly practice began in the sixteenth century, with the implication that no medieval work that represented knights could be critical of knights. In this book I have already taken issue with that notion: in Chapter 3 I considered many 'chivalric' texts from the fourteenth and fifteenth centuries (Lydgate's *Destruction of Thebes* and late medieval Troy Books, for example) that are extremely cautious about a chivalric ethos, and that promote such caution from the perspective of cultivated, prudential, courtly figures, who may or may not be knights. Narratives of societal collapse provoked by chivalric commitment to unwinnable wars may represent knights in combat and love, and they may be directed at knights as much as kings, but they are not 'romances' in the sense that that word will be used in this chapter. On the contrary, these tragic narratives point in precisely the opposite direction from the comic resolutions of romance. Whereas the prudential voice of such texts serves the ends of monarchical survival, romances address a satellite class, owing obeisance to, yet claiming a good measure of independence from, kings.

Eighteenth-, and more so nineteenth-, century scholars tended to include all chivalric works under the title of romance, and tended, too, to conceive of romance in its purest form as medieval. While modern scholarship has of course long abandoned the eighteenth-century identification of romance with non-Chaucerian medieval literature, it remains remarkably unwilling to distinguish categories among works that deal with knights. If a narrative represents knights in combat and love, then it is chivalric, and so continues to be classed as romance.[17] Modern scholarship has also been slow to consider

[17] Derek Pearsall's seminal literary historical articles on Middle English romance work within a very broad definition: 'a narrative intended primarily for entertain-

sixteenth-century examples of chivalric practice and writing.[18] This chapter is designed to reveal the powerful political functions of romance as chivalric comedy, distinct from the chivalric tragedies discussed in Chapter 3. It also reveals the continuities and narrowings of romance writing from the fourteenth century into the Henrician period. I begin by analysing the social logic of romance, using pre-Malorian examples. I then turn successively to the following: the role of romance within the irreducible heterogeneities of Malory's works, where romance is pitched against narratives of regnal collapse; and the political domestication of romance in the Tudor period, particularly as Henry VIII successfully laid claim to being himself the source of chivalric honour.

If, however, romances as a form of comedy are designed to qualify the monarchical interests of 'tragic' narratives, they themselves face challenge from another form of comedy, the wholly anti-chivalric, prudential comedy of bourgeois fiction. In the final section of this chapter I consider the prudential comedy of the *Canterbury Tales* as a sustained though unwinnable offensive against romance; Chaucer can only interrupt romance, and, finally, enlists it himself in much more powerful ways than literary history and criticism have allowed.

II

Romance both represents and itself provokes shame. From the earliest scholarship on the genre, scholars express shame in the pleasure they take in it. Hurd's *Letters* begin with a warning from Tasso not to be seduced into the '*incantato alloggiamento* [the enchanted habitation]' (p. 76) of the *ciance*, or idle stories, of romance.[19] And Warton's *History of English Literature* could have served as a copy

ment, in verse or prose, and presented in terms of chivalric life'. See Pearsall, 'English Romance in the Fifteenth Century', p. 57, and 'Development of Middle English Romance'. For a large-scale application of these broad categories that exposes its unmanageably wide range, see Barron.

[18] For good beginnings, see A. B. Ferguson, *Chivalric Tradition in Renaissance England*, and Anglo (ed.), *Chivalry*.

[19] See also the revealing comments in Letter 6: 'We are upon enchanted ground, my friend; and you are to think yourself well used that I detain you no longer in this fearful circle' (p. 113).

text for Freud's *Civilisation and its Discontents,* since Warton is torn between praise of his own era as 'an age advanced to the highest degree of refinement' on the one hand, and a sense of the profound loss that a 'civilized' rationalism entails on the other. By the revolution of the Renaissance, England has gained good sense, taste, and criticism, but

> in the mean time we have lost a set of manners and a system of machinery more suitable to the purposes of poetry. . . . We have parted with extravagancies that are above propriety, with incredibilities that are more acceptable than truth, and with fictions that are more valuable than reality.[20]

These 'extravagancies' (i.e. romances) are associated in Warton with embarrassing and unspeakable longings, for popish 'superstition' above all, but also for the childish, and for imaginative desire ungoverned by reason.

Twentieth-century scholarship on romance was not of course ashamed of its interest, but it did find discussion of romance embarrassingly difficult, since romances tend to operate below the standard characteristics that activated critical attention. Individual romances, that is, often lack (for example) stylistic density;[21] an implied yet elusive authorial perspective; explicit ethical complexity; resistance to narrative closure; a self-conscious sense of literary tradition, which itself produces a philological care for the preservation of a textual tradition;[22] a named patron;[23] a named author;[24]

[20] Warton, 2. 463.

[21] The most penetrating discussion of the style of romances is by Spearing, 'Early Medieval Narrative Style'. This chapter analyses the style of pre-1350 examples, but its conclusions are relevant for much post-1350 romance.

[22] Just as the plot of romances deals with the irreducible horizontal conflict between cousins, so too do the surviving texts of romances often present irreducibly variant horizontal relationships that prevent any genealogical analysis. For the problems of editing romances, see Edwards, 'Middle English Romance'.

[23] The exceptions are *William of Palerne*, written at the instance of Humphrey de Bohun (d. 1361); Henry Lovelich's *Merlin*, dedicated to Harry Barton, Lord Mayor of London; and John Metham's *Amoryus and Cleopes*, dedicated in 1448–9 to Sir Miles Stapleton and his wife. The patron named in the *Romance of Partenay* is that of the original French text. The author of the English *Partonope of Blois* says that he has been commanded by his 'sovereign' to translate the work into English, but does not unfortunately name the 'sovereign' (l. 2335).

[24] The exceptions are, for good reason, the texts in n. 23, above; a named patron produces a named poet: *William of Palerne* was written by one 'William' (l. 5521); Henry Lovelich (*c.*1420) names himself cryptically as the author of *Merlin* (l. 21956),

and historical specificity.[25] The fact that a sophisticated romance like *Sir Gawain and the Green Knight*, consistently a darling of Anglo-American critics since the mid-twentieth century, has many of these qualities in abundance (even, possibly, the last) merely proved the rule by exception. Above all, however, romances provoked embarrassment or dismissal in modern critics by their apparently uncomplicated acceptance of a tightly governed aristocratic and chivalric ideology, in which nobility of blood wins out over all comers. Even more embarrassing was the fact that romances would seem to have been read by non-aristocratic audiences, apparent victims of an aristocratic ideology.[26] Romances seem, that is, to be shamefully simple works of shamefully popular entertainment.

Romances themselves, of course, deal centrally with shame, and I turn to this aspect of every romance narrative by way of confirming yet complicating their acceptance of an aristocratic and chivalric ethos. A simple tail-rhyme romance, *Sir Amadace*, serves as my example. The work is missing its opening, but its narrative lineaments are entirely clear from its 840 remaining lines; it was probably composed between 1350 and 1400, and survives in two manuscripts, both of the last half of the fifteenth century.[27] An indebted lord, Sir Amadace, is advised by his steward to put off his creditors, but Amadace decides secretly to mortgage his lands and to leave court, not to return until he is out of debt. Before leaving he gives a magnificent feast and distributes many gifts; after having ridden through a forest, he discovers a chapel in which there lies a woman lamenting over a putrid corpse. Despite the intense stench, Amadace enters the chapel, to discover from the woman that she cannot bury her merchant husband, who, over-munificent while he lived, now owes £30 to another merchant who will not allow him to be buried

just as John Metham names himself (l. 2207) as the author of *Amoryus and Cleopes*. The only 'minstrel' poet who rises to the dignity of a name is Thomas of Chestre, author of *Launfal*. Chestre may have written other romances; see Mills.

25 For an impressive attempt to historicize earlier Anglo-Norman and Middle English romance, see Crane, *Insular Romance*; and for the topical references in printed romances, see Cooper, 'Romance after 1400', pp. 698, 707.

26 For the merchant readers and household context of many romance manuscripts, including some evidence of female ownership, see Meale, '"Gode men | Wiues maydenes and alle men"'.

27 For information about the MSS of romances, see Guddat-Figge (ed.).

while the debt is outstanding. Having failed to persuade the living merchant to waive the debt, Amadace not only pays it, but also supplies an extra £10 for a splendid funeral and feast in memory of the dead merchant. Now entirely destitute, he wanders disconsolate in a forest, only to meet a knight who promises to supply him with all his knightly needs, on condition that he later share his winnings with him. A newly equipped Amadace enters a tournament called by a nearby king, pretends that he is a wealthy but shipwrecked prince lacking men, and wins the tournament. He marries the princess, and they have a son. The knight in the forest returns to ask his share; Amadace is only too willing to give it to him, until the knight insists that he does not want the lands and goods, only half Amadace's wife and son. A grieving and recalcitrant Amadace is persuaded by his wife to hold to his covenants, and is about to bisect his wife and child when the mysterious knight stays his hand. The knight declares that he is the merchant, and has come from beyond the grave in gratitude for Amadace's earlier generosity. He leaves; Amadace rebuys his lands, recalls his former household, and becomes king when his father-in-law dies.

On the face of it, this story confirms a simple aristocratic ideology in a simple style and a simple narrative. Amadace's consistently chivalric behaviour, helping women in distress and offering largesse even when it makes him destitute, ensures his eventual happiness and success in a world that seems overwhelmingly hostile. The narrative is circular, beginning and ending in a noble environment, and that structural circularity encodes a deeply conservative ideology: the return to noble status, that is, is premissed on never being anything less than noble. The world of this comic story is providential, where everyone has a place to which they will eventually and rightly return. The narrative structure is not at all driven by the central figure's self-improving work or shrewdness of calculation. On the contrary, all Amadace must do is to manifest what he already is at the beginning (i.e. noble) in order to ensure his return to noble status. The narrative is driven, that is, by what it always and already knows, and so is not concerned with personal 'development' so much as with class display: Amadace must simply demonstrate his innate nobility for the narrative to return to its noble beginnings. The operations of narrative under such an ideology are a kind of shadow-boxing, since the apparent destitution of the noble figure will always be the premiss of return to noble wealth. Chance is given such high profile in narratives of this kind precisely to disguise the fact that success is genetically programmed, and does *not* depend on chance. This is a providential world, in which noble figures always end up where they belong, regardless of chance; the dice always finally roll their way. Nobility that admits of no real chances is emphasized by that with which it contrasts: the mean merchant who will not release the widow from her debts; the ungrateful guests at the funeral feast who dismiss Amadace's generosity by saying that he won the money easily, and so spends it easily (ll. 340–2). Merchants live in a world of commodities and exact accounts, while nobles inhabit a world of gifts and munificence.[28] At the heart of this contrast, indeed, lies the repulsive, putrid, and dead merchant.

I have just given an account of a wish-fulfilment narrative, in which obstructive realities evanesce in the face of very powerful mythic structures. That is indeed the way the story ends, and the way it would, apparently, have itself read. It seems to me, however, that this narrative is susceptible of a very different reading. While on the one hand the merchant's rotting corpse insists on the absolute difference between the merchant and the knight who 'lived happily ever after', on the other one could read the hideous corpse as a decoy, designed to disguise what turn out to be striking, unavoidable, and shameful similarities between merchants and knights in this narrative. The one point where this similarity is absolutely unavoidable is at the climax, where the knight must commodify his own wife and son. Unless he act like a merchant, and pay back exactly what he promised, *without the possibility of paying more*, then his world will collapse. Reassertion of the enclosed system of noble generosity in *Amadace* can only be made by a preparedness to accept all that threatens enclosure. Thus the reintegration of social units depends on a readiness to break the most profound bonds of that very social unit. The story might evoke the catastrophes of history, and especially the slaying of kin, only to avert them, but those catastrophes can be averted only by a readiness to accept a logic (here a mercantile

[28] For a pentrating analysis of commodity and gift in this romance, see Putter, 'Gifts and Commodities'.

logic) that is diametrically opposed to the model of order the narrative as a whole upholds.

Once we have recognized this unavoidable identity between knight and merchant, we can see many other, much less spectacular examples of it: the merchant is said to have an income of £300 (l. 142), which turns out to be exactly Amadace's own annual income (l. 388); the merchant dies in debt precisely because he has, by his wife's account, acted like a fool: 'He cladde mo men agaynus [in preparation for] a Yole | Thenne did a nobull knyghte' (ll. 158–9). From this it would provisionally appear that only the noble Amadace can act with unstinting liberality and gain from it, while a merchant who acts in the same way will suffer. But even this affirmation of the unbridgeable merchant–knight opposition is put into question by the final sequence, where the dead merchant returns from the grave as a white knight. This narrative expresses shameful secrets even as it would disguise them: not only is Amadace dependent on a merchant's loans, and not only must he be prepared to pay them back to the letter, but the merchant himself can become a knight. Amadace's initial account of why he has been so generous, indeed, acknowledges this very possibility: he says of the dead merchant that 'he myghte full wele be of my kynne' (l. 209). By the same token, Amadace must act like a merchant: when he arrives without men at the tournament, he performs a confidence trick by *pretending* to be a noble prince (ll. 553–64). This story can insist very heavily on one ideology only by registering the necessity of its obverse. It only appears to confirm Auerbach's influential point that romances disguise the socio-economic basis of the society they represent;[29] a more reflective reading reveals a confession of the intimate connection between knighthood and merchants.

And just as knights are revealed to be dependent on merchants, so too are they dependent on women. This romance plays out the standard narrative topos of the knight helping a widow in distress, and that of the knight fighting for the hand of the princess. Both these actions tend, however, to disguise the fact that it is more the women who are helping the knights in distress than vice versa: Amadace's initial act of pity leads to his access to merchant wealth, which leads

[29] Auerbach, 'Knight Sets Forth'.

to his wedding with the princess and the long-term solution to the problem of his poverty. In reality late medieval noble and gentry women were indeed married primarily with the property interests of their larger families in mind; romances often not only recognize that link, but also empower women readers by underlining male dependence on female wealth.[30]

III

Modern scholarship has counted eighty-eight 'romances' extant in 'codices dating from the second half of the thirteenth century up until 1534/5'.[31] The initial date simply marks the first instances of roughly datable Middle English romances, while the terminal date here is the death of the printer Wynkyn de Worde, a date significant for romance production and printing, since de Worde was by far the most prolific printer of romances.[32] This tally, which already excludes Scottish romances, would be significantly reduced to about forty if we were also to make two further exclusions. In the first place, for the purposes of this chapter on comedy, I exclude many works that do not conform to a very specific tripartite narrative pattern characteristic of romance. This comic pattern is visible in the narrative of *Sir Amadace*: a state of actual or implied integration gives way to a state of disintegration, submission to the tests of which is the premiss of return to a state of integration.[33] For the purposes of this history, I also exclude works that are definitively written pre-1350, such as the many romances in the so-called Auchinleck manuscript (written *c.*1330).[34] The figure of forty would rise back to

[30] For the household context of romances and their relation with historical marriage practices, see D. Starkey, 'Age of the Household'.

[31] Citation from Meale, 'Caxton, de Worde and the Publication of Romance', p. 285. For a helpful division of 'romances' into broad chronological bands, see 'Romances', in Severs and Hartung (eds.), I. 13–16. For more specific lists of prose romances, see P. A. Scanlon, and Keiser, 'Romances'. For bibliography on romances, in addition to Severs and Hartung (eds.), vol. I, see Rice (ed.).

[32] For which see Edwards and Meale.

[33] By far the best account of the story structures of romance is by K. Hume. I restrict my discussion of 'romance' to her 'Type A' (pp. 161–3). See also Brewer, 'Nature of Romance'.

[34] The romances that appear in the Auchinleck MS (National Library of Scotland, MS Adv. 19.2.1) are listed in Guddat-Figge (ed.), 121–3.

between fifty and sixty within the period of this history were we to include, as we should, romances embedded in larger works by Gower, Hoccleve, Lydgate, Chaucer, and Malory.[35]

I address the romance production of the authors just named later in this chapter. If we restrict ourselves for the moment to the almost wholly anonymous corpus of chivalric comedy written between 1350 (bearing in mind that dating is often very slippery indeed) and the terminal point of this history, we can generalize from the reading of *Amadace* to generate a model for reading these works, all of which are designed to manage noble, or at least 'gentle', shame. In so doing, they modify and redirect the explosive forces of the chivalric ethos described at the beginning of this chapter.

As will be obvious from the plot of *Amadace*, stories of this kind generate narrative out of clear oppositions. In *Amadace* the principal opposition is clearly that between merchants and nobles, but stories can be generated from any number of possible contraries: daughters and fathers; non-Christians and Christians; higher and lower nobility; provincial and metropolitan courts; sons and fathers; sons and mothers; women and men; wild and cultivated; human and animal. In most narratives a primary opposition is reinforced by many other correlative oppositions: thus in *Sir Eglamour* (*c.*1350), the principal source of frustrated desire is that of the lower-born knight Eglamour for the higher-born Cristabelle, daughter of the Earl of Artois. Before these lovers can marry, with Eglamour becoming earl of Artois, the

[35] The romances I am working with for this chapter are, therefore, as follows. I largely follow the broad dates of composition as given in Severs and Hartung (eds.). Composed 1350–1400: *Sir Isumbras*, *Sir Eglamour of Artois*, *Gamelyn*, *Chevalere Assigne*, *Athelston*, *Apollonius of Tyre*, *Sir Gawain and the Green Knight*, *Le Bone Florence of Rome*, *Sir Cleges*, *Ipomadon*, *Sir Degrevant*, *Sir Triamour*, *Sir Amadace*, *Generides*, *Robert of Sicily*, *Sir Launfal*, *Emaré*, *Sir Gowther*, *The Earl of Toulous*, *Sir Torrent of Portyngale*, *Syre Gawene and the Carle of Carleyle*, Chaucer's tales of Knight, Man of Law, Wife of Bath, Clerk, Squire, Franklin, and *Sir Thopas*, and Gower's tales of Florent, Constance, and Apollonius of Tyre. Composed 1400–1500: Lydgate's *Fabula duorum mercatorum*, and *Guy of Warwick*, Hoccleve's tales of Jereslaus' wife and of Jonathas, Lovelich's *Grail* and *Merlin*, *Lyfe of Ipomydon*, *The Avowynge of King Arthur*, *King Ponthus*, *Amoryus and Cleopes*, *Eger and Grime*, *The Weddynge of Sir Gawen and Dame Ragnell*, Malory's romances, the prose *Merlin*, the prose *Ipomedon*, *Paris and Vienne*, *Blanchardyn and Eglantine*, *Partonope of Blois*, *The Grene Knight*, *The Squire of Low Degree*, *The Romans of Partenay*. Composed 1500–50: *Valentine and Orson*; *Knight of the Swan*; the prose *William of Palerne*.

following obstacles must be overcome: a giant, a wild boar, and a dragon must be killed by Eglamour, in three ostensibly impossible challenges set by Cristabelle's (incestuously?) possessive father; Cristabelle and her illegitimate child must endure exile in a boat; the child must be separated from its mother, captured as he is by a griffin before being deposited with and adopted by the king of Israel; Cristabelle, suffering exile in Egypt, must be married to her son who, now 15, has won her hand in a tournament; Eglamour must fight his son, whom he conquers, for Cristabelle's hand (the truth about the son having been discovered in time). Thus the central opposition in this narrative, that between the higher and lower nobility, awakens the spectre of a wide range of subsidiary oppositions, many of which are potentially shameful, such as father–daughter and son–mother incest; parricide; and illegitimate birth. The premiss of Eglamour's absorption into the higher nobility is not so much his virtue; on the contrary, a series of fundamentally illegitimate desires must be expressed and nearly fulfilled as a condition of reaffirming and enlarging the social order. The social order is enlarged, since by the end the lower nobility has been absorbed into the higher, but that absorption is underwritten by violence and transgression both within and outside the family. The violence and transgression turns out to be constructive, and to unwrite myths of parricide and incest that shadow such narrative. Violence and transgression are, however, equally unavoidable: preparedness to break the social order is the condition of its stability and reformation. These stories operate on a level deeper than ethics, since rationally explicable ethics are themselves a resource of the civilized order. The very premiss of these stories is that the obvious resources of the civilized order are incapacitated by challenges that necessitate the near transgression of fundamental taboos; they must express 'extravagancies beyond propriety' in Warton's perceptive words. Moral readings that posit heroes or heroines as exemplary of a given virtue tend in my view to miss the point and power of romance, even where the name of the hero or heroine personifies a virtue, such as 'Constance'. These narratives address what might be called social ecologies, which exist prior to morality.

Shameful contact with all that is other to the noble order is a constant feature of these stories. Explicitly incestuous desire generates the narrative of *Emaré*; borrowing a horse from a mayor's daughter is the condition of wealth that must remain hidden in *Launfal*; in *Octavian* the noble hero must become apprenticed to a butcher, from whom he borrows rusty armour before he can regain his royal status, just as the hero of *Isumbras* must become a blacksmith before he can reassemble his noble family; recuperation of noble identity and noble marriage in *Lybeaus Desconus* is premissed only on the fair unknown's kissing a serpent woman; the king in *Robert of Sicily* must become the court fool and eat with the dogs; nobles take the disguise of, and are transformed into, wild animals in *William of Palerne*; the hero and heroine of *Generides* must disguise themselves as a leprous beggar and a laundress before they can be reunited; idolatry is the prelude to reintegration in the very strange *Amoryus and Cleopes*; Melusine in the *Romance of Partenay* is at once the source of wealth and weekly a serpent whose husband must not but does look at her in her serpentine form;[36] in the extraordinarily sophisticated *Partonope of Blois* the hero shamefully exposes his lover; Gawain's preparedness to marry a repulsive old hag in public is the condition of her transformation into a beautiful young woman in *The Wedding of Sir Gawain and Dame Ragnell*; necrophilia of a kind is a condition of social mobility in *The Squire of Low Degree*, as filial violence is in *Sir Degrevant*.

A rather sophisticated model of human identity emerges from these romance narratives: the 'civilized' order cannot survive by rigid reassertion of its own norms against that which threatens it; in any case these threats often completely outscale the obvious resources of the 'civilized' world. On the contrary, the civilized order survives only by entering into, and having commerce with, all that threatens it, even to the point of the barbarism of almost killing one's own family. That subtle account of the civilized order emerges only structurally, however, in the oppositional contrasts and secret identifications that emerge across whole narratives.[37] In most romances these

[36] I acknowledge that *Partenay* does not quite fit my definition of romance, since the family is not reunited (the wife must leave after her husband's indiscretion, and the father orders the death of his aptly named son 'Horrible'). It is, however, fundamentally a narrative of family foundation and extension, relying on the narrative energies of romance. There is a prose version, printed in the early 16th cent.; see *Melusine*, ed. Donald.

[37] The best structuralist analysis of Middle English romance is Wittig.

more subtle meanings cannot and, indeed, must not be explicated by the narrators themselves, since romances deal with shameful secrets. One condition of dealing with those secrets is that they be kept secret as far as possible, at best presented in displaced and disguised form. By the very same token, the shameful secrets are never simply discarded, since they provide the energies by which the narrative achieves circularity. For this reason romances tend not to be characterized by explicit and ethical narratorial comment, since the meanings are structural, and better left unspoken.

The importance of structural meanings also accounts for the wide range of style and metre in which romances can remain powerful. More than a fifth of *Sir Amadace*'s lines are formulaic;[38] any reading that sought meaning from the densely patterned verbal texture would be badly disappointed. These works gain their power from the oppositions of identity and otherness they evoke and rearrange, and that power often survives the stylistically and metrically thin surface they often present.[39] For this reason, too, these stories can work perfectly well as oral presentations in which stylistic density is impossible.

These narratives cannot be described as reactionary and conservative in any simple way. Some Middle English narratives normally classed as romances, and especially works from the Charlemagne cycle, do work within basic oppositions without ever seriously engaging the 'other' (usually 'Saracens').[40] But these gung-ho, action-movie style narratives do not share the basic circular pattern of romance narrative; they are instead late remakes of *chansons de geste*. The circular pattern of romances does indeed return to beginnings, and so appears to be conservative in its attempt to close out history and change from the romance world. But, as we have seen, the movement to home base will always have encountered and recognized all that is other to value and order as defined by that ending. The return implies a conservatism; the provisional encounter with

[38] For the statistics, see ibid. 18.

[39] For the stylistic thinness and its implications, see Spearing, 'Early Medieval Narrative Style', and Wittig, ch. 1. Romances appear in the following prosodic forms: tail-rhyme; four-stress couplet; five-stress couplet (Chaucer); seven-stress couplet; alliterative long line; rhyme-royal; prose.

[40] Thus e.g. *Firumbras*, *Otuel and Roland*, *The Sowdone of Babylone and of Ferumbras His Sone Who Conquerde Rome*.

the other implies a reformist conservatism. That merchants and women read these narratives is entirely in keeping with the way in which such stories centrally and consistently address the dependence of knights on merchants and women.[41] One of the most sophisticated of the Middle English romances, *Partonope of Blois*, indeed, is not only about a knight's dependence on a woman; it is also addressed to a woman, and consistently gives voice to the heroine's shrewd and often moving account of the feminine predicament in a chivalric world.[42] Romances may be the product of chivalric society, but they do not promote the violent 'ethics' of chivalry in any simple-minded way.

Romances are only apparently about individual fulfilment. A more reflective reading reveals that they are about groups, and that individual heroes or heroines can only reaffirm their lost identity by acknowledging and enlarging the group to which they belong by 'nature'. That moments of moving anagnorisis, or recognition, always signal the end of romances implies that individual fulfilment can only be premissed on social reintegration. These narratives work to define what might be called a social ecology, since the individual trajectory necessitates that a whole system readjust and provisionally reform itself, where the readjustment involves both victims who must be ejected from the system, and new arrivals who deserve accommodation.

This structural bonding applies not only to the society represented within such stories, but also to the narrative technique of the stories themselves and to the social relation of narrator and audience. In the stories themselves recapitulation is a consistent feature of their narration. This is not simply because recapitulation serves the needs of an aural audience, but also because nothing is left behind or out in these narratives in which everything has its place. The social relation of narrator and audience serves the same ends of societal bonding. In most verse romances the narrative voice addresses a listening

[41] *Sir Degrevant* not only represents the dependence of knights on women in its narrative, but may also have been copied by women; see Edwards, 'Gender, Order and Reconciliation'.

[42] *Partonope of Blois*, ed. Bödtker, ll. 5517–73, 5883–6067, and esp. 10699–10800. The narrator also forcefully attacks clerics for their criticism of women: ll. 6759–96.

audience, even when such address seems evidently a fiction.[43] And the narrative voice is not ironic, since irony (i.e. saying one thing and meaning its opposite) implies social division in the necessity to cater for one audience while really addressing another. While historical 'irony' is the necessary concomitant of romance narrative's social displacements, irony of that kind has only a provisional hold on the narrative, and is always ironed out as figures return to their 'proper' place. Such a return to propriety, however, equally neutralizes any narratorial irony. Precisely because the oppositions of romance are so deep, narrator and audience are both involved in the act of recognition and reintegration.

Romances, then, are designed to address the internal, structural tensions of groups. The tragedies discussed in Chapter 3 address the violence of external war, and the ways in which that violence can produce civil destruction. Romances, by contrast, represent the ways in which the controlled expression of civil violence within social groupings can serve finally to reintegrate them. The groups so reintegrated are themselves various. Families often dominate, and are never wholly absent, since whatever the action of a romance, its resolution will imply nobility of blood.[44] But romances cannot help but evoke the larger political order, precisely because their resolutions restore the pattern of whole societies. I turn to some examples of more obviously political romances by way of concluding this section on largely anonymous verse romance. Whereas romances are dismissed as the reactionary expression of a chivalric class out of its historical depth, I argue here that these narratives are extremely sensitive to the dangers of self-enclosed and unthinking reaffirmations of chivalric and noble self-sufficiency. My two examples, *Gamelyn* and *Sir Gawain and the Green Knight*, stand at either end of a spectrum of metropolitan versus provincial romance settings.

Gamelyn (*c.*1350, 902 lines in roughly seven-stress couplets) tells the story of a younger son who is cheated out of his inheritance by his oldest brother. In a society that practises primogeniture, younger brothers will always be an energetic and potentially disruptive social

[43] For the ficitivity of audiences in Middle English romance, and the dangers of accepting the fictional as the historical audience, see Pearsall, 'Middle English Romance and its Audiences'.

[44] For the notion of family romance, see D. Brewer, *Symbolic Stories*.

type. Many romances tell the story of younger brothers (Malory's Gareth, for example) who marry into land and wealth. Gamelyn, by contrast, fights for his paternal inheritance, since his father has insisted on sharing his land and goods, against the determinations of his executors, who had intended to leave Gamelyn dependent on the generosity of his brothers. The oldest brother's exclusion of Gamelyn forces him into increasingly illegal violence, which starts with Gamelyn breaking into and exhausting the brother's stores, then attacking the brother's monastic guests, who have sided with the oldest brother, before attacking the sheriff's representatives come to apprehend him. Forced to flee to the forest as an outlaw, he becomes king of the outlaws, before returning to attack his brother, who has become sheriff in the meanwhile. The second brother stands in as bail for Gamelyn while Gamelyn returns to the forest, gathers his men, and returns to court to hang the justice, his brother the sheriff, and the twelve corrupt jurors who would have hanged him. Gamelyn and his men go to the king, who pardons them, and makes Gamelyn and the second brother justices.

This is clearly the narrative of an aggressive gentry society, where the practice of law is underwritten by physical violence. The narrative does insist on a nobility of blood ethos: Gamelyn's first act of rebellion is to refuse to serve food, by declaring his gentle birth, 'born of a lady and geten of a knight' (l. 108). And the forest turns out to be less a place of lawlessness, than of true law governed by a 'king' of noble birth; Gamelyn is confident that the leader of the outlaws will feed him 'if that he be heende [noble] and come of gentil blood' (l. 663). Equally, the narrative can only reach closure by acknowledging the king's supremacy. But if *Gamelyn* reaffirms the power of a gentry society's blood and declares its allegiance to the king, it does so in the most unsentimental way. The narrative turns on Gamelyn's dependence on the Steward: the very figure who does supply food, and with whom Gamelyn had rejected affinity, turns out to be the one on whom he is most dependent. *Gamelyn* does not pause anxiously over this recognition of weakness: the hero offers the Steward half his lands, and goes on spectacularly, if provisionally, to attack the entire structure of provincial justice and society. Gamelyn takes an especial pleasure in aggressing monks, who are in complacent league with the corrupt oldest brother. While a sentimental reading would have it that the values of true justice are rediscovered in the forest and serve finally to reform and reconfirm the king's justice, a more plausible reading would argue that the 'justice' that issues from the forest barely avoids replicating the thuggery to which it is ostensibly opposed. This narrative claims, as local gentry did indeed claim in the fourteenth and fifteenth centuries, to take charge of local justice.[45] It does so by making unembarrassed alliances with the non-gentle, and unembarrassed displays of premeditated violence.[46] If the fundamental story of monarchy from the twelfth to the sixteenth centuries is the story of gradually monopolizing legitimate violence, *Gamelyn*'s final royal gesture only masks a more powerful claim to legitimate violence exercised against the king's representatives. *Gamelyn* takes very little care to disguise secrets that might be shameful to 'gentle' society.

If *Gamelyn* is romance serving the interests of provincial gentry society, *Sir Gawain and the Green Knight* (*c.*1390, 2,530 alliterative lines) would seem to be at the other extreme of the network that linked provincial gentry to the crown. Whereas *Gamelyn* begins in the provinces, and moves to the royal court only at its end, *Gawain* begins and ends in a royal court. And on the face of it, *Gawain* would seem to restore both a royal and a chivalric identity to its own plenitude at the poem's end. All the court laugh at what they take to be Gawain's excessive shame, and decide to wear the sash with which Gawain has returned from his adventure, as if they were forming an order of knighthood. The motto, indeed, that follows the poem in the manuscript was the motto of the Order of the Garter, 'Hony Soyt Qui Mal [Y] Pence' ('Shame be to the one who thinks ill of it'). This Order was established in 1348–9 by Edward III, in a move designed to cement the loyalties of his great magnates to the crown.[47] Whereas knighthood originated as a centrifugal force, by the fourteenth century kings were beginning to deploy chivalric symbolism within a monarchical system. If that cannot help but admit a kind of shame by admitting the king's need, the Order's motto both expresses and contains that shame in its circular and belted form.

Like the motto and circular shape of the Garter, the poem itself

45 For which see Kaeuper, pp. 176–81.

46 For the romance in its historical context, see Scattergood, '*The Tale of Gamelyn*'.

47 J. Vale, pp. 81–91.

both expresses and contains royal shame. While the contrasts of romance narrative in *Sir Gawain and the Green Knight* seem to expel all that threatens the court, the narrative's more complex operations serve consistently to collapse those oppositions. All that seems most protected is invaded by that which threatens it, and vice versa. Readers discover this most powerfully at the Green Knight's cave, ostensibly the site of devilish and barbaric practice. Gawain's readiness to submit to that barbarity, however, transforms the monstrous Green Knight into the most subtle of moral commentators, who argues that Gawain has only failed a little, and entirely forgivably, in accepting the sash. Thus the readiness to incur catastrophe produces its opposite, a statement of the civilized order. While in *Sir Amadace* this moment leads quickly forward to the resolution, in *Gawain* it leads backwards. We realize that Gawain's real test is not here at the cave, but has already happened, in the castle of Bertilak. That sudden inversion of violence and ethical delicacy, then, merely evokes another such inversion in Fit 3, where we see that the bedroom was the wild place, not so much the extraordinarily violent hunting scenes. These inversions imply the invasion of the apparently protected and enclosed courtly spaces by their opposite. The very name of the castle, 'Hautdessert', itself declares the inseparability of wild and ordered: the name may mean both 'high reward', and 'extremely uncultivated place'.[48] This recognition only underlines the shame of Gawain as royal representative, since in the ostensibly provincial castle, in a society that advertises itself as uncultivated, Gawain has been successfully hunted like an animal in the most sophisticated way. The dead fox, indeed, with whom Gawain is most fully identified, is unceremoniously stripped of his fur by a joyful provincial hunting party (l. 1921).

Gawain's own shame cannot be contained as a personal failing, unrelated to the royal court. Arthur's court consistently fails to appreciate the gravity of Gawain's experience, and agrees to wear what he regards as a mark of shame, as a communal badge of honour. By the apparently rigid terms of the pentangle, which Gawain wears as the court's representative, he has failed. The pentangle's positivist terms would have it that any failure in fidelity is as

[48] If the name 'Hautdessert' applies to the Green Chapel, then the force of the contradictory meanings simply reverses itself.

significant as any other, regardless of the magnitude of the breach, or of its motivation. So in a shame culture the small wound that Gawain bears in the flesh of his neck might stand synecdochally for very much more. This poem contains many asymmetries that turn out to be equatable: one man's words can overpower the renown of the whole Round Table (l. 314); a huge pile of slain deer is deemed to 'equal' one kiss (l. 1390). So a small and finely calibrated cut in the neck might point to the collapse of Arthur's kingdom: the poem begins, after all, with reference to the fall of Troy, provoked by Aeneas, who was 'tried for his trichery, the trewest on erthe' (l. 4). Whether we read the adjectival phrase in that line as applying to 'trichery' or to Aeneas, it weaves treachery and fidelity inseparably, and points both backwards to the fall of Troy, and forwards to Gawain as the 'trewest' traitor 'on erthe'.

The poem, indeed, never escapes a sense of threat. The most intensely minatory moment, Gawain waiting for the axe to fall, is never fully contained, since it evokes other moments in a widening circle: the hunted Gawain under threat in the bedroom, while sharp weapons are being wielded on flesh outside in the forest; the giant axe hung above Arthur's head once the Green Knight has gone; and the fall of Troy, a reference to tragic narrative that begins and ends the poem, reminding us that Arthur's kingdom did indeed fall. And if this poem about a young king was in fact written late in the reign of Richard II, we are permitted to reflect that in 1387 the child-king Richard was engaged in civil war with his magnatial competitors, who finally toppled him in 1399.[49]

Nothing in this poem stays still for long. However much it may point outside the closed circle of romance to regnal collapse, its commitments to social reintegration are finally sustained, though only by extending the resources of chivalric romance. The most obvious way in which the provincial 'other' is absorbed is at the opening feast. Just as Richard II and Henry IV both staged a theatrical challenge to their authority by having a knight ride into the coronation feast and challenge anyone who disputed the title of the new king, so too is the feast of Arthur actually permitted to proceed by the irruption of the Green

49 Richard II seemed rather to accentuate his youth, as in e.g. the Wilton Diptych (painted, probably, in 1396, when Richard was 30), where he is depicted as a beardless youth. See Gordon.

Knight.[50] Threatening otherness also acquiesces to the larger system of Arthur's authority in the revelation that Arthur's half-sister Morgan had generated the whole performance in spite: the Other turns out to be part of the family. These points might suggest that it is a measure of a royal court's power theatrically to produce challenges to its own authority; the fact remains, nevertheless, that Gawain has, or had, a cut in his neck: something beyond the reach of the court has inflicted a certain damage, and that small flesh wound may implicate very much more. Only by extending the resources of romance to include a pentitential ethics can the narrative contain all that threatens royal authority. The Green Knight, who describes his action in explicitly penitential terms (ll. 2390–4), articulates a penitential, self-regulating morality, by which, and only by which, the explosive force of shame can be managed. In retrospect, even the pentangle's uncompromising ethical system contains its opposite, since the last aspect described is 'pité, that passes alle pointez' (l. 654). No point in the wholly rigid and symmetrical pentangle should pass any other point, whether not or we understand 'poyntez' here literally or figuratively. Only pity, which takes individual circumstances and motivations into account, can admit of gradations of punishment, unlike shame. But pity implies a pentitential ethics, in which the individual accepts a privately administered and regulated account of self-worth. The finesse of the Green Knight's calibration offers an alternative to aristocratic shame. And so in this poem a penitential ethics, quite distinct from both the prudential and the chivalric ethics described above, serves the ends of chivalric self-regulation.[51] The final citation of the Garter motto acknowledges yet interiorizes shame ('hony soyt qui mal y *pence*'), at which point shame becomes self-regulating guilt.[52]

While romances tend to set a chivalric society very definitely in the 'medieval' past, governance of chivalric society was very much a

[50] For the interruption to Henry IV's coronation feast, see Harder, who does not seem to be aware that this challenge was routine at coronation feasts. For what may be an eyewitness account of the bungled ritual at the coronation of Richard II, see Thomas Walsingham, *Historia Anglicana*, 337.

[51] For the other penitential romances (*Guy of Warwick*, *Gowther*, *Isumbras*, *Robert of Sicily*), see Hopkins.

[52] For a fuller version of this argument, see Putter, '*Sir Gawain and the Green Knight*', ch. 5.

contemporary issue for later fourteenth-century kings. As I argued in Chapter 1, Geoffrey of Monmouth was himself a 'medievalist', insofar as he writes a narrative that fills in the large tract between the fall of empire and the rise of new monarchies. The very word 'romance', originally designating romance languages, itself invokes a Roman past only to insist that power has now moved West, into post-imperial forms. The majority of Middle English romances, and most obviously the Arthurian examples, are self-consciously set within fluid, post-imperial political orders. This is true, for example, of the brilliant *Partonope of Blois* (12,195 lines in four-stress couplets, translated into English in the first half of the fifteenth century from a late twelfth-century French original). Whereas tragic narratives represent a definitive exodus from the fall of Eastern empire, *Partonope* reverses the movement by allowing the powers of romance to recuperate all that has been lost from the imperial East.

If, however, romances tend to set royally regulated chivalric societies in the very distant past, in actual fact it was only in the middle of the fourteenth century that English kings began successfully to regulate chivalric society. Not only did Edward III create the Order of the Garter in 1348–9, but in the same years he also allowed squires to bear heraldic arms,[53] and established the Curia militaris, a chivalric court designed to settle and regulate chivalric disputes.[54] Only in the late fourteenth century did English kings begin to grant arms themselves;[55] and the first document establishing a system of royal jurisdiction and visitation over the distribution of armorial bearings in England dates from 1417. Issued by Thomas Duke of Clarence and written in French, it specifies that each of the four so-called 'Kings of Arms' in a given 'province' should know all the 'noble and gentle' residents in that area; that the names and arms of those noble and gentle families be registered; and that each officer of arms frequent 'honeste places et bonne compaignie', and apply himself to read 'livres de bonnes moeurs, eloquence, croniques actes et gestes d'honneur faictz d'armes'.[56]

[53] Given-Wilson, *English Nobility*, p. 70.

[54] Wagner, *English Genealogy*, p. 120. For Edward III's Arthurian displays, see also R. S. Loomis, 'Chivalric and Dramatic Imitations', 1. 79–97, and Juliet Vale.

[55] Wagner, *Heralds and Heraldry*, p. 66.

[56] Cited from ibid. 137–8. Mervyn James thinks the document may be spurious; see James, 'English Politics', p. 328.

In establishing these controls, the Lancastrian prince is attempting to manage a large and powerful body of families: by the end of the fourteenth century in England the nobility was defined primarily by its ownership of land. It was divided into the sixty or so very great landowners, the nobility *stricto sensu*, while knights, squires, and gentlemen, as many as 9,000 families, comprised the 'gentry'.[57] From the perspective of contemporary royal regulation of chivalric society, we can see that the tensions between metropolitan and provincial courts in both *Gamelyn* and *Gawain* were issues of pressing concern for late medieval kings. *Sir Gawain and the Green Knight* is written in an alliterative metre, and in north-western dialect. Recent scholarship has rightly argued that there is no reason why *Gawain* cannot be a London, or perhaps a Westminster, poem, since so much other alliterative poetry is produced in London. The poem is also conversant with the world of mercantile values.[58] All the same, it does represent a provincial court that happens to be every bit as sophisticated as its royal counterpart, and it is written in a non-metropolitan dialect. *Sir Gawain and the Green Knight* insists that kings must be prepared to see beyond the theatrics of royal spectacle to the powerful network of chivalric society outside Westminster. Richard II, who was dependent on his bodyguard of Cheshire archers in late fourteenth-century London, may have appreciated the force of this lesson.[59]

IV

Late medieval romance, then, negotiates between different poles of power; the king may be the point of departure and return for many romances, but the genre is primarily designed to offer space to the satellite figure of the knight, on whom the king is revealed to be dependent; and the knight's own position is itself revealed to be dependent on his dealings with women and merchants in particular. While the genre ostensibly promotes the interests of knights, their

[57] Given-Wilson, *English Nobility*, ch. 3.
[58] Putter, '*Sir Gawain and the Green Knight*', ch. 5, and Mann, 'Price and Value'.
[59] For which see Bowers, '*Pearl* in its Royal Setting', pp. 115–19.

success is always premissed on a complex interaction with other social forces internal to a given society.

If romance is fitted to address tensions internal to a social system, how well does it cope with civil war? In this section I answer this question by turning to Malory's *Works*, a large set of prose works, translated for the most part from thirteenth-century French sources by Sir Thomas Malory, and finished, in prison, in 1469–70. Malory's central and single near-perfect romance, the only narrative sequence for which no source has been found, 'The Tale of Sir Gareth of Orkney', balances the centrifugal and centripetal forces of his other works. It also exposes, however, why romance cannot constrain the internecine fraternal forces by which both Arthurian and late fifteenth-century English society is broken from within.

Late medieval kings presided over a society whose most powerful forces were geared for war. They were therefore faced with a choice between civil and foreign war. The pattern is quite simple: Edward III, Henry V, Edward IV, and Henry VIII chose wars against France, while Richard II, Henry IV, and Henry VI (all peacemakers with France) were confronted by civil war.[60] The pattern becomes more complex and interesting when we consider that these two kinds of war provoke each other: civil wars may be provisionally resolved by foreign conquest, but the enormous expense of maintaining foreign conquest, and the social disruption provoked by servicing war, themselves provoke civil war. That is what Lydgate predicts in his *Troy Book* (1412–20), and that is what effectively happened after the death of Henry V: the lands gained in France by Henry's conquests had all been lost by 1453; the first battle of the civil war known as the Wars of the Roses was in 1455.

Immediately after that sequence of civil wars, and just before another in 1485, we can see the same pattern reasserting itself. A speech made on behalf of Edward IV to the Commons in 1472 itself makes precisely the points I have just made with crystal clarity. It was made after eighteen years of civil war, in which two kings had been deposed, one of whom had been murdered. In 1472 Edward IV, who

[60] These choices are not of course immutable, but I describe the main thrust of policy for each king. See Keen, for the period up to the reign of Henry VII. For Henry VIII's duplicitous and aggressive dealings with France, see e.g. Scarisbrick, *Henry VIII*, ch. 2.

had returned from his deposition in 1470, is now secure as king, but only, the speaker insists, as long as he declares war on France. No one has escaped the trouble of recent history, he begins, but now the problem is 'rotely taken awey and extincte, so that there can be lefte no colowr or shadowe . . . in any mannys mynde but that our Soverayn Lord is in dede . . . sole and undoubted Kyng'. No sooner does he make this affirmation, however, than he qualifies its confidence: there is many a 'perilous wounde left unheled', and the kingdom is full of 'the multitude of riotous people'. Considering the inveterate nature and extensiveness of this violence, the speaker concedes that the 'rigour of the lawe' should not be applied, since it would result in the decimation of the population, and render the realm vulnerable to foreign attack by the Scots, Danes, and French. No, the only solution is to set the riotous and idle multitude, under the leadership of the King, the Lords, and the 'Gentils', to the work of 'werre outward', in which many 'gentilmen, as well yonger brothers as other, myght there be worshipfully rewarded'. War will best serve for 'pacifieng of the londe inwards', since, 'be it well remembred, how that it is nat wele possible, nor hath ben seen since the Conquest, that justice, peax, and prosperite hath contenued any while in this lande in any Kings dayes but in suche as have made werre outward'.[61]

This speech was made just two or so years after Malory finished his sequence of Arthurian works. Its tone is militant and externally aggressive, and thereby provides a convenient contrast with Malory's finally melancholic presentation of defeat in France, as Lancelot parcels out the territories that England had lost by 1453.[62]

The speech's call to outward aggression for the purpose of inward peace also contrasts with Malory's use of romance as an alternative way of imagining pacification of the 'londe inwards'. Romances tend, as we have seen, to begin and end with the *loci* of central authority, leaving a large space for the operations of both illicit pleasure and constructive violence within that frame. The structure of Malory's *Works* presents the same broad pattern, since the outer panel deals with Arthur's rise to national and then international

[61] *Literae Cantuarienses*, ed. Sheppard, 3. 282. For the follow-up to this policy (the invasion of France, which ended in the treaty of Picquigny in 1475), see Keen, pp. 475–8.

[62] Malory, *Works*, ed. Vinaver, rev. Field, 3. 1204–5.

power, while the final sequence traces the retreat from that power into the tragedy of civil war from which the story had begun. Between those outer panels stands a series of romances, each exploring in its own way how the balance of inward power may be sustained within Arthur's imperial success. The narratives of Lancelot, Gareth, Tristram, the Grail, and finally Lancelot and Guinevere each seek the resolutions of romance, by way of containing the very energies that Arthur's external success has unleashed.

To put the matter in this admittedly simplifying way may imply that Malory conceived of his work as one book. The structural alterations Malory makes to his sources in the early works, especially the postponement of Arthur's fall in the Emperor Lucius section, and the broad pattern of rise and fall in the work as a whole, make the argument that Malory conceived of the whole book within one broad strategy unassailable. This is not at all, however, to suggest that Caxton was right to reduce the book into a single narrative disposition. On the contrary, there are radical heterogeneities between the different parts of the one book, and these are themselves, in my view, part of Malory's strategy. In their heterogeneity, they are more like the chivalric compilations of powerful gentry families, the so-called 'Grete Bokes' of chivalry, than they are like the other prose romances printed by Caxton, to be discussed below.[63] Malory's *Works* are, one might say, the *Canterbury Tales* of chivalric literature: one broadly conceived work in which heterogeneous sequences are strategically juxtaposed.[64]

Each sequence has its own specificity, but the broadest terms of this heterogeneity are history and romance, which are most starkly evident in the differences between 'The Tale of the Noble King Arthur and the Emperour Lucius' and 'The Tale of Sir Gareth of Orkney'. These two narratives represent different genres of writing: they have quite distinct structures, which themselves serve quite distinct ideological ends. The structure of 'Lucius' is linear, tracing a pattern of imperial conquest, while 'Gareth' is circular, beginning and ending

[63] For 'Grete Bookes' of chivalry and Malory's relation with them, see Cherewatuk.

[64] For a clear account of the one/many book/s debate for Malory's work/s, see Meale, '"Hoole Book"', pp. 3–6. For an excellent example of scholarship that does recognize the heterogeneity, see Riddy, *Sir Thomas Malory*.

with Arthur. 'Lucius' is focused on the person of the king and his success: Arthur is larger than life, he takes on fights himself, and all relationships within this narrative are political; by the time the narrative is finished, all relationships are also vertical, from the victorious king downwards. In 'Gareth' the king is very much in the background, as kings are in all romance; the focus is instead on the satellite figure, Gareth. Relationships are primarily horizontal, and form a pattern of male combat and heterosexual love leading to marriage. By asserting himself in horizontal relationships, Gareth rearranges vertical relationships: when he returns at the end, Arthur, earlier the parental provider, now 'wepte as he had bene a chylde', while Gareth's mother sinks in a swoon. Even the geographical coding is different in both narratives: Arthur traverses recognizable European territory on his way to France and then Rome, while Gareth must find his way to a British castle besieged by a 'tirraunte', the Rede Knight of the Rede Laundys, of whom not even Arthur has heard.[65] The first of these narratives serves a monarchical, centralizing ideology, while the second serves the ideology of both magnates and gentry: Gareth is himself a magnate, and his power is finally constituted by the smaller knights whom he has defeated, as they return at the end to form his household.

On the face of it, romance is the subservient obverse of imperial conquest narratives, since the one pacifies the 'lond inward', while the other engages those energies for 'werre outward'. Certainly 'Sir Gareth' promises to hold its place within a larger monarchical system, by consistently applying a principle of blood's nobility to order internal conflict, and by acknowledging Arthur's authority as the source of that nobility. The entire story of 'Sir Gareth' is marked by moments of hiding or disclosing name, precisely because disclosure of name equally discloses a hierarchy of blood. The narrative can only begin, indeed, by Gareth hiding his name, and pretending to no higher ambition than to be a kitchen boy. Once his adventure begins, he reveals his name only to those whom he cannot defeat (i.e. Lancelot) or to those whom he has already defeated. Refusal to disclose the name leads invariably to violence, a violence that issues in

[65] Malory, *Works*, ed. Vinaver, I. 296. Further refs. to this edn. will appear in the text.

Gareth's victory and the disclosure of his name and lineage. Disclosure of name produces, correlatively, reconciliation and the winding down of narrative. This applies to Gareth's fights not only against knights external to the Round Table, but also against Arthur's own knights; in the tournament called by Arthur he insists on further repression of his name: 'I woll nat be knowyn of neythir more ne lesse, nothir at the begynnynge nother at the endyng' (I. 345). As long as anonymity is preserved, significant violence remains possible, and the narrative remains unclosed. In the tournament itself, Gareth changes colour by virtue of the ring given him by his future wife Lyonesse, such 'that there myght neyther kynge nother knyght have no redy cognyssauns of hym' (I. 348). Forgetting his magic ring after his final victory, Gareth is discovered; his name is publicized as widely as possible, with the herald now shouting '"This is sir Gareth of Orkenay in the yealow armys!"' (I. 351), thus bringing the tournament to an end.

Each fight is consistently resolved by manifesting Gareth's royal birth, whereby levels of physical power and birth, both encoded in Gareth's name, are identified: '"Thow lyest!"', Gareth says to one of his adversaries, '"I am a jantyllman borne, and of more hyghe lynage than thou, and that I woll preve on thy body"' (I. 304). Almost whenever Gareth is named, his kin is identified at the same time; his proper name is inseparable from the collectivity to which he belongs, a collectivity that is defined by its royal blood: '"Wete you well, he is a kynges son and a quenys, and his fadir hyght kynge Lot of Orkeney, and his modir is sistir to kyng Arthure, and he is brother to sir Gawayne, and his name is sir Gareth of Orkenay"' (I. 329). If power and birth are coterminous, then this narrative does not trace any moral trajectory, and cannot be described, despite appearances, as a story of becoming. Instead, Gareth rather manifests what he already is. For this reason, again despite appearances, there are no chances, or *aventures*, in this story, since Gareth's progress is genetically determined. This point is made from within the story when Gareth defeats the Black Knight. The scoffing Lyonet accompanying him dismisses the victory as 'myssehappe'; Gareth replies by courteously using Lyonet's word 'hap', meaning 'chance', in such a way as to point to its irrelevance: '"for ever ye sey that they woll sle me othir [or] bete me, but howsomever hit *happenyth* I ascape and they lye on the ground"' (1. 304, my emphasis). The story is designed to demonstrate and to reiterate what it knows from the beginning: Gareth's nobility. This nobility both permits Gareth's erotic pleasure and guarantees his marital success with Lyonesse, the wealthy and noble woman in whose service he undertakes his adventures. Only the power relations around Gareth change, relations that are established by the noble figure simply manifesting his disguised, innate superiority by strategic violence. Precisely because name so thoroughly encodes innate quality, it must be disguised for the narrative to 'happen' at all.[66]

This romance would seem, then, to balance the centrifugal claims of chivalry carefully with the centripetal claims of monarchy. It recognizes the need for Gareth to manifest his power outside the ambit of Arthur's power, and it allows a space for both female and male erotic pleasure. That violence and even illicit pleasure finally, however, buttress both Gareth and Arthur: the pleasure leads to marriage, and the violence brings the defeated knights within Gareth's newly formed household, and so within the ambit of the Round Table. The narrative understands a knight's dependence on women, and the king's dependence on knights brought in from outside, but it equally underlines the superiority of the king's power.

'Gareth' is as fully achieved as romance can be, but Malory leaves a small loose end in it, from which, in part, the entire system of Arthur's court unravels. Once Gareth has defeated knights of the Round Table, except for Lancelot, the story would seem to have nowhere further to go. It does take one further, final step, however, in which Gareth encounters his older brother in a violent, anonymous, and unresolved individual combat, the only unresolved fight in the Gareth sequence.[67] In the story as a whole, the carefully graded pattern of violence begins with common thieves, moves to knights exterior to the Round Table, almost culminates with knights of the Round Table, but can only end as Gareth moves as close to himself as possible, in a fight with his own brother. Gawain and Gareth's

[66] The previous two paragraphs are largely drawn from Simpson, 'Violence, Narrative and Proper Name'.

[67] For the story pattern of older and younger brother conflict (and Gareth's earlier conflict with Gawain in this tale), see Nolan, '*Tale of Sir Gareth* and *Tale of Sir Lancelot*'.

fight is both the logical consequence and the undoing of romance. Social gradation in this narrative is achieved by constructive violence premissed on degrees of nobility; the Gareth–Gawain fight must be unresolved, because there can be no genetic distinction between them. So while this rigorously systematic narrative follows through to the place it must end, with Gareth's violence exercised ever closer to himself, it also points to the unresolvable difference of fraternal combat. The fight ends peaceably, but by the end of the narrative Gareth, devoted to Lancelot, is withdrawing from Gawain's company, 'for he [Gawain] was evir vengeable, and where he hated he wolde be avenged with murther: and that hated Sir Gareth' (1. 360).

A system of primogeniture made distinctions between the genetically identical at precisely the point where a system of nobility of blood could least afford distinction. Fraternal relations were clearly therefore a source of serious disruption in chivalric society. The 1472 speech cited above, for example, feels the need to cater for the violent energies of 'gentilmen, as well yonger brothers as other'. To say that the entire system of Arthur's kingdom unravels from the moment of Gareth's unresolved fight with Gawain is to point forward to future catastrophe. It points especially to the unresolvable dispute between Gawain and Lancelot in the final sequence, where Gawain refuses to forgive Lancelot for Lancelot's accidental murder of Gareth. The crucial vulnerabilities in Arthur's power take the form of horizontal rivalries, and especially between Lancelot and Gawain.

More broadly, the fraternal aggression that 'Gareth' cannot absorb is symptomatic of the incapacities of a comic mode across the whole of Malory's *Works*. The very neatness and narrative rigour of 'Gareth' point to the messiness of its adjacent narratives, focused on the royal adulterers Lancelot and Tristram respectively, which seek yet fail to be romances. In the honour culture of the 'brotherhood' of the Round Table, the best knights have nowhere to go but against the society at whose apex they stand. So Lancelot must simultaneously be the source both of greatest stability and anarchy, loving the king's wife and fighting his knights. The narrative of Tristram not only threatens to pull Arthur's kingdom into the instability of Cornwall; the adultery that generates the narrative also issues in unfinishable, repetitive, and horizontal rivalries between men. Whereas earlier French Tristan narratives splinter into ever smaller units as they replicate the identity crises of adulterous love, Malory's version becomes unmanageably long, as it pursues the male rivalries that are embedded in yet unresolvable in this romance narrative.[68] Romance in Malory is haunted by the fate of Balan, the hero and victim of the second narrative in the very first sequence of stories. In a story of unmitigated disaster and consistently malign chance,[69] Balan unwittingly kills his own brother Balyn. Not only are their names nearly indistinguishable, but after their fight so too are their very faces unrecognizable: Balan lifts the visor of his moribund brother, but he 'myght not know hym by the vysage, it was so ful hewen and bledde' (l. 57). The fate of Balan is not unlike the fate of the 'maleureux' Malory, who wrote his book in prison after, it seems, having changed sides with Warwick in a civil war which itself threatened to obliterate the difference, but not the hostility, between 'brothers'.[70] Like 'Tristan', Malory's very name signals the impossibility of romance.[71] Certainly the eternal promise of romance to hold history at bay is finally broken in the *Works*, since the recollection of Henry V's victories in the 'Lucius' sequence is balanced by the recollection of Henry VI's losses in France in the final sequence. The intervening romances have failed to do their work of containing the energies of 'gentilmen, as well yonger brothers as other'. We can only gauge the force of that failure by distinguishing between different, and finally opposed, kinds of chivalric writing within Malory's *Works*.

V

The knight Malory may not have survived the civil wars, but his merchant printer William Caxton certainly did. Caxton was born between 1415 and 1424, and died in 1492. He therefore lived through at least seven regnal changes, and despite his apparently

[68] Examples of the splintering of the Tristan and Isolde story in earlier French and Anglo-Norman narrative are as follows: Marie de France's *lai Chevrefoil*, and the *Folie Tristan* texts, of both Oxford and Berne.

[69] For which see Mann, '"Taking the Adventure"'.

[70] For Malory's extraordinarily violent career, see P. J. C. Field.

[71] The etymology of 'Malory' is 'maleureux', or 'unlucky'; see P. J. C. Field, p. 38.

close relations with Yorkist kings and magnates,[72] he remained productive as a publisher of books, often with explicit Tudor connections, up to his death in the reign of Henry VII.[73] Although he cannot have planned the near coincidence, Caxton happily released *The Noble and Joyous Booke entytled Le Morte Darthur*—his title for Malory's *Works*—on the last day of July 1485, three weeks before the Welsh Henry Tudor's victory in the Battle of Bosworth. It is plausible that Caxton's failure to name a Yorkist patron for the work is tactical; whereas Caxton freely uses the names of kings in his prologues, *Le Morte Darthur* was prepared at the instance of 'many noble and dyvers gentylmen of thys royame'.[74] However much he may simply be placing his bets both ways here, Caxton's packaging of chivalric matter, including his romances, was, however, very much in keeping with the Tudor centralization of chivalry.

Romance survives the Tudor revolution. While the events of the 1530s and 1550s provoked the radical limitation or the official repudiation of many varieties of Middle English writing, romance continued to be produced. The *Works* of Malory, in Caxton's ver-

[72] Caxton's dedications are conveniently gathered in *Caxton's Own Prose*, ed. Blake. I list the following dedications to, commissions from, and claims of 'protection' from Yorkist royals and magnates, with date and relevant page numbers of *Caxton's Own Prose*, ed. Blake, in parentheses. Dedicated to Edward IV: *Siege of Jerusalem* (1481, pp. 141, 142). Executed under the 'protection' of Edward IV: *Mirror of the World* (1481, p. 119); *Of Old Age, Of Friendship and Declamation of Noblesse* (1481, p. 122); *Polychronicon* (1482, p. 132); *Siege of Jerusalem* (1481, p. 141). Dedicated to Prince Edward: *Jason* (*c.*1477, p. 104). Commissioned by Margaret Duchess of Burgundy: *History of Troy* (1473, p. 97). Dedicated to Richard III: *Order of Chivalry* (*c.*1484, p. 127). Dedicated to George Duke of Clarence: *Game of Chess* (1474, p. 85). Dedicated to Lord Hastings: *Mirror of the World* (1481, p. 115). Commissioned by Earl Rivers: *Cordial* (trans. Rivers, 1479, p. 70); *Dicts or Sayings of the Philosophres* (trans. Rivers, 1477, p. 73); *Moral Proverbs* (1478, p. 119). Commissioned by the Earl of Arundel: *Golden Legend* (1483, p. 96). None of these claims should be taken at face value, and may encompass a wide range of relationships, some of which, and especially claims of 'protection', may be very vague. For caution about Caxton's claims to patronage, see Blake, 'William Caxton: A Review', pp. 9–14.

[73] For Caxton's life, see Blake, *William Caxton*. The Tudor dedications and commissions are as follows (year and relevant page number of *Caxton's Own Prose*, ed. Blake in parentheses). Dedicated to Prince Arthur: *Eneydos* (1490, p. 81). Commissioned by Queen Elizabeth and Margaret, Duchess of Somerset: *Fifteen Oes* (1491, p. 83). Dedicated to Margaret, Duchess of Somerset: *Blanchardyn and Eglantine* (*c.*1489, p. 57). Commissioned by Henry VII: *Fayttes of Armes* (1489, p. 81).

[74] For the relation between Caxton's publication of Malory and the battle of Bosworth, see Blake, 'Caxton Prepares his Edition', p. 206.

sion, were themselves reprinted in every century except the eighteenth until and including the twentieth.[75] Certainly the genre was subject to attack first by the medieval Church, and later by humanists and Protestants, but the market for romance remained viable, cultivated as it was by enterprising commercial printers.[76] In the first place, the genre did not activate any sustained official campaign, possibly for many of the same reasons that it often fell below scholarly notice in the twentieth century: romance occupies a low place in the literary system.[77] Mainly, however, romance flourished across the entire period of this history by absorbing and acknowledging attack with insouciant confidence. Just as the condition of success for a romance hero or heroine is that they patiently submit to that which threatens them, so too do romances adapt to new discursive, commercial, and political environments. Discursively, they might acknowledge their often liminal ethical credentials by citing St Paul to the effect that all that is written is written for our instruction (2 Tim. 4: 16), even the libidinal narrative of romance;[78] or they might fit penitential recuperation to the pattern of romance narrative;[79] or they remain romance in the guise of hagiography.[80]

Commercially, romance adapts to new markets precisely because

[75] For a list of editions from 1485 to 1983, see Parins (ed.), pp. 40–4.

[76] For late medieval preachers' attacks on the reading of romance, see Spencer, pp. 36, 90–1. For humanist attack, see Ascham's comments cited in Parins (ed.), pp. 56–7, and Richard Hyrd's translation of Vives's *Instruction of a Christen Woman* (?1529), cited in Cooper, 'Romance after 1400', pp. 694–5. Puritan reading of Malory required expurgation, for an example of which see L. B. Wright, *Middle Class Culture*, p. 394.

[77] The raid made in 1569 on the antiquary John Stow's house, in search of illicit texts, is instructive. The romances found ('Sir Degory, Tryamoure etc') are dismissed as 'folish and fabulous bokes of olde prynte'. The religious matter, by contrast, is reported as incriminating: 'He hath besides . . . old phantasticall popishe bokes prynted in the olde tyme. . . . His bokes declare him to be a great favourer of papistrye'. Cited from Stow, *Survey of London*, ed. Kingsford, vol. 1, pp. xvi–xvii.

[78] Thus the Prologue to *Partonope of Blois*, ed. Bödtker, ll. 1–63. In the Preface to *Blanchardyn and Eglantine* Caxton argues that romance reading provides models of courage and fidelity for the young, both men and women. He defends romance by saying that it is just as profitable for the young, 'as it is to occupye theym and studye overmoche in bokes of contemplacion' (*Caxton's Own Prose*, ed. Blake, p. 58).

[79] Thus e.g. *Sir Gowther*, *Isumbras*, *Robert of Sicily*, Lydgate's *Guy of Warwick*, *Valentine and Orson*.

[80] Thus e.g. Chaucer's *Man of Law's Tale* and Gower's Constance narrative (*Confessio Amantis*, 2. 587–1598).

romance narrative itself often recognizes the power of merchants. Even if the speech to the Commons of Parliament in 1472 I cited above encouraged a war policy to be conducted by knights, the speech itself was, however, principally designed to persuade merchants, who made up a significant proportion of the Commons in late medieval parliaments.[81] All late medieval kings wanting to wage foreign war were heavily dependent on merchants not only for large-scale credit, but also for revenues from both taxation and the commodities market, especially wool.[82] This structure of society, in which merchants formed an intrinsic part of the chivalric and military system, is acknowledged in many romances, though not in those by Malory. It is far too powerful not to survive the arrival of Henry VII and the revolutionary regime of his son. Caxton himself aimed at this parliamentary society made up of both merchants and knights. His press was in Westminster, and in one instance at least he hired a shop for the period of parliament.[83] Although he addresses 'the knightes of Englond' in many of his prologues, encouraging them to 'rede the noble volumes of Saynt Graal, of Lancelot, of Galaad, of Trystram, of Perse Forest, of Percyval, of Gawayn and many mo',[84] he is also offering the same material to a mercantile audience. Prior to print, many of these romances, in French, had been part of a luxury commodities market open only to the upper nobility;[85] Caxton may himself have traded in such goods,[86] but now he offered them at affordable prices, in English, to a larger audience. And if nobles were dependent on merchants, the reverse was also true: Caxton, after all, was and remained principally a merchant, and while his books must have been bought by mercantile readers, his most explicit address is to a chivalric class. This remained true after the accession

[81] For which see A. L. Brown, 'Parliament, *c.*1377–1422'; and Myers.

[82] See esp. Kaeuper, ch. 1.

[83] For which see Blake, *William Caxton*, pp. 31–2.

[84] *Caxton's Own Prose*, ed. Blake, p. 126.

[85] For examples of books owned by the upper nobility in the 15th cent., and the overlap with Caxton's production, see Kekewich. There are also strong areas of overlap between the Burgundian ducal library and Caxton's output, for which see Blake, *Caxton and his World*, p. 70. This may not imply Caxton's direct access to that library (Blake, 'William Caxton: A Review', p. 14), but it does demonstrate that Caxton was printing works, for a wider audience, that corresponded to the tastes and possessions of the upper nobility.

[86] Blake, *William Caxton*, pp. 17–18.

of Henry VII: while Caxton had produced some chivalric material before 1485, including *The Order of Chivalry* dedicated to Richard III in 1484, and while he had clearly prepared the Malory collection before Bosworth, the bulk of his specifically chivalric translations were produced after the accession of Henry VII: *Paris and Vienne* (1485); *Charles the Great* (1485); *Blanchardyn and Eglantine* (1488); *Fayttes of Armes* (1489); *Four Sons of Aymon* (1489); and *Eneydos* (1490).[87]

The marketing of printed romances for mercantile audiences is even clearer in the business practices of Caxton's successor, Wynkyn de Worde, who took over Caxton's press in 1492 until his death in 1534/5. Richard Pynson, the other main successor to Caxton in the English booktrade, relied principally on the secure market of official sponsorship; he produced official publications (yearbooks, statutes, liturgical books) and became King's Printer in 1508. De Worde, by contrast, developed a commercial market.[88] One index of this is that he moved the Caxton press from Westminster to Fleet Street in 1500; another is that he produced some 'popular' verse romances. Caxton himself had been rather wary of older vernacular English literature, relying on the few big names of Chaucer, Gower, and Lydgate; all his romances, apart from Malory's *Works*, are translations from French. De Worde seems to have shared Caxton's caution before leaving Westminster, producing as he did a large folio *Canterbury Tales* and an edition of Malory's *Works*. He continued to produce prose romance after leaving Westminster, but unlike Caxton he also printed a number of Middle English verse romances in this period, including both earlier fourteenth-century works like *Apollonius of Tyre*, *Bevis of Hampton*, *Sir Degaré*, *Torrent of Portyngale*, and *Ipomydon*, and rather more sophisticated fifteenth-century productions like *Generides* and the extraordinary *Partonope of Blois*.[89] In producing these romances de Worde was relying on 'traditions of popularity close to those of Middle English manuscript culture';[90] and by appealing to a mercantile readership he was also feeding a market that had already in the fifteenth century been one consumer

[87] For the dates of Caxton's entire output, see ibid. 51–63.

[88] For the activities of both Pynson and de Worde, see Edwards and Meale.

[89] Meale, 'Caxton, de Worde and the Publication of Romance', 288–9.

[90] Edwards and Meale, pp. 118–19.

of Middle English verse romances.[91] The design of a page printed for this market was clearly designed to mimic the effect of a luxury manuscript, but to make it available to a much wider audience, as in Figure 6, the title-page of, appropriately, the *Squire of Low Degree*, a narrative about upward social mobility.[92]

Romance, then, is an unkillable genre. It survived the medieval 'period' in both low and high form, both the popular versions of Middle English romances found in the Percy folio (*c.*1650), or, say, Spenser's Protestant and courtly *Faerie Queene* (1589–96).[93] Self-consciously archaic romance even bears the weight of Shakespeare's near-final reflections on his entire dramatic career, in the 'old wives' tales' of the late plays, the *Winter's Tale*, *Cymbeline*, and *Pericles*, the last of which is introduced by 'Gower' in recollection of one source for the play, Gower's own beautiful Apollonius romance (*Confessio Amantis*, 8. 271–2008).

If for later Tudor and Jacobean writers romance is a permissible channel back to the repressed pre-Reformation past, Spenserian romance nevertheless bears the imprint of the Tudor centralization of chivalry around the person of the monarch. This centralizing process began with Caxton's homogenization of Malory's *Works*, includes Hawes's 'indoctrination' of chivalry in his *Pastime of Pleasure* (1506) (ll. 372–2912)[94] and, in the period of this history, reaches its culmination in what Mervyn James has called Henry VIII's 'nationalization of honour'.[95] I turn to this process by way of completing these sections on chivalric comedy, before turning in my final section to Chaucer's comedic works.

Both Henry VII and Henry VIII deployed Arthurian materials for their own propaganda. That Henry VII, with his Welsh ancestry, should have named his first son Arthur would itself seem to imply an obvious appeal to Arthurian precedent for a victorious Welsh ruler. There is, however, some evidence to the contrary. Because Arthurian

[91] Meale, '"Gode men | Wiues maydenes and alle men"'.

[92] See Lerer, *Courtly Letters*, pp. 82–5 for the reuse of this frontispiece, originally used by de Worde, in a wide range of works.

[93] For the popularization of romance, see Pearsall, 'English Romance in the Fifteenth Century', pp. 64–6. For the contents of the Percy folio, see Guddat-Figge (ed.), pp. 151–9.

[94] Hawes's poem narrates the education of the chivalric hero, which includes a training in the liberal arts.

[95] James, 'English Politics', pp. 328–9.

Fig. 6. Anonymous, *The Squire of Low Degree*, n.d., frontispiece.

references were transformed into classical and astronomical references in poems on the birth of Arthur and in the pageant welcoming Katherine of Aragon as Arthur's future wife in 1501, scholars have argued that the early Tudor kings did not make very much of the Arthurian connection.[96] This position needs now to be nuanced, particularly with regard to Henry VIII's use of Arthur. At moments when the 'imperial pretentions of the English crown were at stake', Arthur was deployed: this is true of Henry's claims to both religious and military jurisdictions, as we have seen in Chapter 3.[97] The Act of Appeals of 1533 declares that 'by diverse sundry old authentic histories and chronicles it is manifestly declared and expressed that this realm of England is an empire',[98] and John Leland's presentation of Arthur, *Assertio inclytissimi Arthuri* (1544) was clearly designed for propagandistic and imperialist ends. Earlier in the early 1520s, as Henry manoeuvred against France, he had used Arthuriana, including the Round Table, as part of his diplomacy with the Spanish.[99]

Henry's use of Arthur for diplomatic and propagandistic purposes was primarily shaped to the ends of an aggressive foreign policy; in a literary history, it is, therefore, more relevant to the history of tragic narrative than to comedy. Domestically, however, Henry sought control over the entire chivalric system. In 1530 a dispute between two of the king's heraldic officers was resolved by Henry claiming a direct prerogative over the granting of arms. He instituted a system of visitation, whereby the king's so-called King of Arms, or chief heraldic officer in a given area, was 'to reforme all false armorye and Armes devysed without auctoritie'. The officer was to 'deface' these illegitimate arms, wherever they appeared, whether in stone, plate, or windows. This chivalric iconoclasm was the obverse of Henry's new chivalric creations. The King of Arms was entitled to distribute arms according to the 'grace vertue or connynge [knowledge]' of potential recipients, as long as they were not rebels, heretics, or 'issued of vyle blood'.[100] In defining this system Henry was clearly perfecting the visitations envisaged in the 1417 document cited

96 Anglo, '*British History*'; and Carlson, 'King Arthur'.

97 The citation is from D. Starkey, 'King Henry and King Arthur', p. 193.

98 Cited from Scarisbrick, *Henry VIII*, pp. 272–3.

99 D. Starkey, 'King Henry and King Arthur', p. 194.

100 Wagner, *Heralds and Heraldry*, pp. 9–10. Ch. 9, below, offers an account of the controversy that gave rise to the commission of 1530.

above, but he also massively extended the system. Now Henry claimed the sole right to distribute arms, and he did so on the basis of service rather than blood. Earlier, medieval claims to nobility of soul had been made in *opposition* to claims to nobility through blood.[101] The 1530 document certainly registers the possibility of 'nobility of soul' (i.e. service to Henry), but does so by incorporating it *within* the system of blood. It also made the king the sole arbiter of nobility, the font of a 'state-centred honour system'.[102]

One 'Caxtodunus' (i.e. Caxton) had prompted Leland to search out 'authentic' remains of Arthur.[103] I end this section by considering some of the ways in which Caxtonian romance is consonant with the Henrician centralization of chivalry. Caxton famously reduced the eight narrative sequences of Malory's *Works* into one work; he ordered it into twenty-one books, each subdivided into chapters, a fact that did not occur to scholars until the discovery of a prior version, the so-called Winchester manuscript, in 1934. This meant that Malory's *Works* were read for 450 years as a single book and under a title that pointed the whole book to Arthur.[104] Caxton also removed explicits within the *Works* that mention the author (i.e. Books 4 and 7), and he deletes mention of Malory as prisoner in other explicits.[105] His other main change to Malory's text was to rework the language of the second book in detail, ironing out the powerful alliterative traces that remained from Malory's own reworking of the alliterative *Morte Arthure*. The cumulative effect of these changes was to bring the whole work under the appearance of a single monarchical perspective; to expel language that did not conform to the 'London' standard that Caxton himself was shaping;[106] to repress reference to the authorial 'knight prisoner' of the recent civil wars; and, above all, to homogenize Malory's sequence of generically discrepant chivalric narratives. The new *ordinatio*, or organization, of Malory's *Works* is made to look identical with the layout of Caxton's other, generally Burgundian prose romances, like

[101] For examples and further reading, see Simpson, *Sciences and the Self*, p. 295 n. 23.

[102] James, 'English Politics', p. 338.

[103] Parins (ed.), p. 53.

[104] Ibid. 40–4.

[105] Blake, 'Caxton Prepares his Edition', pp. 203–7. For a scholarly edn. of Caxton's print, see Malory, *Caxton's Malory*, ed. Spisak.

[106] Issues of standardization arise explicitly in Caxton's prologues; see e.g. his Prologue to *Eneados* in *Caxton's Own Prose*, ed. Blake, pp. 78–81.

Blanchardyn and Eglantine, which *is* narrated from a single perspective.

My argument is not that Caxton is in any simple way a Tudor propagandist. It is true that he made, as one might expect of a merchant understandably interested in survival, explicitly favourable comments about the Tudors. The rose imagery in *Blanchardyn and Eglantine* is, for example, given a specifically Tudor spin,[107] and he also declares that he produced books specifically at the request of Henry VII.[108] The book in which the details of Henry's command to translate are most specific is *The Book of Fayttes of Armes and of Chivalry*, a chivalric manual translated from Christine de Pisan's own early fifteenth-century French compilation. This work in no way promotes a centrifugal chivalric ideology; instead it offers specific instruction in military strategy, and a précis of the international laws that should govern war. In its commitment to centralized monarchy, it is positively hostile to chivalric ideology in many ways, arguing, for example, that trials of combat usurp the function of the king's justice.[109] And in his Prologue to this work Caxton is unusually frank about the bases of Henry's power, to which Caxton presents himself as a humble servant: Caxton has not 'herd ne redde', he says, 'that ony prynce hath subdued his subgettis with lasse hurte' than Henry Tudor.[110]

Caxton's 'centralization' of Malory is not, however, so much a sign of intimacy with or direct subservience to the new Tudor king, as of the logic of printing. New technologies of expanded reproduction always involve problems of control. In the matter of romance writing, Caxton's own proactive response both to those problems and to his chosen market was to produce romances in which knights are thoroughly self-regulating and subservient to royal governance. This is most obviously true of his translation *Paris and Vienne* (published in December 1485). This prose romance tells the story of the love between the Princess Vienne and her slightly less noble lover Paris. This discrepancy of status drives the narrative until its final resolution, as in many of the romances we have considered in this

[107] Cooper, 'Romance after 1400', p. 707.

[108] *Fayttes of Armes* (1489); see *Caxton's Own Prose*, ed. Blake, p. 81.

[109] *The Book of Fayttes of Armes and of Chyvalrye*, ed. Byles, pp. 258–61.

[110] *Caxton's Own Prose*, ed. Blake, p. 82.

chapter. The discrepancy, however, is relatively small: Paris's family forms part of the princely visiting circle, rather in the manner of a Stendhal novel, and the decorous movement towards resolution of a small courtly society serves at the same time as a model of courtesy. There certainly is intra-family dispute (Vienne is imprisoned by her princely father). But the narrative decorum is strictly verisimilar, and the artistic energy in this work goes into the composition of letters, cited in full, and extended speeches of persuasion; the plot is entirely secondary to the models of courtesy that the story occasions.

Paris and Vienne was produced only five months after Caxton's *Morte Darthure*. The two prose works, along with Caxton's other prose romance, *Blanchardyn and Eglantine* (1488) are given chapter headings and are therefore each presented as one work. While this is entirely in keeping with the single perspective and narrative coherence of the later works, it disguises the heterogeneities between Malory's narrative sequences, and so disguises the huge difference in kind between Malory's *Works* and these decorous productions. Henry Watson's translation of the prose romance *Valentine and Orson*, produced for Wynkyn de Worde in 1503–5, may contain more risqué 'extravagancies' of nobles become wild men, but all these long prose romances imply readers with a great deal of time, and they all capitalize on the now private experience of a long read to instruct in matters of courteous conduct. As Caxton himself says in the Prologue to *Blanchardyn and Eglantine*, the work is 'honeste and joyefull to all vertuouse yong noble gentylmen and wymmen for to rede therin, as for their passe-tyme'. It teaches 'yonge ladyes and damoyselles' in particular to 'lerne to be stedfast and constaunt' to their lovers.[111] The book was sent to Margaret Beaufort, mother to Henry VII, and Caxton declares that the Duchess had commanded him to translate it. This should not necessarily, however, be mistaken for the personal relationship of writer and patron in a manuscript culture, since Caxton stands between two literary systems, that of aristocratic patronal power and mercantile enterprise.[112] If the book

[111] *Caxton's Own Prose*, ed. Blake, pp. 57–8.

[112] For which see Summit, 'William Caxton, Margaret Beaufort'. MS culture could also work by explicitly addressing a noble patron and a wider audience. *William of Palerne* e.g. is commissioned by Humphrey de Bohun, but written for an English-speaking audience (ll. 164–9).

was indeed commanded by the King's mother, then she too understood the communal potential of printed books. That greater power of distribution, however, equally required the centralization of romance. The word 'romance' derives from 'Rome', the imperial source of the romance languages. 'Romance', then, the space of libidinal errancy, actually contains a recollection of its opposite, the centre of power to which errancy must finally return. By the early sixteenth century, romance is recalled back within reach of a new imperial centre.

VI

The Host in Chaucer's *Canterbury Tales* (1390s) interrupts Chaucer's own performance, the *Tale of Thopas*, principally because the tail-rhyme metre is intolerable, but also because it contains nothing of 'murthe or . . . doctrine' (7. 935). In response Chaucer tells the *Tale of Melibee*, a prose narrative in which narrative itself is almost entirely overborne by deliberation. The contrast between these two tales is extreme in every way. *Thopas* is designed for entertainment; addresses a listening audience in a metrical scheme and with a lexical choice adapted for aural reception; evokes a general literary tradition of chivalric romance; and narrates impetuous action in search of chivalric honour. *Melibee* is designed for instruction; requires private reading for full absorption; is written in an abstract, philosophical prose; precisely cites a range of classical, biblical, and later medieval *auctoritates*; and tells a fundamentally anti-chivalric story, in which the very impulse for sequential narrative is constrained at every point by rational deliberation. While the rich and powerful Melibee, whose daughter Sophie has been subject to aggression, wants to take vengeance to save his honour from public shame, his wife Prudence carefully deflates his aggression and redirects it to the constructive ends of civic harmony and reconciliation.

The contrast between these two tales is comically extreme. Whereas the action of *Thopas* is predicated on *aventures* that disguise an inevitably providential world, the action of *Melibee* relies on nothing but prudential deliberation. In *Thopas* the hero is 'fair and gent' (7.

715), the son of a lord, and if the tale had been allowed to proceed, his actions would inevitably have confirmed and extended his familial power. Melibee, by contrast, is wealthy, but his wealth is labile, and his extended family nebulous: they are, as Prudence warns, 'but a fer kynrede; they been but litel syb to yow' (7. 1375). Human groupings in this narrative are dependent not on lineage but rather on human covenants. Survival in the world of *Melibee* requires rational deliberation on how to bring an apparent catastrophe to a 'good conclusion and to a good ende' (7. 1727), whereas Thopas (whose very name invokes the magical properties of stones) will be dependent on an 'elf-queene' (7. 788). And rational deliberation in the second tale requires professional technologies: it is an 'advocate' who first warns Melibee against a rash response, while Prudence acts in the manner of a professional in conflict resolution. She both advises Melibee to take counsel, and herself skilfully practises the art of counsel, knowing when to speak and when to stay silent.[113] Whereas romance eschews rational reflection, *Melibee* is dominated by it. The very structure of the narrative, indeed, itself implies a form of self-reflection, since Melibee's household is also the 'household' of his psyche: Melibee (whose name means 'honey drinker') represents the will, who has drunk too deep on the 'hony of sweete temporeel richesses' (7. 1411), so much so that his higher wisdom is seriously wounded. He can regain access to that higher wisdom by consulting the prudential wisdom of his wife Prudence, whose gender is, in the literal narrative, not merely grammatical (7. 1069–1111).

Chaucer's choice of tales for himself is characteristically self-deprecating, since both are such extreme examples of their kind that neither has any chance of winning the Canterbury competition. The contrast may be comically extreme, but Chaucer is investing heavily in it by advertising his own comic affiliations. For all its pedestrian rigour, *Melibee*, beside the heading of which Chaucer's portrait is placed in the Ellesmere manuscript, addresses the entirely serious issue of civic reconciliation, and it does so by implicitly dismissing the absurd pretensions of romance to do the same thing. Chaucer commits himself here to a serious assault on the premisses of romance, by promoting nobility of soul above nobility of blood; professional

113 See Wallace, *Chaucerian Polity*, pp. 232–4.

technology above magic in the service of a providential order; and prudential management of social conflict above the pretentions of chivalric violence to create social order. Chaucer promotes, in short, a bourgeois comedy, in which fullness of self is achieved through reflective exercise of professional technologies.[114]

Pitched in this way, the competition between a chivalric and a prudential comedy looks to be over before it has begun. *Thopas*, that is, is so clearly a burlesque of the metrical and narrative techniques of a recognizable form of Middle English romance, many examples of which exist prior to the *Canterbury Tales*. Certainly critics since at least the eighteenth century have read the contest off in this way. Richard Hurd uses the example of the 'manifest banter' of *Thopas* in his *Letters on Chivalry and Romance* (1762) to illustrate how the 'immortal genius' of Chaucer saw into the 'impertinences of books of chivalry'. Describing Chaucer as wholly exceptional to the currents of his own time, 'so superior is the sense of some men to the age they live in', Hurd says that in *Thopas* Chaucer 'not only discerned the absurdity of the old romances, but has even ridiculed them with incomparable spirit'.[115] Twentieth-century professional Chaucerian scholarship, also anxious to assert Chaucer's novel and extraordinary status, took much the same line, arguing that Chaucer repudiated English romance, the one tradition of English poetry from which he might, a priori, have drawn. Developing the words of one critic that Chaucer was 'biting the hand that fed him', one scholar accentuated the hand metaphor by arguing that Chaucer was 'snapping it off at the wrist'.[116] The manuscript collocations of Chaucer's works would seem to support arguments for an apartheid between Chaucer and romance, since works by Chaucer appear in only four manuscripts with verse romances (not including *Gamelyn*, which spuriously appears only in *Canterbury Tales* manuscripts as the tale of the Cook).[117] And whereas Chaucer is a dominant figure for many

[114] Even if the premisses of fabliau are non-chivalric, that still leaves the question of its audience open. See Hines, pp. 23–5 for scholarship on the audience of fabliau.

[115] Hurd, *Letters on Chivalry*, ed. Morley, pp. 146–7.

[116] See, respectively, D. Brewer, 'Relationship of Chaucer', and Spearing, *Medieval to Renaissance*, p. 35. Brewer's article stresses more the feeding than the biting.

[117] Edwards, 'Gender, Order and Reconciliation', p. 63 n. 23.

fifteenth-century non-chivalric writers, chivalric romanciers operate without extended reference, if any at all, to Chaucer. Malory is one example among many, while the author of *Partonope of Blois* is the single important exception.[118]

It may be true that Chaucer's relation to English romance is condescending, despite the fact that he is stylistically indebted to popular romance in English in his earlier works composed in four-stress couplets.[119] In what remains of this chapter, however, I argue that the relation of Chaucer with romance more generally is more accurately described by the notion of 'interruption' and readaptation than that of total rupture. As we have already seen in this chapter, romance is an unkillable genre, capable as it is of resurfacing under new conditions, and flexibly acknowledging as it does all that threatens it. Chaucer has two romances interrupted in the *Canterbury Tales* (*Thopas* and the *Squire's Tale*), but he acknowledges the power of romance even as he interrupts it; he also has recourse to the comic structures of romance to express his own most profound and daring reflections on the political order. The interruption of the Squire's own romance by the Franklin itself encapsulates the irresistible pull of the genre. The Squire chooses romance even after the Knight, his father, has seriously questioned the possibility of chivalric comedy in his tale; not only that, but the Squire's own tale threatens never to end; if the Franklin interrupts him for this reason, it is equally true that the Franklin himself tells a romance, reformulated to suit the needs of a different social gradation. In distinction to the promise of prudential comedy to make a 'good conclusion and . . . a good ende', romance in the *Canterbury Tales* threatens never to end, and can at best be interrupted by the clean endings of fabliaux (short, often bawdy stories of wholly prudential comedy written in a low style). And besides, Chaucer also reveals that professional technologies may themselves lead to unending narratives, as in the *Canon's Yeoman's Tale*, where alchemical experiments 'concluden in multiplicacioun' (8. 849).[120]

[118] For remarks about what amounts to the rather low indebtedness of 15th-cent. romance to Chaucer, see Pearsall, 'English Romance in the Fifteenth Century'; for the exceptional case of *Partonope of Blois*, see Windeatt, 'Chaucer'.

[119] Brewer, 'Relationship of Chaucer'.

[120] For which see Patterson, 'Perpetual Motion'.

Chaucer was surrounded by romance. It was not only a well-represented secular genre in English writing prior to Chaucer, but writers of secular poetry contemporary with, and immediately after, Chaucer all took the genre seriously. It is true that neither Gower, Hoccleve, nor Lydgate make any extended use of Arthurian material,[121] and each of these poets from a non-chivalric class was extremely wary of unbridled chivalric practice; each did, however, write romances. The anti-chivalric Lydgate's single comic romance revealingly treats of the fidelity of two merchants,[122] while Hoccleve deploys romance within his *Series* to create a playfully unpredictable voice in a text that promises to placate its women readers: the first has a woman heroine while the second is dominated by a wily prostitute.[123] At the same time, the first in particular (that of Jereslaus's wife) is a fable of virtue disbelieved being finally restored to social credit, a fable that suits the needs of the estranged Hoccleve. By far the most powerful investment in romance is made, however, by Gower in the *Confessio Amantis*, in which romances are strategically placed constructively to redirect the destructive forces of Ovidian elegy. Whereas the Ovidian tales consistently end in catastrophe and often in bestial transformation, the romances (i.e. Florent in Book 1, Constance in Book 2, and Apollonius in Book 8) are narratives of social reintegration. The last of them, indeed, bears the weight of Gower's politics, as the (notably unchivalric) King Apollonius is restored both to his own kingdom and to that of his wife, but only after having been restored to life by his daughter, and having recovered his wife, both of whom he had thought dead. Precisely because Gower's politics are rooted in the integration of the whole body, romance answers to his political vision more fully than the explicitly political discourse of Book 7. Romance must both acknowledge erotic desire, and nearly incur social transgression before the body politic can be reintegrated. It therefore serves Gower's 'body politics' in an especially apt and rich way: political reintegration is not a matter of abstract reason dominating the desires of the whole body; on the

[121] The only narrative Lydgate devotes to Arthur is, significantly, of his fall; see Lydgate, *Fall of Princes*, 8. 2661–3204.

[122] *Fabula Duorum Mercatorum*, in Lydgate, *Minor Poems*, pt. II, ed. MacCracken, no. 21.

[123] The tales of *Jereslaus' Wife* and of *Jonathas*, both in Hoccleve's *Series*.

contrary, and as in romance structures themselves, the rational order must have commerce with all that threatens it.[124]

None of Gower's romances relies on chivalric violence, and only one involves a knight (Florent). Gower is not promoting a chivalric ethos through romance, but he does rely powerfully on romance as a response to the political and emotional predations of Ovidian elegy. Almost all Chaucer's writing before the *Canterbury Tales* is heavily indebted to traditions of elegy; does romance provide an escape route from elegy for Chaucer as it does for Gower? Or is romance as roundly rejected as *Thopas* would have us believe?

The most obvious point of connection between Ovidian elegy and romance in the *Canterbury Tales* is the Prologue to the *Man of Law's Tale*. Asked to tell a tale, the Man of Law hesitates to respond, since, he says, Chaucer has 'toold of loveris up and doun | Mo than Ovide made of mencioun | In his Episteles' (2. 53–5). He then catalogues many of the women to whom narratives were devoted in the *Legend of Good Women*, along with some other abandoned Ovidian heroines. About to narrate the story of another heroine, we can see a filiation running throughout Chaucer's entire oeuvre here: the Man of Law narrates an alternative to the elegiac *Legend of Good Women*, which itself was written in penance for *Troilus and Criseyde*, which, in turn, massively expands the narrative predicaments of Dido in Book 1 of the *House of Fame*. In fact the Man of Law tells a romance, the narrative of Constance, who must endure a variety of separations from successive husbands before she can finally be reunited with her Roman family.[125]

The Man of Law's choice of genre might suggest that Chaucer is, like Gower, adopting romance as an alternative to elegy, and as an alternative to the history of female oppression evident in that Ovidian narrative filiation that runs back to the beginning of Chaucer's career. This judgement would be premature, since the Man of Law is

124 See Chs. 4 and 5, and Dimmick, '"Redinge of Romance"'.

125 The *Man of Law's Tale* fits the providential comic pattern of romance in every way; for the history of debate about its genre, see Pearsall, *Canterbury Tales*, p. 260. In all the discussion of the *Canterbury Tales* below, I cannot hope to set my argument within the precise context of the voluminous debates of Chaucerian scholarship. I restrict myself to signalling especially pertinent discussions. For an admirable guide to the scholarship, see Cooper, *Canterbury Tales*.

rather presented as a poor reader of Gower, and the romance he tells replicates the narrative of female oppression expressed by Ovidian elegy. Chaucer has the Man of Law take especial pains to distinguish Chaucer's work from that of Gower: the Man of Law praises Chaucer for not having told stories of 'unkynde abhomynacions', mentioning in particular the incest narratives of Canacee and of 'Tyro Appollonius' (2. 77–89). Both these narratives do appear in the *Confessio*, (3. 143–360 and 8. 271–2008) and critics have descried in these lines a dispute between Chaucer and Gower. The more likely force of these lines is that the Man of Law is a poor reader of Gowerian romance, since Gower's Apollonius story is precisely an *anti*-incest narrative. And however much the story told by the Man of Law is not explicitly incestuous, it has direct connections with tales, like the romance *Emaré*, that are. In the Man of Law's romance Constance is made relentlessly to serve the interests of central, Roman power. She is twice married, first to the Sultan of 'Surrye' and then to the Anglo-Saxon king of Northumbria, to whose kingdom she has floated by chance, having been expelled from the land of her first marriage. This realistically implausible geography only makes sense as a cultural geography, wherein Constance traces the boundaries of, and bears the power of, Roman Christianity. Women in this narrative must either be expelled from its Rome-centred ecology, or serve it unswervingly: the mothers of both kings are unremittingly hostile to the Christian princess, while Constance herself returns repeatedly to her father. Unlike the incest narrative of *Emaré*, in which the daughter's marriage finally rehabilitates and distances her incestuous father, the *Man of Law's Tale* has Constance return twice to her father, begging him to recognize her and begging him, even after she has been reunited with her husband, to send her 'namoore unto noon hethenesse' (2. 1112); after her husband's death, she returns a second time to Rome and to father, having 'scaped al hire aventure' (2. 1151). The child she bears to the English king also returns to Rome, to succeed his grandfather as emperor. Constance exports Roman power and imports male rulers; she herself remains wholly within the ambit of patriarchal power. Ovidian elegy may express the victimization of women by the forces of imperial power, as in the case of Dido for example; romance, in the Man of Law's hands, promotes female subservience under the aegis of Christian expansionism. Romance does not necessarily offer an escape from elegy.

What Chaucer, as distinct from the Man of Law, makes of this deployment of romance is unrecoverable. The plurality of voices in the *Canterbury Tales* renders each tale provisional, though not at all necessarily ironic. The *Canterbury Tales* is not short of poor male readers (e.g. the Host, January, Pluto); it is at least plausible to argue that the Man of Law's critique of what are apparently Gower's incest stories is strategic: the Man of Law repudiates incest narratives only to reproduce one.[126] If from one perspective the providential comedy of romance in this tale does not offer any real alternative to elegy, it is consonant with the first group of tales, which collectively mount a powerful critique of providential comedy, and especially of chivalric romance. It does this first by undoing the very possibility of chivalric romance in the *Knight's Tale*, and then by offering an alternative to both romance and elegy in the prudential comedy of fabliaux.

The chance of the Knight pulling the short straw to tell the first tale might seem providential, since it apparently allows 'natural' social decorum to preside over the literary decorum of the *Canterbury Tales*. It is, indeed, a perfect motif of romance narrative itself, since chance returns the noble figure to his 'proper' place in such a way as to undo the operations of chance. This sense of a providential order is powerfully present in the tale itself, especially in its ending, where Theseus articulates the philosophical order of the romance world. The universe is governed by a First Mover, named by Theseus as 'Juppiter', 'the prince and cause of alle thyng, | Convertynge al unto his propre welle' (1. 3036–7). 'Propriety' is the desired end-point of all romances, and propriety implies the fit insertion of the ethical and the political within the larger pattern of 'nature'. 'What', asks Theseus after the tribulations of a romance narrative that ends in marriage within the political order, 'may I conclude of this longe serye, | But after wo I rede us to be mery?' (1. 3067–8).

The phrase 'longe serye' at the end of a Theban narrative that

[126] The most spectacular example of a poor male reader in the *Canterbury Tales* is that of Pluto, who declares that he has one million stories at the ready to prove the inconstancy of women, a statement made only a few lines after we have been referred to another story, that of the rapist Pluto (4. 2222–48). See Mann, *Geoffrey Chaucer*, p. 65.

promises the closure of romance might, however, give us pause. For at the very beginning of his *Thebaid*, which recounts the catastrophic and miscegenated history of Thebes, Statius pauses to ask how he might begin his Theban narrative of 'fraternas acies', since 'longa retro series' (I. 1–7): the catalogue of catastrophe is so long and goes so far back into history that it is difficult to know how to begin. The optimistic, romance ending to the Theban narrative of the *Knight's Tale* ends with an invocation of the larger narrative cycle whose patterns of fraternal strife the *Knight's Tale* replicates *in parvo*. The romance ends, then, by invoking the world of tragic narrative that romance is designed to recuperate from the ravages of time. Can the micro-history of the *Knight's Tale* reverse the endless history of chivalric disaster that stands behind it?[127]

Certainly Theseus has managed to relocate the story from Thebes to Athens, and he designs Athens in such a way as not only to contain violent chivalric impulses, but also to imply numinous and symmetrical relations between the earthly and the heavenly orders. The theatre built for the fraternal tournament mirrors key relations in the universe, with its inbuilt temples of Mars, Venus, and Diana. And even if these are potentially violent forces, their conflict is to be viewed from a higher perspective, 'That whan a man was set on o degree, | He letted nat his felawe for to see' (I. 1891–2). This recognition yet containment of violent forces is very much in keeping with the operations of romance, but in this narrative there are at least two obstructions to any satisfying romance resolution. In the first place, the heroes are cousins who wear 'oon armes' (I. 1012), identical in all except the astrological force in whose name they fight; romance, as we have already seen, has a fatal flaw when it comes to the genetically identical, since one must lose and so undermine the very ground of providential narrative. Secondly, the apparent symmetries between the earthly and universal orders turn out not to square. There are three generations on earth (the lovers, Theseus, and Egeus) and three in the heavens (Venus, Juppiter, and Saturn). Whereas Theseus has it that Juppiter is prince and king of heaven, in fact it is the grandfather figure in the heavens, the malign Saturn, who resolves

127 For the recursive pull of disastrous Theban history in *Anelida and Arcite*, *The Knight's Tale*, and *Troilus and Criseyde*, see Patterson, *Chaucer and the Subject of History*, chs. 1–3.

a battle in which there can be no just winner. The First Mover figure should not be identified with the planetary influence Juppiter, despite the fact that Theseus calls the First Mover 'Juppiter'. The planetary influence, faced with dispute between Venus and Mars, 'was bisy it to stente [stop]' (I. 2442).[128] All the same, Chaucer invites the confusion, and in any case the malign, outermost planet Saturn, whose course 'hath so wide forto turne' (I. 2454), gives the appearance of being the dominant force.

Once Arcite has been tossed from his horse and mortally wounded by the fall, the tale breaks up into modes foreign to romance: an extraordinarily materialist and detached description of Arcite's physical deterioration (I. 2743–61) is followed by an elegiac complaint by the dying hero, complaining of his solitary death, 'in his colde grave | Allone, withouten any companye' (I. 2778–80). Chivalric loneliness and humiliation, indeed, is the leitmotif that the concluding sequences seem unable not to express. Even as Theseus praises the knights in the tournament, he insists rather too much on the fact and so implicitly denies that it is no shame to have been beaten; there is no 'disconfiture'

> . . . to be lad by force unto the stake
> Unyolden, and with twenty knightes take,
> O persone allone, withouten mo,
> And haryed forth by arme, foot and too. [toe]
>
> (I. 2723–6)

The rhetorical figure of *occupatio* (pretending not to discuss something in such a way as to draw attention to it) dominates this penultimate sequence: Theseus wants to pass over the shame and humiliation of defeat, just as the Knight wants, yet seems unable, to pass over the description of Arcite's funeral (I. 2919–66), in which the woodland gods are 'disherited of hire habitacioun' (I. 2926). However much, in short, the *Knight's Tale* gestures at and even rationalizes a romance resolution, it cannot help but point towards the larger narrative pattern of chivalric disaster to which it belongs. This is certainly the way Lydgate read the tale, when he continued the *Canterbury Tales* in 1422–3: a pale and melancholy figure,

[128] Mann, 'Chance and Destiny', pp. 89–90. For the astrological system of the *Knight's Tale*, see also Minnis, *Chaucer and Pagan Antiquity*, ch. 4.

Lydgate tells the tragic narrative of Thebes leading up to the events of the *Knight's Tale*, which thoroughly forestalls whatever philosophically optimistic gestures the *Knight's Tale* might make.[129]

Chaucer's fictional departure from London in the late 1380s may have resonances with his strategic withdrawal from the royal bureaucracy in a brief period of civil war. In 1387 Richard II's magnatial relations, partly in aggrieved response to Richard's anti-war policies, had mounted a brief and successful civil war against the king, which led to a purge of royal appointees in 1388. Chaucer himself resigned a royal annuity in 1388, and in the period leading up to 1387 seems voluntarily to have resigned his controllerships of wool and petty customs. When Richard regained control in 1389, Chaucer was reappointed to the royal household, as Clerk of the King's Works.[130] Although the *Knight's Tale* was written in the 1380s and only later inserted into the *Canterbury Tales*, its Theban narrative of warring cousins and the humiliations of chivalry must have had new resonance in its new context, just as Lydgate's Theban prequel in 1422–3 warns chivalric readers of civil war. Precisely because, however, the road between London and Canterbury is figured as a space of leisure in which the pressures of the 'real' world are temporarily allayed, we should be wary about making very specific cases for Chaucer's historical interventions.

For all that, the *Knight's Tale* is set in a new and refreshing context, which does offer alternatives to Theban chivalry. However much political pressures may be set at a distance, the tale-telling involves its own alternative 'political' organization, and itself produces tales whose 'politics' are strictly non-chivalric and non-providential. The pilgrims form a composite group, 'by aventure yfalle | in felaweshipe' (I. 25–6). This 'aventure' may be underwritten by a larger providential and cosmic order in which humans seek their health in spring, but for the entire time of the pilgrimage the pilgrims accept the provisional, covenantal order of the journey, in which all are potentially equal and potentially winners of the literary competition.[131]

129 See Ch. 3, above, and Simpson ,'"Dysemol daies"'.

130 For which see Strohm, *Social Chaucer*, pp. 36–41.

131 For the egalitarian institution of the fraternity as a model for the Canterbury pilgrims, see Wallace, *Chaucerian Polity*, ch. 2.

This order of provisionality is equally an interruption of literary as much as social hierarchies, and the occasion for alternative models of comedy to assert themselves against romance. This assertion is felt most fully and explicitly in the fabliaux, whose own order is in keeping with the order of the pilgrimage itself, based as both are on the model of 'quitting', in the archaic sense of 'repaying', or 'getting even'. Thus the tales of Miller, Reeve, Friar, Summoner, Merchant, and Shipman each operate on the basis of a trading whose rules are guaranteed by nothing more than human wit. The *Knight's Tale* implies a melancholic acceptance of the fact that the political order can only ever be constructed, arbitrary as it is to the order of the universe; the fabliaux, by contrast, celebrate that makeshift, provisional order, since it gives scope for the exercise of a worldly and self-interested prudence, and produces new hierarchies founded on gradations of professional skill. Familial and mythic providential orders in such tales are, indeed, asserted only to be exploited or denied. Nicholas exploits the providential order of salvation history and divine floods in order to sleep with Alison. John the carpenter building tubs to escape the flood evokes Noah, and Absolon the competitor plays the part of Herod in mystery plays (I. 3384). The evocation of these powerful male figures from salvation history is made only for them to be marked out as victims in the new order ruled finally by Alison, the only one who escapes suffering and shame altogether. In the *Merchant's Tale* providential orders are powerfully evoked to be denied: January's enclosed paradisical garden witnesses January's humiliation; its visitation by the mythic figures of Pluto and Proserpine only magnifies domestic dispute into cosmic proportions. Whereas the mythic structures of romance absorb domestic violence, in this tale it is the other way around: January and May's own names imply the Proserpine seasonal myth, but that myth is figured as a narrative of ineluctible domestic dispute involving male rapacity and female cunning. The need for domestic cunning becomes the single rule of the natural order.

The possibility of hierarchies based on prudential cunning and trading skills allows a very wide competition in which anyone can win. Women in particular come out consistently on top, and university learning is no guarantee of superior wit. Trade itself embraces a wide range of social environments, from manorial and artisanal milieux at one end of the scale in the tales of Miller and Reeve, to the world of high finance and international money markets in the *Shipman's Tale*. The kind of trade differs accordingly, from the simple exchanges and technologies involved in milling in the *Reeve's Tale* to the abstract system of large profits and currency dealing in the tale of the Shipman. In the simpler economic environments there are winners and spectacular losers, while the more complex and abstract trading in the Shipman's St Denis allows everyone to win in its utterly unashamed celebration of the triumphant power of trade to commodify anything and therefore everything.[132]

Chaucer's extraordinarily sophisticated and committed welcome to this genre in the *Canterbury Tales* opens up refreshing stylistic and ideological possibilities. Fabliau's genuinely funny prudential comedy offers a powerful and coherent alternative to the providential comedy of romance, allowing virtually unlimited entry into the world of the self-made, and rich possibilities for the expression and resolution of social rivalries. The bulk of the Canterbury pilgrims have no claim on nobility of blood, and many of the portraits are, indeed, indebted to the world of the fabliau, just as the tale-telling 'quitting' of the *Canterbury Tales*, in which anyone could win, is itself based on a fundamental motif of fabliaux. Without wishing to diminish this comedy, in what remains of this chapter I suggest that it is never more than an interruption of romance, on whose power Chaucer relies for the most daring of his political tales, the *Clerk's Tale*. I approach that conclusion with brief discussions of romance as deployed by the Wife of Bath and the Franklin.

The opposition between aristocratic and bourgeois comedy is nowhere so stark as between the Wife of Bath's Prologue and her Tale. In the Prologue the Wife articulates a marital biography that is in every way sceptical of the mythic resolutions of romance as downright dangerous. Marriage is wholly a matter of business, and business is threatened whenever love is involved. 'Al is forto selle', she declares (3. 414), in the footsteps of La Veille in Jean de Meun's section of the *Roman de la Rose* (*c.*1275). Chaucer translated this work, which itself explodes the ideology of romance while pretending merely to finish one. The Wife is a particularly well-informed

[132] The evergreen study of Chaucer's style in the fabliaux and its philosophical implications is Muscatine. See also Hines.

yet sceptical reader of biblical texts, and her expert yet wholly self-interested interpretations imply an acute eye for the operations of ideology in texts. What is made to look natural by the artist (e.g. the frightened lion) is designed to mask the opposite reality; so, she argues, narratives designed to naturalize the wickedness of women have been written by 'clerkes . . . withinne hire oratories' (3. 694). The Wife's sceptical and philological textual approach makes her choice of romance (Arthurian romance at that) all the more surprising, particularly as the narrative has all the appearance of self-deluding wish-fulfilment of exactly the kind that romances are supposed to offer. She tells the story of a male rapist who escapes capital punishment by discovering from an ugly old woman what women most desire (i.e. power over their husbands), on condition that he marry the old woman. Married, she offers him the choice of having her old, ugly, and faithful, or beautiful and faithless. By abjuring the choice and therefore granting power to his wife, she transforms into a beautiful, noble, and faithful wife, obedient to his every desire. By having power, the old woman is transformed into a young and beautiful woman who abjures that very power. Is this a wish-fulfilment or the representation of wish-fulfilment? Is the Wife just as acute a reader of Arthurian romance as she was of the biblical texts she cited in her Prologue, or is she its victim?

That the question is irresolvable itself points to the abiding power of romance. Certainly the Wife would seem to demystify romance, by at once setting the story 'in th'olde dayes of the Kyng Arthour . . . manye hundred yeres ago' (3. 85763) and by beginning with a rape. Sophisticated writers of romance express a subtle awareness of chivalric violence towards women, even as the stories claim to represent knights helping women.[133] The Wife takes the lid off that myth directly, by having the knight casually rape a woman as the story's

[133] *Ywain and Gawain*, a 14th-cent. (pre-1350) translation of Chrétien de Troye's *Yvain* (late 1170s) is a good example, in its representation of the noblewomen reduced to the level of exploited industrial cloth workers by the rashness of their adventurous king. They produce cloth for nobles, an example of which is visible in the enclosed orchard adjacent to their workshop, in which the rash king is read a romance by his daughter as they sit on a splendid cloth. See *Ywain and Gawain*, ed. Friedman and Harrington, ll. 2957–3067. *Yvain* was the very example chosen by Auerbach ('Knight Sets Forth') to exemplify his point that romances disguise the socio-economic sources of the aristocratic world.

opening event. Moreover, the Wife has the old wife articulate precisely the central points of humanist objection to chivalric and romance ideology. Whereas the young knight grieves above all for the shame incurred by his family in this marriage, the old woman reproaches him by citing what secular, non-noble clerics had said throughout the later medieval period: that nobility is entirely a condition of soul, wholly unrelated to birth. She also praises voluntary poverty and the respect due to age. Just as the Wife is an acute operator in, and exposes, the gender bias of biblical textuality, so too does she strike at the gender and class presuppositions of romance with humanist accounts of the potential nobility of all humans. The argument that the Wife is better described as the critic of Arthurian romance than its self-deluded victim therefore appears strong. In the same way that a wide range of anti-chivalric, broadly 'humanist' late medieval and early modern writers dismissed or avoided Arthurian romance, the Wife's Tale exposes a deep fault-line between a secular clerisy and chivalric ideology.

In the light of this chapter's broader account of romance, however, an alternative account is possible. As we have seen, the abiding power of romance lies in its recognition of ideological fluidity. Certainly romances characteristically end with a reaffirmation of a conservative social order premissed on nobility of birth. They can reach that position, however, *only* by encountering and having commerce with all that threatens it. Romances cannot be described as simplistic purveyors of a chivalric ideology, since the very premiss of the aristocratic order in these narratives is recognition of its obverse. This fluid relation between different social systems resolves the Wife's Tale, and in so doing the tale works wholly within the dynamic of romance. The very condition, that is, of the knight's power at the end of the narrative is his powerlessness: he is dependent on women above all, but the story must also recognize the coherence of an entirely non-aristocratic social and ethical order before it can end. At the heart of the plot, indeed, is the knight's obligation to hold to a promise given to one outside the chivalric system. The interactive relation of ostensibly opposed forces in romance here offers an alternative to the marital relations of relentless domination by one side or another evident in the Prologue. Within the terms of that Prologue, the Wife's only possible response to the relentless anti-feminist satire of Jankyn's composite volume is to tear out its pages. The romance she tells is more complex and interactive in its account of chivalric education.

Although he does not give it an Arthurian setting, and he does not have it begin with a rape, Gower also tells broadly the same story in the *Confessio Amantis* (1. 1407–1861) as the Wife. Neither does Gower have the old woman articulate humanist arguments against a chivalric ethos, and, as throughout the *Confessio*, he uses the four-stress couplets characteristic of one kind of 'popular' romance. In so doing Gower is less embarrassed about recognizing his affiliations with simpler, prior traditions of English romance, but the comparison serves to underline that Gower, who also promotes a nobility of soul ethos,[134] deploys this narrative in ways that are at least consistent with the Wife's own more complex narration. In both, that is, the aristocratic fidelity to humbling and potentially shameful pacts with the non-noble is the condition of aristocratic restoration.

Once that point has been made in the *Canterbury Tales* it is repeated and its force expanded. Certainly romance continues to be interrupted in the tales, with the Wife's Tale followed by the Friar and Summoner's; the Clerk followed by the Merchant; and the Squire's apparently unendable effort is interrupted by the Franklin. The Franklin's interruption is, however, less of a stop to than a reformulation of romance. That the non-noble gentry figure of the Franklin should tell a story of aristocratic restoration is unsurprising, but he tells it in such a way as to open the very bases of chivalric comedy up to a non-chivalric class. The magician displays his powers to Aurelius by conjuring up visions of aristocratic parks, filled with deer, 'knyghtes joustyng in a playn' (5. 1198), and a vision of Dorigen. This mirage of wish-fulfilment is rudely broken, however, by the magician clapping his hands Prospero-like, to reveal his study, 'ther as his bookes be' (5. 1207). In contrast to the undiscriminating fascination with the marvellous in the *Squire's Tale*, the magic in this tale is professionally produced, and in any case gives way to the greater marvel of human, not merely aristocratic, generosity. If aristocrats act like urban professionals by submitting themselves to the 'truthe' of pre-established covenants, then urban professionals

[134] See *Confessio Amantis*, 4. 2269–77.

act like aristocrats, practising a liberal generosity beyond desert. This generous extension of romance has provoked many critics to argue that Chaucer is satirizing the Franklin for his class aspirations; such a response exposes not only the class anxieties of modern critics, but also their misunderstanding of the real dynamics of romance, which are always engaging the providential and the aristocratic with their obverse.[135]

The delicate comedy of the *Franklin's Tale* explicitly acknowledges a tradition of Breton lays (5.709–15), beautiful translations of which into English exist from the early fourteenth century.[136] Chaucer is possibly citing one such romance in the Prologue,[137] which also implies his interest in varieties of romance, including English examples. If, however, romance can reintegrate the 'gentil Britouns in hir dayes' (5. 709), how successfully can it manage pressingly contemporary Lombard tyrants? I end this chapter by suggesting that Chaucer risks a great deal by relying on romance to broach this question in the *Clerk's Tale*. He translated the English story principally from Petrarch's Latin text (1373–4), itself translated from Boccaccio's Italian vernacular version in *Decameron*, 10. 10 (1349–51). Petrarch (d. 1374) wrote this at the very end of his life, after a career spent since 1353 in the service of despotic governments. Chaucer, who himself travelled both to republican Florence in 1373 and to despotic Milan in 1378, takes up the tale of Griselda, then, within a broad grid of oppositions: republicanism versus despotism; vernacular versus Latin.[138]

At very first glance, the Clerk's narrative of patient Griselda is what may be called a reformist romance: the enclosed world of nobility is both reconstituted and reformed by acknowledging its dependency on all that it repudiates. Before the 'pitous day' of the tale can have its 'blisful ende' (4. 1121), the aristocratic figure must incur various dangers: recognizing nobility of soul, family separation, and near father–daughter incest. This interpretation faces an immediate and insurmountable obstacle, however: in this case the tests that

[135] For scholars who dismiss the Franklin as a *parvenu*, see *Riverside Chaucer*, ed. Benson, p. 895.

[136] For which see Spearing, 'Marie de France'.

[137] Laura Hibbard Loomis, pp. 18–23.

[138] For a full discussion, see Wallace, '"Whan she translated was"'.

premiss return to the aristocratic order are themselves the product of the aristocratic 'hero', so much so that he ceases to be the hero at all. Like the Wife of Bath's romance, this story is seen entirely from the perspective of the woman, who suffers the tyranny of the aristocratic order. Petrarch's own way of reformulating yet preserving aristocratic authority and its demand for unswerving obedience is to allegorize the story, using the example of a woman only to deny that contemporary women could be capable of following her. He effectively makes God a despotic ruler, who tempts us not in order that he should know our souls, since he knows them already, but simply in order that we should know our own weakness.[139] Petrarch, an ardent admirer of Augustine, instates an inscrutable and omniscient God, whose only interest in tempting us is that we recognize our weakness, which his omniscient intelligence already knows. Petrarch the humanist in the service of despots, then, reinscribes relations of political tyranny into a theological reading of the tale, creating a convergence of Augustinian theology and political subservience of a kind commonly found in later Protestant theology.[140]

Chaucer retains this interpretative swerve away from the literal story: just as a woman was so patient 'Unto a mortal man, wel moore us oughte | Receyven al in gree [good spirit] that God us sent' (4. 1150–1). In the larger narration of the *Clerk's Tale*, however, this abstraction from the literal Griselda is unworkable. Chaucer consistently stresses Walter's pathological, tyrannical, and needless obsession with testing (e.g. 4. 456–62; 621–3; 696–700), no trace of which appears in Petrarch. If Walter is a God figure, then God is also pathological, even more so since he already knows the result of his testing. In exposing the implications of this theological allegorization, Chaucer may merely be bringing to light implications that are already embedded in Petrarch's version. The result of this new emphasis in Chaucer is, however, to incapacitate the allegorical reading, and to return us to the literal level of the romance.

If we cannot avoid the literal level, then must we not also abandon any notion that this story is a romance? Griselda's patience is to a despotic regime; the 'happy' ending exemplifies nothing more, it

139 See Severs, p. 330.

140 For examples of which see Ch. 7, below.

could be argued, than the happiness of subjects who do submit themselves totally to the inscrutable desires of tyrants. This reading has powerful authority from within the tale, since how is Griselda's obedience different, it could be asked, from the brutal henchman whom Walter sends to take Griselda's daughter? Like Griselda, he too is entirely obedient to the wishes of tyrannical masters: 'men moote nede', he says, 'unto hire lust obeye' (4. 531). If Chaucer abandons Petrarch's allegorical reading, are we therefore left with a fable recommending obedience to tyrants? Is this romance in its most authoritarian form?

As we have seen throughout this chapter, romances represent interactive relations between ostensibly opposed systems, in such a way as to produce accounts of the social order that are often irresolvably poised between obverse possibilities. While tyranny and blind obedience do not stand in any tension at all, tyranny and passive resistance do. What distinguishes Griselda from everyone else in the tale is her freely given commitment to stand by a given social order. By maintaining that commitment, it could be argued, Griselda not only preserves her dignity, but also humanizes Walter. In this reading it is not Griselda who is helplessly obedient, but Walter himself, who cannot help but submit to pathological and vicious desire; he is, by the Clerk's account, like those who 'kan nat stynte of hir entencion, | But, right as they were bounden to that stake, | They wol nat of that firste purpos slake' (4. 703–4). Unlike the Clerk himself who promises obedience to the Host in the tale-telling competition 'as fer as resoun asketh, hardily' (4. 25), Griselda's obedience knows no conditions except that it be freely given, even if this means accepting wholly unethical impositions. This in itself is parallel to another theology, developed especially in the fourteenth century, whereby God freely commits himself to the order of penitence, whereby he promises to reward humans who do their best.[141] According to this reading it is Griselda, not Walter, whose actions have divine resonances, but they do so most fully only as long as we read her actions literally. By this reading the tale is a radically Christian defence of passive resistance, whereby a fundamental faith in human goodness rides out and finally exhausts human pathologies. But this radical

[141] See Ch. 7, below. See also Mann, 'Parents and Children', pp. 178–83.

Christianity also reveals romance at its furthest reach; it reveals, indeed, that the Christian narrative is itself a romance.

Certainly fifteenth-century writers did not think of Chaucer as primarily a romancier. The wonderful early fifteenth-century spurious continuation of the *Canterbury Tales*, the *Tale of Beryn*, marks the tension between a providential and a prudential comedy neatly. The story has an envelope romance in which the noble Beryn is finally restored to his noble status through marriage. Beryn survives the intervening period of test, however, through the purely prudential actions of a suitably named 'Geoffrey' on Beryn's behalf. Geoffrey ruthlessly manipulates legal procedure in the corrupt city in which Beryn has lost all his goods with the result of finally marrying Beryn to the princess of the city whose legal practice has itself been purified by Geoffrey's legal manipulations. The outer envelope of the story *is* a romance, but that narrative hardly touches the inner narrative of professional skill that permits the romance resolution. Beryn himself, for example, never remotely understands or masters the legal trickery of his honest professional ally.

In its thoroughly divided affiliations to both romance and to prudential comedy, *Beryn* is a shrewd response to the *Canterbury Tales*. In the rest of the fifteenth century, however, romance won out against prudential comedy. Only in Caxton's extraordinarily accomplished and funny translation *Reynard the Fox* from the Dutch (1481) do we find anything with the power and refreshing bite of Chaucer's fabliaux,[142] or of the *Nun's Priest's Tale*, where, like the fox, the narrative forever escapes the predations of moralizing interpretation. From this account of Chaucer's romances, however, we can see that Chaucer's own deployment of romance is much less hostile to the genre than criticism would have us believe. Only romance can deal with the most dangerous questions, and this is true not only of Chaucer but also of many other writers of romance, especially before, but also after him.

142 *The History of Reynard the Fox*, ed. Blake. I regret that limitation of space precludes discussion of this brilliant work. For the very sparse history of the fabliau in English after Chaucer, see Hines, pp. 259–60.

7

Edifying the Church

After four chapters devoted to secular writing, I turn now to varieties of religious literature, beginning with the fundamental and forever contentious question of the Church itself. What is its function? Who comprises the true Church? Where is it? Should it own property? The central discussion of this chapter contrasts evangelical ecclesiology with the way in which the Church is represented in *Piers Plowman*. The broad contrast that emerges points to the profound delusions of evangelical theology. Despite its superficially demotic tone and its laudable promotion of the vernacular, this theology centralizes grace in the hands of God, and consequently demolishes institutional and historical stabilities. Centralization and demolition of this kind find striking parallels in the cultural centralizations and literal demolitions of Henrician England. In *Piers Plowman*, by contrast, grace is managed in a thoroughly decentralized way, dependent for its distribution on both the initiative of the individual Christian and the integrity of an Apostolic, demotic Church.

I

Thomas Wyatt's *Paraphrase of the Penitential Psalms* traces a singularly lonely process of atonement between the sinner and his God. Writing between 1534 and 1542, Wyatt follows his Italian source in imagining a biographical context for King David's inspired composition of the seven so-called 'Penitential Psalms' (Psalms 6, 31, 37, 50, 101, 129, and 142 in the Vulgate Bible). David falls in love with Bathsheba, conspires in the death of her husband, is reproached by the prophet Nathan, and immediately withdraws 'into a dark cave | Within the ground, wherein he might him hide' (ll. 60–1).[1] Here David is imagined singing psalms of repentance to an injured, omnipotent, and entirely silent God.

Of course all acts of repentance evoke the past in order to delete it, and so penitence is ideally a kind of self-consuming autobiography. King David's sins are indeed entirely consumed, but so too, in the process, is King David himself. The unspecified narrator declares that none of the king's meritorious deeds has any bearing whatsoever on the recompense that he receives from God:

> But when he weigh'th the fault and recompense,
> He damn'th his deed and findeth plain
> Atween them two no whit equivalence;
> Whereby he takes all outward deed in vain
> To bear the name of rightful penitence,
> Which is alone the heart returned again
> And sore contrite that doth his fault bemoan,
> And outward deed the sign or fruit alone.
>
> (ll. 648–55)

In this poem the asymmetries between God and the sinner are so great and unmediated as to render the king's own 'outward deeds' wholly insignificant. So far from having any power to persuade the 'perfect intelligence' (l. 222) of God, good deeds become, in this theology, mere signs of decisions having already been taken, the fruits of God's prior election; the conversion of the single life is itself converted into God's own initiative: 'all the glory of his forgiven fault | To God alone he doth it whole convert' (ll. 658–9). While the narrative apparently marks a moment of conversion in history from one kind of life to another, in a deeper sense the individual's history is pre-empted by the sheer concentration of power and initiative in God's hands. It is God who gives the sinner power and voice to declare his unworthiness in the first place: '. . . Of thyself, O God, this operation | It must proceed by purging me from blood' (ll. 490–1). In addition, God's power beggars the civil processes of

[1] All citation of Wyatt's poetry is from Wyatt: *The Complete Poems*, ed. Rebholz.

law whereby an accused person might justify him or herself before a judge:

> . . . And after thy justice
> Perform, O Lord, the thing that I require;
> But not of law after the form and guize
> To enter judgement with thy thrall bondslave
> To plead his right, for in such manner wise
> Before thy sight no man his right shall save.
>
> (ll. 731–6)

King David's isolation, then, is not merely physical; he is also cut off from the assurances of prior virtue, just as he can make no appeal to the insurance of due legal process. In the face of God's inscrutable presence and power, the purchase of individual biography on God is invoked only to be dismissed: even virtuous 'outward deeds' are taken by God 'as sacrifice [his] pleasure to fulfil' (l. 507). Nothing but grace, or God's unprovoked, unmerited gift, defines the relation between sinner and God, as David unhesitatingly recognizes: 'For on thy grace I wholly do depend' (l. 758). Grace, in this account, renders the virtuous accretions of the individual life entirely redundant, or at best a 'sacrifice'.

If, as is probable, the poem was written after 1536, its acceptance of God's grace as the sole ground of justification before God was an official doctrine. The Ten Articles of 1536, the first official formulary of the Church of England, represent a careful, if finally incoherent, compromise between radical and conservative views. Despite their attempt to preserve some sense of historical continuity, their understanding of grace equally points the way to a radical break with what has been humanly instituted. The Articles are divided into those 'commanded expressly by God', and those that 'have been of a long continuance for a decent order and honest policy, prudently instituted and used in the churches of our realm'. The five articles specifying what is 'necessary' marked a sharp break with traditional doctrine, since only three sacraments are specified: baptism, penance, and the Eucharist. The account of penance begins traditionally enough, by saying that whoever should do proper penance will 'without doubt attain remission of their sins, and shall be saved'; the substance of the article, however, rather destroys penance. It defines an evangelical notion of God's election, whereby through faith the penitent 'must conceive certain hope . . . that God will forgive him his sins, and repute him justified, and of the number of His elect children, not for the worthiness of any merit or work done by the penitent, but only for the merits of the blood and passion of our Saviour Jesu Christ'.[2] The article on justification corroborates the definition, and thereby diminishes the status, of penance: sinners attain justification 'not as though our contrition, or faith, or any works proceeding thereof, can worthily merit or deserve to attain the said justification; for the only mercy and grace of the Father, promised freely unto us for His Son's sake, Jesu Christ, and the merits of His blood and passion, be the only sufficient and worthy causes thereof'.[3]

Such a view of grace explosively disrupts historical continuities, in both selves and institutions. It is symptomatic of this disruptive power that the remaining five articles (concerning the use of images, the honouring of saints, praying to saints, 'rites and ceremonies', and purgatory) should be corralled off as qualitatively different from the 'necessary' articles. These others are defended as merely 'laudable custom', but the form of the defence merely marks out their vulnerability: each of these 'laudable customs' was, indeed, to be abolished as positively idolatrous within just over a decade of their defence in 1536.

After Wyatt's death, Surrey understood Wyatt's Psalms to be an attack on the concupiscence of Henry VIII. By presenting the 'lyvely faythe and pure' in David's 'swete returne to grace', Wyatt had, by Surrey's account, offered a mirror wherein rulers might see the 'bitter fruit of false concupiscence' and be woken out of their 'synfull slepe'.[4] Certainly the years 1534 to 1542 provided ample justification for such an attack, since in those years Henry had executed two wives and divorced a third (a fourth had died in childbirth). The fact that the poem circulated only in manuscript may also suggest the need for secrecy, until its first printing in 1549.[5] Surrey's interpretation is entirely plausible, but it is worth remembering that Wyatt's

2 Cited from *English Historical Documents*, ed. Williams, 5. 799.

3 Ibid. 802.

4 Surrey, 'The Great Macedon', in Henry Howard, *Poems*, ed. Jones, no. 31.

5 *RSTC* 2726.

own position with regard to Henry across these years was not so different from David's with regard to God. Wyatt was twice imprisoned in the years 1536 to 1541, the first time on account of his relation with Queen Anne, and the second on charges of having treasonously slandered the King with a few intemperate words. He escaped death by an apparently very narrow margin in 1536, and in 1541 his careful defence may never have been delivered, since he was excused without trial, 'yelding himself only to His Majesties marcy'.[6] Like David, Wyatt had nothing else to fall back on save his sovereign's grace.

Even with that grace, however, David in Wyatt's poem exercises extreme caution with words. He wants to repeat his entreaty to God,

> And so he doth, but not expressed by word.
> But in his heart he turneth and poiseth
> Each word that erst his lips might forth afford.
> He points, he pauseth, he wonders, he praiseth
> The mercy that hides of justice the sword.
>
> (ll. 517–21)

David's verbal vigilance evokes Wyatt's own position in 1541. In 1534 the definition of high treason had been for the first time explicitly extended to verbal utterance. It became an act of high treason to pronounce the king a heretic, schismatic, tyrant, infidel, or usurper of the crown 'by expresse writinge or wordes'.[7] Wyatt was himself arraigned on precisely the charge of treason for malicious words in 1541, and his defence scrutinizes the enormous difference a single word or syllable can make: 'And besydys that, yt is a smale thynge in alteringe of one syllable ether with penne or worde that may mayk in the conceavinge of the truthe myche matter of error.'[8] Both Wyatt and David operate in a context where the penalties for infringing the exiguous confines of the Word are severe.

Without pursuing the biographical freighting of Wyatt's poem, I underline the striking parallels between the new-made evangelical, penitent David and the courtier Wyatt: both inhabit worlds of 'extremity', to use Wyatt's own word (l. 110), in which the power

[6] Wyatt, *Life and Letters*, ed. Muir, p. 210.
[7] *SR*, 26 Henry VIII, ch.13, (3. 508); see further Bellamy, p. 31.
[8] Wyatt, *Life and Letters*, ed. Muir, p. 197.

relations between lord and servant are massively disproportionate. On the side of the servant stands fault, 'beastliness' (l. 739), and a dependence on the lord for the very impulse to confess his unworth; on the side of the lord stands pure grace, wholly unconstrained by claims of any kind. Between the two there is 'no whit equivalence' (l. 650). Of course it is implausible that Henrician courtiers actually believed that such political relations were desirable, but these were, paradoxically, precisely the spiritual relations that courtiers such as Wyatt actively embraced. Evangelical spirituality is intensely centralized: all initiative rests in the hands of God, whose omnipotence must not be infringed by any 'legal' claims that a defendant's works might bring, and in whose grace the single virtue of faith must trust, despite all appearances to the contrary.

The claim that Protestant spirituality is centralized sits uneasily with influential traditions of Protestant historiography. The Henrician Reformation has had powerful defences as a popular movement: from John Foxe's *Acts and Monuments of the English Martyrs* (first published in 1563), through James Froude's twelve-volume *History of England from the Fall of Wolsey to the Defeat of the Spanish Armada* (1856–70), to A. G. Dickens's *The English Reformation* (1964), historians have presented the English Reformation as a fundamentally progressive movement, in which the popular will has triumphed over the authoritarian and corrupt institution of the medieval Church. Whether from the perspective of commitment to Protestant theology, or to a nationalist conception of the Anglican Church, or to a progressivist, evolutionary conception of history, or to liberal championing of individual conscience above oppressive institutional control, the Reformation by these accounts was a progressive and entirely positive historical turning point.[9] This tradition has, of course, been met with opposition at a variety of historical moments: first compiled with the support of Archbishop Laud, Peter Heylyn's *Ecclesia Restaurata* (1661) argued that the Anglican Church was not the product of popular protest, but was rather a purified Catholic and Apostolic Church with proper and powerful continuities with the pre-Reformation Church; just prior to the Catholic Emancipation Act of 1829, William Cobbett's *A History*

[9] For J. A. Froude, see J. W. Burrow, chs. 9 and 10.

of the Protestant Reformation in England and Ireland (1824–7) attacked the Reformation on the grounds of its alleged impoverishment of the people by the destruction of institutions of poor relief;[10] contemporary with the Oxford Movement, S. R. Maitland's publications between 1837 and 1849 sought to discredit Foxe as a historian; and in the later twentieth century the work of revisionism grew in substance, as Eamon Duffy's *The Stripping of the Altars: Traditional Religion in England 1400–1580* (1992) built on the work of Scarisbrick and Haigh.[11]

The business of this literary history is clearly not to broach questions of the popular will directly from the kind of evidence marshalled by Duffy, for example (namely churchwardens' accounts, wills, archaeological remains, liturgical aids). I will, however, be looking to a range of vernacular texts across the period that address questions of the church's institutional history and/or legitimation. I argue that the concentration on the person of the king in English Reformation literature and polemic was in no way accidental to the structure of English evangelical theology. The many sixteenth-century calls for absolute obedience to the royal will represented not only a practical political necessity but also the coherent result of an evangelical conception of divine grace, whose overwhelming force etiolates the Church to the profit of the State. Wyatt may, as Surrey suggests, be registering protest against Henry in the *Penitential Psalms*, but the evangelical form of that protest equally neutralizes it, since evangelical theology, in Henrician England at any rate, played directly into royal interests.

This is the principal argument of the chapter with regard to the sixteenth century; it will be balanced by contrast with the very different account of the institutional distribution and management of divine grace in the late fourteenth-century set of texts known as *Piers Plowman*. Here I will be arguing that *Piers Plowman* was prophetic, looking forward as it did to Reformation theology. Even as it prophesied such a spirituality, however, it also recoiled from it: *Piers Plowman* both foresaw and forestalled the Reformation, by offering

10 For Cobbett, see Chandler, ch. 2.

11 Scarisbrick, *Reformation*, and Haigh (ed.). For convenient surveys of Reformation historiography, see O'Day, and Haigh, 'Recent Historiography of the English Reformation'.

a reformation of its own in which grace is distributed in a wholly decentralized way.

For reasons we shall look to in a moment, non-Lollard fifteenth-century works have very little role to play in representing the Church as an institution. The proto-Protestant movement Lollardy, sometimes known as Wycliffism, was the ostensibly popular theological movement that flourished in the early fifteenth century; it drew inspiration from the writings of John Wyclif (d. 1384). Once the contrastive relation between the reformist spirituality of *Piers Plowman* and the revolutionary spirituality of the sixteenth century has been brought into focus, I situate Lollardy within that contrast.

II

Wyatt's *Penitential Psalms* represent a break with the devotional and literary past. Whereas these psalms had been built into devotional books of hours in earlier practice, here they are presented, in their 1549 printing, at any rate, as a whole book. And whereas Wyatt's Italian source is in prose, he translates the psalm sequences themselves into *terza rima*, a form not used in English before Wyatt, with the exception of a short experiment by Chaucer. Despite this, echoes of an earlier metrical tradition and an earlier English vernacular approach to questions of God's forgiveness might be just audible. David 'doth measure | Measureless mercies to measureless fault' (ll. 525–6): line 526 conforms to a classical alliterative line (aa/ax), while the following lines not only deploy alliteration, albeit within a pentameter line, but also evoke *Piers Plowman* verbally. David has a vision of the Annunciation and Crucifixion, when

> He seeth that Word, when full ripe time should come,
> Do way that veil by fervent affection,
> Torn off with death (for death should have her doom),
> And leapeth lighter from such corruption
> Than glint of light that in the air doth lome. [shine]
>
> (ll. 703–7)

These lines possibly evoke Will's vision of the Annunciation and Crucifixion in *Piers Plowman*, when Christ must rest within Mary

'Til *plenitudo temporis* tyme comen were | That Piers fruyt floured and felle to be rype' (B.16. 93–4), just as line 705 has debts to the kind of chiastic alliterative practice we find in Langland in these lines, for example: 'And that was tynt thorugh tree, tree shal it wynne, | And that Deeth down broughte, deeth shal releve' (B.16. 140–1).[12]

If these are indeed echoes of *Piers Plowman*, they are frustratingly fragmentary. This obliquity and lack of deep contact with *Piers* is, however, characteristic of a tradition of evoking the poem in the sixteenth century. *Piers* remained fundamentally unassimilable within any English tradition in the fifteenth century and again, for much more complex reasons, in the sixteenth. In the fifteenth century the kind of discourse represented by *Piers Plowman* was effectively proscribed by both ecclesiastical and parliamentary legislation. In the sixteenth century we might expect a revival for the poem, since readers clearly did see in it a prophetic voice heralding the triumphal arrival of Protestantism. There was indeed a revival of sorts, but one, as we shall see, that was incapable of deploying anything like the full force of the earlier poem.

Piers Plowman was not the only pre-Reformation work to be rescued by reformers. Henry VIII himself was, it seems, interested in deploying proto-Protestant, Wycliffite material for his own purposes in 1530. He sent a letter to the Convocation of the University of Oxford, requesting that the 'articles for which Wyclif was condemned by the university' (in 1382) be sent him.[13] Between 1530 and 1550 a variety of texts that were presented as Wycliffite were published both abroad and in England. Some of this material was genuinely Wycliffite, and, when presented as part of a sixteenth-century text, clearly demarcated to serve in new conditions.[14] Some was only probably genuine, but apparently rewritten in parts to make it suit the needs of the present. That is true of the anti-papal *Ploughman's Tale*, first printed in 1536, probably as part of an official propaganda

[12] Compare also the image of light leaping with *Piers Plowman*, B.5. 495: 'And the light that lepe out of Thee, Lucifer it blent'. I am indebted to Colin Burrow for the suggestion that Wyatt may have echoed Langland. Editions of the B and C versions from which I cite are Langland, *Vision of Piers Plowman: the B-Text*, ed. Schmidt and Langland, *Piers Plowman: The C-Text*, ed. Pearsall.

[13] *L&P Henry VIII*, 4/3.

[14] See Hudson, '"No Newe Thyng"'.

campaign.[15] This text was soon afterwards published as part of the *Canterbury Tales* in order to appropriate Chaucer for the evangelical cause,[16] just as the Lollard *Jack Upland* (written between ?1389 and 1396),[17] was attributed to Chaucer in its 1536 printing.

This is a relatively small haul of material, numbering no more than eleven or so quite short texts, but the consequences of its deployment could be momentous, particularly in the case of the attributions to Chaucer, whereby the great pre-Reformation poet became a champion of the Reformation. The strategy of these revivals of Lollard matter is clearly to legitimate Henrician, or at least evangelical, interests. This is true of officially sponsored or condoned publications, like the *Ploughman's Tale*, but also of works published before it became officially allowable to promote such doctrine. Thus in Jerome Barlowe's *A proper dialogue betwene a gentillman and a husbandman*, published in Antwerp in 1530, the gentleman and husbandman agree on the rapacity of the clergy, and on the desirability of clerical disendowment. The gentleman has his own version of fifteenth-century history, as he argues that Henry V's persecution of Lollards was the cause of England's disastrous military history for the rest of the fifteenth century. The husbandman is no less conversant with Lollard history, since he produces 'a remenant' of a tract 'above an hundred yere old' (p. 149). After reading the 'olde fragment' together, the gentleman approves of it thus:

> Yf soche auncyent thynges myght come to lyght
> That noble men hadde ones of theym a syght
>   The world yet wolde chaunge peraventure
> For here agaynst the clergy can not berke [bark]
> Sayenge as they do thys is a newe wercke
>   Of heretykes contryved lately.
>
> (p. 165)[18]

[15] See Wawn, 'Chaucer, *The Ploughman's Tale* and Reformation Propaganda'.

[16] Hudson, 'John Stow (1525?–1605)', p. 59.

[17] For the revised dating, see Hudson, *Premature Reformation*, p. 97.

[18] Compare, too, the prefatory remarks to *The prayer and complaynte of the plowman* (Antwerp, 1530; London, 1531), a probably authentic Lollard work, described by its 16th-cent. printer as 'a Holy Relique' (A5). The printer claims that the text was written not long after 1300, and that he has printed it 'in his awne olde English' in order to demonstrate that 'it ys no new Thinge, but an olde practyse of oure Prelates . . . to defame the Doctrine of Christe'.

The fact that official printers were themselves drawing on Lollard works within six years of this remark proves the gentlemen's acuity.

By far the largest scale revival of pre-Reformation material, however, was that of *Piers Plowman*. The bibliographer Leland, writing *c.*1540, clearly knew, but presumably had not read, *Piers*, since he confuses the *Ploughman's Tale* with *Piers Plowman*, calling it 'fabula Petri Aratoris', and attributing it to Chaucer. Bale, by contrast, clearly had read the poem, and, after confessing a certain ignorance about the author, whom he calls 'Robertus Langelande', says in his *Catalogus* (1557–9):

> this much, however, is clear, that he was among the first disciples of John Wycliffe, and that he published in a fervour of spirit a pious work in English, under pleasant rhetorical colours and allegories . . . which he called The Vision of Piers Plowman . . . In this erudite work, beside the various and delightful allegories, he prophesied many things, which we have seen come to pass in our own days.[19]

Unlike Leland, Bale was writing after *Piers Plowman* had been printed: the evangelical printer and poet Robert Crowley published the book twice in 1550, with the first print going through three imprints.[20] Despite some annotations that point to *Piers* as prophetic, Crowley himself was less inclined to read the poem as prophecy, and more as offering a powerful example of courageous protest, whose force was still relevant.[21] 'Loke not upon this boke . . . to talke of wonders paste or to come, but to amend thyne owne misse.' All the same, Crowley certainly enlisted *Piers* as an exemplary document of the evangelical tradition: he correctly guessed that Langland wrote at the end of the fourteenth century, when, he goes on to say,

> it pleased God to open the eyes of many to se hys truth, gevyng them boldenes of herte, to open their mouthes and crye oute agaynste the worckes of darcknes, as dyd John Wicklefe . . . and this writer.[22]

[19] John Bale, *Scriptorum . . . catalogus*, p. 474. Bale's comments are also available in the inestimable bibliography of DiMarco.

[20] Bale knew MSS of the poem; see *Index*, ed. Poole and Bateson, p. 383.

[21] While J. N. King is the best single book on Reformation literature, King's arguments about Crowley's understanding of *Piers Plowman* as prophetic (pp. 319–39) are overstated. For Crowley's edn., see Thorne and Uhart.

[22] *The Vision of Pierce Plowman, nowe the seconde time imprinted by Roberte Crowley* (1550), fo. ii^{r}. For Crowley as editor, see C. Brewer, ch. 1.

Crowley's readiness to use *Piers* for its power to affect the present was matched in a small series of polemical works that appeared in London very close to Crowley's editions: *I playne Piers which cannot flatter* (?1547); *Pyers plowmans exhortation unto the lordes, knightes and burgoysses of the parlyamenthouse* (1550); and *A godly dyalogue and dysputacyon betwene Pyers plowman, and a popysh preest* (1550).[23] Like Chaucer, then, Langland became, for a brief period from the death of Henry VIII until the Marian reaction in 1553, a critical representative of the enlightened few from 'the dercke and unlearned times', who had seen through to the evangelical future.[24] Given Chaucer's Protestantization, and the ascription of the *Ploughman's Tale* to him, Chaucer and Langland briefly converged, indeed, as Reformation prophets.[25] In my view, however, none of the works that claims inspiration from *Piers*, let alone any prior 'ploughman' material from the 1530s, made any serious engagement with Langland's poem.[26] The following two sections explore the reasons for the incapacity of fifteenth- and sixteenth-century writers to write anything remotely on the scale, or with the discursive richness and configuration of *Piers Plowman*.

III

My own view is that *Piers Plowman* ceased to exert any real pressure on later literature because changes internal to the structure of theology and politics rendered the poem, despite the evident desire of later writers to deploy it, effectively unreachable. The withering of the *Piers* tradition, however, also requires a brief conspectus of an 'external' force, that of censorship, across the period 1350 to 1550.

For the entirety of these centuries writing that broached questions of ecclesiastical legitimacy operated within severe official limitations.

[23] Respectively, *RSTC* 19903a, 19905, and 19903. See further Hudson, 'Legacy of *Piers Plowman*'.

[24] The citation is from Robert Braham's 1555 Preface to Lydgate's *Troy Book*, reprod. in *Lydgate's Troy Book*, ed. Bergen, pt. 4, pp. 60–5 (at 65).

[25] A point made by Bowers, 'Piers Plowman and the Police', p. 42. This article is more generally indispensable to the study of *Piers Plowman* reception up to 1550.

[26] These texts are discussed below, with the exception of Hugh Latimer's 1548 'Sermon on the Plowers'.

The severity was registered on the latter edge of the period, in the first year of the reign of Edward VI (1547). Edward's first parliament published a statute that carefully set about deleting prior statutes. Statute claims more permanence than most forms of discourse, and so the matter of dismantling prior legislation is a delicate business. The Edwardian Act begins by recognizing that in times of emergency, strict laws are necessary;[27] Henry VIII, indeed, made laws that might seem 'verie streighte, sore, extreme and terrible' both to foreigners and to the King's own subjects. If in a tempest, the Act goes on, heavy protection is in order, so too in fair weather a light garment may be worn. Accordingly, 'none acte dede or offence, being by Acte of parliament or statute made treasone or petit treasone by wordes, writing, ciphring, dedes or otherwise . . . shalbe taken . . . to be highe Treason or petit treasone, but only such as be treason under 25 Edward III' (i.e. an Act defining treason made in 1352). The Act then goes on to repeal Acts made in the following years: 1382 (a Ricardian statute prohibiting the preaching of heresies 'in markets, fairs, and other open places');[28] 1414 (an Act made in the second year of the reign of Henry V, directing those responsible for royal justice to search out 'all them which hold out any error or heresies, as Lollards, and which be their . . . common writers of such books, as well of the sermons as of their schools, conventicles, congregations, and confederacies');[29] 1534 (an Act affirming the previous two statutes, yet excusing attacks on the 'Bishop of Rome' from imputation of heresy);[30] 1539 (Henry's attempt to turn the clock back on the advances of evangelical doctrine, known as the Act of Six Articles);[31] and 1542 (the statute banning Tyndale's Bible and 'all other bookes and wrytinges in the English tongue teaching . . . any matiers of Christen religion' contrary to the doctrines established by the King in 1540).[32] The years 1352 and 1547, then (almost exactly the boundaries of this history), mark key events in the history of censorship, whereby the statute of Edward VI attempts to return to the status-quo of Edward III.

27 *SR*, 1 Edward VI, ch. 12 (4/1: 18–22).
28 *SR*, 5 Richard II, 2, ch.5 (2. 25).
29 *SR*, 2 Henry V, 1, ch.7 (2. 187).
30 *SR*, 25 Henry VIII, ch.14 (3. 454–5).
31 *SR*, 31 Henry VIII, ch.14 (3. 739–43).
32 *SR*, 34 Henry VIII, ch.1 (3. 894–7).

The series of statutes explicitly mentioned in the legislation of 1547 offers a thumbnail sketch of the shape of censorship across the period. The first Act of 1382 was made in the context both of the Peasants' Revolt of 1381, which had been associated with heresy, and of the Oxford Blackfriars' Council of 1382, in which Wycliffite heresies were condemned.[33] While that statute directed its attention rather broadly to preaching of heresies, without having a name for the heretical movement, the Henry V statute of 1415 has a much sharper sense both of the target ('Lollardries'), and of attacking an organization capable of producing, disseminating, and teaching written materials. It was also made in the context of, and underwritten by, two recently promulgated and draconian pieces of legislation, the 1401 statute *De Haeretico Comburendo* (*Concerning the Burning of Heretics*) and the English Church's own complementary legislation published in 1409, known as Arundel's *Constitutions*.[34] The 1401 legislation permitted the burning of heretics for the first time in England, and allowed that once an ecclesiastical body had determined heresy, the heretic would be handed over to the secular authority, who shall 'receive, and them before the People in an high Place do to be burnt, that such punishment may strike fear to the minds of other'.[35] Heresy was defined as preaching or writing anything 'contrary to the Catholic faith or Determination of the Holy Church', and making conventicles or schools.

Archbishop Arundel's *Constitutions* of 1409 drastically widened the scope of what could be regarded as heretical: no one was to preach without licence; preachers were to conform their matter to their audience, being sure not to address matters fit for the clergy to the laity; no one was to question the sacraments of the Church; no schoolmaster was to teach boys in his charge about the sacraments; no unauthorized person was to read the books of Wycliffe; no one was to translate Scripture into English; and among the remaining injunctions, one specifies that no one was to affirm anything contrary to good morals, even if such an affirmation could be defended by 'a certain skilfulness of words or terms'.[36] From this point until

[33] For the decisions of the Blackfriars' Council, see *Concilia*, ed. Wilkins, 3. 157–8.

[34] Available in, respectively, *SR*, 2 Henry IV, ch. 15 (2. 125–8), and *Concilia*, ed. Wilkins, 3. 314–19.

[35] *SR*, 2 Henry IV, ch. 15 (2. 128).

[36] *Concilia*, ed. Wilkins, 3. 317.

the 1530s the punitive state and ecclesiastical legislation of the early fifteenth century holds, even in the 1520s under pressure from the Lutheran heresy.[37]

In the 1530s, however, altogether new forms of legislation appeared, which revealed a convergence of heresy and treason. Certainly in the late 1520s ecclesiastical legislation had proscribed sets of Lutheran and evangelical English books. This legislation was targeted specifically on heresy, and saw a genealogy between 'the old and damnable Wycliffite heresy' and its 'pupil, the Lutheran heresy'.[38] In 1529 and 1530 this ecclesiastical legislation found state support in a royal proclamation proscribing the dissemination of the same books outlawed by the ecclesiastical injunctions, and prohibiting scriptural translations.[39] After the break with Rome, however, the initiative for defining heresy is found rather in statute than in ecclesiastical injunction. Thus the 1534 heresy Act specifies that no attacks on the Bishop of Rome and his spiritual laws 'which be repugnant or contrariant to the laws and statutes of this realm or the king's prerogative royal', shall be regarded as heretical,[40] while, as we have seen, the 1534 treason Act makes it high treason either to write or say anything to the effect that the king is a heretic, schismatic, tyrant, infidel, or usurper. Heresy (a crime against the Church) and treason (a crime against the king) become more difficult to distinguish in this decade since, as the opening formula of the 1539 statute has it, the 'king's most excellent Majesty is by God's law supreme head immediately under Him of this whole Church and Congregation of England'.[41] All the Henrician statements (in 1536, 1538, 1539, and 1542) of official theology figure theological doctrine as issuing from the king, and in so doing make the distinction between heresy and treason a very fine one. The Edwardian 1547 statute clearly wishes to abolish both the anti-Lollard legislation of Henry V, and the anti-Protestant legislation of Henry VIII. Despite the fact that it was targeted at heresy, however,

[37] The arrival of Lutheran texts in England prompted Wolsey to circulate a first list of Lutheran errors in 1521; see ibid. 690–3.

[38] See ibid. 711, and, for lists of proscribed books, ibid. 706–7 (1526); 719–20 (1529); 727–37 (1530); and 737–9 (1530).

[39] *Tudor Royal Proclamations*, ed. Hughes and Larkin, 1. 181–6 (1529), no. 122; and 193–7 (1530), no. 129.

[40] *SR*, 25 Henry VIII, ch. 14.7 (3. 455).

[41] *SR*, 31 Henry VIII, ch.14 (3. 739).

the Edwardian Act was headed 'An act for the repeal of certain statutes concerning treasons'. By doing so, it acknowledged the Henrician blurring of treason and heresy; it also reinstated the normal meaning of treason by reverting to the 1352 definition, which had nothing to say about heresy or doctrinal orthodoxy.[42]

However obnoxious the action of the censors was, one can see why religion was such an explosive topic across the period. Most obviously, the laity were intensely concerned since the eternal fate of their souls was at issue. Not much less obviously, huge property holdings and financial systems were at stake, made vulnerable to moral more than legal attack. As early as the Blackfriars' Council in 1382, convened to target Wyclif, the opinions proscribed as errors include the following: 'that temporal lords may, at their own discretion, appropriate the temporal goods of ecclesiastics who are habitually immoral'; and 'that tithes are pure charity, and that parishoners may withhold them from sinful curates, and confer them to others as they wish'. The same council declared heretical the assertion that it was contrary to Scripture that ecclesiastics should have any possessions.[43]

Both Lollard and Protestant polemicists were acutely aware of the secular attractions of their programmes for ecclesiastical disendowment. In his *Supplicacyon for the Beggars* (1528), Simon Fish encouraged Henry to reflect on the implications for his own military power of the disendowment of the regular religious, who possess 'nighe unto the half of the hole substaunce of the realme' (p. 4); this same strategy had been used, with more precise financial calculations, in the Lollard Disendowment Bill of 1410.[44] These attractions may explain why extremely powerful lords like Richard II's uncle John of Gaunt were sympathetic to Wyclif and his followers in the 1380s, no less than why Tudor landowners were equally sympathetic to Henrician disendowment when precisely this policy was put into action in 1530s. The Church's vulnerability on this front

[42] For the 1352 treason statute, see *SR*, 25 Edward III, 5, ch. 2 (1. 319–20), and Bellamy, 9–12.

[43] *Concilia*, ed. Wilkins, 3. 157.

[44] The Lollard Disendowment Bill is available in *Selections from English Wycliffite Writings*, ed. Hudson, pp. 135–7. For discussion of the Lollard bill, see Hudson, *Premature Reformation*, pp. 114–16.

equally explains why it should have enacted such draconian legislation from 1401 so consistently up to 1534, at which point the State took over. Just as institutions tend to be prepared to censure and kill for doctrinal issues, so too do they censure and kill over matters of property.

Until 1534 when treason and heresy begin to blur, ecclesiastical and state legislation against heresy is much more coherent, draconian, and consistently applied than legislation against writing ill of the king in purely political complaint.[45] Public displays of official punishment for heresy, in the form of burnings, both of books and of people, are frequent in periods of intense doctrinal dispute, especially between 1520 and 1558.[46] Public execution for treasonous writings or speech against the king is much rarer until Henry VIII activated his extended treason legislation in the 1530s. Certainly there are public executions of those who challenged the king's authority or legitimacy across the entire period, but fears of widespread dissent, both written and spoken, centre on doctrinal issues and the rebellion that such dissent may provoke, as in the Pilgrimage of Grace of 1536.[47]

This point is essential to the history of 'literature' across this period. It alerts us to the fact that the discursive conditions for different kinds of writing can be radically different. Regiminal writing, for example, certainly negotiated real dangers in addressing and correcting its royal readers, but the audience of such writing was necessarily rather limited, unlike the audience of religious matter. Thus the state's increasingly invasive control of printing, after a first proclamation of 1530, was provoked by fear of the dissemination of theological rather than strictly political books.[48] From the earliest

[45] For the purely secular legislation, see Simpson 'Constraints of Satire', p. 17; see also Scase, '"Strange and Wonderful Bills"'.

[46] In the earlier period of persecution, there were many fewer burnings of people; two people were burned in the reign of Henry IV.

[47] Even though the uprising seems not to have been primarily motivated by religious grievance, it was read by later commentators as if it had been; see e.g. the argument of Aston, 'Lollardy and Sedition'.

[48] See *Tudor Royal Proclamations*, ed. Hughes and Larkin, I. 193–7, no. 129 (1530), which prohibited the printing of 'any books in the English tongue concerning Holy Scripture'; I. 270–6, no. 186 (1538), which prohibited unlicensed printing of Scripture, and required all licensed books to print 'cum privilegio regali ad imprimendum solum' on the title-page; *SR* 34/35 Henry VIII, c. 1 (1543), which for the first time

anti-Lollard legislation, legislators across this period were acutely conscious that theology had a very wide appeal, and that issues of heresy were also, immediately, issues of textual production and dissemination. When Henry issued a proclamation in 1539 attempting to repress theological dispute, for example, the text betrayed acute anxieties about, if not impotence in the face of, popular theological discussion. While the King had hoped that permission to read Scripture in English would have produced meek readers in his people, instead he finds to his consternation that

> each of them dispute so earnestly against the other of their opinions as well in churches, alehouses, taverns, and other places and congregations, that there is begun and sprung among themselves slander and railing each at other as well by word as writing, one part of them calling the other papist, the other part calling the other heretic.[49]

By this account, England had become a hothouse of theological dispute, wherein the proper bounds and proper language of learned dispute had been swept aside by popular ferment. As far as popular unrest, the dissemination of books, and organized systems of surveillance go throughout this period, the hottest issue of all was religion, not politics as narrowly defined.[50]

The dangers of writing or printing theologically dangerous material were especially acute in the vernacular. Wyclif's Latin writings attracted censure from the first papal injunctions against his doctrines in 1377, but the problem of heresy soon became closely associated with the use of English for any theological discussion, let alone speculation, especially from the 1409 *Constitutions*. The dangers of entering the discursive field of vernacular theology at any point were neatly expressed by the licence granted by Archbishop Tunstall in 1528 to Thomas More, granting him the right to read books adjudged heretical.[51] Even to touch the subject as an official

specified penalties for printers of illicit matter; and *Tudor Royal Proclamations*, ed. Hughes and Larkin, 1. 373–6, no. 272 (1546), which required the printer to identify himself, the author of the book and the date of publication. Each of these pieces of legislation specified theological matter as the source of danger. For a conspectus of censorship and legislation concerning printing, see Loades, chs. 8 and 9.

49 *Tudor Royal Proclamations*, ed. Hughes and Larkin, 1. 284–6, no. 191.

50 For the system of Tudor surveillance, see Elton, *Policy and the Police*.

51 *Concilia*, ed. Wilkins, 3. 711–12.

opponent at the highest level required official permission. This licence was granted in a period of high tension, but throughout the period 1350 to 1550 writers in the vernacular very often expressed fear at the dangers they were incurring, whether the writer was a Lollard, a Protestant, or one of their opponents. Writers in this field were acutely sensitive to legislation surrounding the publication of dangerous matter; from *Piers Plowman* forwards, indeed, statute law was one of the most proximate discourses to any discussion of ecclesiastical legitimacy.[52] Awareness of the dangers of speaking was most obviously and unsurprisingly characteristic of Lollards in the fifteenth century, and of evangelical writers up to the death of Henry VIII. Such awareness was also found, however, in thoroughly orthodox writers like the blind poet John Audelay who, writing about 1426, expressed fears that he, like anyone else who dared criticize the Church, would be branded as a heretic and burnt as a 'lollere'. No one dares speak, he says,

> Fore dred of the clerge
> Wold dampnen hem unlaufully
> To preche apon the pelere, [pillory]
> And bren hem after too.[53] [burn]

Likewise, and tragically, the orthodox Reginald Pecock's intellectual honesty in confronting the Lollards head-on, in a very precise vernacular prose, ended with his own conviction for heresy in 1457.[54]

Vernacular religious writers dealt with these challenges in a variety of ways. Most simply, they avoided sacramental controversy and ecclesiological issues altogether, and remained 'within reason' by writing wholly devotional and/or penitential matter. Thus Nicholas Love's *Mirror of the Blessed Life of Jesu Christ* of *c.*1410, which was published with Archbishop Arundel's approval, restricted itself to the kind of discourse acceptable to the censor: devotional, bodily, almost wholly unspeculative, and engaging in discussion of the

[52] This is a large and unexplored topic. For a stimulating beginning with regard to *Piers Plowman*, see Middleton, 'Acts of Vagrancy'.

[53] Audelay, *Poems*, ed. Whiting, no. 2, ll. 673–6, p. 34.

[54] For Pecock, see Hudson, *Premature Reformation*, pp. 55–8, and 440–3; and Scase, *Reginald Pecock*. For the official association of heresy with use of the vernacular, see Hudson, 'Lollardy: The English Heresy?'.

Eucharist only to defend an entirely orthodox position.[55] I shall deal with this corpus of matter in Chapter 8; there we shall see that, even if issues of ecclesiastical authority are subliminally present, the posture of such works was one of submissive vernacular and lay piety.

When writers did engage directly with ecclesiological issues, they may have exercised a self-censorship. Such a self-denying ordinance would offer a plausible explanation of the changes from the B- to the C-Text of *Piers Plowman*, written on different sides of the English Uprising of 1381, when 'Piers Plowman' had been so effective a rallying cry of the rebels that 'Per Plowman' appeared listed as one of the leaders of the uprising in a later account.[56] The C-Text omits some of the more explosive episodes from the B-version, notably Piers's tearing of the pardon and, what is perhaps more subversive, Piers's abandonment of ploughing, as he disputes with a priest (B.7. 115–39).[57]

Anonymity was also a marked characteristic of theologically sensitive writing; even if 'William Langland' really was the name of the poet of *Piers Plowman*, he never anywhere says so in the poem, and instead thematizes the name so as to imply a dispersed or common authorship, the 'will' of the whole 'land', whereby the poem's readership ideally becomes its author.[58] Lollard writers also relied on anonymity and common authorship. So too did later evangelical writers who deployed the name 'Piers Plowman', in defiance of the 1546 prohibition on omitting the author's name from printed books.[59] The joint effect of legislation on heresy and on illicit printing clearly also provoked the printing of evangelical (and Lollard) books either abroad, sometimes with a misleading place of publication, or in England with false places of publication, especially after the 1526 printing of Tyndale's New Testament in Germany.[60]

[55] The phrase 'within reason' is frequently used in Nicholas Love's *Mirror of the Blessed Life of Jesu Christ* to delimit the scope of legitimate interpretation: see Simpson, 'Desire and the Scriptural Text', p. 235. For a wide-ranging account of the effects of Arundel's *Constitutions*, see Watson, 'Censorship and Cultural Change'.

[56] See Hudson, 'Legacy of *Piers Plowman*', p. 252; Hudson also surveys the ways in which the rebels themselves cited Langland's poem; see also Justice.

[57] It is also possible that the A version of the poem is a bowdlerization and simplification of the B version; see Mann, 'Power of the Alphabet'.

[58] See Simpson, 'Power of Impropriety'.

[59] For Lollard anonymity, see von Nolcken, '"Certain Sameness"'. For the 1546 royal proclamation requiring printers to specify authorship, see *Tudor Royal Proclamations*, ed. Hughes and Larkin, 1. 373–6, no. 272.

[60] See A. Hume.

Perhaps the most profound effect of the severity of censorship throughout this period was, however, the suppression of fiction. However much the author of *Piers Plowman* expressed his sense of the dangers of writing as he did,[61] the poem itself manifests a profound and daring commitment to fiction, since Langland's own creations, both Piers and Will, themselves enter the textual landscape of biblical narrative.[62] Equally, the poem manifests just as daring a commitment to impersonation: dialogues in this text are characteristically conducted between two competing voices, often unpoliced by obvious authorial guidance. Striking and dangerous views are expressed, concerning, for example, the disendowment of the Church, or the uselessness of any virtuous moral effort whatsoever, in contexts where the authorial position is not at all clear. Of course this may in itself have been a way of avoiding censorship, by disclaiming responsibility, just as the use of dreams might have displaced responsibility from an author. Tactics of this kind were, however, spotted early by the censors and largely abandoned early by dissident voices. Arundel's *Constitutions* specified, as we have seen, that nothing contrary to good morals was to be written, not even if it could be defended by 'a certain verbal or terminological dexterity'. Lollard and Protestant writers had reasoned objections to the 'imagination' in any case, and may therefore have had other reasons for rejecting fiction.[63]

Whatever the reason, from the early fifteenth century, with some notable and courageous exceptions, both fiction and impersonation were eschewed in theologically dissident material, reappearing only after the 1547 relaxation of censorship in, for example, the lamely ironic dialogues of Luke Shepherd, [64] or the brilliantly ironic *Praise of Folie* by Erasmus, the English translation of which was first published in 1549.[65] Irony reappeared at the same moment that

[61] See Simpson, 'Constraints of Satire'.

[62] See J. A. Burrow, *Langland's Fictions*.

[63] Lollard rejections of fiction are frequent; see e.g. the rejection of 'fabulacion' in *Middle English Translation of the 'Rosarium Theologie'*, ed. von Nolcken, p. 73. For the larger evangelical rejection of the imagination, see Simpson, 'Rule of Medieval Imagination'.

[64] For a higher valuation of Shepherd, see J. N. King, pp. 252–70.

[65] By the time it was translated into English in 1549, much of the force of Erasmus's ecclesiastical satire had been completely transformed by changes that had occurred since Erasmus began the work in 1509.

censorship was relaxed. In place of irony and impersonation were stability and consistency of utterance, more often than not in prose, without any developed claims to fictional creation. Thus for example Reginald Pecock, an extreme instance of discursive sobriety and caution, rejected 'worldly trouthis, oolde rehercellis, strange stories, fablis of poetis, newe inventiouns', with their 'curiose divisyngis and . . . newe langage forgyng', as wholly erroneous paths to divine truths. Furthermore, whereas a text like *Piers* is explicitly addressed (if at all) to an unspecified 'us', with 'lered men' or 'ye rich' sometimes imagined as observers of the text, later Protestant polemic generally had great clarity of address, very often directed as it was to parliament or to the king himself. The threatening pressures of statute reproduced the discursive stabilities of statute.

IV

Piers Plowman itself, then, just as much as its demonstrable *Nachleben* up to 1550, is unintelligible without reference to a legislative environment that sought to constrain writing that directly challenged ecclesiastical authority. Even if the poem's final version must have been written not long after 1388, the conception of the work was generated from the late 1360s, prior to the thoroughly organized campaign of state legislative censorship that began in 1382 and found very explicit and terrible form in 1401. By exactly the same token, the poem found a large-scale readership again in almost the same moment that those strictures were relaxed: Crowley's ability to print the poem was surely due to the extraordinary if short-lived florescence of printed Protestant matter after the deregulation of 1547, which permissive environment also produced the works mentioned above that explicitly evoke *Piers*.

In looking to censorship we look to a history, or an implied history, of suppression, disappearance, and silence. Censorship, however, does not sufficiently account for the weak reception of *Piers Plowman* up to 1550, since the more significant disappearances across that period were not provoked externally. They were rather produced by deeper changes in what Michel Foucault would call the 'archaeology of knowledge', or the relation of discourses that allows and disallows discursive configurations. In *Piers Plowman* we see a particular configuration of theology, ecclesiology, and politics that had become impossible from the 1530s. Of course every historical moment is unrepeatable, and all historiography is necessarily the story of unrepeatability. The 'unrepeatability' of *Piers* nevertheless merits especial attention for two reasons: on the one hand, the poem itself prophesied the future, and on the other, that very future attempted to reinvoke the poem. From the 1520s, however, attempts to reinvoke this poem's power failed, since an evangelical theology of grace so profoundly disrupted institutional and personal histories as to render the poem irretrievable. And however much that evangelical theology was heterodox until 1547, its centralization of grace's distribution by God found unexpected consonance with the centralization of secular grace in the person of Henry VIII.

As we have seen, some influential Protestant readers read *Piers Plowman* as prophetic. Just as Chaucer was taken by many Tudor readers as an outstanding exception to the darkness of his own period, so too was Langland regarded as exceptional to his own time and prophetic of the enlightened age to come. This response is most obviously and influentially true of Bale, according to whom Langland 'prophesied many things, which we have seen come to pass in our own days'. In a sense, Bale is, I think, correct. I do not mean to say this with regard to the explicitly prophetic passages in *Piers Plowman*, and not even the ones that struck Tudor readers with especial force, like the prophecy in Passus B.10 about a king who will put regular religious 'to hir penance—*ad pristinum statum ire*' (B.10. 319), which Crowley not unreasonably glossed with 'The suppression of Abbayes'. Bale is correct, rather, in the deeper sense that Langland's poem is so acutely aware of the pressures on the institution of the Church that it is capable of recognizing whence change is likely to come. The changes that were institutionalized in the 1530s and again in the reign of Edward are not without their historical precedents; even if the combination of intellectual and institutional factors in the late fourteenth century was not such as to produce the radical changes of the 1530s and 1540s, many of the elements of that change were available. If all historiography is the story of disappearance, it is equally the story of the future imagined. I want first to trace that 'prophetic' quality by looking to Langland's theology, and from there to the ecclesiology, economics, and politics that flow from the theology. For each of these discussions I compare Langland's case with examples from 1520 to 1550, and in each case I argue that Langland does indeed 'foresee' the Reformation, but equally recoils from, and attempts to forestall, it.

The fifty-five surviving full manuscripts of *Piers Plowman* can be sorted into four versions, at least three of which appear to be authorial. The shorter A-Text (*c.*2,500 lines) may be a prelude to, or an abbreviation of, the B-Text, much larger in conception and correspondingly longer (*c.*7,200 lines); this text would seem to have been written *c.*1377–80. The C-Text is slightly longer than B, with some major structural additions and deletions, and hundreds of minor alterations; it must date from after 1388.[66] Recent scholarship has argued for a further and first authorial version, known as the Z-Text, after the manuscript siglum by which it is known.[67] In this chapter I will refer to and cite from B, with occasional stated reference to C. The poem is a dream poem, and is divided into eight visions and twenty passus (Latin 'steps'; sing. 'passus'; pl. 'passūs'), in the B-Text, where one vision will usually extend across more than one passus. We cannot be certain who read this poem, but the evidence points to a wide readership. The number of manuscripts is large, implying some powerful patronage. The quality of the manuscripts is not, however, of the deluxe standard often used for the texts of Chaucer and Gower, for example. Langland seems certainly to have had readers who worked within the London bureaucracy, a key and understudied readership of both secular and religious vernacular texts. His readership was not restricted to London, to the powerful, or to men: many manuscripts are locatable from their dialect in the Malvern area; 'Piers Plowman' was a rallying cry in the English Uprising of 1381, and the text appeared in a will being bequeathed to a woman.[68] The poem's imagined audience would seem to be theologically sophisticated, but debarred from the higher reaches of Latin learning. This is the audience, ranging from civil servants,

[66] This dating is dependent on references to a 1388 statute in the C version, a point first made by Hanna, *William Langland*. For the strongest argument in favour of single authorship, see Kane.

[67] William Langland, *Piers Plowman: The Z Version*, ed. Rigg and Brewer.

[68] See Kerby-Fulton and Justice.

to priests, to merchants and artisans, that Lollard writing also attracted.

(*a*) Works, Grace, and Predestination

Passus 19 of *Piers Plowman* imagines the actual building of the Church by Piers Plowman, who works under the inspiration of Grace. In the next and final passus that Church is invaded and corrupted from within. The poem ends in this strikingly unresolved way, as Conscience, the presiding spirit of this renovated Church, abandons it:

> 'By Crist!' quod Conscience tho, 'I wol bicome a pilgrym,
> And walken as wide as the world lasteth,
> To seken Piers the Plowman, that Pryde myghte destruye,
> And that freres hadd a fyndyng, that for nede flateren [income]
> And countrepledeth me, Conscience. Now Kynde me avenge,
> And send me hap and heele, til I have Piers the Plowman!'
> And siththe he gradde after Grace, til I gan awake.
>
> (B.20. 381–7)

In a variety of ways this passage appears strikingly to confirm Bale's understanding of the poem as prophetic. The individual conscience leaves the institution of the material Church, which has been corrupted from within by the regular religious, appealing to a model of lay spirituality and simplicity for the foundation of a new church. And just as grace is central to the Lutheran theology of sixteenth-century reformers, so too does Conscience cry after grace: salvation, in this scene, has become entirely a matter of the individual's unmediated dependence on God's gift, and is no longer the product of ecclesiastical mediation. Even if this climactic and enigmatic passage may seem triumphally to herald a new form of unmediated, lay spirituality, I want nevertheless to argue that for Langland this is a moment of terrible despair, and an admission of at least provisional defeat for the ambitious project of his poem. The central effort of *Piers Plowman* is to imagine the metaphorical construction of a reformed Church. With the heterogeneity of discursive materials at his disposal, the Church so constructed is unashamedly a *bricolage*, but its *raison d'être* is nothing if not to dispense the sacrament of penance. The Church's failure to dispense penance provokes Conscience's pilgrimage into the wide world outside the Church, and leaves nothing between him and God but grace alone.

Retracing some of the steps by which Conscience arrives at this point reveals not only how catastrophic this moment of departure is, but also the acuity with which Langland foresees and forestalls critical features of a Protestant spirituality.The first two visions of the poem are devoted to the life of society, and focus respectively on the processes of secular and of spiritual law. In the second of these visions the penitential impulse of a whole society to seek pardon from God is, characteristically for Langland, transformed into an action of communal labour in the production of food, under the direction of the ploughman Piers (Passus 5). This enterprise, however, collapses as the workmen refuse to contribute to the communal action of penitential labour; in the place of that steadying system, labour economics become vulnerable to the violent boom and bust conditions of material plenitude and dearth (Passus 6). Only after the collapse of this penitential labour does the pardon arrive as a document from God in his aspect of justice, or 'Truthe'. The Pardon itself says only this (citing the Athanasian Creed, cited in Latin in the poem): 'Those who do well will go into eternal life; | Those who do badly will go into eternal flame' (B.7. 110a–b). This, of course, is no pardon at all, since it restates the ground rules of justice that pertain *before* a pardon becomes necessary. God as Justice goes back to first principles, however unnerving they may be.

Piers and a priest jointly read and dispute the meaning of this austere document, until Piers, in an astonishing moment (that was cut from the C-Text), tears the document in two and abandons his role on the field of labour:

And Piers for pure tene pulled it atweyne [anger]
And seide, '*Si ambulavero in medio umbre mortis*
Non timebo mala, quoniam tu mecum es'.
'I shal cessen of my sowyng,' quod Piers, 'and swynke noght so hard,
Ne aboute my bely joye so bisy be na more;
Of preieres and of penaunce my plough shal ben herafter.
(B.7.115–20)

(Latin: 'if I should walk in the middle of the shadow of death, I shall fear no evil, for you are with me'.)

This passage has been interpreted as a radical affirmation of the centrality of grace;[69] just as in Protestant theology, so too in its long Pauline and Augustinian prehistory: works stand helpless before God's justice. Piers recognizes this and abandons his works; by the same token he seems equally to abandon any confidence in the institution of the Church: his is the voice of theologically sensitive lay spirituality, rejecting the obtuse ecclesiastical establishment with its complacent expectation of pardon. Piers seems to rely wholly on faith, even in the darkness of the valley of the shadow of death, and to invoke God's grace through private penance. Here, too, we have another moment of abandonment like Conscience's at the end of the poem; and like the later moment, this leave-taking represents a rejection of institutional mediation, a faithful throwing of the self onto God's mercy, and a corresponding reliance on grace. Certainly Crowley read this section in precisely this way. Immediately after Piers's rejection of works, Will wakes up and muses upon his dream, declaring that Christians should not rely on pardons (B.7. 168–95); Crowley glosses this in characteristically evangelical fashion: 'And that to truste for salvation in workes, is but a vayne thing.'

Langland's poem *refutes* this position of grace alone; before looking to that refutation, we should briefly characterize the *sola fides* Lutheran theology that appeared in England from the mid-1520s. In 1573 John Foxe edited a very large folio volume *The Whole Works of W. Tyndall, Iohn Frith, and Doctor Barnes, Three Worthy Martyrs*.[70] Each of these three had been burnt at the stake, Tyndale (1494–1536) in Germany, while Frith (1503–33) and Barnes (1495–1540) were condemned and burnt in England.[71] For Foxe these three theologians have become the intellectual heroes of the English Reformation, and I restrict my characterization of English Reformation evangelical theology up to 1550 to their works, despite differences of emphasis both among them and between them and Luther. Tyndale's full translation of the New Testament was first

69 Baker, 'From Ploughing to Penitence'.

70 *RSTC* 24436.

71 The two important books on these thinkers are as follows: Clebsch, and Trueman.

published in 1526 in Worms; his two most important theological works were published in Antwerp in 1528, *The Parable of the Wicked Mammon*, and *The Obedience of a Christian Man*. Barnes's *Supplication unto King Henry the Eighth* was published in 1531 (Antwerp) and revised in 1534 (London). Frith had translated works of Luther into English; some of his principal theological works were written in the Tower, before his burning in 1533.

The most insistent theme in these theological works is the uselessness of works before the standards of God's justice. Tyndale often denies that 'a man with works deserveth eternal life, as a workman or labourer his hire or wages.'[72] Given the humanly irredeemable enslavement of the human will, humans must in no way depend on the righteousness of their works before God. Justification can be achieved not through human effort, but is rather a matter of divine election and grace, which is itself predicated on Christ's merits before God, as distinct from any human merits. Tyndale returns repeatedly to the ensuing centrality of faith:

> That faith only before all works and without all merits, but Christ's only, justifieth and setteth us at peace with God, is proved by Paul in the first chapter to the Romans . . . For in the faith we have in Christ and in God's promises find we mercy, life, favour, and peace. In the law we find death, damnation, and wrath . . . In the law we are proved to be the enemies of God, and that we hate him. For how can we be at peace with God and love him, seeing we are conceived and born under the power of the devil, and are his . . . captives and bondmen . . . so that it is impossible for us to consent to the will of God.[73]

In this theology faith is the pre-eminent bond between humans and God. Of course all Christian theology places a high premium on faith, but when works are of no value, then faith in God's grace, or gift, becomes the only source of conviction and hope. Establishing a relationship with this God is less a matter of working in the world towards a future reconciliation, and more the trickier, psychological matter of persuading oneself that God has already made a positive decision.

The value of good works is, indeed, wholly redefined. Now they have no purchasing power on God, and serve only as signs of a prior

[72] Cited from Tyndale, *Parable of the Wicked Mammon*, p. 82. [73] Ibid. 47.

election, signs that serve to certify the sinner of his or her election. The key events of history have, in a profound sense, already happened, and pre-empt any action in the sinner but the psychological challenge of self-assurance that he or she is among the elect:

> . . . thou mayest not imagine that our deeds deserve the joy and glory that shall be given unto us . . . I cannot receive it of favour and of the bounties of God, freely, and by deserving of deeds also. But believe as the gospel, glad tidings and promises of God say unto thee; that for Christ's blood's sake only, through faith, God is at one with thee, and thou received to mercy, and become the son of God . . . Of which things the deeds are the witnesses; and certify our consciences that our faith is unfeigned.[74]

Despite this stress on prior divine decisions and the signs that might confirm them, however, the Christian must in no way be confident in the evidential signs that would justify such decisions, since they have been taken by a wholly inscrutable God:

> of the whole multitude of the nature of man, whom God hath elect and chosen, and to whom he hath appointed mercy and grace in Christ, to them sendeth he his Spirit; which openeth their eyes, sheweth them their misery . . . Then lest they should flee from God by desperation, he comforteth them again with his sweet promises in Christ; and certifieth their hearts that, for Christ's sake, they are received to mercy, and their sins forgiven, and they are elect and made the sons of God . . . Now may not we ask why God chooseth one and not another; either think that God is unjust to damn us afore we do any actual deed . . . Our darkness cannot perceive his light. God will be feared, and not have his secret judgements known.[75]

This theology redefines the spiritual life as a psychological field of action, in which the sinner struggles to believe in his or her election by a wholly unaccountable and inscrutable sovereign. Desperation, self-hatred, and hatred of God form the negative side of this spiritual psychology's circuit, the other side of which is exultant gratitude and readiness to convert. Because everything is in God's gift, the Christian's only field of action is emotional response.

For Langland, too, the collapse of worldly action also provokes a psychologization of theology. Precisely given the failure of work in the world, and the world's apparently incorrigible wilfulness, the will itself becomes the locus of an extended psychoanalytical drama

[74] Tyndale, *Parable of the Wicked Mammon*, p. 71. [75] Ibid. 89.

from Passus 8 of the poem until the refoundation of the Church in Passus 19. While God's pardon starkly demands the performance of good action in the world, the preceding ploughing scene has proven nothing if not the wilful human incapacity to meet the unmitigated standards of God's justice. The key aspect of the dreamer's psyche, then, the will—the loving, desiring part of the soul—suddenly becomes the poem's central problem and potential solution. Across Passus 8–13 Will interrogates the rational powers of the psyche of which he is a part, along with the educational institutions that train the reason. This is literally a psychoanalytical drama, in a pre-Freudian sense: the parts of the the soul are separated out, and questioned each in turn. Will poses to each the question posed so urgently by the non-pardon: 'what is Dowel?' How, Will is asking, do Christians deserve salvation?

The answers he receives from representatives of the reason are depressing. 'Dowel', each says in turn, 'is to doon as law techeth' (B.9. 200). Thought, for example, says simply, and apparently uncontentiously, that Dowel accompanies whoever 'is trewe of his tunge and of his two handes, | And thorugh his labour or thorugh his land his liflode wynneth' (B.8. 80–1). However, Will knows (and who better?) that the law is precisely what humans are incapable of obeying. After all, Thought's reasonable definition of basic good action in the world has already been found to be radically inadequate by Piers, who has rejected a life of labour and winning 'liflode'. Will himself repeatedly disrupts the calm complacence of rational faculties by citing scriptural texts that deny the possibility of doing well: 'Sevene sithes [a day], seith the Book, synneth the rightfulle' (B.8. 22); 'For the sothest word that ever God seide was tho he seide *Nemo bonus* [no one is good]' (B.10. 440).

These passus of psychological interrogation also represent, as they must, educational institutions and texts that train the psyche. Will meets personifications of preliminary education (Study) and of higher, theological investigation (Clergy and Scripture) in Passus 10. If, however, these passus represent a process of education, they do so in order to question the whole enterprise of that education.[76] Will has a rooted conviction that no one is indeed good enough to meet

[76] For which see Simpson, *Piers Plowman*, ch. 4.

the standards of God's justice through works; this provokes him to reject both education and moral effort altogether. He dismisses Scripture's teaching in this way:

> 'This is a long lesson,' quod I, 'and litel am I the wiser!
> Where Dowel is or Dobet derkliche ye shewen.
> Manye tales ye tellen that Theologie lerneth, [teaches]
> And that I man maad was, and my name yentred [entered]
> In the legende of lif longe er I were, [Book of Life]
> Or elles unwritten for som wikkednesse, as Holy Writ witnesseth:
> *Nemo ascendit ad celum nisi de celo descendit*'.
>
> (B.10. 371–6a)

(Latin: 'No one ascended to heaven unless s/he descended from heaven')

From this point until the end of the passus (B.10. 376–475a) Will progressively and spectacularly demolishes the ethical grounds of learning by pointing to examples both of great scholars who have been damned, and of simple illiterates who have been saved: none is 'sooner ysaved . . . Than plowmen and pastours and povere commune laborers, | Souteres and shepherdes' (B.10. 459–61). If good works cannot satisfy God, then the good work of learning itself is also useless. While the lay student Will presents himself as submissively searching out clerical instruction in this vernacular poem, the actual process of that cursus threatens to demolish both the authority and the very point of a spiritual education.

The doctrine articulated by Will is that of predestination, according to which God prejudges souls either to salvation or damnation before humans act in the world. In expressing the doctrine Will cites the 'Austyn the olde' as the 'doughtieste doctour', and the principal teacher of the Church (B.10. 452–3). However much Will misapplies the particular quotation he cites here,[77] the invocation of Augustine by the will is peculiarly apt in this doctrinal context. Augustine, who witnessed the invasion of Rome by barbarian armies in 410, developed for Christian theology the theories both of the will's inherent sinfulness and of God's predestination of souls.[78] In a period of political collapse, Augustine's theology imagines, as two sides of the same

[77] C. D. Benson, 'Augustinian Irony'.

[78] For Augustine's critical contribution to the theory of the will, see Dihle. For the theory of soteriology (or salvation) more generally, see McGrath.

theological coin, both an omnipotent God whose prerogatives can in no way be infringed by the claims of the law, and an inherently sinful human will. It is precisely these two conceptions, duly extended, that stand at the heart of Lutheran theology, certainly as that theology was expressed in Luther's *Bondage of the Will* (1525).[79] If imperial Rome is the inspiration of humanist writing in the sixteenth century, it is rather the theological culture of the Roman collapse four hundred years later that inspires sixteenth-century Protestant writers.

English reformers unquestionably accepted Luther's Augustinian-predestinarianism. Tyndale does not produce sustained reflections on predestination, but his acceptance of the doctrine is visible in, for example, the citations from the *Parable of the Wicked Mammon* cited above. John Frith, however, did produce a full discussion of predestination. He cites St Augustine carefully throughout, as in this passage, for example:

> St Austin saith, Some man will affirm that God did choose us, because he saw before that we should do good works; but Christ saith not so, which saith, Ye have not chosen me, but I have chosen you; for (saith he), if he had chosen us because he saw before that we should do good works, then should he also have seen before, that we should first have chosen him, which is contrary to the words of Christ.[80]

Like evangelical theologians, then, Langland's Will/will articulates a profound doubt about the will's capacity to justify itself before God; and that doubt leads directly both to a deep scepticism about the value of works, and to an acceptance of God's monopoly on spiritual initiative. By the end of Passus 10 Will is no longer asking what 'do well' is, and how good action might satisfy God. Instead he abdicates responsibility for moral action by affirming that all the key decisions have been taken by God 'longe er I were', and that those decisions are written into God's unreadable and secret 'Book of Life'. At this depressing cul-de-sac the authorial section of the A-Text of the poem ends, for whatever reason. How does the B-Version resolve this impasse?

In the following passus, Will, almost uniquely in medieval poetry,

[79] Trueman, pp. 56–72.

[80] *A Mirour to Know Thyself*, 4. 267. This text was written 1532–3.

falls into a dream within a dream. There are two such dreams in *Piers Plowman* (B.11. 4–404, and B.16. 18–166), and in each Will receives liberating illuminations. In the Passus 11 dream, after a period of 'recklessness' (the predictable result of a belief in predestination), he suddenly confronts Scripture's austere text, the parable of the wedding feast that ends 'Many are called but few are chosen' (Matt. 22: 1–14). The stark polarities of this text refuse to allow any careless negligence, and Will trembles in his heart as to 'wheither I were chose or noght chose' (B.11. 117). In the dialogue that follows, however, Will himself challenges this purely passive conception of salvation, whereby the Christian can only guess at whether or not he or she has been chosen by God. Instead, Will affirms the possibility of negotiated atonement between humans and God. He says that Christians are unable to renounce their legal rights before God, in the same way that even a runaway serf cannot escape the legalism of his status:

> Ac he may renne in arerage and rome fro home, [run · debt]
> And as a reneyed caytif recchelesly aboute. [foresworn wretch]
> Ac Reson shal rekene with hym and rebuken hym at the laste,
> And Conscience acounte with hym and casten hym in
> arerage, [settle accounts]
> And putten hym after in prison in purgatorie to brenne, [burn]
> For his arerages rewarded hym there right to the day of dome,
> But if contricion wol come and crye by his lyve [unless]
> Mercy for his mysdedes with mouthe or with herte.
>
> (B.11. 129–36)

This passage recapitulates the threats of depair and damnation in which the previous passus have seemed imprisoned: the serf's 'rechelessness' evokes Will's ethical scepticism, while the prison evokes the constant theme of human legal incapacity before God, whereby 'few are chosen'. The speech as a whole, however, also opens up liberating possibilities, since it affirms a legal mechanism whereby the runaway serf might, through his own initiative, reinstate himself in his lord's favour. Langland makes comparison with contemporary statuted labour laws, whereby runaway serfs would be imprisoned. The statutes of 1349 and 1351 (made immediately after the labour chaos provoked by the plague of 1348) stipulate that the serf shall be imprisoned until he should be able to find a surety, or bail; the reformulation of this statute in 1360 revokes the possibility of bail.[81] Langland's spiritual analogy of lord–serf relations, then, is more forgiving than the secular labour laws in force in the 1370s, since God as lord does permit the possibility of bail, on the 'surety' of the serf's contrition. The analogy is not only more generous than contemporary labour laws; it also mitigates the absoluteness of divine law cited from Athanasian Creed in the pardon, which has it that those who do well will be saved, and those who do evil damned.

Langland's strategic comparison with statuted, positive law opens up the possibility of God and humans entering into negotiation, whereby the legal ruptures of the past can be restored through a pact of atonement. This realm of positive law recognizes the likelihood of failure, yet also sees the possiblity of future reconciliation achieved by the joint initiative of the disputants. Certainly Scripture agrees with the lay figure Will:

> 'That is sooth,' seide Scripture; 'may no synne lette [prevent]
> Mercy, may al amende, and mekenesse hir folowe; [if]
> For thei beth, as oure bokes telleth, above Goddes werkes:
> *Misericordia eius super omnia opera eius.*'
>
> (B.11. 137–9a)

(Latin: 'His mercy is above all his works')

In having Will confront Scripture, Langland is representing an act of reading. There are certainly proto-Protestant aspects to this scene, since the lay figure Will confronts the largely vernacular text of the Bible without ecclesiastical mediation.[82] The theological perceptions to which this lection leads Will are, however, in stark contrast to Protestant positions: Scripture has it that the future is open; because the works of penance have real purchase on God, he is open to persuasion.

Even more striking here is the vernacular elaboration of the scriptural text: Scripture interprets herself, as it were, by affirming not only that God's mercy is above all his works, but meekness is also. God's mercy, indeed, is activated only on condition that humility accompany it. Meekness, or humility, can only be a *human* attribute

[81] *SR*, 34 Edward III, ch. 9 (1. 366).

[82] For the representation of Will as reader more generally, see Simpson, 'Desire and the Scriptural Text'.

in this context. Scripture extends the sense of the Psalm text (Ps. 144: 9), then, by affirming that both mercy and humility are above the normal operation of God's workings, and that mercy is dependent on an activating *human* humility. The human may be a serf in this analogy, but the lord attends upon the serf. Whereas Tyndale and Wyatt deny that a Christian can plead with God as a 'thrall bond-slave' pleading his right, Langland affirms precisely those rights. At the very heart of Langland's theology stands a patient, activating human humility. And if Langland foresees a Protestant theology of grace alone, wholly dependent on God's prior election, so too does the narrative of his poem swerve away from that belittling possibility to affirm human initiative.

(*b*) The Church

One could follow the consequences of this liberating perception, as Langland explores in particular the historical limits and basis of this new dispensation of mercy. He looks both to the virtuous pagan to affirm the worth of his just intent (Passus 12), and, more centrally, to the dynamic of Hebraic history (Passus 16–18), leading up to the great atonement scene of Passus 18, where Will witnesses Christ laying the legal foundations for the new legislative dispensation between humans and God. The striking differences of emphasis between Langlandian and Protestant theology have, however, been made, and I now turn to the institutional consequences of Langland's theology, comparing those with the institutional consequences of a Protestant notion of grace.

Will's liberating perception about the possibility of human reconciliation with God is made outside the Church: Will reads the vernacular Scriptures for himself, without clerical mediation. What implications, however, does Will's perception have for the institution of the Church? Holy Church is the first figure Will confronts in this poem (Passus 1), and when he does so the imposing figure of the Church claims an interpretative and moral authority over the entire 'field of folk' that Will has observed in the Prologue. While Langland never explicitly rejects the authoritarian figure of Holy Church represented in Passus I, the narrative strategy of the poem is to expose the shortcomings of institutions precisely by acts of apparent submission. This is true of educational institutions in Passus 8–14, for example, in which Will is educated only to expose the limitations of academic education. The poem's satirical strategy is, however, reformist rather than damnatory: it circles back to revisit and reform institutions whose inadequacy has been exposed. Is this also true of the Church? As with Langland's theology, does he foresee and forestall Protestant positions in his understanding of ecclesiology?

Langland certainly offers a powerful critique of ecclesiastical practices in the second vision (Passus 5–7). The prologue might expose the corruption of friars and pardoners, but only in the second vision does Langland systematically expose the complacent negligence of the contemporary Church. Once Piers tears the pardon and Will wakes from his vision, Will hastens to offer his orthodox credentials: he affirms that the Pope has power to grant pardon, and 'so I leve leelly [faithfully]', he says, that pardons, penance, and prayers save souls that 'have synned seven sithes dedly' (B.7. 177–9). All this, however, before an outright attack on the uselessness of 'a pokeful of pardon . . . ne provincials lettres' on the Day of Judgement (B.10. 182–201); and all this before he begins the next vision by arguing that even the just man sins seven times per day, and so cannot be saved. The ploughing of the half-acre in Passus 6 exposes the debilitating way in which the official forms of penance have been dislocated from communal labour relations. Ploughing, with all the communal relations that sustain it, is for Langland what constitutes real penance, not going on pilgrimage to Rome or Jerusalem.

The critique of pilgrimages certainly 'foresees' Protestant critique and satire; by 1538, indeed, the attack on pilgrimage is an official doctrine. Cromwell's 1538 Injunctions instruct priests that 'if ye have heretofore declared to your parishoners anything to the extolling or setting forth of pilgrimages, feigned relics, or images, or any such superstitions, ye shall now openly afore the same recant and reprove the same'.[83] Langland's critique of the institutional Church becomes much stronger and more systematic than satirizing pilgrimages, however. If in Passus 1 Holy Church instructs the individual soul, by Passus 15 this relationship has been reversed: now it is the individual soul, Anima, who delivers the most far-reaching critique

[83] *English Historical Documents*, ed. Williams, 5. 813.

of the Church of Christendom. The very projection of this critique has a Protestant flavour, since the individual soul is now in a position to critique the institution: after his long psychoanalysis (Passus 8–14), Will now confronts the whole soul of which he is a part, in what is a moment of psychosynthesis. Anima's primary point is that the Church has declined from its originary foundations. Just as holiness emanates from the Church, so too 'out of Holy Chirche alle yveles spredeth | There inparfit preesthoode is, prechours and techeris' (B.15. 92–6). This very lack in the Church is itself the justification of Langland's own poem, since the poem fills, from a lay perspective, a discursive vacuum that should be filled by those very preachers and priests. Anima sets the decline of the Church within the frame of the foundational moments in Church history: he cites the desert fathers, the founders of European monasticism, and of English Christianity, when Pope Gregory converted 'al that marche' (B.15. 445), as well as the founders of the fraternal orders. Since the Emperor Constantine's endowment of the Church in the fourth century with 'londes and ledes [men], lordshipes and rentes', the Church has been poisoned by greed; this produces the poem's most outspoken and daring call for ecclesiastical disendowment; lords should take the wealth of ecclesiastics by force:

> Taketh hire landes, ye lordes, and let hem lyve by dymes; [tithes]
> If possession be poison, and inparfite hem make,
> Good were to deschargen hem for Holy Chirches sake.
>
> (B.15. 563–5)

Attacks of this kind on the corrupting temporal wealth of the Church form the staple fare of much later evangelical polemic. Certainly by 1536 the moral justification for the disendowment of monasteries had become part of the official discourse of statute.[84] Before this date, when such opinions were heterodox, front-line polemicists had made the same attacks. Simon Fish's lively and proscribed *Supplicacyon for the Beggars* (1528), for example, devotes many pages to enumerating the Church's infinite and illegitimate sources of income, the prime examples of which are the 'exaccions' paid 'to delyver our soules out of the paynes of purgatori'. Fish goes

[84] Thus e.g. *SR*, 27 Henry VIII, ch. 28 (3. 575) (1536), which opens by declaring the 'manifest synne, vicious carnall and abhomynable lyvyng' of the smaller abbeys.

on to deny the existence of purgatory, saying instead that it is 'a thing invented by the covitousness of the spiritualitie, only to translate all kingdomes from other princes unto theim, and that there is not one word spoken of hit in al holy scripture.' (p. 10).[85] Like Langland's Anima, tracts of this kind also cite key points in Church history, when the Church gained an improper control over secular wealth.[86]

If Langland shares with later evangelical polemicists a deep mistrust of ecclesiastical endowment, however, the similarity leads to entirely different institutional consequences. The Lutheran theology that influenced English theologians has, as I argued above, an inscrutable God at its centre. It is God who elects, for unsearchable reasons, the saved. And the body of the saved constitutes the true Church. At a stroke, this conviction profoundly modifies the Church's status in the world, reducing it as it does to an unreadable sign of God's bounty rather than the actual channel between God and humans. Robert Barnes, for example, defines 'the universall church', in his tract *What the Church is*, as standing 'in the election of all faythful men, throughout the whole worlde, whose head and spouse is Christ Iesus':

> whether they bee Iew or Greeke, kyng or subiect, carter or Cardinall, butcher or Byshop, tancardbearer or cannelraker, free or bounde, Frier or fidler, Monke or miller: if they beleeve in Christes word, and sticke fast to his blessed promises, and trust onley in the merites of his blessed bloud, they bee the holy Church of God, yea and the very true church afore God . . . Boast, crake, blast, blesse, curse till your holy eyes start out of your head, it wil not helpe you, for Christ chooseth his church, at his iudgement and not at yours. (p. 244)

A passage of this kind has a superficially demotic sense, demolishing as it does boundaries that might discriminate between degrees of membership of the Church, and mocking the ecclesiastical instruments that pretend to make those distinctions. Just as it demolishes the Church's power to elect its members, so too, however, does Barnes deprive the butcher or miller themselves of the power to choose. Membership of this Church, and the very existence of this

[85] The document proscribing this text is reprod. in *Concilia*, ed. Wilkins, 3. 706–7. Wilkins's dating of 1526 must be incorrect.

[86] Thus e.g. Fish, *Supplicacyon*, ed. Furnivall, p. 5.

Church, is wholly a matter of God's prior election. The material Church that has developed in history, indeed, loses all legitimacy in this theology, since 'the Church' becomes an ideal form in the mind of God. Accordingly, as in the case of individual salvation, the force of God's grace is so overwhelming as to destroy the claims of the material, historical church to act as any kind of channel for humans to negotiate with God.

The status of the Church before God in this theology is effectively reduced, indeed, to the status of individuals before God, since the true Church is nothing but the congregation of the elect, whose anterior election the material Church can in no way affect. And as with the virtuous accretions of the individual life before God, the historical accretions of the material Church are dissolved by the direct and powerful solvent of divine grace. Any number of evangelical tracts attack the material objects and practices of the visible church, the world of 'men's dreams, traditions, imaginations, inventions, ceremonies, and superstition'.[87] From the perspective of Protestant ecclesiology, we can see that these attacks are not only underwritten by popular distaste of material wealth and display; they are also, more profoundly, underwritten by a complete distrust of human, historical enterprise.

If that is the ecclesiological direction taken by Protestant theology, what of Langland, who is equally hostile to the Church's temporal wealth? In the C-Text, the speech of Anima is spoken by a figure called Liberum Arbitrium, free will, the spokesman for the soul's highest power. Liberum Arbitrium, like Anima, encourages temporal lords to dispossess the Church (C.17. 227–32). Before this speech, however, Will has asked him for a definition of 'Holy Church'. This is how Liberum Arbitrium responds:

. . . 'Charite,' he seide;
Lief and love and leutee in o byleve and lawe, [belief · one · fidelity]
A love-knotte of leutee and of lele byleve, [faithful]
Alle kyne cristene clevynge on o will, [one]
Withoute gyle and gabbynge gyve and sulle and lene.' [deception · sell · lend]

(C.17. 125–9)

[87] William Tyndale, *A Prologue upon the Epistle of St Paul to the Romans*, in *Work of William Tyndale*, ed. Duffield, pp. 120–46 (at 135).

This definition of the Church stands in the starkest contrast with the Protestant conception. It is true that Langland does not identify the Church with its material instantiation, but neither does he identify it with an idea in the mind of God. Instead, the Church is given a psychological, volitional location. And this psychological disposition has immediate material results, since charity expresses itself as cooperation in the exercise of material life: charitable giving, selling, and lending are at the heart of this construction of the Church. Just as Langland's theology recognizes the virtuous accretions and intentions of a single life, so too is his Church the sum of those charitable and material accretions. The connection between the individual and the institution is, indeed, visible in this very passage, since the Church is defined as all Christians cleaving 'in one will': from this perspective the poem's problematic protagonist Will becomes the poem's solution, a solution which is at once personal and institutional. By volunteering his own identity to the corporate body of Christians, Will constitutes the Church.

This conception of the Church finds its fullest representation in Passus 19, where Will witnesses the construction of the Church under the papal direction of Piers Plowman. This ecclesiastical construction gains its legitimacy from Christ's act of Atonement, which Langland has represented in Passus 18. At the beginning of Passus 19 the figure Conscience explicates Christ's merciful yet just intervention in history, affirming that Christ's *best* act was to found the Church. In Protestant theology Christ's merits allow for the possibility that sin will not be imputed to individual Christians. In Langland's poem, by contrast, Christ's best act is to allow individuals to merit salvation through penance. Just before Christ's Ascension, he

> . . . yaf Piers power, and pardon he grauntede:
> To alle maner men, mercy and foryifnesse;
> [To] hym, myghte men to assoille of alle manere synnes [absolve]
> In covenaunt that that thei come and knewliche [acknowledge
> to paye satisfactorily]
> To Piers pardon the Plowman—*Redde quod debes.* [for the pardon
> of PP]
>
> (B.19. 184–8)

(Latin: 'Repay what you owe')

Passus 8–10 had stressed that 'Dowel' was to obey the absolute standards of God's law. Here, 'Dobest' is seen to abrogate that strict demand, and to institute a modified standard of justice, whereby the Christian can be saved if he or she 'repays what s/he owes' through penance. Salvation is ultimately dependent on Christ's freely given act of Atonement, but immediately dependent on the choice of individual Christians. That gracious irruption into history certainly disrupts the prison-bound pattern of human history, but it also inaugurates the new, human history of the Church. The sacraments, and especially the sacrament of penance, are not merely signs of prior decisions in this instutition; on the contrary, they are functional practices for negotiating with God. The Church's legitimacy is identifiable in this system not with God's inscrutable election of the saved, but rather with its distribution of penance in particular. For the individual Christian, history remains open to individual effort, and is not wholly subject to the inscrutable movements of grace.

The most remarkable aspect of Langland's Church is unquestionably its pope, Piers Plowman. 'Piers' clearly evokes the Apostle Peter, the first bishop of Rome, and Langland's Church is clearly a return to a primitive Apostolic, but Roman tradition. Piers's Christian name thus overlays Langland's scene onto a resonant biblical subtext. His occupation, however, insists on the connections between penance and the material life of society. Like the Apostle Peter (Matt. 16: 18–19), Piers has power to bind and unbind, absolving sinners of the guilt of sin, though not from the satisfaction (here 'dette') that true penance requires:

> Thus hath Piers power, be his pardon paied,
> To bynde and unbynde bothe here and ellis,
> And assoille men of alle synnes save of dette one. [the need to make satisfaction]
>
> (B.19. 189–91)

Whereas the connection between works and salvation has been deeply contested in the course of the narrative, here instead the poem's climactic moment triumphantly affirms the possibility of doing well, and of being saved through penance. Full absolution, however, involves not merely the contrition and confession of the sinner, but also the satisfaction of good works—the 'dette' that remains even after absolution. Piers's status as a ploughman insists on the intimate connection between hard, humble, and materially essential labour on the one hand, and the possibility of earned salvation on the other. Certainly this Church is profoundly reformed, embodied as it is by the humble worker who is at the same time its papal head. The whole thrust of Langland's theology points back to work, which is where the poem now turns, in the imagined scene of a newly founded Church as a Barn of Unity, 'Holy Chirche on Englissh' (B.19. 331), into which Piers brings the fruit of material and spiritual labour.

(*c*) Labour and Politics

Material labour necessitates political relationships. In *Piers Plowman* this is most pressingly evident in the ploughing scene of Passus 6. The ploughing begins with a knight offering to plough himself, if Piers will teach him how (B.6. 21–3). This remarkable offer implicitly recognizes the equality of Christians in a penitential context; Piers, however, courteously declines the offer, and reinstates a conservative model of social relations. He promises to work for the knight, on condition that the knight protect Holy Church and enforce the sanctions of justice against 'wastours and . . . wikked men that this world destruyeth' (B.6. 28). This conservative model of social relations recapitulates the model first proposed in the Prologue, with an important difference. In the Prologue an ideal commonwealth is imagined, in which the king, knighthood, and clergy ordain that the commons should be responsible for the production of food, whereupon the commons 'for profit of al the peple plowmen ordeyned | To tilie and to travaille as trewe lif asketh' (B. Prol. 119–20). This is the conservative manorial, agrarian model we find in Passus 6, with the difference that in Passus 6 the model is produced from the bottom up.

Top down or bottom up, however, this backward-looking model fails. Writing in a period of severe labour unrest, culminating in the English Uprising of 1381, Langland represents the legal powerlessness of the knight as the labourers refuse to work. Waster 'let light of the lawe, and lasse of the knyght' (B.6. 168), leaving the labour market wholly unconstrained by either penitential or legal sanction. The only effective force remaining is Hunger, by whose power 'derthe [is] justice' (B.6. 327), and who rules the boom and bust world of a labour market impelled by material desire alone (B.6. 171–329).

At this point, as we have seen, Langland's poem loses confidence in labour altogether, as Piers abandons the field of work. Until the Atonement of Passus 18, indeed, the poem cannot regain its confidence in the value of labour, since the intimate connection between penance and works seems to have been broken. Even when Will is persuaded of the possibility of divine charity, his understanding of that divine patience itself requires acts of human patience and abnegation. Thus the figure of the active life, Haukyn, accepts the advice of Patience to give up the active life and cast himself wholly upon the providence of God (Passus 14). Once, however, penance is reinstated as the central institutional channel whereby humans can satisfy a modified spiritual justice, then labour equally reassumes a central function. In Passus 19 Piers returns to plough in the field at whose centre stands the Barn of Unity. His work is not purely spiritual, and the labour relations imagined are no longer exclusively those of the agricultural manor. In a Pentecostal action that evokes the foundation of the Apostolic Church (Acts 2: 1–4), Grace distributes crafts to different groups. These gifts are anchored in another biblical text, Corinthians 12: 4–11, where Paul lists the gifts of evangelization. Piers's workers receive some of these evangelical gifts in Passus 19 (the powers of preaching and prophecy for example), but for the most part the crafts distributed are practical skills, to be deployed prudentially in the world. Lawyers, merchants, husbandmen, fishermen, artisans, and legal officials are, for example, among those who receive Grace's gifts. Whereas God as Truthe, or justice, had provoked the labour relations of manorial society, the dispensation of a merciful Christ produces an entirely different set of labour relations. Now Langland imagines a much more complex variety of occupations, embracing urban as much as agricultural crafts; and the relations between them are no longer hierarchical. As with the lay fraternities that flourished in this period, and upon which Langland models his society, I think, the relations in this society are horizontal and fraternal. Although some crafts might be 'cleaner' than others, Grace encourages them all to relate as brothers: 'Loketh that noon lakke oother, but loveth alle as bretheren' (B.19. 256).[88] Political and legal functions are certainly imagined in Grace's division of crafts, but no king appears; the reformed Church is the central institution in this great scene, and the communal labour relations produced by this Church require only the king Conscience: 'Crouneth Conscience kyng, and maketh Craft youre stiward' says Grace (B.19. 258).

Langland's understanding of both labour relations and ecclesiology, then, springs from his theology. A theology of modified justice, freely instituted by Christ, requires an institution for the dispensation of grace; this institution itself produces an egalitarian society whose commitment to spiritual sustenance equally underwrites its commitment to labour in the material world.

How do Henrician evangelical writers imagine the politics of labour relations? Is it the case there, too, that a conception of the Church equally produces a politics? The most consistent theme of Henrician theological polemic is its insistence on obedience to the king. This insistence is found in both heterodox and orthodox texts. Thus Tyndale's heterodox tract *The Obedience of a Christian Man*, published abroad in 1528 and immediately proscribed, coincides with Bishop Stephen Gardiner's orthodox *Oration of True Obedience*, published in Latin in 1535 in the wake of John Fisher's execution.[89] Heterodox or orthodox, these tracts have one central theme, which is that disobedience to the king, even should the king be a tyrant, is tantamount to disobedience to God. Tyndale the committed reformer is more extreme on this point than the doctrinally conservative Gardiner arguing for royal supremacy, but the convergence of argument is clear from the fact that Gardiner's text itself became heterodox, as it was translated into English by Protestant exiles in 1553. Tyndale argues that there can be no distinction between judgement of the king and God: 'He that judgeth the king judgeth God; and he that layeth hands on the king layeth hand on God; and he that resisteth the king resisteth God, and damneth God's law and ordinance.'[90] The duty of obedience extends to tyrants, since

[88] For the London context of this scene (and especially for fraternities), see Simpson, '"After Craftes Conseil"'. For fraternities more generally, see Scarisbrick, *Reformation*, ch. 2.

[89] The proscription first appears in *Concilia*, ed. Wilkins, 3. 706–7.

[90] Tyndale, *Obedience of a Christian Man*, p. 177.

the tyrant has been appointed by God, and is better in any case than a weak and effeminate king:

> though he be the greatest tyrant in the world, yet is he unto thee a great benefit of God, and a thing wherefore thou oughtest to thank God highly. For it is better to have somewhat, than to be clean stript out of all together . . . Yea, and it is better to have a tyrant unto thy king than a shadow . . . A king that is soft as silk, and effeminate . . . shall be much more grevous unto the realm than a right tyrant.[91]

In subjection to tyrants, Tyndale goes on to argue, Christians should not be like the child, who, 'as long as he seeketh to avenge himself upon the rod, hath an evil heart'. On the contrary, Tyndale enjoins submission: 'if we . . . meekly knowledge our sins for which we are scourged, and kiss the rod, and amend our living; then will God take the rod away, that is, he will give the rulers a better heart'.[92]

The simplest explanation for this insistence on obedience to kings and even to tyrants is political strategy. From very early in the persecution of Lollardy, heresy had been associated with sedition.[93] It was certainly in the interests of the Church to promote such an association, since the king should be persuaded that doctrinal heterodoxy threatened his own jurisdiction. By the same token, serious chances of practical success in any programme of ecclesiastical disendowment clearly depended on the support of the king; it was in the interests of reformers to promote the idea that the king's jurisdiction would be enlarged by the application of their programme of change. One can see this strategy in action in, for example, Simon Fish's *Supplicacyon for the Beggars*, which, while heterodox, and while explicitly proscribed, in 1529 came, by Foxe's account, into the hands of Henry VIII. The King was interested and impressed by the tract, since it insisted both on ecclesiastical infringement of royal prerogative, and on the enormous material opportunities offered the monarch by disendowment.

Promotion of royal supremacy was not merely, however, a matter of strategy. For non-evangelical proponents of royal supremacy in matters of religion, the question is one of geographical and jurisdic-

[91] Tyndale, *Obedience of a Christian Man*, p. 180.
[92] Ibid. 196.
[93] Aston, 'Lollardy and Sedition'.

tional unity. Thus Stephen Gardiner argues that if the king is the head of the realm, then his subjects are subject to him 'in all one kind of subieccion, that is to say for Goddes sake'.[94] Gardiner's position does not do away with the material church, but it divides the Church into national groupings: 'the churche of Englande is nothing elles but the congregation of men and women . . . united in Christes profession . . . and of the place it is to be named . . . as is the churche of Fraunce the churche of Spayne and the churche of Rome'.[95]

For properly evangelical thinkers there are scriptural and theological grounds for their more thoroughgoing promotion of obedience to royal authority. The section on obedience to 'Kings, Princes and Rulers' in Tyndale's *Obedience* begins with an extensive citation from the text of Romans, the book he elsewhere calls 'the principal and most excellent part of the new Testament':[96]

> Let every soul submit himself unto the authority of the higher powers. There is no power but of God: the powers that be are ordained of God. Whosoever therefore resisteth the power, resisteth the ordinance of God. They that resist shall receive to themselves damnation.[97]

Like Gardiner, Tyndale does have some sense of geographical jurisdiction: 'one king, one law is God's ordinance in every realm'.[98] But the real pressure behind Tyndale's abolition of jurisdictional diversity is his understanding of the Church's own lack of institutional authority. The true Church, for Tyndale, is the congregation of the faithful, and its material instantiation on earth has no independent authority at all, being not merely subject to the temporal power, but having no power of its own whatsoever. Tyndale glosses Paul's statement that 'there is no power but of God' accordingly: 'By power understand the authority of kings and princes.'[99]

Protestant theology, ecclesiology, and, politics, then, were each highly centralized, and they jointly operated so as to efface jurisdictional and institutional boundaries. What effect did this have on

[94] Gardiner, *Oration of True Obedience*, p. 95.

[95] Ibid. 95.

[96] *Prologue upon the Epistle of St Paul to the Romans*, in *Work*, ed. Duffield, p. 120.

[97] Rom. 13: 1–2; Tyndale, *Obedience of a Christian Man*, p. 173.

[98] Tyndale, *Obedience of a Christian Man*, p. 240.

[99] Ibid. 179.

Protestant conceptions of labour? I conclude the principal part of this chapter by looking briefly to the Piers Plowman tracts and some related material by way of answering this question. What we observe in these reinvocations of Piers is a total incapacity to harness the power of the earlier poem. As in English evangelical theological writing of this period, these tracts suggest no connection whatsoever between labour and penitential payment to God. Labour in these works has been fundamentally disconnected from theology, and becomes instead a matter of social policy. Equally, they manifest no connection whatsoever between labour practices and the Church; labour is, rather, wholly a matter of the secular power. Correlatively, the address of these texts is to secular powers, either king or parliament, not to the commonwealth as a whole. Whereas *Piers Plowman* imagines, and indeed promotes, a labour structure being generated from the bottom up, the organization of work in these later tracts is projected as wholly in the decision and initiative of the king or parliament.

The only tracts that explicitly use the name 'Piers Plowman' in their title were each published in the deregulated period 1547 to 1553. *A Godly dyalogue and Dysputacion Betwene Pyers Plowman, and a Popysh Preest* (*c.*1550) is entirely doctrinal in interest. A learned ploughman refutes the arguments of an ignorant priest concerning transubstantiation. The text is wholly in prose, and bears only the faintest trace of *Piers*: the ploughman is theologically learned, and he defeats a priest in argument, which might recall the tearing of the Pardon scene, but there are no deeper strategic or stylistic borrowings from Langland's poem. *Pyers Plowman's Exhortation unto the Lordes of the Parlyamenthouse* (*c.*1550) is, by contrast, wholly unconcerned with doctrinal issues, and focuses instead on the problem of unemployment. Workers have been made unemployed since the dissolution of the monasteries and the ensuing enclosures of pasture land by the new landlords. The author proposes protectionist economics and the conversion of more wasteland for arable purposes. The only resemblance to *Piers Plowman* here is the posture of plain speaking; the author describes his writing as 'the naked trueth in rude wordes' (Bii^{r}). Piers remains an undeveloped voice, the platform for the presentation of policy to help the poor. A third 'Piers Plowman' tract is slightly more complex, with slightly more connection to the fourteenth-century text. *I Playne Piers which can not flatter* (*c.*1547) is written in prose, although it is verbally indebted to the verse *Ploughman's Tale*. This work does imagine a world in which 'a pore plowman of pope myght get the keys' (Aiii^r^), but the position is unquestionably evangelical, celebrating as it does the death of More and Fisher, 'the chefe pyllars of the vyperous generacion', and lamenting the burning of Tyndale and the banishment of Coverdale. Its central complaint is against the constraint of Bible reading enacted in the 1542 legislation. There is some development of the persona of the ploughman: he is represented working and writing, but the fiction is minimal, and the voice wholly unequivocal.

Although these are the only texts since the late fourteenth-century *Pierce Plowman's Crede* to use the name 'Piers Plowman', they stand in a tradition of sorts with some 'ploughman' material produced or at least printed earlier in the reign of Henry VIII. The *Praier and Complaynte of the Plowman* (printed abroad in 1531) is almost certainly an early fifteenth-century Lollard text against clerical abuses, with no relation to *Piers Plowman* whatsoever beyond the opposition of a ploughman's virtue and ecclesiastical corruption. *A proper dialogue betwene a gentillman and a husbandman* (*c.*1531) has a husbandman and a gentleman agree on the desirability of lay scriptural reading, and incorprates a genuinely Lollard prose text on disendowment. The main text is in verse, with no verbal or stylistic debts to *Piers Plowman*. Neither does the *Ploughman's Tale* (published 1536) have any significant connections with *Piers*, beyond the sporadic use of alliteration and the association of anticlericalism and a ploughman. This text is also largely made up of early fifteenth-century anti-papal and broadly anti-ecclesiastical material, reframed so as to suit Henrician conditions.[100]

Stylistically, verbally, and thematically, then, all these texts have the slimmest of connections with Langland's poem. Neither do they deploy Langland's characteristic satiric strategies, of pretending submission in order to expose a discursive vacuum in official discourse that will be filled by the text itself. Most significantly, however, they collectively represent a splintering of the discursive constellation that was *Piers Plowman*. For reasons we have examined in this chapter,

[100] Chaucer, *The Plowman's Tale*, in *Complete Works*, ed. Skeat, suppl. vol. See also Wawn, 'The Genesis of the *Plowman's Tale*'.

the particular configuration of theology, ecclesiology, labour theory, and politics was simply unavailable to these authors. Because their fiction is so thin a veil for fairly standard ecclesiastical satire, they are not significantly different from *Rede Me and be not wrothe* (published Strasburg, 1528), whose ecclesiastical satire and pleas for Scripture in English are put into the mouths of two priests' servants. The humble position of the protagonists lays claim to a popular voice, in the way of the ploughman material, but nothing is and can be made of the labour of these servants. And because they are wholly dependent on the king for any change, neither are these texts significantly different from the unofficial evangelical policy papers directed at the king or parliament from the late 1520s, like Fish's *Supplicacyon* (1528); *A Supplicacion to our moste Sovereign Lorde King Henry the Eyght* (1544); Henry Brinkelow's virulent *Complaint of Roderyck Mors* (*c.*1542); and *A Supplication of the Poore Commons* (1546). Of these, Brinkelow attacks Henry VIII most explicitly, claiming that the bishops have made Henry a pope (p. 35); he attacks the rent rises on the expropriated monastic lands, the enclosures, and the cruelty of the Court of Augmentations, the body responsible for managing the expropriation of the monasteries. Like many other works of the 1540s and 1550s, Brinkelow laments the rapacity of the new order, and, even as a committed reformer, looks back nostalgically to the monasteries, when 'every man knoweth that many thowsandes were well relevyd of them', whereas now 'I do not heare tell that one halpeny worth of almes or any other profight cometh unto the peple' from the lords who have bought up the monasteries and enclosed their lands (p. 33). Brinkelow's solution for these ills is, however, more of the same: he proposes a complete Protestant programme of reform, without recognizing that the concentrations of power that the Protestant revolution created have exacerbated the very problems of poverty of which he complains.

V

The decades 1370–90 and 1520–53, then, offer rich areas for the study of ecclesiological writing, both imaginative and practical. The other especially important body of vernacular texts within the centuries of this history was that produced by the Lollard movement, largely in the period 1380–1415. The importance of this movement came into much sharper focus in the last twenty years of the twentieth century, as the work of Anne Hudson in particular revealed a movement that was both theologically articulate, and extraordinarily well organized and prolific in the matter of vernacular textual production.[101] A literary history is clearly not the place for any extended account of this movement, whose writings almost without exception set out to be discursively stable, unimaginative, and instrumental. One critical question should, however, be answered before I end this chapter with a short sequence of individual works across the period 1350–1550. What is the relation between Lollardy and *Piers Plowman*?

A number of studies tried to answer this question. After isolating some areas of theological overlap, this scholarship tended to concur with David Lawton, who had argued that the influence is from Langland to the Lollards rather than vice versa: 'The issue is really that Lollards had Langlandian sympathies.'[102] I agree that Langland draws on a matrix of theological and ecclesiological issues prior to Lollardy. He may also have written for the kinds of audience to which Lollardy appealed. The Lollards did not, however, have Langlandian sympathies. One or two areas of doctrinal overlap aside (especially disendowment, and the desirability of vernacular Scripture), the Lollards were, in fundamental respects, wholly at odds with *Piers Plowman*. I say this not because Lollard texts consistently rejected both fiction, and 'dremes', and not because I find no reference to, or evocation of, *Piers Plowman* in any explicitly Lollard prose text. The profound difference, a difference that emerges much more clearly in the light of the contrast between *Piers Plowman* and

[101] For Lollard history and textual production, see Hudson, *Premature Reformation* (for textual production, esp. pp. 106–8, and ch. 5). The seriousness with which Lollards set about producing large and high-quality texts is attested by surviving numbers of the Wycliffite Bible (250) and the Wycliffite Sermon Cycle of 294 sermons (31), for which last point, see *English Wycliffite Sermons*, 1, ed. Hudson, pp. 189–207.

[102] D. Lawton, 'Lollardy and the *Piers Plowman* Tradition', p. 793; Bowers, 'Piers Plowman and the Police'; for more cautious assessments, which cover almost all the possible areas of doctrinal overlap, see Gradon, and Hudson, *Premature Reformation*, pp. 401–8. For a wholly sceptical view, largely the one proposed here, see von Nolcken, '*Piers Plowman*, the Wycliffites, and *Pierce Plowman's Crede*'.

sixteenth-century evangelical theology, centres on the conception of the Church.

Anne Hudson is correct in describing the Lollard movement as the 'premature Reformation', insofar as all the key elements of evangelical theology are present to Lollards, even if not systematized or emphasized in the same way. For Lollards, largely inspired by their intellectual mentor Wyclif (d. 1384), God has chosen whomsoever he wished to be saved; the body of these elect make up the true Church; the material Church loses much of its sacramental function; and the king, to whom complete obedience is owed, should appropriate the material Church's wealth.[103] In particular, Lollard texts were very clear about the whereabouts of the true Church, and who was in it. The Church, for Lollards, was the 'congregation of trew men predestinate and iustified'.[104] Wyclif was an extreme idealist in the philosophical sense, believing that entities, including the Church, exist eternally and unchangeably in the mind of God. To suggest otherwise would be to abrogate divine omnipotence and omniscience, since it would concede that God is not in full possession of the future. This massive centralization of initiative in the hands of God must put the power of the sacraments, and especially penance, under extreme question.

Lollard texts remained unclear on this point,[105] but they were not at all unclear about the nature and membership of the true Church. The representative text *The Lanterne of Light* (*c.*1415), for example, is structured around a division of the three churches: the true Church, the material Church, and the Devil's Church. The material Church contains members of both other churches, and the anonymous author takes especial care to caution against certainty in the matter of sorting Christians into the other two churches: 'Noon may discryve thise twoo parties verrili iche from othir wandiryng in this secounde chirche for licknessis that thei usen' (p. 48).[106] Once he has cautioned against certainty, however, the author generates the rest of

[103] The broad doctrinal coherence of the Lollard movement is articulated by Hudson, *Premature Reformation*, chs. 6–8.

[104] *Rosarium Theologie*, ed. von Nolcken, p. 67.

[105] For an example of the lack of clarity, see Sermon 55, in *English Wycliffite Sermons*, 2, ed. Gradon, 1–5.

[106] Very much the same argument about the Church can be found e.g. in the Lollard text known as 'The Church and her Members'.

his substantial text precisely out of conviction about who belongs to which church. The surest sign of belonging to Christ's Church is to be persecuted, but there are many other signs: many of the normal practices of the material Church, indeed, are taken as sure signs of reprobation.

This certainty about who belongs to the true Church characterizes the address and satiric posture of very many Lollard texts. Whereas Langland's poem is addressed to an indeterminate 'us', ideally designed to embrace his whole imagined readership, Lollard polemical texts are written by and for a very specific 'us', distinguished even in the earliest examples from the 'heretics', 'hypocrites', and 'servants of the fiend' who people the 'synagogue' of the material Church.[107] Exclusivity of address also characterizes the non-conversation of Lollard 'dialogue'. In, for example, the *Testimony of William Thorpe* (*c.*1407, a text printed in 1530 and incorporated by Foxe in 1563 in his *Acts and Monuments*), Thorpe represents his inquisitor Archbishop Arundel demanding that he 'be gouerned bi holi chirche'. Thorpe replies with apparently confident obedience: 'Ser, al my wille and purpos is and euer schal be, I triste to God, to be gouerned bi holi chirche' (p. 51). Such confidence is based, however, on Thorpe's alternative meaning of 'holi chirche', which he has already defined: 'the feithful gederinge togidre of this peple, lyvynge now here in this liif, is the holi chirch of God, fightinge here in erthe ayens the fend [devil] and the prosperite of this world and her fleischli lustis' (p. 32). God's own prejudicial act of having already written the names of the faithful 'in the book of liif' leads directly to Thorpe's own prejudicial mode of 'argument', a mode that works by assertion rather than engagement. Of course the same is true of the inquisitorial archbishop, and I may be doing nothing more than describing the inevitable features of highly polemicized and dangerous confrontation, in which both sides manipulate openings offered by their opponents to press their own unbending position.[108] That is certainly true, but I am also suggesting that this mode is built into Lollard theological conviction.

The same is true of the closed system of Lollard ecclesiastical

[107] For the Lollard manner of address, see von Nolcken, '"Certain Sameness"'.

[108] For the discursive features of polemical attack in these texts, see Barr, ch. 4.

satire. Langland's satire is certainly generated by an explosive anger; the poem nevertheless submits that anger to the discipline of patience, a discipline informed by theological sensitivity to the generosity of divine patience. The resultant satire is reformative rather than damnatory: if God is prepared to 'suffer' the sinfulness of humans, in the hope of their reformation, then so too should the satirist temper his own judgement.[109] Thus Langland's satire circles back on itself, recuperating that which it had seemed to reject. Lollard satire is, by contrast, unequivocal and damnatory. Of course this, too, is partly a matter of the extremely threatening environment in which Lollard authors wrote, particularly after 1401; it is more centrally a matter of their theological conviction about membership of the true Church. Their God has already made up his mind, and so have they. This absolute division of the Christian living in the present into the saved and the damned prefigures later Protestant representations of the true and false Church, divided on the model of pre-Reformation accounts of the Last Judgement (Fig. 7).

In the brief sequences that follow, I use this distinction to discriminate between pre- and post-Lollard writing: the work written out of an earlier theological environment is designed to embrace new members of an enlarged material Church; post-Lollard ecclesiological writing, with some exceptions, is designed to exclude the reprobate. The contrast is very sharp in the first pairing of late fourteenth-century texts.

(*a*) *St Erkenwald* and *Pierce Plowman's Crede*

These two texts are possibly very nearly contemporary. *St Erkenwald* (352 lines) may be associated with the London revival of the cult of that saint in 1386, while *Pierce Plowman's Crede* (850 lines) was certainly written after 1393 and probably before 1400. Both were written in alliterative meter, *St Erkenwald* in the 'classical' meter characteristic of north-western poetic productions, while *Pierce Plowman's Crede* uses the looser alliterative structures of *Piers Plowman* and other south-western, predominantly satirical

109 'Who suffreth more than God?', says Reson in *Piers Plowman* (B.11. 379); see Simpson, 'Constraints of Satire'.

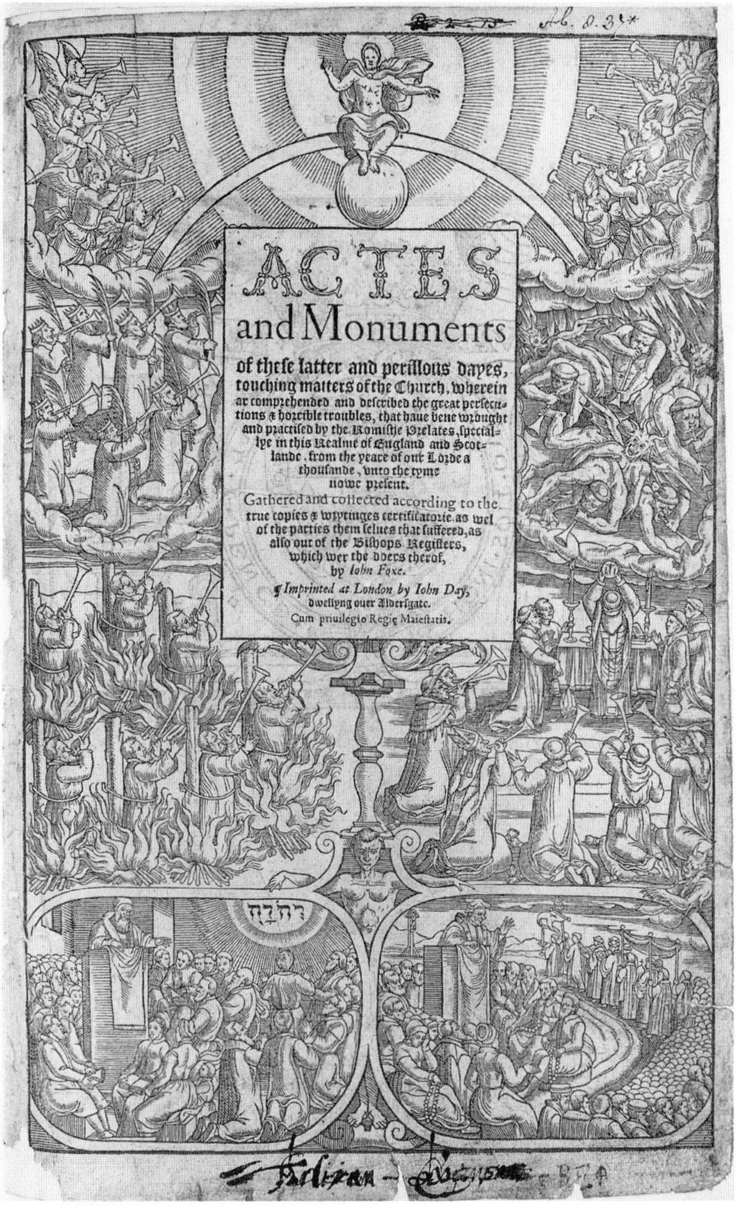

ACTES
and Monuments
of these latter and perillous dayes,
touching matters of the Church, wherein
ar comprehended and described the great persecu-
tions & horrible troubles, that haue bene wrought
and practised by the Romishe Prelates, special-
lye in this Realme of England and Scot-
lande, from the yeare of our Lorde a
thousande, vnto the tyme
nowe present.
Gathered and collected according to the
true copies & wrytinges certificatorie, as wel
of the parties them selues that suffered, as
also out of the Bishops Registers,
which wer the doers therof,
by *Iohn Foxe.*
¶ *Imprinted at London by Iohn Day,*
dwellyng ouer Aldersgate.
Cum priuilegio Regiæ Maiestatis.

Fig. 7. John Foxe, *Acts and Monuments* (1563), title page.

texts. Despite their dialects, both poems have clear London affiliations. On the face of it, the slightly later text is much more heavily indebted to *Piers Plowman*. Unlike later sixteenth-century Piers texts, the *Crede's* debts to *Piers Plowman* go much further than simple name-dropping. The poem's satire traces a path forged by *Piers*: the apparently naïve narrator's desire to know his Creed generates the narrative; his search for authoritative sources of instruction takes him to the friars, each order of which venomously attacks the other instead of teaching the narrator. This vituperation at once attacks the friars out of their own mouth, and legitimates the poem itself as filling the vacuum of authority created by the friars. That vacuum is filled, as it is in *Piers*, by the simple yet theologically sophisticated ploughman, who himself attacks the friars before teaching the narrator his Creed. Certainly sixteenth-century readers saw this poem as a companion to its greater predecessor: the 1553 print as well as the two sixteenth-century manuscript copies all append the poem to *Piers Plowman*.

If the *Crede*, as *Piers*, moves to the margins for authority, *St Erkenwald* is by contrast situated at the heart of London official religion, in St Paul's, and one of its heroes is the bishop of London. While workmen in seventh-century London re-edify St Paul's from the pagan temple it had been, they discover, as they dig deep to lay the foundations, a beautiful coffin inscribed with unintelligible letters and containing a splendidly dressed and perfectly preserved corpse. The archaeological discovery provokes interpretative confusion, which is resolved only by Bishop Erkenwald, whose inspired intercession brings the corpse to life to speak for himself. A pagan judge has been discovered, whose own story of faithful adherence to his own form of pre-Christian justice moves the bishop to baptismal tears: the judge receives his belated baptism, and his soul is received into heaven even as his corpse and garments turn instantly to ash.

For all the obvious connections between the *Crede* and *Piers*, *Erkenwald* shares with *Piers* an embracing Christianity derived from an earlier, pre-Wycliffite theological environment. The main theological controversy in earlier fourteenth-century England had been between so-called 'semi-Pelagians', who upheld the powers of individuals to contribute to their own salvation by works (within God's freely established dispensation of mercy), and those, like Bishop

Bradwardine (*c*.1300–49), who upheld the absolute power of God.[110] These issues were a matter for legislation right up to the *Piers Plowman* period, since a mandate sent by Archbishop Simon Langham to the Chancellor of Oxford in 1368 labels the following conclusions as errors: that 'adult and rational Muslims, Jews and pagans, who never have had, nor will have the act or habit of the Christian faith, [can] be saved'; or that 'anyone can be saved through their unaided, natural powers'.[111] These positions are not themselves unequivocally upheld by either *Piers* or *Erkenwald*: in *Piers* the saved pagan Trajan might say that he was saved by his 'pure truthe', and not through any 'preiere of a pope' (B.11. 155), but this claim cannot be taken readily as authorial; and in *Erkenwald* the baptismal, sacramental tears shed by the bishop are a necessary premiss of salvation. Both poems nevertheless express a profound commitment to the solidarities of human justice: in *Erkenwald* the bishop's tears are only shed, and the barriers of history only transgressed, in response to a purely human justice; and in *Piers* God's respect for human efforts to 'do-well' through 'truthe' (i.e. justice) is nearly the deepest conviction of the poem: 'Ne wolde nevere trewe God but trewe truthe were allowed' (B.12. 287). Both these texts, like Gower's accounts of Constantine and Constance in Book 2 of the *Confessio Amantis* (1390), represent historical continuities between 'pagan' and Christian culture.

The pagan judge in *Erkenwald* is discovered in the foundations of the 'New Werke' of St Paul's. As the workmen 'dalfe so depe into the erthe' to be sure of the 'fundement' of the new building (ll. 41–6), they discover an anterior civilization; and before they can proceed with the new foundation, that older culture must be absorbed rather than simply destroyed. Like almost all Lollard texts, the *Crede* is also deeply concerned with foundations, and with the 'grounding' of the Church. This takes the form of attacking the false foundations of the friars, where 'foundation' refers both to the institutional basis and the material buildings of the friars, with their elaborate architecture and splendid stained glass. Both the institutions and the buildings

110 For Langland as a 'semi-Pelagian', see Adams; for a view that sees Langland's soteriology as entirely orthodox and conservative, see Minnis, 'Looking for a Sign'. For theologians of the *via moderna*, including Ockham and Holcot (previously but unhelpfully called 'Nominalists') see McGrath, pp. 166–72.

111 *Concilia*, ed. Wilkins, 3. 76.

are dismissed as an unnecessary excrescence in and on the Church. The frequent relaying of the material foundations of these churches is provoked by the 'dygginge devel' who 'dissaveth [deceives] the chirche' (ll. 504–5). So where the foundational complexity of Christian history is figured through the metaphor of architecture in *St Erkenwald*, the *Crede* reverses the same figural scheme: this poem lines buildings up in its destructive sights in order to get back to the unequivocal simplicity of secure scriptural grounding (though without recognizing that the Creed is not itself scriptural). Grace is redistributed outside the Church in the earlier poems in such a way as to relativize authority; the *Crede* simply relocates spiritual authority in the person of the ploughman, and excludes one large segment of the material Church from the true Church. *Pierce Plowman's Crede* is itself an exceptional Lollard text, insofar as it does explicitly evoke *Piers Plowman* in a variety of ways: it adopts a fictional frame; it is in verse, unlike the vast bulk of Lollard writing; and it does employ impersonation and a satiric strategy directly indebted to the earlier poem. Despite these apparent gestures towards *Piers*, it marks a radical narrowing of the project of *Piers Plowman* in the simplicity of its polemical message, and a reversal of *Piers* in its ecclesiological exclusivity.

(*b*) John Audelay's *Marcol and Solomon*

Fifteenth-century writers broaching ecclesiastical matters tended to keep their heads well down. By 1415 the Lollard movement seems to have been driven underground, and certainly by 1440 had stopped producing books on the extraordinary scale of the years since 1380.[112] The reaction to Lollardy was so draconian, however, as to repress almost all orthodox vernacular representations of the Church as well. Conditions for imaginative representation in the vernacular were inauspicious on every front: Archbishop Arundel outlawed the treatment of theology in the vernacular, and Lollards rejected fiction in any case. Certainly there are devotional texts and saints' lives (to be treated in Chapter 8), and treatments of the individual Christian life, as in Lydgate's translation *The Pilgrimage of*

[112] Hudson, *Premature Reformation*, ch. 10.

the Life of Man (*c.*1426).[113] But writing that addresses the Church as an institution in the vernacular is either narrowly polemical and orthodox, or wholly unimaginative in its attempt to address Lollardy. Bishop Reginald Pecock (*c.*1395–1460) alone exemplifies the second of these alternatives, and also exemplifies the dangers of saying anything about such matters, since he was himself convicted of heresy in a thoroughly abject attempt of Henry VI to bolster his failing authority in 1457. Examples of the narrowly polemical in verse are Hoccleve's *Remonstrance against Oldcastle* (1415), and Lydgate's *Defence of Holy Church* (*c.*1415). The *Remonstrance* is Hoccleve's most narrowly based poem (perhaps the only poem he wrote as an unequivocally official poet), where he speaks in direct address to Oldcastle as a spokesman for the King, presumably soon after the so-called Oldcastle Rising of January 1414. Hoccleve ostensibly attempts to persuade Oldcastle to revert to orthodoxy on doctrinal grounds, while Lydgate simply encourages the King to persecute Lollards, using Old Testament exempla. Both poems tread potentially dangerous ground, even in their statement of orthodoxy, since Hoccleve is obliged to insist on the superiority of papal over monarchical jurisdiction (ll. 305–16), and Lydgate points to the downfall of kings who appropriated church property (ll. 134–47). Both, nevertheless, bristle with official threat: Lydgate insists that the King 'distroye' Lollards, while Hoccleve repeatedly reminds Oldcastle that 'in the fyr yee feele may the sore' (l. 320).

All these texts attempt to speak with a singular and wholly orthodox voice. If that is the discursive response we might expect to legislative danger, then John Audelay's almost wholly unnoticed yet brilliant poem *Marcol and Solomon* (1,013 lines) is all the more remarkable for its discursive fluidity.[114] Audelay had served as a chaplain to Lord Lestrange, who in 1414 had been appointed to search out Lollards in Shropshire.[115] By the time Audelay was writing (*c.*1426), he seems to have become blind and deaf, and to have

[113] For a comprehensive list of works produced, see Watson, 'Censorship and Cultural Change', pp. 859–64.

[114] Audelay, *Poems*, ed. Whiting, no. 2. The individual poem has no editorial or authorial title; my title *Marcol and Solomon* is invented by analogy with the titles of *Solomon* dialogues in Old English. Audelay seems to entitle the whole collection *The Council of Consience* in no. 18, l. 417, p. 146.

[115] See M. Bennett.

retired to Haughmond abbey near Shrewsbury. His own poem explicitly courts the dangers of anti-Lollard persecution: any honest priest incurs the wrath of his fellow priests, who accuse him of being a Lollard (l. 133), just as any secular who criticizes the clergy is taken to be burnt as a Lollard (ll. 669–76). The poem has good reason to express these anxieties, since it also presses some Lollard positions of its own, concerning the 'grounding' of ecclesiastical institutions (ll. 315–20), church endowment (ll. 456–68), and pluralities and the secular service of clerics (ll. 728–53). Despite its evident and explicit orthodoxy on key sacramental issues (ll. 780–857), this text dares to agree with Lollard critique of ecclesiastical wealth, and to do so in an explicitly Lollard vocabulary. The poet even names himself (l. 1008).

How does Audelay avoid censure? He brilliantly exploits a traditional discursive position, that of the fool, Marcol, who writes to a wise man, Solomon. The poem is written in the voice of Marcol, on behalf of 'homle hosbondusmen' (l. 68), and it manages to unwrite itself as it broaches dangerous territory: Marcol is not so much making this complaint as asking the wise man, Solomon, to pass it on to official audiences. Exploiting this provisional address, Marcol does nevertheless speak to powerful audiences, both secular and ecclesiastical, though in a shifting, fragmented way. Marcol's voice is a kind of funnel, through which scraps of reported speech, including prophecy and official legislation, flow. The verse form is itself fragmented, divided as it is into thirteen-line stanzas, which often change voice and audience without warning. The larger effect of the poem is, however, a 'praise of folly', since authority accrues to the fool Marcol's voice in many ways: it is courageous, metrically proficient, and subtle in its allusive use of Latin Scripture. Marcol is also extremely well read in *Piers Plowman*, since the poem is brimming with citation of the earlier text. And like *Piers Plowman*, this poem's constantly shifting audience finally forms one audience, a Church from which no one is irredeemably excluded.

(*c*) Skeltonics

While discursive conditions in the latter half of the fifteenth-century were entirely unpropitious for the production of overtly anti-ecclesiastical satire, resources of the kind deployed by Audelay resurfaced in the new theological environment of the 1520s to 1550s. As the ecclesiological situation changed rapidly, however, the same popular verse form was exploited by entirely opposed 'popular' voices. John Skelton's *Colin Clout* (1,265 three-stress lines, written 1521–2), for example, parades both its metrical incivility and the fiction of its unlearned origins in its very title: 'Colin' derives from Latin *colonus*, 'smallholding farmer', while 'clout' evokes the 'tattered and jagged, | Rudely rayne-beaten' metrical 'patches' of which the poem is constructed.[116] Like Audelay, Skelton positions himself outside the Church and addresses it in what is perhaps the last orthodox example of traditional anti-ecclesiastical satire. Scraps of different voices are ventriloquized by Colin, including prophecies and official threats against the very kind of discourse practised by the poem itself. Wolsey is the prime target, but the episcopate, schoolmen, and the friars are also attacked, no less than the laity who promote heresy.

Skelton's narrator claims to be the only truth-telling voice and imagines the voices of official anger raised against him, ordering him to be set 'fast by the fete' (l. 1166). So far from suffering for this work, however, by 1523 Skelton was obsequiously praising Wolsey in the dedication of his *Garlande of Laurell*, in which Skelton shamelessly trumps his own fame as an official poet laureate. By 1528 he is actively fulfilling that role in the *Replycacion*, a poem, sumptuously dedicated to Wolsey, mocking two recanting heretics. That much narrower, partisan, and official tone characterizes the sudden raising of the stakes in 1529, the year that also marks the beginning of Thomas More's own voluminous attack on evangelical doctrine with his *Dialogue concerning Heresies*. From that year until 1558 at least, the discursive conditions for those writing about the Church were extremely treacherous, since the content of orthodoxy itself became uncertain. And if Skeltonic verse form had been used in 1521 to defend orthodoxy, by 1534 the same form was being used to exuberant effect for precisely the opposite position: *The Image of Ipocrisy* (written between 1529 and 1534)[117] is a verbal tour de force of evangelical mockery, in which the author correctly predicts that

[116] Citation of *Colin Clout*, ll. 54–5, is from Skelton, *The Complete English Poems*, ed. Scattergood, pp. 246–78.

[117] In Skelton, *Poetical Works*, ed. Dyce, 2. 413–47.

what is regarded as treason and heresy now will soon change: 'Then shall we here and se | In Christianitye, | Whether youe or we | The very traytours be'.[118] When that prophecy had indeed come true in the reign of Edward VI, Skeltonics are being used again, in, for example, Luke Shepherd's puerile anti-Catholic railings, or the more serious *Vox Populi Vox Dei*.[119] In that poem the two-stress form is once again used to express the popular voice, but that voice now confronts evangelical disillusion. In what is possibly a very distant echo of *Piers Plowman*, the poet complains that 'lady mesteres Mede' expels the poor tenant farmer. Here, however, as in other examples of evangelical disillusion like Brinkelow's *Complaint* or Crowley's moving and intelligent *Philargyrie* (1551),[120] the complaint has no other resources than to rely on the king for what has turned out to be the deterioration of social conditions: 'we have banyshed superstycion, | But styll we kepe ambycion | We have sent awaye all cloysters, | But still we kepe extortyoners.'

[118] Skelton, *Poetical Works*, ed. Dyce, p. 420 (the poem has no line numbering).
[119] Ibid. 400–13.
[120] *RSTC* 6089.5.

8

Moving Images

In this chapter I consider a range of late medieval and early modern 'devotional' writings; I do so precisely in order to question the imputation of *naïveté* that the 'devotional' label evokes. These kinds of writing served a wide variety of often overlapping discursive ends, especially national, institutional, and those of the household, where the pressures were most insistently on the politics of gender. Whatever the discursive end served by this writing, the issue was consistently one of jurisdictions: what liberties have been established, what jurisdictions have been redrawn, by the action of Christ or the saint, and by the remembrance of that action? The three broad areas of writing considered are as follows: saints' lives; 'visionary' writing;[1] and religious lyrics. I consider these discursive areas together partly by way of highlighting their broad similarities of strategy; in particular, I argue that they are all significantly related to the image and/or relic's power to move. The discussion of the reformist impulse embedded in much devotional writing necessarily involves, of course, consideration of the revolutionary impulse behind the removal and destruction of images from the later 1530s.

I

A royal proclamation of 1538 struggled to police remembrance. On the one hand it preserved a set of liturgical practices as long as they served as a token of remembrance. On the other, it specified that

[1] In not using the word 'mystics', I follow, despite his title, Watson, 'Middle English Mystics', pp. 539–40.

Thomas Becket was to be deleted from the national memory. Images and pictures of Becket were to be taken down throughout the whole realm; his festival days were not to be observed, and his name was to be 'erased and put out of all the [liturgical] books', with the 'intent that his grace's loving subjects shall be no longer blindly led and abused to commit idolatry as they have done in times past'.[2]

This proclamation was generally conservative in aim, as Henry attempted to rein in the revolutionary forces his break with Rome had unleashed earlier in the decade, right up to 1538. Even in its preservation of 'laudable ceremonies' such as 'the bearing of candles upon the day of the Purification of Our Lady', however, the question of remembrance was critical to royal control. The King's subjects could practise these ceremonies, and all like them that have not been 'abrogated nor abolished' by the King, 'so as they shall use the same without superstition, and esteem them for . . . tokens, and signs to put us in remembrance of things of higher perfection, and not to repose any trust of salvation in them'. Power was relocated in this newly conceived liturgical practice: no longer were the King's subjects to regard these ceremonies as the conduits of divine power; instead they were signs alone of a power that had receded from the material world and was no longer immanent in the world of human practice. The proclamation made the present an area of remembrance alone, rather than a field through which the energies of the past continued to flow.

This reconception of the past emptied the present, material world of its inherited numinous power. It thereby offered intellectual justification for the massive destruction of the material edifice of cultic practice that had already taken place in 1538, the high point of Henrician iconoclasm. The very objects that had been regarded as both the channel of divine power, and as human memorials, became themselves images of death and pure materiality, deserving only of the hammer. Already in Henry's 1536 Injunctions to bishops, priests were prohibited from showing 'any images, relics, or miracles for any superstition or lucre'.[3] By 1538 the prohibition was much stronger: all visible cult of the saints before their images was forbidden, and all images that are 'abused with pilgrimages or offerings

[2] *Tudor Royal Proclamations*, ed. Hughes and Larkin, 1. 276.

[3] *Visitation Articles and Injunctions*, ed. Frere and Kennedy, l. 5.

. . . ye shall, for avoiding that most detestable sin of idolatry, forthwith take down and delay [destroy]'.[4] These injunctions prepared the way for the fully fledged Edwardian iconoclastic programme; in 1551 a statute ordered that parsons were to 'cause to be defaced and destroyed' any image of 'stone, tymber, allebaster or earthe, graven carved or paynted'.[5]

These Injunctions, the Articles on which they are based, and almost all theoretical discussion of images in the period of this history adopted a condescending posture towards images.[6] Images were either idolatrous, and had led the 'rude people' into superstition,[7] or else they were at best, in the words of the 1538 Royal Injunctions, 'books of the unlearned men, that can no letters, whereby they might be otherwise admonished of the lives and conversation of them that the said images do represent'.[8] This last defence, by far the most common throughout the entire medieval and early modern periods, assumed that actual books are the most sophisticated and powerful form of communication, one that anyone would choose were they able to read. It also assumed that saints' images ideally serve purely devotional ends, as, according to the Ten Articles of 1536, 'representors of virtue and good example, that they may also be by occasion the kindlers and stirrers of men's hearts, and make them often to remember their sins and offences'.[9] This condescending posture to the King's 'loving subjects' was also found in the 1538

[4] Ibid. 38.

[5] *SR*, 3 and 4 Edward VI, ch. 10 (4. 110–11). For the history of legislation on iconoclasm in these centuries, see Aston, *England's Iconoclasts*. Archbishop Cranmer had already in Feb. 1547 required the destruction of all images in churches; see Cranmer, *Miscellaneous Writings*, ed. Cox, pp. 509–11.

[6] For the defence of images, from the 14th to the 16th cents., see Aston, *England's Iconoclasts*, and further bibliography. The exceptions to this condescending posture towards images are, in my view, the powerful defences of images by Bishop Reginald Pecock in his *Repressor of Over-much Blaming of the Clergy* (*c*.1449), and by Thomas More in his *Dialogue concerning Heresies* (1529).

[7] Cited from the Ten Articles of 1536, in *English Historical Documents*, ed. Williams, item 112, 5. 795–805.

[8] *Visitation Articles and Injunctions*, ed. Frere and Kennedy, l. 38. This defence has a very long history, going back at least as far as Gregory the Great's defence of images as books to the unlearned, written in 560; see Aston, 'Devotional Literacy', in her *Lollards and Reformers*, p. 115.

[9] Ten Articles of 1536, in *English Historical Documents*, ed. Williams, item 112, 5. 795–805.

proclamation that permitted the continuance of certain liturgical practices.

The condescension is, however, belied by the same proclamation's treatment of Becket, which exposed a deeper understanding of the power of images and of saints. Most obviously, the proclamation exposed an understanding that the lives of saints excite much more than simple devotion and penitential grief. Recollection of the saints was also deeply political, insofar as their lives, and especially their deaths, redrew the boundaries of State and Church power. Becket's stand against Henry II in the 1160s established a critical division of powers in England, which Henry VIII wished to efface. The promulgation has it that Becket 'stubbornly' withstood the 'wholesome laws established against the enormities of the clergy by the King's highness's most noble progenitor, King Henry II'; so far from being a saintly martyr, Henry has decided that 'there appeareth nothing in his life and exterior conversation whereby he should be called a saint, but rather esteemed to have been a rebel and traitor to his prince'.[10]

The most remarkable thing about this proclamation is that it begins itself to become an anti-saint's life. In the very act of effacing Becket, the proclamation brings him to life, in a replay of the moment of his death. The declarative procedure of the official document gives way momentarily to narrative as it relates Becket's last moments, and implicitly exonerates his killers. The 'gentlemen' sent by Henry II to the archbishop counsel him to

> leave his stubbornness and to avoid the commotion of the people risen up for that rescue; and he [Becket] not only called the one of them bawd, but also took Tracy by the bosom and violently shook and plucked him . . . so that upon this fray one of their company . . . struck him, and so in the throng Becket was slain.[11]

Official proclamation, then, has recourse to narrative to rewrite a critical moment in Church–State relations. Whereas the lives and images of Becket represent him kneeling in prayer, face to the altar and back to his killers, this story represents him as a ruffian killed by temperate 'gentlemen' in a confused mêlée.[12] In the later Middle

[10] *Tudor Royal Proclamations*, ed. Hughes and Larkin, 1. 276. [11] Ibid.

[12] For the image of Becket patiently suffering martyrdom, see e.g. Laurence Wade, 'Life of Thomas Becket' (1497), ll. 1933–2009.

Ages especially, saints' lives themselves formed part of a variegated discursive environment, including many official documents that constituted the case for canonization;[13] here an official document momentarily reverts to narrative, as the declarative gives way to the persuasive. In so doing the statute both recognized the power of the saint, and could not help bringing him back to a political life of sorts. In the very act of deleting Becket's 'images and pictures' the still image moves into the action of narrative, which itself cannot omit mention of the 'people risen up for that rescue'.

The powerfully political consequences both of martyrdom, and of popular devotion to the images of that martyrdom, are everywhere apparent in the traces we have of the attempt to erase Becket's memory. No official documents survive, curiously, concerning the destruction of Becket's shrine.[14] An almost certainly spurious document of 1538, probably the product of papal propaganda, recorded the citation and judgement against Becket in a state trial. Becket was to be brought back from the dead for trial by Henry: 'We cite and call you to our supreme court, Thomas . . . '. No one having appeared to defend Becket, he was adjudged guilty as rebel and traitor to the King; his name was accordingly to be erased from liturgical books, and his bones exhumed and publicly burnt.[15]

However much this document is untrustworthy as an account of an actual trial, it deployed almost exactly the verifiable terms in which Henry did attempt to obliterate Becket from the historical record. Aside from the 1538 proclamation that branded Becket as a 'rebel and a traitor', a royal circular to Justices of the Peace in 1538 charged them to suppress the talk of those people who complained that Henry was taking away the liberties of the realm originally fought for by Becket; instead 'bishop Becket of Canterbury, which they have tofore called Saint Thomas', demanded these liberties 'traitorously against the law of the realm'.[16] Wriothesley's *Chronicle*, written during the relevant years, tells us that the bones of Becket were burnt by Cromwell; at St Thomas of Acres church in London,

[13] For which see Vauchez.

[14] See Butler, p. 114.

[15] *Concilia*, ed. Wilkins, 3. 835–6. For the spuriousness of the document, see *L&P Henry VIII*, 13/2. 133. For the papal bull of 1538, which also makes mention of Becket's trial, see *Concilia*, ed. Wilkins, 3. 840–1.

[16] *L&P Henry VIII*, 13/2. 1171.

furthermore, Becket's image, along with all the glass that depicted him, and the image of his martyrdom at the altar, were taken down, 'so that there shall no more mention be made of him never'.[17]

The attempt to police remembrance between 1536 and 1538 was, then, unsurprisingly incoherent, given the sheer difficulty of the job. On the one hand, the popular custom was retained as popular, as long as the past stayed still, and as long as it did nothing but excite personal devotion. Images could be reverenced, as long as they were considered merely semiotic, signs alone that carry none of the power of the past into the present, and as long as they remained within the discourses of emotion and personal piety. On the other hand, the treatment of Becket in the 1538 proclamation clearly exposed an awareness that none of these constraints on images would hold. The ferocity of the attempt to obliterate Becket's memory clearly betrays the following understandings: that the past will not stay still, and that its consequences continue to flow into the present; that the saint's life and its images will not remain within the discourse of the devotional, the emotional, and the penitential; and that 'popular' practice deserves not so much condescension as the closest political scrutiny and governance.

By relying so heavily on the image, the works considered in this chapter incur the charge of unsophistication and simplicity. Just as images themselves were defended as 'books' for the illiterate, so too are these books ostensibly directed to the intellectually unsophisticated, who are represented as incapable of abstraction and so reliant on the physicality of corporal images. Nicholas Love, in his *Mirror of the Blessed Life of Jesus Christ* (c.1410) articulated the limitations of this audience very clearly. His book is written for 'symple creatures the whiche as childryn haven nede to be fedde with mylke of lyghte doctryne and not with sadde [substantial] mete [food] of grete clargye'. This kind of reader must rely on corporal images. To those of 'symple undirstondyng'

is more spedefull [profitable] and more sykere [certain] than is hyghe contemplacion of the godhed ande therfore to hem is pryncipally to be sette in mynde the ymage of crystes Incarnacion passion and Resurreccion so that

[17] Wriothesley, *Chronicle of England during the Reigns of the Tudors*, ed. Hamilton, I. 87.

a symple soule that kan not thenke bot bodyes or bodily thinges mowe have somwhat accordynge unto is [his] affection where with he maye fede and stire his devocion. (p. 10)

This division between the bodily and the abstract was at once a linguistic, a psychological, and, very often, a gender division. Writing of this kind is in English, precisely insofar as it was directed at readers without Latin. It was also designed to provoke specific psychological reactions and not others: these are 'devoute ymaginacions and likenessis', (p. 10) which provoke emotional responses. Love very carefully fenced in this emotional, devout imagining from its potentially doctrinal consequences: his readers may, he says, 'imagine by reson . . . not by errour affermyng bot devoutly ymagining and supposyng' (p. 74). And these two controls, of language and psychological effect, imply an audience of laity, and of women in particular: writing of this kind was frequently designed to appeal to non-religious, and especially to women, readers. The very text that Love is translating, the *Meditationes Vitae Christi* (mid-fourteenth century), was written for 'a religiouse woman', and she is encouraged to model herself on St Cecilia, who always bore the Gospel in her bosom. Love wrote for a lay audience, of 'lewde [unlearned] men and women' (p. 10). Love's verbal images are of a piece with the visual religious culture of late medieval England, in which viewers of an image were encouraged to identify with the suffering of viewers represented within the image itself, as in Figure 8.

This material presents itself as devotional, emotive, lay, vernacular, largely non-ecclesiological, and, often, written for a feminine readership. This self-presentation has had one of two effects in its modern reception. Scholarship has until recently tended to relegate it to the background of the literary history of religious writing of the period, singling out only the 'mystics' as worthy of serious attention, and even there rigorously excluding the 'hysterical' (i.e. Margery Kempe) from the truly 'mystical' (e.g. Julian of Norwich).[18] An alternative approach has been to deploy much of this material (and not

[18] There are, of course, some rare exceptions. For women saints' lives, see the excellent book by Winstead, *Virgin Martyrs*. Two excellent studies are devoted to the religious lyric: Woolf, *English Religious Lyric*, and D. Gray, *Themes and Images*. For a call to reintegrate visionary writing into the field of 'vernacular theology', see Watson, 'Middle English Mystics'.

Fig. 8. The Crucifixion. Alabaster panel, late fifteenth century, English.

the 'mystics') as exemplary of 'traditional religion', of the first importance precisely as an unproblematic index of popular practice.[19] My discussion of this material after my chapter on the Church might itself imply that I, too, regard this material in the second rank of 'reformist' writing, insofar as devotional writing apparently disowns any interest in the front line of ecclesiological politics of the kind so insistently and dangerously raised in the works discussed in Chapter 7. Those works, correlatively, do not focus on the lives of saints: *Piers Plowman* groups saints at only one moment (B.15. 223–317), but the saints are chosen almost entirely because they are founders of religious orders.

I readily acknowledge the less overtly ecclesiological nature of the texts discussed in this chapter. Nevertheless, critical jurisdictions were being challenged by them. Given the intense scrutiny of any religious matter written in English after Arundel's *Constitutions* of 1409, even the most apparently anodyne devotional matter in English had an ecclesiological resonance.[20] It did so even by avoiding any concern with ecclesiological and sacramental issues. In this chapter as a whole, however, I consider the range of discourses activated by the devotional. I look especially to works that actively exploit the secondary status of ostensibly naïve devotional writing to express complex notions of geography, history, textuality, and selfhood. Many of these texts are avowedly 'orthodox', but, as we shall see, such texts are capable of obliquely expressing grief at the way the heterodox are being persecuted. And many of these texts that promote the cult of saints are, strangely, rehearsals for the sixteenth-century persecution of that same cult. Some professions of *naïveté* might prove to be accurate, but none will be taken at face value. My assumption will be that images and relics are by nature extremely powerful, and that works that parade their simple reliance on a visual mode might be taking cover under the 'inferior' status of the image as conferred by a dominant clerical and Latinate tradition.[21]

[19] The best example is Duffy. For a penetrating critique of this approach, see Aers, 'Altars of Power'.

[20] For Arundel's *Constitutions*, see Ch. 7, above; for the dangers of any theological matter in English, see Hudson, 'Lollardy: The English Heresy?'.

[21] For a broadly applicable critique of scholarly dismissal of 'popular' religious practice, see P. Brown, ch. 1.

I do not, by and large, consider the most obviously reformist writing of the period here, that of Lollards, precisely because Lollards rejected the discourses I here discuss.[22] By not discussing Lollard texts here I do not intend to imply that the devotional texts on which I focus are the expression of a timeless 'medieval' devotion. On the contrary, they contributed to the construction of a spiritual practice that had to operate within very tightly governed, historically specific constraints. The production of saints' lives in such profusion in the fifteenth century, especially in East Anglia, might, for example, have been a response to Lollardy and the measures taken to repress it.[23] The Henrician repression of religious images and the instauration of the sacral image of the king was not in any way the first irruption of 'history' into an otherwise ahistorical structure of cultic practice; on the contrary, that very conflict between Church and State, and the competition between images of State and Church power, was repeatedly rehearsed and reflected on in fifteenth-century saints' lives. By the same token, the Henrician claim to geographical sovereignty, which was followed up by John Foxe's massive project to sacralize England with its own set of national martyrs (his *Acts and Monuments)*, was also repeatedly contested in saints' lives especially, given their intensely historical and geographical consciousness.

II

Suffering produces biography. In Chaucer's *Legends of Good Women* (first composed ?1386–8) the women whose lives are recounted are all victims. Each of them has been abandoned as a relic, something left over and behind. As relics they become numinous, or relics in the religious sense. In that poem the cult of relics itself produces further suffering, and further lives, since Chaucer is charged by Cupid with improperly adoring the image of Alceste, and

22 More discussion of Lollardy can be found in Ch. 7, above. For the range of Lollard hostility to images, see Aston, *England's Iconoclasts*, ch. 4. For Lollard rejection of devotional reflection on the wounded Christ, see Aers and Staley, ch. 2.

23 For the records of contemporary heresy trials in Norwich, see *Heresy Trials in the Diocese of Norwich, 1428–1431*, ed. Tanner.

subjected to a trial during which his own authorial biography comes to light (F.414–41), and by whose sentence the rest of his authorial life is spoken for: he must write the lives of women who loved well, 'al hire lyves', says Alceste, 'while that thou lyvest, yer by yere' (F.480–5). The proper cult of images is rigorously policed in that poem, but even as Cupid seeks to suppress anything outside the jurisdiction of his desire, 'heterodox' sequences in the lives both of the 'saints' and of their new author rise irrepressibly to the surface.[24]

Chaucer's awareness of the ways in which adoration of the relics of martyrs evokes further lives is most fully expressed, of course, in the *Canterbury Tales*, where the pilgrims recount their narratives on the way to Canterbury cathedral, 'The hooly blisful martir for to seke, | That hem hath holpen whan that they were seke' (1. 17–18). However much the presence of the martyr is very much in the background of the *Tales*, his suffering activates the extraordinary range of discourses within which the pilgrims relate their stories. Whole lives are, furthermore, most sharply felt when relics and the suffering of the saints are at issue. The Second Nun, for example, tells the story of St Cecilia. She begins her Prologue by associating the 'werkis' of faith with her own 'werk' as a writer, in such a way as to make the terms of authorship resonate with the terms of penitential effort across a whole life: she asks her audience to 'forgive' her lack of authorial skill, and bids them 'my werk amende' (8. 64–84). Traces of Chaucer's own biography might just survive in this Prologue, since the narrator describes her/himself, in a plea for the Virgin's merciful intercession, as an 'unworthy sone of Eve' (8. 62). Chaucer had written a life of St Cecilia before the *Canterbury Tales*; he was also released from a charge of having raped a woman named Cecily in 1380.[25] The Pardoner, too, is at the same time a figure whose biographical angularities extrude most painfully into the Canterbury pilgrimage, and who trades with the signs of past suffering. His relics are fakes, pure materiality posing as the numinous; precisely for this reason the Host would inflict a martyrdom on the Pardoner himself,

[24] For which see Simpson, 'Ethics and Interpretation'.

[25] See *Legend of Good Women*, F.426 for Chaucer's reference to a pre-*Canterbury Tales* life of Cecilia. For Chaucer's release from the charge of rape, see Cannon. The female saints' lives written by Bokenham, discussed below, are a good example of saints being chosen whose names correspond with those of women in the poet's circle.

in an aggressively materialistic parody of the saint's spiritual suffering:

> I wolde I hadde thy coillons in myn hond [testicles]
> In stide of relikes or of seintuarie.
> Lat kutte hem of, for I wol thee helpe hem carie;
> They shal be shryned in an hogges toord!
>
> (6. 952–5)

'Improper' adoration of the saint's suffering is a powerful sign of fetishized and habitual reduction of a whole life to idolatrous praise of the material. As in the *Legend of Good Women*, improper adoration of the martyr itself evokes the threat of a new spectacular and public martyrdom.

Suffering also evokes the larger historical and geographical jurisdictions that suffering changes. The *Canterbury Tales* begin with the geography of sainthood: pilgrims move 'from every shires ende | Of Engelond to Canterbury' (1. 15–16), and this broad spiritual geography is redefined and contextualized as the tales proceed: the Knight's battles draw the violent boundaries of Christendom (1. 51–67); Constance's marital suffering in the *Man of Law's Tale* equally traces the potential spiritual dominion of Rome, a dominion that finally excludes North Africa, but includes Northumbria; the action of the *Second Nun's Tale* occurs in the suburbs of early Christian Rome in the time of persecutions; and the anti-semitic *Prioress's Tale* takes place in a Christian-Jewish community in the Middle East, though it ends with an invocation of Hugh of Lincoln's 'martyrdom' 'but a litel while ago' (7. 686). The English martyrdom to which the Prioress refers was supposed to have happened in 1255, about midpoint between the anti-Semitic massacres of the late twelfth century, and the expulsion of Jews from England in 1290.[26] The geography of martyrdom is also, then, a cultural geography, contextualizing England within a larger spiritual map of co-religionists and those defined as spiritual enemies. By the same token, martyrdom takes place at, and provokes, the turning points of history. This is most obviously true of Christ, but the layerings of Christian history visible in the *Canterbury Tales* are each marked by exemplary suffering: Cecilia suffers in the time of persecutions in third-century Rome; Constance

[26] For which see Stacey.

marks the period of Anglo-Saxon conversion in the seventh century; Becket's martyrdom in the twelfth century inaugurates a high water mark of ecclesiastical power; Hugh of Lincoln's thirteenth-century martyrdom invokes the Jewish pogroms of the later twelfth century.

These moments of historical transition occur by transforming the living pantheon of gods, by which state power is underwritten, into dead matter. Thus Chaucer's Cecilia mocks the pagan judge Almichius who orders her to sacrifice to the pagan gods as a mark of obedience to the state. Cecilia replies that the judge must be blind, since he fails to see that the gods are nothing but stone:

> That ilke stoon a god thow wolt it calle. [same]
> I rede thee, lat thyn hand upon it falle [advise]
> And taste it wel, and stoon thou shalt it fynde. [feel]
>
> (8. 501–3)

Refusal to bow down before these insensate images is the decisive moment that transforms the saint's own body itself, in the eyes of her pagan persecutors, into matter deserving of nothing more than burning. The saint's survival of her torment, in turn, insists on the materiality of the images, and the deadness of the political order that rests upon their cult.

Chaucer explored these themes in a theological environment of relative freedom; even if the heterodox theological movement of Lollardy began in the last twenty years of Chaucer's career, it was not at this early stage implacably opposed to the cult of images, and neither did the state immediately define its own cultic interests in stark opposition to those of the Lollards.[27] Both these conditions altered after 1400: as Lollardy became a fully-fledged vernacular movement, so too did it express a sustained hostility to the cult of saints through their images; and the Lancastrian regime, needing to create internal enemies to buttress its own shaky legitimation, targeted Lollards as both heretical and seditious.[28] Hagiography produced under Lancastrian rule was, therefore, a double-edged

[27] For the conditions of censorship, see Ch. 7, above, and, esp., Watson, 'Censorship and Cultural Change'. For Wyclif's moderate views on images, see Aston, *England's Iconoclasts*, pp. 98–104.

[28] For Lancastrian interests in targeting Lollardy, see esp. Strohm, *England's Empty Throne*, ch. 2, and further references.

weapon: on the one hand, it ostensibly withdrew from front-line ecclesiastical politics into 'popular' devotion. On the other, the very narratives to which the orthodox had recourse were insistently about a frequent event in Lollard trials: the confrontation of state and ecclesiastical power with heroic figures who refuse to adore insensate images upon which those powers are founded. In their heroism, that is, the saints could look very much like Lollards. The orthodox haven could turn out to reproduce ecclesiological battle lines in oblique form.

(*a*) Saints' Lives: Institutional Jurisdictions and Geographical Mapping

In this sub-section I focus on the themes of geographical and institutional jurisdiction in some fifteenth-century saints' lives. My examples here and in the following sub-section are mostly drawn from the century or so between the *Constitutions* of Archbishop Arundel in 1409 and the Act of Supremacy in 1534, principally because, within the period 1350–1550, these years witnessed the most significant attempts to populate England with saints whose lives were written in English. Of course earlier periods had witnessed the project of supplying saints in the vernacular, from, notably, the translation of Bede's Latin *Historia Ecclesiastica* (early eighth century) into Anglo-Saxon in the ninth, to Aelfric's *Lives of the Saints* in the late tenth, and then to the *South English Legendary* in the late thirteenth, centuries.[29] Within the centuries of this history, however, for the related reasons of both heterodoxy and of national consciousness, the period from Arundel to the Act of Supremacy is the significant one for vernacular hagiography. The Act of Supremacy in 1534 blocked the normal route of saints into England; the cultural vacuum it created produced, just after and outside the period of this history, Foxe's enduringly influential replacement of imported saints with an almost all-English cast in his *Acts and Monuments* (first edition 1563). Foxe's collection of English martyrs modelled itself on medieval hagiographies, since, for Foxe, 'the goodes and ornamentes of the Church chiefly . . . consiste . . . in the bloud, actes and lyfe of

[29] One might also include the less ambitious early 14th-cent. *North English Legendary*, ed. Horstmann.

Martyres'. Despite its models, Foxe's massive documentary effort implicitly consisted, however, in the repudiation of the 'actes and lyfe' of martyrs who had not died either for the primitive or the English Protestant Church.[30]

Osbern Bokenham (1393–*c.*1467) composed a set of women saints' lives, his *Legendys of Hooly Wummen*, between 1443 and 1447 (10,617 lines, in a variety of metres). The first saint whose life he relates is St Margaret, the patron saint of childbirth. A frequent element in the narration of a saint's life is the translation of the saint's body, and Bokenham includes a detailed itinerary of Margaret's body in its westward journey. The saint herself died in Antioch, in defiance of state power, in the period of Christian persecutions. Upwards of seven hundred years later in 908, Antioch is subject to civil war, and the state power destroys the church built in honour of Margaret. Augustine, a Pavian abbot resident in Antioch decides to flee the destruction, but he divulges his plan to two helpers to take the body of Margaret with him, 'of summe relykys to make a translacyon' (l. 1034). They dig 'so depe' that they finally find the body, aided by divine inspiration, whereupon they take it to Brindisi in southern Italy, having first broken up its silver casing and replaced it with a wooden one for fear of discovery. The plan is to transport Margaret to Pavia, but on the way north through Italy they donate a rib to a church newly dedicated to the Virgin before travelling on to an abbey in the 'vale of Palantes', where Augustine dies. The monks accept the relics, but their own church is itself subject to destruction and civil war, such that 'this place desolat | Withinne a fewe yerys was, and stood aloon' (ll. 1188–9). The body is then removed to a church dedicated to the Virgin at Ruyllyan and reposes there for a hundred years before that church is also destroyed and its site soon entirely overgrown. Not until 1405 is a divine vision vouchsafed to two Neapolitan hermits who finally persaude an abbot to provide the resources to discover the body. While the body is being taken to the abbey of Montefiascone, just north of Rome, it becomes so heavy that its bearers decide that this is the place for a church, which, after yet more vicissitudes, is built there, where the body of Margaret still reposes at the time Bokenham writes (ll. 939–1400).

30 Citations from Foxe, vol. 1, p. vii.

This travel narrative reveals a rich conception of history as itself an act of translation. There can be no direct access to the past in this narrative: the numinous archaeological testimony of the past is accessible only through a mixture of human effort and divine intervention. Finding it involves both digging and visions, and moving it involves loss: the silver casing must be broken up, and the saint is one rib short by the time she arrives in Montefiascone. Her translation is subject to the ongoing ravages of a carefully dated human history, which itself is recovered in the story of the martyr's body. The itinerary reveals a movement from East to West, and a refusal on the saint's part to move any further than Rome. However much that might imply, as it does, an affirmation of Roman spiritual power, Bokenham's own textual translation itself affirms the ongoing movement of the past into Bokenham's England. Bokenham himself had been at Montefiascone in *c.*1438, where he learned Margaret's life 'Bothe be scripture and eek be mowthe', and whence he brought the text back to England (ll. 104–22). This 'England' is most immediately Bokenham's own religious house, the Augustinian friars based at Clare in Suffolk, which, he tells us earlier, possesses the sacred relic of Margaret's foot (ll. 135–8); this is, indeed, the specific reason for Bokenham making 'thys translacyon . . . | Into oure language' (ll. 124–5).

The textual translation into English is, then, of a piece with the corporal translation of the saint, and no less subject to further, local ravages of place and time. Bokenham refuses to divulge his name for fear of being attacked by Cambridge readers, and, like a pilgrim, he is exhausted by the business of writing. He needs a rest, he says, before going from the saint's life to her translation, since he has so overworked himself and his pen that as it writes it 'doth blot, | And in my book maketh many a spot' (ll. 903–4). Writing the saint's life evokes the translator's own life, and the obstacles of malice and exhaustion that will block the passage of the life. At one point he even says that he would be better advised to stop writing 'and suche as ys amys | To reformyn in my lyvynge' (ll. 1418–19), before taking courage by asking Christ and Mary to accept his good 'intention' in writing.[31] He equally reveals the resources that will promote the

[31] Issues of artistic creation as potentially immoral rise in the trial of William Thorpe, where Arundel is quoted as saying that foreign sculptors or painters confess

ongoing work of translating the saint: Margaret herself prays before she dies for those who 'Other [either] rede, or wryte, or other do teche [cause to be taught]' her suffering, and she promises to intercede especially for women in childbirth, 'oppressyd wyth peyne and grevaunce' (l. 842). This evocation of a female readership points to the readers to whom Bokenham also appeals, a set of East Anglian women patrons, some of whose names and whose daughters' names are paralleled by those of the women saints in the collection.[32]

Bokenham, then, connects a community of secular women in England with a female saint in Antioch, with Rome as the meeting point in a journey that takes more than a millennium. In England the saint's force is felt along the networks of noble and gentry families in East Anglia, via the mediation of religious houses in both Clare and Cambridge. This specific *institutional* deployment of both imported and local saints, both relatively recent and after a long 'translation', is a common phenomenon of fourteenth- and fifteenth-century hagiography. It continues right up to and including the first third of the sixteenth century, when the pressure to produce national saints in the vernacular became stronger, even before 1534.

Thus a 658-line life of St Anne is composed in rhyme-royal stanzas for a community of religious men to be read on 'this day', by which is presumably meant the feast of St Anne, introduced into England in 1378;[33] a metrically simpler and shorter life of St Anne in four-stress quatrains is addressed to 'soveregns and serys', and prays in conclusion that Mary and her mother 'maynteyneth this gild', by which must be meant a parish guild of the kind that flourished from the middle of the fourteenth century, many of which were dedicated to either St Anne or the Virgin;[34] the life of Robert of Knaresborough

and take penance before beginning artistic work, praying the priest that the artist should have grace 'to make a faier and a devoute ymage'. See Thorpe, pp. 57–8. Correlatively, Lollards attack artists themselves; see e.g. *Heresy Trials in the Diocese of Norwich*, ed. Tanner, 148 and 160.

[32] For which see Edwards, 'Bokenham's *Legendys of Hooly Wummen*'.

[33] *The Life of St Anne*, item 2 in *The Middle English Stanzaic Versions of the Life of St Anne*, ed. Parker.

[34] Ibid., item 3, l. 453. See further Gibson, *Theatre of Devotion*. For a full list of parish guilds (dating especially from the middle of the 14th cent.), including many dedicated to the Virgin, and some to St Anne, see Westlake, app. For parish guilds more generally, see Scarisbrick, *The Reformation*, ch. 2.

(d. 1218), is recounted in a later fourteenth century promotion of the Order of the Holy Trinity;[35] in the 1430s John Lydgate produced two large-scale hagiographical works for monastic patrons, one for his own abbot, William Curteys of Bury St Edmund's (*Saint Edmund and Saint Fremund*, 1434–6), [36] and one for the humanistic abbot of St Albans John Wethamstede (*Saint Albon and Saint Amphibalus*, 1439);[37] the Augustinian friar John Capgrave presented his *Life of St Norbert* (1440), the twelfth-century Flemish founder of the Premonstratensian Order, to the abbot of the Norfolk house of that order;[38] in 1451 the same author wrote a prose life of Gilbert of Sempringham (d. 1189), patronized by the master of the Order of Sempringham, and written for the 'solitarye women . . . whech unneth [hardly] can undyrstande Latyn'; he also wrote a life of the founder of his own order, St Augustine, for a female patron;[39] Laurence Wade, a monk of Canterbury, wrote an English life of Becket in 1497;[40] and Henry Bradshaw's *Life of Saint Werburge of Chester* (1513) was printed by Pynson in 1521.[41] Bradshaw was a monk of the abbey of St Werburge in Chester; he also wrote the *Life of Saynt Radegund* (also printed in 1521), patron of the convent of St Radegund in Cambridge that had recently been transformed into Jesus College.[42]

Saints, then, served local institutional needs. The monks of Shrewsbury, in need of some relics, imported only a small part of the Welsh saint Winifred, as recounted in Caxton's 1485 prose version.[43] In the same way religious institutions of many kinds, from

[35] *The Metrical Life of St Robert of Knaresborough*. The work consists of 1,010 lines, in four-stress couplets, with irregular alliteration.

[36] This ambitious work consists of three books, totals 3,695 lines, and is written in rhyme-royal stanzas. Complete texts survive in twelve MSS; see Pearsall, *John Lydgate: a Bio-Bibliography*, p. 75.

[37] This equally ambitious work is 4,713 lines long, is divided into three books, and is written in rhyme-royal stanzas. It survives in five MSS; see Pearsall, *John Lydgate: a Bio-Bibliography*, pp. 74–5.

[38] This consists of 4,109 lines in rhyme-royal stanzas. Only one MS survives.

[39] John Capgrave, *Lives of St Augustine and St Gilbert of Sempringham*, ed. Munro, p. 61. Two MSS had survived until the Cotton fire, only one of which remains intact. Both works are in prose; the life of Augustine is heavily indebted to Augustine's autobiography, the *Confessions*.

[40] Wade, 'Life of Thomas Becket'. In his edn., Horstmann cites only one MS; the work is written in six-stress, seven-line stanzas, and consists of 2,303 lines.

[41] *RSTC* 3506; 5,566 lines in rhyme-royal stanzas.

[42] Ed. F. Brittain, *RSTC* 3507.

[43] *RSTC* 25853.

small parish guild to powerful monastery, required the lives of the saints whose suffering underwrote the jurisdiction and liberties of their own foundation. In Lydgate's *Albon and Amphibalus*, for example, King Offa's translation of the British saint's body in 793 marks the foundation of St Alban's; Lydgate takes care to underline the 'privilegis, fredam, and liberte' that are granted to the new foundation by the pope, along with the 'libertees and fraunchises ful roiall, | Perpetually boundid' granted by the king (3. 1401–1414). These local jurisdictions have the power to resist metropolitan domination. Thus, for example, Lydgate relates that a late eleventh-century bishop of London granted permission for the body of St Edmund, the ninth-century king of East Anglia martyred by the Danes, to be translated to Bury. The bishop tries surreptitiously to redirect the relics to St Paul's, but the coffin refuses to budge; 'Yt stood as fix as a gret hill of stoon' (3. 1351), until it is pulled in the right direction, after which the relics finally arrive in Bury in 1095 to be placed in the new foundation of Bury St Edmund's, Lydgate's own house.

As local historical liberties were being confirmed in these narratives, however, national histories were also being told. Telling the stories of martyrs also involved precisely dated periods of national persecution or invasion. Reading a sequence of saints' lives produces a clearly defined sense of a set of historical horizons, from the persecution of British Christians in the time of Diocletian (Albon), to the period of Saxon invasion and settlement (St Werburge), to Danish invasions of the ninth century (Edmund). Even if Lydgate, for example, produced hagiography for local monastic foundations, these are of such national importance as to attract and require royal defence. The life of St Edmund ends with Lydgate's plea to Henry VI to be 'dyffence and champioun' to the monastery at Bury (where Henry had in fact stayed from Christmas 1433 to April 1434), just as the life of Albon ends with strikingly national imagery:

> Be glad and mery, this tytle is riche and good,
> Lond of Breteyn, callid Brutis Albioun,
> Which art enbawmyd with the purpil blood
> Off blissid Albon, prynce of that regioun.
>
> (31366–9)

Collections of national saints began to appear in the vernacular as early as the first half of the fifteenth century as in, for example, the collection of eight saints' lives in prose in Southwell Minster MS 7, where six of the eight saints are either Saxon or British.[44] Only in the sixteenth century, however, did stridently national saints' lives appear, such as Alexander Barclay's *Lyfe of St George* (printed by Pynson in 1515), which ends by praying St George to preserve 'his' realm 'in peas and unyte | Represse rebellers and men presumptuous | Defende thy prynce from all adversyte'.[45] The *Kalendre of the Newe Legende of Englande*, printed in 1516, restricts itself to what it calls 'English' saints, and its definition of 'English' has imperial pretensions.[46] The treatise, says the author, may rightly be called the calendar of England, because the 'most part of tho sayntes . . . were eyther borne in this realme or were abydynge therin and . . . these other countreys, Irelande, Scotlande and Wales, of veray ryght owe to be subiecte and obedyent to this realme of Englonde' (p. 46). The saints, he insists, are a national resource. Whereas the other nations of the British Isles honour national saints, in England, for whatever reason, 'fewe people . . . have devocyon to any of thyse blessyd seyntes that have laboured for the welthe of the people in this realme in tyme paste'. This failure to cultivate national saints is equally a failure to exploit a national resource, since the saints certainly respond to prayers, 'and we maye not dowte but they be redye to pray for us if we do worship theym and calle unto theym by our prayer for helpe' (pp. 44–5).

The specifically English and nationalist collection of saints in the *Kalendre* pointed forward to Foxe's 'elect nation' of *Acts and Monuments*.[47] By the same token it contrasted with the much broader geographical and temporal embrace of the *Legenda Aurea* (second half of the thirteenth century), an embrace that extended from North

44 See Nevanlinna and Taavitsainen, pp. 50–1.

45 *RSTC* 22992.1 (Pynson, ?1515), ll. 2682–4. The whole work consists of 2,715 lines in rhyme-royal stanzas. Lydgate's life of St George was, by contrast, produced for a more local group, the guild of Armourers in London; see *The Legend of St George*, in *Minor Poems*, pt. 1, no. 33 (245 lines in rhyme-royal stanzas).

46 *RSTC* 4602; this work is a translation and précis of the *Nova Legenda Anglie*, printed by de Worde in 1516, *RSTC* 4601.

47 For the history of England as the 'elect nation' in Protestant propaganda, see Collinson, ch. 1.

Africa and the Middle East to the whole of Europe, and moved from the earliest Christian martyrs to relatively modern saints like St Francis (d. 1226). This great, crowded collection of Christian saints was translated into English twice in the fifteenth century, in the 1438 *Gilte Legende* and in Caxton's *Golden Legende* (first printed in 1483, though reprinted seven times until 1527).[48] While both the *Kalendre* of 1516, and Foxe's martyrology (1563) promote the impression that England was the source of saints, the translations of the *Legenda Aurea* imply that saints are themselves translations, carried across into both England and English from the geography and languages of Christian history. Even those lives that do promote specifically British martyrs deployed typology so as to imply the ongoing action of biblical events in an English landscape. Thus Lydgate's *Albon*, for example, ends, as we have seen, with a sense of Britain enclosed and protected, 'embalmed' as it is by Albon's blood; Albon's martyrdom, however, is preceded by a typological scene that imports and pathetically inverts the triumphalism of Moses' crossing the Red Sea. As the crowds rush eagerly to witness the 'uncouth spectacle' of Albon's martyrdom (2. 1530), they overbear a bridge and drown, at which sight Albon prays successfully for their recovery; just as God helped the victorious Moses, so too does he respond to the prayer of Albon:

> For he that made, maugre Pharaoo [despite]
> His peeple of Israel to passe the Red See
> With drye foot, the same Lord also,
> Whil that Albon kneelid on his knee,
> Prayeng, the Lord of grace and of pite
> Grauntid the peeple to have inspeccioun
> And passe the river to seen his passioun.
>
> (2. 1605–11)

The moment of crossing the river becomes itself a moment in which the translation of biblical events into an English topography is represented.

Like most romances, the vast majority of saints' lives are set in a

[48] For details of English versions of the *Golden Legend* see D'Evelyn, 'English Translations of *Legenda Aurea*'. There were eleven editions and/or reprints between 1483 and 1527; *RSTC* 24877–80.

post-, or at least late, imperial world, in which the boundaries between state and ecclesiastical power are fluid. In the eighteenth-century historiography of saints, indeed, the post-imperial cult of saints was itself regarded as a symptom of a political breakdown of sorts, by which the 'Monarchy of heaven . . . was degraded by the introduction of a popular mythology which tended to restore the reign of polytheism.'[49] When in the sixteenth century Henry VIII claimed imperial powers over the British Isles, one consequence of that claim was the need to control the jurisdictions of saints. Lives of saints were being printed right up to the Act of Supremacy, in both reprints of Caxton's *Golden Legende*, and in the lives of individual saints, such as the 1531 reprint of Lydgate's *Life of Our Lady* by Redman, or the 1534 edition of Lydgate's *Saint Albon and Saint Amphibalus* by the monks of St Alban's. (Lydgate's closing address to Henry VI in the original of this text was replaced by a badly timed address to Henry VIII as the new protector of the monastery.)[50] The first Royal Injunctions of 1536 began, however, by proclaiming that 'the Bishop of Rome's pretensed and usurped power and jurisdiction within this realm' has been abolished, and went on to confirm instead the 'King's authority and jurisdiction within the same, as of the Supreme Head of the Church of England'.[51] An essential part of that newly claimed jurisdiction was the governance of saints, whose power had been imported from such a wide geography. That 'all superstition and hypocrisy . . . may vanish away', the king's subjects were not to 'set forth or extol any images, relics, or miracles for any superstition or lucre, nor allure the people by any enticements to the pilgrimage of any saint' unless such cultic activity had previously

[49] The citation is from Gibbon, p. 359.

[50] Lives of the following saints in verse were printed: George (Pynson, ?1515); Radegunde (Pynson, *c.*1525); Werburge (Pynson, 1521); Ursula (de Worde, ?1509); *Life of Our Lady* (Caxton 1484, Redman 1531); St Alban (Redman, 1534); Joseph of Arimathea (Pynson, 1520); Margaret of Scotland (Rastell, *c.*1530); Margaret (Pynson, 1493, Redman, ?1530); Thomas Becket (Rastell, *c.*1520); Petronilla (Pynson, ?1495). In prose the following were printed: Bridget (Pynson, 1516); Jerome (de Worde, ?1499); Joseph of Arimathea (de Worde, 1511); Edward the Confessor (de Worde, 1513); Katherine of Alexandria (Pynson, ?1520, Waley, 1555); Katherine of Siena (de Worde, ?1492); Nicholas of Tollentino (de Worde, ?1525); Winifred (Caxton, 1485). I am extremely grateful to A. S. G. Edwards for help on these matters. For full details, see D'Evelyn, 'Legends of Individual Saints'.

[51] *Visitation Articles and Injunctions*, ed. Frere and Kennedy, i. 3.

been approved by the king.[52] In the same year many saints' festivals were abolished; by 1538 all visible cult of the saints was prohibited, and the invocation of the saints was supressed from the litany.[53]

Even after the Edwardian statute of 1551 commanding the total destruction of the images that blur the king's own jurisdiction, however, new images, modelled on the pattern of the old, filled the vacuum caused by destruction. This was most obviously true of the royal image, which during the reign of Elizabeth replaced cultic images by taking pride of place in thousands of churches, even if frequent examples of such substitution had already taken place in Henry's reign.[54] Such substitution belies the description of the period as iconoclastic in temper: mid-sixteenth century iconoclasts destroyed one set of images so as to make way for another. The same Edwardian statute that commanded the destruction of all religious images, for example, made specific exception for 'any image or picture . . . [made] only for a momument of any kinge, Prince, Nobleman or other dead person, which hath not bene comonly reputed and taken for a saincte', a spectacular example of which royal iconography can still be seen in and on King's College chapel, Cambridge.[55] This connection was not lost on those who objected to the destruction, such as William Ludelam, the hermit of St Thomas' chapel in Chesterfield, who, in a report to Cromwell dated July 1538, is reported to have remarked that 'if a man will pluck down or tear the king's arms he shall be hanged, drawn and quartered'; what punishment, he asks, is fit for the man who 'doth pluck down churches and images'? The king, after all, 'is but a mortal man as we be'.[56]

This pattern of deploying the structures of the past to efface the past is already visible in William Thorpe's account of his trial (composed ?1407). Wyclif and Lollards dismissed post-biblical saints,[57] and certainly Thorpe is hostile to the images of the saints, and to the artists who fabricate them, who deserve penance for the 'synful and veyn craft of kervynge, yetynge [casting in metal] or of peyntynge

[52] Ibid. 5.

[53] For which see Duffy, 392–408.

[54] For a general survey of royal arms in churches, see Cautley; see also Collinson, p. 118.

[55] *SR*, 3 and 4 Edward VI, ch. 10 (4. 110–11).

[56] *LP Henry VIII*, 13/1. 1345.

[57] See Hudson, *Premature Reformation*, pp. 302–3.

that thei haden usid [practised]'.[58] At the same time, the very model informing Thorpe's own account of his interrogation by a blustering yet very threatening Archbishop Arundel is that of saints' lives, in many of which the saint confronts an exasperated persecutor in intellectual debate, just as Anne Askew's account of her trial is modelled on that of saints in the same position.[59] In the sixteenth century the practice of deploying the model of the saint's life in order to obliterate the memory of those lives produced the massive project of Foxe's *Acts and Monuments* (1563). Foxe recounts in elaborate and juridical detail the trials, including that of Thorpe, and the martyrdoms of English Lollards and Protestants; this Protestant and nationalist version of the *Golden Legend* comes replete with its own calendar of 'martyrs' and 'confessors'.

(*b*) Saints' Lives and Historical Transition: Women Suffering History

The lives of saints did not only map institutional and topographical jurisdictions. They also marked, and sometimes initiated, the limits of political power by effecting critical historical transitions. A simple life of St Cristina (528 lines in eight-line stanzas), translated from the *Legenda Aurea* by one William Parys while he was imprisoned by Richard II between 1397 and 1399, illustrates the point in very simple if powerful form.[60] Cristina is herself imprisoned in a tower by an overbearing father, who fills the tower with idols of the gods, to whose service he commits an unwilling daughter. Cristina's first act of decisive rebellion against the patriarchal order is to smash the idols; she flings them from the window of her high tower, and 'bryste ther legges and armes in too'. She then proceeds to strip them, by picking off the 'plates of silver and golde, and casting them to the poor' (ll. 129–36). Her enraged father immediately orders Cristina herself to be stripped, scoured, and drowned with the most spectacu-

[58] Thorpe, *Testimony*, p. 58.

[59] Bale, *Examinations of Anne Askew*; Bale, who intersperses his own comments into his 1546 edn. of Askew's own writing, explicitly compares Askew to martyrs in the primitive church (pp. 10–13).

[60] The work consists of 528 lines in octave stanzas. See further Winstead, *Virgin Martyrs*, pp. 83–4.

lar violence. Before she can be beheaded by paternal order, however, her father is found dead. The judge who replaces him orders that Cristina be led naked through the city to the temple of Apollo; the women of the city having been outraged by this, Cristina commands the statue of Apollo to self-destruct: 'Apolyne felle ther downe one the stone | In poudire, ther alle mene myghte see' (ll. 365–6). This act of cultic destruction itself provokes the death of the second judge, who is replaced by a third. Further tortures manifest the indestructible vivacity and fertility of Cristina's body: from severed breasts flows milk not blood; she not only continues to speak after her tongue has been cut out, but she uses it to blind her persecutor by tossing it at his eye.

The lurid energy of this short narrative derives from its interactions of living and dead bodies. The stripping and breaking of the idols immediately provokes the stripping and dismemberment of the virgin iconoclast. Whereas, however, the idols remain inert matter, susceptible of material destruction, Cristina's own numinous and naked body repeatedly reaffirms its indestructible and inexhaustible vivacity. Around the central opposition between the living body of Cristina and the inert bodies of the idols forms a larger gender divide between the patriarchal male judges and the women outraged by Cristina's treatment by the judge Dyons: 'Vengeance, Dyons', they cry, 'on the betyde! | Thou dos alle womene shame this daie' (ll. 359–60). The larger resources of female energy exhaust the male tormentors so much that two die in the process of trying to kill Cristina (in Bokenham's version the tally is three). This exhaustion of male aggression equally marks the founding of a new historical order: the patriarchs of Diocletian's third-century persection die no less surely than the cultic images upon which their power rests are reduced to rubble.

William Parys, the imprisoned translator of this life, perhaps saw himself as heralding a new order; he describes himself as the only man still loyal to his master Thomas Beauchamp, an Appellant Lord imprisoned by Richard II in 1397, and prays to Cristina for deliverance, which in fact came with the overthrow of Richard II in 1399.[61] That might be the specific political impetus for this saint's life, but

[61] See Winstead, *Virgin Martyrs*, pp. 83–4.

the stripping and breaking of images, in the name of a new order, is perhaps the most constant feature of the lives of saints; it is certainly very prominent in mid-fifteenth- and early sixteenth-century lives of women saints. In Bokenham's *Legendys of Hooly Wummen* (1443–7), for example, the following saints either break images, or otherwise insist on their insensate materiality: Cristina, Agnes, Dorothy, Mary Magdalene, and Cecilia. In John Capgrave's great *Life of St Katharine of Alexandria* (*c*.1445, 6,882 lines, in rhyme-royal stanzas, divided into five books), as in the Bokenham examples, the key test of orthodox submission to the pagan imperial order is a readiness to acknowledge the pagan pantheon's images. After the tyrannical Emperor Maxentius has decided that the cult and 'dew rente' of the old gods must be renewed (4. 305), Katharine of course refuses. She confronts Maxentius directly with a double and unresolved attack on the idols by which he is surrounded: they are either devils, or else they are irredeemably dead matter:

> Thi goddis arn devellis, and thi preestis eke
> Disceyvouris of the peple, right for covetyse; [deceivers]
> Thei wote as weel as I, though men hem seke, [know]
> These maumentis I mene, thei can not sitte ne ryse; [idols]
> Thei ete not, thei drynke not in no maner of wise;
> Mouth wythoute speche, foot that may not goo,
> Handes eke have thei and may noo werk doo. [also]
>
> (4. 589–95)

Likewise in Barclay's *Life of Saint George* (1515), the saint follows up his victory over the dragon by having the people destroy their pantheon: 'olde Idollys of fendes infernall | They threwe to the grounde and brake them everychone' (ll. 1122–3).

In this sub-section I attend to the ways in which historical transition is figured in the lives of women saints in particular, since in these narratives it is women especially who suffer and provoke painful historical transitions. Saints' lives oscillate between mutilation of the bodies of idols and virgin saints by way of figuring the breakdown of the old order and the living, resurgent energies of the new. This representation of historical *transitus* is partly a matter of mapping the decisive historical articulations for Christianity, but also, more pressingly I suggest, a way of reflecting on the pressures for a new order within fifteenth-century English culture itself. While on the face of it saints' lives mark a retreat in the fifteenth century from the front line of ecclesiological politics into a realm of popular and naïve devotion, in fact these narratives repeatedly represented exactly the pressing and intensely topical issues of popular cult. Lollard polemicists were arguing precisely what the heroic saints of these ostensibly orthodox narratives argue to the death: that the images of the divine worshipped by the people are in fact entirely dead matter, whose cult only exploits the poor by diverting the resources of relief from them. And just as the heroic saints replayed the action of Lollards, so too did their hapless persecutors face the problems of managing heterodox and potentially destabilizing forces. There could be no escape from the literally burning issues of Lollard persecution, in an environment in which even an ostensibly orthodox text, by virtue of its very orthodoxy, engaged in dialogue with its opponent.

By way of focusing the representation of women as the bearers of the new order in fifteenth-century texts, I begin with a sixteenth-century example, written in a moment of extremely stressful and momentous historical transition. The point of framing the discussion with a sixteenth-century example is to suggest that mid-sixteenth-century historical transition can only be managed by focusing on women and their images as signs of the very materiality the new Henrician order will strip and dispose of.

At 9 a.m. on 13 February 1542 Henry Parker, Lord Morley's daughter Lady Rochford was beheaded in the Tower of London, preceded by Queen Catherine Howard. She had been convicted of treason and sentenced to death on account of her complicity with Catherine Howard's reputed affairs while she was queen. A statute of 1542, asking that both women be 'convicted and attainted of Highe Treasone', describes Lady Rochford as 'that bawde the Lady Jane Rochford'.[62] The charges laid against the queen's reputed lovers are more specific about Jane Rochford: Thomas Culpepper and Francis Dereham , 'the better to pursue their carnal life . . . retained Jane Lady Rochford . . . as a go-between to contrive meetings in the Queen's stole chamber and other suspect places; and so the said Jane falsely and traitorously aided and abetted them'.[63]

[62] *SR*, 33 Henry VIII, ch.21, art. 1 (3. 857).
[63] *LP Henry VIII*, 16. 1395.

Less than a year after the execution of his daughter, in, almost certainly, New Year 1543,[64] Morley presented to the King a book of exceptional women, a translation into English prose of Boccaccio's *De claris mulieribus* (produced, in Latin prose, between 1361 and 1375).[65] In it he closely translated into English prose the first forty-six of the one hundred and four lives contained in Boccaccio's Latin original. The presentation of this work surely stood in significant relation to the execution of Lady Rochford. Morley had attended the House of Lords for each reading of the bill passed in 1542 to attaint his daughter and Queen Catherine.[66] If the Act legislated so as to punish both queenly lasciviousness and failure to report it, then the translation enlisted humanistic learning to align itself, at a discreet historical distance, with the legislation. The book itself (now Chatsworth, Duke of Devonshire, MS Safe 3C) is a deluxe volume, significantly more expensive than any other surviving Morley presentation volumes. New Years' gifts served as part of a system of exchange between monarch and subject,[67] whereby, in Morley's words in his Preface to another translation, a subject, 'althoughe he had grevously offendid your Highnes . . . he were sure to go from you ioyous and mery awaie, so moche of grace resteth in that roiall harte of yours'.[68] If Morley, the father of a reputedly immoral daughter punished by the king, should present a book largely concerned with control of women so soon after his daughter's execution, then it is manifestly implausible that there be no significant connection.[69] On the contrary, Morley's humanist translation actively participates in

[64] For the dating, see Carley, 'Writings of Henry Parker', p. 43.

[65] See Branca, p. 110. An earlier, much livelier translation of the *De claris mulieribus* had been made in the mid-15th cent.; see *Die Mittelenglische Umdichtung von Boccaccio's 'De claris mulieribus'*, ed. Schleich. The text survives in a single MS. For comparison of this and Morley's translation, see Simpson, 'Sacrifice of Lady Rochford'. The discussion of Morley's work here is abbreviated from this article.

[66] See Miller, p. 157.

[67] For the importance of presentation MSS in this period, see Carlson, *English Humanist Books*, pp. 8–12. For an account of a New Year's gift-giving, see D. Starkey (ed.), *Henry VIII*, pp. 126–8.

[68] The citation is from Morley's translation of Plutarch's lives of Scipio and Hannibal; see *Forty-Six Lives, translated from Boccaccio's 'De Claris Mulieribus' by Henry Parker, Lord Morley*, ed. Wright, p. 162. All future references to Morley's translation of *De claris mulieribus* will be made in the body of the text.

[69] See further Carley, 'The Writings of Henry Parker', p. 43.

exactly the discursive environment of these executions, by way of implicitly assuring the King of the justice of his daughter's death.

Morley actively promotes the notion that he is writing in, and contributing to, a moment of decisive historical change and novelty. Translating a printed book produced for an impersonal readership, Morley personalizes his work as a special, manuscript gift to Henry, whose initials are inscribed into the first letter of the text, and whose presence as reader continues to be felt from that initiating moment.[70] Morley's whole sense of literary tradition, indeed, is intimately linked with Henry as imperial patron. In the Preface he accordingly links his source text with Roman imperial power. The height of Latin writing was achieved 'in the greate Augustus days', and continued to decline from that point on, until 'the greate empyre of Rome decayde' over six or seven hundred years, by which time the Romans were 'as barbarouse as the best'. The renovation of letters occurred in Italy, he goes on, in the time of Edward III, who held 'the septre of thys imperiall realme, as your Grace nowe doth;' in this time three Italian writers, Dante, Petrarch, and Boccaccio restored letters, so that, in the case of Petrarch at least, there is hardly any 'noble prynce in Italy, nor gentle man' who is without a copy of his vernacular works (pp. 1–3). This standard recitation of humanist literary ideology quietly insinuates, as it usually does, that Henry is the new Augustus; that cultivation of literature and imperial power are mutually sustaining; and that the renovation of imperial letters is about to begin in England.[71]

Morley makes no references to an English literary lineage, not even in his translation of Petrarch's *Trionfi*, a work one of whose central themes is poetic fame and tradition.[72] For Morley, as for other Henrician propagandists, the renovation of English letters is phoenix-like, without English parentage.[73] Even the Italian works that he does claim as sources are miracles of nature, denying their lineage: no sooner, in the same preface, does Morley claim that

[70] The opening page of Morley's text (f. 1a) is reproduced as the frontispiece to Wright's edition.

[71] Certainly Morley makes no reference, here or elsewhere in his oeuvre, to a pre-Henrician English literary tradition. For the gift of a spiritual work to Princess Mary, see *Forty-Six Lives*, ed. Wright, p. 168.

[72] Henry Parker, *Lord Morley's 'Tryumphes of Fraunces Petrarcke'*.

[73] See Ch. 4, above.

Dante shaped his 'maternal eloquens' than he neutralizes the maternal reference by claiming that Dante's poetry 'semyd a myracle of nature' (p. 2).

This neutralization of feminine power is everywhere apparent in the lives of the women that Morley chooses to narrate. So far from it being the case that the resistant power of these women marks new historical possibilities, Morley takes the occasion of writing female biography to undo the historical significance of women in human and divine history. This is especially clear in his euhemeristic treatment of female gods among the pagan pantheon. Throughout the series there runs an undercurrent of euhemeristic comment, the effect of which is to demystify the divine attractions of women. Divinity is denied to all the goddesses to whom a life is devoted. About Venus, for example, it is said that 'sum calleth hyr a hevenly woman, commen downe from the lappe of Jupiter to the earthe, and, brifly, all they, blyndyd with theyr oune folyshnes, all though they knewe well ynoughe that she was a mortall woman, yet they affirmede hyr to be an immortall goddesse' (p. 30).[74] Euhemerism is so relentless, in fact, that it incurs the possibility of undoing the very project of isolating exceptional women: Boccaccio must have recourse to what the 'poetes have founde . . . to feyne' as the premiss of his narrative (p. 71), but no sooner has he included goddesses on the basis of poetic myth than he strips away the myth to reveal an altogether mortal and fallible woman, whose failures are, in Boccaccio's eyes, rather predictable and *un*exceptional. Thus Venus herself, very much a 'mortall woman', 'coulde not resyste suche fylthynes, thoughe she were accomptyd Jupiters doughter and taken as oone of that moste venerable sorte emonge the best' (p. 30). Concluding the narrative of Venus, Boccaccio pursues his demystification as far as it will go: Venus is reported to have been the first person to set up 'these comune baudes houses' (p. 32). In what is surely a significant addition to this story of a 'baude' considered with veneration by virtue of her father's status, Morley slightly alters his source in its last words. Whereas Boccaccio ends by lamenting the fact that the lascivious ways instigated by Venus penetrated 'ad Ytalos usque [*as far as Italy*]', Morley adds 'and dyvers countres moo' (p. 32).

[74] For euhemerism, the theory that the gods are 'recruited from the ranks of mortal[s]', see Seznec, ch. 1. Citation from p. 11.

If the goddesses are stripped of their mystique to reveal an altogether less palatable reality, the same is true of many of the women about whose mortality there was never question. The second narrative in the collection, for example, is that of Semiramis, which evokes, possibly, not only the accusations concerning 'bawdes' in the Catherine Howard executions, but also the convictions of incest in the Boleyn scandal. Semiramis, despite being a remarkable queen after her husband's death by 'takynge to hyr mans hert', nevertheless falls prey to an unquenchable lasciviousness 'in usynge hirself moste unhappely in fleshly lustes'. Not only did she act 'more beastly then womanly in the company of corrupte bawdes', but, what is worse, she committed incest with her own son. Boccaccio and Morley are ready to describe feminine success in the public world as the result of women adopting a masculine spirit, but feminine sins remain feminine, proof that women make poor rulers. As Boccaccio says in another narrative, women's pride is intolerable, since they are inclined by nature to pride; those who are not are 'more apte to vertue then to rule' (p. 54).

Morley writes to an imperial patron, then, and he invokes a brilliant new Augustan age. In doing so, however, he dismantles the pantheon that underwrites the imperial model; he focuses especially on the fact that the female gods are merely powerful and lascivious human women who have been ideologically elevated to divine status through popular acclaim. And just as works of famous historical lives press forward into the famous lives of the present, so too does Morley imply that these wholly fallible, non-iconic women serve as appropriate models for the women of Henry's court, amongst whom he expects the book to be circulated (p. 3). Henry's own power, Morley implies, is underwritten by nothing but itself: these divine women who might serve as the benchmarks for a new order are returned to a tawdry human world in which they act poorly. Their iconic status is dismantled even as Morley chooses them as 'exceptional' women. In so doing, Morley implicitly condones Henry's own treatment of famous women after a decade in which Henry had divorced two wives, and executed two more (one had died in childbirth).

Morley presented his work of famous women in 1542, only eight years after the Act of Supremacy. Morley did give a pre-Henrician spiritual work by Richard Rolle (the commentary on the Psalms) to Princess Mary in these years, offering it as 'an olde boke and to the fyrst sythe [sight] a cast away', and declaring that he does not know either who wrote this 'rude Psalter' or when it was written (pp. 168–9). In addressing the King, however, Morley could not afford to recognize any pre-Henrician English literary tradition of religious writing; certainly in the matter of exemplary lives, he chose wholly non-Christian examples, since, presumably, the lives of women saints had become treacherous territory after the previous five years of iconoclasm, and the questioning of saintly intercession since 1536. By 1550, indeed, the statute commanding the destruction of all images in churches also commanded that all service books, including 'legends', 'be forbidden, to be utterly abolished, extinguished, and forbidden for ever to be kept or used in this realm'.[75]

If Morley stripped his classical feminine icons, the iconoclasts had themselves been stripping the images of women saints in the previous five years. On 13 June 1538 Hugh Latimer, previously bishop of Worcester, wrote to Cromwell about the image of the Virgin at Worcester. He derisively called the image 'our great Sibyll', and asked that Cromwell 'bestow her to some good purpose'. The profitable end to which Latimer wished to consign the image is a public and exemplary burning of the kind, and in the place, assigned to heretics. A month earlier Latimer had preached at the burning of the recusant friar John Forrest, who was burnt at Smithfield on 22 May 1538 along with 'an idol that was brought out of North Wales . . . which the people . . . honored as a sainct'.[76] In June Latimer wants the image of the Virgin to be given the same treatment, since

> she hath been the devil's instrument to bring many, I fear, to eternal fire; now she herself, with her old sister of Walsingham, her young sister of Ipswich, with their other two sisters of Dongcaster and Penryesse, would make a jolly muster in Smithfield. They would not be all day in burning.[77]

Latimer's language about these images of the Virgin figures all that is idolatrous as simultaneously feminine and diabolic, so both recalling the reported Lollard insult of 'the wyche of Walsyngham', and

[75] *SR*, 3&4 Edward VI, ch.10 (4. 110).
[76] Wriothesley, 1. 80.
[77] *L&P Henry VIII*, 13/1. 1177.

presaging the campaign of witch-burning that began in the later sixteenth century.[78] Even as he derides the images, he nevertheless attributes to them a real power, just as he invests them with a juridical personality by imagining their burning at Smithfield, the place of execution for heretics.

It is not certain what ultimately happened to the images to which Latimer refers,[79] but the same uneasy mixture of derision and anthropomorphism is evident in the comments of witnesses to their treatment by iconoclasts. The image at Walsingham and its chapel were stripped of gold and silver on 14 July 1538;[80] on 18 July 1538, a John Husee reports that 'our late lady of Walsingham' has been brought to Lambhithe to Cromwell and many other prelates, 'but there was offered neither oblation nor candle. What shall become of her is not yet determined.'[81] Later in the same month one of Cromwell's officers hauntingly reports from London that he has received 'the image of our lady that was at Ipswich, which I have bestowed in your wardrobe of beds. There is nothing about her but two half shoes of silver and four stones of crystal set in silver.'[82]

The very Church of Rome was itself conceived in these years as a corrupting, feminine force, whose idolatrous images provoked licentiousness. Describing the Roman Church as the whore of Babylon was the staple attack by the reign of Edward, but a gendering of the Roman and English Churches as respectively female and male is also found in Henrician documents. William Barlow, the Bishop of St David's, wrote to Cromwell in August 1538 that he has ordered the 'idolatrous images' to be taken down throughout Wales, and that 'Welsh rudeness' will soon be 'framed to English civility'. 'Rudeness' and 'civility' are immediately gendered, as Barlow goes on to say that Wales has 'always been esteemed a delicate daughter of Rome resembling her mother in idolatry, licentious living, deceitful pardons'. He

78 For a report of the Lollard insult, see Knighton, *Chronicle, 1337–1396*, ed. and trans. Martin, p. 297. Large-scale persecution of 'witches', and statutes specifying penalties for witchcraft are all post-medieval; see *SR*, 33 Henry VIII, ch. 8 (1542), (3. 837); 5 Elizabeth 1, ch. 16 (1562), (4/1. 446–7); 1 James 1, ch. 12 (1604), (5.1028–29).

79 See Dickinson, p. 65.

80 *L&P Henry VIII*, 13/1. 1376.

81 Ibid. 1407.

82 Ibid. 1501. For Latimer's stripping of the image of the Virgin at Worcester in August 1537, see ibid., 12/2. 587.

concludes his report by attacking the cult of St David, who, he says, probably never existed.[83]

The strippings of the Virgin in 1538, the suppression of female monastic houses mostly in 1536, and the derisive gendering of the Roman Church occur within a few years of Redman's printing of Lydgate's *Life of Our Lady* in 1531.[84] Lydgate wrote this work almost certainly for Henry V in ?1416–22;[85] an extraordinary forty-two manuscripts survive, and Caxton also printed it twice in 1484.[86] The work is unquestionably produced within the context of a Lancastrian, anti-Lollard orthodoxy: it was almost certainly produced for Henry V; it draws extensively on the *Meditationes vitae Christi*, the translation of which had been officially approved by Archbishop Arundel in 1410;[87] and Lydgate is fierce in his attack on Lollardy in roughly contemporary works, such as *A Defence of Holy Church* (1413). If Lydgate himself is writing in a period of threatened change, however, he deploys the image of the Virgin in exactly the opposite ways from Latimer's figuration of the superstitious, idolatrous and destested past as feminine. Lydgate's Mary figures historical continuities between Christianity on the one hand, and both Hebraic and classical pagan cultic practice on the other. The work is certainly a statement of orthodoxy, but orthodoxy, unlike its Wycliffite opponent, favours the layering of historical practices in which the structure of many pasts remains visible in the present.

The *Life of Our Lady* is a work of high ambition. Lydgate divides its 5,932 lines, written in rhyme-royal stanzas, into six books, each devoted either to a section of the life of the Virgin (Books 1–2), or to a feast day in which the Virgin features prominently (Books 3–6).[88] Narrative is frequently overborne by sequences of highly wrought, intensely imagistic Marian invocation, or equally imagistic typologi-

[83] Ibid. 13/2. 111.

[84] *RSTC* 17025. The following paragraphs about Lydgate's *Life of Our Lady* are drawn from Simpson, 'Rule of Medieval Imagination'.

[85] For the arguments about dating, see *Critical Edition of John Lydgate's 'Life of Our Lady'*, ed. Lauritis et al., pp. 7–8, and Pearsall, *John Lydgate: A Bio-Bibliography*, pp. 19–20.

[86] *RSTC* 17023 and 17024.

[87] For the text of Arundel's 'imprimatur', see Nicholas Love, *Mirror*, ed. Sargent, p. 7.

[88] For the logic and structure of the work, see Hardman, 'Lydgate's *Lyfe of Our Lady*'.

cal prefiguration of the birth of Christ. Here I focus on Book 6, 462 lines devoted to the Feast of Candlemas, which falls on 2 February. It deals with the 'purification' of the Virgin, forty days after giving birth. Lydgate begins with a description of the Purification taken from Luke 2: 22–40, before allegorizing the two birds required as oblation in the Hebraic rite. He then gives a historical account of the rite of bearing candles, before allegorizing the candles in conclusion.

The *Legenda Aurea,* upon which Lydgate is dependent for much of the material in Book 6 of the *Life of Our Lady*, says that the Church established the custom of bearing candles for the purpose of abolishing 'erroneous custom'.[89] In Lydgate's version the 'erroneous custom' is certainly described, but its 'error' feeds into the present by way of transformation rather than abolition. In ancient Rome, he tells us, everyone went in pairs every five years on 1 February

> To Februa of olde fundacion—
> That modir was to Mars omnipotent—
> In whose honoure this procession
> Ordeyned was by greate avysement. [deliberation]
>
> (6. 316–19)

Februa, it was supposed 'in her [their] opynyon', could intercede for the Romans, 'thorough her helpe and mediacion' (6.327). After the Romans had converted to Christianity, they retained this rite,

> For olde custome is harde to putte away,
> And usage grevythe folkes full sore
> To do away that thei have kepte of yore.
>
> (6. 341–3)

Pope Sergius, observing the danger of the pagan rite, worked 'this ryte to chaunge into the honoure | Of our lady' (6. 348–9), to the end that, throughout the world, men and women should come bearing candles to the 'Temple' and make their offering, 'in honour oonly of the hevenly quene | That best may be our mediatrice | To hir son' (6. 357–9).

Lydgate's cultural archaeology here provides historical depth for one of the fifteenth-century Church's principal feast days, in which

[89] See Jacobus de Voragine, *Golden Legend: Readings on the Saints*, trans. Ryan, p. 148.

every parishioner participated by carrying a candle to Church, and offering it, with a penny, at Mass.[90] Many parish fraternities, most dating from the latter half of the fourteenth century, were dedicated to the Purification of the Virgin. Such guilds for which returns were made in 1388 were concentrated in the east of England, and included the influential Candlemas Guild at Bury St Edmund's, the site of Lydgate's own monastery.[91] Many of these guilds performed processions, such as the Guild of the Purification based at great St Mary's in Cambridge, or performances of the Virgin's purification and presentation of Christ at the Temple, such as the theatrical event performed by the Guild of St Mary in Beverley in Yorkshire. In this performance, each brother and sister of the fraternity would gather at a certain distance from the church. The women followed a woman of the guild designated to play the Virgin bearing a simulacrum of the infant Jesus, while the men followed those members of the guild who played the roles of Joseph and Simeon, all processing to the high altar to enact the Purification, 'bini et bini in ordine sobrio et moderato gressu' ('two by two at a sober and moderate step').[92]

Some voices nearly contemporary with Lydgate's *Life of Our Lady* attack physical representations of Old Testament scenes, since such enactment reverses the dynamic of salvation history by returning the present back onto the past. Thus one author of the probably Wycliffite *Tretise of Miraclis Pleyinge* (early fifteenth century) argues that theatrical representations of Old Testament scenes destroy belief in Christ, 'and is verre goinge bacward, fro dedis of the spirit to onely signes don after lustis of the fleysh' (ll. 526–34).[93] Lydgate's own account of the Purification goes one step further 'backward' in his account of the rite: not only does he explain the Hebraic rite of the birds brought by the Virgin to the Temple, but, as we have seen, he also attaches the fundamental structure of the parish procession and performances to the Roman ritual in which everyone went 'tweyne and tweyne a paas [step]' (6. 314). Not only does he go backward, but he is unembarrassed about going back-

90 See Duffy, p. 16.

91 See Westlake, *Parish Guilds of Medieval England*, app., which lists eleven guilds specifically dedicated to the feast of the Purification. For the important Candlemas guild in Bury, see Stratham, pp. 138–44.

92 For the full document, see Young, 1. 252–3.

93 See further Nissé.

ward to the 'flesh', or at least the maternal; unlike his source, Lydgate underlines the evident parallels between the maternal Februa as intercessor with her son and the Virgin as mediatrix, in a work that might itself be directed at women readers (5. 379–427). The Christian ritual bears within itself, then, different pasts, both Jewish and Roman, by which it is structured, and which it, in turn, transforms. Allegory might transform the significance of those cultic pasts, but it cannot help preserving their memory at the same time.

In the last three books of the *Life of Our Lady* Lydgate provides the rationale for certain feasts in the Christian calendar, revealing as he does the cultural archaeology of 'olde custome' behind these celebrations. Even as he does so, however, he exposes the fragility of those cultural passages by which the picture of the past is transmitted to the present. Lydgate's mode in this work is intensely visual, insofar as he repeatedly dwells on standard iconographic images (e.g. 3. 246–52). So far from relying on visual images for any direct access to the past, however, he also dwells on the fragile opacity and rhetoricity of those visual images. In the conclusion to Book 5 devoted to the Epiphany, for example, he grieves not so much for what he sees (a queen in an ox's stall), as for *how* he sees, or fails to see, the 'showing' of the Epiphany:

> But o, alas, ther is but a lykenesse
> Of portrature that doth us grete offence,
> For we may not have full the blissednesse
> Of thy visage ne of thy presence;
> And so to us grete harme doth aparence,
> Whan that we sene of our desyre we fayle,
> We may well pleyne but it may not avayle.
>
> (5. 638–44)

In this poem pictures are in no way condescended to as the sign of 'popular' and illiterate culture; on the contrary, the 'picture' is indistinguishable from the text itself. However feeble it might be, and however much it insists on absence as much as presence, it is the only 'figure' by which that layered past can be re-entered.

In Lydgate's poem, then, Mary acts as a kind of historical intercessor, since her life mediates between different historical dispensations. This historical intercession produces an accretive history, within which Christian practice builds onto prior dispensations. In the *Life of Our Lady*, however, there is another model of historical transition, one effected by demolition rather than accretion. On the night of the Nativity, Lydgate tells us in Book 3, the Temple of Romulus in Rome collapsed; the repository of the old order's cultural strength conveniently acknowledges its exhaustion by self-destructing: the temple in which 'the statue stode of myghty Romulous' 'to grounde fel adoune, | Pleyne with the erthe, wast and desolate' (3. 1072–8). Apollo had orginally prophesied that the temple would last until a virgin gave birth, and so its builders, mistakenly thinking the temple to be indestructible, inscribed its eternity over the entrance. On the site where the temple and its idol collapsed, a church dedicated to Mary and Christ has been built. Even if the old order prophesies its own collapse, and so in some way participates in the construction of the new order, this model of historical transition requires the material demolition of the old order.

Demolition is a powerful motif in mid-fifteenth-century female saints' lives, in which, as we have seen, refusal to bow down before material idols, and readiness to break them, is the acid test of Christian resistance. By way of concluding this section, I turn to John Capgrave's very remarkable *Life of St Katharine* (*c.*1445), in which the pressures of Lollard iconoclasm are obliquely registered in the representation of the virgin saint. Unlike his other hagiographical works, Capgrave's *Katharine*, also much longer than the other works, has no named patron. In it Capgrave exploits to the full the potential paradoxes of virgin hagiography, a genre officially designed to promote orthodox devotion, but whose heroines are powerfully and consistently resistant to the pressures of persecution. They resolutely refuse both to marry and to adore the pantheon of their powerful male suitors.[94] In so doing, they provoke a violent historical transition that demands the destruction of images. The lives of these saints themselves initiate long histories of translation and accretion: Capgrave narrates, for example, the complex process by which the text of Katharine's life was written in Greek, long buried, and finally translated into Latin and English (1. 43–252). However much the history of the saint's *Nachleben* through time and space is one of

[94] For the specific features of female, as opposed to male, saints' lives, see Heffernan, p. 185.

accretion, the saint's own history involves the destruction of historical monuments and images.

As with Parys's life of Cristina, Capgrave's life of the virgin martyr Katharine marks the boundaries of political jurisdictions by destroying the images upon which the old order is founded. The work is divided into five books, narrating respectively Katharine's education as a princess, daughter to the King of Alexandria; her debate with the Alexandrian parliament in which she, as queen, refuses to take a husband; her spiritual marriage with Christ; her debate with the fifty pagan philosophers on the virtues of Christianity versus paganism; and her martyrdom. Book 4 begins with the successful invasion of Katharine's realm by the Emperor Maxentius, exiled from Rome; if that book relates a point of political transition in which Katharine is defeated, however, the work as a whole traces the defeat of that political order and its icons in the martyred Katharine's triumph. At the end of the work the injustice of Katharine's torture provokes popular conversion, which itself is marked by iconoclasm:

> Many of hem that herden hir thus speke,
> Were converted to crist, oure saveour;
> Ful prevyly her maumentis dede thei breke [idols]
> Whiche that thei hadde in ful grete honour.
>
> (5. 1233–6)

And, as with the life of Cristina, Katharine's boundless energies exhaust and depress her male persecutors. The Emperor Maxentius having executed his own convert wife, and thereby having been rebuked by his disgusted, convert general, falls into deep depression of 'very malencoly': 'O me most wretched of alle men that leve! | Wherto brought nature me onto lyf?' (5. 1604–5). The old order collapses inwardly, its energies and judicial resources exhausted. Martyrdom only provokes more converts.

On the face of it, representing the collapse of the imperial Roman order before the power of its Christian rival is equally a statement in favour of the orthodox ecclesiastical order of mid-fifteenth-century England. Capgrave was a figure of real consequence in that order, being prior provincial of the Augustinian friars between 1453 and 1457. He was also closely aligned with the Lancastrian regime, having dedicated a series of exegetical works in Latin to Humphrey

Duke of Gloucester from 1439, and a work in praise of Henry VI, the *De Illustribus Henricis*, to that king in 1447. Capgrave also successfully negotiated his transition to the reign of Edward IV, by presenting the new king with his *Abbreviacion of Cronicles* in 1461. That work contains attacks on the Lollards as 'erroneous dogs' (p. 197). Unlike Bishop Reginald Pecock, who was condemned for heresy in 1457 after having attempted to confront the Lollards directly with a rebuttal in English, Capgrave's exegetical works in Latin and apparently pious saints' lives in English would seem to fit perfectly with the Arundelian theological orthodoxy established in 1409.[95]

In fact, however, the *Life of St Katharine* is an insistently double-edged work, which walks the finest of lines between maintaining orthodoxy and grieving for the violence that such maintenance incurs. Just as Katharine's pagan persecutors grow faint, so too does Capgrave's narrative insistently reflect on the diminishing legitimacy of an orthodoxy maintained by violence. These reflections pertain both to the narrative devoted to Katharine's own rule (Book 2), and to the representation of Katharine's realm under foreign domination (Books 4 and 5). The parliamentary debate of Book 2 is extraordinarily spirited, in which both Katharine and her male counsellors mount vigorous arguments respectively for and against female rule, the first such debate in English.[96] Katharine, still a pagan, first responds to the parliamentary speaker's request that she marry by privately reflecting on the difficulty of her predicament. Recalling Criseyde's similar soliloquy in *Troilus and Criseyde* (2. 694–812), she reflects that she had intended to 'leve [live] now at myn eese', but that were she to marry she must abandon 'my stody and myn desyre, | My modir, my kin, my peple'. Marriage means the end of reading and the beginning of hunting, a sport she detests: 'I muste leve stody and wash myn book in myre, | Ryde oute on huntynge, use al newe atyre' (2. 183–9). This dislike of witnessing violence is precisely her principal vulnerability as a queen without a husband. Her first opponent in the debate is a plain speaking lord, who insists that Katharine marry, since she could not endure the public executions of traitors,

[95] For the details of Arundel's *Constitutions*, see Ch. 7, above.

[96] Winstead, 'Capgrave's Saint Katherine'. See also Winstead, *Virgin Martyrs*, pp. 167–77.

To see the bowailes cutte oute of his wombe [bowels · stomach]
And brent before hym, whil he is on lyve, [burnt]
To see men be served as thei serve a lombe, [lamb]
Thurgh-oute his guttes bothe rende and ryve, [pull and tear]
To see hem drawe oute be foure and be fyve.
Your pytous herte myght not see this chaunce,
For it would make you to falle in a traunce.

(2. 267–73)

A second lord follows up this point by arguing that Katharine lacks the courage to punish wrongdoing, either in men, wives, or virgins, 'with deth and vengeance'. Katharine subtly and adroitly withstands the verbal onslaught of her male counsellors across the 1,498 lines of Book 2, resolutely parrying their claims that a woman, and especially a woman devoted to private reading and study, is incapable of rule. At one point she drops the pretence of merely delaying marriage by saying that she will never marry, however much the lords may 'karpe, stryve, clatere, and creke' (2. 1106). Only at the end of the book does she mockingly relent, by saying that she will only marry a man superlative in all respects, who is also immortal (2. 1373–1456).

This last hostage to fortune turns out, of course, to be claimed, since Katharine does marry Christ in the following book, a turn of events that makes Katharine the 'victim' of her own intellectual skill. That historical irony is, however, a minor effect of the debate, which much more powerfully underlines the violence inherent in the daily exercise of power, a violence to be visited upon both the ruler's own subjects and potential foreign enemies. This masculine assertion of the inherent, grinding discipline of violence is rebuffed by Katharine. She concedes that she would not be able to witness 'swiche bocherye' as they describe; in the case of incorrigible criminals, she would have deputies supervise the executions, but she would be certain to exercise more mercy in any case. Rather than fainting before public executions, she would forgive the traitor; she immediately caps this point in her characteristically shrewd way by pointing out that her father did precisely this to some of the very men who oppose her now: 'loke weel abowte, for somme of hem ben here | Whiche were thus saved' (2. 424–5).

The conduct of secular power in Capgrave's *Katharine* is powerfully considered, then, well before any issues of heresy arise. While

Katharine's is by far the more civilized position, the narrative unblinkingly registers the force of her male interlocutors' arguments, since Katharine's realm is indeed successfully invaded. If Book 2 is double-edged in its defence of rule by a woman, so too do Books 4 and 5 cut both ways in their treatment of heresy. If Book 2 expresses a kind of grief at the violence of secular power, these books express a similar grief at the treatment of heretics. For in these books Katharine the deposed queen is on trial for heterodox religious positions, particularly concerning the worship of images. Most strikingly, Katharine acts like a Lollard, while her pagan opponents propose arguments strikingly similar to those of fifteenth-century defenders of images; the corollary of these resemblances is that her persecutors resemble nothing more than the persecutors of Lollardy. In short, we observe in the *Life of St Katharine* a strange swapping, or at least blurring, of positions: by the mid-fifteenth century the ostensibly orthodox heroine speaks strangely like those 'erroneous dogs' the Lollards, while her persecutors cannot help but resemble the orthodox Lancastrian establishment.

In Book 5 the persecutor Maxentius offers to make an image of Katharine, 'a solenne ymage like an empresse; | As liche as craft wil countirfete your face | It shal be made' (5. 401–3). It will be made of metal; anyone who fails to reverence the image shall fall 'in grete offens', while anyone who seeks intercession from the image shall be granted forgiveness; a temple of marble will be built around it. In response, Katharine mocks the idea by insisting on the material deadness of the proposed image. No one, she taunts, is capable of making the eyes of such an image see or its tongue speak; it will be 'insensible, | Stonde liche a ston' (5. 470–1). Katharine's attack on her own image has strange parallels with the account in Henry Knighton's *Chronicle* (late 1370s–1397) of two hungry Lollards searching for firewood in a chapel, who come across an old wooden image of St Katharine. They mock its insensibility by adopting the position of tormentors: if the head bleeds when the axe strikes, then they will convert; if it responds like wood, then they will burn it to heat their soup (pp. 296–8).[97] Knighton generalizes from the incident to say that Lollards hated and attacked images, preaching that they

[97] See further Stanbury.

were idols and spurning them as mere simulacra (p. 296). Clearly this attack on images remains a vibrant part of Lollardy: in the heresy trials of Norwich between 1428 and 1431, many defendants repudiate the veneration of images.[98] The deposition against Margery Baxter, for example, claims that she held that some of the devils who fell with Lucifer entered into and remain within the images that stand in churches, such that the people who worship them commit idolatry.[99]

The question of idol worship becomes, indeed, the central issue out of which the theological debate of Book 4 issues. Katharine is aroused from her study by the noise of sacrificial ritual in honour of Maxentius, and refuses to honour the gods by which the Emperor is surrounded in all his ersatz glory (4. 358–427); she has even less respect for idols than Margery Baxter, since she argues that they are entirely insensate, and that the pagan gods were in any case mere humans elevated to the status of gods (4. 554–602). Out of this confrontation about the damaging stupidity of honouring mere 'stookes', or pieces of wood (4. 701), issues the theological debate between Katharine and fifty pagan male philosophers. This debate mirrors the wholly secular debate of Book 2 between Katharine and the male counsellors. It also confronts issues of representation in images, with one of the pagan philosophers conceding that the images of the gods are themselves mere matter, but that they still deserve to be honoured, since 'they ben but figures, | Representynge other-maner thyng'. Arguing in exactly the terms used by defenders of anti-Lollard orthodoxy, he argues that they are honoured 'not for her cause, but for signifycacion | Of the worthy whom thei represent', and are designed only to provoke 'devocion' (4.1492–1512).[100] Katharine concedes this point, but goes on to reply that the lives of the gods are in any case vicious. The next philosopher's argument retreats to the fall-back position that the gods are physical allegories of elemental forces, but Katharine beats him back too, by arguing that such forces are but the shadow of truth (4. 1562–1631). At this point the chastened and converted philosophers ask for a theological

[98] For many examples of which, see the references listed in *Heresy Trials in the Diocese of Norwich*, ed. Tanner, p. 13.

[99] Ibid. 49.

[100] For the defence of images, see Aston, *England's Iconoclasts*, *passim*.

lesson, to which request Katharine replies with a serious and detailed account of Trinitarian and soteriological theology. Even the recently converted Christians who have previously bowed to 'maumentis' now grieve at their idolatry, 'demyng hemself ful worthy grete penauns' (4. 1827). The debate ends with the conversion of the philosophers; even the lords threaten to kick down their pagan idols (4. 2094–2100).

This settled debate is itself unsettling in the context of its production in English. Its most obviously surprising aspect in a mid-fifteenth-century environment of theological repression is its serious defence of pagan religion. Just as the male counsellors mount a plausible case against the rule of a female scholar in Book 2, so too do the pagan philosophers thoughtfully explicate the sophisticated logic of pagan religion in Book 4. Even more surprising, perhaps, is the theological articulation of Christianity in sophisticated, vernacular terms in a text designed to be read 'of man, of mayde, of wyf' (1. 66). Not only that, but the defence is one that could appeal to Lollards, since it makes no reference to ecclesiological or sacramental issues; and many of the issues about which Lollards did care passionately, like the worship of images, are themselves part of Katharine's *own* arsenal against idolatrous religion. It would be impossible, indeed, for Katharine to mount a defence of honouring images, given the ferocity of her attack on precisely that practice, including an extended critique of honouring her own image. In some ways this saint's life promotes, remarkably, a version of Christian practice that is not itself dependent on honouring the saints.

Capgrave was not adopting Lollard positions; his formally dialogic text, nevertheless, obliquely exposed the grounds and methods of orthodoxy for inspection. Most simply, the text cannot help put into sharpest relief questions concerning the management of heterodox positions. In the late antique world of the poem, Katharine represents the heretic; Maxentius her persecutor repeatedly recognizes that he has made a mistake in handling the matter in such a public way, since his own people begin to 'despise | Alle my goddis', and the Christians 'han caught boldnesse' (4. 736–49). Finally this poor exercise of heresy-containment ends, as we have seen, in exhausted and solitary depression; like many of the lives in Bokenham's collection, Capgrave's serves as an extended reflection on how to manage heterodoxy.[101] More forcefully, the text is powerfully if not quite unreservedly behind a theologically educated and articulate woman. Attacks on Lollard women who, despite having 'thin wits' wish 'argumentes [to] make in holy writ', are common in earlier anti-Lollard polemic.[102] Capgrave's text might acknowledge that Katharine's bookishness makes for bad foreign policy, but it unquestionably celebrates her passionate devotion to learning, and traces her training and growth as an intellectual.[103] Capgrave's own work, indeed, is itself a cultivation of learning, since it offers a sophisticated account of both pagan and Christian theology to vernacular readers, both 'mayde' and 'wyf'.

Most strikingly of all, the courage persecuted Christians require is explicitly linked to the courage of Lollards. In Capgrave's earlier *Life of St Norbert* (1440), the saint is arraigned for heresy, having been caught preaching without licence. The bishops judge that it is 'grete presumpcioun | That swech a lewid man in despite of hem alle | Shuld preche in here diosise' (ll. 325–7). They summon him as a 'heretike', and charge him with slandering their own authority, and wearing simpler clothes than was fit for a priest. Norbert replies by redefining true religion as practising the seven works of mercy, and he defends both preaching and simple clothing by reference to the Gospels (ll. 349–85). These charges made against Norbert, and his mode of answering, have close parallels with Lollard trials. If the early twelfth-century Norbert himself is excused, and goes on to become a great saint, Katharine, who lives in a period of much greater cultural transition, is instead martyred. Strikingly, though, the position of the persecuted early Christians in this narrative is explicitly linked to that of the Lollards. In Book 3 the hermit Adrian is charged by the Virgin Mary to seek out Katharine in preparation for Katharine's wedding with Christ. The Virgin tells Adrian that he will find Katharine in her private study, normally prohibited to men, reading.

[101] For the same kind of reflection, see Bokenham's life of Agnes, in *Legendys of Hooly Wummen*, ed. Serjeantson.

[102] Citations from Thomas Hoccleve, *Remonstrance against Oldcastle*, ll. 145–52. See further Aston, 'Lollard Women Priests?'.

[103] See e.g. 2. 533–67; 1324–52. For Katharine's bad foreign policy, see Winstead, 'Capgrave's Saint Katharine'. Capgrave's life of Augustine is also the biography of an intellectual.

Adrian is to have no fear before Katharine's questions, since the Virgin will inspire him 'To yeve hir answere to every questyon'. She cites Christ's words to the disciples in Mark 13: 9–11, with an interesting twist:

> 'Whan ye stande', he seyde, 'before the doom [judgement]
> Of many tyrauntis, and ye allone yourselve,
> Thow thei you calle lollard, wytche or elve,
> Beth not dismayed, I shal geve you answere,
> Ther can no man swiche langage now you lere. [teach]
>
> (3. 325–9)

These are *Christ's own words*, as reported by the Virgin. The Virgin herself promises Adrian eloquence in his own vernacular: you shall have, she says, 'in thi langage | Swiche wonder termes' (3. 330–1). Katharine herself appeals to precisely this text from Mark before her encounter with the pagan philosophers, when she prays to God that she should have the same capacity to answer as did the Apostles, to whom no one could reply, 'neither of the secte of hethen ne of heresye' (4. 1169). For Capgrave's orthodox readers 'heresye' denoted Lollardy; by the time they reached this point in the text, that denotation might not be so evident.

After the Act of Supremacy in 1534, then, saints became extremely treacherous territory. In the 1470s Caxton had printed saints' lives as popular, and entirely safe material; he did not print *Piers Plowman*. After 1534 that situation was reversed: no longer were lives printed, and treatment of the saints was more a matter of official injunction, designed to limit their cult in favour of royal jurisdiction. Women's lives were used by Morley to celebrate the momentous change of Henrician empire, but those lives were non-Christian, and they were stripped of whatever numinous power they possessed.

By contrast, the lives of women saints in the fifteenth century suffer and provoke historical change as heroines. Some fifteeenth-century orthodox writers deployed the lives of women saints to figure historical change in terms of transformation and translation. Lydgate's life of Mary revealed the layerings of cultic practice from other religions that Mary herself mediates to Christian culture, just as Bokenham's lives often related the complex process of translation by which both the body and text of the saint had been carried across inhospitable terrains of time and space. Even if, however, all these saints initiate accretive histories, some of the women martyrs do so by physically attacking the icons of previous cultural orders. In the context of fifteenth-century orthodox repression of Lollard iconophobes and iconoclasts, these ostensibly orthodox narratives of heroic iconoclasm occasionally even threatened, as in the case of Capgrave's *Katharine*, to countenance the position of the heterodox, and to question the violence with which the heterodox were being persecuted. Whereas saints' lives were defended across almost the entire period of this history, up to the Injunctions of 1538 at any rate, as stirrers of pious and lay devotion, it will be clear how they consistently engaged much less manageable forces. These narratives enact complex mapping of state and ecclesiastical jurisdictions; some of them produce sophisticated vernacular theologies; and many of the women's lives in particular both reflect on the management of popular heretical movements, and rehearse the moment at which the images of the Christian saints will themselves be demolished.

III

If painful historical transitions tend to centre on the deployment of images, the same is true of the painful if illuminating moments of individual lives. In this section I turn to the irreducibly visual focus of visionary writing produced in the period of this history, by way of arguing that women writers in particular exploit the ostensibly 'popular' and devotional status of images to produce exploratory vernacular theologies.

Images create societies around them, and so marginalized writers deploy them to initiate or reorganize their relations with readers. Thomas Hoccleve's *Lerne to Die* (938 lines in rhyme-royal stanzas) is a good example. This work forms part of the royal bureaucrat Hoccleve's so-called *Series*, a miscellaneous sequence of works published in *c.*1420 after he had suffered a period of mental instability about six years earlier. In the *Complaint* and *Dialogue* that open the *Series*, Hoccleve complains of being, effectively, a dying author, since his friends refuse to believe that he is cured of his madness. His problem now is not so much madness as the debilitating isolation of being thought unstable; if he goes to Westminster his colleagues search for signs of madness in his face, and if he stays away they say that he has 'fallen in agayne' (l. 182). In this no-win position Hoccleve desires nothing more than death, to 'crepe into my grave' (l. 261).[104] In the *Dialogue* that follows this opening *Complaint*, Hoccleve declares to his friend that he intends, by way of penitential recompense to God, to translate a work called 'lerne for to dye' (l. 206). The friend's first response is to dissuade him from trying, since the work will drive him mad.

As both person and author, then, Hoccleve is dying. The friend, finally persuaded of Hoccleve's stability of person, encourages him to write, and in this reconstruction of a life and society Hoccleve relies powerfully on images. However much the tract on dying is presented as a recompense to God for having cured Hoccleve, it is also the very means to cure, since it reconstructs the image of the dying Hoccleve himself in the minds of his readership. The text is presented in the voice of the young seeker after wisdom, who, in order to learn to die, is told by Wisdom to 'Beholde now the liknesse and figure | Of a man dyynge and talkynge with thee' (ll. 85–6). The text that follows consists mainly of the dialogue between the young man and the image of a dying man he constructs in his own 'conceit' (l. 88). The dying man acts exactly like Hoccleve himself had done earlier in the *Complaint*, since he complains of his terrible isolation before death, and of the fact that he is 'nat reedy [ready] in the grownd to creepe' (l. 182). His friends will not pray for his soul, and in his torment, he is even unsure of the solidity of his own thought, since he cannot be sure whether or not his repentance is real or merely imagined (ll. 358–64). The weirdly reflexive quality of this image at the extremity of life is heightened by its own encouragement to the young man: he is to imagine, the *image* says, his own soul crying to him in purgatory, begging him not to allow it to suffer torment in 'this hot prison' (l. 504). The image in the young man's mind, then, provokes the young man to call up another image, and this further image, itself in torment, pleads for an act of friendship: 'Nat knowe y frendshippe or to whom it strecchith' (l. 511).

This text presents images of extraordinary and tormented solitude, but the effect of this in the *Series* as a whole is to reconstruct

[104] For Hoccleve's predicament in the *Series*, see Ch. 5, above.

friendships and readerships through the imagination. The horrified young man observes the abject image dying before his very eyes, crying out as it falls over the brink of life into the flames of a friendless torment: 'heere y die in thy presence' (l. 740); having witnessed this, he promises to learn to die, and avers that he could never forget the image of the dying man, since it is so 'deepe enclosed' in his mind (l. 759). By the same token, Hoccleve's readers cannot forget this text, nor its likenesses to Hoccleve's own situation: Hoccleve, too, complains of the torment of solitary friendlessness; he too is ready to die; and he too has been 'sore sett on fire, | And lyved in great torment and martire' (ll. 62–3). Whereas the young man is powerless to help the friendless image as it slides over the edge into torment, Hoccleve implies that his readers *can* reach out to the living Hoccleve and reincorporate him into a society of friendly readers.

This social reincorporation not only uses images, but it also implies that social relations are fundamentally rooted in images. In the *Complaint* Hoccleve unconvincingly pretends not to set much store by 'the peples ymagination, | Talkynge this and that of my sycknesse' (ll. 380–1), but his real problem is certainly with what would now be called his 'image'. While in the *Complaint* he says that he is unable to prevent men from imagining whatever they will about him (ll. 197–8), his strategy in *Lerne to Die* is directed precisely at the redirection of imagination. Social relations, this text implies, are grounded in imaginative apprehension of another's situation, and the imagination requires images. The social imagination is at once the sensual, and especially the visual, imagination.[105] Not only that, but images are the surest way of reconstructing social relations out of breakdown: experiencing the simplified, collateral relationships of images returns humans to the social world of real persons with a renewed confidence.

The social function of images is everywhere apparent and implicit in late medieval society, in the works of both those who defend and use images, and those who would destroy them. This social function is very often grafted to a religious model, or set in a religious context. Hoccleve himself has the image of Chaucer limned in his *Regement of Princes*, and defends the image by reference to those of the saints.

[105] For the theory of the social imagination, see Simpson, *Sciences and the Self*, ch. 6, and pp. 252–71.

Although Chaucer is a dead author, Hoccleve resuscitates him by a likeness, 'That thei that have of him lest thought and mynde, | By this peynture may ageyn him fynde' (ll. 4997–8). Hoccleve no sooner instates the image of the absent Chaucer than he defends it by reference to 'the ymages that in the chirche been' (l. 4999): they too provoke thought of absent presences. However much its function within the *Series* might be to reinstate Hoccleve socially within a textual and personal community, *Lerne to Die* is itself translated from part of a devotional source in Latin, the Rhineland visionary Henry Suso's *Horologium Sapientiae* (*c.*1335).[106]

In late medieval testamentary practice we can see that this connection between remembrance of the saints and of persons through images is not merely a matter of parallelism. Very often testators bequeath to their church sacral images through which they will themselves be remembered. On the death of her husband in 1470, Alice Chester (d. 1485) of All Saints' Bristol provided for 'in carved work a tabernacle with a Trinity in the middle over the image of Jesus, and also at her own cost had it gilded full worshipfully'; she also had the altar of the Virgin gilded, along with the imagery of 'Our Lady, Saint Katherine and Saint Margaret'. These and many other of her benefactions are recorded in a 'book of good doers', though Alice and her husband's memory is by no means dependent on this book: she has the images produced in order to have 'both their souls prayed for specially amongst all other good doers', and she donated a rich hearse cloth on which was written, in gold letters and poor Latin, 'Orate pro animabus Henricus Chestre et Alicie uxoris eius' ('pray for the souls of Henry Chester and his wife Alice').[107] Prominently displayed words, whereby every funeral became a way of recalling these generous donors, preserve their memory, but the church itself is also richly decorated with sacral images that are designed to recall not only the saints but also their donors. Examples of this kind could be multiplied very many times: just as Hoccleve preserves and reshapes his image in a dying text, so too do wealthy donors throughout late medieval England attach their memory to the sacral images they have endowed.[108] Apart from the many images donated by John

[106] For an account of Suso's fortunes in England, see Lovatt, 'Henry Suso'.

[107] Cited from *Pre-Reformation Records of All Saints', Bristol*, pt. I, ed. Burgess, pp. 15–17, and 28–9.

[108] For some outstanding examples, see Gibson, *Theatre of Devotion*, ch. 4.

Baret of Bury St Edmund's (d. 1463) to the church of St Mary, for example, he asks in his will that an image of the Virgin be moved 'just to the wal on the south syde where as Marie Mawdelyn stondith, and that ymage to be set just ageyn the peleer there I was wont to sitte, her visage toward the Savyour' (pp. 38–9).[109]

The wills of Alice Chester and John Baret imply metonymies, or associational habits, between the saint, his or her image, and the person who donates the image to the church. Those metonymies underlay the vast system of testamentary bequest in the two centuries leading up to the 1530s, but they also underlay the arguments of those who objected to images. In wishing to do away with images, that is, Lollards, and later evangelical iconoclasts, were equally objecting to a particular kind of society. The author of *Pierce Plowman's Crede* (*c.*1390), for example, attacks the friars for encouraging images of donors in windows, in which St Francis himself enfolds the donor in his cope and presents him to the Trinity (ll. 118–29); in observing the friars' splendid church, the narrator observes the windows shining with 'shapen sheldes [heraldic shields] to shewen aboute, | With merkes [badges] of marchauntes y-medled bytwene' (ll. 176–7). Merchants and aristocrats donate the images, so the poem implies, at the expense of the poor. This account of an unjust circulation of wealth would have it that the money has stopped at the image, when it should move on to the *real* image of Christ, which turns out to be the starving peasant to whom the narrator finally moves. This implicit argument preserves the notion of metonymic relation between the divine, the image and the human, but relocates the metonymy by identifying image and human: because humans are the *real* image of God, cultic images in the normal sense should be both bypassed and destroyed.

This argument was explicit in many Lollard works against images, in which their material deadness was stressed by comparing them with the living pain of 'the true image of God'; material images 'neither thirsteth nor hungreth nor feeleth any coldness neither suffreth disease, for they may not feel nor see nor hear nor speak nor look nor help any man of any disease'.[110] Reginald Pecock in his

[109] Baret was an associate of Lydgate; see Pearsall, *John Lydgate: Bio-Bibliography*, pp. 37–8, and docs. 20–2.

[110] Cited in Aston, *England's Iconoclasts*, p. 119.

defence of images (*c.*1449) argued that images evoke the saints in the way that portraits evoke absent friends, and thereby provoke viewers to love and serve them better;[111] the Lollard writer just cited relied on the same associative logic to destroy material images in favour of worshipping God in his 'quick [living] image' of the poor. Whereas Hoccleve's *Lerne to Die* implied that images play an essential and reconstitutive role in human relationships, Lollard authors, along with their evangelical followers in the sixteenth century, insisted on the self-sufficiency of human relationships unaided by the sharpening, collateral simplifications of the image.

Both these irreconcilable positions, which continued to clash right up to More's defence of images in 1528, preserve a sense of the immense power of images, a power that is at once sacral and social.[112] I turn now to some examples of devotional writing that deploy sacral images in ways that are also social. Reliance on the 'naïve' and 'popular' medium of the image is a source both of new theologies and of new social forms. I begin with Nicholas Love's prose *Mirror of the Blessed Life of Jesus Christ* (*c.*1410), a work that apparently seeks to repress novelty in both theology and society. Closer inspection reveals, however, an unexpectedly liberal reading practice, and an implicit invitation to transgress the bounds that the work apparently wishes to preserve.

Love's work was enormously popular, surviving as it does in upwards of fifty-six manuscripts; it was printed by Caxton in 1484, and went through eight more printings by various printers before 1530.[113] Despite the fact that Love was a Carthusian, an order whose austere spirituality militated against images, he produced a work of Franciscan spirituality, directed to lay readers and heavily reliant on images. Love consciously builds on a pattern of clerical cultivation of lay spirituality in the vernacular, whose sources might be conveniently dated from the Fourth Lateran Council of 1215, and whose

111 Reginald Pecock, *Repressor of Over Much Blaming of the Clergy*, I. 136–99 and 267–74. Discussed in Aston, *England's Iconoclasts*, pp. 147–54.

112 More's defence of images can be found in his *Dialogue concerning Heresies* (1529). The 2nd edn. (1532) included a rebuttal of *The Ymage of Love*, by John Rickes (*RSTC* 21472). For discussion, see Aston, *England's Iconoclasts* 174–81, and Trapp, 'Thomas More and the Visual Arts', pp. 48–54.

113 See Salter, and Love, *Mirror*, ed. Sargent, pp. lxi–xii. For a bibliographical survey of Love, see Nolan, 'Nicholas Love'.

ongoing results in England within the period of this history include works of lay instruction such as *The Lay Folk's Catechism* (*c.*1357);[114] the immensely popular *Pricke of Conscience* (*c.*1350), surviving in about 127 manuscripts; and penitential, catechetical treatises in prose like Chaucer's *Parson's Tale*, the *Speculum Christiani* (*c.*1360–80), and the nine English versions of *Somme le Roi* (1279) by the Dominican Lorens d'Orléans, from the *Ayenbite of Inwit* in 1340 to Caxton's *Royal Book* in *c.*1486.[115] Works of this kind were recopied and revised throughout the fifteenth century, and so too did the new Henrician order devise basic catechetical works after the Act of Supremacy, in *The Bishop's Book* (1537) and its conservatively revised version, *The King's Book* (1543).[116] Already, however, in the second half of the fourteenth century programmes of basic catechetical and penitential instruction in the vernacular had produced more sophisticated vernacular spiritual works; these texts clearly register and contain lay pressures to assimilate the religious practice of professional religious.

Examples of these more sophisticated works include the *Abbey of the Holy Ghost* (*c.*1350–75),[117] and the *Epistle on the Mixed Life* of Walter Hilton (d. 1396).[118] The first of these constructs a figurative 'abbey' in the psyche of its lay reader, while the second exhorts its reader to remain within the active life while practising some aspects of the life of contemplative withdrawal. These works both cultivate and constrain lay spirituality by restricting the lay eye to the image, and by prohibiting the lay mind from abstract reflection. Hilton, for example, instructs his lay reader to meditate in 'the ymaginacioun of the manheed of oure Lord', but not to 'seke knowynge or feelynge more goosteli of the Godhede' (p. 129).[119]

114 For a review of works of lay instruction and their cultural function, see Woods and Copeland, pp. 390–406. For a bibliographical survey of such works, see Raymo, and Jolliffe.

115 For versions of *Somme le Roi*, see *Book of Vices and Virtues*, ed. Francis, introd. See also *Speculum Christiani*, ed. Holmstedt.

116 *RSTC* 5163 and 5168 respectively; see Duffy, pp. 400–1, and 427–30.

117 For discussion of the interface between claustral and lay piety in the period, see Sargent, 'Contemplative Literature and Bourgeois Piety'.

118 For Hilton's other writings and further bibliography, see *English Mystics of the Middle Ages*, ed. Windeatt, pp. 292–4. The *Epistle on the Mixed Life* was printed by Pynson (1506), *RSTC* 4602. 2, and three more times up to 1533.

119 Tracts of this kind continued, of course, to be written right up to the dissolu-

By the time Love was writing in the early fifteenth century, there also existed, of course, Lollardy, the very powerful and heterodox movement of lay theological activity in the vernacular. Being primarily focused on theological and ecclesiological issues, Lollardy had moved quite outside the devotional and penitential limits that clerical cultivators of lay spirituality had sedulously defined. Love was therefore poised in the *Mirour* between contradictory impulses, writing a work that opens the Gospels up for a lay readership's participation, at the same time as he constrains the very ends to which that participation might lead. The constraint is not only explicit in the sequences directed against Lollard doctrines, marked 'contra Lollardos' in the margins, but more profoundly in the extreme care with which he shepherds the Gospel text within strictly imaginative and moral limits. Scenes from Christ's life are drawn from the Gospels and deployed so as to provoke emotional sympathy and moral reflection, but not abstract theorizing of any other kind. Love describes the Temptation of Christ, for example, by drawing on both the Gospels and St Bernard, and by encouraging his readers not to enquire into what 'diverse doctors' have written about the event. Instead they should consider how easy it is for humans to be tempted when Christ himself was: 'We' should also 'take gude hede and behold . . . inwardly oure lord Jesu etyng alone . . . and thenk we devoutly by ymaginacion tho thinges that folowen here aftur, for thei ben ful faire and stiryng to devocion' (p. 74).

Once these constraints have been established, however, Love allows an imaginative freedom to his readers. Even if the Gospels do not say what Christ ate in the desert, 'we mowe [may] here ymagine by reson and ordeyne this worthy fest as us liketh [as we please]'. This freedom to imagine extends to more significant matters than Christ's diet: with reference to the Lord's Prayer, for example, Love says that the person who reflects deeply on this prayer and says it with devotion shall 'fynde in his soule, whan god wole gife his grace, with gret likynge diverse undurstandyng therof most pertynent to his desire and that othere than is written in the comune exposicion therof' (p. 86). Within the vernacular, lay realm of devotional experience Love is unexpectedly liberal: Scripture is not at all held within

tion of the monasteries; see e.g. the works of Richard Whitford of Syon abbey, listed in Hogg, pp. 164–6.

a lexical straitjacket; instead whenever what is written in the book cannot be 'proved' by reference to Scripture, then it shall be 'taken none otherwyes than as a devoute meditacion, that it *might* be so spoken or done' (p. 11; my emphasis).

The sense of possibility in this text profers new horizons to its imagined textual community. The Gospel text becomes an imaginative field in which lay readers can themselves participate, by virtue of the historical foreshortening of which the imagination is capable. Each of Love's readers is encouraged to make 'the in thi soule present to thoo [those] thinges that bene here writen seyd or done of oure lord jesu, and that bisily, likyngly and abydyngly, as thei [though] thou herdest hem with thi bodily eres, or sey [saw] thaim with thin eyen don' (p. 13). Even this formulation puts the work's status as text in question, since the text is composed of what is 'written, said or done', while the reader is to re-present the action and so to de-textualize it; written narrative becomes a theatrical event in which the reader participates almost as an equal with the biblical players. Just as Langland's Will inhabits a biblical landscape in *Piers Plowman*, so too do Love's readers become participants in the wholly open biblical text they witness as living theatre. Words evoke moving pictures in such a way as to dissolve the textuality of words.[120]

Love's de-textualization of the Gospels into seen events permits audiences officially denied access to Scripture an even greater authority: they can claim visual experience of divine events. So far from being a repressive or obfuscating cultural act, in my view this gave women in particular access to a new and powerful form of authority, whereby textuality could be achieved by consistently appealing to non-textual experience.[121] Certainly the most striking aspect of almost the entire range of visionary writing in England from the late fourteenth century until the execution of the visionary Elizabeth Barton in 1534 is the near monopoly held by women writers.[122] If many fifteenth-century saints' lives in English are about

[120] For Love's dramatic sense of 'devout imagination', see Beadle, '"Devout ymaginacioun"'.

[121] For female reading and ownership of Love's work, see Meale, '"oft sithis with grete devotion"'.

[122] For the execution of the visionary Elizabeth Barton as part of the 1534 censorship campaign, see Devereux.

women, many of the visionary works translated into English in that century are *by* near-contemporary women, many of whom had themselves been canonized as saints. Translations into English from the pan-European phenomenon of late medieval female visionary writing were made in the fifteenth century, such as the *Revelations of Saint Birgitta*, and the *Liber Celestis* both by St Bridget of Sweden (1302–73),[123] the *Orchard of Syon*, by St Catherine of Siena (d. 1380); the *Revelations* of St Elizabeth of Hungary (1297–1338); and the *Booke of Ghostlye Grace* of Mechthild of Hackeborn (1241–98).

These works demonstrably appealed to a female readership: the works of Catherine of Siena and Bridget of Sweden listed here were, for example, translated in the first place for the Bridgettine nuns of Syon abbey, founded in 1415. The Rule of this community allowed the nuns 'as many [books] as they will' for the purposes of study;[124] the *Mirour of Oure Ladye*, written in prose for the Syon nuns between 1415 and 1450, gives specific directions on the selection of different kinds of book for different purposes and states of mind, and the ways in which they should be read (pp. 65–71).[125] Even if, however, this community of women readers formed a spiritual élite, the kind of works they read were indistinguishable from the reading matter of devout laywomen.[126] And even if devout laywomen like Margery Kempe (*c.*1373–*c.*1439) could not read, their broadly understood 'literacy' gave them access to a wide range of devotional matter, some of which was written by women.[127] Margery compares the quality of her intimacy with God favourably with that of other visionaries whose works she knows: 'sche herd nevyr boke, neythyr Hylton's book, ne Bridis boke, ne Stimulus Amoris, ne Incendium

123 For the late medieval apostolic women's movements, see Glasscoe, pp. 38–41 and further references. This book is also a general introduction to many of the writers discussed below.

124 Cited from Hutchison, p. 217.

125 Discussed in Hutchison.

126 See esp. Riddy, '"Women Talking about the Things of God"'; in the same volume see also Meale, '" . . . Alle the bokes that I have of latyn"'. Also Hutchison, and Erler.

127 For women's literacy in this period, see Boffey, 'Women Authors and Women's Literacy'. For a newly enlarged definition of literacy that is necessary in dealing with matter of this kind, see Aston, 'Devotional Literacy'. An excellent application of this broader definition can be found in Wogan-Browne, 'Apple's Message'.

Amoris, ne non other that evyr she herd redyn that spak so hyly of lofe of God' as her own conversations (bk. 1, ch. 17, p. 115).[128] At one point when her clerical scribe begins to disbelieve the authenticity of her visions and weeping, he is persuaded of their authority by reading the life of the visionary Mary of Oignies (d. 1213); the *Prick of Love*, *Incendium Amoris* of Richard Rolle (d. 1349); and the writings of Elizabeth of Hungary (1. 62, p. 296).[129]

Works of this kind deploy distinctive authenticating devices, characteristic of those who have been excluded from the processes of textual transmission to which clerical writers appeal. Whereas the male, clerical writers of saints' lives considered above appeal principally to textual and Latin sources that have survived the ravages of long stretches of time, these texts appeal to what has been seen immediately through inspiration. The representation of books within these visions itself implies the secondary status of material books; Bridget of Sweden, for example, has a vision of the Book of Life, which is, she is told, 'not write [written] as the scriptur that is and was nott, bot the scripture of this book is alway';[130] earlier she sees a book whose words speak, which speaking in turn becomes something seen: 'which boke, and the scriptur therof, was not write with ynke, bot ych worde in the boke was qwhik and spak itself . . . No man redde the scriptur of that boke, bot whatever that scriptur contened, all was see[n]'.[131] The words of God, which almost entirely constitute Bridget's own text, are fundamentally present: God repeatedly introduces his speeches with the words 'I am', insisting on his existential presence and accessibility.

Such visions in turn become the source of textual authority for male, clerical writers: Nicholas Love, for example, appeals to the *Revelations* of St Elizabeth of Hungary to authenticate his account of the Virgin's life between the ages of 3 and 14, since the Virgin herself relates her biography to Elizabeth in that work.[132] Certainly, then,

[128] For further references to St Bridget, see bk. 1, chs. 20 and 58.

[129] Some of the works to which Margery refers here became available in English translations: for Mary of Oignies, see 'Life of Mary of Oignies', in Horstmann (ed.), 'Prosalegenden', pp. 134–84. For the English trans. (*c.*1370–1400) of the *Stimulum Amoris*, see *Prickynge of Love*, ed. Kane. For Elizabeth of Hungary, see *The Two Middle English Translations of the Revelations*, ed. McNamer.

[130] St Bridget of Sweden, *The Revelations*, ed. Cumming, p. 86.

[131] Ibid. p. 68. [132] Nicholas Love, *Mirror*, p. 18.

women write out of repressive conditions, without access to the legitimating resources of a Latinate and text-derived culture; for all that, these women writers discover non-textual routes into areas of high textual authority, as can be seen in Figure 9, where St Bridget writes not out of books, but rather from direct vision. By way of completing this discussion of vernacular visionary writing, I turn to two East Anglian visionaries: the first known woman writer in the English vernacular, the remarkable Julian of Norwich (*c.*1343–after 1416), and her slightly younger contemporary, the first writer of autiobiography in English, the no less remarkable Margery Kempe of Lynn. In both cases I argue that reliance on a visionary mode at the same time negotiates the obstacles of clerical culture and creates new textual communities.

Julian experienced her visions in 1373, at the age of about 30, before the arrival in England of the works of Bridget of Sweden, Catherine of Siena, and Mechthild of Hackeborn from the 1390s.[133] The record of her revelations exists in two prose versions, one considerably shorter than the other. The shorter version has been assumed until recently to have been written in 1373, and the longer version some twenty years later, after Julian had meditated on the meaning of the visions; it has been argued that the dating should be set to a slightly later period (1380s and *c.*1415), which makes better sense of Julian's cautious comments about her orthodoxy.[134] Whatever the precise historical context of Julian's writing, she is extraordinarily conscious of the fragility of her claims to textual authority. She calls herself 'unlettered'; she makes no textual references at all, except to the story of St Cecilia she heard told in church;[135] and, particularly in the shorter text, she insistently acknowledges the authority of 'Holy Church'. Julian exploits, however, these very disclaimers to insist on an extraordinary, alternative authority. Early in the shorter text she pauses to disclaim any status

[133] For the arrival of work by Continental women visionaries, see Watson, 'Composition', p. 653. For a bibliographical survey of studies on Julian, see von Nolcken, 'Julian of Norwich'.

[134] Watson, 'Composition'.

[135] Julian of Norwich, *A Book of Showings*, ed. Colledge and Walsh, 1. 204–5. All further references will be to this edn., and will be made in the body of the text, by part and page number. References to pt. 1 are to the shorter version, and to pt. 2 to the longer version.

Fig. 9. St Bridget receiving her Revelations. *Dietary of Gostly Helth* (1520).

as a teacher: 'for I meene nought soo, no I mente nevere so; for I am a womann, leued [ignorant], febille and freylle'. No sooner has she made this disclaimer, however, does she turn it to her advantage, by immediately going on to claim divine authority: 'Botte I wate [know] wele, this that I saye, I hafe it of the shewynge of hym that es soverayne techare' (I. 222).

This strategy of capitalizing on her very weaknesses to generate astonishing strengths applies in many ways to the *Showings*, but nowhere more insistently than in the matter of seeing. As I suggested above, throughout the period of this history the visual is characterized as the realm of the unlearned because it is restricted to the corporal and fleshly. The visual is deployed in official religious practice to provoke powerful feelings of devotional piety and penitential regret, but precisely as such it precludes abstract thinking. Julian herself appears to accept these strictures, and to underline the consistency of her practice within the experiential limits established by the *Meditationes Vitae Christi* (Love's Latin source, to which Julian must surely have had access).[136] Already at the very beginning of the shorter version she declares her desire to have been present at the Crucifixion with Mary Magdalene and 'othere that were Crystes loverse, that I myght have sene bodylye the passion of oure lorde that he sufferede for me' (I. 201–2). Determination not to exceed the bounds of the experiential and the visual even threatens to become a kind of disobedience: at one point Julian has a 'profyr' in her reason, 'as yf it hadde beene frendlye'. This voice commands Julian to look up from the Cross to God the Father in heaven. She intuits that there is nothing between the Cross and heaven that would impede her vision of the presumably abstract essence of the Godhead. Despite this, she refuses to look up, so apparently refusing to obey God himself: 'Naye, I may nought, for thowe erte myne heven'. Her rationale for this steadiness of visual focus on the corporal presence of Christ is a feeling of security in corporality: 'I wyste wele whilys I lokyd upponn the crosse I was sekyr [secure] and safe' (I. 236). On the face of it this statement refers to Julian's feeling of psychic protectedness within her vision, but it is also a 'political' statement: Julian is 'safe' from persecution in the increasingly dangerous atmo-

[136] For the influence of the *Meditationes* in 15th-cent. visionary writing, see Despres.

sphere of official persecution from the early 1380s as long as she keeps her head down, as it were, looking at the earthbound and wounded image of the crucified Christ and not presuming to 'look' at God's transcendent being.

Within the security of this corporal vision, Julian does in fact 'see' abstract ideas, but even here she refuses to distinguish the abstract from the corporal: both are things 'seen'. The first sequence of the revelations begins with a crucifix being proferred her at what she thinks is the moment of her death; the vision proper begins as this image suddenly moves, and Julian sees the 'rede blode trekylle downe fro undyr the garlande, alle hate [hot], freschlye, plentefully and lyvelye' (1. 210). Concurrent with this bodily sight Julian sees a 'gastelye [spiritual] sight'. She 'sees' that Christ is our clothing, since love 'wappes us and wyndes us, halses us and alle be teches us. ('encloses us, encircles us, embraces us and guides us'). *Within* this vision she sees a little thing no larger than a hazelnut, lying in the palm of her hand, which might easily fall; she is told that it is all that is made. Here, too, she 'sees' that God made it, that he loves it, and that he 'kepes' or protects it. The penultimate sequence of the revelation is a vision of the Virgin, who, Julian 'sees', is of greater worth than all other things that God made. The final sequence, concurrent with all the rest, is the bodily sight of the copiously bleeding head of Christ (1. 207–17).

This vision is in fact rigorously analytical, hierarchizing as it does all creation within a scale of createdness, and readily recognizing the unsettling fragility of that created universe, which must be 'noughted' by those who desire access to the transcendence of God. Julian, however, resists the potential intellectual violence of this vision, since she refuses to 'nought' the created universe, seeing instead that it is loved and preserved by God precisely by virtue of its createdness. This refusal to 'nought', or destroy, the material turns out to be an undoing of conceptual hierarchy: Julian concludes the first vision by listing what she 'saw', juxtaposing corporal sights and concepts.[137] She both 'sees', for example, the wounded Christ, all creation, and the fact that God loves and preserves his creation. The list is an analysis that undoes analysis, since the physical sights have

[137] The most penetrating discussion of Julian's exegetical modes is Watson, 'Trinitarian Hermeneutic'.

no lesser status as things 'seen' than the meanings those sights show forth. As she says about a later vision in the longer text, she is incapable of separating the meanings of the revelation from 'the hole revelation fro the begynnyng to the ende' (2. 520). Even words themselves are things seen. In the sixteenth revelation of the longer text, she relates that God revealed words that disown the immaterial properties of words: 'then shewed oure good lorde wordes fulle mekely, without voyce and without openyng of lyppes' (2. 645–6).

As many scholars have argued, Julian does not in fact rely heavily on the image of the wounded Christ, and her habit of mind is just as insistently analytical as it is resistant to analysis. Out of this tension arises a theology whose sometimes radical conclusions are inseparable from its serenity.[138] Although Julian clearly exploits a 'devotional', vernacular, feminine position to produce a deeply considered theology, it would, however, be a mistake to drive too deep a wedge between Julian's visionary practice and that of, say, Love's *Mirror*: Julian's theology does not merely exploit the visual; as a fully incarnational theology that finally refuses to separate flesh and spirit it is grounded in the visual. Julian is rather accepting the liberal invitation of the tradition to which Love's text belongs. The fact that Love so insistently shepherds his text to keep it within the bounds of the emotional and the domestic itself implies that these very visual experiences invite a range of more challenging responses.

Julian's envisioned theology also creates a new textual community. Out of the very discursive weakness of her position as a women writer, dependent on the seen rather than the read, she implies a body of readers whose communal authority is no greater or less than her own. Towards the end of the revelations in both texts Julian reports that after the penultimate vision, in embarrassment and shame, she dismissed her visions as 'ravings' to the priest at her bedside, certain that he would not believe her (1. 266, 2. 633). Christ answers these doubts, sitting in Julian's soul as in the middle of a city, which is at once his 'hamelyeste hame', and restoring her by promising that she 'schalle nought be overcomenn' (1. 268–9). The political and domestic location of this vision implies that Julian will not be overcome in the social and political world to which her visions are

[138] See Aers and Staley, ch. 3.

consistently addressed. From the first vision that address is made precisely by way of both undoing and establishing her own discursive authority. After the concluding analysis of that vision she turns to the question of its status, in answer to which she evokes her community of readers by claiming and disclaiming propriety over her vision: 'Alle that I sawe of my selfe, I meene in the persone of alle myne evynn cristene [my fellow Christians], for I am lernede in the gastlye schewynge of oure lorde that he meenys so' (1. 219). The very syntax of this sentence proffers, only to withdraw, the singularity of Julian's status: Julian saw it herself, and she is instructed by God, but that 'self' is immediately reformulated to include all her fellow Christians, just as what she learns from God is precisely that her learning is common. Julian is acutely aware of the ontological implications of this claim: the vision is, she says, 'comonn and generale as we ar alle ane, and I am sekere [certain] I sawe it for the profytte of many oder'(1. 220). The very acknowledgement of weakness again turns into a reformulated, communal account of strength: her weakness is no greater than everyone's, just as her strength consists in her fundamental identity with her potential readers: 'in generalle', she says, 'I am in anehede [unity] of charyte with alle myne evynn cristene' (1. 220). The ostensibly unlettered act of seeing the divine implies for Julian no less than an ontology of communal reading and writing, in which her readers participate in the construction of a book that is begun, 'but . . . not yet performyd' (2. 731).

Whereas Julian's inclusive vision implicates all her 'evene christians' as both her audience and co-visionaries, the survival of her work is in fact very fragile. Only one manuscript of the shorter version, written in the middle of the fifteenth century, survives; the three full witnesses of the longer text were produced by recusant communities in the seventeenth century.[139]

By around 1413, however, when Julian was an enclosed anchoress in Norwich, she was clearly a person to whom an entirely lay woman could successfully appeal for authoritative confirmation of authentic spiritual experience. Margery Kempe of Lynn, a wife, mother of fourteen children, and a failed brewer, visited Julian at about this time to assure herself that there was no deception in her visions.

[139] See Julian of Norwich, *A Book of Showings*, ed. Colledge and Walsh, 1. 1–10.

Unlike many of Margery's modern religious readers, Julian is calmly confident of the authenticity of Margery's experience. Because Margery's text appears, unlike Julian's, so unintellectual and so unstrategic, it has fallen victim to 'experts' who either dismiss it as not authentically mystical, and/or redescribe it as symptomatic of psychological hysteria.[140] While I cannot help myself feeling a perhaps condescending sympathy for Margery as she practises her exhausting *thérapie par l'espace*, in the brief discussion that follows I read her work as Hoccleve wished his readers would read the *Series*, not as a symptom whose diagnosis confirms the technical mastery of the reader, but in a rather more friendly way as the revealing expression of suffering and its therapy.[141]

Like her contemporary Hoccleve, Margery relies on images to reconstitute her relation to her world, and in so doing she begins to reconstitute that world. The *Book of Margery Kempe* was finally written, after a complex and obstructed scribal history, about 1438 by a priest acting for Margery, who could not herself write. Whereas Julian begins from powerful corporal sights as a way of positioning herself always to 'see' deeper, more abstract visions, Margery takes literally directions of the kind made by Love to lay readers to make themselves present in, and to re-enact, biblical scenes.

In chapters 78–81 of Book 1, for example, Margery describes how she would see the liturgical ceremonies of Easter Week; she brings each liturgical gesture to life to create an entire pictorial and dramatic sequence of the week, from Palm Sunday to the resurrected Christ's meeting with Mary Magdalene. These scenes together constitute an astonishingly vivid and powerful set of speaking *tableaux vivants*, drawn either from the theatrical mystery cycles and/or from sequences of painting, examples of which Margery would almost certainly have seen in her pilgrimage to Italy, which included a visit to Assisi. She accompanies the Virgin, for example, to the Mount of Olives, and there witnesses exactly the dramatically charged scenes of arrest of the kind painted by Giotto and Duccio:

And than com a gret multitude of pepil wyth meche lyght and many armyd men wyth stavys, swerdys, and polexis to sekyn owr Lord Jhesu Crist, owr

[140] For the squeamish and fastidious reception of Margery Kempe, see Hirsch.

[141] The citation is drawn from P. Brown, p. 87.

merciful Lord as a meke lombe seying onto hem: 'Whom seke ye?' Thei answeryd wyth a scharp spiryt, 'Jhesu of Nazareth'. Owr Lord seyd ayen, 'Ego sum' (I. 79, p. 343).

Margery deploys the imagination not so much to foreshorten historical distance as to traverse it altogether. In this she is not naïve; on the contrary, she is simply experiencing biblical texts within the single level of interpretation, the moral, to which she as a lay person should, by Love's account at any rate, restrict herself.

Julian's exegesis of her vision of the lord and servant moves between the historical, the allegorical, and the moral (or tropological) levels of interpretation.[142] Margery, by contrast, remains within the moral level, the whole point of which is to efface historical distance, and to render the historical event in as immediate and morally relevant a way as possible. In Norwich, for example, she sees a *pietà*, an image of the Virgin cradling Christ on her lap after the Deposition. In response to Margery's sudden burst of tears at this sight, the priest of the church tells her that 'Ihesu is ded long sithyn [since]'. Margery's reply rebukes the priest by restating the fundamental injunction of tropological interpretation: 'Sir, hys deth is as fresch to me as he had deyd this same day, and so me thynkyth it awt to be to yow and to alle Cristen pepil. We awt evyr to han mende [mind] of hys kendnes and evyr thynkyn of the dolful [painful] deth that he deyd for us' (I. 60, p. 150).

Margery's 'reading' within the affective, moral level is so intense as to revivify and in part reconstitute the social and political world she inhabits. As we have seen, Lollard writers insist that imagistic metonymies should be restricted to apply between humans, the only true 'images' of God, and God himself. For Margery, by contrast, the rich stock of material images she has encountered constantly feeds into and sensitizes her vision of humanity. Whenever, she tells us, she saw a wounded man or animal, or a man beating a child or whipping a horse, she 'thowt sche saw owyr Lord be betyn er [or] wowndyd lyk as sche saw in the man er in the best' (I. 28, p. 69). This often spectacular sensitivity affects and in part readjusts the repressive ecclesiastical world she inhabits. Christ himself tells Margery

142 The simplest introduction to the vast topic of fourfold exegesis is Thomas Aquinas, *Summa Theologiae*, ed. Gilby, I. 36–41, and Ch. 9 below.

both that he is pleased that she is obedient to the Church, and that, since he is above the Church, she should disregard ecclesiastical absolution from going on pilgrimage and go to Rome and Compostela (I. 72–3, pp. 320–4). Five times she is accused, and twice formally arraigned for heresy, threatened in each case with burning.[143] In each of these dangerous encounters Margery, who courageously plays the role of Christ before Pilate and Herod, capitalizes on her position as both obedient to the Church and as somehow above it. By criticizing the Archbishops of both Canterbury and York in what turn out to be interviews from which she escapes without punishment, she lays successful claim, in the presence of the very sources of repression, to an authoritative lay spirituality. Even if we were not to credit the details of her own account of these interviews, the very existence of her book makes the same claim.

The most powerful way in which Margery reconstitutes the social world is, however, in her recapitulation of the lives of women saints. It is revealing that the first autobiography in English should generate itself on the model of the 'lives' of saints, and especially of women saints, whose exemplary suffering produces a coherent biographical narrative. Those lives preserve patriarchal models, of, for example, marriage to Christ, only by the most strenuous rejection of those same models in the material world. Margery relives this aspect of the saint's life: like Sts Cecilia and Elizabeth of Hungary, she negotiates a celibate life with her husband; Margery chooses to do this on Midsummer Eve, the day reserved for feminine disruption (I. 11).[144] This results in her marriage with Christ in the presence of a crowd of divine sponsors including Sts Katherine and Margaret (I. 35, p. 87), and the scene of Christ's promise of wedded, sensual intimacy with Margery (I. 36, p. 90). Margery's 'life' is thus generated out of precisely the structural tension that produces a saint's biography: the community of heaven is constructed on the model of, yet serves to critique, the rejected secular community.[145]

Precisely because Margery's life is so rooted in a very specific if

[143] See I. 13 (Canterbury), I. 16 (Lambeth), and I. 47–9 (Leicester, *c.*1417), I. 52 (York); I. 53 (Hessle).

[144] For the feminine disruption of Midsummer Eve, see e.g. William Dunbar's *Tretis of the Twa Mariit Wemen and the Wedo*, l. 1.

[145] For a sharp definition of this model that nevertheless argues that Kempe's practice can never break the 'mould of . . . submission', see Beckwith.

largely hostile social world, her imagination of the heavenly alternative is all the more passionate and socially precise. This newly formed spiritual community is also fundamentally feminine in structure: at one point Christ thanks Margery for her generosity in offering her soul as the space for *sacra conversazione*: Christ is there in Mary's arms, who suckles him; she is welcomed by Mary Magdalene, since she mediates most powerfully for Margery, and by the whole court of heaven. This court is both welcoming and welcomed, and is dominated by the suffering women saints, Katherine, Margaret, and 'alle holy virginys, that . . . shulde arayn the chawmbre of thi soule wyth many fayr flowerys and wyth many swete spicys that I [Christ] myth restyn therin' (1. 86, p. 210).

Margery also relives the textual history of the lives of the saints. After the death of Bokenham's St Margaret, the textual history of her life into the English vernacular involves, as we have seen, wearisome traversings of space, time, and language, from the East to a final resting place in England. Margery recapitulates both the journeys and the difficult textual history. Like Bokenham later she worries that her writing is taking her away from the proper business of penitential prayer, only to be answered by Christ that he is well pleased with her participation in the arduous business of writing her life (1. 88, pp. 379–82). Just as saints' lives must be translated across many languages, Margery's life must be passed from her oral account first to a German-speaking scribe whose English is near incomprehensible, before it can be retranslated, with great difficulty and only aided by divine grace, by another priest. The single copy of the whole book that survives, only discovered in 1934, is written by another scribe.[146]

The most remarkable thing about Margery's life, however, is the long and arduous pilgrimages that produce extended narratives of rejection by humans and welcome approval by the court of heaven. Between 1413 and 1415 she travelled to Jerusalem via Rome; in 1417 to Santiago; and in 1433–4 at the age of about 60 and with very little means of support she set off to Danzig via Norway, returning via pilgrimage sites in Pomerania and at Aachen. The lives of the women saints, as we have seen, come into focus as they destroy the

[146] For a lucid account of the writing of Margery's work, see Boffey, 'Women Authors and Women's Literacy', pp. 162–3. For a penetrating theoretical account of Margery's status as writer, see Lochrie.

icons of the paternal order and thereby create the conditions for their own iconization and translation. Margery's own life is produced by reversing the movement of this translation: she takes herself across exhausting terrain back to the site of the saint, where she dramatically enters a past triggered by relics or images, and often becomes a relic of sorts herself, by being left behind by her fellow travellers. Margery's own arduous entry into the privileged world of textuality is premissed on her readiness of access to the non-textual world of the seen and experienced. The exemplary suffering of her own life is an unfolding of the suffering implicit in images.

In his *Confutation of Tyndale's Answer* (1532), Thomas More hankers after an age of innocence, in which English lay readers were unbothered either by the works of 'heretics' or of their respondents. Instead, he advises them to read what he takes to be classics of the devotional tradition in English, which are also in conformity with 'the catholike faithe of thys 1500 yere'. The unlearned should be reading 'suche englishe bookes as moste may noryshe and encreace devocion. Of which kind is Bonaventure of the lyfe of Christe, Gerson of the folowyng of Christ and the devoute contemplative booke of Scala perfectionis' (pref., pt. 1, 37). The works to which More refers here are, respectively: Love's translation of the *Meditationes Vitae Christi*, the original of which was once ascribed to the thirteenth-century Parisian theologian Bonaventure (*c.*1217–74), but which was in fact written *c.*1350–80; the *Imitation of Christ*, often ascribed to the Parisian theologian Jean Gerson (1363–1429), and now ascribed to the Netherlandish canon regular Thomas à Kempis (1379–1471); and the *Scale of Perfection* by Walter Hilton (d. 1396), canon of the Augustinian priory of Thurgarton in Nottinghamshire. More's account of that vernacular tradition is misleading in one respect. Certainly Love's work had been printed by Caxton in 1486, and had been taken up by both Pynson and de Worde, the latter of whom issued it four times between 1500 and 1530. De Worde printed the *Scale* in 1494 at the request of Lady Margaret Beaufort, and the work was reissued four more times before 1533.[147]

[147] In 1501 de Worde also printed a summary version of the *Book of Margery Kempe* (*RSTC* 14924). For the printing of visionary writing produced earlier in the 14th and in the 15th cents., see Keiser, 'Mystics and Early English Printers'.

The *Imitation of Christ*, however, had had a very restricted circulation before its first printing in 1502. Why was this so, and why did the *Imitation*, alone among pre-Reformation vernacular works and translations, survive the 1530s in non-recusant circles?[148]

From the late fourteenth century at least some clerical vernacular writers express a deep distrust of the imaginative affectivity of vernacular visionary and devotional writing. The author of the late fourteenth-century *Cloud of Unknowing*, for example, attacks as no less than heretical those false contemplatives who are 'enflaumid with an unkyndely hete of compleccion' (p. 86), which must be a critique of the kind of bodily and intensely affective spirituality shaped by Richard Rolle (d. 1349).[149] Evangelical polemicists dismissed the whole culture of affective devotion as, in the words of Thomas Cranmer (1489–1556), an expression of 'all manner of superstition and idolatry'; its corrupt tendency to worship creatures is found especially in 'fond women, which commonly follow superstition rather than true religion'.[150] Within that environment specific visionary works by women are, for example, dismissed as 'the ravings of a little woman' (Bale's descripton of Bridget of Sweden's *Revelations*).[151] This tradition is alive in the twentieth century, and has shaped reception of Margery Kempe in particular. Referring to works like the *Cloud* as contributing to a 'stream of pure spirituality', David Knowles argued that from the early fifteenth century this stream was 'contaminated' by 'a more emotional and idiosyncratic devotion manifesting itself in visions, revelations and unusual behaviour'. For Knowles this contaminating current is entirely feminine, produced by women saints like Bridget of Sweden, and expressed most fully in England by Margery Kempe.[152]

As exemplified by the *Cloud of Unknowing* at any rate, Knowles's tradition of 'pure spirituality' is austere and radically hostile both to images and the imagination. The *Cloud*-author's spirituality places

148 For the narrow circulation of the *Imitation of Christ* in the 15th cent., see Lovatt, '*Imitation of Christ*'. See also Sargent, 'Minor Devotional Writings'.

149 For the hostility to visionary experience in the late fourteenth century, see Watson, 'Composition', pp. 646–8. For a bibliographical introduction to the *Cloud*-author and an account of the other tracts he wrote, see Minnis, '*Cloud of Unknowing*'.

150 Cranmer, *Miscellaneous Writings and Letters*, p. 179.

151 See Bridget of Sweden, *Revelations*, ed. Cumming, p. xxix.

152 Knowles, 2. 222–3.

God's transcendence at its centre, and subjects the world of created things and language to the desconstructive pressure of that immaterial transcendence. The only certainty offered by language and images is that they must fail to gain access to God, and so should be used, if at all, only to be broken in recognition of their inadequacy.[153] The *Cloud*-author's hostility to images is epistemological rather than theological, but it amounts to a kind of interior iconoclasm, since the true contemplative is to undo the very processes of both imagination and thought in the psyche, by way of approaching purest being. Whereas Julian refuses to exercise the intellectual violence of 'noughting' the world, the *Cloud*-author's contemplative is to 'distroie this nakid wetyng [knowing] and felyng of thin owen beyng' (p. 83). The radically philosophical, ahistorical nature of the *Cloud*-author's God produces a correlatively elitist text, which is directed to a 'privy' audience of single persons, who must read the work in order from beginning to end.[154] In keeping with its elitist posture, it lays all power in the hands of God's grace: knowledge of God is granted by God to whatever soul he wishes to grant it, 'withoutyn any deseert of the same soule' (p. 69).

The *Cloud* survives in seventeen manuscripts, some of which were connected to Carthusian houses in both Yorkshire and London.[155] Carthusian environments probably also produced the first translation of the *Imitation of Christ* in the mid-fifteenth century; a second translation was printed by Pynson in 1503, and a third translation, possibly by Richard Whitford, a Bridgettine monk of Syon abbey, was printed in 1531.[156] The first translation circulated in a very small group of readers within the Bridgettines and the Carthusians.[157] The heroic resistance of Bridgettine and Carthusian monks from Syon abbey and Sheen to Henry VIII's claim to the headship of the Church

[153] For an example of the *Cloud*-author's aggression towards the imagination, see *Cloud of Unknowing*, ed. Hodgson, pp. 22–3. It is no paradox that his use of language is imaginative, since he uses images in order to break them; see J. A. Burrow, 'Fantasy and Language'.

[154] Ibid. 1–2 (for reading directions in the *Cloud*), and 135 (*Book of Privy Counselling*).

[155] For the seventeen MSS of the *Cloud*, see ibid. pp. ix–xxvi.

[156] For the first translation, see Thomas à Kempis, *Imitation of Christ*, ed. Biggs. See *RSTC* 23954.7 for Pynson's edn. of 1503, and *RSTC* 23961 for the first printing of Whitford's translation.

[157] Lovatt, '*Imitation of Christ*', p. 114.

of England is well known. That resistance is not without its historical ironies: the religious houses from which these men came were founded by Henry V by way of harnessing powerful monastic foundations to royal interests; furthermore, the very spirituality of these houses, austere and isolating as it was, was not out of keeping with evangelical spirituality. The *Imitation* was popular from its printing of 1503, of which eight reprints were made up to 1528, but its popularity remained undiminished across the 1530s and well beyond: Whitford's own translation was reprinted twelve times up to 1585, and competed with other translations throughout the sixteenth century.[158] More's statement that the *Imitatio* was a classic of vernacular spirituality is incorrect: unlike the other two books mentioned by More, the *Imitatio* expresses a chaste, austere, and largely imageless spirituality; it enjoyed no popularity until the arrival in England of the *devotio moderna*.[159] This chaste spirituality, with its generally chaste prose, is also found in More's own *Dialogue of Comfort* written in the Tower in 1535 as More awaited execution.

Paradoxically, More's own chaste and Carthusian spirituality itself converges with its evangelical enemy. Certainly by the mid-sixteenth century evangelical authors were deploying the works of Erasmus, More's friend and exponent of 'Christian humanism', on the side of an imageless spirituality.[160] For More, as for his ostensible enemy John Ryckes, the author of the *Ymage of Love* (1525), the truest account of God is imageless.

IV

The topic of religious lyrics is far too large to cover in any detail here.[161] I focus on some characteristic and not-so-characteristic examples by Lydgate that demonstrate not only that lyrics work wholly within traditions of the lay-directed, affective image

[158] For the fifty-one editions between 1503 and 1639, see *RSTC* 23954.7–23993.

[159] For which see McConica.

[160] See e.g. *A dialogue . . . of two persones . . . intituled the pilgremage of pure devotyon* (*RSTC* 10454).

[161] The best accounts, for both variety and function, are Woolf, and D. Gray, *Themes and Images*.

described above, but also that these very traditions absorb the lives of the learned.

Lydgate wrote many such lyrics, and he often provides the directions by which they should be read. To the text of one direct, dramatic address by Christ from the Cross, for example, is appended an envoi that instructs the poem to have itself hung 'affore Iesu', and to have each passer-by read it once a day.[162] In another work Lydgate has the authorial voice represented as a reader, whose meditative reading produces a new work. During a wakeful night, the author opens a 'contemplatiff' book; s/he turns the leaves randomly and comes across an image of the *pietà*. Admiring the paintwork, which 'by crafft was agreeable', the reading author also observes how grief-stricken the Virgin is. Reading further, 'by aventure', s/he also begins to read the text, and, finding it 'dyd myn herte good', 'took a penne, and wrott in my manere | The said balladys, as they stondyn heere', after which we read the newly translated text.[163] This subtle account of the interaction of personal grief, imagistic therapy, and writerly activity has it that images create an author's work from an author's own 'peyne'. Another set of reading instructions within a *pietà* poem also expresses how personal biography is activated by focusing on images and on text that becomes image. If the passer-by is moved by the image she or he is to run to a priest and confess; after this experience, the viewer is to 'enprynt thes wordes myndly thy hert wythin', and 'thynk how thow seest Cryst bledyng on the tree'. The short poem ends with a defence of images, arguing that they arrest us in such a way that 'holsom storyes thus shewyd in fygur | May rest with us with dewe remembraunce'.[164] That remembrance is not only of the historical narrative depicted, but also of the viewer's own moral history.

Texts of this kind have been taken as exemplary of the impersonal posture of medieval authorship: the 'I' of such texts is deliberately undifferentiated so as to allow anyone to occupy its position, and so we should not read such texts, it has been argued, as expressions of personal feeling, but rather as exercises for any reader to use.[165] In

162 Lydgate, *Minor Poems*, pt. 1, no. 42, p. 221.
163 Ibid., no. 51, p. 269.
164 Ibid., *Minor Poems*, no. 62, pp. 297–9.
165 Thus Woolf, pp. 5–8.

conclusion to this whole chapter, I turn to one final 'moving image', that of Lydgate's *Testament*, by way of arguing that Lydgate identifies his 'will' wholly with this ostensibly naïve tradition, in such a way as both to evoke and efface an entire life in an image. Whereas Margery Kempe unfolds her life out of sacral images, Lydgate folds his life back into an image. And whereas Margery enters the world of textuality from her experience of images, the learned Lydgate's *Testament* seeks to undo its own documentary status by bringing an image to life.

The *Testament* (?1449) presents itself as a complex document, inserted into an intensely documentary, textual culture. It models itself on the testament, or 'laste wille', appointing Jesus to be 'chief surveiour', or executor (l. 211).[166] The debts that the testator must pay are, however, moral debts, and in this discursive environment the document of the 'last wille' is directed to a further trial in which texts will be necessary. Lydgate must make a 'reckenyng'; without the support of Jesus, he will be drawn into the devil's 'danger', or jurisdiction, by 'overstreite audite' (l. 222). Thinking on his past life, personifications of Remembrance and Regret come to his bed, and present him with 'a wooful bille' of his past sins (ll. 262–75). His hope rests in the 'document' of the crucifixion, with which Christ paid for the ransom of humanity, 'sealed with five woundes' (l. 69), a document that Lydgate wishes scarified on his own heart: he wishes Jesus to enter his heart, 'more nere than my sherte | With aureat letres, grave there in substaunce' (ll. 507–8), or he desires that the word 'Jesus' be imprinted at the centre of his psyche, 'in length and brede like a large wounde' (l. 594). The very name 'Ihesus' is itself textualized, whereby each letter serves as a cue for a historical and moral reading of Christ (ll. 169–192).

Surrounded by texts as he is, Lydgate writes his own document, which is very self-conscious of its documentary status. The text is made up of five movements, which deploy rhyme-royal for the two narrative sequences and an octave stanza form for petitionary and declarative passages. One sequence has each stanza introduced by, and liberally translate, a line of address from the Psalms, in Latin. The very dividedness of this text declares its documentary status, but

[166] Lydgate, *Minor Poems*, pt. 1, no. 68. The *Testament* was printed by Pynson in ?1520, *RSTC* 17035.

it also implies a problem of narrative. This is a text that cannot really begin, since Lydgate himself is broken; he describes himself as a 'broken house' and a 'reven cheste' (ll. 553–4); whereas the standard testament speaks from a stable discursive position, grounded in a first-person voice, this testament cannot generate consistent biographical narrative without at once provoking the need for intercession. Even the opening formula of a will, in which the testator is named, here gives way to an extended reflection on the name of Jesus.[167] More than once does the text begin, promising 'to write a trites [treatise] of surfetes' at line 238, only to mark the real beginning with a cross at line 418. The two sequences of biographical narrative cannot consitute the required document, since their record of scholarly indolence and wilfulness merely underlines the need for a different kind of document, in which Christ deletes Lydgate's biography.

That document is indeed produced as the final sequence of this complex collage; this 'document' not only undoes the past, but undoes the very documentary culture within which the poem situates itself. In the penultimate sequence Lydgate describes his education, and especially underlines his lack of application in learning to read and in committing himself to his monastic profession. He was, he says, like the 'image of Pygmaleon, | Shewed lyfly, and was made but of ston' (ll. 696–7). The final sequence, however, effectively does away with reading altogether as the central biographical experience, and institutes the visual in its place. Lydgate remembers a crucifix he saw when he was 15, 'myd of a cloyster, depicte upon a wall' (l. 743), beside which was written the one word '*vide* [Behold!]'. Only now, in his 'last age', does Lydgate understand the 'sentence' or meaning of this experience, and so he begins his text again, for the last time. This final act of writing returns to a visual experience of childhood, since Christ speaks from the Cross, in what could have been an independent lyric, and recounts his own passion narrative as something seen and present: almost every sentence begins with Christ's command to 'behold' or 'see'. The fact that Christ himself speaks the final sequence of the 'last wille' implies that Lydgate's own life has been absorbed by Christ's; and the fact that Christ is made visually present

[167] For literary versions of the will or testament in this period, see Boffey, 'Lydgate, Henryson, and the Literary Testament'.

implies both that the recounting of Lydgate's past has become redundant, and that the documentary status of his text is entirely overborne by the dramatic, present, *seen* experience of the 'popular' image.[168]

The destruction of images from 1538, then, was equally an attack on various forms of community. Not only did such iconoclasm attack lay bequest of images that developed especially from the fourteenth century, whereby donors would leave a residue of their own memory in sacral images; it also attacked participation in, and creation of, new bodies of writers and readers, particularly women, who claimed access to the privileged realm of textuality via the direct and dramatic experience of the visual. That iconoclastic campaign also consigned the visual to the realm of the dangerous and seductive. Whereas fifteenth-century learned writers had acknowledged the power and even primacy of the ostensibly naïve realm of the visual, from the sixteenth century the visual became rigidly 'popular', from which it quickly became the realm of 'superstition' and 'idolatry'.

[168] Sections of Lydgate's poem became, in turn, themselves a visual image, painted as they were in the Clopton chantry chapel at Holy Trinity church, Long Melford, Suffolk. See Trapp, 'Verses by Lydgate'.

9

The Biblical

John Foxe movingly narrated the life and death of William Tyndale (*c.*1494–1536), an 'Apostle of England', in his *Acts and Monuments* (1563). After the account of Tyndale's strangulation and burning, Foxe says that it would take too long to recite 'the worthy virtues and doings of this blessed martyr', but he does permit himself one 'miracle' narrative. Resident in Antwerp, Tyndale asked to attend a dinner party at which a conjuror had been employed to perform tricks; 'through his diabolical enchantments of art magical', this magician would 'fetch all kinds of viands and wine from any place . . . and set them upon the table'. In the presence of Tyndale, however, the juggler's work goes for naught: 'At last, with his labour, sweating and toiling, when he saw that nothing would go forward, but that all his enchantments were void, he was compelled openly to confess, that there was some man present at supper, who disturbed and letted [hindered] all his doings' (5. 129). Immediately after this miracle story, Foxe turns to Tyndale's books, and especially his translation of the New Testament. In answer to his many enemies with their 'slanderous tongues and lying lips', Tyndale responded with 'faithful dealing and sincere conscience', declaring, for example, that he never altered 'one syllable of God's word against my conscience'. The books are no less sincere and straight dealing than the man: just as Tyndale's translated Bible neutralized the juggling enchantments of the popish clergy, so the story implies, so too did the very presence and unfeigned simplicity of his person undo the conjuror's 'diabolical enchantments'. Tyndale was a simple, entirely readable man, just as he produced a simple, entirely readable text.

Simplicity, indeed, is the leitmotif of Foxe's entire account of

Tyndale. In his early career Tyndale attempted to persuade his patrons and their clerical guests 'simply and plainly'. When checked, he would 'lay plainly before them the open and manifest places of the Scriptures'. By the premature end of his career he had lost none of this simplicity, despite the fact that it exposed him. One Henry Philips, a hypocrite pretending friendship to entrap him, had no difficulty insinuating himself into Tyndale's confidence. The imperial soldiers commissioned to arrest Tyndale 'pitied to see his simplicity when they took him' (5. 123). Above all, the texts that Tyndale himself translated and wrote were themselves simple texts designed for simple people. Whereas, in the manner of the hapless conjuror, the 'pharisaical clergy' did all they could to blind simple readers to biblical truth, Tyndale opened up the plain text. The clergy would, by 'juggling with the text', 'darken the right sense with the mist of their sophistry, and so entangle those who rebuked or despised their abominations . . . and . . . would so delude them in descanting upon it with allegories, and amaze them, expounding it in many senses laid before the unlearned lay people, that . . . [thou] couldst . . . not solve their subtle riddles' (5. 118–19). Tyndale cuts through this web of deceit by turning Scripture 'into the vulgar speech, that the poor people might also read and see the simple plain word of God' (5. 118).

Praise of textual simplicity was equally praise of the literal sense of Scripture as its *only* sense, a point with a long history of Protestant polemic ahead of it. Foxe's account of clerical sophistry 'descanting upon [Scripture] with allegories' was in fact drawn from Tyndale's own prose, in a passage where Tyndale had himself insisted that Scripture 'hath but one simple, literal sense, whose light the owls cannot abide'.[1] Throughout his prefaces Tyndale warns his reader to 'beware of subtle allegories',[2] since allegory is the surest tool the clergy can wield to preserve their own power over and possession of Scripture. 'Here a man had need to put on all his spectacles, and to arm himself against invisible spirits', he says about 'false allegories': they can prove nothing, and are useful only as a teaching device, used to 'declare and open a text', by the use of analogy.[3]

[1] 'The Preface of Master William Tyndale that he made before the Five Books of Moses called Genesis' (1530), in *Tyndale's Old Testament*, ed. Daniell, pp. 3–4.

[2] 'A Prologue into the Second Book of Moses called Exodus', ibid. 84.

[3] 'A Prologue into the Third Book of Moses called Leviticus', ibid. 148.

Nineteenth-century Anglican historians repeated and elaborated this 'common-sensical' insistence on the improbability of allegory. Frederic Seebohm, for example, with his passionate belief in the compatibility of science with the 'honest facts' of religion, described allegoresis of the Bible, derived from a sense of its 'magic sacredness and absolute inspiration', as a 'strange theory', carried out to 'absurd length' by scholastic theologians.[4] In the late twentieth century, too, the tradition of textual simplicity was very much alive, in accounts both of Tyndale and of post-Reformation biblical criticism generally. David Daniell, for example, approvingly cited Tyndale's own statement that 'Scripture hath but one sense which is the literal sense. And that sense is the root and ground of all, and the anchor that never faileth'.[5] Or John Barton, championing a post-Reformation exegesis, the only exegesis truly to be called 'biblical criticism', declared that such criticism is 'concerned with the "plain sense" or "natural" sense of the text'. Biblical criticism aims to 'let the text speak through the stifling wrappings of interpretation with which it had been surrounded'.[6]

In this chapter I have no reason to take issue with Foxe's account of Tyndale's courage and heroic simplicity of person; nor do I question the fact that allegorical exegesis was taken to implausible lengths by some (though not scholastic) pre-Reformation exegetes.[7] I also readily concede that the pre-Reformation Church often controlled the reading of Scripture in thoroughly oppressive ways. Many examples of pre-Reformation biblical writing reveal, however, that the biblical text is in no way 'simple', that its meaning cannot be 'plain', and that the text cannot simply 'speak for itself' through direct, unproblematic access. Certainly Tyndale's achievement in particular, along with that of the translators of the Wycliffite Bible, was a very extraordinary and by any modern standards laudable step in the direction of widening access to the Bible. A widened access to the Bible, however, did not in itself do away with problems of con-

[4] Seebohm, 124. For much more sophisticated 19th-cent. biblical criticism, see Drury (ed.).

[5] Daniell, p. 239. The citation is from Tyndale's *Obedience of a Christian Man*, p. 304.

[6] Barton, p. 17.

[7] Scholastic theologians themselves held by the principle that theological and doctrinal arguments could be generated only from the literal sense of Scripture. For the history of this idea, see Minnis, '"Authorial Intention" and "Literal Sense"'.

trolling the text's meaning in any simple way; on the contrary, it is precisely in such moments that the real complexity of biblical meaning makes itself felt most pressingly.

Unlike Tyndale, many pre- and anti-Reformation biblical theorists and users recognized the inevitable primacy of what would now be called the interpretative community (in this case the institution of the Church), and therefore recognized the primacy of interpretation in constructing the text of Scripture. For such a textual community the Bible was one tool in a larger arsenal of homiletic resources, such as preaching and penitential instruction. Pre-Reformation readings from the Bible were absorbed into the larger educational project of the institution in a wide variety of forms, and each of these gave high profile to commentary on the biblical text. The relationship between text and commentary can be seen at a glance, for example, in the format of any sermon or penitential treatise, where the often rubricated biblical citations are isolated in a surrounding sea of commentary and exhortation, as any selection from, say, Chaucer's *Parson's Tale* will demonstrate. The coherence of biblical narrative, what Tyndale calls the 'process, order and meaning of the text',[8] was entirely broken up in this textual and institutional culture, subordinated as it was to the larger coherence of an institutional programme of teaching. This textual culture frankly accepted interpretative and textual accretion by biblical readers: rereadings of the Bible produced parabiblical rewritings (parallel to yet different from the biblical text), where the interpreter's own spiritual needs, or those of his audience, permitted rearrangement of and addition to the scriptural text.

Post-Reformation practice, by contrast, deployed forms of *elimination* in getting back to the true, 'plain' sense of Scripture by scraping away what one scholar called the 'encrustations of centuries of turgid and stagnant religious doctrine'.[9] Such elimination was both interpretative and philological: just as the evangelical interpreter eliminated allegorical traditions, so too the Reformation philologist eliminated disposable readings in his establishment of the true text of Scripture.[10] Reformation biblical scholars gave primacy to the text of Scripture above the institution of the Church, and so

[8] Tyndale, 'Preface . . . that he made before . . . Genesis', p. 3.

[9] Ginsburg, p. 48.

[10] For the eliminative practice of humanist philology, see Grafton, e.g. pp. 27, 57–8.

eliminated all interpretations and, furthermore, all liturgical ceremonies that were not grounded explicitly in Scripture.

The contrast I have just made in the previous two paragraphs between pre- and post-Reformation treatment of the Bible is more or less a restatement of the standard account of biblical reception in these centuries. I repeat the standard position here partly by way of promising to confirm it in the chapter that follows: in pre-Reformation practice the coherence of the biblical text *was* compromised by its subordination to institutional demands in many discursive forms. And in many cases this accretive form of biblical reception was also closely policed by ecclesiastical authority.

This chapter will, however, also revise the standard contrast in three principal ways. First, rather than describing biblical theory as pre- and post-Reformation, it is instead the case that two traditions, one 'orthodox' and the other evangelical, run parallel across this entire period, and that the orthodox position turns out to be surprisingly liberal, in theory at least. Secondly, I explicate the exploratory ways in which certain pre-Reformation 'literary' texts receive the Bible. In works like *Piers Plowman*, Julian of Norwich's *Showings*, and *Pearl*, for example, the Bible is received and remade in an accretive, dialogic way. Finally, I argue that Tyndale's own Bible, no less than many other post-Reformation examples of biblical reception, cannot avoid its subjection to the accretive pressures of the highly charged social world into which it was delivered. The actual conditions of textual reception never allow a text to remain 'plain'. A text, and especially a text with as much authority as the Bible, is, instead, always subject to appropriative governance by readers and institutions. The attempt to repress allegory altogether creates unbearable prohibitions for the reader. This repression must either be compensated for by the admission of allegory through more clandestine routes, or must implicitly threaten much of the Old Testament with irrelevance. Even as post-Reformation biblical philologists attempted to shear away the accretions of biblical commentary to expose the bedrock of biblical narrative, so too did they threaten the Bible's relevance to contemporary readers. The apparently commonsense position that there is only one, literal sense turned out, we shall see, to produce its own severe difficulties. Both pre- and post-Reformation readers needed the Bible to speak to present desires;

pre-Reformation practice was less embarrassed about representing the reader actively constructing the biblical text to serve those desires.

I

Before we look to actual biblical translation and adaptation, however, two preliminaries are advisable: on the one hand I offer a brief account of strictly biblical translation through the period of this history, and on the other I sketch the main positions of biblical debate, which tend to be made within three sets of decades. Those debates might seem extraneous to a literary history, but theorists in the 1390s, the 1440s, and the 1530s argued for a profoundly historical reception of the Bible, which frankly recognized the ways in which the Bible needs to be remade by human intervention. Pre- or anti-Reformation theorists throughout the period 1370–1535 effectively justified the reader's active intervention in the remaking of the biblical text. That account of the Bible's historical reception itself makes it possible to link subjects normally given quite separate treatment: strict translation of the Bible and the manifold ways in which the Bible was received in 'literary' texts.

First, then, a brief account of strictly biblical translation, whose great moments can be stated quite simply. Translation of sections of the Bible into English had of course been made prior to the period of this history: there were many scriptural poems in written Old English; in the late tenth century Aelfric had translated, or rather adapted, the Heptateuch into Old English, at the same time as a full translation of the Gospels was produced.[11] Anglo-Norman versions of the Psalter were written in the twelfth century. In the late twelfth century Orrm translated and harmonized Gospel readings used in the Mass; and in the first half of the fourteenth century Richard Rolle (d. 1349) produced a translation of and gloss on the Psalter in English prose,[12] which was still being used, by both heterodox and

[11] For a conspectus of pre-Wycliffite scriptural translation and adaptation, see Shepherd. For a wider conspectus, see Lawton, 'Englishing the Bible'. A bibliographical guide is available in Muir.

[12] For which see Watson, *Richard Rolle*, pp. 242–8.

orthodox readers, in the fifteenth century.[13] The lively *Cursor Mundi* (written between 1300 and 1350) can hardly be described as a biblical translation, for all its inclusion of biblical narrative: it produced and rearranged narrative ultimately drawn from the Bible simply as sourceless and unquestionable history.

Within the centuries of this volume, there were two major periods of biblical translation. In the last two decades of the fourteenth century translators working broadly within the movement that soon after came to be known as 'Lollardy' produced two versions of the entire Bible known as the 'Wycliffite Bible', translated from the Latin Vulgate Bible of Jerome (fourth century). The first was a strictly translated version, so strict as to obstruct easy access; the second offered the same text in a more syntactically flexible rendering. No fewer than two hundred and fifty manuscripts of this translation survive, containing part or, in twenty-one instances, the whole Bible (Fig. 10).[14] The Wycliffite Bible suffered prohibition within thirty years of its production, in the *Constitutions* of Archbishop Arundel (1409), one article of which prohibited the translation of Scripture into English and the possession of such material.[15] In the last decade of the fourteenth and in the early fifteenth century translations of the Penitential Psalms (nos. 6, 31, 37, 50, 101, 129, and 142, by the Vulgate numbering) also appeared: those of Thomas Brampton and Richard Maidstone in verse, and the prose translation and commentary of Dame Eleanor Hull.[16] John Lydgate also produced versions of some psalms.[17]

Very limited licensed reading of the vernacular scriptures would seem to have been permitted even under the draconian strictures of the *Constitutions*,[18] but no new translation of Scripture was pub-

[13] For orthodox use, see *Mirour of Oure Ladye*, ed. Blunt, p. 3. For the Lollard use, and the 'immense popularity' of Rolle's Psalter, see Alford, 'Richard Rolle'.

[14] For a conspectus of scholarship on the Wycliffite Bible, see Hudson, *Premature Reformation,* pp. 228–47.

[15] For theology in the vernacular as the especial target of the *Constitutions*, see Hudson, 'Lollardy: The English Heresy?'.

[16] Maidstone *Penitential Psalms*, ed. Edden; Brampton, 'Metrical Paraphrase', ed. Kreuzer; and Hull, *Seven Psalms: A Commentary on the Penitential Psalms*, ed. Barratt.

[17] *Minor Poems*, pt. 1, nos. 1, 3, 16 (stanzas 12–20), and 17. 2 (stanzas 12–18). See Kuczynski, pp. 135–48.

[18] See *Mirour of Oure Ladye*, p. 3: 'Of the psalmes I have drawen but fewe, for ye

Fig. 10. Page from the Wycliffite Bible (later version), Prologue to Romans. Cambridge, Cambridge University Library MS Dd.1.27 (2), fo. 474v (*c*.1430).

lished until the extraordinary New Testament of William Tyndale. This great text, translated from Greek, with aid from Luther's German translation, was published in Worms in 1526 (revised in 1534).[19] Tyndale's Pentateuch, translated from the Hebrew with Luther's German also serving, arrived in England from Antwerp in 1530; in the following year, probably, Tyndale published a translation of Jonah.[20]

Like its Wycliffite predecessors, Tyndale's translations were also subject to censorship, although in this case, where the printing of bibles made them readily reproducible in much larger numbers, the response was more rapid. In a proclamation of 1530 the King declared that he would institute an officially approved translation, only so long as his 'people do utterly abandon and forsake all perverse, erroneous, and seditious opinions, with the New Testament and the Old corruptly translated into the English tongue now being in print, and that the same books and all other books of heresy . . . be clearly exterminate and exiled out of this realm of England forever'.[21] For all that, it was Tyndale's version that provided the basis for the sequence of full Bible translations that appeared in quick succession from the mid-1530s: the Coverdale Bible in 1535, and both the officially approved translations, the 'Matthew Bible' of 1537 and the Great Bible of 1539. In 1530 George Joye's translation of the Psalter into English prose also appeared.[22]

Issues of large moment are clearly involved in the translation of Scripture into the vernacular. When a book has the authority of Scripture, ostensibly written as it is by God himself, then its translation enacts a massive transference of discursive power, away from one set of readers to another, who had previously been excluded

may have them . . . out of Englisshe bibles if ye have lysence therto.' The *Mirour* was written between 1415 and 1450.

[19] A New Testament fragment translated by Tyndale had been published in 1525.

[20] For the sources of Tyndale's biblical translations, see Daniell, pts. 2 and 4.

[21] *Tudor Royal Proclamations*, ed. Hughes and Larkin, 1. 196, no. 129 ('Prohibiting Erroneous Books and Bible Translations').

[22] For a detailed bibliography of printed Bibles in English, and accounts of their dependency on previous Bibles, see Darlow and Moule (eds.). The accounts of dependency on Tyndale's work should be supplemented by reference to Daniell, *William Tyndale*, pts. 2 and 4. For a bibliography of English Psalm versions 1530–1601, see Zim, app. The Continental context of early 16th-cent. biblical scholarship is lucidly presented by Bentley.

from discursive authority. Translation into the vernacular also enacts a massive transference of authority to the language itself, away from the learned languages previously reserved for arcane discourse. To put the matter in this way is equally to say that scriptural translation into the vernacular is a profoundly 'democratizing' act, redistributing discursive power on a massive scale. This is certainly true, but when we look to the disputes that scriptural translation provoked, we find, curiously, that the democratic, or at least conciliar, arguments were deployed by those who spoke for an ideal orthodoxy, *against* those who had translated Scripture. To these debates I now turn, since they pave the way for consideration of the dialogic, accretive reception of Scripture we observe in pre-Reformation culture.

There are three high points of debate, which I discuss in reverse chronological order: the More–Tyndale controversies between 1529 and 1533; Reginald Pecock's *Repressor of Over Much Blaming of the Clergy* (*c.*1449), directed against fundamentalist Lollard opponents; and the contrasted positions of John Wyclif and William Woodford, propounded between 1376 and 1397. The first two debates listed here are conducted in English, the last in Latin. Taken together, these three confrontations produce a surprisingly consistent picture: on the side of orthodoxy stand More (who represents an orthodoxy about to become heterodox), Pecock, and Woodford, against their evangelical opponents Tyndale, unnamed Lollards, and Wyclif. Across the 150-year span of these disputes the battle is conducted from consistent lines: the 'orthodox' argue that scriptural meaning is the product of human convention, and is dependent on the decision-making powers of human institutions for its formulation. Their fundamentalist opponents argue instead that human decisions must derive from Scripture and Scripture alone. For the orthodox Scripture is the product of history; for their evangelical opponents history should be the product of an inviolable Scripture.

More's voluminous, intense, and relatively brief engagement with Tyndale occurred between 1529 and 1533, a period largely coinciding with More's chancellorship. More's posture in this debate is generally described as manic, of a piece with his generally virulent pursuit of heresy. Certainly *The Confutation of Tyndale's Answer* (1532–3) is a rambling and repetitive work, but the first salvo in the campaign is anything but rambling and manic. More's *Dialogue concerning Heresies* (1529) is a deeply thoughtful dialogue between a young man of Protestant sympathy (the messenger from a friend of More) and More himself.[23] Although More certainly 'wins' the debate, the discussion across the four books of the dialogue moves with extreme care and courtesy, with powerful arguments being put for both sides, through a series of contentious issues: veneration of images; the relative authority of Scripture and the Church; the status of the Church; vernacular translation of Scripture; and the persecution of heresy.

The sequence of issues raised reveals their interconnectedness: the non-scriptural credibility of the saints leads into the institutional faith Christians have in the Church to determine the meaning of Scripture, which itself leads to the central question of the Church's status as a whole, and finally to the ways in which it exercises its authority. The end point of the dialogue condones the persecution of heresy, and so would seem to confirm More's position as the humanist turned illiberal persecutor. The road by which More arrives at that position is characterized, however, by fundamentally conciliar and consensual convictions. It could be argued that More the humanist of *Utopia* was in fact much more illiberal than More the Catholic apologist of the *Dialogue*.

With regard to the status of Scripture, More's central argument in the *Dialogue* is that Scripture is a historical body of documents, bequeathed by God to humans and thereafter in the keeping of, and subject to, human and institutional decisions made in the course of Christian history. His opponent argues that Scripture is simple and plain, and that it delivers its own meaning without human intervention: 'Me thynketh', he says, that 'the text is good ynough and playne ynoughe nedynge no glose yf it be well consydered & every parte compared with other' (p. 168). More's response is to argue that nothing is so plain as not to require a gloss of some kind; even the plainest assertions imply intuitive understandings upon which they rest: 'Harde it were', he says, 'to fynde any thynge so playne that it shold nede no glose at all' (p. 168). More's defence of glossing here derives from an understanding of linguistic meaning itself, rather

[23] For larger accounts of the confrontation, see esp. Greenblatt, *Renaissance Self-Fashioning*, ch. 2; Hecht; and Cummings.

than from any wish to preserve the Church's control of interpretation for its own sake.

From this critical hermeneutic observation, More argues that even the collation of one biblical text with another, in the process of elucidating meaning, itself amounts to a gloss. And from here he extends the ways in which we are subject to uncertainty about biblical meaning. How do we know that a given scriptural author really wrote a given book, when there are many books that have 'false inscriptions'; some parts of Scripture have perished or been corrupted; the Church has had to reject many works from the canon in order to arrive at the 'sure undoubted trewe':

> And therefore sayth saynt Austyne I sholde not byleve the gospell but yf it were for the chyrche. And he sayth good reason. For were it not for the spyryte of god kepynge the trouthe therof in his chyrche who could be sure whiche were the very gospels? (p. 181)

More begins, then, from a deep sensitivity to the fragility of the scriptural text and the possibility of error in the explication of its meaning. The only assurance he can have that the scriptural text and its understanding are reliable is by appeal to the guardianship of the Holy Spirit working through history. More's concept of faith is therefore central to his argument, but it is a faith grounded in historical and consensual decisions rather than an inspirational faith intervening so as to disrupt historical continuities.

He asks his interlocutor how he comes to know that the matter of the Gospel is true. The young man articulates More's very point in his answer, relying as he does on an account of faithful transmission of truth across time. God did not tell him that the Gospel is true directly, 'mouthe to mouthe', but, he says,

> he hath told it to other in the begynnynge . . . and after that it was ones knowen the knowledge wente forthe fro man to man. And god hath so wroght with us that we beleve it bycause the hole chyrche hath alway doen so before our dayes. (p. 180)

This is the heart of More's own position. He believes in the judgement of history, because he believes in the consensual decision-making processes of the Church, guided as they are by the Holy Spirit. He does not, he insists, appeal to the judgement of only one or two learned men, but to 'the consent and comen agrement of the olde holy fathers', and 'the comen consent of the chyrche' (p. 169). There is an element of grace in this position, but it is a grace that manifests itself in conciliar rather than personal experience; its authenticity can be proved only by its duration across the history of the Church.

Tyndale's response, *An Answer to Thomas More's Dialogue* (1531), met More head on. More himself had not at all restricted himself to the question of whether or not Scripture should be available in the vernacular, and in any case argued, with certain qualifications, in favour of such a project, despite his hostility to Tyndale's own translation. Like More, Tyndale addressed the larger questions involved, especially those about the relative priority of Scripture and the Church, and the means we have of interpreting Scripture reliably. His response was not at all based on philological arguments about the greater confidence readers might now have in establishing the text of Scripture, with the recovery of Greek and Hebrew learning. Tyndale was well placed, after all, to make such a riposte, but he clearly recognized that the real question is the theoretical one about Scripture's autonomy from, or dependence on, the Church.

The essence of Tyndale's opposition to More lay, in my view, in their differing conceptions of how we know what we know about Scripture. More and Tyndale *shared* a view that Scripture is not self-sufficient, but that it requires a prior authorization. Whereas More located that prior authorization in the conciliar decisions of the Church, however, Tyndale located it in the inner conviction of the individual reader. There are, he says in the *Answer*, two kinds of faith, 'an historical faith, and a feeling faith'. Faith of the historical kind 'hangeth of the truth and honesty of the teller, or of the common fame and consent of many', whereas a 'feeling faith' derives from personal experience (1. 5–51). When applied to Scripture, Tyndale dismissed the value of historical faith, since it is 'but an opinion, and therefore abideth ever fruitless'; feeling faith, on the contrary, is derived from direct divine intervention in the spirit of individual readers:

But of a feeling faith it is written (John vi), 'They shall be all taught of God.' That is, God shall write it in their hearts with his Holy Spirit . . . And this faith is none opinion; but a sure feeling, and therefore ever fruitful. Neither hangeth it in the honesty of the preacher, but of the power of God, and of the Spirit: and, therefore, if all the preachers of the world would go about to persuade the contrary, it would not prevail. (1. 51)

This understanding of the authenticity of personal conviction does away both with numbers and with historical precedent.

From it Tyndale generates his account of the absolute priority of Scripture above the Church: 'Wherefore, if the word beget the congregation, and he that begetteth is before him that is begotten, then is the gospel before the church' (1. 24). Conciliar arguments cut no ice with Tyndale at all: on the contrary, he argues that 'general councils of the spirituality' are no different from secular councils, dominated as they are by a few 'wily foxes', such that 'no man dare say his mind freely and liberally, for fear of some one and of his flatterers' (1. 159); council members are 'beguiled with subtle arguments and crafty persuasions'. More and Tyndale have entirely different conceptions of conciliar process and their application across time: More trusts historical decisions with a 'historical faith', given his sense of the fragility of Scripture isolated from an interpretative community; Tyndale, by contrast, distrusts decision-making processes and so trusts the text, with a 'feeling faith'. Historical accretion is for More the very stuff of belief, whereas for Tyndale it must be eliminated. One trusted committees, while the other did not.

If we move back in time from the heat of the Tyndale–More controversy, we find very similar positions being propounded in the middle of the fifteenth century, by Reginald Pecock (*c.*1395–*c.*1460), Bishop of St Asaph and then of Chichester.[24] Pecock's views are striking, principally because he is considerably more confident even than More in the powers of human reason, and in the necessity of applying what he calls 'the lawe of kinde writen in mennis soules with the finger of God'.[25] Pecock, almost uniquely among orthodox spokesmen throughout the fifteenth century, attempted to confront Lollards on their own ground, by replying to them in English, and by deploying logical argument. The strategy failed, not only because appeal to logic of the kind Pecock made was unlikely to persuade Lollard opponents, but also because Pecock was himself charged and convicted of heresy. Precisely because he articulated Lollard pos-

24 For Pecock's career, see Scase, *Reginald Pecock*.

25 Pecock, *Repressor of Over Much Blaming of the Clergy*, 1. 20.

itions, in English, albeit in order to refute them, he attracted the attention of a failing king, Henry VI, on the lookout for scapegoats. In 1457 he was charged with heresy, forced to recant, and resigned his bishopric.

Like More, Pecock asserted Scripture's insufficiency without the aid of humanly instituted rules for its interpretation and application. So many aspects of modern life, he argues, are not grounded in Scripture, such as codes of dress, hairstyle, the use of clocks, culinary practices. These examples are designed to expose the historical simplicity of only permitting that which has been grounded in Scripture, since times change and many modern practices were clearly unforeseen by scriptural writers. Having prepared the ground, Pecock then capitalizes by making a much more telling point: there is no mention anywhere in Scripture that Scripture 'schulde be write in Englisch tunge to lay men, or in Latyn tunge to clerkis'. With regard to all these practices, none of which is mentioned in Scripture, Pecock concludes that

> No governaunce or treuthe is expressli groundid or witnessid in Holi Scripture, which mai not be knowen bi the Scripture aloone, without more sett therto of propocisiouns in the resoun of him which redith and undirstondith there in Scripture. (1. 121–2)

Pecock has no wish to question new practices not sanctioned by Scripture; on the contrary, he chooses them as inevitable aspects of modern life precisely in order to underline the necessity of living by reason, outside the bounds of what Scripture determines. This strategy is especially wily with regard to the translation of Scripture. For on the one hand he implicitly *condones* Scriptural translation (something he does explicitly elsewhere), and so creates common ground with his Lollard opponents. On the other, by the very same move he cuts the ground from under those opponents, since Scripture itself does *not* explicitly sanction the Scriptures in English. Proponents of *scriptura sola* cannot ground their translation of Scripture on Scripture; they must instead appeal to natural reason.

Pecock proclaims his faith in reason above revelation boldly. He says that the greater part of divine law 'is groundid sufficiently out of Holi Scripture in the inward book of lawe of kinde [nature] and of moral philosophie, and not in the book of Holi Scripture' (1. 39–40). Even for those who believe in the separate grounding of Scripture, he urges tolerance for the separate jurisdiction of reason: they should allow Scripture to remain 'withinne his owne termys and boundis, and not entre into the boundis and the right of lawe of kinde' (I. 70). His programme for the laity and his discursive mode derive coherently from this persuasion: he wishes that the rules of formal argument were available in English, by way of promoting the quality of public debate, and his own mode is thoroughly grounded in the rules of dialectic. He gives a full account of the positions he wishes to contest, and contests them with syllogistic reasoning. This confidence in reason is also a confidence in the councils on whose communal practice of reason governance of both Church and State is founded. Thus, by way of analogy with Scripture, he proffers examples of documents whose authority derives not from their status as documents, but rather from the decisions of councils upon which their authority rests. If the king of England, for example, were to send letters from Gascony bidding his subjects to obey specified laws, the force of those laws derives not from the letter itself. The laws are not grounded in the letter, even a letter written by the king himself; the laws are instead grounded in prior communal decisions: 'for her ground is had to hem bifore thilk epistle of the King, and that bi acte and decre of the hool Parliament of Englond which is verry ground to alle the lawis of Englond, though [even if] thilk [that] epistle of the King . . . had not be writun' (I. 22).

However much the depth of Pecock's confidence in reason is unparalleled in debates of this kind, he was not without predecessors in arguing that Scripture can be mediated only by the rational reflection of conciliar bodies. Neither were his Lollard opponents, whom he reliably reports to believe in a *scriptura sola* position, without predecessors. The Pecock debates had their origins, within an English context, in the debates about biblical meaning generated by John Wyclif in the last three decades of the fourteenth century.

Wyclif's *De veritate sacrae scripturae* (1377–8) offered the reverse image of Pecock's position. Wyclif argues that all philosophy is contained in Scripture; that Scripture stands alone, prior to and above any human interpretative or philological intervention; and that reading Scripture is a matter of reading the literal level alone, inspired by God. He so distrusts the human enterprise, indeed, that he recasts the very notion of Scripture: no longer are the sacred writings instantiated in books 'made with the skins of dead animals', subject as those material objects are to decay and fragmentation.[26] Wyclif's view is instead an ultra-realist one, whereby Scripture is an idea in the mind of God. His argument, then, led away from philology (unlike that of his immediate followers, who translated the Bible into English), just as his hermeneutics rejected interpretative tradition and appealed instead to inspiration. Wyclif did indeed claim, like his evangelical followers, that Scripture had only one sense, the literal. He incorporated all the obviously figurative passages of the Bible into his theory, along with the mystical senses as traditionally defined, by arguing that these, too, are literal *to the mind of God*, a mind to which the inspired reader will have access through inspiration.

This reading practice has institutional implications: whereas More and Pecock's hermeneutics were embedded within a larger defence of the Church as an institution, Wyclif's hermeneutics did away with conciliar tradition. And so a treatise on Scripture also turns to the explosive subjects of ecclesiastical property not sanctioned by Scripture. That institutions stand or fall by modes of reading is implicit in the range of topics covered by the *De veritate sacrae scripturae*. Possession of the text determines control of material possessions.

Wyclif's main academic opponent in such debates was the Franciscan polemicist William Woodford, to whose arguments I briefly turn by way of concluding this conspectus of biblical hermeneutic controversy. Woodford's arguments, made in Latin between 1376 and 1397, cohere with those of Pecock and More. Regarding himself as living in an old world, he is deeply conscious of the fragility of Scripture in its material history and of its malleability as an object of hermeneutic study.[27] The material Bible suffers many defects and contains many things that are not necessarily worthy of faith; the canon is itself constructed on labile grounds; fixing biblical meaning is an uncertain business; and using the Bible as an infallible guide in the present is dangerous, since what was fit at the time of biblical writing is now inappropriate, since times have changed. So Woodford, with his profoundly historical sense of the contingency of

[26] Wyclif, *De veritate sacrae scripturae*, I. 108–9 and 114–15. For a lucid account of Wyclif's hermeneutics to which the following discussion is indebted, see Ghosh, 'Eliding the Interpreter'.

[27] For Woodford's hermeneutics, see Ghosh, 'Contingency and Christian Faith'.

biblical truth, naturally turns to the importance of councils. His solution is essentially the same as More's: the durability of a properly made decision must serve as a guide to truth. If the council was legitimately constituted, guided by those expert in theology, and conducted without fear or favour, then its determinations are to be accepted, especially if the Church persists in such determination without objection from those skilled in theology.[28]

Protestant treatment of the Bible has generally been considered genuinely 'historical', as opposed to a naïve and ahistorical pre-Reformation approach. Certainly Reformation philology does attempt to apply one form of historicism to the biblical text, to which I will return later in this chapter. If we restrict ourselves to the great confrontations concerning biblical meaning, however, then two points in particular have emerged from the preceding discussion. First, the strict contrast between pre- and post-Reformation thought needs to be redrawn: the contrast is between an evangelical approach to biblical truth and an approach grounded in the ongoing history of conciliar decisions. These traditions both run right across the period of this history. Secondly, historical understanding of the Scriptures, and their place in the Church, is to be found on the *anti*-evangelical side. For these writers the text of the Bible is subject to material degradation across time; the applicability of scriptural truth to new historical situations is in constant need of accretive adaptation; biblical meaning can only be persuasively elucidated by communal and temporally durable means. Against them stand those of evangelical persuasion, who, in their theoretical statements at least, do all they can to preserve the simplicity of the biblical text by extracting it from history. For these authors the Bible is whole unto itself, without need of any apparatus for its interpretation; its plain, literal meaning is directly perceptible by divine inspiration. Of course the extremity of that position might be strategic: evangelical writers faced a large and powerful enemy, and their line of attack had to be designed to strike with maximum effectiveness. Neither is the position without force: intense and personal reading experience often presents itself as offering an especially privileged access to a text, beyond the constraints of any textual community. For all that, the position remains ahistorical.

[28] Ibid. 18.

II

However much the arguments of More, Pecock, and Woodford stress conciliarism, their reliance on institutional grounding for scriptural authority can easily tip over into authoritarian positions. A paradox haunted More's discussion of the ways in which authority is grounded. His position derived from a sense of the contingency of Scripture in history: he respects the decisions of history so much, that is, precisely because Scripture does not and cannot stand alone, hermetically sealed against historical forces. That very respect for historical sanction, however, prohibits him from acknowledging historical novelty. The only way he could confront novelty was to dismiss it as, implicitly at least, not itself a historical phenomenon. The very structure of the *Dialogue* exposes this paradox, moving as it does from a profoundly historical and conciliar sense of the Church to a justification for the persecution of heresy. Within the very structure of the *Dialogue*, that is, More moves from a liberal account of historical precedent to an illiberal resistance to historical novelty. For More this decision has an immediately practical upshot, since More was himself responsible for the persecution of heretics, a responsibility he assumed with enormous and fierce energy.

For Pecock and Woodford, too, the maintenance of institutional authority in the matter of scriptural and doctrinal meaning had its dangers. Pecock could have had no theoretical response to the council that convicted him of heresy, and Woodford's civilized account of conciliar decision-making looks sadly out of touch with realpolitik by the time of the 1401 statute *De Heretico Comburendo* or Arundel's *Constitutions* of 1409. The first of these statuted the burning of heretics for the first time in English history, while the second, among its many depressing prohibitions, forbade the translation of Scripture into the vernacular. The existence of two hundred and fifty manuscript copies of the Wycliffite Bible attests to the fact that the Lollard movement was in every way a historical phenomenon, and in no way dismissible as an eccentric freak. The response of the conciliar bodies of early and late Lancastrian England to this powerful force was outright repression.

In this section I consider vernacular works preceding and immediately following the *Constitutions*, focusing especially on the liberties with which these texts deployed biblical material and modes of reading the Bible. In Chapter 8 we considered visionary material, much of it dating from after 1409. In a sense the *Constitutions* legislated for a discursive shift in vernacular theological writing, by prohibiting the complex and theological reception of biblical matter by vernacular writers, and by instituting new ground rules, whereby only bodily, imaginative responses to Scripture were permitted. Of course some writers managed to work biblical matter in exploratory ways in the fifteenth century, such as John Audelay,[29] and many dramatists, whose work will be discussed in the next chapter. More characteristic is Nicholas Love's *Mirror of the Blessed Life of Jesus Christ* (*c.*1410), which was given a licence by Archbishop Arundel, for the purpose of the 'edification of the faithful and the confutation of . . . Lollards' (p. 7). The work was discussed in Chapter 8; here one need only recall the opening account of its discursive limits to confirm its studiously pious and bodily approach, broaching theological matters only to attack Lollard positions. The work is, by Love's account, more profitable than 'high contemplacioun' of the Godhead; it is directed to those 'simple soules' 'that kan not thenke bot bodyes or bodily thinges', in order that such a person 'mowe have somwhat accordynge unto [h]is affection where with he maye fede and stire his devocion' (p. 10).

For all its repeated calls to remain within the bounds of imaginative reflection on Scripture, always 'within reason', Love's text nevertheless exercises, as we saw in Chapter 8, considerable freedom within those limits. Each of the reflections that make up the work, one for each day of the week, is motivated by Gospel accounts of Christ's life, but the text is not at all restricted to the Gospel account. Wherever, we are told in the Prologue, the text may not be 'prevet [proven] by holi writ or groundet in expresse seyinges of holy doctors, it s[h]al be taken none otherwyse than as a devoute meditacion' (p. 11). Given that freedom, the text very often encourages the reader to read, or rather see into, the strictly scriptural account, and to embroider it with his or her own imagination.

The unexpected freedoms we find in Love's text are of an altogether less daring kind than the modes of biblical reception to be

[29] Audelay, *Poems*, esp. no. 2.

found in late fourteenth-century works. The freedom to read into the text encouraged by Love, is, however, consistent with the anti-evangelical positions discussed above, just as it is consistent with the later fourteenth-century texts. As will be already evident, the anti-evangelical position across these centuries recognized that scriptural meaning only exists through what one scholar has called 'a complex interaction between the scriptural words and the various prerogatives of individuals, institutions and traditions'.[30] This is not a reading culture that demands philological expertise from the reader to perceive the true intention of the original text; on the contrary, this textual culture is fundamentally directed to what modern criticism would call 'reader-response': the acid test of a good reading is not that the reader has perceived the original intention of the biblical text, but rather that the reader has become a better person for having read.[31] Another way of putting that point is to say that the original intention of God in writing Scripture was in any case to promote charity, and if the interaction of text, institution, and reader produces that result, then the reader has indeed 'perceived' the original intention.[32] A textual culture of this kind will not be philologically over-anxious about the text of Scripture, since it is concerned to promote what the Church regards as *implicit* in Scripture. Other texts can, and indeed must, serve in promoting the realm of the scripturally 'implicit'. Neither will such a textual culture be especially anxious about the canon of Scripture itself, since the point of Scripture is not to produce better philologists, but better Christians. The boundaries of what Scripture is will be much less sharply defined, merging as they do the Scriptures themselves and patristic writings.[33] In an environment where not everyone can read, 'Scripture' will also include visual material.

[30] Ghosh, 'Contingency and Christian Faith', pp. 4–5.

[31] The rhetorical purpose of Scripture, designed as it is to appeal to readers, and to different kinds of reader with different styles, is central to 13th-cent. scholastic accounts of biblical style. See Minnis, *Medieval Theory of Authorship*, ch. 4, esp. pp. 126–7.

[32] For the key Augustinian text, see Augustine of Hippo, *On Christian Doctrine*, trans. Robertson, 3. 15, p. 93. For discussion see Copeland, pp. 154–8.

[33] Abelard's *Sic et Non* (1122–44) attempts to distinguish the relative authority of Scripture and patristic writings; the need to do so implies a prior equality of status; see Minnis and Scott (eds.), pp. 87–100. For Aquinas's understanding of the integral relation of *sacra scriptura* and *sacra doctrina*, see Persson, ch. 3.

If that description of a pre-Reformation textual culture explains aspects of Love's work, much more so does it account for the sometimes relaxed, sometimes daring absorption of biblical matter and modes into pre-Arundelian vernacular English writing between the 1360s and 1409, to which I now turn. Evidence that citation and deployment of Scripture can be made with apparent freedom is readily available in a variety of works written before 1409. Certainly Chaucer seems careful not to question biblical authority in the *House of Fame*, a poem in which all secular literary sources are subject to scepticism. In the *Canterbury Tales*, however, he freely deploys Scripture within the narrative texture of different tales, most vibrantly in the representation of women readers. Whereas in the post-Arundel climate of 1415 Hoccleve commands Lollard women who 'wole argumentes make in holy writ' to sit down and spin instead, since their wit is 'to feble to despute of it',[34] Chaucer represents women as deft and well-informed readers of Scripture. The Wife of Bath no less than Proserpine in the *Merchant's Tale* deploys Scripture in shrewd ways to counter patriarchal dominance in marriage and textual authority. In alliterative poetry, too, works like *A Pistel of Susan* (championing a woman protagonist in the vernacular), *Patience*, and *Cleanness* each manifest an intimate knowledge, and a confident freedom in the adaptation of, scriptural narrative.

Perhaps the most daring of these pre-Arundelian works is *Piers Plowman*, whose narrative effectively recounts the education of the biblical reader, in its larger narrative of the edification of the Church. The Latin Scriptures are caught in their transition into English by this poem, as perusal of any folio of a *Piers Plowman* manuscript will testify: lines of Latin, many of them scriptural quotations, are often set off from the English by being highlighted in various ways,[35] while the English will often translate the Latin in poetically mobile ways. The Latin Scriptures are used for a variety of purposes, including doctrinal instruction, satire, and prophecy. More profoundly, the narrative through Passus 8–18 of the B-Text traces the education of a biblical reader, whose success as a reader depends on seeing beyond the literal level of the biblical text.

[34] *Remonstrance against Oldcastle*, l. 149.

[35] For examples of the highlighting, see Benson and Blanchfield.

In Passus 8–10 Will repeatedly cites biblical passages whose literal sense prohibits salvation for all but the perfect. The so-called Pardon of Passus 7 puts into stark profile the severity of the literal text. This is not exactly a scriptural text in the post-Reformation sense, but an article of the Athanasian Creed, which states that all who do well will be saved, and those who do ill will be damned (B.7. 110a–b). Piers Plowman himself responds to this stark text, sent from Truthe, in an apparently tangential, allusive way. He responds powerfully, by tearing the pardon in two, but so far from being defeated by the severity of the literal text, he instead cites (in Latin) scriptural passages that offer hope in the midst of darkness: '*Si ambulavero in medio umbre mortis | Non timebo mala, quoniam tu mecum es*' ('if I should walk in the middle of the shadow of death, I shall fear no evil, for you are with me'; Vulgate Psalm 22: 4) (B.7. 116–17).[36] And so far from attempting to fulfil the strictness of the literal pardon's injunctions about working well, Piers instead abandons work in the world, citing a Gospel text from Matthew (6: 25) that promotes faithful abandonment to God's provision of material needs: '*Ne soliciti sitis*, he seith in the Gospel' ('Be not solicitous . . .') (B.7. 127). If Piers is the spiritual ideal of this poem, then this passage already implies that literal reception of God's dicta is inadequate. Piers reads the threatening text by drawing on other, more hopeful texts. Piers knows his Bible well, citing from both Old and New Testaments in Latin; but his strength as a reader derives more from the goodness of his will and the strength of his faith rather than any philological commitment to the literal truth of divine words.

Will himself finally practises the same allusive, dynamic, and hopeful reading of Scripture, but not before he is nearly submerged by a scholastic commitment to the literal force of biblical texts by which he is, apparently, damned. '*Sepcies in die cadit iustus*' ('The just man falls seven times each day'; Prov. 24: 16) (B.8. 21); '*Nemo ascendit ad celum nisi de celo descendit*' ('No one has ascended to heaven who did not descend from heaven'; John 3: 13) (B.10. 376a), which Will takes to refer to predestination; 'For the sothest word that ever God seide was tho [when] he seide *Nemo bonus*' ('No one

[36] All citation from *Piers Plowman* is from William Langland, *Piers Plowman: The B-Text*, ed. Schmidt.

is good'; Luke 18: 19) (B.10. 440): in each of these statements Will insists on the literal force of the divine text, good scholastic student that he is. The problem with these literal readings is that they deny the value, or even the possibility, of good works done towards salvation. These texts, taken literally, and taken with the relentlessly literal Pardon, offer a bleak prospect: the pardon demands good works, and these texts deny the possibility of good works. One scriptural text confronts others, each of them, apparently, inescapably literal in its force. The only escape routes from that confrontation are either despair, or a new kind of reading. Will despairs in Passus 10, but in Passus 11 begins to read in a more liberating, satisfying way. His crucial encounter with Scripture herself was discussed in Chapter 7; the key point in this context is that, in a moment of near desperation as to his own salvation, Will responds to Scripture's austere text in Piers's allusive, glancing manner of biblical reading. 'Many are called but few are chosen' is a poor text from which to generate an account of Christ's salvific generosity, but this is precisely what Will does, by recalling other, more emotionally powerful biblical texts that promise salvation: '*O vos omnes sicientes, venite . . .*' ('O all you who thirst, come to the waters . . .'; Isaiah 55: 1) (B.11. 121). Will also recalls contemporary statuted labour laws that promise some kind of redemption for the runaway serf, until Scripture herself agrees with Will, by citing this text from Psalm 144: 9: '*Misericordia eius super omnia opera eius*' ('His mercy is above all his works'; (B.11. 139a). This critical breakthrough in the poem's theological argument is also a moment of dialogic reading, where the reader responds to one literal scriptural text by evoking other, more satisfying passages from the Scriptures, in such a way that Scripture itself swings behind Will. Scriptural reading is, by this account, a matter of satisfying one's deepest, best desires by collation of one scriptural text with another. To remain within the realm of the explicitly literal is to remain locked within irresolvable and destructive tension.

Will is this poem's main protagonist, and his very name, an English equivalent of Latin *voluntas*, designates that part of the soul that generates the best kinds of reading. The will, as the soul's loving, desiring power, cannot be satisfied with the texts of Truth, framed as those texts are within a wholly literalist, rational, explicit textual practice.[37] And so the text of Scripture cannot, as it is in evangelical theory, be conceived as whole unto itself in its literal statement. It requires instead the active engagement of individual readers who construct the text's meaning within new historical environments. It is no accident, therefore, that Will's interpretation of Scripture should itself be part of the representation of Scripture: this is a reading culture that is wholly unembarrassed about placing the reader in the scriptural picture. The following sequences of the poem, up to and including Passus 18, enact this increasingly deep, dynamic, and allegorical reading of Scripture, in which Will even enters the biblical landscape. In Passus 13, at the Feast of Conscience, Will practises a monastic, ruminative reading of Scripture, as he 'eats' painful scriptural texts at the feast. And in Passus 16–17 he encounters Old Testament figures, as he journeys towards Jerusalem to witness Christ's atonement. He encounters Abraham, or Faith, who is followed by Moses, or Hope, who is succeeded by the Good Samaritan in his act of charity. Will is *part* of Scripture at this point, as he moves dynamically through history towards a renewed understanding and vision of Christ. The old dispensation is itself made part of the Christian story through its allegorization. Just as Will has exercised faith and hope towards his charitable reading of Scripture, so too does he reread the Old Testament in precisely these terms. And however much the Samaritan is drawn from a New Testament parable, Will engages with, or reads, him figurally, as a final deferment of the vision of the truest charity in Christ, whom Will sees directly in Passus 18.

For all its daringly personal engagement with Scripture, Will's reading does not take him outside the Church. On the contrary, Will's participation in biblical narrative serves to lay the foundation for a renewed Church, of whose building's fabric Scripture is part rather than the foundation. The poem itself even begins to imitate biblical sequence in its narrative of the Atonement and of the establishment of the institution. Will witnesses the events of the Crucifixion and Atonement 'soothly, *secundum scripturas*' (B18. 112), in a sequence modelled on the Gospel account of Easter Week, and on

[37] For Langland's representation of voluntarist reading, see Simpson, 'Desire and Scriptural Text'.

the apochryphal Gospel of Nicodemus, translated into Middle English in a number of versions.[38] From here he moves in Passus B.19 to a Pentecostal scene modelled on Acts 2: 1–4, and on 1 Corinthians 12: 4–11, in which Langland's fictional creation Piers astonishingly merges with the historical figure of St Peter as the first Pope. The scenes of the decay of the Church in Passus 20 are inspired at key moments by Gospel and Pauline accounts of the last days. *Piers Plowman* is itself, then, a vernacular Scripture, rewriting its own narrative into Scripture and vice versa. The scriptural poem so produced reimagines the Church as a barn designed to receive the harvest of Piers, but the poem seeks ideally to incorporate both itself and Scripture into that vernacular Church. Piers calls upon Grace to build the barn, in response to which Grace provides the materials of Christ's passion,

> And therewith Grace bigan to make a good foundement,
> And watlede it and walled it with hise peynes and his passion,
> And of Holy Writ he made a roof after,
> And called that hous Unite—Holy Chirche on Englissh.
>
> (19.327–31)

For Langland, then, Scripture answers to human need. It is not 'grounded' in itself, so much as in the reformed reading will, that power of the soul that is itself grounded in Christ's charity. Certainly Will's reading of Scripture reforms the Church, but Scripture is itself brought within the structure of that Church.

Julian of Norwich also deploys scriptural modes both to edge beyond and to reimagine the institution of the Church. As we saw in Chapter 8, she repeatedly hastens to display her credentials as a devout believer in the Church's teaching, and even then within the limited, visual field of Christ's human suffering: she 'leevyd sadlye alle the payntyngys of crucyfexes that er made be the grace of god aftere the teachynge of haly kyrke to the lyknes of Crystes passyonn' (1. 202). These affirmations are especially marked in the Shorter Version of her *Showings*. In her deployment of scriptural mode, however, she both tests and reforms the authority of the Church.

Julian says that she feels 'safe' in the 'person' of her fellow

[38] See D'Evelyn and Foster.

Christians (1. 221); this sense of being preserved, or 'kept', to use her own frequently used word, underwrites the most radical of her theological perceptions, especially when she challenges the Church. The great fourteenth revelation of the Lord and the Servant does not appear in the shorter version, perhaps because it was dangerous. God sends the vision to resolve Julian's sense of contradiction between the divine love for humans that she consistently witnesses in her visions on the one hand, and the Church's teaching on sin and divine readiness to blame on the other: 'For I knew be the comyn techyng of holy church . . . that the blame of oure synnes contynually hangyth uppon us . . . .Then was this my merveyle, that I saw oure lorde god shewyng to us no more blame then if we were as clene and as holy as angelis be in hevyn' (2. 511). In answer to this discrepancy between what Julian sees in her visions and the teaching of the Church, God sends her the 'mysty example' of the Lord and the Servant, a very simple narrative with very few variables: a servant, clad in a labourer's tunic, stands just to the side of a seated lord, who commands him to go on an errand. In loving haste to fulfil the lord's will, the servant falls into a mire. He is unable to raise himself and suffers great pains, the worst of which is his inability to turn to his lord.

Despite her intimate knowledge of Scripture, Julian does not cite Scripture explicitly, making only occasional and imprecise references to a scriptural author; neither does this revelation have a scriptural source.[39] Her detailed reflection on it is, however, inconceivable without a confident understanding of biblical exegesis. For however much Julian must present herself as excluded from textual traditions, and reliant instead on direct visionary experience, as with Langland she nevertheless produces what is effectively a form of para-scriptural writing. Almost twenty years after first having this vision, Julian says that she received divine instruction as to its meaning. By looking very closely at the details of the 'misty example', she comes to an understanding that the servant was Adam, the Lord God. The servant who falls down on the business of his lord falls precisely because he is too eager to fulfil his lord's will: the servant 'stertyth and rynnyth in grett hast for love to do his lordes wylle. Anon he fallyth in a slade

[39] For Julian's knowledge of Scripture, see ibid. 43–7.

[slough], and taketh ful grett sorow' (2. 514–15). Julian's most authoritative editors insist that 'there can be no doubt' that the fallen servant represents the suffering Christ,[40] which flatly contradicts Julian's own primary interpretation, which is that the servant 'was shewed for Adam' (2. 519). Julian's exegetical refusal to cast any part of her vision aside, however, finally does produce what Colledge and Walsh describe as 'the Church's' interpretation in their edition: some aspects of the servant do not correspond to Adam, which pushes Julian to recognize that in the servant 'is comprehendyd the second person of the trynyte' (2. 532). Julian's own exegetical practice here is one of 'preserving', or 'keeping', a practice that preserves the consubstantiality of the human and the divine, by linking Adam and Christ. Just as Adam fell, so too did 'the godhede sterte fro the fader in to the maydyns wombe, fallyng in to the takyng of oure kynde, and in this fallyng he toke grete soore' (2. 540). Before making the figural connection with Christ, however, Julian dwells on the good will of the servant as Adam, almost retrospectively transferring Christ's goodness back onto Adam. What justifies this daring transference?

Julian applies standard modes of biblical interpretation to her own parable, to produce a vernacular version of a daring theological position. Pre-Reformation biblical readers understood the events of the Old Testament as allegorical prefigurations of the events of the New, as can be seen in visual terms in the *Biblia Pauperum*. The historicity of the Old Testament is not destroyed by this method of allegorization, so much as fulfilled. Julian's interpretation of her vision does precisely this, to produce a reading of Adam's fall that is at once historical and sympathetic. Not only, Julian implies, was Adam's fall fulfilled by Christ, but the first fall takes on some of the qualities of the second, particularly because Julian dwells on the goodness of the fallen servant as the fallen Adam before she reveals the Christological interpretation. Certainly Julian draws on the theological tradition of the *felix culpa*, or 'happy fall', whereby Adam's fall is regarded as in some way positive given its result. Whereas, however, the tradition of the *felix culpa* puts an optimistic accent on Adam's sin by pointing to its consequence of Christ's redemption, Julian

[40] Ibid., 2. 513 n. 3, and 515 n. 15. For a full discussion of the fourteenth revelation, see Baker, *Julian of Norwich's* Showings, chs. 4 and 5.

focuses rather, to my knowledge uniquely, on the attempted *propriety* of Adam's fall. The simply stated yet radical essence of her position is, to cite a statement that is made in the shorter text, that 'synne is behovelye' (1. 244),[41] by which I take Julian to mean that sin is (somehow) 'fitting'. The worst thing about the fall is the servant's inability to see his lord, and the lord himself sympathizes with the condition of the good-willed but over-eager servant. Julian's question about blame and punishment is answered by her understanding that 'oonly payne blamyth and ponyschyth, and oure curteyse lorde comfortyth and socurryth' (2. 523).

Julian's application of the modes of biblical interpretation to her own vision has institutional consequences, redefining as it does the nature of the Church by redefining the nature of suffering. The serene perception of Adam's goodness produces the extended reflections on Christ as mother; Julian ends the vision by warning against any reader taking this vision 'syngularly to hym selfe', since 'it is generall, for it is oure precious moder Cryst, and to hym was this feyer kynde dyght [prepared] for the wurshyppe and the nobly of mans makyng' (2. 613). Like the regular religious, Julian disowns what is 'proper' or singular, and this reformed version of the 'common will' and common ownership is a remarkable declaration of the 'behovely' propriety of theological discourse by vernacular witnesses. The para-scriptural reading enlarges and feminizes the generality of the Church.

If Julian writes a kind of para-Scripture indebted to the modes of scriptural interpretation, the same is true of *Pearl*, also written, presumably, within the last two decades of the fourteenth century, by (again presumably) the same poet who wrote *Sir Gawain and the Green Knight*. Unlike Julian, however, the *Pearl*-poet makes explicit, extended, and confident reference to Scripture, in a variety of ways. The poem is in some ways a *cento,* or collage, of scriptural citation, ranging from the importation of very large blocks of scriptural narrative, to the small-scale yet explicit citation of Scripture in theological argument, to the silent embedding of what are certainly scriptural sources into the texture of narrative. The author demonstrates a fluent and wide knowledge of the Vulgate, drawing as easily from

[41] Colledge and Walsh gloss 'behovelye' as 'necessary', *Showings*, ed. Colledge and Walsh, 1. 244. I read it as shading into 'appropriate'; see MED, sense (b).

the Psalms and Isaiah as from the Gospels, the Pauline Epistles, and Revelations. The extended account of the New Jerusalem (ll. 867–1123), for example, is modelled directly on John's vision of the heavenly city in Revelations. This long citation of a biblical vision authorizes the poem's own visionary mode, just as the very structure of the New Jerusalem, with its twelve gates and twelve foundations, determines the poem's own limits, with its 1,212 lines, beautifully arranged, by a complex metrical pattern, into 101 stanzas.

Pearl narrates the visionary meeting of a grieving father with the redeemed soul of his 2-year-old daughter, in which the daughter chastises her father: he should stop grieving for the 'pearl' of what was his natural, 'privy' daughter, and focus instead on the pearl of his own soul, which is 'commune' to all the saved. This is, then, a poem of pain, and Scripture is deployed to painful, salutary effect. If *Piers Plowman* and Julian domesticate Scripture within the generous terms of their own theologies, *Pearl*, by contrast, stresses the austere otherness of Scripture. Whereas the father insists on familial, private, 'natural' values, the daughter shatters such familiarity by insisting on the universal, the public, and the spiritual. The provisionally cruel essence of her position lies in her point that by grieving for the loss of that singular 'pearl', the father is *un*natural: 'Thou art no kynde jueler', she says (l. 275). One's truest nature is spiritual; attachment to the merely natural in fact distracts one from recognizing the deepest form of one's identity.

The reader participates in this disruptive reconstruction of identity by empathy with the narrator father, caught as he is between feelings of recognition and alienation. 'I knew hyr wel, I hade sen hyr ere' he says as soon as he sees the maiden, but his impulse to call out to her is checked by the strangeness of the surroundings: 'To calle hyr lyste con me enchace, | Bot baysment gef myn hert a brunt. | I segh hyr in so strange a place' (ll. 173–5).[42] The poet enlists Scripture in this dialectic of strangeness and familiarity, of 'missing and meeting' (cf. l. 329), by placing it on the side of disconcerting *un*familiarity and *im*personality. The daughter recounts, for example, the Parable of the Vineyard, by way of dismissing the father's objection that his daughter has not worked long enough in the 'vineyard' of the world

[42] 'I was urged on to call to her, but confusion delivered such a blow to my heart, since I saw her in so strange a place.'

to have deserved her crown in heaven (ll. 501–76). She absorbs St Paul's conception of the corporate nature of the Church into the poem's own version of spiritual courtliness, to berate her father's spiritual discourtesy (ll. 457–68). And finally she appears in the mystical procession of 144,000 virgins in the New Jerusalem (modelled on Revelations), barely distinguishable from any other in her resplendent, courtly clothes: 'And coronde wern alle of the same fasoun, | Depaynt in perlez and wedez qwyte [white garments]' (ll. 1101–2).

The poet also absorbs modes of reading Scripture into the texture of his own fiction, especially with regard to its central image, the pearl. He delights in strategically revolving words and images in such a way as to invest them with different meanings in close succession, and applies this technique within the structure of each five-stanza group of stanzas, linked as they are by one theme word. He also applies it to the image of the pearl across the whole poem. The first line of the poem is echoed yet altered by the last: 'Perle, pleasaunte to prynces paye' (l. 1), 'And precious perlez unto his paye' (l. 1212). The first line expresses devotion to a single pearl, possessed by the father, whereas the last marks the narrator's acceptance of his identity with every other Christian soul; and these souls are now the 'homly hyne [domestic servants]' of the Lord who manifests himself in the sacrament of the Eucharist ministered daily by the priest. Just as the poem effects a painful shift from earthly to heavenly attachments, so too do the referents of the pearl shift across the poem, from the earthly and literal to the spiritual. In so doing they imitate the constant move in scriptural exegesis, from 'carnal', literal readings to the fruitful, 'mystical' meanings buried within. The critical turning point is itself made by reference to the parable of the pearl of great price (Matt. 13: 45–6), 'the joueler gef fore alle hys god' (l. 734):

> For it is wemlez, clene, and clere, [spotless]
> And endelez rounde, and blythe of mode, [expression]
> And commune to alle that ryghtwys were. [righteous]
>
> (ll. 737–9)

This is the pearl of salvation that must be 'bought' by the dreamer himself; learning this point is dependent on learning to apply modes of reading Scripture to the world at large.

Vernacular scriptural writing before the *Constitutions* of 1409 manifests, then, an extraordinary confidence, ranging as it does from the stricter translations such as we find in *Patience* and *Cleanness*, to the daring appropriations of Scripture and scriptural mode found in works like *Piers Plowman*. Many of these works confirm the anti-evangelical theory considered above: they represent Scripture as secondary, grounded as it is in the divine *voluntas*; precisely because of this, they feel free to work within a realm of what might be called 'para-scriptural' narrative; they freely represent the reader and interpreter of Scripture within their representations of Scripture itself; and they bring Scripture within the fabric of the communal institution of the Church, even if in some cases they refigure the Church at the same time. Above all, they represent reading as a matter of improving the will of the reader: when it comes to a choice between a literal understanding of a biblical text that provokes despair and a hopeful interpretation that sustains readerly desire, these texts choose the latter. This textual culture is focused on receivers of grace rather than the literal intentions of texts, and one may receive grace in a variety of ways. As Walter Hilton says in his *Epistle on the Mixed Life* (?mid-1380s), the fire of love for God in each soul needs to be nourished, but it can be fed with wood of diverse kinds:

> And so it is good that eche man in his degree, after that he is disposed, that he gete him stikkes of o thing other of another—either of preieres, or of good meditaciouns, or reding in hooli writte, or good bodili worchynge—for to nourische the fier of love in his soule. (p. 121)

III

More's sense of biblical meaning is, as we have seen, rooted in its historical reception. This position is profoundly historical, but the history is focused rather on reception than on originary truth. A philological approach to the Bible is also profoundly historical, but the definition of history itself is recast: the philologist's enterprise is in this tradition devoted to understanding the originary moment of textual production. Such pursuit of the past must threaten, however, to render the past wholly irrelevant. For the more one elucidates the pastness of the past, and its difference from one's own culture, the more the past becomes a wholly foreign country. The harder the philologist pursues the past, that is, the more it will elude his grasp. This tension between the past as wholly relevant and wholly foreign is embedded within humanist culture, with, as one scholar puts it, some humanists wishing to 'make the ancient world live again, assuming its undimmed relevance and unproblematic accessibility', while others seek to 'put the ancient texts back into their own time, admitting . . . that success may reveal the irrelevance of ancient experience and precept to modern problems.'[43] The great philologist Erasmus himself felt the tension between these two models. On the one hand he produced the first modern edition of the Greek New Testament (1516), while on the other his earlier comments about scriptural exegesis favoured a wholly allegorical, non-literal interpretation, designed to bring the text into the hearts of modern readers. Thus in his *Enchiridion Militis Christiani* (?1503, translated into English by 1534), he describes the literal sense of Scripture as 'harde' and 'unsavery', but, he says, 'get out the spiritual sence and nothyng is more sweter nor more full of pleasure and swete juice' (p. 45). Among scriptural exegetes, Erasmus encourages his readers to choose those who 'go *farthest* from the lettre . . . for I see the divines of later tyme stycke very moche in the lettre and with good wyll gyve more study to subtyle and disceytfull argumentes than to serche out the misteryes' (p. 49; my emphasis).

Tyndale's late fourteenth-century Wycliffite predecessors were able to balance this need for contemporary relevance and philological accuracy. Certainly the project of translating the whole Vulgate Bible into English required an immense philological effort, both of collating Latin bibles and producing an idiomatic yet faithful translation. The Prologue of the Wycliffite Bible declares that the 'symple creature' who was responsible for the translation 'hadde myche travaile, with diverse felawis and helperis, to gedere manie elde biblis . . . and to make oo Latyn bible sumdel trewe'.[44] On the other

[43] Grafton, 26–7. See also Eisenstein, I. 367: 'Vernacular Bible translation took advantage of humanist scholarship only in order to undermine it by fostering patriotic and populist tendencies.'

[44] *Holy Bible . . . made from the Vulgate by John Wycliffe and his Followers*, ed. Forshall and Madden, I. 57.

hand, the aim of the translation is to serve the needs of contemporary readers, to alter the situation whereby only a 'fewe pore men and idiotis' have access to the truth of Scripture, as against the 'many thousinde prelatis and religiouse' (I. 30).

These two demands, of fidelity to both the text and the audience, can be met through the hermeneutic stance of the same Prologue. Whereas Wyclif had insisted that there was only one biblical sense (the literal), the translators of the Wycliffite Bible staked out an interpretative programme very much within the main lines of late medieval biblical scholarship. In keeping with a standard scholastic principle, they argued that the literal sense is foundational, but this does not in any way do away with biblical allegory or the need for an active interpreter who can construct biblical meaning. The Psalter teaches the mysteries of the Trinity and the Incarnation (I. 37); in Ecclesiastes Solomon speaks through the voice of many persons, not necessarily approving those opinions (I. 41);[45] the Song of Songs teaches the 'greet prevytees of Crist and of his chirche' (I. 41). There follows a traditional account of the fourfold scheme of biblical interpretation, with three mystical senses (the allegorical, the moral, and the anagogical) all dependent on the literal (I. 53).[46] And all this is underwritten by appeal to Augustine's influential account of biblical reading as a process of inducing charity in the heart of the reader (I. 44–5). If, says Augustine, anything in the Bible does not produce a charitable reading literally, it is to be regarded as figurative: 'if it seemith to comaunde cruelte, either [or] wickidnesse, either to forbede prophit [what is profitable], either good doinge, it is a figuratijf speche'.[47] This mode of reading is not at all held in thrall to the literal sense; on the contrary, the reader is encouraged to come to the text with a pre-given, charitable understanding of what it will mean. Anything in the biblical text that fails to produce that meaning is to be read allegorically, and worked at until it should produce its real, charitable meaning.

45 For the scholastic awareness of multiplicity of voice in the Bible, and the possibility of irony, see Minnis, 'Theorizing the Rose'.

46 For a readily accessible account of the fourfold system, see Aquinas's account, in Minnis and Scott (eds.), pp. 241–3.

47 The citation is from Augustine of Hippo, *On Christian Doctrine*, trans. Robertson, Bk 3. 15.

The Wycliffite Bible has, then, a flexible response to the dilemma of philological accuracy and contemporary relevance. Tyndale's prologues, by contrast, manifest deep and unresolved tensions between those two ideals. As with the Wycliffite translators, he is committed to both. He encourages his reader to think 'that every syllable pertaineth to thine owne self',[48] and he passionately wants a Bible open to 'all manner of persons, men, women, young, old, learned, unlearned, rich, poor, priests, laymen, lords, ladies, officers, tenants, and mean men, virgins, wives, widows, lawyers, merchants, artificers, husbandmen', as Thomas Cranmer puts it in his preface to the Great Bible of 1540.[49] The wonderfully supple, plain prose of Tyndale's translation addresses precisely that range of audience, excluding no category of reader.[50] He is also committed to philological accuracy, in practice most obviously by his recourse to the Greek text of the New Testament and to the Hebrew for the Pentateuch, but also in theory in his Prologues. The very first paragraph of the Prologue to the 1526 New Testament offers a flurry of grammatical terms by way of justifying Tyndale's own translation of Greek tenses.[51] In the Prologue to the Pentateuch this commitment to philology threatens to become a form of disciplinary punishment. Tyndale does not recognize the authority of the institution of the Church; he does however submit the book to those who 'submit themselves to the word of God, to be corrected of them', and he freely concedes the right of such readers to burn his translation if they can produce another, more correct translation from the Hebrew.[52]

How does Tyndale reconcile these potentially divided commitments, to philological accuracy to the text as a historical object on the one hand, and to the need for every reader to take 'every syllable' as relevant to themselves on the other? He certainly does not have recourse to the flexible system of interpretation adopted by the translators of the Wycliffite Bible. On the contrary, his interpretative

48 Tyndale, 'Preface . . . before . . . Genesis', p. 8.

49 Cranmer, *Prologue or Preface . . . made by Thomas, Archbishop of Canterbury*, p. 121. This is the preface to the 2nd edn. of the Great Bible.

50 For the style and translation practice of Tyndale's Bible, see Partridge, ch. 4, and Daniell, *William Tyndale*, pts. 2 and 4.

51 *Tyndale's New Testament*, p. 3.

52 'Preface . . . before . . . Genesis', in *Tyndale's Old Testament*, p. 6.

mode is determined by his philology: by Tyndale's account the biblical text has, as we have seen, only one sense, the literal. Tyndale's instinct is to move as little away from the literal sense as possible, and so he focuses on the explicit statements of promise, threat, or contract made between God and humans in the Bible: the good Christian will 'hate himself and . . . desire help, and then comfort himself again with the pleasant rain of the gospel, that is to say, with the sweet promises of God in Christ, and stir up faith in him to believe the promises'.[53] Thus Tyndale takes especial care to give marginal glosses for each of the covenants made by God. Given this predilection for explicit injunction, and his sympathy for Pauline theology, it is unsurprising that Tyndale should settle on Romans as 'the principal and most excellent part of the new testament . . . and also a light and a way in unto the whole scripture'.[54]

Explicit covenants, however, cannot resolve the tension between historical fidelity and contemporary relevance, since they comprise, after all, so little of the whole Bible. To reduce the relevance of the Bible to explicit commandments and promises is to leave most of the narrative unaddressed. In addition to promises, Tyndale will occasionally have recourse to what pre-Reformation exegetes called the tropological, or moral, sense of scriptural narrative to recuperate an Old Testament narrative for contemporary application. Thus Moses is not to be taken as an allegorical type of Christ, says Tyndale, but as a model for all princes to follow in his 'long-suffering and soft patience'.[55]

Neither literal contracts nor tropology, however, can reveal the relevance of the whole of the Bible, and especially the Old Testament, with its large tracts of narrative and ceremonial procedure, for example. Much of the Old Testament itself threatens to become irrelevant, and as it falls into irrelevance, so too does it come to resemble the dead practice of papish religion. Thus the ceremonial injunctions of the Old Testament are to be shunned, since they have been adopted by the Pope, who has become a 'priest of the old law, and hath brought us into captivity . . . under the ceremonies of the old

[53] Tyndale, 'Prologue to the Epistle of Paul to the Romans', in *Tyndale's New Testament*, ed. Daniell, p. 216.

[54] Ibid. 207.

[55] 'Prologue into . . . Exodus', in *Tyndale's Old Testament*, ed. Daniell, p. 85.

law'.[56] Tyndale thus presents the Bible in a paradoxical way, whereby he makes the text available with one hand, and with the other sets it out of reach and relevance. The potential exclusions of this approach are everywhere apparent in his Prologues, which are pressingly, disconcertingly concerned to isolate those who might be excluded from reading the 'simple', and 'plain' scriptural text. The Prologue to the New Testament promises to unlock a Scripture that will, at the same time, lock many readers out. Certainly Jews and the scholastic theologians are excluded immediately:

as Christ testifieth how that the scribes and the Pharisees had so shut it [Scripture] up and had taken away the key of knowledge that their Jews which thought themselves within, were yet so locked out, and are to this day that they can understand no sentence of the scripture unto their salvation, though they can rehearse the texts everywhere and dispute thereof as subtly as the popish doctors of dunce's dark learning, which with their sophistry, served us, as the Pharisees did the Jews.[57]

Tyndale lived in a period of schism, and we might be unsurprised to find him defining his ideal readership by historical and sectarian exclusions. Even that ideal readership, however, is itself threatened by reading the Scriptures. Tyndale warns his 'most dear reader' about the terrible dangers of reading the Bible without true faith. Without this, Bible reading might deceive the reader, and be 'unto thy greater damnation'. The Bible might make a man better, or it might 'make him worse and worse, till he be hardened that he openly resist the spirit of God, and then blaspheme'. The 'just damnation' of the reader whose life is not converted by reading begins 'immediately, and he is henceforth without excuse';[58] or, he says in the same prologue, 'the servant that knoweth his master's will and prepareth not himself, shall be beaten with many stripes'.[59] Biblical experience is, then, by Tyndale's account, an extremely dangerous business, threatened as it is with exclusions at every turn. The very freedoms permitted by the vernacular text incur corresponding, punishing disciplines. Many kinds of reader are automatically and irrevocably excluded, and even those who are not excluded risk incurring the same danger of damnation by reading the biblical text incorrectly.

[56] *Tyndale's Old Testament*, 126.
[57] *Tyndale's New Testament*, p. 3. [58] Ibid. 5. [59] Ibid. 6.

Just as Tyndale appeals to an ideal Church wherewith to exclude the material Church, so does he invoke an ideal reader to exclude or challenge his real readers. At points he even identifies the elect of the true church with the ideal reader of Scripture; God reserved for his elect 'knowledge of . . . his holy Gospel';[60] only the elect are moved by hearing the Gospel, for 'when the evangelion is preached, the Spirit of God entereth into them which God hath ordained and appointed to eternal life'.[61] An elect Church is produced by an elect readership. In this culture reading is elevated into a prerequisite for salvation, but not all readers will be among the elect.

So too does he exclude philological challenges to his text. The Prologue to the second edition of the New Testament (1534) is wholly devoted to an attack on George Joye, whom Tyndale accuses of having played 'boo peep' with the first edition, by changing it without Tyndale's permission. Tyndale appeals to other men to judge whether or not Joye's changes are permissible, but Tyndale is himself in no doubt, for 'if it were lawful after his example for every man to play boo peep with the translations that are before him, and to put out the words of the text at his pleasure and to put in everywhere his meaning . . . that were the very next way to stablish all heresies'.[62] A text that is to be the sole ground of the Church is a text in which every word must be chosen with care, and whose philological credibility is essential, since heresy will now arise from textual dispute. A philological text fears nothing so much as every man inserting 'his meaning', and instead presents itself as inviolable.

No text can of course remain inviolable, and every text, especially the Bible, will be remade by the social world into which it is delivered. Although Tyndale's own New Testament never achieved official recognition in the life of Henry VIII, the concerted official campaign against it was a losing battle, and the text ended up forming the basis of the very official editions that were produced in its wake. Whereas Tyndale's New Testament is a small, modest octavo book, the sequence of Bibles that followed (Coverdale Bible republished in 1537, the so-called 'Matthew Bible' of 1537, and the Great

[60] Tyndale, 'A Pathway into the Holy Scripture' (1525), in *Doctrinal Treatises*, ed. Walter, pp. 1–28 (at 14).

[61] Ibid.

[62] *Tyndale's New Testament*, p. 14.

Bible of 1539) had official sanction and look like it: they are large folio editions, the first and third of which bear images of the King distributing bibles. The most spectacular of these images appears in the Great Bible of 1539, whose frontispiece shows a munificent Henry VIII, immediately below God, distributing the Word of God to his grateful subjects. On the King's right and left respectively, Cranmer and Cromwell receive the text, and pass it down through a hierarchical chain to an adoring people, who all mouth 'Vivat Rex', even the prisoners in the gaol depicted in the bottom right-hand corner of the image (Fig. 11).

This image of a confident king and an adoring, grateful people in one sense represented Tyndale's greatest triumph. At the same time, the image belies the deep uncertainties about biblical translation evident in Henry's proclamations and statutes throughout the 1530s and 1540s. In 1530, under More's chancellorship, the position was one of repression, declaring that for the moment the people shall have Scripture expounded by preachers, even if the King proposes to commission a translation when his people have abandoned their 'perverse, erroneous and seditious opinions', and when the 'corruptly translated' versions now available have been 'exiled out of this realm forever'.[63] By 1538 the ground had shifted: no one shall import or print any books of Scripture with any annotations, unless it has been approved by the King's council; the people are enjoined to 'read and hear with simplicity and without any arrogancy the very Gospel and Holy Scripture'.[64] In the very next year a proclamation expresses fury that this has not happened, and that many readers, clearly evangelicals, do 'wrest and interpret' Scripture so as to subvert the sacraments of the Church. This proclamation imagines an irrepressible explosion of biblical debate, in 'churches, alehouses, taverns, and other places and congregations . . . whereby is like to follow sedition and tumult and destructions', and proceeds to control scriptural preaching and, rather more desperately, reading Scripture 'with any loud or high voices'.[65] By 1541 the King ordered the Great Bible to be placed in every church, to the end that his 'loving subjects' should use

[63] *Tudor Royal Proclamations*, ed. Hughes and Larkin, I. 196, no. 129 ('Prohibiting Erroneous Books and Bible Translations').

[64] Ibid. 272–5, no. 186 ('Prohibiting Unlicensed Printing of Scripture').

[65] Ibid. 284, no. 191 ('Limiting Exposition and Reading of Scripture').

Fig. 11. Hans Holbein. Title-page to the Great Bible (1539).

it 'humbly, meekly, reverently, and obediently', directions consistent with the image of readerly reception in the frontispiece to that edition.[66]

By 1542, however, a repressive statute implied that Henrician subjects were still reading the Bible 'perversely'. Any bibles containing unauthorized material must have their annotations cut or blotted out, and unlicensed preaching of biblical matter is prohibited. There follow very specific directions about the spaces in which certain categories of people can read the Bible: noblemen and gentlemen can read the Bible, or have it read to their families within their house, orchards, or garden; merchants can read it in private; noblewomen and gentlewomen are allowed to read the Bible in private, though not to anyone else; no other woman, and no man below the status of merchant, is permitted to read the Bible, or, presumably, any other books banned by the Act; the 'lower sorte' have so abused it that in future no 'woomen nor artificers, prentices, journeymen, serving men of the degrees of yeomen or undre, husbandmen nor laborers shall reade . . . the Byble'.[67]

Two points emerge from this brief account of Henrician biblical management. In the first place, the hope expressed by official discourse that the Bible will be read 'simply' turns out, as it must, to be delusory. And secondly, the King and his councils have become the institution governing biblical reception, as Christopher St Germain himself recommended.[68] Just as Tyndale must 'let other men judge' in his dispute with Joye, so too Henrician policy had to recognize that the Bible does not stand alone as a 'simple' or 'plain' text; once it is delivered into a social world, it immediately evokes the need for institutional management.

IV

More confessed to weariness and exhaustion in his fight with Tyndale. Precisely because he was committed to an intuitive sense of scriptural content, which is, ideally, loosely defined and a matter of general consensus, More was on the back foot as he explicated

[66] Ibid. 297, no. 200 ('Ordering Great Bible to be Placed in Every Church'), p. 297.

[67] *SR*, 34 Henry VIII, ch. 11 (3. 896).

[68] See Guy, 'Scripture as Authority'.

the force and place of Scripture. In the *Confutation*, for example, he wished not only all 'heretical' books burned, but also that 'myne owne were walked wyth them, and the name of these matters utterly put in oblyvyon' (1. 36). Perhaps More also intuited that he was going to be the spectacular loser in this struggle, in which the combined forces of philology, printing, and an intense demand for bibles were going to win. Tyndale certainly did 'win', his triumph extending into the King James Bible and the massive influence of that text across many centuries.

I turn finally to Surrey's less triumphalist biblical translations, which express a profound delusion and exhaustion while remaining committed to an ideal of evangelical simplicity. The sequences are very free translations and adaptations, using the Latin paraphrases of Campensis (1532) as a guide, of Ecclesiastes 1–5, and Psalms 8, 55, 73, and 88 (Vulgate numbering). All were probably produced in the last years of his life, and the Psalms were almost certainly written in Surrey's final imprisonment before his execution in 1547. In the Ecclesiastes translations, Surrey speaks in the voice of King Solomon to rebuke his own king. The voice expresses a profound weariness and disgust with the trappings of power, and even of royal power. He looks to the 'royall throne wheras that Justice should have sitt; | In stede of whom I saw, with fyerce crwell mode, | Wher Wrong was set, that blody beast, that drounke the giltless blode' (45. 44–6).[69] In rejecting the endless theatre of power's self-interest and injustice, Surrey imagines a communal society and Church. This Church is built with love and 'simple fayth', within which the Lord 'for aye . . . in his woord dothe rest' (46. 54–5). Across these translations, however, this imagined simple faith remains only imagined, whereas in practice the Davidic and Solomonic voice is faced with the reality of endless care. Even Solomon, a king famous for his wisdom, finds that the attempt to solve 'mens follies and ther errors' is 'an endles wourke of payne and losse of tyme' (43. 40), a loss that is inherent in the very nature of the search for wisdom, since he who seeks wisdom, 'The further that he wades ther in, the greater doubts shall find' (43. 42).

[69] All citations are from Surrey, *Poems*, ed. Jones, cited by item and line number. Jones does not print Eccl. 5, for which see Henry Howard, *Poems*, ed. Padelford, pp. 107–8.

Both the Ecclesiastes and the Psalm translations are a very fluid form, capable of shifting easily between theological and political discourse, and, in Surrey's hands, frequently personal in reference. Where the Ecclesiastes material ranges across worldly affairs in the voice of the king, however, the Psalm material is intensely personal, bewailing, as the Psalmic voice does, the total isolation of the speaker in an entirely hostile world. Earlier, pre-Reformation 'translations' of the Penitential Psalms, such as those mentioned earlier in this chapter, had the effect of domesticating the extremity of the Psalmic voice by importing a specifically Christian and forgiving God into the perspective of the speaker's world. Wyatt's *Penitential Psalms* and Surrey's Psalm texts, by contrast, make no such allowance for the spiritual comfort of the speaker.[70] On the contrary, both these bodies of Psalm adaptation represent a voice wholly isolated by a hostile social world, and wholly dependent on, yet unforgiven by, a relentlessly punishing God. Both writers use the Psalms to explore relations of power in situations of extreme need. In the face of the urgent, dependent voice crying out from a duplicitous and threatening world, God himself is anything but simple and direct. Instead he withdraws into impenetrable silence, failing to disclose his award either of grace or damnation to the solitary voice.

Surrey's Psalmist complains to God as a suitor, pleading for justice in the face of enemies thronging close about, 'Buckled to do me scathe, so is their malice bent' (55. 4). This menacing social environment of what Surrey's psalmist calls 'our town' has its own malicious code, which he has broken. He has 'decyphred', that is, the civic malaise, whereby Guile and Wrong guard the walls, Mischief the market place, 'whilst wickidness with craft in heapes swarme through the strete' (55. 14–17).[71] Declared enemies are the least of his problems: much harder to decipher are the actions of his 'old fere [companion] and dere frende', the one to whom he had confided his 'secreat zeale to God' (55. 25). In this social world, whose literal surface is anything but 'plain' and 'simple', the Psalmist appeals to God as the one source of his comfort. To the 'lively name' of God he appeals with a 'lively voyce', as one of the 'elect'. This very appeal is

[70] For discussion of Wyatt's *Penitential Psalms*, see Ch. 7.

[71] For the biographical context of the psalm translations, see Brigden, 'Henry Howard, Earl of Surrey'.

made, however, only by way of signalling its uncertainty. Why, the Psalmist begs, does God forbear to appear in defence of his own,

> To shewe such tokens of thy power, in sight of Adams lyne,
> Wherby eche feble hart with fayth might so be fedd
> That in the mouthe of thy elect thy mercyes might be spredd?
> The flesche that fedeth wormes can not thy love declare,
> Nor suche sett forth thy faith as dwell in the land of dispaire.
> In blind endured herts light of thy lively name
> Can not appeare, as can not judge the brightnes of the same.
>
> (48, 19–26)

The very formulation of the appeal to this God threatens, then, to expose its groundlessness, since God does not respond. The more silent God is, the greater the intensity of appeal, but this in turn merely underlines the undeniable possibility that God is silent precisely because the speaker is *not* one of the 'elect'. Having deciphered the malicious craft of his social world, Surrey is left facing an even more impenetrable God. The hermeneutic challenge posed by this God is that the Psalmist should continue to interpret God's apparent punishment and apparent rejection of the sinner as the surest sign of his ultimate favour: the Psalmist complains his woe from a bottomless pit, where 'O Lorde, thow hast cast me hedling to plese my fooe' (48. 9). The paranoiac mentality is of course characteristic of Psalmic discourse generally: it runs, as it must, through George Joye's powerful translations of the entire Psalms. In Surrey's intense and few translations that posture is put in especially vivid relief. Surrey, no less than many pre-Reformation adapters of biblical matter, appropriates biblical matter to his own historical world. In that world, however, the word of God remains locked and hidden, inaccessible to interpretative scrutiny. Given the sinner's uncertainty as to his own salvation, he must implicitly distrust the sincerity of his own voice; confidently declaring 'thy worde', even in the very act of biblical translation, must remain only a future possibility:

> And my unworthye lypps, inspired with thy grace,
> Shall thus forspeke thy secret works, in sight of Adams race.
>
> (49. 65–6)

10

The Dramatic

Thomas More's *History of Richard III* (1513) presents the Duke of Gloucester taking possession of the kingdom as an elaborately staged theatrical exercise. Richard is offered, but refuses the crown. The offer being repeated, he 'saw there was none other way' but to accede, at which point he makes an elaborate, ostensibly unscripted speech of gracious acceptance. Unspecified enthusiasts immediately raise a cry of 'Kyng Richard, Kyng Richard!'; the lords approach the new-made king, and the people depart, 'talkyng diversly of the matter every man as his fantasye gave him'. More reserves his own views of this cheap spectacle, or rather puts them into the mouths of the people, by way of underlining the fact that the royal display fooled nobody. Some said that it was bizarre that a matter so clearly scripted should be so laboriously played out as spontaneous action. Others concede the necessity of performance for the sake of propriety: a bishop whose seals have been paid for is nevertheless required to refuse his bishopric twice, and only accept the third offer, as though unwillingly. So too, a shrewd though cautious popular witness is reported as saying,

in a stage play all the people know right wel, that he that playeth the sowdayne [sultan] is percase a sowter [shoemaker]. Yet if one should can so lyttle good [be so ignorant], to shewe out of seasonne what acquaintance he hath with him, and calle him by his owne name whyle he standeth in his magestie, one of his tormentours might hap to breake his head, and worthy for marring of the play. And so they said these matters be Kynges games, as it were stage playes, and for the more part plaied upon scafoldes. In which pore men be but the lokers on. And thei that wise be, wil medle no farther (pp. 80–1).

On the face of it, this passage registers popular shrewdness, but more deeply exposes quiescence. Of course the humble spectator raises the very real possibility that King Richard is in fact a very ordinary man, like the shoemaker who plays the sultan. He also recognizes, however, that it is dangerous in any circumstances to break a theatrical illusion: if the local players will 'break the head' of an audience member who destroys the suspension of disbelief, all the more so will the king's men punish the breaker of royal performances. King's games are played 'upon scafoldes', where More puns powerfully on the notion of the scaffold as both 'stage' and place of execution. Break the royal performance, the pun implies, and the scaffold of the stage becomes the scaffold of punishment.

More's finally quiescent imagined spectator performs the desired work of this royal theatre. Precisely by being an acute witness to the truth of the matter, the spectator buries that truth. He understands, that is, that this performance less represents the Duke of Gloucester's accession as king than it advertises threat not to break the new king's fictions of legitimacy. To understand the real nature of the play is to understand and to absorb a threat of punishment, of having one's head broken by the 'tormentours'. The sceptical perception that the performance was a sham might offer resistance of sorts, but that resistance has already absorbed a threat of punishment. The resistance, then, is the very condition of success for the royal theatre: the best spectator will understand that the performance is a sham, but will further understand that he must in no way expose it as such.

In this case, then, spectatorial resistance is the very condition of successful royal theatre. Throughout the last decades of the twentieth century, theatre scholarship reiterated that perception. Royal display, including theatrical display, in early modern England itself depended, so scholars argued, on resistance of sorts.[1] Certainly the perception was a rich one, since it invited us to see theatre proper within a spectrum of practices designed to display royal power, from royal entries to public executions. Its notion of power, however, was a peculiarly self-enclosed one, whereby a single putative source of power always holds all the cards. Whatever the apparent signs of opposition, they finally turn out to be no more than reflexes of that

[1] The seminal essay is Greenblatt, 'Invisible Bullets'.

infallible source of governance; the signs of opposition are, indeed, the condition of governance, since they serve to disguise the deeper, more subtle operations of a central Power. The audience in such formulations is always and already co-opted by the performance.

This understanding of power's circulation developed from within the study of early modern theatre. Whether it holds good for the theatrical practice of the whole of that period I leave to the judgement of others. In this chapter, however, I argue that the amateur cycle-play tradition that began in the later fourteenth century offers a very different model of power relations between actors and audience. This amateur theatrical tradition cannot be understood within a model of either power, or of resistance to power, that places all initiative in one hand. On the contrary, these plays were produced out of, and themselves represent, a complex set of jurisdictions, across which cultural power is widely dispersed. As the productions of urban craftsmen and possibly women, they did indeed project a telling critique of their cultural competitors, and especially of those who abuse their control of legitimate violence. If More's imagined scene reveals that the king is in fact a very ordinary man, it also refers to an amateur theatrical tradition in which very ordinary men play the king, in which the 'sowter' plays the sovereign, not to speak of many ordinary men playing Christ. As we shall see, very ordinary men also played the roles of powerful and corrupt bishops in this drama. If they offered resistance to royal and ecclesiastical power, however, 'mystery' plays also implicated themselves in the operations of power. Boundaries between actors and audience are much less clearly demarcated in this drama: precisely because this was an amateur, self-generated tradition, the heroes and tormentors on the stage also express the potential heroism and viciousness of the audience. These are plays in which a given community stood in judgement not only over its competitors, but also over itself.

The enormous variety of vernacular theatrical tradition in this period can be broadly divided into two currents, the amateur and the professional. Those two currents ran throughout and beyond the years 1350–1550, but by the last quarter of the sixteenth century the amateur theatre was entirely dismantled. Within the period of this history, the forces of theatrical centralization won out over powerful sources of devolution. The sixteenth-century professional theatre was London-based, and centred on the person of the monarch; it moved indoors, and was performed by professionals who worked under ecclesiastical or noble, sometimes royal patronage; at times they worked, as we shall see, as an arm of a government seeking to effect a cultural revolution. This theatre did seek to co-opt audiences for specific programmes, often by advertising the spectacle of punishment. And, as we shall see, it was sometimes directed against the amateur theatre of 'rude mechanicals', from whose tradition the professional theatre had drawn much of its energy.

I

Before King Herod goes to bed in the York play of 'Christ before Herod', performed by the litsters, or dyers, he harangues his audience, demanding silence:

> Pes, ye brothellis and browlys in this broydenesse inbrased,
>   And freykis that are frendly your freykenesse to frayne,
> Youre tounges fro tretyng of trifflis be trased,
>   Or this brande that is bright schall breste in youre brayne.
>   Plextis for no plasis but platte you to this playne,
> And drawe to no drofyng but dresse you to drede,
>   With dasshis.[2]

The stage villain Herod's demand for silence is at once ridiculous and resonant, evoking as it does other, less comic demands for silence in fifteenth-century York. Most immediately, within the fiction of the play, Herod is addressing the men of his own household, 'my men and of my menye [household]' (*York Plays*, 31. 23), demanding that they keep quiet while he sleeps. As Herod addresses that aristocratic household, this urban play mockingly deploys an enriched, metrically exaggerated form of alliterative poetry to deflate aristocratic pretension. The call to silence is not at all restricted, however, to the

[2] 'Silence, you wretches and scum contained in this open space, and you men who are friendly, [in order] to control your boldness, restrain your tongues from idle chatter, or else this sword shall cut through your head. Don't fight for places, but fall down to this ground, and make no disturbance but remember instead my blows.' *York Plays*, ed. Beadle, 31. 1–7. All further citations are from this edition, cited in the body of the text by play and line number.

fictional space of the stage. The fictional space of these plays insistently serves as a synecdoche for larger social spaces. For the reference to 'this broydnenesse', or 'broad space', in the first line clearly designates the acting space in the street of York where the play is being performed. The playwright is obviously capitalizing on the need to get the audience's attention and silence by giving full vent to Herod's magnificent bombast. He is also telling them not to fight for places ('plextis for no placis'), but to settle down peaceably and enjoy the performance. However much the call for a submissive audience is certainly comic here, it resonates with the problem of public order on Corpus Christi Day, when the plays were performed. Records from York clearly indicate, unsurprisingly, that public drunkenness and disorder often marred the long summer day of performance in a crowded city.[3]

If Herod's call evokes problems of civic order, I also suggest that the cumulative force of these calls for silence also evokes, at an outer reach, national calls to silence on certain issues. As we have seen in Chapters 7 and 9, the *Constitutions* of Archbishop Arundel in 1409 forbade, among other things, translation of the Scriptures into the vernacular, and the assertion of anything 'contrary to good morals'.[4] As we shall see, all the York plays take liberties with a translated Scripture, and certain plays in the York and Wakefield cycles in particular act out dramas of interrogation and punishment that address critical prohibitions in fifteenth-century English society. I will not be arguing that the plays are themselves expressive of Lollard positions; their inclusive theology is far too broad-based for that to be true. I will be arguing that the plays often provoke sharply critical reflection on royal and episcopal mechanisms in the prosecution and management of 'sedition' and 'heresy'. Along with many other orthodox fifteenth-century religious texts, the cycle plays addressed an environment constrained by censorship and repression.[5]

Even as the plays insistently open with a demand for silence, they

[3] See e.g. Johnston and Rogerson (eds.), 1. 43, ll. 10–11, dated 1426.

[4] *Concilia*, ed. Wilkins, 3. 317.

[5] I therefore disagree with the consensus that has grown in the wake of Watson's excellent article 'Censorship and Cultural Change'. While Watson very convincingly argues that vernacular theology of a certain kind diminishes sharply after 1409, this is not the end of powerful vernacular theology; we should rather look for such theology in different places. See also Ch. 8, above.

are powerfully expressive of an urban, lay culture that is as sharply critical of adjacent institutions as it is of itself. Such will be the principal argument of this chapter's discussion of mystery plays. To make this argument is to agree with what has become a central persuasion in drama scholarship, that the cycle plays did not develop organically out of liturgical drama. They did not move steadily from altar to nave, and from there to market square, outside the space of the Church altogether. E. K. Chambers stated the argument in favour of such an evolution most forcefully, in his monumental work of 1903, but his position was successively dismantled by scholarship on drama in the excellent books of Hardison and Kolve from the mid-1960s.[6] Whereas Chambers had argued that the cycle drama was born 'in the very bosom of the Church's own ritual',[7] later twentieth-century scholars placed increasing emphasis on the plays as a separate dramatic phenomenon.[8] The cycle drama was produced, they argued, in response to the introduction of the Feast of Corpus Christi into the English Church in 1318. By the later fourteenth century the plays had attached themselves to the procession of Corpus Christi, which was a silent, outdoor procession through urban centres, designed to show forth the miracle of the Host throughout salvation history.[9]

However much mid-twentieth-century scholarship dislodged the idea that cycle drama derived from liturgical practice, it remained wedded to the idea that such drama was a fundamentally ecclesiastical production, designed to promulgate basic scriptural narratives and homiletic truths. Rosemary Woolf, for example, thought that the Church attached the cycles to the procession simply because it wished to capitalize on the 'propagandist ceremony' of the procession to further its 'chief object', which was the 'devotional education of the bystanders'. This account of the cycle plays' purpose is in fact very old. It can be found whenever the plays' status comes under

[6] Hardison, Essay 1; and Kolve.

[7] Chambers, 2. 2.

[8] Though there were clearly connections between liturgical and cycle drama. See the instances of vernacular liturgical plays from Shrewsbury in *Non-Cycle Plays and Fragments*, ed. Davis, pp. 1–7, which, as Davis points out, have close connections with the York shepherds' play (p. xvii).

[9] Luckily, the programme of a Corpus Christi procession survives; see Lydgate, *Minor Poems*, pt. 1, no. 11.

question for any reason, as in the early fifteenth-century *Tretise of Miraclis Pleyinge*, hostile to the plays (ll. 179–85), or in sixteenth-century defences of the plays against Protestant attack. Neither is such an account of the plays' purpose and direction implausible: the fourteenth and fifteenth centuries in England witnessed a massive ecclesiastical effort to 'vernacularize' religion at a popular level.[10]

Such an account falls short, however, in various ways. As massive an undertaking as the performance of a cycle must have involved many institutions, not simply the Church: taking over the space of a city for a day or more must, for example, have answered to other than simply devotional interests. The pride and status of individual crafts was clearly involved, just as the status and identity of the whole city was focused by the plays.[11] The cycles were clearly important economically, too: they brought large influx of trade into the city over the period of their performance.[12] Many interests, not simply ecclesiastical and devotional, were served by such a large event. As the proclamation of the Chester plays in 1531–2 says, the plays are to be performed 'not only for the augmentation and increase of the holy and catholick faith . . . and to exhort the mindes of comon people to good devotion and holesome doctrine therof, but also for the common welth and prosperity of this citty'.[13]

The argument that the Church used the plays to instruct a simple laity in simple devotion also falls short of the nature of the texts themselves. Certainly the cycle plays would be unimaginable without the grand project of lay instruction mounted by the Western Church in the later Middle Ages. The plays themselves, however, do not project themselves as occasions for 'instruction'. Precisely because the Church had been so successful in vulgarizing the basic narrative of salvation history, the materials for that history were available for use by lay writers in the fifteenth century.[14] Counter to the thrust of much scholarship on the plays, the cycles are not, I sug-

[10] For which see esp. Ch. 8, above.

[11] For the seriousness with which York civic officials treated texts, recording the order and script of the plays, see Beadle, 'York Cycle', pp. 90 and 95.

[12] For the economic importance of cycle and many other forms of medieval drama, see Coldewey, 'Economic Aspects'.

[13] Cited in *Chester Mystery Cycle: Essays and Documents*, ed. Lumiansky and Mills, p. 215.

[14] See Clopper, 'Lay and Clerical Impact', p. 116.

gest, primarily devotional, and they do not offer consistent 'instruction' on typological or sacramental matters. Nor do they offer, as *Piers Plowman* does, for example, sustained ecclesiological reflection. Certainly there are devotional, typological, and sacramental aspects to the plays, but their energies are devoted to largely different ends. Typological instruction and devotional responsiveness cannot convincingly account for the project of these plays; they are not, therefore, simple examples of the Church's instruction of the laity.

The cycles are not 'instructional' at all. Instead they offered a space in which the members of many institutions could reflect on their own practice in the active life. Many spiritually sophisticated lay figures in the fourteenth and fifteenth centuries clearly felt the inevitable strains and compromises of the active life, and wished for retirement to the contemplative life of monastic discipline. Impulses of this kind were met by defences of the 'mixed life', that life of activity in the world that nevertheless made room for retirement and spiritual reflection.[15] The plays seem to me to emerge from that sophisticated lay culture, a culture that shaped its own theology of mercy out of its immersion in and knowledge of the rigours of domestic and civic life. The plays take possession of salvation history by writing the pain of family and political life into scriptural narrative. This argument applies especially to the York, Wakefield, and what remains of the Coventry cycles; qualifications need to be made with regard to Chester and stark contrasts with the much more instructional and conservative N-Town cycle.

Before giving substance to this proposition, however, we should pause to absorb some key historical information about the cycles. Four complete 'Corpus Christi' cycles survive, those of York, Wakefield (sometimes called the 'Towneley' Cycle),[16] Chester, and the so-called 'N-Town' Cycle, which derives possibly from Norwich. Two extended plays survive from a cycle in Coventry, and Beverley certainly had a cycle. Single plays that might have formed part of a whole cycle survive from Norwich, Newcastle, and Brome. In addition to the cities just listed, Kendal, Preston, Lincoln, Louth, Ipswich,

[15] See e.g. *Abbey of the Holy Ghost*, and Walter Hilton, *Epistle on the Mixed Life*, in *English Mystics*.

[16] For conclusive arguments that the 'Towneley' cycle derives from Wakefield, see Martin Stevens, pp. 97–109.

and Worcester each had plays that were called 'Corpus Christi' plays, even if no plays survive. Though not associated with Corpus Christi, Cornwall and London both had cycles. The Cornish cycle, performed in Cornish, lasted three days, and London's performance of scriptural plays was performed over several days at Skinners' Well.[17]

The plays were called 'Corpus Christi' plays because, as has been mentioned, they seem to have had their origins in the outdoor procession associated with that feast; in each cycle except N-Town they were at least originally performed on the day of Corpus Christi, the Thursday after Trinity Sunday, which fell between 21 May and 24 June. The midsummer date is essential, since the plays were outdoor events, whose performance lasted a long summer's day or days, beginning at first light.[18] They were performed on mobile wagons (or 'pageants'), and each of the fifty or so plays (in York, for example) was performed at different stations throughout the city. The dramatic action of a whole cycle of Corpus Christi plays has an immense reach, comprising as it does the narrative of the world from the Fall of the Angels to the Last Judgement. Each cycle has a small selection of Old Testament plays, before presenting a concentrated sequence of events in the life, death, and resurrection of Christ, and ending with scenes from the Apostolic life and the Last Judgement. Individual plays often have a basis that is ultimately scriptural, though the scriptural passages are mediated by vernacular retellings of scriptural narrative, such as the *Stanzaic Life of Christ*. The form is remarkably confident in adapting scriptural texts, or in deploying apocryphal material such as the Harrowing of Hell.

A Corpus Christi sequence had, then, an extraordinarily ambitious spatial and historical scope: it occupied an entire city as its theatrical space, and it promised to re-enact the history of the world

[17] For the Cornish drama, see Murdoch. For the key documents regarding London scriptural drama, see Lancashire (ed.), pp. 112–13.

[18] The only scholar to have proposed that the plays were performed indoors, before city dignitaries, is Nelson. Nelson's arguments about the organizational difficulties of moving the required number of wagons, in true processional form, through the streets of York, and performing the plays within tolerable limits, are impressive. If one imagines a mobile audience, the difficulties he proposes are less insuperable. I do not find that the documents he offers for evidence of indoor performance lead inevitably to that conclusion.

from beginning to end. Theatre of this kind demanded massive organization and expense, and was dependent on the cooperation of many interlocking institutions. The cultural conditions for such cooperation came into being rather precisely within the historical bounds of this history. The massive plague of 1348, which had less virulent though serious successors in the later fourteenth century, created a huge labour shortage, which itself created the conditions of social mobility and a movement to towns.[19] This development might have been damaging to rural landlords, but for peasant and larger urban populations the last half of the fourteenth and the fifteenth centuries were times of relative prosperity, despite local variation, and despite a waning of fortunes towards the end of the fifteenth century.[20] It may be significant that fifteenth-century aristocratic fiction, such as the narratives of Troy and Camelot, is predominantly tragic; however much urban theatre stresses the pain of social existence, it is finally comic and immensely confident.

The late fourteenth and fifteenth centuries were also times of new social formations. While religious fraternities and craft guilds certainly pre-dated the mid-fourteenth century, they flourished from 1350 until 1547, when they were abolished. The first were largely self-help and charitable organizations, often parish-based, and they replaced some of the functions of family in urban centres.[21] They were self-regulating and operated on the basis of gender equality.[22] Membership of a trade guild, by contrast, was rather determined by professional skill; these organizations, variously called 'mysteries' (from Latin *ministerium*), 'crafts', or 'guilds', controlled the practice and demarcations of different trades within urban centres. In some cities such as York, for example, they were deeply enmeshed in the governance of the city.[23] Relations between different crafts were often contentious and sometimes violent.[24] These organizations

[19] See Coldewey, 'Economic Aspects'.

[20] See Bolton, ch. 8.

[21] For the culture of fraternities, see Simpson, '"After Craftes Conseil"', and further references. See also Wallace, *Chaucerian Polity*, pp. 75–97.

[22] For the ordinances of fraternities, as collected in 1388, see *English Gilds*, ed. Smith.

[23] For the rapid growth of trade guilds in the latter half of the 14th cent., see Platt, p. 136, and Bolton, ch. 8. For the governmental structure of York, see Martin Stevens, pp. 23–4.

[24] See esp. Bird.

were responsible for the production of the Corpus Christi plays; very often the specific play was chosen for its relevance to a particular craft: the York shipwrights performed one of the Noah plays, while the thatchers were responsible for the Nativity, which took place in a badly thatched stable.

Cycle plays seem to have been well underway by the 1370s, when surviving documents first refer to them, although it seems certain that they were considerably enlarged in the fifteenth century. The texts of some of the cycles seem to have been written wholly in the fifteenth, or even the sixteenth, century.[25] The whole performance, then, was a model of civic cooperation, though the plays were themselves often the occasion of dispute between crafts, as one or other became unable to mount an expensive production.[26] The essential organizations for the production of these plays, then, were not ecclesiastical; they were urban, secular, and grounded in forms of labour. In 1426 a York friar, one William Melton, expressed his approbation for the instructive effect of the plays but petitioned that they be moved to the day before Corpus Christi, lest they distract from the central religious observation of the day. The city, whose governing class was drawn from the crafts, apparently agreed, but in fact continued to hold both events on the day of Corpus Christi. By 1468 the two were separated, but it was the procession that was moved to the day after the feast.[27]

[25] That the York cycle developed between 1415 (the first full record of the order of pageants) and 1463–77 (the date of the one MS of the whole cycle), see Beadle, 'York Cycle'. For Wakefield's emergence as an urban centre, and the likely date of the plays in the last quarter of the 15th cent., see Martin Stevens, ch. 2. Chester was possibly written between 1500 and 1550; see *Chester Mystery Cycle: Essays and Documents*, ed. Lumiansky and Mills, p. 48. The MS of the N-Town cycle was written between 1468 and 1500; see Fletcher, p. 164. The plays themselves probably derive from earlier in the 15th century.

[26] For the best account of the Corpus Christi day events as expressions of the corporate identity of medieval urban centres, see Mervyn James, 'Ritual, Drama and the Social Body'. There are many records of dispute between crafts about the costs of production; see e.g. Johnston and Rogerson (eds.), I. 45, dated 1428.

[27] For the discussion of 1426, see Johnston and Rogerson (eds.), I. 41–3. For the failure to enact the agreement, see Alexandra Johnston, 'Procession and Play of Corpus Christi'.

II

If the plays were not primarily 'instructional', then how did they project themselves? Such a question cannot be simply answered with regard to such a large corpus of material; each cycle has upwards of forty to fifty plays, and the surviving cycles differ significantly each from the other. In this section I discuss three ways in which these plays addressed their audiences. First, they offered pointed critique of royal and episcopal management of new forms of lay spirituality. Secondly, the communities that mounted these plays were also powerfully self-critical of their own domestic and labour practices. Finally, they mounted a theology of labour at whose centre stands the practice of mercy in the active life. I draw my examples from the York and Wakefield cycles especially.

In each of the cycles the many plays devoted to the interrogation and torture of Christ all represent Christ overturning received structures of power. Herod's opening call to silence in the York play of 'Christ before Herod' is met, indeed, with Christ's silence. So far, however, from being a submissive silence, Christ's refusal to talk entirely reorganizes the relations of power that the play so brazenly advertises in its opening.

After Herod goes to bed for a peaceful night's sleep he is disturbed by the arrival of Pilate's men, who bring the prisoner Christ; they gain entry to Herod's court by first promising some 'fun' with the prisoner whom, before the judgement of any trial, they openly intend to execute. Herod at first refuses anything to do with Pilate's men, until the messengers flatteringly insist on Pilate's recognition of Herod's jurisdiction in Galilee. Once the point about jurisdictional boundaries has been made, the 'fun' of some late evening torture mixed with a trial of sorts begins: 'we shall have goode game with this boy' (*York Plays*, 31. 165). Through Herod the playwright promises a play within a play, with Christ providing the entertainment. In vain Herod cajoles and threatens Christ by way of getting the performance going, only occasionally asking the questions proper to a trial. By refusing to play, however, Christ himself redraws the jurisdictional boundaries of theatricality itself, for in the face of Christ's deafening silence it is Herod and his henchmen who are themselves finally reduced to the level of the court's unwitting fools. Precisely by attempting to make a spectacle of Christ by having him don a fool's robe (in this case a white robe, following the Gospel of Luke), they become the spectacle themselves. There *is* a play within this play, but Christ is its director. By realigning the force lines of Herod's theatre of trial and torture, Christ realigns the force lines of secular society. Herod's opening boasts of absolute power are dwarfed by the very thing that that pretended power began by demanding: silence.

The cycle plays are populated by tyrants, such as Pharaoh, Herod, sometimes Pilate, and Augustus. These tyrants may open plays with the bombast we love to hate in stage villains, but their actions in society are far from being comically ridiculous. On the contrary, they command terrible violence against civilian populations, such as the Slaughter of the Innocents, and they are presented by means of powerful and deliberate anachronism. So far from being naïve, this anachronism instead advertises the force of the plays' ineluctible critique of contemporary lords. They and their henchmen sometimes deploy Anglo-Norman usages, in the style of a fifteenth-century English aristocracy, and their alliterative grandiloquence is set up as the high vernacular style of a Northern aristocratic and gentry society.

These plays subject feudal and royal lords to critique; they do the same to bishops. Annas and Caiaphas, the Pharisees responsible for Christ's conviction, are in the York and Wakefield plays also presented with a very deliberate anachronism. Caiaphas, for example, threatens Christ by marking his episcopal status: 'Lad, I am a prelate, | A lord in degré' (*York Plays*, 21. 222–3), and peppers his speech with specifically Christian asservations, such as 'As ever syng I mes [mass]' (21. 231). As in York's Herod, the Wakefield 'Buffeting' play also represents a private scene of Christ's interrogation. In this case the interrogators are bishops rather than a king, and their problem is to find a charge that will persuade the secular authority to execute Christ. The encounter between Christ and the bishops, surrounded as they are by their torturers, veers menacingly between different models. Strictly an examination scene, it is also a game in which Christ is to play 'King Copyn'; his refusal to play provokes, however, a third model, in which we are allowed to witness illegal yet judicial torture. Caiaphas is represented as a manic hooligan, desiring only to inflict savage violence on Christ, and restrained by Annas, who counsels him to remember his ecclesiastical role: 'Sir, thynk that ye ar | A man of holy kyrk; | Ye shuld be oure techere, | Mekenes to wyrk' (21. 300–3).

Each of the social models underlying this play (examination, game, and illegal torture) demands a victim, yet once again Christ refuses to play. Instead he restructures the relations of power and weakness by allowing his tormentors to speak for themselves, declaring their own impotence and his power. The torturers open the play by recounting Christ's miracles of healing, and so unwittingly declare Christ's divinity and their own exhaustion. In the examination itself, Caiaphas articulates a principle of canon law, that '*Omnis qui tacet* | *Hic consentire videtur*' ('anyone who remains silent seems thereby to be complicit').[28] Christ himself speaks only once in this play, crucially to confirm a truth already articulated by his enemies. Asked by Annas to say whether or not he is the Son of God, Christ replies succinctly. He confirms his interrogator's own witness of truth, and promises a future spectacle of his own: 'So thou says by thy steven [voice], | And right so I am; | For after this shall thou se | When that I com downe | In brightnes on he [high], | In clowdys from abone [above]' (21. 363–8). This play ends with the gratuitous permissible violence of the torturers. Annas manages to restrain the psychopathic Caiaphas from murdering Christ there and then, but permits the 'new play of Yoyll', a popular Christmas game involving beating about the head.[29]

The Wakefield 'Buffeting', then, works to expose episcopal brutality in the pursuit of 'heresy'. It does so not only by highlighting the anachronisms of the Pharisees as bishops, but also by underscoring the precise mechanisms of fifteenth-century English law in the prosecution of heresy. The 1401 statute *De heretico comburendo* specified that heresy was now to be punished by the secular authorities, since the Church had no power to effect the death penalty.[30] In this play Annas, no less concerned to nail Christ than Caiaphas, restrains the violence of his fellow bishop by stating the legal

[28] The maxim also appears in *Mum and the Sothsegger*, l. 745. For a possible source, see *Piers Plowman Tradition*, ed. Barr, p. 326.

[29] For the evidence aligning trials in the plays with contemporary legal practice, see Pamela M. King, 'Contemporary Cultural Models'.

[30] For the statute, see McHardy.

position: 'Sir, take tent [pay heed] to my sawes: | Men of temporall lawes, | They may deme sich cause; | And so may not we' (21. 400–3). Bishops nevertheless conducted the preliminary examinations for heresy, and such examinations were an essential part of the judicial process that led towards capital punishment. Episcopal menace and impotence are both on show in reported examination scenes written by Lollards from early in the fifteenth century.

Thus the Lollard William Thorpe represents his interrogator Archbishop Arundel as himself desiring only to inflict violence on his victim in a private examination, but held back by legal restraint. At one point in the trial Arundel exclaims that 'the king doith not his dever [duty] but if [unless] he suffre thee to be deemed!'[31] At another the Archbishop, 'as if he hadde ben angrid', crashes his fist down on a cupboard, and threatens to have Thorpe executed; the attendant clerics step in to play the nice and nasty roles of interrogation, played by Annas and Caiaphas respectively in the Wakefield plays: 'thei spaken to me manye wordis ful plesyngli, and also other wise, manassynge me and conseilynge me ful bisili to submytte me, either ellis, thei seiden, I shulde not ascape ponyschinge over mesure'. Thorpe clearly imagines himself as playing the role of Christ in this scene; cycle drama of the kind just described would seem to enable that understanding of his role.[32]

Secular power stands menacingly just beyond the horizon of the episcopal examination in both cycle plays and Lollard accounts of interrogation. After representing these two arms of law acting separately, the cycle drama brings them together on stage in the management of heresy. In the York play of the Resurrection, for example, the focus is not, astonishingly, on the Resurrection itself. On the contrary, secular and episcopal management of the Resurrection occupies centre stage, as Pilate consults his bishops in the matter of containing and manipulating the latest news about Christ. Whereas each of them had demanded silence from the audience in earlier plays, in this play they want initially to impose silence on themselves. 'Nevene [discuss] it no more' Annas counsels Pilate, and if any 'rebelles wolde ought rise', then hold them until the next sitting of

[31] Thorpe, *Testimony*, p. 80.

[32] Ibid. 88. Connections of this kind have been discussed by Kendall, pp. 57–8.

the court, 'and than make ende' (*York Plays*, 38. 19–35). The news, however, rises inexorably around them. The centurion enters to announce his faith in the risen Christ, in response to which a rattled Caiaphas begins a single speech by saying that there is no call to 'neven this noote [discuss this matter]' any further. He ends with a flat contradiction of his first response: 'To neveyn this noote mythynke moste nede | And beste to do' (38. 125–43). By the end of the play itself, after the soldiers sent to guard Christ's tomb have confessed the truth, Pilate and the bishops are paying them to keep quiet: 'ne of this sight that ye gonne see | Nevynnes it nowthere even ne morne' (38. 440–1). As in the earlier plays, bishops and secular rulers are calling for silence; now, however, the silence is fragile, and evidently about to be swamped by the rising tide of articulate testimony.

In representing royal theatre the plays resist it. Herod's attempt to mount a theatre of cruelty and submission collapses entirely, and in so doing the cycle play takes possession of royal theatricality itself. Certainly late medieval cities *did* perform for monarchs, by mounting spectacular if unashamedly kitsch receptions for monarchs entering cities. Royal entries of this kind developed in England from the reign of Richard II, and so coincided with the emergence of the cycle plays.[33] Royal entries were often performed at moments of especial strain between monarch and city, as in Richard II's entry to London in 1392, or Henry VII's welcome by the cities of York and Worcester in 1486, after those cities had backed Richard III against the victorious Henry.[34] These performances pulled out all the stops in praising monarchs: in the performance of 1390, for example, Richard entered London represented as Christ entering the bridal chamber of his spiritual bride in the heavenly Jerusalem. There are certainly connections between these civic displays of self-interested adoration and the mystery plays: in a welcome of Queen Margaret to Coventry in 1456, the first to hail her presence were the prophets Isaiah and

[33] For royal entries in England, see Kipling, *Enter the King*.

[34] For the text of Richard II's 1392 entry to London, see Richard Maidstone, *Concordia*, ed. Smith, and Lancashire (ed.), under 'London', pp. 176–7. See also Lerer, 'Chaucerian Critique'. For fascinating texts of Henry VII's welcome by the penitent cities of Worcester and York, both of which had supported Richard III, see, respectively, Klausner (ed.), 406–11, and Johnston and Rogerson (eds.), 1. 137–52.

Jeremiah. Just as prophets in both surviving Coventry plays prophesy and celebrate the birth of Christ, so too did these prophets celebrate the birth of Prince Edward: 'Like as mankynde was gladdid by the birght of Jhsus, | So shall this empyre joy the birthe of your bodye'.[35] And the plays themselves have their own royal entry, as Christ enters Jerusalem.[36]

The royal entries worked hard to paper over the embarrassing difficulties between city and monarch. The cycle plays, by contrast, consistently and explicitly represent the difficulties of ruling elites, especially in the management of popular religious movements. The development of a secular and professional theatre in the sixteenth century is often hailed as a moment of liberation from a religious theatre governed by an oppressive Church. From the evidence of the cycle plays we can already see the weakness of that position. These plays took street audiences indoors, to witness the spectacle of interrogation as a menacing game played by sadistic kings and bishops. The Elizabethan legislation of 1559 that prohibited the issuance of licences for plays that dealt with matters of religion or the governance of the state was almost certainly not directed at the mystery plays; it seems not to have been observed in any case.[37] The reign of Elizabeth did nevertheless witness the disappearance of the religious theatre; from the perspective of the plays considered here, one can see why monarchs and bishops may have wished to silence such a theatre.

III

By strategic use of anachronism, then, the cycle plays certainly projected a penetrating critique of institutions adjacent to, and standing over, the urban matrix of craft guilds. As I argued above, recent accounts of control and resistance often tend to place all the initiative in one hand. If the cycle plays cannot be absorbed into a model of

[35] *Two Coventry Corpus Christi Plays*, ed. Craig, app. 3, p. 110.

[36] For the York Christ's entry to Jerusalem as a royal entry, see Martin Stevens, pp. 51–2.

[37] The legislation can be found in *Tudor Royal Proclamations*, ed. Hughes and Larkin, 2. 115–16. See further White, *Theatre and Reformation*, pp. 59–60.

royal or episcopal control, does that mean that their energies are wholly devoted to resistance? Craft guilds were themselves powerful organizations, which regulated labour and in some cities controlled city government. In this section I argue that the full force of this Christian comedy can be understood only so long as one registers the plays' critique of the very society and institutions that produced them. Cycle drama reinscribes the received narratives of biblical history with the contemporary pressures not only of secular and episcopal power. It also adapts scriptural narrative to make it resonate with both the trials of domestic life and the corrupting brutalities of labour itself. A model of monolithic power and oppositional 'resistance' belittles the complexity of outward and inward critique in these plays.

In the tilethatchers' York Nativity play, Mary and Joseph enter Bethlehem searching, but unable to find, lodging 'this nyght | Within this wone [dwelling]' (*York Plays*, 14. 6–7). Drama is literally a (re)presentation, and the high incidence of deictics in these opening lines most immediately serves drama's principal need, to create an illusion that the action is happening right now: historical time must become stage time. In the cycle drama, however, deictics tend not to delimit the fictional space of the action to the stage itself. On the contrary, they revealingly extend the space of fiction and play across the whole city, which is, after all, the true stage of this drama. 'For', says Joseph,

> . . . we have sought bothe uppe and doune
> Thurgh diverse stretis in this cité.
> So mekill pepull is comen to towne [many]
> That we can nowhare herbered be,
> Ther is slike prees. [such a throng]
>
> (14. 8–12)

The Corpus Christi plays attracted many non-citizens to the cities of their performance.[38] Joseph and Mary thus replicate the experience of their audience, many of whom will themselves have anxiously sought accommodation in the crowded streets of York. The city and its citizens effectively become themselves the subject of this pathetic

[38] For strangers coming to cities for Corpus Christi plays, see e.g. Johnston and Rogerson (eds.), 1. 43, dated 1426.

scene, but they are presented in a quietly critical light. Joseph remarks that the roof of the stall in which they take refuge is broken. This is an inside joke about the tilethatchers, of a kind with Noah's remark in the shipwrights' play of the flood, when he complains to God that he knows nothing of shipbuilding.

These insider jokes are quietly funny, but inside jokes cannot remain inside in these plays for long, precisely because this drama undoes boundaries between inside and outside, between the fictional space and the real city. The area in which Christ could not find shelter is at once an imagined Bethlehem and a real York. The fluidity with which scriptural narrative is suddenly the narrative of fifteenth-century urban and manorial life generates self-criticism of different intensities. In domestic narratives male weakness is exposed fairly gently for the most part, whereas other narratives expose the alienation of labour from its brutal human effect in searingly critical ways.

Let us begin with the exposure of men. Male organizations were responsible for the production of these plays, but the crafts were closely related to, and in some cases overlapped with, religious fraternities, which practised a gender equality. Women figure very prominently in the action of the plays, and women possibly played the women's parts.[39] The plays give extraordinary prominence to domestic life in their reception of scriptural narrative, and women hold centre stage in many of the dramas of family life, such as Eve, Noah's wife, Elizabeth, Mary, and the mothers defending their children against Herod's mass murder. In the Apostolic plays, when the social structures on stage are evangelical rather than familial, women continue to play critical roles. In almost all these plays the women are the heroines, who set into sharp contrast the exhaustion, the blindness, and sometimes the brutality of men. In the slaughter plays the brutality is that of thugs and henchmen of feudal aristocrats, but for the most part male weakness in these plays is that of *l'homme moyen sensuel*.[40]

[39] The evidence for women actors in the mystery plays is not abundant, but there is some. Chester assigned the Play of the Assumption of the Virgin to the 'wyfus of the town', for which see Bevington, p. 79.

[40] For an excellent discussion of the cycle plays' presentation of 'natural man', see Kolve, chs. 9 and 10.

The most daring appropriation of Scriptural narrative is the comic play of 'Joseph's Trouble with Mary', which appears in all four complete cycles. In the York play, for example, Joseph opens the play by lamenting his own impotence, and the shame he feels at his wife's pregnancy. He fears lest anyone should ask him to prove his own fatherhood, and is equally unwilling to defame his wife 'with any man': 'I mon noght scape withouten schame. | The childe certis is noght myne; | That reproffe dose me pyne | And gars [causes] me fle fra hame' (*York Plays*, 13. 54–7). Dialogues with both Mary's handmaidens and Mary herself fail to persuade Joseph of the strange truth. He translates that truth into wonderfully compacted jokes whose comedy he cannot appreciate: denying that an angel is responsible for Mary's pregnancy, he invokes popular stories of men dressed as angels betraying women: 'Nay, some man in augellis liknesse | With somkyn gawde has hir begiled' (13. 136–7). Joseph remains locked in his shame, embarrassment and fear of the law, determined to flee to the wilderness, until the angel comes to him in sleep. The angel resolves the marital dispute, Joseph is reconciled with Mary, and the play ends with the impotent and exhausted Joseph reassuming his burdens, his pride protected by a shrewd wife. Mary denies that Joseph requires forgiveness, and so Joseph takes up the heavy pack for the journey to Bethlehem: 'Till Bedlem bus [behoves] me it bere, | For litill thyng will women dere [vex]; | Helpe up nowe on my bak' (13. 303–5).

The play ends, sure enough, with patriarchal structures intact, but fully revised. Patriarchy here is quietly revealed as a structure designed to disguise male impotence and exhaustion. The marriage between old Joseph and young Mary is no less improbable than the cultural marriage of fabliau and scriptural narrative; both marriages reveal, however, that the ostensibly weaker partner is the real source of strength.

In these plays, too, then, what should remain silent is open to view. In the Coventry weavers' play of the Purification Joseph initially refuses to search out the two doves required for the rite, pleading old age. From the stage Joseph addresses all the men of the audience, encouraging them to speak up about the pain and travail of marriage: 'How sey ye all this company | That be weddid asses well asse I? | I wene that ye suffur moche woo . . . Speyke men, for schame! |

Tell you the trothe ase you wel con!'.[41] This comic call ostensibly asks the men in the audience to engage in some conventional wife-berating; the play as a whole, however, articulates a larger truth about male vulnerability that the men might rather wish to conceal.

This exposure of male vulnerability is especially pronounced in the Joseph and Mary plays, but even in the more traditionally patriarchal Old Testament plays the women expose the rigours of patriarchy. Thus in the wonderful single survivor from Northampton, a play about the sacrifice of Isaac, Abraham is fearfully and rightly worried about what Sara will think of his willingness to sacrifice their only son at God's behest. That reflection puts maximal pressure on the apparent brutality of God's pact with Abraham. Or in the Noah plays Noah's wife, in refusing to enter the ark, would seem to be a butt of conventional anti-feminist satire. The York, Wakefield, and Chester Noah plays nevertheless reveal the reasons why Noah's wife might be infuriated by her husband's dealings with God. In York she says that Noah is always at work, without telling her what he's been up to; this will strike chords with the married couples of the audience, particularly as Noah has been at it for one hundred years (*York Plays*, 9. 113–34). And the wife is, reasonably, unwilling to enter the ark without her 'commodrys [gossips, close friends] and cousynes bathe' (9. 143). In the Wakefield Noah play the dispute between Noah and his wife is so violent as to beggar simplistic anti-feminist responses. The play represents the stress and emotional mess of a fraught familial moment of getting ready for a journey, which degenerates into spectacular domestic violence in front of the children. The husband threatens to beat the wife, and the wife wishes the husband dead; each partner appeals respectively to the wives and husbands in the audience for support.

Domestic violence in which men are thoroughly implicated, then, stands at the turning points of Old Testament history. After Christ's Resurrection family structures are replaced on stage by evangelical groupings who prepare for the apostolic life, but here, too, women play critical roles so as to expose the blindness of their fellow apostles. At the end of the Wakefield Thomas play, for example, Thomas

[41] *Two Coventry Corpus Christi Plays*, ed. Craig, ll. 463–74. All further references will be made by line number in the body of the text.

apologizes to Christ and begs his mercy for his disbelief. He should also, the play makes clear, be apologizing to women, just as should Peter and Paul. For the play begins with Mary Magdalene announcing to Peter and Paul that Christ is risen. The chief apostles meet her announcement with a disbelief underwritten by anti-feminism. Women believe anything. Paul is the first to expose the grounds of his disbelief: 'And it is wretyn in oure law, | 'Ther is no trust in womens saw, | No trust faith to belefe' (*York Plays*, 28. 29–31). And so he goes on, concluding that women are fickle 'in word and thought'. Of course these same apostles later in the same play recognize the truth of Mary's witness, but even after their conversion doubting Thomas dismisses the other male apostles' credulity as feminine: they are like women, 'lightly oft solaced' (28. 404).

As the productions of male organizations, then, the cycle plays are reflexively critical of patriarchy. They are also powerfully self-critical in their presentation of labour, especially in those plays where the focus is on workmen. Thus in the York Crucifixion play we observe not tyrants or vicious bishops, but rather humble soldiers who do the practical jobs of punishment. Like many of the plays in the cycles, this play is clearly relevant to the craft responsible for its staging, since it was performed by the pinners, or nail makers, who in this play must nail Christ to the Cross. At the centre of the play they complain about the way their labour is damaging them physically; a failed attempt to lift the crucified Christ produces nothing but shoulders out of joint and breathlessness in these 'wight' or strong men (*York Plays*, 35. 188–206). This little moment may be taken as exemplary of the representation of labour in these plays, since, for all the pride in the labour of a given craft, the plays equally underline the ways in which a purely material practice of labour is brutal and damaging. Near the beginning of the cycles, in Adam and Eve's expulsion from Paradise, they are promised hard labour: in the Chester play, for example, God insists that the earth will be cursed in Adam's work, and 'with greate travell behoves thee | one earth to get thy livinge'.[42] The plays are acutely conscious of the ways in which 'greate travell' demeans and brutalizes.

[42] *Chester Mystery Cycle*, ed. Lumiansky and Mills, 2. 326–8. All further references will be made by play and line number in the body of the text.

The York Crucifixion play represents the alienation of labour and technology from their brutal effects in searingly powerful ways. Like the pinners performing their play, the workmen on stage have only a limited time to do their work and they open by stressing the deadline: 'This dede on dergh [extended time] we may not drawe' (*York Plays*, 35. 2). For the workmen are proud of their skill as artisans, and annoyed at the carelessness of the artisans who bored the holes on the Cross. For the holes are too far apart, and so demand a terrible pulling of Christ's arms to stretch him to the required fit. Because Christ is laid out flat on the stage, the audience sees only the workmen at work, and hears them complain about the poor work of their fellow craft. Within the limitation of that vision, the audience provisionally wishes only that the hole borers had done their job more carefully. The pinners' work is, however, subject to pressure from another sense of 'work'. They insist that their 'wirkyng be noght wronge' (35. 26), or, once the nail pierces the bones and sinews of the stretched arm, they express their satisfaction: 'This werke is wele' (35. 104). Even as Christ asks God for their forgiveness, however, they also unthinkingly accuse Christ of 'wikkid werkis' (35. 66).

These workmen enjoy an evident solidarity; they also want to do a job well. The processes of their labour are, however, dwarfed by a larger, ethical account of 'works'. That larger perspective is dramatically visible once Christ is raised. The workmen ask him how he admires 'this werke that we have wrought' (35. 249), but Christ's address is to 'Al men that walkis by waye or strete', cautioning them to be sure that they shall 'no travayle tyne [waste]' (35. 253–4). The speech of the elevated Christ is a massive break in the fictional bounds of the stage: Christ speaks to the audience in the 'street' as much as to the workmen, and beyond them to all who behold the spectacle of the crucified Christ. The playwright brilliantly renews a biblical topos of devotional poetry ('O all you who pass by') in the context of the street theatre.[43] In theatrical terms, Christ's speech effects a radical alienation effect, prohibiting the audience from immersion in the stage illusion. The point of the theatrical alienation is to underline the more significant alienation of labour from its larger ethical meaning.

[43] The biblical source is Lam. 1. 12. For the use of this text in religious lyrics, see Woolf, pp. 42–5.

IV

The cycle plays, then, were capable of penetrating reflection on the institutions out of which they emerged, both the institutions responsible for the execution of secular and ecclesiastical law, and the labour organizations of late medieval cities. Pilate begins the Wakefield flagellation play with a metaphor that expresses the relentless lack of pity characteristic of both law and labour: 'For like', he says, 'as on both sydes the iren the hamer makith playn, | So do I, that the law has here in my kepyng' (*York Plays*, 22. 14–15). Reflection on the exhausting, relentless, and finally melancholy nature of the active life is given extraordinarily high profile in these plays: the literally and thematically central scenes of interrogation and punishment show the hammer of law and labour being wielded with regularity. In this section I turn to the plays' account of how the active life might find energies within itself that are capable of turning the hammer of the world aside.

If the plays represent Christ as the victim of interrogation, trial, and punishment, then the cycle as a whole takes care to represent Christ's own trial and punishment of mankind at the Last Judgement. The argument of this chapter so far has been that the cycle plays of York and Wakefield are not primarily sacramental or devotional. They do occasionally make sacramental references, though only very occasionally and with nothing like the insistence of the Corpus Christi procession or, as we shall see, *The Croxton Play of the Sacrament*. And if they frequently draw on the modes of devotional writing that dwell on Christ's suffering, they do so within a larger reflection upon the social structures that produce that pain. Within the light of that argument, it is significant that the conclusion of the plays should focus so insistently upon a theology of social practice, rather than liturgical practice or private devotion. Whereas the sacrament of the Eucharist in particular became an instrument for separating the faithful from the heretic in fifteenth-century England, Christ's discriminations of sheep from goats in the Last Judgement plays are made on the basis of individuals' applied acts of mercy. Thus Christ cites himself from the Gospel of Matthew (Matt. 25: 31–46) in a final dissolution of the boundary between stage and audience so characteristic of this drama. Christ will save those who exercised mercy to the Christ in each suffering human: 'Whanne I was wille [desolate] and werieste | Ye herbered me full hartfully; | Full gladde thanne were ye of youre geste, | And pleyned [sympathized with] my poverté piteously' (*York Plays*, 47. 293–6). Just as the plays themselves presented many bodies playing Christ, so too do they promote a notion of the divisibility of Christ in each suffering human.

The cycles do not of course leave this account of socially active mercy until their final play, and neither do they restrict this point for what is effectively, for all its grandeur, an instructive mode. I complete this discussion of the cycle plays by looking to the action of mercy in the profound Wakefield Second Shepherds' play. This play might on the face of it seem to provide perfect exemplification of Marx's dictum that religion is the opium of the people. The play begins with the shepherds complaining of their exploitation, and ends with the resolution of that exploitation as they give what little they have to the newborn Christ. The Wakefield playwright knows very well how painful it is for agricultural workers to give of their earnings: in the Cain and Abel play, Cain's refusal to tithe is an entirely plausible account of a peasant worker refusing Church taxation. He also knows how oppressive is the life of such a labourer: this play begins with the first shepherd complaining privately of the oppression of landlords, who not only take his equipment, but also threaten him if he complains. The precise representation of manorial life in the Wakefield cycle may indeed derive from the manorial organization of that town, unlike the self-governing city of York.[44] This precisely realized account of manorial oppression is resolved at the play's end, however, by the shepherds' voluntarily giving the Christ child what little they can spare—a bob of cherries, a bird, a ball. The shepherds answer, then, to the robbery of their own lords by giving material gifts to yet another lord.

A materialist account of this play is not at all eccentric to its representation of manorial life, but it finally falls seriously short of the play's own account of materiality. After the opening complaints of the shepherds, the thief Mak arrives, promising friendship and complaining of his domestic situation, with a voracious wife and so many children to feed. Once the sheep has been stolen and taken home,

[44] For the civic structure of Wakefield, see Martin Stevens, pp. 126–7.

Mak returns to the shepherds in the fields, pretending to have slept all night with them. He then returns home, followed soon after by the shepherds in search of their sheep. Gil his wife has in the meanwhile disguised the sheep as a newborn child and pretends herself to be suffering from the pains of childbirth. The shepherds are tricked until, as they go, they remember that they have not given the child a present. The child's especially long nose being discovered, the sequence ends with the shepherds tossing Mak in a sheet as a punishment; the play ends with the shepherds being called by the angel to Bethlehem and giving their gifts to the newborn Christ.

The key moment in this sequence is not when the shepherds give to the newborn Christ. It is, instead, when they remember to give to Mak's 'child'. This play is pressingly aware of the ways in which members of an oppressed society oppress each other in turn. If the lords oppress the peasants, the first two shepherds oppress the third; the second shepherd feels oppressed by his wife; Mak exploits the trust of the shepherds. What drives this oppression amongst the oppressed is, unsurprisingly, hunger: the third shepherd is hungry, and Mak is tormented by the insatiable hunger of his many children, so much so that he wishes himself in heaven, where no children weep. Even as the hungry shepherds have been robbed of their sheep, however, they return to give to the newborn child, and out of that act of generosity emerges the giving at Christ's nativity. The structure of this play implies less that Christ came to help the starving than that the generosity of the starving produces Christ. Christ's presence in this play does not in any way dissolve the material world; on the contrary, Christ is born out of the relentless imperatives of that material world, precisely because one small act of generosity has turned those relentless imperatives aside.

The Christian comedy of this play takes possession of official discourses through the force of what might be called its materialist spirituality. Within the play, the shepherds take possession of the official sanction of law, which hovers threateningly at the edge of this play, since the penalty for sheep-stealing was hanging. Instead of hanging, they toss Mak in a sheet. Popular appropriation of official discourse also characterizes the play's own practice. For there are typological and sacramental resonances here, since Christ is the Lamb of God, the sacrifice adumbrated by Isaac as he is replaced by the animal, and Christ is the lamb whose flesh Christians eat in the Eucharist. Mak's wife at one point promises to eat the child in her cradle if she has tricked the shepherds. The force of this compacted comment dissolves the boundaries between official discourse and its parody, since, in the larger structure of the play, Gil will indeed 'eat the child' precisely because she has sinned. This 'official' account of Eucharistic practice can only work, however, through its popular parody. Eating the Eucharist is intimately related to, and finally inseparable from, feeding a family.

V

In the mystery plays the operation of mercy serves to recuperate the old, and all those who are exhausted by the relentless pressures of the active life. Even as the audience members witness Christ's future separation of the saved and the damned in the Last Judgement, they are themselves, in the present of the play's performance, offered the chance of inclusion among the saved. Before the Crucifixion the aged Simeon in the York Purification feels rejuvenated by the promise of the newborn Christ: 'Nowe am I light as leyf on tree, | My age is went, I feyll no fray, | Methinke for this that told is me | I am not olde' (*York Plays*, 17. 346–9). And after the Crucifixion Christ harrows Hell, drawing the souls of the faithful from darkness. Christ also draws the Old Testament into the New, just as the formal practice of the plays draws much that is textually and culturally discarded into a newly formulated urban spirituality. Old Testament and wholly apocryphal narrative is freely included and transformed by a promise of salvation that is at once ethical and cultural: those who thought they were for ever in Hell can be saved, just as the forms of popular culture can take possession of the streets of great cities.

Let us now turn, for contrast, to the professional theatre, both post- and pre-Reformation. For there, instead of ethical and formal inclusiveness, we observe instead exclusions, or inclusion through severe disciplines and punishments. If the mystery plays took possession of official punishment, the professional theatre enforced it. I begin with John Bale's own version of the mystery cycles, for there we can see in very sharp form a new, exclusionary historical practice whose exclusions are at once formal and doctrinal. The exclusions are so sharp, indeed, that Bale must paradoxically repudiate the doctrine and form of the very drama upon whose energies he is dependent.

A policy document of around 1538, probably written by Richard Morison, encouraged Henry to countenance plays. The propaganda machine of the enemy is so powerful, the document avers, that Henry needs to counter-attack. The Pope has his own interests 'inculked and dryven into the peoples heddes, tought in scoles to children, plaied in playes before the ignorant people'. So, too, Morison argues, Henry should himself promote 'playes, songes and books . . . specyally whan they declare eyther the abhominacion of the bisshop of rome . . . or the benefittes browght to thys realme by your graces tornyng hym and hys out of it'.[45] Morison's suggestion is straightforward enough, but he cannot help but acknowledge a problem with it, that any such propaganda will carry other dangers. It may be that Henry simply does not like drama at all—plays are to be tolerated, says Morison, 'thowghe som thyng in them [is] to be misliked'. From the evidence of the slightly later legislation of the 1540s, it is indeed clear that Henry was sensitive to drama (though not, apparently, to cycle drama), and wished to control it.[46] Morison's unspecified worry about what might be distasteful in the drama at least suggests that the real problem is contamination by the very modes one wishes to repudiate. It is very difficult, he says, 'to make any thyng ayenst papists so perfecte as you woll not fynd faut with it'. That this is what worries him is also suggested by the propagandistic processional modes he goes on to outline, since these are modelled on ecclesiastical processions, but now given a nationalistic content.

Morison was secretary to Thomas Cromwell from the mid-1530s; if he promoted the idea of anti-papal plays, then it is entirely possible that John Bale wrote them, since, as seems to be the case, Bale too was in the pay of Cromwell in the late 1530s. The troupe 'Balle and his felowes' played before Cromwell more than once between 1538

[45] The quotations from Morison in this para. are from Anglo, 'Early Tudor Programme', p. 178.

[46] *SR*, 34–5 Henry VIII, ch. 1 (3. 894–5), and *Tudor Royal Proclamations*, ed. Hughes and Larkin, 1, 341–2 (dated 1544). This legislation is discussed below.

and 1539, and scholars now identify Bale's troupe with the company 'Lord Cromwell's Players'.[47] Certainly plays by Bale survive from the 1530s, both his *King Johan* and his mini-cycle of religious plays. Many other plays, often about the life of Christ and apparently offering a Protestant answer to the cycle plays, have not survived.[48] I turn now to Bale's 'mini-cycle', comprising *God's Promises*, *Johan Baptystes Preachynge*, *The Temptation of Our Lord*, and the *Three Laws*.[49] For in these plays we observe precisely Morison's fear of contamination by a detested model upon which one is nevertheless reliant.

The basic instructional strategy of these plays is to identify the immediate past with the fallen past of the Old Testament, so repudiating both. Thus in *God's Promises* Bale's Old Testament God consistently feels ill at the prospect of Israel's obstinate worship of idols that are clearly the idols of the pre-Reformation Church:

> Discontent I am with you beastes of Gomorra,
> And have no pleasure whan I your offerynges se.
> I abhorre your fastes and your solempnyte.
> For your tradycyons my wayes ye set apart.
> Your workes are in vayne: I hate them from the hart.
>
> (ll. 691–5)

The very title of this play is Tyndalian, as is its contradictory posture towards the past. Old Testament history is recounted not to be recuperated; on the contrary, that history is a narrative of catastrophe and divine repugnance at idolatry and faith in works. Precisely as such, Old Testament history serves to attack the immediate past, too, since God's visceral repudiation of idolatry is clearly a repudiation of the cultic practice of the pre-Reformation Church within which Bale had himself been trained, and in which he was still living as he wrote.

The only way in which history can be recuperated is via the narrow path of lonely heroism and foresight. *God's Promises* consists of a

[47] See White, *Theatre and Reformation*, pp. 16–17.

[48] For a precise account of Bale's dramatic output, see Bale *Complete Plays*, ed. Happé, 1. 8–9.

[49] Edited ibid., vol. 2. All of these plays except *Johan Baptystes Preachynge* were printed in Wesel in 1547. All further citations of the text itself are from this edn., cited in the body of the text.

series of dialogues between God and individual just men: Adam, Noah, Abraham, Moses, David, Isaiah, and John the Baptist. Pater Coelestis is on stage at every moment, and the only way his interlocutors interact with him is occasionally to restrain his vengeance; otherwise they receive his threats of extermination and spectacular punishment. Thus Moses and God:

Pater Coelestis: Nevyr wyll I spare the cursed inyquyte
Of ydolatrye for no cause—thu mayst trust me.
Moses Sanctus: Forgeve them yet, lorde, for thys tyme if it maye be.
Pater Coelestis: Thynkest thu that I wyll so sone change my decre?
No, no, frynde Moses, so lyght thu shalt not fynde me.
I wyl ponnysh them: all Israel shall it se.

(ll. 507–12)

Only the few just, capable of foreseeing the brilliant new law of Christ, are to be saved. In *Three Laws* Moses describes himself as a 'blind cripple' wandering alone and abiding the time of grace (l. 1266).

Old Testament history survives, then, only in the person of the single survivor, the Pauline figure whose authenticity can be guaranteed only through persecution. Bale himself clearly saw himself in precisely these terms, and may be writing himself into the part of the persecuted John the Baptist in *Johan Baptystes Preachynge*. That play begins with John the Baptist preaching to '*turba vulgaris* [vulgar crowd]'; after the central action of the persecution of John the Baptist for his preaching of the 'newe learnynge', the play ends with Bale's own epilogue, preaching the same thing. Certainly Bale did see himself as a new St Paul, and his expulsion as a dramatist by the '*turba vulgaris*' of Kilkenny, Ireland, contributed to his sense of evangelical mission. Sent to Kilkenny as bishop of Ossory in the reign of Edward VI, Bale recounts that, after the death of Edward had been announced, the accession of Mary was celebrated with great liturgical pomp. Bale tried to counter the celebration by mounting a performance of Bale's 'cycle' plays, 'to the small contentacion of the prestes and other papistes there'.[50] All this is shortly before Bale fled Kilkenny for Dublin and further misadventures in fear for his life.

[50] *Vocation of Johan Bale*, p. 59. Bale compares himself explicitly and at length with St Paul, pp. 33–4.

Bale's drama has been described as the first genuinely 'popular' theatre. His expulsion by the *turba vulgaris* of Kilkenny is itself, rather, a response to Bale's own expulsion of the 'popular'.[51] The most obvious such expulsion is that of apocryphal matter. The text of Scripture supervises these plays, with all the non-scriptural scenes that appear in the mystery plays, such as the fall of the Angels, removed. Whereas the cycle plays give a very cursory account of the Old Testament by restricting themselves to a few grand encounters that extend no further than Exodus, apart from some prophet plays, Bale tries to squeeze in as much summary as possible. Bale's bibliographical instincts take over in *God's Promises*, whose seven acts offer a small course in the shape of the Old Testament, with whole stanzas devoted to summarizing sequences of books. Christ himself enunciates the principles of this biblical pedagogy in *The Temptation of Our Lord*, where he debates points of Scripture with Satan. When Satan tempts Christ by citing a passage of Scripture, Christ responds with an axiom of evangelical reading practice: 'In no wyse ye ought the scriptures to deprave, | But as they lye whole so ought ye them to have' (ll. 215–16). Christ himself is held to the command of Scripture here: if he ignored scriptural injunction by following Satan, he would incur God's wrath. In the *Three Laws*, indeed, Evangelium becomes itself the hero of the play, the indestructible survivor of the catastrophe of history. These plays are so dominated by the authority of Scripture that fidelity to that pre-dramatic text effectively pre-empts the dramatic itself. 'Drama' becomes instead the occasion for scriptural summary.

Not only does Bale proscribe the textually 'popular' from the stage, but he actively demonizes popular practice on stage. In the second act of *Three Laws* Infidelitas attacks Natural Law with her minions Idolatry and Sodomy. Idolatry is associated especially with peasant magic and feminine midwifery, which uses charms, 'with crossynges and with kyssynges'. She is to be 'decked like an olde wytche' (p. 121). Her appearance heralded new legislative control of midwifery in Henrician England, as well as the campaign against old women on charges of witchcraft that reached its height in the later

[51] For description of Bale's drama as 'in the popular manner', see the otherwise excellent Bevington, p. 51.

sixteenth century.[52] Sodomy figures both as a standard evangelical attack on private religions, and as a subset of idolatry, since idolatry itself is, and spawns, unnatural confusion of proper semiotic practice: 'The gentyles after Idolatrye | Fell to soch bestyall Sodomye | That God ded them forsake' (ll. 604–6). Sodomy's first appearance on the English stage, to my knowledge, is itself consonant with the Henrician statute against 'buggery', the first statute in English law of its kind.[53] Whereas the charms and popular practice of the Second Shepherds' Play are finally absorbed into a renewed and much broader theological understanding, in Bale's plays the popular is a sure sign of satanic enormity.

The representation of history within Bale's plays is, then, parallel to the plays' own historical posture. We see, that is, single Old Testament figures on stage represented as the lonely survivors of a catastrophic history, and their heroism is defined precisely by their rejection of their own times. So too does Bale's drama stand formally in relation to the cycle plays as a survivor who rejects the tradition out of which it grew. And beyond the plays, so too does Bale himself present his own life as a narrative of persecution by a corrupt and misguided world. His survival of that persecution and his rejection of the culture of his youth guarantees the authenticity of his faith.

That argument holds for the contrast between Bale's mini-cycle and the cycles of York and Wakefield, and the surviving plays of the Coventry cycle. Before leaving cycle drama altogether, however, some qualification should be made with regard to the Chester and N-Town cycles. Those cycles are unquestionably born out of a pre-Reformation theological and social matrix, but they do in some respects offer the resources for a much more aggressively didactic drama of the kind Bale writes. The Coventry, York, and Wakefield plays each represent lay appropriation of clerical learning, and each equally represent the arrogance of academics, especially in the plays devoted to the boy Christ's encounter with the doctors in the temple. The Coventry weavers' play is especially revealing here, as Joseph is afraid to go up to the doctors to ask about his son: 'With men of myght durst I neyver mell [talk]. | Loo! Dame, how the sytt in there

[52] See *Visitation Articles and Injunctions*, ed. Frere and Kennedy, 1. 58, for evangelical control of midwifery.

[53] *SR*, 25 Henry VIII, ch. 6 (3. 441).

furis [furs] fyn!' (*Coventry Plays*, 1039–40). By contrast, Chester and the N-Town plays are much more clearly aligned with an academic and clerical posture of lay instruction. This is evident not only in their very explicit teaching on the sacraments, but also in their much more consistently underlined typology. In the N-Town New Testament plays the playwright stresses sacramental theology of baptism, penance, and the Eucharist much more consistently than do the York and Wakefield cycles.[54] Chester does the same, though begins earlier, with Melchisedech's offer of bread and wine to Abraham (*Chester Cycle*, 4. 65–80).

It may also be relevant that the N-Town cycle gives much higher profile to obedience in the Old Testament plays of Noah, and Abraham and Isaac, where the York and Wakefield cycles present conflict. In the context of East Anglia, where Lollardy was especially active, it is also significant that criticism of 'bishops' is very muted. One Pharisee is a model figure, and when Annas and Caiaphas appear the playwright takes especial care to insist that they be dressed in the costumes of the old law.[55] Whereas York and Wakefield deploy anachronism in highly strategic ways so as to critique contemporary institutions, N-Town seeks to neutralize any potential criticism of its contemporary episcopate.

Chester above all, however, manifests a concerted deference to academic learning and frequently gestures to the presence of written, scriptural authority beyond the bounds of, yet constraining, the action on stage. Anxieties about the match of Scripture and plays were clearly alive in the later stages of the play's history, as it came under evangelical scrutiny. The Banns that must have been produced shortly before the plays were closed in 1575 are very defensive about the antiquity of the cycle and its value. The presenter quickly warns that the plays sometimes intermingle 'onley to make sporte | Some thinges not warranted by anye wrytte'. He hastens to assure his enlightened audience that they should in no way compare the plays

[54] e.g. 22: baptism; 27: Last Supper; 35: Harrowing of Hell. The York Cycle misses a leaf for the Last Supper, which was possibly removed deliberately in the sixteenth century. Some important evidence is therefore missing. See *York Plays*, ed. Beadle, pp. 230–1.

[55] *N-Town Play*, ed. Spector, vol. 1. A model bishop appears in Play 14. Play 26 specifies old law costumes for Annas and Caiaphas, p. 252.

with the 'age or tyme wherein we presentlye staye— | But to the tyme of ignorance whearin we doe *straye*'.[56]

That such anxieties should be expressed about the Chester cycle is ironic, since the plays of that cycle, more than any other, allude to the para-text of Scripture around the drama. Thus in the Barbers' play of Abraham, after the priest Melchisedech exchanges offerings with Abraham and Lot, a mounted Expositor interrupts the action without any pretence of maintaining the dramatic illusion: 'Lordynges, what may this signifye | I will expound yt appertly – | The unlearned standynge hereby | Maye knowe what thjis may bee' (*Chester Cycle*, 4. 113–16). He goes on to explain that the gift of bread and wine signifies the New Testament; so too after the non-sacrifice of Isaac, he interrupts to shepherd learned interpretation: 'This deede yee seene done here in this place, | In example of Jesus done yt was' (4. 464–5). In these and many other instances in the Chester cycle, the dehistoricized, learned voice stands outside the action of the historical moment to instruct the audience.[57] The Chester plays were possibly produced from Chester's monastery of St Werburgh, the site of the first station; this might account for the high profile of the learned in the Chester plays. It may also be relevant that the form of the plays in which they survive seems to derive from the period 1500–50, later than any of the other cycles and possibly written, then, in an environment of heightened consciousness about the boundaries and interpretation of Scripture. In any case the role of Expositor, drawn from the mystery plays, provides the cue for 'Baleus prolocutor' who instructs his own *turba vulgaris* at the beginning of each play in the Bale 'mini-cycle'.[58]

Bale's strained relation to the cycle plays in the late 1530s is symptomatic of later evangelical hostility to the amateur drama of the cycles. The mystery plays are historically inclusive; ready freely to reinscribe Scripture with apocryphal and anachronistic material; centrally committed to a soteriology of works. For all these doctrinal and cultural reasons the plays became increasingly fragile from the

[56] *Chester Mystery Cycle: Essays and Documents*, ed. Lumiansky and Mills, pp. 285–6; my emphasis.

[57] Other instances of such an expositor in the Chester cycle are found as follows: plays 5, 6, 8 (partially held within the action of the play), 12, and 22.

[58] York is not wholly without its Doctor (Play 12), but he has a much lower profile. Wakefield has no Doctor play.

Act of Supremacy until their disappearance within a few years, from 1569 to 1576. I end this section with a discussion of why the cycle plays survived so long.

Corpus Christi drama had attracted powerful if isolated critique from evangelical writers in the pre-Reformation period. The late fourteenth-/early fifteenth-century *Tretise of Miraclis Pleyinge* attacked the plays by arguing that they 'reverse' Christ in many ways. The dispute imagined by this text is a copybook instance of the hermeneutic confrontation discussed in Chapter 9. The Lollard author imagines an opponent, who argues that the plays should be criticized only insofar as they are contrary to *belief*. The author responds by saying that they can be countenanced only if they are *grounded* explicitly in Christ's sayings. They are not so grounded: they only play at miracles, whereas Christ's were true; they joke about God; they detract from the serious business of penance; they add or subtract from Christ's words; they encourage expense that would be better directed to the poor. Most damagingly, they are idolatrous: they move in reverse from the New Testament, constituting 'a verre goynge bacward from dedis of the spirit to onley syngnes don after lustis of the fleysh' (ll. 526–34).

Strangely, however, the plays did survive until the 1570s. Given the massive rupture provoked by the cultural revolution of the 1530s for almost each mode of writing considered in this history, why should the cycle plays have alone survived so long? That they were closed down in the 1570s by government fiat was argued persuasively by Gardiner in an excellent book of 1946. For Chester, York, and Wakefield he cites incontrovertible evidence of centralized and evangelical effort to ban the plays, contrary to a strong local desire to keep them going, in the 1560s and 1570s. Gardiner's argument has been qualified by more recent scholars, who point to the economic crises of the sixteenth century, crises that militated against the expensive mounting of cycle drama by guilds.[59]

On the whole, though, I think Gardiner's arguments about a 'top-down' evangelical and governmental suppression of the drama remain persuasive. The dating of the plays' demise also sits well with the arguments of Collinson about the second wave of iconoclastic

[59] Coldewey, 'Economic Aspects', p. 88; and Bills.

activity in Reformation England, which began towards the 1580s.[60] The real question, though, is rather why they survived so long. Evidence that they were adapting to circumstances in the face of evangelical hostility can be seen in the way some plays are dropped, or in the way a cycle moves to a less contentious date in the calendrical year. Thus in York the plays representing the death, assumption, and coronation of the Virgin were excised between 1548 and 1553, in the reign of Edward VI.[61] The Chester cycle had moved from Corpus Christi to Whitsun as early as 1521, but in 1575 it was moved again to an entirely secular feast on midsummer. Small-scale adaptation, however, cannot account for the survival of such large and visible enterprises. Neither can the argument that they were simply so popular that central control was unable to handle them.[62] Central government had, after all, demolished popular liturgical practice in the 1530s.[63] Governments could dismantle popular practice when it was not constrained by intervening institutional barriers. I offer two suggestions.

In the first place, the plays were the production of civic institutions, which were not under direct royal command in the way the Church theoretically was from 1534. Tudor monarchs depended on the good will and taxation of great urban centres, and could not command cultural practice there in the way they could theoretically control ecclesiastical practice after 1534. As we have already seen, the production of Corpus Christi plays was a matter of intense civic pride, by way of promoting the prestige of the city, spiritual considerations aside. The plays themselves provided a sense of the continuities of civic history and identity. When the plays were under threat, for example, one possible line of defence was the historical one, that the plays were and should continue to be performed 'according to the auncyente and lawdable usages and cutomes there hadd and used fur above remembraunce'.[64] Each of the five texts of the Chester cycle was copied after the final performance of the plays,

[60] Collinson, ch. 4.

[61] *York Plays*, ed. Beadle, pp. 459–60.

[62] As argued by Dutton, 'Censorship'.

[63] Duffy.

[64] *Chester Mystery Cycle: Essays and Documents*, ed. Lumiansky and Mills, p. 224. The citation is from a document defending the mayor's decision to mount the plays as a corporate decision, dated 1575.

between 1591 and 1607, by copyists clearly interested in preserving important documents of civic history.

Secondly, some of the cycles were not, as I have argued in this chapter, wholly at odds with the *entire* evangelical programme. John Foxe's single story of John Careless, the Protestant weaver released in 1553 from prison in Coventry for a day to perform in the Corpus Christi play, is itself an insufficient basis on which to mount a case for evangelical sympathy for the plays.[65] Defences of the plays made in Chester when the plays were under serious attack are slightly stronger evidence for a potential source of such sympathy. Thus the Late Banns from Chester invoke a putative author of the cycle, the prolific fourteenth-century monk Ranulph Higden, who deserves praise for having made available 'storyes of the testamente' at a time when they were 'in common Englishe tonge never reade nor harde'. According to this account the monk ('and noe moncke', the author hastens to add) risked execution for having set out 'parte of good belefe'.[66] Such a defence pictures Higden as a proto-Protestant, risking his life to promulgate Scripture. It is of course made in an especially defensive document, and is useful as the kind of argument that might retrospectively be drawn on to defend the plays from radical evangelical attack.

More persuasive, perhaps, is the evidence from the plays themselves. As we have seen above, the York and Wakefield cycles in particular promote a vernacular theology that is seriously critical of academic, episcopal, and royal repression of new religious movements. The point that the plays are not themselves Lollard cannot be overstressed, but they do emerge from the same cultural pressures that produced Lollardy. Even so, by the late 1570s such overlaps are fine points now lost from view as the plays fell victim to a more radical iconoclastic pressure. By 1609, after listing the order of the 'Whitson plays', an antiquarian author in Chester concludes his discussion of the mystery plays thus:

[65] Though White does begin from that episode to mount an excellent, wider case for a moderate Protestant reception of the plays; see his 'Reforming Mysteries' End'. For a ground-breaking argument about how the plays should be historicized according to different moments of their reception, see also Emmerson.

[66] *Chester Mystery Cycle: Essays and Documents*, ed. Lumiansky and Mills, pp. 285–7; the citation is from the Late Banns, ll. 18–27.

And we have all cause to power [pour] out oure prayers before God that neither wee nor oure posterities after us maye nevar see the like abomination of desolation with suche a clowde of ignorance to defile with so highe a hand the most sacred scriptures of God. But, oh, the merscie of God: for the tyme of oure ignorance, he regardes it not.[67]

VI

Lydgate's *Troy Book* (1412–20) describes the building of Priam's royal palace in the new Troy, with a theatre attached, that comedies and tragedies might be performed. The palace is perfectly round, and whoever wished to take its measure would be obliged first to enter via the space of the theatre. From the theatre, the admirer of Priam's palace would ascend to the walls, where he would see 'the boundis of many regioun, | And provincys that stond rounde aboute' (2. 941–61).[68] Whereas the mystery plays, as I have argued, resist appropriation by any royal ideology, early Tudor drama takes place very much within the bounds of the king's inspection. England's first professional theatre opened, in Whitechapel, in 1567, which coincides with the end of the cycles in York (1569), Wakefield (1576), and Chester (1575). Scholars have made a good deal of the fact that the suburbs of London, particularly Southwark, were outside the jurisdictional bounds of the cities of either London or Westminster.[69] Southwark is a good deal closer to London, however, than either York or Wakefield. Here I plot some of the movements towards the more centralized, professional theatre from the reign of Henry VII to 1547. In Section VII, I turn to pre-Reformation professional theatre. In both these areas we find a professional, troupe theatre clearly aligned with the disciplinary interests of sponsoring institutions.

[67] Ibid., pp. 265–6.

[68] See Ch. 2, above.

[69] See Mullaney, who seems unaware of a popular, non-metropolitan theatre; thus on p. 8 he says that 'of all the arts, drama is the most social, indeed the most metropolitan'. On p. 9 we read that 'popular drama in England emerged as a cultural institution only by . . . dislocating itself from the strict confines of the social order and taking up a place on the margins of society, in the Liberties located outside the city walls'. For the first commercial theatre opening in 1567, and not 1576 as is usually stated, see Gurr, p. 13.

Henry VIII was certainly interested in the theatre. A letter of 1535 tells a remarkable story of Henry walking ten miles at 2 a.m., and travelling thirty miles in all to see a play based on the Apocalypse. Henry concealed himself by getting into a secret position where he could see everything. Before the play was over, however, he is said to be 'so pleased at seeing himself cutting off the heads of the clergy, that in order to laugh at his ease, and encourage the people, he discovered himself'.[70] The letter goes on to suggest that the play informed policy, since Henry sent off bills in accordance with this interpretation of the book of Revelations.

Not all the drama of Henry's reign so gratified the King. This is unsurprising, since Henry's own views on ecclesiastical reformation themselves changed. Thus the 1542 statute for the 'Advancement of True Religion' prohibited the printing or playing of any 'printed bookes printed balades playes rymes songes and other fantasies' that run counter to more conservative policy since 1540.[71] In 1544 a proclamation expressed concern that 'manifold and sundry interludes' are being played 'in suspicious, dark, and inconvenient' places in London. All plays were accordingly banned in London, except those performed in the houses of noblemen, the lord mayor, sherrifs, aldermen, gentlemen, or in the halls of 'companies, fellowships or brotherhoods'. The only outdoor theatre permitted was that sanctioned by historical usage.[72] This sharpening of theatrical regulation continued in the reigns of Edward, Mary, and Elizabeth: an Edwardian proclamation of 1551 declared that all play scripts had now to be approved by the Privy Council;[73] a Marian proclamation of 1553 prohibited the printing and playing of any 'interlude' without royal licence;[74] and some further Elizabethan legislation culminated in the establishment of the office of Master of the Revels in 1579.

None of this legislation seems to have been aimed at Corpus Christi plays; it had in its sights rather the highly polemicized, small-

[70] *L&P Henry VIII*, 8. 949. For many other instances of Henry 'suddenly discovering himself' in theatrical ways, see Lerer, *Courtly Letters*, 39–41.

[71] *SR*, 34–5 Henry VIII, ch. 1 (3. 894–5).

[72] *Tudor Royal Proclamations*, ed. Hughes and Larkin, 1. 341–2.

[73] Ibid. 517. For discussion, see White, *Theatre and Reformation*, p. 57.

[74] *Tudor Royal Proclamations*, ed. Hughes and Larkin, 2. 5–8. For discussion of the Tudor regulation of printing dramatic texts, see Greg Walker, *Politics of Performance*, app. 1.

troupe drama of religious policy, a drama that also had the printing press at its disposal. Insofar as cycle drama was embedded in a specific economic matrix, its aim was not to sell itself so much as to bring trade to its city and to produce what might be called cultural capital for that city. 'Our pleyeinge is not to get fame or treasure', as the Late Banns in Chester put it.[75] No early printer chose to print cycle plays. In the professional theatre the situation was very different. There the printing and selling the play itself was part of the economics of play production, from what was probably the first printing of a dramatic text in English, John Rastell's printing of Henry Medwall's *Fulgens and Lucrece* between 1512 and 1516.[76] The legislative materials cited in the previous paragraph were mostly concerned with the printing of play texts as much as with their production.

Royal scrutiny of theatre; the determination to bring it indoors within reliable playing spaces; and the determination to oversee its printing: all this implies a rebellious theatre. Given that the legislation post-dated the Act of Supremacy and was directed often explicitly at a polemical religious theatre, it seems clear that the legislation was indeed addressing evangelical theatre of the kind Bale produced, in a changed climate when that drama had become unacceptable.

When we look to the actual drama that survives from the reigns of Henry VII and Henry VIII, however, we observe a largely deferential drama working within very tightly defined theatrical and discursive spaces. The theatrical space was the dining hall, for performance probably between courses of a meal (thus the term 'interlude'). The theatrical and discursive space was determined by dependence on powerful patronage. In some cases this drama was produced for performance within the king's household; even when it was produced in other great households, or even when it expressed criticism of royal policy, it was nevertheless extremely careful in its alignment with royal interests. Dramatic activity in the reigns of Henry VII and Henry VIII occurred in a variety of institutions, including the royal court, ecclesiastical households, the Inns of Court, schools and

75 *Chester Mystery Cycle: Essays and Documents*, ed. Lumiansky and Mills, p. 294, l. 209.

76 For the economics of printing drama, see Greg Walker, *Politics of Performance*, ch. 1.

universities, and, in one instance at least, the private, household theatre of the dramatist and printer John Rastell.[77]

Despite the range of institutions, this drama was focused principally on the person of the king. If the hidden Henry VIII was gratified to see 'himself cutting off the heads of the clergy', he and his father would have been equally gratified by much of the surviving drama of their reigns. For that drama too was one of crime and instructional punishment, performed within well-defined institutional spaces by small professional troupes dependent on either royal patronage or royal toleration.[78] The modes of this drama were twofold: one used a comic and instructional mode derived from earlier professional theatre, and the other the form of the debate.

The instructional comic mode has a tripartite structure, of ideal state, degradation of that ideal state, and restoration through instruction and absorption of moral lessons. The central, wayward section of the play is the space for 'popular' dramatic action, as the vice figures exercise their control over the protagonist. This dramatic structure employs a concomitant linguistic structure. Just as the protagonist of such drama undergoes a fall from and rise back to an officially acceptable position, so too does the linguistic level of the play shift accordingly. It moves from official discourses and a high style, to a lower register of 'popular', often scatological language, before recovering the official, often Latinate register to end. A switch of dress code also accompanies the switch of linguistic register, as the protagonist changes from proper to improper costume. That central space is often also distinguished from official discourse by the adoption of simpler metrical structures than the graver, more complex prosody of official discourse. Theatre of this kind deploys and repudiates theatre itself, since the middle section of the play is at once the most 'merry', the most dramatic, and the least desirable. In most plays of this kind the action is manageable by a small troupe of actors, with not all the actors on stage at any one time, allowing the same actor to assume different roles.[79]

77 For the range of institutions sponsoring drama, see Bevington, chs. 3 and 4. For the theatrical space of the indoor hall, see Twycross, pp. 66–83.

78 The phrase 'crime and punishment' applied to the morality plays is drawn from Wickham, *Medieval Theatre*, pp. 112–21.

79 Bevington provides the best account of the dramaturgy of Tudor drama.

There are many simple instances of this extraordinarily resilient dramatic structure, and they are usually directed at a youthful audience. The appeal of drama to youth, and the effectiveness of instructing youth by drama are consistent preoccupations of both regulators and playwrights throughout this period. Henry's own legislation restricting the printing and playing of interludes was above all concerned about the corrupting effect of theatre on 'the youthe of this realme', who were led astray by 'light, idle and evil-disposed persons', to 'all proneness, proclivity, and readiness of divers and sundry kinds of vice and sin'.[80] Whatever the political climate, dramatists drew on this structure to address a wayward youth, allowing their audience a certain enjoyment of waywardness within the central section of the play before restraining its excesses by its end. Henry Medwall (b. 1461) deploys this structure twice, in both acts of his interlude *Nature* (1490–1500; printed *c.*1530), where the repeated descent and rise of the Mankind figure is rather the descent and rise of a youth being trained for the rule of a large household.[81] Plays about and directed to youth later in Henry VIII's reign, and in the reign of the young Edward VI, use the same dramatic structure for entirely different, even opposed ends. Whereas earlier youth plays worked within an unsurprising hierarchy of riotous youth and sagacious, pious age, evangelical drama reversed this. Thus *Lusty Juventus* (published between 1547 and 1553) appealed, as revolutionary art does, to youth *against* age. In this play it is Hypocrisy who encourages youth to obey age; this Youth does, only nearly to incur damnation. The play ends with a prayer for the long life of the evangelical and very youthful King Edward.[82]

Early in Henry's reign, too, youth took centre stage. The youth in question was often, however, Henry himself, to whom such plays were directed, and in whose presence drama had diplomatically to create a space to speak. Skelton's *Magnificence* (?1515–16; printed 1530) is on the face of it an economic narrative about the

[80] *Tudor Royal Proclamations*, ed. Hughes and Larkin, I. 341. The 1542 statute referred to above also makes specific reference to the effect of drama on youth.

[81] Medwall, *Plays*, ed. Nelson. The edn. contains two plays, *Fulgens and Lucrece*, and *Nature*. All further citations from these plays will be taken from this edition, and be cited by line number in the body of the text.

[82] R. Wever, *An Interlude called Lusty Iuventus*, ed. Thomas. Thomas argues for a Henrician date, but this is surely an Edwardian play.

Aristotelian virtue of liberality, the exercise of which guarantees the king's magnificence. Whereas the comedic dramatic structure of fall and rise had previously been applied strictly within a moral discourse, Skelton transferred it to an action that is at once ethical and economic. The king Magnificence initially banishes Fancy, the psychological figure who plays the court fool and encourages free spending. With the help of Counterfet Countenance and other vice figures, however, the king is persuaded to spend without restraint. Measure experiences the nightmare of the courtier, being suddenly banished from court, and leaves Folly in charge. Adversity marks Magnificence's nadir, warning the audience from the example of a prostrate and humiliated Magnificence. Despair and self-knowledge is a prelude to salvation, which is at once emotional and economic.

That economic plot is indeed the play's centre, but a larger plot focused on the discursive freedoms of the play itself encircles it. The productive balance of economic forces, this play implies, is itself dependent on the proper balance of discursive freedoms. What is required is by no means total discursive liberty. Instead, just as economic health demands a balance between liberality and avarice, so too must the kingdom's verbal economy be checked by a measured freedom.

Thus the play opens with an argument between Felicity and Liberty, in which Liberty complains of censorship: he has been 'lockyd up and kept in the mew', and is afraid to talk now lest 'he sholde be maskyd | in a payre of fetters or a payre of stockys' (ll. 30–5).[83] This is not, however, the prelude to an argument in favour of total verbal freedom; on the contrary, it is rather a defence of this play's and this playwright's freedom, since, as Felicity says, by complete liberty 'is done many a great excesse' (l. 53). Addressing the young king on whom Skelton is dependent for patronage clearly demands the performance of careful verbal protocols, and Skelton must promote the limitation of verbal liberty in order to justify his own. This strategy is visible in the play's own account of playing, since Skelton manages to associate playing with vice, and yet defend the utility of his own play. The central action of the play is dominated by the vices, court

[83] The text is cited from John Skelton, *Complete English Poems*, ed. Scattergood.The play has 2,572 lines.

figures who depend on disguise and who deploy the forms of court foolery. For all its critique of playing, however, the play insists that play itself, or this play, at any rate, is the proper thing wherewith to catch the conscience of the king. Fancy is the psychological faculty that initiates the king's fall, but it is equally the first to warn the king of what is awry (ll. 1843–74). The entire action of the play takes place within a space bounded by threatened and imagined punishments. In the represented action of the play, however, only the king is punished, even being offered 'the knyfe and . . . halter' to commit suicide by Despair (l. 2317). Finally, of course, the king escapes that punishment, and the play as a whole advertises the king's power to punish 'improper' verbal freedom and action.

Magnificence seems surely designed for an indoor performance before the king. Of course the king's household was not the only court to enjoy theatrical entertainment, but even the drama of those extra-royal courts could be focused on the person of the king. Thus the household of Henry Percy, fifth Earl of Northumberland, is recorded to have employed players, and one of the plays that seems certainly to derive from that household is *Youth* (1513–14, printed in 1532–3).[84] The play is a simple and short (795 lines) conversion narrative of a youth, who passes from dissolution to 'good contrition', and so effectively ceases to be youth at all. Directed primarily at his own son, Percy also critiques the new king's own cult of youth and high expenditure. Even if the play is critical of, and written outside the ambit of the royal court, it is nevertheless focused on the person of the king.

Much more interesting is *Hick Scorner* (1514, printed 1516), whose personification allegory is more closely localized, in the low-life world of London and its prisons. On the face of it this is another narrative of fall and rise, with Free Will as the protagonist, brought low by the machinations of Hick Scorner and his vice figures, including Imagination and a corrupted Free Will. The play's most obvious strategy is to use religion as a counter to social corruption. The picture of London is so murky and threatening, however, that religion

[84] See *Two Tudor Interludes: 'The Interlude of Youth'; 'Hick Scorner'*, ed. Lancashire. For the Percy connection, see pp. 27–9. All further citations from both these plays will be taken from this edn., and cited by line number in the body of the text.

is more of a relief from a claustrophobic world than a positive alternative. While the play promises paradise at its end, its more powerful residue threatens hanging. Free Will celebrates his escape from Newgate prison by the corrupt offices of Imagination, but the gallows humour of the play as a whole underlines the shady, unsteady world of 'court's estate'. The prisoners of Newgate, all facing hanging, are compared with the servants of a noble household, with their livery collars: Imagination says he was placed in prison 'among the thickest of the collar' (l. 239).

This macabre moral plot is not on the face of it political, but Ian Lancashire's excellent edition clarifies the insistently topical undertow of the play. Written probably for Henry VIII's intimate Charles Brandon, Duke of Suffolk, whose Southwark manor was opposite the Marshalsea prison, the play is also a political allegory about Henry VIII's enemy Richard de la Pole, the then current Yorkist pretender to the throne. While plays of this kind normally offer a complete resolution in their conversion, in this play only Free Will and Imagination convert, while Hick Scorner disappears from an action dominated by the menacing atmosphere of Chaucer's *Pardoner's Tale*, upon which the play draws heavily. This early Henrician play offers less the promise of moral conversion to youth than it advertises imprisonment and horrible death to Henry's enemies.

If the lurid, murky action of *Hick Scorner* turns the attention of its audience inward to the prisons of London, the instructional project of John Rastell's *Four Elements* (*c.*1518; printed *c.*1519) is very definitely outward. Rastell (*c.*1475–1536) is not an extraordinary playwright, even if his career is very remarkable in other respects, as barrister, printer, entrepreneur, engineer, and evangelical convert. Rastell's single play is in structure a simple morality play, distinguished by its fresh content.[85] It too presents an action of rise, fall, and rise again, but the trajectory here is between knowledge of the world through experience and 'studious desire' at the one pole and ignorance at the other. The player Ignorance wittily boasts that his

[85] John Rastell, *Three Rastell Plays*, ed. Axton. The edn. contains *Four Elements*, *Calisto and Melebea* (a proficient dramatic version of the Spanish text *La Celestina*), and *Gentleness and Nobility*. Any citations from these plays will be taken from this edition, and cited by line number in the body of the text. For Rastell's extraordinary life, see pp. 4–10.

power is greater than that of the kings of England and France; in England alone he has a retinue of five hundred thousand souls (ll. 1135–50). We do not know how this play ends, and to whom it was explicitly directed. Certainly it proposes an educational programme focused principally on geography; one of its props is evidently a newly printed and huge world map,[86] with which Experience instructs Studious Desire.

That pedagogy implies an ideal audience of youth and their instructors, but Rastell also takes care to advertise this programme to the king's economic interests. For America appears on stage for the first time in English theatre here, pointed out by an enthusiastic Experience: 'And that contrey is so large of rome, | Muche lenger than all cristendome' (ll. 741–2). No one, says Experience, can 'imagine' what commodities lie within this enormous land, at which point he curses the sailors who have robbed English entrepreneurs of the chance of being the first to 'take possessyon' of America, a reference to Rastell's own failed investment in commercial exploration to North America in 1517. Rastell also takes care to fill out the territorial project with ideological justification, by pointing to the desirability of converting the inhabitants of America to 'live more vertuously' (l. 777). The play, then, is ultimately directed to a royal audience, advertising 'the boundis of many regioun' that might be Henry's if he invests in expeditions of the kind Rastell himself had funded.

Instructing the young Henry VIII might be a permissible posture for playwrights early in his reign, especially playwrights like Skelton who had served as Henry's tutor before he became king. Later in Henry's reign such direction was obviously more difficult. In his revised *Three Laws* (originally written between 1534 and 1536, and revised in 1548), Bale ends with praise of Henry VIII for having banished idolatry and 'fowle Sodomye' from England, before going on to pray long life for King Edward, and that God be the 'directour' of Queen Catherine and the Lord Protector (ll. 2034–5). Bale might rather be praying that the play itself be the 'director' of policy, since in both this play and more explicitly in his *King Johan* (*c.*1534) he seeks to influence the king. In the history play Bale directs the king by

[86] Ibid., p. 131.

devising a more complex form of the instructional, comic plot, for he applies this comic structure to what is fundamentally a tragic plot line. Throughout the play King John is an increasingly lonely figure, successively abandoned by all except the powerless voices of the widow England and Veritas the historical expositor. King John dies, drugged by a monk, near the end of the play. Like Bale's other heroes, then, King John is wholly isolated in his time, aware of the way of the future but unable to enact it.

Bale is not writing antiquarian drama, however, so much as a pressingly polemical policy document of sorts. He accordingly champions the figures of the present who transform the tragedy of King John into a comedy of King Henry. Nobility, Civil Order, and Clergy, all of whom had abandoned King John, return in the play's close to offer their support to Imperial Majesty, who thanks Verity for having reformed them. This play is not directed at the common viewer, since 'Commonalte' is represented only once to be immediately dismissed as blind and poor, a hopeless stooge of papal propaganda. The play is rather directed at its final hero, Imperial Majesty, as he banishes the Pope, the 'slauterman of the devil' and assumes absolute control. That absolute royal control of the dramatic action is explicated as the play's own political ideology, as Verity promotes a doctrine of total obedience to kings, a doctrine shared by orthodox and heterodox in the 1530s and 1540s.[87] 'He that a prince resisteth doth dampne Gods ordynanuce' (l. 2352).[88]

Bale writes this play, then, by imagining a hidden Henry gratified by seeing himself 'cutting off the heads of the clergy'. Bale's manipulation of the instructional form of this comedic structure is adroit, since he manages to offer policy to a king at the height of his powers without appearing to do so. The enlightened and enlightening figure at the end of this play is the king himself.

If the drama of comedic instruction draws on a pre-Reformation dramatic tradition, the other main dramatic form in early Tudor England that survived in print is rather derived from scholastic environments of learned disputation. I end this section by looking to a series of debate plays produced between the last decade of the

[87] For which see esp. Ch. 7, above.

[88] The play is edited in Bale, *Complete Plays*, ed. Happé, vol. 1.

fifteenth century and the Act of Supremacy. The dialectic 'action' of these plays offers space for the play of wit, in which witty players claim prestige and promotion on the basis of their exercise of dialectical skill more than, even against, nobility of birth. Like the instructional plays, however, they too are the product of, and address, very small coterie audiences whose consciousness is never far from the business of gaining royal favour. These often claustrophobic plays are about promotion within closely defined institutional spaces, and that promotion is often achieved by finely targeted penetrations, either intellectual or sexual.

The most complex of these plays is the earliest, Henry Medwall's *Fulgens and Lucrece*, written and performed in the 1490s within the hall and household of Cardinal Morton, whom Medwall served as notary public.[89] The central action of the play is a debate between Lucrece's two suitors, the nobly born Cornelius and the nobly spirited Gaius, each of whom promote their respective claims. That part of the drama is based on John Tiptoft, Earl of Worcester's translation (*c.*1460) of Buonaccorso da Montemagno's *Controversia de Nobilitate*, a translation that had been printed by Caxton in 1481.[90] Praise of nobility of spirit above nobility of blood derived from riches is an ancient debate in Western Europe, and reappears whenever two closely related phenomena occur: the expansion of education and of administrative bureaucracies. Both expansions occurred in early Tudor England, and were encouraged by Tudor monarchs who needed to draw on resources outside the aristocracy. Medwall's play is careful not to dismiss the claims of blood allied with wealth altogether, but Lucrece opts for the non-aristocratic Gaius.

Were that the whole plot, it would represent a moderate but clear defence of nobility of spirit above blood. It is not, however, by any means the whole plot, since Medwall introduces a sub-plot of the two male servants, A and B, competing for the attentions of Lucrece's maid Joan. A and B also serve as expositors on the play; at the beginning of the second act A tells us that amongst the 'matter

[89] For Medwall's career, which coincides precisely with the fortunes of his patron Cardinal Morton, see Medwall, *Plays*, ed. Nelson, pp. 3–16.

[90] For Tiptoft and his translation (1460) of Buonaccorso da Montemagno's *De Nobilitate* (*c.*1428), see Tiptoft, 'Of True Nobility', in Mitchell, *John Tiptoft*, app. 1.

principal' of the play is mixed some 'dyvers toyes' designed to 'stir folk to mirth and game' (2. 22–3). The 'mirth' they introduce is, however, so insistent and so directly pertinent to the main plot that what is ostensibly the sub-plot cannot help but modify the simplicities of the main plot, even as it would dismiss itself as irrelevant mirth.

The servants begin the drama as spectators, but Medwall deploys them brilliantly both to introduce the play and to sketch what is after all a spatial synecdoche for the central issue of the whole piece. For, despite the dangers of stepping up onto the playing space itself, these servants do precisely that, in such a way as to confuse the distinction between fictional and 'real' action. Already, then, the play presents promotion across apparently insuperable barriers, but in so doing it qualifies any simple version of nobility of soul. For the significantly anonymous A and B achieve their promotion by pretending to be what they are not, and even in their pretence they are to imitate actors. They also are out wholly for themselves: 'This gere shall us both avaunce' (1. 393). The servants inhabit a world of material necessity, and their promotion mirrors that of Gaius, even as he achieves his promotion by dismissing riches and denying their importance. Once on stage and promoted, the servants must then compete between each other for the goods of court life. The debate between the two main male protagonists is a matter of intellectual thrust and parry, judged by Lucrece, but the sub-plot offers a pre-play of that in apparently comic but insistently anal terms.

Joan insists that they are to demonstrate their prowess in order that she can make her choice, and so they enact a mock tournament, in a game version called 'fart-prick-in-cul' (1. 1167). A is wounded in the 'arse', and invites his lord Gaius to put his 'nose therin, | Even up to the harde eyes!' (1. 1270–1). This play offers models of servant-class misunderstanding of the educated: whereas Cornelius orders B to remind Lucrece of how he threw her musk-ball into the hole of the hollow ash, B garbles the message to produce an account of Lucrece kissing Cornelius 'on the hole of thars' (1. 289). The pressure of anal reference, and the pressure of the sub-plot threatens to overcome the clearly defined intellectual world of humanist engagement ostensibly at the play's centre. Finally this play suggests that successful promotion in court is a matter not merely of intellectual penetration; it is also a question of sexual, and especially anal, penetrations within an enclosed yet closely observed society of male competitors.

The other surviving Henrician debate interludes were written by John Heywood (*c.*1497–1580), son-in-law to John Rastell. By far the most intellectually exhilarating of these is *Gentleness and Nobility* (*c.*1523, printed *c.*1525), revealingly anonymous, but plausibly attributed to Heywood. *Fulgens and Lucrece* might be very tentative about stating arguments in favour of nobility of soul against that of blood, but its positions are tame compared with the radical dismantling of noble pretension in this play. A Knight and a Merchant begin by arguing their respective claims to nobility. In itself this argument is fresh, given that the debate is not the old one between *miles* and *clericus*, or soldier and scholar; here the merchant lays claim to nobility on the basis of his and his ancestors' practical contribution to the commonwealth. All this, however, is dimissed as 'bybbyll babbyll', as the idle chat of the chattering classes by the real force in this play, the Ploughman. The Ploughman's impulse to stage an implicitly revolutionary violence is rechannelled into a debate in which the Ploughman is by far the most convincing and intellectually forceful figure. Not only, he argues, is he the most self-sufficient, appealing to a standard Stoic definition of nobility; more refreshingly, he destroys the Ciceronian understanding of human governance. Cicero argued that strife originally arose in the state of nature about the division of goods, at which point the noblest and most eloquent devised the laws of human society. This position, put complacently by the Knight, is totally dismissed by the Ploughman, who puts instead the Machiavellian position, that 'all possessions began first of tyranny', and that laws were made only as a defence of extorted property (ll. 597–613).[91] The Ploughman does not stop there, either: like Thomas Starkey he endorses the election of governors on the basis of commitment to the interests of the commonwealth. He goes yet further and argues that these elected rulers should enjoy their wealth only for the term of their lives, without passing it to their children.[92] Finally the Ploughman brings Knight and Merchant together into a defensive solidarity by dismissing even the form of the play itself: nothing

[91] For the text of Heywood's plays, see Heywood, *Plays*, ed. Axton and Happé.

[92] For Thomas Starkey, see Ch. 5, above.

will ever change by idle debate alone, and besides, he has work to do. The play ends with a Philosopher setting forth a moderate version of the Ploughman's position.

Debate plays work powerfully as drama partly through the seriousness of the debate, and partly through the ways in which alliances and dispersals on stage underline the social import of the intellectual debate. In my view none of Heywood's other interludes manages this in the way of *Gentleness and Nobility*. *Witty and Witless* (*c.*1525) expresses a paradox, that the superiority of the witless life, and the endless pain of the witty life, can only be perceived by the use of wit. The praise of folly can only be made by those who cannot themselves enjoy folly. The debate in the *Pardoner and the Frere* (?1529) between those figures is strangely not resolved by the entry of the Parson; this is conventional pre-Reformation anti-ecclesiastical satire, rather than satire with an evangelical inflection. The *Play of Love* (1529), performed at the Inns of Court, sounds all the paradoxes of a rational approach to its fundamentally irrational subject.

Only Heywood's *The Play of the Wether* (?1533) approaches intellectually engaging themes in a witty way. Suitors approach Jupiter with exclusive and self-centred appeals for weather that will suit them. However much these appeals are amusing in their cumulative selfishness, the politics they underwrite are finally absolutist. On the basis of petition, the king alone is to make the decision. The only space for counsel is one for Mery Report, a figure for Heywood himself, who gains promotion in Jupiter's court as the play begins. The other plays by Heywood (*Johan Johan*, *c.*1526–30 and *The Four PP*, ?1531) are not formally debates, but agonistic verbal competitions, in the first of which a husband is mocked and humiliated by his wife and her adulterous lover, the local priest, and in the second of which a series of charlatans compete to tell the tallest story, before the humble Pedlar brings the play to rest with his statement of traditional religion. Heywood was clearly a survivor himself: he produced court entertainment for four monarchs, before finally dying in exile in 1580. He survived by playing Mery Report, providing entertainment within very restricted discursive limits.

The Pardoner in Heywood's *The Four PP* easily recognizes the Devil in Hell, because, he says, 'oft in the play of Corpus Cristi | He hath played the devyll at Coventry' (ll. 831–2). This is a tolerant joke, and expresses none of the complex hostility and dependence expressed in Bale's play cycles. The remark in this context nevertheless alerts us to the sharpest contrasts between different dramatic forms considered in this chapter. One form is non-metropolitan, amateur, played in the street, and as critical of its own exercise of power as it is of royal and episcopal power; Tudor household drama is, by contrast, metropolitan, professional, played indoors, and extremely cautious under the eyes of its powerful patrons.

VII

The distinction just made implies a historical contrast between what the modern director Peter Brooke calls a 'rough' (medieval) theatre and a highly professionalized and inhibited (Tudor) theatre. There is much truth in that, insofar as there was a broad movement, across the centuries of this history, towards a metropolitan, professional, and much more highly regulated drama. Such a historical contrast is, however, an oversimplification, since it implies that there were no court entertainments, and no interludes, in the pre-Reformation period. It is true that no texts survive, but the evidence for professional court drama is available elsewhere.

The festive events of *Sir Gawain and the Green Knight*, for example, evoke both royal Christmas entertainments and the legitimating theatre of coronations of medieval kings. Late medieval kings did spend the twelve days of Christmas in lavish style.[93] And just as the Green Knight enters the feast theatrically dressed so as both to astonish and frighten, as 'mon most [the tallest man]' (l. 141), so too were frightening theatrical false heads common in late medieval England around Christmas. City ordinances prohibited the wearing of these socially disruptive costumes.[94] The most striking theatrical feature of the opening scene is, however, its connection with the coronation challenge of English medieval kings, whereby a knight was required

[93] See Given-Wilson, *Royal Household*, p. 41.

[94] See Lancashire (ed.), items 890, 921, 922, 935. Item 922 (London, Christmas 1418) prohibits anyone walking at night 'in eny manere mommyng, pleyes, enterludes, or eny . . . disgisynges', with pretended beards, painted visors, or 'disfourmyd or colourid visages'. The Green Knight offends in many respects.

to ride into the coronation feast and demand a fight with anyone who challenged the king's right to rule.[95] The Green Knight rides into the hall, and challenges the legitimacy of the king, whose youth, along with the youthfulness of his court, is stressed above all: the transgressive visitor wears no armour, since 'hit arn aboute on this bench bot berdlez chylder' (l. 280).[96] Hovering between the theatrical and the 'real', the Green Knight puts in question the court's power to generate only legitimating theatre. For whereas no one was expected to challenge the newly crowned king's knight, the Green Knight insists on playing a 'real' version of another theatrical tradition, an execution game involving a green man,[97] all the while calling it 'a Crystemas gomen [game]' (l. 283). The Green Knight offers brilliant children's theatre, expert as he is in the calibration of threat, astonishment, and playfulness.

Courts, however, desire the power to construct the world in their own image, and they do so by rendering threat theatrical: theatrical threat acknowledges the existence of external danger, but simultaneously neutralizes it by insisting that danger is a performance alone, and that it is 'not really happening'. Thus Arthur reabsorbs the Green Knight's transgressive irruption into the court by redescribing it as part of the 'laykyng [playing] of enterludez' that befits Christmas entertainment (l. 472).

Evidence of this kind suggests that court interludes survive from the early sixteenth century precisely because printing these otherwise ephemeral plays became both possible and part of the economics of production. If court interludes do not survive from the period prior to the introduction of printing, the texts of some religious plays that have precisely the same structure as many court interludes do survive. Whereas many chapters of this book have pointed to a total rupture between pre- and post-Reformation, the drama offers a different picture. Certainly the *content* of Tudor instructional interludes might be different, but the comic structure of rise, fall, and recovery is taken over very directly from a medieval theatre of instruction, which is also a professional troupe theatre. The habit of

[95] For this practice and its relevance to *Sir Gawain and the Green Knight,* see Simpson, 'Chaucer's Contemporaries'. This para. is drawn from this article.

[96] 'There are only beardless children at this table'.

[97] Wickham, *Medieval Theatre*, pp. 133–6.

calling one form the 'interlude' and the other the 'morality play' has tended to disguise the continuity. I close this chapter by briefly considering four plays of this kind, before ending with a discussion of the most spectacular of the non-cycle, non-morality plays, *The Croxton Play of the Sacrament*. If I have been suggesting that the medieval theatre is a theatre of broad inclusion, each of these plays in its own way qualifies that. Each specifies the strict and sometimes punishing disciplinary regimes that an official position demands of its audience.

Like the conservative N-Town cycle, and like many smaller plays and fragments that have survived, *The Castle of Perseverance*, *Mankind*, and *Wisdom* are all of East Anglian origin.[98] They are preserved in a single codex, assembled by an East Anglian antiquarian, Cox Macro (1683–1767). Each is distinctive in various ways: *The Castle* (*c.*1440; 3,649 lines) astonishes in the ambition of its staging; the manuscript preserves a diagram of the outdoor, fixed set, with a castle in the centre, sourrounded at the points of the compass by God (East), the World (West), Hell (North), and the Flesh (South). The play follows the life and death of Mankind, as he is drawn between different poles of influence, especially that of covetousness, who has his own separate station. *Wisdom* (*c.*1460–5; 1,163 lines) is distinctive for its appeal to the contemplative life. As we have seen, the cycles are very definitely addressed to the active life; so too are *The Castle* and *Mankind*. *Wisdom*, by contrast, has the devil himself tempt Mynde with the promise of the *vita mixta*. 'Lewe yowr stodyes . . . Yowr prayers, yowr penance . . . And lede a comun lyff' (ll. 470–2), he persuasively suggests. The relatively sophisticated psychology and theology of this play, coupled with its distrust of the mixed life, imply that this was monastic drama. This is corroborated by several links with Bury St Edmunds. *Mankind* (*c.*1465–70; 914 lines) is striking for the scatological vigour of its language and its racy interactions between devils and audience.

For all their separate distinctions, these plays share a fundamental

[98] For the density of drama in East Anglia, see Coldewey, 'Non-Cycle Plays'. For the 'morality' plays, see Pamela M. King, 'Morality Plays'. The three plays are edited in *Macro Plays*, ed. Eccles. *Wisdom* also appears in one other MS, containing a variety of other dramatic types; see *Late Medieval Religious Plays of Bodleian MSS Digby 133 and E Museo 160*, ed. Baker et al.

commitment to the didactic, instructional mode discussed above. Like many Tudor interludes, they are comic in two senses: they end happily, with protagonists personally and institutionally reintegrated, and they aim to be funny. Their humour is reserved for the central section, dominated by vice. Social, linguistic, prosodic, and dress codes drop down the scale so as to provide irreverent burlesque of the sober official positions from which these plays tend to begin. The space of the comic in that sense is always, however, strictly policed and bounded: protagonists return chastened to recognize the truth of an official ecclesiastical position, having recognized that wayward comedy leads finally to moral and legal nightmare. The only real exception to this structure is *Everyman* (late fifteenth/early sixteenth century; printed 1512–15), whose sober beauty contrasts with the spectacular disciplines of the troupe plays. Almost certainly translated from a Dutch original, *Everyman* addresses the life of those successful in the world as they must leave their financial reckonings and make another, moral settling of accounts. As each 'friend' in turn abandons Everyman on the point of death, the dialogue gains its poignancy from the way in which everyday affirmations of solidarity break in the presence of death. Like the other 'morality' plays, *Everyman* promotes a sacramental theology, focused especially on penance. Acceptance of that theology occurs not through a lurid, 'merry', and bewildering experience of sin, as in the other 'morality' plays; instead Everyman works to reconstitute his biography, discovering that Good Deeds is his only true friend who will accompany him on his perilous journey.

Literary history normally distinguishes two main streams of medieval drama, the cycle plays and the 'morality' plays. More recent scholarship has revealed that the incidence of drama throughout English villages and urban centres was astonishingly dense, and that the range of dramatic kind was wide.[99] One of the few non-cycle, non-morality examples of this drama to have survived is the brilliantly dramatic and darkly threatening *Croxton Play of the Sacrament* (1461), another product of East Anglia.

Set in the Middle East, the play tells the story of a rich Christian

[99] See Coldewey, 'Economic Aspects', who clarifies just how important drama was to the parish economy.

merchant who agrees to sell a Eucharistic host to some Jews. The Jews are fascinated by this strange and charismatic object, seeing it wholly from the outside in such a way as to defamiliarize it altogether. Just as fifteenth-century Lollards ridiculed Eucharistic transubstantiation, so too these Jews are baffled by Christian belief: Christians 'believe on a cake—me thynk it is onkynd'.[100] The Jews test the host's vivacity by nailing it to a post to see if it bleeds and tossing it in an oven. These tests have spectacular and lurid results: one Jew's hand is pulled off as he tries to pull it away from the nailed host, and Christ bursts out of the oven door in which the host has been imprisoned. This is literally a play about reincorporation, since the hand is restored to the converted Jew at the end of the play. That final reincorporation of the single body equally imagines the reincorporation and enlargement of the body of believers, since the Jews are all converted. That reintegration of the body of the faithful can only occur, however, through spectacular violence. Eucharistic belief became a key litmus test of faith in post-Arundelian England, and failure to pass that test could and did lead to the stake.[101] In this play the Eucharist itself brims with a terrible violence, repaying the violence done against Christ with its own savage exactions. The Eucharist is an unbreakable body that itself breaks bodies. The play is astonishing dramatically, with its stage metonymies of both Crucifixion and Resurrection, but its dramatic effects point to a threatening sacramental theology.[102]

No play could more sharply reveal, by its contrast, the light sacramentalism of the mystery cycles of York and Wakefield. The theology of this play is about specific standards of belief, not at all about works. Like the later Tudor interlude, and like the pre-Reformation drama of instruction, this play offered inclusion to an audience principally by advertising the punishments awaiting those who decline the invitation.

[100] See *Play of the Sacrament*, in *Non-Cycle Plays and Fragments*, ed. Davis, l. 200. The play has 1,007 lines.

[101] See e.g. the opening of Thomas Hoccleve's *Regement of Princes*, which recounts the burning of John Badby for his refusal to acknowledge transubstantiation.

[102] For the public disciplines of both legal and dramatic punishment in 15th-cent. England, see Lerer, ' "Representyd now in yowr syght" '.

Envoi

Convinced that our periodic terms had become straitjackets, I began writing this book with the no doubt hubristic intention of dissolving the boundary lines between 'medieval' and 'Renaissance' or 'Early Modern' altogether. The process of writing confirmed the conviction about the straitjacket, but persuaded me that dissolution of the boundary line would be a misrepresentation of history. Despite the many connections between 'medieval' and 'early modern' culture, despite the self-interested exaggerations of difference between the two periods by scholars since the sixteenth century, there are, I am now convinced, very significant changes of cultural practice in the first half of the sixteenth century. In sum, each chapter has argued that the sixteenth century witnessed a contraction and simplification of a much more complex 'medieval' jurisdictional field.

That there was such a thing as the Middle Ages and a 'Renaissance' might seem a dispiritingly familiar conclusion for such a long book to have reached. The definitions of the differences offered by this book are, however, rather unfamiliar. The central perception of the book is as follows: concentrations of power that simplify institutional structures also simplify and centralize cultural practice, by stressing central control, historical novelty, and unity produced from the top down. That perception could be tested against a wide range of cultural practices, from architecture to philology.

In the field of literary history, the main features of 'medieval' cultural practice turn out to be as follows: a sense of long and continuous histories; an accretive reception of texts, where the historicity of the reader receiving the old text is not at all suppressed; clearly demarcated and unresolved generic, stylistic, and/or discursive divisions within texts; and, above all, an affirmation of the possibility of human initiative, whether in politics or theology. Later medieval English, no less than European, society was characterized by a complex set of adjacent, overlapping institutions, each with its own history, and each often competing for cultural power. Such institutional complexity in England developed, in part at least, within the period of this history: fraternities, guilds, and parliament all, for example, became culturally active and articulate after 1350. I have called this culture 'reformist' by way of accentuating its inherently self-regulating energies.

By contrast, 'cultural revolution' has been used to imply the wide range of cultural practices characteristic of those moments, sometimes actual, sometimes imagined, in which power is suddenly centralized. Legitimation of such newly centralized power demands both repudiation of the old order and a vigorous affirmation of novelty. Because accretive reception of texts implies historical continuity, a revolutionary order must repudiate such reception; it must institute in its place the possibility of complete textual recovery of a founding text in its original purity, whether that text be the *Aeneid* or the Bible. A revolutionary order must also stress its own unity, a unity that flows from a central, organizing source. In literary practice the effects of this will be disciplined observation of stylistic and discursive coherence. Above all, revolutionary texts tend to stress central intelligence and initiative: whether in politics or in theology, the first half of the sixteenth century witnessed a newly conceived transcendence of power.

Long traditions praise both 'Renaissance' and 'Reformation' as moments, or a moment, of liberation. This book is clearly sceptical of that case. By contrast, many chapters have observed sudden repressions of evolving traditions. Some kinds of writing (i.e. elegy; romance; hagiography) survived the abrupt changes of the late fifteenth and early sixteenth centuries, though in markedly more controlled forms. Some authors (especially Chaucer) survived, though in politically or theologically corrected form. Most of the literary traditions discussed in this book did not, however, survive: 'Aristotelian' politics; Langlandian ecclesiology; a feminine visionary mode; parabiblical invention: some of these became difficult after the 1410s, and each impossible after the 1530s. Given its strong institutional base, guild-produced religious drama survived the 1530s, but was abolished in favour of a London-based, carefully secular, professional theatre by the 1570s.

Long traditions also posit the shift from medieval to early modern as an inevitable, natural historical break. This book has instead attempted to historicize both the shift and the forms of understanding that flow from it. Each chapter, that is, has defined the historical prism through which we understand the shift from medieval to early modern. The sixteenth, eighteenth, and nineteenth centuries turn out to be as much a part of 'medieval' studies as the strictly medieval centuries of this history.

By redescribing the relation between 'medieval' in positive, and 'early modern' in rather more negative, terms, I may seem to express a nostalgia for the 'medieval'. This book emphatically does not, however, belong to that nineteenth-century tradition of both recusant and high Tory nostalgia for the Middle Ages. These chapters express no nostalgia for a hierarchical Middle Ages in which a rich and comforting consciousness of communal identity was enjoyed at the expense of any liberties. On the contrary, the book rather describes medieval literary practice as less hierarchical, more decentred, than its early modern counterpart. The later medieval ages presented by this book win admiration not for the values of coherence and unity, but rather for divided jurisdictions, unresolved juxtapositions, accretive *bricolages*, and the affirmation of human initiative.

The book, indeed, expresses no nostalgia for the Middle Ages whatsoever. Historical change has the indisputable advantage of having happened. And in England the concentration of political, religious, and cultural power in fewer hands happened in the sixteenth century for many reasons. Given the urgent need for redescription, this book has been primarily descriptive, rather than addressing the causes of cultural change. Certainly this consideration of literary practice would lead to other forms of history that might illuminate the powerful forces leading to the concentrations of cultural power and the sharpening of cultural disciplines in the sixteenth century.

One would want, for example, to consider the history of population and prices, both of which rose dramatically in the sixteenth century, and both of which exerted inevitable pressures. Given England's religious secession from a continental tradition in 1534, one would also want to pursue the history of surveillance, which responded to newly created threats from both without and within. Certainly an extended spy network is demonstrably characteristic of English society for the first time under Thomas Cromwell. One would also want to understand the cultural implications of printing in more depth. Most obviously, newly enlarged modes of textual reproduction themselves produced newly vigilant modes of scrutiny. The 1546 proclamation demanding that the author's name be printed on all books was, for example, designed for the purposes of surveillance. A little less obviously, the technological revolution of the word effected by printing contributed to the centralization of the language, through the production of books in London for a national market. This led to the relegation of non-London literary dialects and metrical forms (notably alliterative poetry) to the status of 'regional' poetry. Less obviously still, printing may, for all its inestimable benefits, have produced its own excesses, particularly in the destruction of images. The phenomenon of iconoclasm is almost by definition excessive to need; one could be saved by the Word without smashing images. Finally, of course, one would want to recognize that the impulse to a 'revolutionary' culture is not exclusively a Henrician phenomenon. Claims to cultural monopoly are found earlier in the period of this history (Arundel's *Constitutions* for example), just as Lollardy manifests some features of a revolutionary cultural practice. And if the printing press created its own revolutionary pressures, those pressures pre-date Henry VIII.

The medieval is defined in Western culture by contrast with both classicism and Protestantism. The stakes of the inexhaustible renegotiation among these terms are, then, rather high at any given moment. In this book I hope not to have reinstated the oppositions simply by reformulating them. A reader might reflect that a good deal of the book's energy has indeed been directed to that end. Even books that make a strong case are, however, properly transitional. Cultural history necessarily provokes the exhilarating yet always unfinished experience of unwriting and rewriting ourselves.

Regnal Dates

The reader may find the following regnal dates useful:

Edward III	1327–77
Richard II	1377–99
Henry IV	1399–1413
Henry V	1413–22
Henry VI	1422–61
Edward IV	1461–70
Henry VI	1470–1
Edward IV	1471–83
Edward V	1483
Richard III	1483–5
Henry VII	1485–1509
Henry VIII	1509–47
Edward VI	1547–53

Author Bibliographies

The literary production of the years 1350–1550 cannot be identified with the production of nameable authors, since so much literary work was produced anonymously. Thus very many romances, many works of political protest, Lollard works, and some mystical treatises were all deliberately, for distinct but meditated reasons, anonymous. Many other works (especially the cycle drama) were produced collaboratively by men and women whose names remain, for the most part, inaccessible. The concept of authorship did nevertheless certainly exist in this period, in different forms and within different systems of literary production; the following list provides points of entry for broadly literary authors who wrote in the vernacular, about whose lives and/or works we have knowledge. Some Scots poets, whose work has high profile in this history, and some non-literary writers whose work was of vital importance for literature, also appear. The bibliographical information consists, for the most part, of editions of principal works in English, a biography where appropriate, and a very preliminary secondary bibliography, itself in the form of guides where appropriate. An asterisk beside an edition cited designates the edition from which a text has been cited in the body of the book. Full details of secondary sources appear in the Works Cited list.

Ashby, George (*c.*1390–1475)

Ashby served, for forty years by his own account, as Clerk to the Signet to Henry VI and Margaret of Anjou. In 1463 he was in the Fleet prison, where he wrote *A Prisoner's Reflections*. The texts *The Active Policy of a Prince* and *Dicta Opiniones Diversorum Philosophorum*, usually regarded as distinct, may be part of the same work, written as advice to Edward, Prince of Wales, also in 1463.

***George Ashby's Poems*, ed. Mary Bateson, EETS, ES 76 (Kegan Paul, Trench and Trübner, 1899)

Scattergood, John, 'The Date and Composition of George Ashby's Poems'

—— 'George Ashby's *Prisoner's Reflections*'

Audelay, John (d. soon after 1426)

Very little is known about Audelay, and most of what is known derives from what he says in his own texts. In 1417 he is named in the retinue of Lord Lestrange in an account of an incident in London; in 1424 he was appointed as chantry priest in the Augustinian abbey at Haughmond, near Shrewsbury. Blind and deaf, he finished his *Concilium consciencie* in 1426.

**The Poems of John Audelay*, ed. Ella Keats Whiting, EETS 184 (Oxford University Press, 1931)

Bennett, Michael, 'John Audelay: Some New Evidence' (1982)

Bale, John (1495–1563)

Bale was born in Cove, Suffolk. After having been sent at the age of 12 to the Carmelite Friars in Norwich, Bale began his study at Jesus College, Cambridge in 1514; he was admitted to the degree of Bachelor of Divinity in 1529, by which time he had produced works on Carmelite authors and history. He was appointed successively as prior of Carmelite friaries at Maldon (*c.*1530), Ipswich (1533), and Doncaster (1534), the year in which he was also admitted to the degree of Doctor of Divinity. In 1536 he left the Carmelites to become a parish priest in Suffolk, and by 1539 he was imprisoned at Greenwich, after complaints about his evangelical preaching. Rescued by Cromwell, he married in that year. *King John* appeared in 1538, along with *Three Laws, John Baptist's Preaching, The Temptation of Christ,* and *God's Promises*. With the fall of Cromwell in 1540, Bale fled to Amsterdam, moving to Wesel in 1546, where he published the first version of *Anne Askew*. He published the *Summarium* in 1548, and his edition of John Leland's *Laborious Journey* in 1549. Having returned to England on the accession of Edward VI, he was appointed bishop of Ossory in Ireland in 1552, whence he escaped to Wesel in the following year after the accession of Mary I. His autobiographical *Vocation* was published in 1553, and his *Catalogus* in 1557 and 1559 (Basel); he returned to England under Elizabeth.

**Illustrium maioris britannie scriptorum, hoc est anglie, cambrie, ac scotiae, summarium* (Wesel and Ipswich, 1548)

**The Laboryouse journey and serche of Johan Leylande for Englandes antiquitees* (R. Jugge, 1549) (*RSTC* 15445) (repr. in facs., Amsterdam, 1975)

**Scriptorum illustrium maioris brytannie, quam nunc angliam et scotiam*

uocant, catalogus (John Oporinus, 1559; both the 1557 and 1559 vols. are printed in this book) (repr. in facs., 2 vols., 1971)
**The Complete Plays of John Bale*, ed. Peter Happé, 2 vols., Tudor Interludes, 5 (Brewer, 1985)
**The Vocation of Johan Bale*, ed. Peter Happé and John King (Medieval and Renaissance Texts and Studies, 70; 1990)
**The Examinations of Anne Askew*, ed. Elaine V. Beilin (Oxford University Press, 1996)

Happé, Peter, *John Bale* (1996)

Barclay, Alexander (*c.*1475–1552)

Probably born in Lincoln, he was admitted to the degree of Doctor of Divinity, at either Oxford or Cambridge. Barclay was a priest in the college of Ottery St Mary, Devonshire, where in 1508 he published his translation of the *The Ship of Fools*. Not long after 1516 he was a monk at Ely, where he wrote his *Eclogues* and the *Life of St George*. He clearly adapted to the new dispensation, being presented with vicarages in 1546 and a rectory in London in 1552.

**The Ship of Fools*, ed. T. H. Jamieson, 2 vols. (William Paterson, 1874)
**The Eclogues of Alexander Barclay*, ed. Beatrice White, EETS 175 (Oxford University Press, 1928)
**Lyfe of St George*, ed. William Nelson, EETS 230 (Oxford University Press, 1955)

DNB

Barnes, Robert (1495–1540)

Born near Lynn, Barnes was by about 1512 an Augustinian friar in Cambridge, later prior of that house. He became a Doctor of Divinity in 1523. He was charged with heresy in 1525; although he abjured, he was nevertheless imprisoned for a short while. Between 1528 and 1531 he resided in Germany, where he was acquainted with Luther. During the 1530s he was engaged on various missions to Germany on behalf of the Crown. In 1530, however, again accused of heresy, after initially retracting he preached Lutheran doctrine. He was burned in July 1540. His *Supplication to King Henry VIII* was first published in 1531.

**The Whole Workes of W. Tyndall, Iohn Frith, and Doctour Barnes* (John Day, 1573)

DNB

Bokenham, Osbern (b. 1393–?1467)

Born in Bokenham, Norfolk, Bokenham was a bachelor in Cambridge by 1423, and referred to as *magister* from 1427. By 1427 he was a member of the Augustinian priory at Clare in Suffolk. He made at least two trips to Italy in the 1430s. The *Legendys of Hooly Wummen* were composed, for a circle of powerful East Anglian women, between 1443 and 1447.

**Legendys of Hooly Wummen*, ed. Mary S. Serjeantson, EETS 206 (Oxford University Press, 1938)

DNB

Edwards, A. S. G., 'The Transmission and Audience of Osbern Bokenham's *Legendys of Hooly Wumen*' (1994)

Bradshaw, Henry (d. 1513)

Born in Chester, he entered the Benedictine monastery of St Werburgh, Chester as a child. He studied at Gloucester Hall, Oxford, before returning to Chester, where he wrote the *Life of St Werburgh* and, possibly, the *Life of St Radegund*.

**Life of Saint Werburge of Chester*, ed. Carl Horstmann, EETS 88 (Trübner, 1887)

**Life of Saynt Radegund*, ed. F. Brittain (Cambridge University Press, 1926)

DNB

Brinkelow, Henry (d. 1546)

Born in Berkshire, Brinkelow was briefly a Franciscan friar before leaving the order to marry and become a London mercer. He was for a time in exile. He wrote satires under the name Roderick Mors. His *Complaint of Roderyck Mors* was published in 1545.

**Henry Brinkelow's Complaint of Roderyck Mors*, ed. J. Meadows Cowper, EETS, ES 22 (Trübner, 1874)

DNB

Capgrave, John (1393–1464)

University-educated (Cambridge BA in 1423; Doctor of Divinity 1427), Capgrave was an Augustinian friar at Lynn. He was ordained as priest in 1417, and became Prior Provincial of his order in England, 1453–7. He visited Rome in 1449. Patronized by Humphrey Duke of Gloucester and Henry VI, he wrote theological, historical, and hagiographical works in both Latin and English. His principal English work is his *Life of St Katharine* (*c.*1445).

**Life of St Katharine of Alexandria*, ed. Carl Horstmann, EETS 100 (Kegan Paul, Trench and Trübner, 1893)

**John Capgrave's Lives of St Augustine and St Gilbert of Sempringham*, ed. J. J. Munro, EETS 140 (Kegan Paul, Trench and Trübner, 1910)

**Life of St Norbert*, ed. C. L. Smetana, Studies and Texts, 40 (Pontifical Institute of Medieval Studies, 1977)

**John Capgrave's 'Abbreviacion of Cronicles'*, ed. Peter J. Lucas, EETS 285 (Oxford University Press, 1983)

Seymour, M. C., *John Capgrave* (1996)

Winstead, Karen, 'Capgrave's Saint Katherine and the Perils of Gynecocracy' (1994)

—— *Virgin Martyrs* (1997)

Caxton, William (b. between 1415 and 1424; d. 1492)

In 1438 Caxton was apprenticed to a London mercer, and in 1453 formally accepted to the livery of the Mercers' Company. By this time he was already active in the Low Countries. Between 1462 and 1470 he served as the Governor of the English Nation in Bruges. Having learned how to print in Cologne, he published the first printed book in English in 1473/4, a history of Troy that Caxton had himself translated. In 1476 he returned to England, and set up his press at Westminster, where he published the first book in English to be printed in England in 1476. Between this date and his death in 1492, Caxton's printing output was enormous. He translated or edited at least thirty-two of these books himself; he was also responsible for editions of works by Chaucer, Lydgate, John Tiptoft, and Malory. The list of his translations and works that follows is very selective; for a full list of works translated and printed by Caxton, see Blake, *William Caxton*, below.

**The Curial, Made by Maystere Alain Charretier*, ed. Frederick J. Furnivall, EETS, ES 54 (Trübner, 1865)

**Paris and Vienne*, ed. MacEdward Leach, EETS 234 (Oxford University Press, 1957)

*'Life of Saint Winifred', in Carl Horstmann (ed.), 'Prosalegenden', *Anglia*, 3 (1880) (Item 1, at pp. 295–313)

**Caxton's 'Eneydos'*, ed. W. T. Culley and F. J. Furnivall, EETS, ES 57 (Trübner, 1890)

**The Recuyell of the Historyes of Troye, translated by William Caxton*, ed. H. Oskar Sommer, 2 vols. (Trübner, 1894)

Caxton's Malory, ed. James W. Spisak, 2 vols. (University of California Press, 1983)

**The History of Reynard the Fox*, ed. N. F. Blake, EETS 263 (Oxford University Press, 1970)

**Caxton's Own Prose*, ed. N. F. Blake (Deutsch, 1973)

Blake, N. F., *William Caxton* (1996)

—— *Caxton and his World* (1969)

Charles d'Orléans (1394–1465)

The nephew of Charles VI of France and the son of Louis of Orléans and Valentina Visconti, Charles d'Orléans was orphaned and widowed by the time he was 15. In 1415 he was captured at Agincourt, and spent the following twenty-five years in captivity in England. His second wife died during his captivity, and he remarried in 1440. Between 1432 and 1436 he was under guardianship of William de la Pole, Earl, later Duke of Suffolk. He composed in Latin, French, and English. His English writing consists of an extended sequence of lyrics.

**Fortunes Stabilnes: Charles of Orleans's English Book of Love, A Critical Edition*, ed. Mary-Jo Arn (Medieval and Renaissance Texts and Studies, 138; 1994)

Spearing, A. C., 'Prison, Writing, Absence' (1992)

Chaucer, Geoffrey (*c*.1340–1400)

Chaucer was born into a family of London vintners; almost certainly educated in London, by 1357 he had entered the service of Elizabeth de Burgh, Countess of Ulster; in early 1360 he is recorded a member of a military expedition to France, part, possibly, of the retinue of Lionel, son of Edward III and husband of Elizabeth de Burgh. In 1366 he was given permission to travel through Navarre, and in the same year married Philippa, daughter, probably, of Sir Gilles de Roet, a knight of Hainault in the service of Queen Philippa. Chaucer is recorded as a member of the royal household in 1367, and may have studied law at one of the Inns of Court during these years. Blanche, Duchess of Lancaster and wife of John of Gaunt, died in 1368, and Chaucer's elegy *The Book of the Duchess* was almost certainly written soon after this. In 1372–3 Chaucer travelled on the king's business to Genoa and Florence, and would have encountered the great vernacular poetry of Dante, Boccaccio, and Petrarch.

In 1374 Chaucer was granted an annuity by Edward III, leased a home over Aldgate, and was appointed as a Controller of Customs, with a further controllership added in 1382. During the years of these appointments (1374–85) he made many diplomatic journeys to the Continent, including a mission to Milan in 1378. He was also released, in 1380, from legal redress by Cecilia Chaumpaigne in respect of her *raptus*, probably meaning 'rape'. These are almost certainly the years in which Chaucer wrote the following works: *House of Fame*, *Parlement of Foules*, *Troilus and Criseyde*, along with his prose translation of Boethius' *Consolation of Philosophy*.

The mid-1380s saw Chaucer strengthen his connection with Kent: in 1385 he was appointed to a peace commission for that county, and in 1386 as one of the county's two members of the House of Commons. In 1386 he gave up the lease on his Aldgate home, and in 1387 his wife may have died. The *Legend of Good Women* was first produced, along with initial work on the *Canterbury Tales* in these years. In 1389 Chaucer re-entered royal service as Clerk of the King's Works (until 1391), and as a deputy forester. After the deposition of Richard II in 1399, Henry IV renewed and increased grants from Richard II; in the same year Chaucer took a lease on a house beside Westminster abbey, where he was buried, according to the later inscription on his tomb, on 25 October 1400.

**The Riverside Chaucer*, 3rd edn., gen. ed. Larry D. Benson (Oxford University Press, 1987)
Cannon, Christopher, '*Raptus*, in the Chaumpaigne Release' (1993)
Pearsall, Derek, *The Life of Geoffrey Chaucer* (1992)

Cooper, Helen, *The Canterbury Tales* (1989)
Minnis, A. J., *The Shorter Poems* (1995)
Strohm, Paul, *Social Chaucer* (1989)
Windeatt, Barry, *Troilus and Criseyde* (1992)

Clanvowe, John (*c.*1341–1391)

In the 1360s and 1370s, Clanvowe fought in French campaigns led by John of Gaunt; in 1373 he entered the service of Edward III, continuing in the service of Richard II after the death of Edward. He was accused of being a Lollard knight by contemporary chroniclers. He wrote at least two works, the ascetic religious text *The Two Ways* and the courtly *Book of Cupide* (between 1386 and 1391). In 1380 he stood witness to the release of Chaucer from prosecution on a charge of *raptus*.

**The Works of Sir John Clanvowe*, ed. V. J. Scattergood (Brewer, 1965; repr. 1975)

Patterson, Lee, 'Court Politics and the Invention of Literature (1992)

Coverdale, Miles (1488–1568)

Born in Yorkshire, Coverdale studied in Cambridge; he was ordained as a priest in 1514, and entered the Augustinian friars in Cambridge. In about 1426 he left the order, and became a secular priest. He spent the years 1528–35 mostly abroad. The bible that appeared in 1535 was produced by Coverdale, on the basis of Latin and German texts, and previous English translations by Tyndale. After Cromwell's fall in 1540, he left for German-speaking territories, returning to an appointment as King's Chaplain in 1548. Having been appointed to the bishopric of Exeter in 1551, he was again in exile in 1555, returning in 1559.

**Remains of Myles Coverdale*, ed. George Pearson, Parker Society (Cambridge University Press, 1864)

Darlow, T. H., and Moule, H. F. (eds.), Herbert, A. S. (rev.), *Historical Catalogue of Printed Editions of the English Bibles* (1968)

DNB

Daniell, David, *William Tyndale: A Biography*, pts. 2 and 4 (1994)

Cranmer, Thomas (1489–1556)

Cranmer was a student at Cambridge between 1503 and 1511, when he took his BA. After his MA in 1515 he became a fellow of Jesus College. After declaring his support for the royal divorce, Cranmer was sent on diplomatic missions in the early 1530s, before his appointment as archbishop of Canterbury in 1532. Throughout the reigns of Henry VIII and Edward VI he served as a dutiful instrument of royal desire. In 1548, a commission presided over by him produced the first English prayer book, the Book of Common Prayer, which was formally instituted in 1549. Having supported the cause of Jane Grey after the death of Edward VI, he was tried for and convicted of treason, though pardoned by Mary. In 1555, however, he was tried for and convicted of heresy. Despite having signed six retractions of evangelical views, Cranmer was still sentenced to be burnt. Expected to sign a seventh at the pyre prepared for his burning, Cranmer instead retracted his retractions, and was burned.

**Miscellaneous Writings and Letters of Thomas Cranmer*, ed. John E. Cox, Parker Society (Cambridge University Press, 1846)

MacCulloch, Diarmaid, *Thomas Cranmer* (1996)

Selwyn, D. G., 'Thomas Cranmer's Writings: A Bibliographical Survey' (1993)

CROWLEY, ROBERT (*c.*1518–1588)

Born in Gloucestershire, Crowley studied at Magdalen College, Oxford. Between 1549 and 1551 he printed a version of the metrical psalms, his own verse, and two editions of *Piers Plowman*. He was appointed deacon in 1551, and was thereafter a professional ecclesiastic, except for a brief period in Germany during the reign of Mary. His own works include *A Petition Against the Oppressors of the Poor Commons* (1548), *Epigrams* (1550), and *Philargyrie* (1551).

**Philargyrie of Greate Britayne* (1551), ed. W. A. Marsden (facs. edn. Emery Walker, 1931)

**The Select Works of Robert Crowley*, ed. J. M. Cowper, EETS, ES 15 (Trübner, 1872)

DNB

DOUGLAS, GAVIN (*c.*1475–1522)

The third son of the fifth Earl of Angus, Douglas was educated at St Andrews between 1489 and 1494, and ordained priest by 1494. After various ecclesiastical appointments, he became provost of St Giles, Edinburgh *c.*1501. His major poetry was written before the battle of Flodden in 1513: *The Palice of Honoure c.*1500–1, and the *Aeneid* translation, which was finished only a few weeks before Flodden. In 1514 he was appointed as archbishop of St Andrews, but ejected by competitors, and in the following year became bishop of Dunkeld. In 1520 he took refuge from civil strife in Scotland in the court of Henry VIII, where he had no success in pursuing his political objectives. He died of plague in London. His is the first translation of the *Aeneid* into any dialect of English.

* *Virgil's 'Aeneid', translated into Scottish Verse*, ed. David F. C. Coldwell, 4 vols., Scottish Text Society, 3rd ser. 25, 27, 28, 30 (Blackwood, 1957–64)

The Palice of Honoure, in *The Shorter Poems of Gavin Douglas*, ed. Priscilla J. Bawcutt (Scottish Text Society, 4th ser. 3; 1967)

DNB

Bawcutt, Priscilla, *Gavin Douglas* (1976)

Elyot, Thomas (?1490–1546)

Son of Sir Richard Elyot and his first wife Alice Fynderne. He was educated at home, in Wiltshire. In 1511 he became a clerk of assize on the western circuit. In 1523 he inherited a great deal of property, and in the same year was appointed by Wolsey to the post of Clerk of the Privy Council, which post he held until dismissed in 1530. He was knighted in that year. He wrote many works; in 1531 he wrote *The Boke Named the Governour*, dedicated to Henry VIII. *Pasquil the Playne* was written in 1533. In both 1531 and 1535 he served as ambassador to the court of Charles V. He was a friend of Thomas More; after More's execution he was obliged to guarantee his own reformed credentials to Cromwell.

* *Sir Thomas Elyot: A Critical Edition of 'The Boke Named the Governour'*, ed. Donald W. Rude (Garland, 1992)

Pasquil the Playne, in *Four Political Treatises by Sir Thomas Elyot*, ed. Lillian Gottesman (Scholars' Facsimiles and Reprints, 1967)

DNB

Erasmus, Desiderius (?1467–1536)

Born in Rotterdam, Erasmus made his profession as a novice in the order of Augustinian canons in ?1488; he was ordained priest in 1492. Europe's greatest philological scholar, he spent most of his life travelling between England, the Low Countries, France, Switzerland, and Italy. On each of his three trips to England (1499–1500, 1506, 1509–14) he had extensive contact with English scholars, especially More, with whom he translated Lucian in 1506, and to whom his *Moriae Encomium* (*Praise of Folie*, 1511) is dedicated. The editor of many classical texts, his greatest achievement is his Greek edition of the New Testament (1516). His influence in England, as throughout Western Europe, was immense; within the period of this history, his main works are as follows: *Moriae Encomium* (1511; Eng. trans. 1549); *Enchiridion Militis Christiani* (1503; Eng. trans. 1534).

**Enchiridion Militis Christiani: An English Version*, ed. Anne M. O'Donnell, EETS 282 (Oxford University Press, 1981)
**The Praise of Folie, by Sir Thomas Chaloner*, ed. Clarence H. Miller, EETS 257 (Oxford University Press, 1965)

Schoeck, R. J., *Erasmus of Europe* (1993)

Bentley, Jerry H., *Humanists and Holy Writ* (1983)
McConica, James Kelsey, *English Humanists and Reformation Politics* (1965)

FISH, SIMON (d. 1531)

Fish entered Gray's Inn *c.*1525. Having acted in a play performed at Queens' College, Cambridge that ridiculed Wolsey in that year, he fled to the Low Countries. He returned soon after, but fled again in 1527, after having been involved in the sale of Tyndale's New Testament. In 1528, before his return from exile in the following year, he wrote the *Supplication of the Beggars*. He died of plague in 1531.

**A Supplicacyon for the Beggars*, ed. Frederick J. Furnivall, EETS, ES 13 (Trübner, 1871)

DNB

FORTESCUE, JOHN (?1395–?1477)

The son of Sir John Fortescue, Fortescue was born at Norris in Devon. He was admitted to Lincoln's Inn before 1420, becoming Governor in 1428–9, and a serjeant-at-law in 1430. In *c.*1436 he married Isabella Jamys. His appointment as Chief Justice of the King's Bench came in 1442, and he was knighted in the following year. In 1461 he fled to Scotland to join Henry, Margaret, and Prince Edward in Edinburgh; later that year he was named in an act of attainder passed against those who had resisted Edward IV. He remained there until 1463, writing tracts in defence of the Lancastrian legitimacy. In 1463 he accompanied Margaret and Edward to France, where he wrote the *De Laudibus legum Anglie* between 1468 and 1471. After the battle of Tewkesbury (1471), in which Edward was killed and after which Henry VI was murdered, Fortescue submitted to Edward's rule. He retracted his Lancastrian allegiance, was pardoned, and presented Edward with a copy of his *On the Governance of England* (*c.*1471). The attainder against him was reversed.

**On the Laws and Governance of England*, ed. Shelley Lockwood (Cambridge University Press, 1997)
**The Governance of England*, ed. Charles Plummer (Clarendon Press, 1885)
DNB

Frith, John (1503–1533)

Born in Kent, he was educated at Eton and then at King's College, Cambridge, where he took his BA in 1525. In the same year he was appointed as junior canon in Cardinal College, Oxford. After professing evangelical opinions, he was imprisoned in the college, and released in 1528. He left England for Marburg, returning, having married, in 1532. Thomas More issued a warrant for his arrest on charges of heresy in that year; he was arrested while trying to escape to Holland. In June 1533 he appeared before a panel of bishops, by whom he was convicted of heresy, and thereafter burnt in July 1533. He wrote exclusively theological works many of which, including *A Mirror to Know Thyself*, were written in the Tower during his final imprisonment.

**The Works of the English Reformers: William Tyndale and John Frith*, ed. T. Russell, 4 vols. (Palmer, 1831)
The Whole Workes of W. Tyndall, Iohn Frith, and Doctour Barnes (John Day, 1573)
DNB

Gower, John (*c.*1330–1408)

Gower was certainly a landowner in Kent, and it is possible that he held some legal office. From about 1377 he seems to have been in residence at St Mary Overeys in Southwark. In 1398 he married, apparently for the first time. Gower wrote in three languages. His main works are as follows: the Anglo-Norman *Mirour de l'omme* (finished between 1376 and 1378); the Latin *Vox clamantis*, written substantially before 1386; and the *Confessio Amantis*, written in English, and first published in 1390. The first recension of the *Confessio* is dedicated to Richard II. By the time of the third recension (1392–3), Richard has been replaced by Henry Bolingbroke, the future Henry IV, as the poem's dedicatee.

**The English Works of John Gower*, ed. G. C. Macaulay, 2 vols., EETS, ES, 81, 82 (1900–1; repr. Oxford University Press, 1979)

Fisher, John H., *John Gower: Moral Philosopher and Friend of Chaucer* (1965)

Minnis, A. J. (ed.), *Gower's 'Confessio Amantis'* (1983)

Simpson, James, *Sciences and the Self* (1995)

HAWES, STEPHEN (b. *c.*1473, d. ?early 1520s)

Hawes may have studied at Magdalen College, Oxford in 1493; in 1503 he entered service in the court of Henry VII as a groom of the King's Privy Chamber. His *Example of Virtue* was written in 1503–4, and the *Pastime of Pleasure* in 1505–6. The *Comfort of Lovers* (1510–11) is saturated with autobiographical reference of a very obscure kind, suggesting at the very least that Hawes was struggling in the new court of Henry VIII.

**Comfort of Lovers*, in *Stephen Hawes: The Minor Poems*, ed. Florence W. Gluck and Alice B. Morgan, EETS, 217 (Oxford University Press, 1974)

**The Pastime of Pleasure*, ed. William Edward Mead, EETS, 173 (Oxford University Press, 1928)

Edwards, A. S. G., *Stephen Hawes* (1983)

HENRYSON, ROBERT (b. between 1425 and 1435, d. *c.*1505)

Nothing is known for certain about Henryson's life, although circumstantial detail points to his residence at Dunfermline, Scotland, and his profession as a schoolmaster. His three major works are the *Fables*, *Testament of Cresseid*, and *Orpheus and Eurydice*.

**The Poems of Robert Henryson*, ed. Denton Fox (Clarendon Press, 1981)

Gray, Douglas, *Robert Henryson* (1979)

HEYWOOD, JOHN (*c.*1497–1578)

Heywood was born most probably in Coventry, also home of the Rastell family, into which he married. He may have been a student at Oxford from 1513; by 1519 he was a singer in the household of Henry VIII, and by 1522 he was married to Joan Rastell. He began writing plays in about 1525

(*Witty and Witless*), with *Gentleness and Nobility*, *The Pardoner and Frere*, *The Play of Love* and *Four PP*, *Johan Johan*, and *The Play of the Weather* being produced between 1526 and 1533. In 1542 he was implicated with John More in a plot against Cranmer, being indicted at Westminster in 1544; after his pardon in the same year, Heywood recanted at St Paul's Cross. By 1552, under Edward VI, he was groom of the Chamber; at the accession of Mary, Heywood's annuity was renewed. In 1564, after the Act of Uniformity, Heywood and his wife fled to Flanders, refusing to return to England, even with royal permission. He died in Antwerp in 1578.

**The Plays of John Heywood*, ed. Richard Axton and Peter Happé (Brewer, 1991)

HILTON, WALTER (*c.* early 1340s–1396)

Hilton the author of spiritual works is probably to be identified as the bachelor of civil law recorded in Lincoln and Ely in the early 1370s, who was an *inceptor* in canon law in the early 1380s. Probably a hermit until the mid-1380s, Hilton then became an Augustinian canon at Thurgarton in Nottinghamshire. He wrote in Latin and English. His longest English work is the *Scale of Perfection* (no modern edition), the first book of which was possibly written in the mid-1380s. Hilton also wrote works of spiritual advice, including the letter *On the Mixed Life*.

The Scale of Perfection, trans. John P. H. Clark and Rosemary Dorward (Paulist Press, 1991)

**Epistle on the Mixed Life*, in *English Mystics of the Middle Ages*, ed. Barry Windeatt (Cambridge University Press, 1994), 110–36

Minnis, A. J., 'The *Cloud of Unknowing* and Walter Hilton's *Scale of Perfection*' (1984)

Sargent, Michael G., 'Hilton, Walter' (1998)

HOCCLEVE, THOMAS (*c.*1367–1426)

At about the age of 20, Hoccleve became a clerk in the office of the Privy Seal, in which position, resident in London, he remained until his death. He seems to have worked in Westminster and lived in a hostel of the Privy Seal, which was located in the Strand. Between 1399 and 1411 he married. His first datable poem is the *Letter of Cupid* (1402). In his frequently autobiographical poetry, he presents himself as subject to poverty (e.g. *Male Regle*, 1405; *Regement of Princes*, 1411) or nervous breakdown (*Series*, 1420). In addition to the works already mentioned, he wrote shorter devotional and political poems, such as his *To Sir John Oldcastle* (1415).

**Remonstrance against Oldcastle*, in *Selections from Hoccleve*, ed. M. C. Seymour (Clarendon Press, 1981)

The Series, in *Hoccleve's Works: The Minor Poems*, ed. Frederick J. Furnivall and I. Gollancz, rev. Jerome Mitchell and A. I. Doyle, EETS, ES 61 (1892; rev. edn. Oxford University Press, 1970)

**Thomas Hoccleve: The Regiment of Princes*, ed. Charles R. Blyth (TEAMS, 1999)

**Thomas Hoccleve's 'Complaint' and 'Dialogue'*, ed. J. A. Burrow, EETS 313 (Oxford University Press, 1999)

Burrow, J. A., *Thomas Hoccleve* (1994)

Perkins, Nicholas, *Hoccleve's 'Regiment of Princes': Counsel and Constraint* (2001)

Howard, Henry, Earl of Surrey (?1517–1547)

Eldest son of Thomas Howard, later third duke of Norfolk. In 1530–2 he was the companion at Windsor of Henry Fitzroy, illegitimate son of Henry VIII. He married in 1531–2, and in 1532 spent eleven months at the French court. He accompanied his father to suppress the Pilgrimage of Grace in 1536. He was imprisoned for minor disturbances in 1537, 1542, and 1543. In 1545 he was appointed commander of Boulogne, and defeated in a battle of 1546, after which he was replaced in his post by his enemy Edward Seymour. In late 1546 he faced charges of implicitly claiming to succeed Henry VIII, and in January 1547 was formally indicted of high treason. He was beheaded at Tower Hill on 21 January 1547, one week before Henry VIII died. He wrote verse in many genres: Petrarchan lyrics, translations of biblical verse, and a translation of Books 2 and 4 of the *Aeneid* (written after 1538).

**Henry Howard, Earl of Surrey: Poems*, ed. Emrys Jones (Clarendon Press, 1964)

The 'Aeneid' of Henry Howard Earl of Surrey, ed. Florence H. Ridley (University of California Press, 1963)

The Poems of Henry Howard Earl of Surrey, ed. Frederick Morgan Padelford, rev. edn., University of Washington Publications, Language and Literature, 5 (University of Washington Press, 1928)

Cattaneo, Arturo, *L'ideale umanistico: Henry Howard, Earl of Surrey* (1991)

Sessions, William A., *Henry Howard, the Poet Earl of Surrey: A Life* (1999)

Hull, Eleanor (*c.*1395–1460)

Daughter of John (later Sir John) Malet (d. *c.*1395) and his wife Joan Hulle. By 1413 she was married to John (later Sir John) Hull (d. 1420–1), a retainer of John of Gaunt. In 1417 a document refers to her as the servant of Joan the Queen, second wife of Henry IV, and in the same year she was admitted to the confraternity of the Benedictine abbey of St Albans. By 1421 she may have retired to the priory of Benedictine nuns at Sopwell, on the outskirts of St Albans, where she was certainly resident by 1427. In 1453 her only son was killed in the battle of Castillon. She had completed her translations of *The Seven Psalms* between 1449 and 1454. In 1458 she made her will, from which it appears that she was living in the Benedictine priory of Cannington in Somersetshire.

**The Seven Psalms: A Commentary on the Penitential Psalms . . . by Dame Eleanor Hull*, ed. Alexandra Barratt, EETS 307 (Oxford University Press, 1995)

James I of Scotland (1394–1437)

James was the son of Robert III of Scotland; he was born in Dunfermline. After the murder of his only surviving brother David in 1402, Robert III decided to send James to France for safety. In *c.*1406 the ship carrying him was, however, intercepted by English sailors, and James accordingly became the prisoner of Henry IV, remaining in England (and briefly, later, in France accompanying Henry V in triumph) under close custody for the next nineteen years. In February 1424 he married Joan Beaufort, sister of the Earl of Somerset, and set out for Scotland the next day, where he was crowned in Scone in May of that year. He was murdered in 1437. He is almost certainly the author of the *Kingis Quair*, whose date may be as late as 1435.

**James I of Scotland: The Kingis Quair*, ed. John Norton-Smith (Clarendon Press, 1971)

DNB

Kratzmann, Gregory, *Anglo-Scottish Literary Relations 1430–1550* (1980)

JOYE, GEORGE (d. 1553)

Joye took his BA from Cambridge in 1513; from 1517 he was a fellow of Peterhouse. In 1527 he was accused of heretical opinions; cited to appear in Cambridge, he escaped to Strasburg and was resident in the Low Countries until his return to England in 1535. In 1530 he produced his metrical translation of the Psalms, and in 1534 he became the object of Tyndale's anger after his publication, without Tyndale's permission, of a corrected edition of Tyndale's New Testament. In 1542 he fled again to the Continent, returning on the accession of Edward VI.

Zim, Rivkah, *English Metrical Psalms* (1987)

DNB

JULIAN OF NORWICH (*c.*1343–after 1416)

In a period of severe illness in her thirtieth year (May 1373), Julian experienced the visions recorded in the two versions of her *Showings*; in 1388 she experienced one further vision, recorded in the longer version. It is reasonable to suppose that she was well educated in theology. Some time after the revelations, Julian became an anchorite, in a cell attached to St Julian's church in Norwich. Her residence there is attested both by donations and records of a visit by Margery Kempe in 1415. Most scholars believe that the Shorter Text was written soon after the visionary experience of 1393, and that Julian wrote the Long Text in 1393. See Watson below for an alternative dating (1388 and after 1413 respectively).

**A Book of Showings to the Anchoress Julian of Norwich*, ed. Edmund Colledge and James Walsh, 2 pts., Studies and Texts, 35 (Pontifical Institute of Medieval Studies, 1978)

Baker, Denise, *Julian of Norwich's* 'Showings': *From Vision to Book* (1994)

von Nolcken, Christina, 'Julian of Norwich' (1984)

Watson, Nicholas, 'The Composition of Julian of Norwich's *Revelation of Divine Love*' (1993)

KEMPE, MARGERY (*c.*1373–c.1439)

Born in King's (then Bishop's) Lynn, daughter of John Brunham, a prosperous burgess who served five times as mayor of Lynn. Married to John Kempe in *c.*1393, she had fourteen pregnancies until 1413, when she and her husband agreed to end sexual relations. For the next four years, she travelled extensively on pilgrimage to the Holy Land, Italy, Santiago, and to sites in England. She remained in Lynn until *c.*1431, when she made a pilgrimage to sites in Northern Europe. Back in England by 1434, she had the first copy of her autobiographical book (*The Book of Margery Kempe*) written in 1436, adding a second book, which was begun in 1438.

**The Book of Margery Kempe*, ed. Barry Windeatt (Longman, 2000)

Hirsch, John C., 'Margery Kempe' (1984)

Lochrie, Karma, *Margery Kempe and the Translations of the Flesh* (1991)

Langland, William (?1325–?after 1388)

The fifty-eight manuscripts containing whole or part of versions of a poem variously titled but frequently called *Piers Plowman* have generally been ascribed to 'William Langland'. The strongest evidence for the existence of a person properly named thus is a note in Trinity College, Dublin, MS 212, ascribing the poem to him. It is also plausible that the name is thematic, a *nom de plume* signalling the 'uplandish' style of a satirical writer who expresses the 'will' of the land. Three principal versions of the poem can be discerned among the manuscripts, versions that may date from the late 1360s to the late 1380s. Nothing certain is known of the author. From his self-presentation in the poem/s, it is reasonable to assume the following: that he had strong affinities with the Malvern Hills and that he was university-educated, having possibly left university before graduating; and that he spent his working life in London as a clerk in minor orders, associating himself with the area of Cornhill.

Piers Plowman: The A-Version, ed. George Kane (Athlone, 1960)
**Piers Plowman by William Langland, An Edition of the C-Text*, ed. Derek Pearsall (Edward Arnold, 1978)
William Langland, Piers Plowman, The Z Version, ed. A. G. Rigg and Charlotte Brewer (Pontifical Institute of Medieval Studies, 1983)
**William Langland, The Vision of Piers Plowman, A Critical Edition of the B-Text*, ed. A. V. C. Schmidt, 2nd edn. (Dent, 1995)

Hanna, Ralph III, *William Langland* (1993)

Alford, John (ed.), *A Companion to 'Piers Plowman'* (1988)
Simpson, James, *Piers Plowman: An Introduction to the B-Text* (1990)
—— 'The Power of Impropriety' (2001)

LATIMER, HUGH (?1485–1555)

Born in Leicestershire, Latimer was educated in Cambridge, graduating as a BA in 1510, being ordained as a priest soon thereafter. Examined by Wolsey in 1525, he disowned Lutheran opinions. Having publicly favoured Henry's divorce, he was presented to a benefice in Wiltshire, in 1531. The following year he was cited to appear on charges of heresy in London, but submitted to the court. From 1535 until his resignation in 1539, he was active promoting the evangelical cause as bishop of Worcester. Between 1539 and 1547 he experienced short periods of imprisonment, but became court preacher after 1548. He was burnt under Mary in 1555.

**Selected Sermons of Hugh Latimer*, ed. Allan G. Chester (University Press of Virginia, 1968)

LELAND, JOHN (?1503–1552)

Having attended St Paul's School, London, Leland studied at Christ's College, Cambridge, taking his BA in 1522, and being ordained as a priest in 1525. He became the king's librarian in 1530, and is reputed to have been appointed the king's 'Antiquary' in 1533, the first such appointment. The years 1534–43 were spent touring England, gathering material for his various projects. He presented his 'New Year's Gift' in 1545, but became insane before the projects promised therein could be brought to an end. Almost all his works were published posthumously.

**Assertio inclytissimi Arthuri*, in Christopher Middleton, *The Famous Historie of Chinon of England*, ed. William Edward Mead, EETS 165 (Oxford University Press, 1925)

**Commentarii de scriptoribus britannicis*, 2 vols. (Anthony Hall, 1709)

**Naeniae in mortem Thomae Viati equitis incomparabilis* (London, 1542)

**The Itinerary of John Leland*, ed. Lucy Toulmin Smith, 5 vols. (G. Bell, 1907–10)

DNB

Carley, James P., 'John Leland in Paris' (1986)

—— 'John Leland' (1994)

—— 'John Leland's *Cygnea Cantio*' (1983)

Love, Nicholas (d. 1424)

On the formal incorporation of the Carthusian foundation of Mount Grace, Yorkshire, into the order, Nicholas Love was appointed the first prior, having previously been rector. He is the author of the *Mirror of the Blessed Life of Jesus Christ* (*c.*1410).

**Nicholas Love's Mirror of the Blessed Life of Jesus Christ*, ed. Michael G. Sargent, Garland Medieval Texts, 18 (Garland, 1992)
Oguro, Shoichi, Beadle, Richard, and Sargent, Michael G. (eds.), *Nicholas Love at Waseda* (1997)

Lydgate, John (*c.*1371–1449)

Born in Lydgate, Suffolk, Lydgate entered the Benedictine abbey of Bury St Edmund's as a boy. Between 1389 and 1397 he passed through the range of orders from acolyte to priest. Lydgate is not recorded as having taken a degree, but he was certainly in Oxford at Gloucester College, *c.*1406–8, possibly much longer. Lydgate's connection with Prince Henry began before his accession as Henry V: already in 1412 Lydgate began his *Troy Book*, finished in 1420. The *Life of Our Lady* was also written during the reign of Henry V. The *Destruction of Thebes* seems to date from 1421, but may date from just after the death of Henry V in 1422. In 1423 he was appointed as prior at Hadfield Regis, a small Benedictine priory in Essex, but had ceased to be prior by 1429–30, and was permitted to return to Bury in 1434. During the Hadfield period he received commissions for both secular and religious works from a wide range of both courtly and civic figures, including works commissioned from him while he was in Paris as part of an occupying force. In 1431 he began work on his huge translation of *The Fall of Princes*, under the patronage of Humphrey Duke of Gloucester. In the period after his return to Bury, he continued to work on the *Fall* up to 1438, as well as producing some large-scale saints' lives.

**Lydgate's Troy Book*, ed. Henry Bergen, 4 pts., EETS, ES 97, 103, 106, and 126 (Kegan Paul, Trench and Trübner, 1906, 1908, 1910, and 1935)
**A Critical Edition of John Lydgate's 'Life of Our Lady'*, ed. Joseph A. Lauritis, Ralph A. Klinefelter, and Vernon F. Gallagher (Duquesne University Press, 1961)
**The Minor Poems*, 2 pts., ed. Henry Noble MacCracken, EETS, ES 107, 192 (Oxford University Press, 1911, 1934)
**Lydgate's 'Siege of Thebes'*, ed. Alex Erdmann and Eilert Ekwall, 2 vols.,

EETS, ES 108, 125 (Kegan Paul, Trench and Trübner, 1911, 1930; repr. 1960)
**The Dance of Death*, ed. Florence Warren, EETS, OS 181 (Oxford University Press, 1924, repr. 1967)
**Lydgate's Fall of Princes*, ed. Henry Bergen, 4 vols., EETS, ES 121–4 (Oxford University Press, 1911, 1934)
**Saint Albon and Saint Amphibalus*, ed. George F. Reinecke, Garland Medieval Texts, 11 (Garland, 1985)
**Lydgate and Burgh's Secrees of Old Philosoffres*, ed. Robert Steele, EETS, ES 66 (Kegan Paul, Trench and Trübner, 1894)

Pearsall, Derek, *John Lydgate (1371–1449): A Bio-Bibliography* (1997)

—— *John Lydgate* (1970)

MAIDSTONE, RICHARD (b. before 1355, d. 1396)

Born probably in Maidstone, Kent, Maidstone almost certainly entered the Carmelite friary at Aylesford, Kent, which is where he died. He had received his doctorate from Oxford before 1390. He may have served as confessor to John of Gaunt. His *Concordia* dates from 1392, and his Psalm versions were also most probably written in the 1390s.

Concordia: Facta inter Regem Riccardum II et Civitatem Londonie, ed. Charles Roger Smith, unpublished Ph.D. diss. Princeton University, University Microfilms, 1972
**Richard Maidstone's Penitential Psalms*, ed. Valerie Edden, Middle English Texts, 22 (C. Winter, 1990)

DNB

MALORY, THOMAS (d. 1471)

Most scholars agree that Thomas Malory the author is to be identified with Sir Thomas Malory of Newbold Revell, Warwickshire. This Malory was imprisoned several times, in periods varying from a few days to three years. He served in the train of Richard Beauchamp, Earl of Warwick. The crimes of which he was accused in 1450–1 include robbery, cattle-raiding, extortion, rape, and attempted murder. In 1445 he represented Warwickshire in Parliament. He would seem to have supported Warwick against Henry VI in the early 1460s, and again in 1471 against Edward IV. He was excluded from four general pardons made by Edward IV in 1468 and 1470. Some, possibly all the *Works* were written in prison; they were finished in 1469–71.

**The Works of Sir Thomas Malory*, ed. Eugène Vinaver, rev. P. J. C. Field, 3 vols. (Clarendon Press, 1990)

Field, P. J. C., *The Life and Times of Sir Thomas Malory* (1993)

Riddy, *Sir Thomas Malory* (1987)

Archibald, Elizabeth, and Edwards, A. S. G. (eds.), *A Companion to Malory* (1996)

MEDWALL, HENRY (1461–before 1512)

Born in Southwark, Medwall was educated at Eton, remaining there until 1480; he then studied at King's College, Cambridge between 1480 and his sudden departure on 13 June 1483, also the day of the arrest of his prospective patron, Archbishop (later Cardinal) John Morton. Later in life Medwall frequently returned to King's. In 1490 he was ordained to minor orders, and in 1491 granted the degree of Civil Law by the University of Cambridge. In his professional career, Medwall served as notary public, much of the time in the employ of Archbishop Morton. Very soon after the death of his patron Morton in 1500, Medwall was sued in 1501; although he won the case, he lost his job, and was dead by 1512. Both his plays, *Fulgens and Lucrece* and *Nature*, were written between 1490 and 1500.

**The Plays of Henry Medwall*, ed. Alan H. Nelson, Tudor Interludes 2 (Brewer, Rowman and Littlefield, 1980)

MORE, THOMAS (1478–1535)

At the age of 13 More entered the household of John Morton, Archbishop of Canterbury and Lord Chancellor. By 1494 he was a student at the Inns of Court and by 1497 he had met Erasmus, with whom he enjoyed a warm friendship. In 1499 he lived near the London Charterhouse, and took daily part in Carthusian exercises. More married twice, in 1505 and, after the death of his first wife, in 1511. His translations of Lucian date from 1505–6. His life of Pico dates from 1510, the year in which he was appointed under-sheriff of London. In 1515 he spent six months in the Low Countries on diplomatic business, when *Utopia* (1516) was written. By 1519 he was a member of Henry VIII's court; he was knighted in 1521 and appointed Speaker in the House of Commons in 1523. He became Lord Chancellor in 1529, the first lay person to hold that office. As Chancellor he was active as writer and legal official in the persecution of heresy. He resigned in 1532; in 1534 he refused to repugn papal authority. His anti-evangelical polemical writing largely begins from the period of his chancellorship and extends to 1534. In that year he was imprisoned in the Tower on 17 April; here he remained until his execution by beheading on 6 July 1535. During this period he wrote his *Dialogue of Comfort.*

**Life of Pico*, ed. A. S. G. Edwards, in *The Complete Works of St Thomas More*, 1 (Yale University Press, 1997)
**The History of King Richard III*, ed. Richard S. Sylvester, in *The Complete Works of St Thomas More*, 2 (Yale University Press, 1963)
**Translations of Lucian*, ed. Craig R. Thompson, in *The Complete Works of St Thomas More*, 3/1 (Yale University Press, 1974)
**Latin Poems*, ed. Clarence H. Miller, Leicester Bradner, Charles A. Lynch, and Revilo P. Oliver, in *The Complete Works of St Thomas More*, 3/2 (Yale University Press, 1984)
**Utopia*, ed. Edward Surtz and J. H. Hexter, in *The Complete Works of St Thomas More*, 4 (Yale University Press, 1965)
**The Utopia of Sir Thomas More*, ed. J. H. Lupton (Clarendon Press, 1895)
**A Dialogue concerning Heresies*, ed. T. M. C. Lawler, Germain Marc'hadour, and Richard Marius, 2 pts., in *The Complete Works of St Thomas More*, 6 (Yale University Press, 1981)
**The Confutation of Tyndale's Answer*, ed. Louis A. Schuster et al., 2 pts., in *The Complete Works of St Thomas More*, 8 (Yale University Press, 1973)
**A Dialogue of Comfort against Tribulation*, ed. L. L. Martz and F. Manley, in *The Complete Works of St Thomas More*, 12 (Yale University Press, 1976)
**St Thomas More: Selected Letters*, ed. Elizabeth Frances Rogers (Yale University Press, 1961)

Guy, John A., *Thomas More* (2000)

Cummings, Brian, 'Reformed Literature and Literature Reformed' (1999)
Greenblatt, Stephen, *Renaissance Self-Fashioning From More to Shakespeare* (1980)
Hexter, J. H., *More's 'Utopia'* (1952)
Skinner, Quentin, 'Sir Thomas More's *Utopia*' (1987)

Parker, Henry (*c.*1481–1556)

Son of Sir William Parker and Alice Lovel, through whom he inherited his title. By 1496 he had entered service in the household of Lady Margaret Beaufort. Around this time he married Alice St John. Under the continuing patronage of Lady Margaret, he was educated in Oxford after his marriage. He does not seem to have entered service with Henry VIII. In 1523 he went to Germany on diplomatic business. In 1530–1 he was appointed to the commission of the peace in Essex and Hertfordshire. Alone of the eleven peers who were able to sit in judgement on the trial of peers for treason, Morley sat on all six trials, including the trial that convicted his son-in-law; in 1542 he attended the parliamentary sitting at which his daughter was sentenced to death. Morley had family connections with the Boleyns. He dedicated books to Mary as both princess and queen, to Cromwell (a copy of Machiavelli's *Il Principe*), and to Henry VIII. His principal literary works are his translations of Petrarch's *Trionfi* (late 1520s) and Boccaccio's *De claris mulieribus* (1543).

**Forty-Six Lives, translated from Boccaccio's 'De Claris Mulieribus' by Henry Parker, Lord Morley*, ed. Herbert G. Wright, EETS 214 (Oxford University Press, 1943)

**Lord Morley's 'Tryumphes of Fraunces Petrarcke'*, ed. D. D. Carnicelli (Harvard University Press, 1971)

Starkey, David, 'An Attendant Lord? Henry Parker, Lord Morley' (2000)

Axton, Marie, and Carley, James P. (eds.), *'Triumphs of English': Henry Parker, Lord Morley, Translator to the Tudor Court* (2000)

Pecock, Reginald (?1395–?1460)

Born in the diocese of St David's, Wales, and educated in Oxford, Pecock was elected fellow of Oriel College, Oxford in 1414. He was ordained priest in 1421, and in 1431 was appointed to the mastership of Whittington College in the Vintry, London. In 1444 he became bishop of Asaph, Wales, and in 1450 bishop of Chichester. He wrote some works against Lollardy, including his *Repressor*, which was published in *c.*1455. Pecock sought to answer Lollards on his chosen grounds of argument in the vernacular, and succeeded in alienating 'every section of theological opinion in England' (*DNB*). He was convoked before Council in 1457 for heretical views, when he recanted. He resigned his bishopric, and was sent to Thorney abbey, Cambridgeshire, where he was confined to one room and deprived of writing materials until death.

**Repressor of Over Much Blaming of the Clergy*, ed. Churchill Babington, 2 vols., Rolls Series (HMSO, 1860; repr. Kraus, 1966)

Scase, Wendy, *Reginald Pecock* (1996)

RASTELL, JOHN (*c.*1475–1536)

Born in Coventry, where his father was city coroner, Rastell studied law in the Inns of Court, London. In 1504 he married Elizabeth More, sister of Thomas More, and in 1506 succeeded in his father's post, until 1509. In 1510 he opened a printing business; 1512 saw him in the service of Sir Edward Belknap, responsible for provision of military equipment in the French war of 1512–14. He financed a failed voyage to the New World in 1517, and was in 1520 responsible for decorations for the Field of Cloth of Gold, and for devising royal entries in 1522 and 1527. When he built his own house in Finsbury Fields in 1524, he included a stage. By 1529 he was working as a lawyer for Wolsey; he sat in the 'Reformation' Parliament of 1529, adopting evangelical positions. He was imprisoned in 1535, and died the following year. His *Four Elements* (*c.*1518) was printed in *c.*1519. His printing of Henry Medwall's *Fulgens and Lucrece* sometime between 1512 and 1516 was the first printing of a play in English.

**Three Rastell Plays*, ed. Richard Axton, Tudor Interludes 1 (Brewer, Rowman and Littlefield, 1979)

SKELTON, JOHN (*c.*1460—1529)

Born of a Northern, probably Yorkshire, family, Skelton possibly graduated from Cambridge in 1480, and in 1488 the title 'laureate' was conferred on him by the University of Oxford; in 1492 and 1493 respectively the same title is supposed to have been conferred by Louvain University and was conferred by the University of Cambridge. Between about 1496 and 1501 he was tutor to Prince Henry; in 1498 he was ordained as priest. In about 1503, however, he retired to Diss in Norfolk, where he was chiefly resident until 1512; he was rector of Diss until his death. In 1512/13 he assumed the title Orator Regius. From at least 1518 Skelton is recorded as living within the sanctuary of Westminster; he was buried in St Margaret's Westminster. His principal works include *The Garlande of Laurell* (begun to be assembled in 1495); *The Bowge of Courte* (?1498); *Magnificence* (1515–16). His anti-Wolsey satires were written 1521–2; by 1523 he was writing at the behest of Wolsey.

*John Skelton, *The Complete English Poems*, ed. John Scattergood (Penguin, 1983)

Walker, Greg, *John Skelton and the Politics of the 1520s* (1988)

STARKEY, THOMAS (?1499–1538)

Born in Cheshire, Starkey graduated from Magdalen College, Oxford as an MA in 1520–1. After his graduation he went to Italy, where he accepted service in the household of Reginald Pole at Venice and Padua. In 1534 he returned to England, and was appointed as a chaplain to the king. He survived suspicion over his views on the royal supremacy, and his connection with Pole, and was appointed to a London living. His *Dialogue* was never published until the modern editions.

Thomas Starkey: A Dialogue between Pole and Lupset, ed. T. F. Mayer, Camden Society, 4th. ser., 37 (Royal Historical Society, 1989)

* *A Dialogue between Reginald Pole and Thomas Lupset*, ed. Kathleen M. Burton (Chatto and Windus, 1948)

TIPTOFT, JOHN (?1427–1470)

Son of John, Baron Tiptoft, John Tiptoft was educated at Oxford, and succeeded to his father's estates and title in 1443. In 1449 he was created earl of Worcester. As a supporter of Richard, Duke of York, he was appointed treasurer in 1452, and in 1459 nominated ambassador to Pius II. In Italy he mixed with Italian humanists, and translated Cicero's *De amicitia* and Buonaccorso da Montemagno's *Controversia de Nobilitate*. Having returned to England in 1461, he was by 1462 Constable of England, when he gained the nickname 'butcher of England' for the ferocity of his vengeance against enemies of Edward IV. With the brief restoration of Henry VI in 1470, Tiptoft was executed.

*'Of True Nobility', in R. J. Mitchell, *John Tiptoft, 1427–1470* (Longman, Green and Co., 1938), app. 1

Mitchell, R. J., *John Tiptoft* (1938)

TREVISA, JOHN (*c*.1340–before 1402)

Born almost certainly in Cornwall, Trevisa gained his MA from Stapledon Hall (Exeter College), Oxford, where he was a student between 1362 and 1369, before becoming a fellow of Queen's College in the same university between 1369–87, with further residence at Queen's in 1394–6. From 1387 he was in the service of Thomas IV, Lord of Berkeley, to whom he dedicated his translation of the *Polychronicon* in 1387. All his other translations were produced under Berkeley's patronage: the *Gospel of Nico-*

demus, Dialogus inter Militem et Clericum, Defensio Curatorum, De Regimine Principum (1398).

On the Properties of Things; John Trevisa's Translation of Bartholomeus Anglicus 'De proprietatibus rerum', ed. M. C. Seymour et al. (Clarendon Press, 1975–88)
The Governance of Kings and Princes: John Trevisa's Middle English Translation of the 'De regimine principum' of Aegidius Romanus, ed. David C. Fowler, Charles F. Briggs, and Paul G. Remley, Garland Medieval Texts, 19 (Garland, 1997)
Dialogus inter militem et clericum; Richard Fitzralph's Sermon: 'Defensio curatorum' . . . translated by John Trevisa, ed. A. J. Perry, EETS 167 (Oxford University Press, 1925)
The Middle English Harrowing of Hell and Gospel of Nicodemus, ed. W. H. Hulme, EETS, ES 100 (Kegan Paul, Trench and Trübner, 1907)

Fowler, David C., *John Trevisa* (1993)
Hanna, Ralph III, 'Sir Thomas Berkeley and his Patronage' (1989)

Tyndale, William (*c.*1494–1536)

Born in the Welsh Marches, Tyndale gained his MA from Magdalen College, Oxford in 1515. After a period in Cambridge and an appointment as tutor in Gloucestershire from 1521, he came to London in 1523, and, having unsuccessfully sought patronage from Bishop Tunstall, was patronized by Humphrey Monmouth, a cloth merchant. In 1524 he went to Germany, and made the acquaintance of Luther. Tyndale's plans to publish his first English translation of the New Testament at Cologne were thwarted; the full translation was published in 1526 in Worms. In 1528 he published his *Obedience of a Christian Man* and the *Parable of the Wicked Mammon*. In 1530 his Pentateuch was published in Antwerp. He engaged with Thomas More, producing his *Answer* in 1531. In that year Henry VIII demanded the surrender of Tyndale by the emperor. Finally betrayed by Henry Phillips, whom Tyndale had befriended, Tyndale was arrested in May 1535; his trial and conviction for heresy in 1536 preceded his burning on 6 August of that year at Vifvorde.

**Tyndale's Old Testament*, ed. David Daniell (Yale University Press, 1992)
**Tyndale's New Testament*, ed. David Daniell (Yale University Press, 1989)
An Answer to Thomas More's Dialogue, ed. Henry Walter, Parker Society (Cambridge University Press, 1850)

**The Obedience of a Christian Man*, in *Doctrinal Treatises and Introductions to Different Portions of the Holy Scriptures,* ed. Henry Walter, Parker Society (Cambridge University Press, 1848)
**The Parable of the Wicked Mammon*, in *Doctrinal Treatises*, ed. Walter

Daniell, David, *William Tyndale: A Biography* (1994)

Thomas Usk (d. 1388)

Born of a London family, Usk served as secretary to John of Northampton, mayor of London 1381–3. After Northampton's defeat in 1383, Usk and Northampton were imprisoned by the new mayor, Nicholas Brembre. Usk extricated himself by turning prosecutor against his former master. He composed his *Testament of Love* in the period 1384–7, partly as a way of clearing his name. In 1387 he was appointed under-sheriff of Middlesex by Richard II; in the same year, however, he was implicated in the arrest of Nicholas Brembre, and executed in March 1388.

**The Testament of Love*, in Chaucer, *The Complete Works of Geoffrey Chaucer*, ed. W. W. Skeat, suppl. vol. (Clarendon Press, 1897)
The Testament of Love, ed. R. A. Shoaf, TEAMS (Medieval Institute Publications, 1998)

Strohm, Paul, 'Politics and Poetics: Usk and Chaucer in the 1380's' (1990)

Walton, John (fl. 1408–1410)

An Augustinian canon at Oseney Abbey, Oxford, Walton was patronized by Elizabeth Berkeley, daughter of Thomas Berkeley, patron of John Trevisa. Walton may have been responsible for a translation of Vegetius' *De re militari* for Thomas in 1408; his translation of the *De consolatione philosophiae* was dedicated to Elizabeth Berkeley in 1410.

**Boethius: De Consolatione Philosophiae, translated by John Walton*, ed. Mark Science, EETS 170 (Oxford University Press, 1927)

Hanna, Ralph III, 'Sir Thomas Berkeley and his Patronage' (1989)

Whitford, Richard (d. ?1555)

Whitford was elected fellow of Queens' College, Cambridge in *c.*1495, and in 1497–8 he accompanied William Blount, the fourth Lord Mountjoy, to the Continent as his confessor and chaplain. In about 1507 he entered the Brigettine house of Syon at Isleworth, Middlesex, where he lived until the dissolution of the monasteries, composing many devotional treatises, including a translation of the *Imitation of Christ.* After the dissolution he received a pension.

Thomas à Kempis, *The Imitation of Christ*, ed. B. J. H. Biggs, EETS 309 (Oxford University Press, 1997)

DNB

Hogg, James, 'The Brigettine Contribution to Late Medieval English Spirituality' (1982)

WYATT, THOMAS (*c.*1503–1542)

Born at Allington Castle, the son of Henry Wyatt, Privy Councillor to both Henry VII and Henry VIII. In 1516 he is recorded as entering St John's College, Cambridge, and as ewerer extraordinary at the court of Henry VIII. He married Elizabeth Brooke *c.*1520. By 1525 he was an esquire of the royal body; probably in the same year he separated from his wife, whom he charged with adultery. Wyatt served as an ambassador for Henry VIII throughout his career, variously in France, Italy, and Spain. In May 1536 he was imprisoned in the Tower on unspecified charges; it is generally supposed that he was implicated in the wave of arrests following the fall of Queen Anne. By June of the same year, after the executions of Anne and her supposed lovers that Wyatt may have witnessed, he was sent to Allington. As ambassador to the imperial court, compatriots laid charges against Wyatt for potentially treasonous misconduct. Only in 1541, after the fall of Cromwell, Wyatt's protector, was Wyatt arrested on charges of treason. The Crown confiscated the household goods at Allington Castle. Wyatt defended himself in a written defence, which seems never to have been delivered. He was pardoned on the understanding that he had confessed to the charges. In October 1542, riding on the king's business, he died of fever. Wyatt wrote lyric poetry across his career; in *c.*1527 he translated Plutarch's *Quiet of Mind* for Queen Katherine of Aragon.

**Collected Poems of Sir Thomas Wyatt*, ed. Kenneth Muir and Patricia Thomson (University of Liverpool Press, 1969)

Plutarch's Quyete of Mynde, Translated by Thomas Wyatt (facs. edn., Harvard University Press, 1931)

**Sir Thomas Wyatt: The Complete Poems*, ed. R. A. Rebholz (Penguin, 1978)

The Life and Letters of Sir Thomas Wyatt, ed. Kenneth Muir (University of Liverpool Press, 1963)

Thomson, Patricia, *Sir Thomas Wyatt and his Background* (1964)

WYCLIF, JOHN (*c.*1330–1384)

Born probably in Yorkshire, most of Wyclif's adult life was spent in Oxford. He was a fellow of Merton College in 1356, and Master of Balliol in 1360. He gained his doctorate in Theology *c.*1372–3. In 1374 he was granted the Leicestershire benefice of Lutterworth. In 1374 he went to Bruges on diplomatic business, but by 1378 the Pope had condemned his views on civil and divine dominion. In 1381 he was forced to leave Oxford, and retired to Lutterworth. An extreme realist, Wyclif's views were powerfully influential on the Lollard movement. It is generally accepted now that he wrote no works in English.

Thompson, J. A. F., 'Wyclif, John' (1998)

Hudson, Anne, *The Premature Reformation* (1988)

Suggestions for Further Reading

All chapters of this book are quite closely annotated, so as to support argument where necessary. The following suggestions for further reading are therefore brief. They specify works that are of central importance for a subject, whether or not mentioned in the notes. Secondary works on specific authors can be found in the Author Bibliographies, or in the guides listed there.

History of the English Language

The following volumes offer a complete guide:

Blake, N. F. (ed.), *The Cambridge History of the English Language*, 2. *1066–1476* (1992)

Lass, Roger (ed.), *The Cambridge History of the English Language*, 3. *1476–1776* (1999)

Bibliographical Guides

All literary critical and historical work is immediately dependent on the primary work of editors and bibliographers of primary material. The indispensable works of primary bibliography for English writing in this period are as follows:

Beal, Peter, *Index of English Literary Manuscripts*, 1. *1450–1625* (1980)

Blake, N. F., Edwards, A. S. G., and Lewis, R. E. (eds.), *Index of Printed Middle English Prose* (1985)

Boffey, Julia, and Edwards, A. S. G. (eds.), *A New Index of Middle English Verse* (British Library, forthcoming)

Edwards, A. S. G. (gen. ed.), *Index of Middle English Prose*, 12 vols. in progress (Brewer, 1984–)

REED volumes

Ringler, William A. (ed.), *A Bibliography and Index of English Verse: printed 1476–1558* (1988)

—— (ed.) *Bibliography and Index of English Verse in Manuscript, 1501–1558* (1992)

RSTC

Severs, J. Burke, and Hartung, A. E. (gen. eds.), *A Manual of Writing in Middle English 1050–1500*, 7 vols. in progress (1967–)

Periodization

Two key works have been profoundly influential and mutually reinforcing for concepts of the Renaissance and later Middle Ages respectively:

Burckhardt, Jacob, *The Civilization of the Renaissance in Italy*, trans. S. G. C. Middlemore (1958)

Huizinga, Johan, *The Autumn of the Middle Ages*, trans. Rodney J. Payton and Ulrich Mammitzsch (1996)

The periodic presuppositions of both these, and many more, books are revealed in the following:

Ferguson, Wallace K., *The Renaissance in Historical Thought* (1948)

Literary History

The following are each very different in their approach. The first was the greatest work of European literary history in the twentieth century. The other works are restricted to England or Britain.

Auerbach, Erich, *Mimesis: The Representation of Reality in Western Literature*, trans. Willard R. Trask (1968)

Burrow, J. A., *Medieval Writers and their Work: Middle English Literature and its Background 1100–1500* (1982)

Carlson, David R., *English Humanist Books: Writers and Patrons; Manuscripts and Print 1475–1525* (1993)

Fox, Alistair, *Politics and Literature in the Reigns of Henry VII and Henry VIII* (1989)

King, John N., *English Reformation Literature: The Tudor Origins of the Protestant Tradition* (1982)

Pearsall, Derek, *Old and Middle English Poetry* (1977)

Spearing, A. C., *Medieval to Renaissance in English Poetry* (1985)

Stevens, John, *Music and Poetry in the Early Tudor Court* (1961)

Turville-Petre, Thorlac, *The Alliterative Revival* (1977)

Wallace, David (ed.), *The Cambridge History of Medieval English Literature* (1999)

Political and Social History

The following have European perspectives:

Allmand, Christopher (ed.), *The New Cambridge Medieval History*, 7. *c.1415–c.1500* (1998)
Elton, G. R., (ed.), *The New Cambridge Modern History*, 2. *The Reformation, 1520–1559* (1958)
Jones, Michael (ed.), *The New Cambridge Medieval History*, 6. *c.1300–c.1415* (2000)
Potter, G. R. (ed.), *The New Cambridge Modern History*, 1. *The Renaissance 1493–1520* (1957)

The focus of the following is for the most part limited to England:

Elton, G. R., *The Tudor Revolution in Government: Administrative Changes in the Reign of Henry VIII* (1959)
Given-Wilson, Chris, *The English Nobility in the Late Middle Ages: The Fourteenth-Century Political Community* (1987)
—— *The Royal Household and the King's Affinity: Service, Politics and Finance in England 1360–1413* (1986)
James, Mervyn, *Society, Politics and Culture: Studies in Early Modern England* (1986)
Kaeuper, Richard W., *War, Justice and Public Order: England and France in the Later Middle Ages* (1988)
Keen, M. H., *England in the Later Middle Ages: A Political History* (1973)
Lander, J. R., *Government and Community: England 1450–1509* (1980)
Smith, Alan G. R., *The Emergence of a Nation State: The Commonwealth of England 1529–1660* (1984)
Starkey, David, 'The Age of the Household: Politics, Society and the Arts c.1350—c.1550' (1981)
Thomson, John A. F., *The Transformation of Medieval England 1370–1529* (1983)

Religious History

The following offer coverage of the high points of religious and theological controversy in the period. Duffy also offers a picture of what he calls 'traditional religion':

Aston, Margaret, *England's Iconoclasts*, 1. *Laws against Images* (1988)
Brigden, Susan, *London and the Reformation* (1989)
Clebsch, William, *England's Earliest Protestants, 1520–1535* (1964)

Duffy, Eamon, *The Stripping of the Altars: Traditional Religion in England, 1400–1580* (1992)
Haigh, Christopher (ed.), *The English Reformation Revised* (1987)
Hudson, Anne, *The Premature Reformation: Wycliffite Texts and Lollard History* (1988)
Leff, Gordon, *The Dissolution of the Medieval Outlook: An Essay in Intellectual and Spiritual Change in the Fourteenth Century* (1976)
McConica, James Kelsey, *English Humanists and Reformation Politics under Henry VIII and Edward VI* (1965)
Rex, Richard, *Henry VIII and the English Reformation* (1993)
Trueman, Carl, *Luther's Legacy: Salvation and English Reformers, 1525–1556* (1994)

Education

Courtenay, William J., *Schools and Scholars in Fourteenth-Century England* (1987)
Grafton, Anthony, and Jardine, Lisa, *From Humanism to the Humanities: Education and the Liberal Arts in Fifteenth and Sixteenth Century Europe* (1986)
Moran, Jo Ann Hoeppner, *The Growth of English Schooling, 1340–1548: Learning, Literacy, and Laicization in Pre-Reformation York Diocese* (1985)
Orme, Nicholas, *English Schools in the Middle Ages* (1973)
—— *Education and Society in Medieval and Renaissance England* (1989)

The Reception of Texts, including 'Humanism'

Copeland, Rita, *Rhetoric, Hermeneutics, and Translation in the Middle Ages: Academic Traditions and Vernacular Texts* (1991)
Grafton, Anthony, *Defenders of the Text: The Traditions of Scholarship in an Age of Science, 1450–1800* (1991)
Kray, Jill (ed.), *The Cambridge Companion to Renaissance Humanism* (1996)
Minnis, A. J., *Medieval Theory of Authorship: Scholastic Literary Attitudes in the Later Middle Ages* (1984)
Schirmer, Walter F., *Der englische Frühhumanismus* (2nd edn., 1963)
Weiss, Roberto, *Humanism in England during the Fifteenth Century* (1967)

History of Political Thought

Skinner, Quentin, *The Foundations of Modern Political Thought*, 2 vols. (1970)

Wilks, Michael, *The Problem of Sovereignty in the Middle Ages* (1963)

History of the Book

The period of this book covers both manuscript and printed books. Taken together, the last two of the following give an overview of both modes of production; Eisenstein offers a Continental perspective.

Eisenstein, Elizabeth L., *The Printing Press as an Agent of Change: Communications and Cultural Transformation in Early-Modern Europe*, 2 vols. (1979)

Griffiths, Jeremy, and Pearsall, Derek (eds.), *Book Production and Publishing in Britain 1375–1475* (1989)

Hellinga, Lotte, and Trapp, J. B. (eds.), *The Cambridge History of the Book in Britain*, 3. *1400–1557* (1999)

Some areas covered in this book are populated by anonymous writers; general indications for those bodies of work are not, therefore, given in the Author Bibliographies. The following four sections offer such guidance.

Drama

Beadle covers all aspects of medieval English drama; the other two entries give a good map of drama in the early sixteenth century:

Beadle, Richard (ed.), *The Cambridge Companion to Medieval English Theatre* (1994)

Bevington, David, *From 'Mankind' to Marlowe: Growth of Structure in the Popular Drama of Tudor England* (1962)

White, Paul Whitfield, *Theatre and Reformation: Protestantism, Patronage and Playing in Tudor England* (1993)

Romance

The two best guides are as follows:

Cooper, Helen, 'Romance after 1400' (1999)
Field, Rosalind, 'Romance in England, 1066–1400' (1999)

Lollardy

The fundamental work is:

Hudson, Anne, *The Premature Reformation: Wycliffite Texts and Lollard History* (1988)

Popular Devotion

Bynum offers a Continental perspective; Gibson's study is an illuminating case-study of East Anglia:

Bynum, Caroline Walker, *Holy Feast and Holy Fast: The Religious Significance of Food to Medieval Women* (1987)
Gibson, Gail McMurray, *The Theatre of Devotion: East Anglian Drama and Society in the Late Middle Ages* (1989)

There are, of course, many areas that have not received extensive coverage, and some that have not received any coverage at all. The following are worth especial mention.

Prose

Edwards, A. S. G. (ed.), *Middle Engish Prose: A Critical Guide to Major Authors and Genres* (1984)

Historical Writing

Galloway, Andrew, 'Writing History in England' (1999)
Gransden, Antonia, *Historical Writing in England*, 2 vols. (1974–82)
Taylor, John, *English Historical Literature in the Fourteenth Century* (1987)

French and Latin Writing in England

Crane, Susan, 'Anglo-Norman Cultures in England, 1066–1460' (1999)
Rigg, A. G., *A History of Anglo-Latin Literature, 1066–1422* (1992)

Writing in Britain outside England

The following offer useful starting points:

Dolan, Terence, 'Writing in Ireland' (1999)
Goldstein, James R., 'Writing in Scotland' (1999)
Roberts, Brynley F., 'Writing in Wales' (1999)

Works Cited

The Abbey of the Holy Ghost in *Religious Pieces in Prose and Verse*, ed. George G. Perry, EETS 26 (Kegan Paul, Trench and Trübner, 1867), 51–62.

Adams, Robert. 'Piers's Pardon and Langland's Semi-Pelagianism', *Traditio*, 39 (1983), 367–418.

Aers, David, (ed.). *Culture and History 1350–1600: Essays on English Communities, Identities and Writing* (Harvester Wheatsheaf, 1992).

—— 'A Whisper in the Ear of the Early Modernists, or Reflections on Literary Critics Writing the "History of the Subject"', in Aers (ed.), *Culture and History 1350–1600*, 177–202.

—— 'Altars of Power: Reflections on Eamon Duffy's *The Stripping of the Altars*', *Literature and History*, 3rd ser., 3 (1994), 90–105.

—— and Staley, Lynn. *The Powers of the Holy: Religion, Politics and Gender in Late Medieval English Culture* (Pennsylvania University Press, 1996).

Alexander, in *The Romance of William of Palerne*, ed. W. W. Skeat, EETS, ES 1 (Trübner, 1867).

Alford, John. 'Richard Rolle and Related Works', in Edwards (ed.), *Middle English Prose*, 35–60.

—— (ed.). *A Companion to 'Piers Plowman'* (University of California Press, 1988).

Allmand, Christopher (ed.). *The New Cambridge Medieval History*, 7. *c.1415–c.1500* (Cambridge University Press, 1998).

Anglo, Sydney. 'An Early Tudor Programme for Plays and Other Demonstrations against the Pope', *JWCI* 20 (1957), 176–9.

—— 'The *British History* in Early Tudor Propaganda', *BJRL* 44 (1961), 17–48.

—— (ed.), *Chivalry in the Renaissance* (Boydell, 1990).

Aquinas, Thomas. *Summa Theologiae*, ed. Thomas Gilby, 60 vols. (Eyre and Spottiswoode, 1968).

Archibald, Elizabeth, and Edwards, A. S. G. (eds.). *A Companion to Malory* (Brewer, 1996).

Aristotle. **Politica*, ed. P. Michaud-Quantin, in *Aristoteles Latinus*, 29/1 (Desclée de Brouwer, 1961).

ARISTOTLE. *The Politics*, ed. and trans. Stephen Everson (Cambridge University Press, 1988).

ASCHAM, ROGER. **The Schoolmaster*, in *Roger Ascham: English Works*, ed. William Aldis Wright (Cambridge University Press, 1904).

ASHBY, GEORGE. **George Ashby's Poems*, ed. Mary Bateson, EETS, ES 76 (Kegan Paul, Trench and Trübner, 1899).

The Assembly of Ladies. See *The Floure and the Leafe and the Assembly of Ladies.*

ASTON, M. E. 'Lollardy and Sedition, 1381–1431', *Past and Present*, 17 (1960), 1–44.

—— 'English Ruins and English History: The Dissolution and the Sense of the Past', *JWCI* 36 (1973), 231–55.

—— 'Huizinga's Harvest: England and the *Waning of the Middle Ages*', *Medievalia et Humanistica*, NS 9 (1979), 1–24.

—— *Lollards and Reformers: Images and Literacy in Late Medieval England* (Hambledon, 1984).

—— 'Devotional Literacy', in Aston, *Lollards and Reformers*, 101–33.

—— 'Lollard Women Priests?', in Aston, *Lollards and Reformers*, 49–70.

—— *England's Iconoclasts*, I. *Laws against Images* (Clarendon Press, 1988).

AUDELAY, JOHN. **The Poems of John Audelay*, ed. Ella Keats Whiting, EETS 184 (Oxford University Press, 1931).

AUERBACH, ERICH. 'Camilla, or the Rebirth of the Sublime', in Auerbach, *Literary Language and its Public in Late Latin Antiquity and in the Middle Ages*, trans. Ralph Manheim (Routledge and Kegan Paul, 1965), 183–233.

—— *Mimesis: The Representation of Reality in Western Literature*, trans. Willard R. Trask (1946; Princeton University Press, 1968).

—— 'The Knight Sets Forth', in Auerbach, *Mimesis*, ch. 6.

—— 'The Weary Prince', in Auerbach, *Mimesis*, ch. 13.

AUGUSTINE OF HIPPO. *Saint Augustine: On Christian Doctrine*, trans. D. W. Robertson (Bobbs-Merrill, 1958).

AXTON, MARIE, and CARLEY, JAMES P. (eds.). *'Triumphs of English': Henry Parker, Lord Morley, Translator to the Tudor Court. New Essays in Interpretation* (British Library Publications, 2000).

BAKER, DENISE. 'From Ploughing to Penitence: *Piers Plowman* and Fourteenth-Century Theology', *Speculum*, 55 (1980), 715–25.

—— *Julian of Norwich's* Showings*: From Vision to Book* (Princeton University Press, 1994).

BALE, JOHN. **Illustrium maioris britannie scriptorum, hoc est anglie, cambrie, ac scotiae, summarium* (Wesel and Ipswich, 1548).

—— **The Laboryouse journey and serche of Johan Leylande for Englandes antiquitees* (R. Jugge, 1549) (repr. in facs., Amsterdam, 1975).

—— *Acta romanorum pontificum, a dispersione discipulorum usque ad tempora Pauli quarti* (Basel, 1558).

—— **Scriptorum illustrium maioris brytannie, quam nunc angliam et scotiam uocant, catalogus* (John Oporinus, 1559; both the 1557 and 1559 vols. are printed in this book) (repr. in facs., 2 vols., 1971).

—— *Index britanniae scriptorum: John Bale's Index of British and Other Writers*, ed. R. L. Poole and Mary Bateson (1902; repr. Brewer, 1990).

—— **The Complete Plays of John Bale*, ed. Peter Happé, 2 vols., Tudor Interludes, 5 (Brewer, 1985).

—— **The Vocation of Johan Bale*, ed. Peter Happé and John King (Medieval and Renaissance Texts and Studies, 70; 1990).

—— **The Examinations of Anne Askew*, ed. Elaine V. Beilin (Oxford University Press, 1996).

BARCLAY, ALEXANDER. **The Ship of Fools*, ed. T. H. Jamieson, 2 vols. (William Paterson, 1874).

—— **The Eclogues of Alexander Barclay*, ed. Beatrice White, EETS 175 (Oxford University Press, 1928).

—— **Lyfe of St George*, ed. William Nelson, EETS 230 (Oxford University Press, 1955).

BARET, JOHN. *Will, in S. Tymms (ed.), *Wills and Inventories from the Beginning of the Commissary of Bury St Edmunds and the Archdeacon of Sudbury* (Camden Society 49; 1850), 15–44.

BARLOWE, JEROME. **A proper dialogue betwene a gentillman and a husbandman* (1530), repr. in *English Reprints*, ed. Edward Arber, 7 vols. (Edward Arber, 1871), 7. 129–69.

BARNES, ROBERT. ** What the Church is: and who bee thereof, and whereby Men May Know Her*, in Tyndale, Frith, and Barnes, *The Whole Workes*, 242–56.

—— **A Supplication to King Henry VIII*, in Tyndale, Frith, and Barnes, *The Whole Workes*, 183–205.

BARON, HANS. 'The Memory of Cicero's Roman Civic Spirit in the Medieval Centuries and in the Florentine Renaissance' (1938), repr. in Hans Baron, *In Search of Florentine Civic Humanism*, 2 vols. (Princeton University Press, 1988), 1. 94–133.

BARON, XAVIER. 'Medieval Traditions in the English Renaissance: John Stowe's Portrayal of London in 1603', in Rhoda Schnur (ed.), *Acta Conventus Neo-Latini Hafiensis* (Medieval and Renaissance Texts and Studies, 120; 1994), 133–41.

BARR, HELEN. *Signes and Sothe: Language in the 'Piers Plowman' Tradition* (Brewer, 1994).

BARRON, W. J. R. *English Medieval Romance* (Longman, 1987).

BARTLETT, ROBERT. *The Making of Europe: Conquest, Colonization and Cultural Change 950–1350* (Allen Lane, 1993).

BARTON, JOHN. 'Historical-Critical Approaches', in Barton (ed.), *The Cambridge Companion to Biblical Interpretation* (Cambridge University Press, 1998), 9–20.

BASWELL, CHRISTOPHER. *Virgil in Medieval England: Figuring the 'Aeneid' from the Twelfth Century to Chaucer*, Cambridge Studies in Medieval Literature, 24 (Cambridge University Press, 1995).

BAWCUTT, PRISCILLA. *Gavin Douglas: A Critical Study* (Edinburgh University Press, 1976).

BEADLE, RICHARD (ed.). *The Cambridge Companion to Medieval English Theatre* (Cambridge University Press, 1994).

—— 'The York Cycle', in Beadle (ed.), *Medieval English Theatre*, 85–108.

—— '"Devout ymaginacioun" and the Dramatic Sense in Love's *Mirror* and the N-Town Plays', in Oguro et al. (eds.), 1–17.

BEAL, PETER. *Index of English Literary Manuscripts*, I. *1450–1625* (Mansell, 1980).

BEAUNE, COLLETTE. 'L'Utilisation politique du mythe des origines troyennes en France à la fin du moyen-âge', in *Lectures médiévales de Virgile*, Collection de l'École Française de Rome (École Française de Rome, 1985).

BECKWITH, SARAH. 'A Very Material Mysticism: The Medieval Mysticism of Margery Kempe', in David Aers (ed.), *Medieval Literature: Criticism, Ideology and History* (Harvester, 1986), 34–57.

BELLAMY, JOHN. *The Tudor Law of Treason: An Introduction* (Routledge and Kegan Paul, 1979).

BENNETT, J. A. W. 'The Early Fame of Gavin Douglas's *Eneados*', *MLN* 61 (1946), 83–8.

BENNETT, MICHAEL. 'John Audelay: Some New Evidence on his Life and Work', *Chaucer Review*, 16 (1982), 344–55.

BENSON, C. DAVID. 'A Chaucerian Allusion and the Date of the Alliterative *Destruction of Troy*', *N&Q*, NS 219 (1974), 206–7.

—— 'An Augustinian Irony in *Piers Plowman*', *N&Q*, NS 23 (1976), 51–4.

—— *The History of Troy in Middle English Literature: Guido delle Colonne's 'Historia Destructionis Troiae' in Medieval England* (Brewer, 1980).

—— and ROBERTSON, ELIZABETH (eds.). *Chaucer's Religious Tales* (Brewer, 1990).

—— and BLANCHFIELD, LYNNE S. *The Manuscripts of* 'Piers Plowman': *The B-Version* (Brewer, 1997).

BENSON, LARRY D. 'The Date of the Alliterative *Morte Arthure*', in Jess Bessinger and Robert R. Raymo (eds.), *Medieval Studies in Honour of Lillian Herlands Hornstein* (New York University Press, 1976), 19–40.

BENTLEY, JERRY H. *Humanists and Holy Writ: New Testament Scholarship in the Renaissance* (Princeton University Press, 1983).

BEVINGTON, DAVID. *From 'Mankind' to Marlowe: Growth of Structure in the Popular Drama of Tudor England* (Harvard University Press, 1962).

Biblia Pauperum: A Facsimile and Edition, ed. Avril Henry (Cornell University Press, 1987).

BILLS, BING DUANE. 'The "Suppression Theory" and the English Corpus Christi Plays: A Re-Evaluation', *Theatre Journal*, 32 (1980), 157–68.

BIRD, RUTH. *The Turbulent London of Richard II* (Longmans, Green, 1949).

BLAKE, N. F. *Caxton and his World* (Deutsch, 1969).

—— 'John Lydgate and Caxton', *LSE*, NS 16 (1985), 272–89.

—— *William Caxton and English Literary Culture* (Hambledon Press, 1991).

—— 'William Caxton: A Review', in Blake, *William Caxton and English Literary Culture*, ch. 1.

—— 'Caxton Prepares his Edition of the *Morte Darthur*', in Blake, *William Caxton and English Literary Culture*, ch. 14.

—— (ed.). *The Cambridge History of the English Language*, 2. *1066–1476* (Cambridge University Press, 1992).

—— *William Caxton*, Authors of the Middle Ages, 7 (Variorum, 1996).

—— EDWARDS, A. S. G., and LEWIS, R. E. (eds.) *Index of Printed Middle English Prose* (Garland, 1985).

BLOCH, R. HOWARD. *Etymologies and Genealogies: A Literary Anthropology of the French Middle Ages* (University of Chicago Press, 1983).

BLODGETT, J. E. 'William Thynne (d. 1546)', in Ruggiers (ed.), 35–52.

BOFFEY, JULIA. *Manuscripts of English Courtly Love Lyrics in the Later Middle Ages*, Manuscript Studies, 1 (Brewer, 1985).

—— 'Lydgate, Henryson, and the Literary Testament', *MLQ* 53 (1992), 41–56.

—— 'Women Authors and Women's Literacy in Fourteenth and Fifteenth-Century England', in Meale (ed.), *Women and Literature in Britain, 1150–1500*, 159–82.

Boffey, Julia. 'Lydgate's Lyrics and Women Readers', in Smith and Taylor (eds.), i. 139–49.

—— and Edwards, A. S. G. (eds.). *A New Index of Middle English Verse* (British Library, forthcoming).

Boitani, Piero and Torti, Anna (eds.). *Literature in Fourteenth-Century England: The J. A. W. Bennett Memorial Lectures*, Tübinger Beiträge zur Anglistik, 5 (Gunter Narr Verlag; Brewer, 1983).

—— and Mann, Jill (eds.). *The Cambridge Chaucer Companion* (Cambridge University Press, 1986).

—— and Torti, Anna (eds.). *Interpretation: Medieval and Modern* (Brewer, 1993).

Bokenham, Osbern. **Legendys of Hooly Wummen*, ed. Mary S. Serjeantson, EETS 206 (Oxford University Press, 1938).

Bolton, J. L. *The Medieval English Economy 1150–1500* (Dent; Rowman and Littlefield, 1980).

The Book of Fayttes of Armes and of Chyvalrye, ed. A. T. P. Byles, EETS 189 (Oxford University Press, 1932).

The Book of Vices and Virtues, ed. W. Nelson Francis, EETS 217 (Oxford University Press, 1942).

Bowers, John M. 'Piers Plowman and the Police: Notes toward a History of the Wycliffite Langland', *YLS* 6 (1992), 1–50.

—— '*Pearl* in its Royal Setting: Ricardian Poetry Revisited', *SAC* 17 (1995), 111–55.

Bradshaw, Henry. **Life of Saint Werburge of Chester*, ed. Carl Horstmann, EETS 88 (Trübner, 1887).

—— **Life of Saynt Radegund*, ed. F. Brittain (Cambridge University Press, 1926).

Brampton, Thomas. 'Thomas Brampton's Metrical Paraphrase of the Seven Penitential Psalms', ed. James R. Kreuzer, *Traditio*, 7 (1949), 359–403.

Branca, Vittore. *Boccaccio, The Man and his Works*, trans. R. Monges (New York University Press, 1976).

Brewer, Charlotte. *Editing 'Piers Plowman': The Evolution of the Text*, Cambridge Studies in Medieval Literature, 28 (Cambridge University Press, 1996).

Brewer, Derek. 'The Relationship of Chaucer to the English and European Traditions', in D. S. Brewer (ed.), *Chaucer and Chaucerians* (Nelson, 1966), 1–38.

—— (ed.). *Chaucer: The Critical Heritage*, 2 vols. (Routledge and Kegan Paul, 1978; repr. 1995).

—— 'The Nature of Romance', *Poetica*, 9 (1978), 9–48.

——*Symbolic Stories: Traditional Narratives of the Family Drama in English Literature* (Longman, 1980).

BREWER, THOMAS. *Memoir of the Life and Times of John Carpenter, Town Clerk of London* (Arthur Taylor, 1856).

BRIDGET OF SWEDEN. **The Revelations of Saint Birgitta*, ed. William Patterson Cumming, EETS 178 (Oxford University Press, 1929; repr. 1971).

——*The 'Liber Celestis' of St Bridget of Sweden*, ed. Roger Ellis, vol. 1, EETS 291 (Oxford University Press, 1987).

BRIE, F. 'Mittelalter und Antike bei Lydgate', *Englische Studien*, 64 (1929), 261–301.

BRIGDEN, SUSAN. *London and the Reformation* (Clarendon Press, 1989).

——'Henry Howard, Earl of Surrey and the "Conjured League"', *Historical Journal*, 37 (1994), 507–37.

——'"The shadow that yow know": Sir Thomas Wyatt and Sir Francis Bryan at Court and in Embassy', *Historical Journal*, 39 (1996), 1–31.

BRINKELOW, HENRY. **Henry Brinkelow's Complaint of Roderyck Mors*, ed. J. Meadows Cowper, EETS, ES 22 (Trübner, 1874).

BRISCOE, MARIANNE G. and COLDEWEY, JOHN C. (eds.). *Contexts for Early English Drama* (Indiana University Press, 1989).

BROWN, A. L. 'The Privy Seal Clerks in the Early Fifteenth Century', in D. A. Bullough and R. L. Storey (eds.), *The Study of Medieval Records: Essays in Honour of Kathleen Major* (Clarendon Press, 1971), 260–81.

——'Parliament, *c.*1377–1422', in Davies and Denton (eds.), 109–40.

BROWN, PETER. *The Cult of Saints: Its Rise and Function in Latin Christianity* (University of Chicago Press, 1981).

**The Brut, or Chronicles of England*, ed. Friedrich W. D. Brie, 2 vols., EETS, 131, 136 (Kegan Paul, Trench and Trübner, 1906, 1908).

BUNT, GERRIT H. V. *Alexander the Great in the Literature of Medieval Britain*, Medievalia Groningana, 14 (University of Groningen, 1994).

BURCKHARDT, JACOB. *The Civilization of the Renaissance in Italy*, trans. S. G. C. Middlemore (Harper, 1958) (1st pub. in German, 1860).

BURNLEY, J. D. *Chaucer's Language and the Philosophers' Tradition*, Chaucer Studies, 2 (Brewer, 1979).

BURROW, COLIN. 'Horace at Home and Abroad: Wyatt and Sixteenth-Century Horatianism', in Charles Martindale and David Hopkins (eds.), *Horace Made New* (Cambridge University Press, 1993), 27–49.

BURROW, J. A. 'Fantasy and Language in the *Cloud*', *Essays in Criticism*, 27 (1977), 283–98.

——'The Poet as Petitioner', *SAC* 3 (1981), 61–75.

Burrow, J. A. *Medieval Writers and their Work: Middle English Literature and its Background 1100–1500* (Oxford University Press, 1982).
—— *Langland's Fictions* (Clarendon Press, 1993).
—— *Thomas Hoccleve*, Authors of the Middle Ages, 4 (Variorum, 1994).
Burrow, J. W. *A Liberal Descent: Victorian Historians and the English Past* (Cambridge University Press, 1981).
Butler, John. *The Quest for Becket's Bones: The Mystery of the Relics of St Thomas Becket of Canterbury* (Yale University Press, 1995).
Bynum, Caroline Walker. *Holy Feast and Holy Fast: The Religious Significance of Food to Medieval Women* (University of California Press, 1987).
Canitz, A. E. C. 'The Prologue to the *Eneados*: Gavin Douglas's Directions for Reading', *Studies in Scottish Literature*, 25 (1990), 1–22.
Cannon, Christopher. '*Raptus*, in the Chaumpaigne Release and a Newly Discovered Document concerning the Life of Geoffrey Chaucer', *Speculum*, 68 (1993), 74–94.
Capgrave, John. **Life of St Katharine of Alexandria*, ed. Carl Horstmann, EETS 100 (Kegan Paul, Trench and Trübner, 1893).
—— **John Capgrave's Lives of St Augustine and St Gilbert of Sempringham*, ed. J. J. Munro, EETS 140 (Kegan Paul, Trench and Trübner, 1910).
—— **Life of St Norbert*, ed. C. L. Smetana, Studies and Texts, 40 (Pontifical Institute of Medieval Studies, 1977).
—— **John Capgrave's 'Abbreviacion of Cronicles'*, ed. Peter J. Lucas, EETS 285 (Oxford University Press, 1983).
Carley, James P. 'John Leland's *Cygnea Cantio*: A Neglected Tudor River Poem', *Humanistica Lovaniensia*, 32 (1983), 225–41.
—— 'John Leland in Paris: The Evidence of his Poetry', *SP* 83 (1986), 1–50.
—— 'John Leland', in David A. Richardson (ed.), *Sixteenth-Century British Nondramatic Writers*, 2nd ser. Dictionary of Literary Biography, 136 (Gale Research, 1994), 224–9.
—— 'The Writings of Henry Parker', in Axton and Carley (eds.), 27–68.
Carlson, David R. 'King Arthur and Court Poems for the Birth of Arthur Tudor in 1486', *Humanistica Lovaniensia*, 36 (1987), 147–83.
—— *English Humanist Books: Writers and Patrons, Manuscripts and Print, 1475–1525* (University of Toronto Press, 1993).
Carpenter, Christine. *Locality and Polity: A Study of Warwickshire Landed Society, 1401–1499* (Cambridge University Press, 1992).
—— 'Political and Constitutional History Before and After McFarlane', in R. H. Britnell and A. J. Pollard, *The McFarlane Legacy: Studies in Late Medieval Politics and Society* (Alan Sutton, 1995), 175–206.

CASADY, EDWIN. *Henry Howard, Earl of Surrey*, Revolving Fund Series, 8 (Modern Language Association of America, 1938).

CATHERINE OF SIENA. *The Orchard of Syon*, ed. Phyllis Hodgson and Gabriel M. Liegey, EETS 258 (Oxford University Press, 1958).

CATTANEO, ARTURO. *L'ideale umanistico: Henry Howard, Earl of Surrey* (Adriatica, 1991).

CAUTLEY, H. MUNRO. *Royal Arms and Commandments in our Churches* (1934; repr. Boydell, 1974).

CAXTON, WILLIAM (trans.). **The Curial, Made by Maystere Alain Charretier*, ed. Frederick J. Furnivall, EETS, ES 54 (Trübner, 1865).

—— *'Life of Saint Winifred', in Carl Horstmann (ed.), 'Prosalegenden', *Anglia*, 3 (1880) (Item 1 at pp. 295–313).

—— **Caxton's 'Eneydos'*, ed. W. T. Culley and F. J. Furnivall, EETS, ES 57 (Trübner, 1890).

—— (trans.). **The Recuyell of the Historyes of Troye, translated by William Caxton*, ed. H. Oskar Sommer, 2 vols. (Trübner, 1894).

—— (trans.). **Paris and Vienne*, ed. MacEdward Leach, EETS 234 (Oxford University Press, 1957).

—— (trans.). **The History of Reynard the Fox*, ed. N. F. Blake, EETS 263 (Oxford University Press, 1970).

—— *Caxton's Malory*. See Malory, *Caxton's Malory*.

—— *Caxton's Own Prose*, ed. N. F. Blake (Deutsch, 1973).

CHAMBERS, E. K. *The Medieval Stage*, 2 vols. (Clarendon Press, 1903).

CHANDLER, ALICE. *A Dream of Order: The Medieval Ideal in Nineteenth Century English Literature* (University of Nebraska Press, 1970).

CHAPMAN, HESTER WOLFERSTAN. *Two Tudor Portraits: Henry Howard, Earl of Surrey, and Lady Katherine Grey* (Jonathan Cape, 1960).

CHARLES D'ORLÉANS. **Fortunes Stabilnes: Charles of Orleans's English Book of Love, A Critical Edition*, ed. Mary-Jo Arn (Medieval and Renaissance Texts and Studies, 138; 1994).

CHARTIER, ALAIN. *Fifteenth Century English Translations of Alain Chartier's 'Le Traité de l'Esperance' and 'Le Quadrilogue Invectif'*, ed. Margaret S. Blayney, EETS 270 (Oxford University Press, 1974).

—— *A Familiar Dialogue of the Friend and the Fellow*, ed. Margaret S. Blayney, EETS 295 (Oxford University Press, 1989).

CHAUCER, GEOFFREY. *The Complete Works of Geoffrey Chaucer*, ed. W. W. Skeat, 6 vols. and suppl. vol. (Clarendon Press, 1897).

—— *Chaucer's Dream Poetry: Sources and Analogues*, ed. and trans. B. A. Windeatt, Chaucer Studies, 7 (Brewer, 1982).

—— **The Riverside Chaucer*, 3rd edn., gen. ed. Larry D. Benson (Oxford University Press, 1987).

Cherewatuk, Karen. '"Gentyl Audiences" and "Grete Bookes": Chivalric Manuals and the *Morte Darthur*', *Arthurian Literature*, 15 (1997), 205–16.

**The Chester Mystery Cycle*, ed. R. M. Lumiansky and David Mills, 2 vols., EETS, ss 3, 9 (Oxford University Press, 1974, 1986).

**The Chester Mystery Cycle: Essays and Documents*, ed. R. M. Lumiansky and David Mills (University of North Carolina Press, 1983).

Chiàntera, Raffaele. *Guido delle Colonne* (Le Monnier, 1955).

Chrimes, S. B. *English Constitutional Ideas in the Fifteenth Century* (Cambridge University Press, 1936).

Chronicles of the Revolution, 1397–1400: The Reign of Richard II, ed. Christopher Given-Wilson (Manchester University Press, 1993).

'The Church and her Members', in *Select English Works of John Wyclif*, ed. Thomas Arnold, 3 vols. (Clarendon Press, 1871), 3. 338–65.

Clanvowe, John. *The Works of Sir John Clanvowe*, ed. V. J. Scattergood (Brewer, 1965; repr. 1975).

Clark, James M. *The Dance of Death in the Middle Ages and the Renaissance* (Jackson, 1950).

Cleanness, in *The Poems of the Pearl Manuscript*, ed. Andrew and Waldon.

Clebsch, William A. *England's Earliest Protestants, 1520–1535* (Yale University Press, 1964).

Clerk, John. **The Gest Hystoriale of the Destruction of Troy*, ed. G. A. Panton and David Donaldson, 2 pts. EETS 39 and 56 (Trübner, 1869 and 1874).

Clopper, Lawrence M. 'Lay and Clerical Impact on Civic Religious Drama and Ceremony', in Briscoe and Coldewey (eds.), 102–36.

**The Cloud of Unknowing and the Book of Privy Counselling*, ed. Phyllis Hodgson, EETS 218 (Oxford University Press, 1944; repr. 1981).

Coldewey, John C. 'Some Economic Aspects of the Late Medieval Drama', in Briscoe and Coldewey (eds.), 77–101.

—— 'The Non-Cycle Plays and the East Anglian Tradition', in Beadle (ed.), *Medieval English Theatre*, 189–210.

Collinson, Patrick. *The Birthpangs of Protestant England: Religious and Cultural Change in the Sixteenth and Seventeenth Centuries* (Macmillan, 1988).

Concilia Magnae Britanniae et Hiberniae, ed. David Wilkins, 4 vols. (Bowyer, Richardson, Purser, 1737).

Cooper, Helen. 'Wyatt and Chaucer: A Reappraisal', *LSE* 13 (1982), 104–23.

—— *The Canterbury Tales*, Oxford Guides to Chaucer (Clarendon Press, 1989).

—— 'Romance after 1400', in Wallace (ed.), *Medieval English Literature*, 690–719.

—— and MAPSTONE, SALLY (eds.). *The Long Fifteenth Century: Essays in Honour of Douglas Gray* (Clarendon Press, 1997).

COPELAND, RITA. *Rhetoric, Hermeneutics, and Translation in the Middle Ages: Academic Traditions and Vernacular Texts*, Cambridge Studies in Medieval Literature, 11 (Cambridge University Press, 1991).

COURTENAY, WILLIAM J. *Schools and Scholars in Fourteenth-Century England* (Princeton University Press, 1987).

Coventry Corpus Christi Plays. See *Two Coventry Corpus Christi Plays*, ed. Craig.

COVERDALE, MILES. **Remains of Myles Coverdale*, ed. George Pearson, Parker Society (Cambridge University Press, 1846).

COX, JEFFREY N. and REYNOLDS, LARRY J. (eds.). *New Historical Literary Study: Essays on Reproducing Texts, Representing History* (Princeton University Press, 1993).

CRANE, SUSAN. *Insular Romance: Politics, Faith and Culture in Anglo-Norman and Middle English Literature* (University of California Press, 1986).

—— 'Anglo-Norman Cultures in England, 1066–1460', in Wallace (ed.), *Medieval English Literature*, 35–60.

CRANMER, THOMAS. **Miscellaneous Writings and Letters of Thomas Cranmer*, ed. John E. Cox , Parker Society (Cambridge University Press, 1846).

—— *A Prologue or Preface . . . made by Thomas, Archbishop of Canterbury*, in *Miscellaneous Writings and Letters*, ed. Cox, 118–25.

CREWE, JONATHAN. *Trials of Authorship: Anterior Forms and Poetic Reconstruction from Wyatt to Shakespeare*, New Historicism, 9 (University of California Press, 1990).

CRICK, JULIA. *The 'Historia regum Britanniae' of Geoffrey of Monmouth, 3. A Summary Catalogue of the Manuscripts* (Brewer, 1989).

CROWLEY, ROBERT. **The Select Works of Robert Crowley*, ed. J. M. Cowper, EETS, ES 15 (Trübner, 1872).

—— **Philargyrie of Greate Britayne* (1551), ed. W. A. Marsden (facs. edn., Emery Walker, 1931).

CUMMINGS, BRIAN. 'Reformed Literature and Literature Reformed', in Wallace (ed.), *Medieval English Literature*, 821–51.

CUTLER, JOHN L. and ROBBINS, ROSSELL HOPE (eds.). *Supplement to the Index of Middle English Verse* (University of Kentucky Press, 1965).

DANIELL, DAVID. *William Tyndale: A Biography* (Yale University Press, 1994).

DARES. *The Chronicles of Dictys of Crete and Dares the Phrygian*, trans. R. M. Frazer (Indiana University Press, 1966).

DARLOW, T. H. and MOULE, H. F. (eds.), Herbert, A. S. (rev.). *Historical Catalogue of Printed Editions of the English Bibles* (English and Foreign Bible Society, 1968).

DAVENPORT, W. A. *Chaucer: Complaint and Narrative*, Chaucer Studies, 14 (Brewer, 1988).

DAVIES, R. G. and DENTON, J. H. (eds.). *The English Parliament in the Middle Ages* (Manchester University Press, 1981).

DEAN, CHRISTOPHER. *Arthur of England* (University of Toronto Press, 1987).

DEMETZ, PETER, GREENE, THOMAS, and NELSON, LOWRY JNR (eds.). *The Disciplines of Criticism: Essays in Literary Theory, Interpretation and History* (Yale University Press, 1968).

DESMOND, MARILYN. *Reading Dido: Gender, Textuality and the Medieval 'Aeneid'*, Medieval Cultures, 8 (University of Minnesota Press, 1994).

DESPRES, DENISE. *Ghostly Sights: Visual Meditation in Late-Medieval Literature* (Pilgrim Books, 1989).

Destruction of Troy. See Clerk, *Gest Hystoriale*.

D'EVELYN, CHARLOTTE. 'English Translations of *Legenda Aurea*', in Severs and Hartung (eds.), 2.430–9 and 559–61.

—— 'Legends of Individual Saints', in Severs and Hartung (eds.), 2. 440 and 561–637.

—— and FOSTER, FRANCES A. 'Saints' Legends', in Severs and Hartung (eds.), 2. 448–9 and 640–2.

DEVEREUX, E. J. 'Elizabeth Barton and Tudor Censorship', *BJRL* 49 (1966), 91–106.

DICKINSON, J. C. *The Shrine of Our Lady of Walsingham* (Cambridge University Press, 1956).

DICTYS OF CRETE. *The Chronicles of Dictys of Crete and Dares the Phrygian*, trans. R. M. Frazer (Indiana University Press, 1966).

DIHLE, ALBRECHT. *The Theory of Will in Classical Antiquity* (University of California Press, 1982).

DIMARCO, VINCENT. *'Piers Plowman': A Reference Guide* (G. K. Hall, 1988).

DIMMICK, JEREMY. 'Patterns of Ethics and Politics in John Gower's *Confessio Amantis*', unpublished Ph.D. thesis, University of Cambridge, 1998.

—— '"Redinge of Romance" in Gower's *Confessio Amantis*', in Rosalind Field (ed.), *Tradition and Transformation in Medieval Romance* (Brewer, 1999), 125–37.

—— Simpson, James, and Zeeman, Nicolette (eds.). *Images, Idolatry and Iconoclasm in Late Medieval England* (Oxford University Press, 2002).

Doane, A. N. and Amsler, Mark. 'Literacy and Readership', in Szarmach, Tavormina, and Rosenthal (eds.), 425–7.

Dolan, Terence. 'Writing in Ireland', in Wallace (ed.), *Medieval English Literature*, 208–28.

Dollimore, Jonathan and Sinfield, Alan (eds.). *Political Shakespeare: New Essays in Cultural Materialism*, 2nd edn. (Cornell University Press, 1999).

Douglas, Gavin. **Virgil's 'Aeneid', translated into Scottish Verse*, ed. David F. C. Coldwell, 4 vols. Scottish Text Society, 3rd ser., 25, 27, 28, 30 (Blackwood, 1957–64).

—— *The Palice of Honour*, in *The Shorter Poems of Gavin Douglas*, ed. Priscilla J. Bawcutt (Scottish Text Society, 4th ser., 3; 1967).

Dowling, Maria. *Humanism in the Age of Henry VIII* (Croom Helm, 1986).

Doyle, A. I. and Parkes, M. B. 'The Production of Copies of the *Canterbury Tales* and the *Confessio Amantis* in the Early Fifteenth Century', in M. B. Parkes and Andrew G. Watson (eds.), *Medieval Scribes, Manuscripts and Libraries: Essays Presented to N. R. Ker* (Scolar, 1978), 163–210.

Dronke, Peter. *Medieval Latin and the Rise of the European Love-Lyric*, 2nd edn., 2 vols. (Clarendon Press, 1968).

Drury, John (ed.). *Critics of the Bible 1724–1873* (Cambridge University Press, 1989).

Duffy, Eamon. *The Stripping of the Altars: Traditional Religion in England, 1400–1580* (Yale University Press, 1992).

Dunbar, William. *William Dunbar: Selected Poems*, ed. Priscilla Bawcutt (Longman, 1996).

Dutton, Richard. 'Censorship', in John D. Cox and David Scott Kastan (eds.), *A New History of Early English Drama* (Columbia University Press, 1997), 287–304.

Eagleton, Terry. *The Ideology of the Aesthetic* (Blackwell, 1990).

Ebin, Lois A. 'Lydgate's Views on Poetry', *Annuale Mediaevale*, 18 (1977), 76–105.

—— (ed.). *Vernacular Poetics in the Late Middle Ages* (Medieval Institute Publications, 1984).

Economou, George D. *The Goddess Natura in Medieval Literature* (Harvard University Press, 1972).

Edwards, A. S. G. 'The Influence of Lydgate's *Fall of Princes*: A Survey', *MS* 39 (1977), 424–39.

EDWARDS, A. S. G. *Stephen Hawes*, Twayne's English Authors Series, 354 (Twayne, 1983).
—— 'Lydgate Scholarship: Progress and Prospects', in R. F. Yeager (ed.), *Fifteenth Century Studies* (Archon, 1984), 29–47.
—— (ed.). *Middle English Prose: A Critical Guide to Major Authors and Genres* (Rutgers University Press, 1984).
—— (gen. ed.). *The Index of Middle English Prose*, 12 vols., in progress (Brewer, 1984–).
—— 'Some Observations on the History of Middle English Editing', in Derek Pearsall (ed.), *Manuscripts and Texts: Editorial Practice in Later Middle English Literature* (Brewer, 1987), 34–48.
—— 'Middle English Romance: The Limits of Editing, the Limits of Criticism', in Tim William Machan, *Medieval Literature: Texts and Interpretation* (Medieval and Renaissance Texts and Studies, 79; 1991), 94–104.
—— 'Gender, Order and Reconciliation in *Sir Degrevant*', in Meale (ed.), *Readings in Medieval English Romance*, 53–64.
—— 'The Transmission and Audience of Osbern Bokenham's *Legendys of Hooly Wummen*', in A. J. Minnis (ed.), *Late Medieval Religious Texts and their Transmission* (Brewer, 1994), 157–67.
—— 'Fifteenth-Century Middle English Verse Author Collections', in A. S. G. Edwards, Vincent Gillespie, and Ralph Hanna (eds.), *The English Medieval Book* (British Library, 2000), 101–12.
—— and MILLER, J. I. 'Stow and Lydgate's "St Edmund"', *N&Q* 218 (1973), 365–9.
—— and PEARSALL, DEREK. 'The Manuscripts of the Major English Poetic Texts', in Griffiths and Pearsall (eds.), 257–78.
—— and MEALE, CAROL M. 'The Marketing of Printed Books in Late Medieval England', *Library*, 6th ser. (1993), 95–124.
EISENSTEIN, ELIZABETH L. *The Printing Press as an Agent of Change: Communications and Cultural Transformation in Early-Modern Europe*, 2 vols. (Cambridge University Press, 1979).
ELIZABETH OF HUNGARY. *The Two Middle English Translations of the Revelations of St Elizabeth of Hungary*, ed. Sarah McNamer, Middle English Texts, 28 (C. Winter, 1996).
ELTON, G. R. (ed.). *The New Cambridge Modern History*, 2. *The Reformation, 1520–1559* (Cambridge University Press, 1958).
—— *The Tudor Revolution in Government: Administrative Changes in the Reign of Henry VIII* (Cambridge University Press, 1959).
—— *Policy and the Police: The Enforcement of the Reformation in the Age of Thomas Cromwell* (Cambridge University Press, 1972).

—— *England under the Tudors*, 2nd edn. (Methuen, 1974).

ELYOT, THOMAS. *Pasquil the Playne*, in *Four Political Treatises by Sir Thomas Elyot*, ed. Lillian Gottesman (facs. edn. Scholars' Facsimiles and Reprints, 1967).

—— **Sir Thomas Elyot: A Critical Edition of 'The Boke Named the Governour'*, ed. Donald W. Rude (Garland, 1992).

EMMERSON, RICHARD K. 'Contextualizing Performance: The Reception of the Chester *Antichrist*', *JMEMS* 29 (1999), 89–119.

The English Gilds: The Original Ordinances of more than 100 Early English Gilds, ed. Toulmin Smith, EETS 40 (Trübner, 1870, repr. 1963).

English Historical Documents 1485–1558, ed. C. H. Williams, 12 vols. (Eyre and Spottiswoode, 1955–75).

English Wycliffite Sermons, vol. 1, ed. Anne Hudson (Clarendon Press, 1983); vol. 2, ed. Pamela Gradon (Clarendon Press, 1988).

ERASMUS, DESIDERIUS. *A dialogue . . . of two persones . . . intituled the pilgremage of pure devotyon* (London, 1540).

—— *The Praise of Folie, by Sir Thomas Chaloner*, ed. Clarence H. Miller, EETS 257 (Oxford University Press, 1965).

—— **Enchiridion Militis Christiani: An English Version*, ed. Anne M. O'Donnell, EETS 282 (Oxford University Press, 1981).

ERLER, MARY C. 'Devotional Literature', in Lotte Hellinga and J. B. Trapp (eds.), *The Cambridge History of the Book*, 3. *1400–1557* (Cambridge University Press, 1999), 495–525.

Everyman, ed. A. C. Cawley (Manchester University Press, 1961).

FAIRFIELD, LESLIE P. *John Bale: Mythmaker for the English Reformation* (Purdue University Press, 1976).

FERGUSON, ARTHUR B. *The Indian Summer of English Chivalry: Studies in the Decline and Transformation of Chivalric Idealism* (Duke University Press, 1960).

—— *The Articulate Citizen and the English Renaissance* (Duke University Press, 1965).

—— *The Chivalric Tradition in Renaissance England* (Folger Books, 1986).

FERGUSON, WALLACE K. *The Renaissance in Historical Thought* (Houghton Mifflin, 1948).

FERSTER, JUDITH. *Chaucer on Interpretation* (Cambridge University Press, 1985).

—— *Fictions of Advice: The Literature and Politics of Counsel in Late Medieval England* (University of Pennsylvania Press, 1996).

FIELD, P. J. C. *The Life and Times of Sir Thomas Malory*, Arthurian Studies, 29 (Brewer, 1993).

FIELD, ROSALIND. 'Romance in England, 1066–1400', in Wallace (ed.), *Medieval English Literature*, 152–76.

FISH, SIMON. **A Supplicacyon for the Beggars*, ed. Frederick J. Furnivall, EETS, ES 13 (Trübner, 1871).

FISHER, JOHN H. *John Gower: Moral Philosopher and Friend of Chaucer* (New York University Press, 1965).

—— 'A Language Policy for Lancastrian England', *PMLA* 107 (1992), 1168–80.

FLEMMING, J. V. 'Hoccleve's "Letter of Cupid" and the "Quarrel" over the *Roman de la Rose*', *Medium Aevum*, 40 (1971), 21–40.

FLETCHER, ALAN J. 'The N-Town Plays', in Beadle (ed.), *Medieval English Theatre*, 163–88.

**The Floure and the Leafe and the Assembly of Ladies*, ed. D. A. Pearsall, Nelson's Medieval and Renaissance Library (1962; repr. Manchester University Press, 1980).

FORTESCUE, JOHN. **The Governance of England*, ed. Charles Plummer (Clarendon Press, 1885).

—— **On the Laws and Governance of England*, ed. Shelley Lockwood (Cambridge University Press, 1997).

FOWLER, ALASTAIR. *Kinds of Literature: An Introduction to the Theory of Genres and Modes* (Clarendon Press, 1982).

FOWLER, DAVID C. *John Trevisa*, English Writers of the Middle Ages, 2 (Variorum, 1993).

FOX, ALISTAIR. *Politics and Literature in the Reigns of Henry VII and Henry VIII* (Blackwell, 1989).

FOXE, JOHN. **The Acts and Monuments of the Christian Martyrs*, 4th edn., ed. Josiah Pratt, 8 vols. (The Religious Tract Society, 1877).

FRADENBURG, LOUISE O. '"Voice memorial": Loss and Reparation in Chaucer's Poetry', *Exemplaria*, 2 (1990), 169–202.

FRITH, JOHN. **A Mirour to Know Thyself*, in Tyndale and Frith, *The Works of the English Reformers*, ed. T. Russell, 4. 266–77.

FRITZE, R. H. '"Truth hath lacked witnesse, tyme wanted light": The Dispersal of the English Monastic Libraries and Protestant Efforts at Preservation, ca. 1535–1625', *Journal of Library History*, 18 (1983), 274–91.

FRULOVISI, TITUS LIVIUS. *Vita Henrici Quinti*, ed. Thomas Hearne (Oxford, 1716).

FYLER, JOHN. '*Auctoritee* and Allusion in *Troilus and Criseyde*', *Res Publica Litterarum*, 7 (1984), 73–92.

GALLOWAY, ANDREW. 'Writing History in England', in Wallace (ed.), *Medieval English Literature*, 255–83.

Gamelyn, in *Middle English Romances*, ed. Donald B. Sands (Holt, Rinehart and Winston, 1966), 154–81.

GANIM, JOHN M. 'The Myth of Medieval Romance', in R. Howard Bloch and Stephen G. Nichols (eds.), *Medievalism and the Modernist Temper* (Johns Hopkins University Press, 1995), 148–68.

GARDINER, HAROLD C. *Mysteries' End* (New Haven, 1946).

GARDINER, STEPHEN. **The Oration of True Obedience*, in *Obedience in Church and State: Three Political Tracts by Stephen Gardiner*, ed. Pierre Janelle (Cambridge University Press, 1930), 67–171.

GEOFFREY OF VINSAUF. **Poetria Nova*, trans. Margaret F. Nims (Pontifical Institute of Medieval Studies, 1967).

GEORGIANNA, LINDA. 'The Protestant Chaucer', in Benson and Robertson (eds.), 55–69.

GHOSH, KANTIK. '"The fift Queill": Gavin Douglas's Maffeo Vegio', *Scottish Literary Journal*, 22 (1995), 5–21.

—— 'Contingency and the Christian Faith: William Woodford's Anti-Wycliffite Hermeneutics', *Poetica*, 49 (1998), 1–26.

—— 'Eliding the Interpreter: John Wyclif and Scriptural Truth', *New Medieval Literatures*, 2 (1999), 205–24.

GIBBON, EDWARD. *The Decline and Fall of the Roman Empire*, abridged edn., ed. David Womersley (1776–88; Penguin, 2000).

GIBSON, GAIL MCMURRAY. 'Bury St Edmunds, Lydgate, and the N-Town Cycle', *Speculum*, 56 (1981), 56–90.

—— *The Theatre of Devotion: East Anglian Drama and Society in the Late Middle Ages* (University of Chicago Press, 1989).

GILLESPIE, J. L. 'Sir John Fortescue's Concept of Royal Will', *Nottingham Medieval Studies*, 23 (1979), 47–65.

GILLINGHAM, JOHN. 'Crisis or Continuity? The Structure of Royal Authority in England 1369–1422', in Reinhard Schneider (ed.), *Das Spätmittelalterliche Königtum in europäischen Vergleich* (Thorbecke, 1987), 59–80.

GINSBURG, DAVID. 'Ploughboys versus Prelates: Tyndale and More and the Politics of Biblical Translation', *Sixteenth Century Journal*, 19 (1988), 45–61.

GIROUARD, MARK. *The Return to Camelot* (Yale University Press, 1981).

GIVEN-WILSON, CHRIS. *The Royal Household and the King's Affinity: Service, Politics and Finance in England 1360–1413* (Yale University Press, 1986).

—— *The English Nobility in the Late Middle Ages: The Fourteenth-Century Political Community* (Routledge and Kegan Paul, 1987).

Glasscoe, Marion. *English Medieval Mystics: Games of Faith* (Longman, 1993).

Goldstein, James R. 'Writing in Scotland', in Wallace (ed.), *Medieval English Literature*, 229–54.

Gombrich, E. H. 'In Search of Cultural History', in Gombrich, *Ideals and Idols: Essays on Values in History and in Art* (Phaidon, 1979), 24–59.

Gordon, Dillian. *Making and Meaning: The Wilton Diptych* (National Gallery, 1993).

Gower, John. **The English Works of John Gower*, ed. G. C. Macaulay, 2 vols., EETS, ES 81–2 (1900–1; repr. Oxford University Press, 1979).

—— *Confessio Amantis*, in Gower, *The English Works*, vols. 1–2.

Gradon, Pamela. 'Langland and the Ideology of Dissent', *PBA* 66 (1980), 179–205.

Grafton, Anthony and Jardine, Lisa. *From Humanism to the Humanities: Education and the Liberal Arts in Fifteenth and Sixteenth Century Europe* (Duckworth, 1986).

—— *Defenders of the Text: The Traditions of Scholarship in an Age of Science, 1450–1800* (Harvard University Press, 1991).

Gransden, Antonia. *Historical Writing in England*, 2 vols. (Routledge, 1974–82).

Gray, Douglas. *Themes and Images in the Medieval English Religious Lyric* (Routledge and Kegan Paul, 1972).

—— *Robert Henryson* (Brill, 1979).

Gray, Thomas. *Thomas Gray: Works*, ed. John Mitford, 5 vols. (William Pickering, 1843).

Green, Richard Firth. *Poets and Princepleasers: Literature and the English Court in the Late Middle Ages* (University of Toronto Press, 1980).

Greenblatt, Stephen. 'Invisible Bullets: Renaissance Authority and its Subversion, *Henry IV* and *Henry V*' (1985), repr. in Dollimore and Sinfield (eds.), 18–47.

—— *Renaissance Self-Fashioning from More to Shakespeare* (University of Chicago Press, 1980).

Greene, Thomas M. 'The Flexibility of the Self in Renaissance Literature', in Demetz et al. (eds.), 241–64.

—— *The Light in Troy: Imitation and Discovery in Renaissance Poetry* (Yale University Press, 1982).

Griffiths, Jeremy and Pearsall, Derek (eds.). *Book Production and Publishing in Britain 1375–1475* (Cambridge University Press, 1989).

GUDDAT-FIGGE, GISELA (ed.). *Catalogue of Manuscripts containing Middle English Romances* (Wilhelm Fink, 1976).

GUIDO DELLE COLONNE. **Guido delle Colonne: Historia destructionis troiae*, trans. Mary Elizabeth Meek (Indiana University Press, 1974).

GURR, ANDREW. *Playgoing in Shakespeare's London*, 2nd edn. (Cambridge University Press, 1996).

GUY, JOHN A. 'Scripture as Authority: Problems of Interpretation in the 1530s', in Alistair Fox and John Guy (eds.), *Reassessing the Henrician Era: Humanism, Politics and Reform 1500–1550* (Blackwell, 1986), 199–220.

—— *Thomas More* (Arnold, 2000).

HAIGH, CHRISTOPHER (ed.). *The English Reformation Revised* (Cambridge, 1987).

—— 'The Recent Historiography of the English Reformation', in Haigh (ed.), *English Reformation Revised*, 19–33.

HANKINS, JAMES. 'Humanism and the Origins of Modern Political Thought', in Jill Kraye (ed.), *The Cambridge Companion to Renaissance Humanism* (Cambridge University Press, 1996), 118–41.

HANNA, RALPH III. 'Sir Thomas Berkeley and his Patronage', *Speculum*, 64 (1989), 878–916.

—— *William Langland*, English Writers of the Middle Ages, 3 (Variorum, 1993).

HAPPÉ, PETER. *John Bale*, Twayne's English Authors Series, 520 (Twayne, 1996).

HARDER, HENRY L. 'Feasting in the *Alliterative Morte Arthure*', in Larry D. Benson and John Leyerle (eds.), *Chivalric Literature: Essays on the Relation between Literature and Life in the Later Middle Ages*, Studies in Medieval Culture, 14 (Medieval Institute Publications, 1980), 49–62.

HARDIE, PHILIP. 'Ovid into Laura: Absent Presences in the *Metamorphoses* and Petrarch's *Rime Sparse*', *Cambridge Philological Society*, suppl. vol. 23 (1999), 254–70.

HARDISON, O. B. Jr. *Christian Rite and Christian Drama in the Middle Ages: Essays in the Origin and Early History of Modern Drama* (Johns Hopkins University Press, 1965).

HARDMAN, PHILLIPA. 'The *Book of the Duchess* as a Memorial Monument', *Chaucer Review*, 28 (1994), 205–15.

—— 'Lydgate's *Lyfe of Our Lady*: A Text in Transition', *Medium Aevum*, 65 (1996), 248–68.

HASLER, ANTHONY J. 'Hoccleve's Unregimented Body', *Paragraph*, 13 (1990), 164–83.

Hawes, Stephen. **The Pastime of Pleasure*, ed. William Edward Mead, EETS, 173 (Oxford University Press, 1928).

—— **Comfort of Lovers*, in *Stephen Hawes: The Minor Poems*, ed. Florence W. Gluck and Alice B. Morgan, EETS, 217 (Oxford University Press, 1974).

Hay, Denys. *Polydore Vergil: Renaissance Historian and Man of Letters* (Clarendon Press, 1952).

—— 'England and the Humanities in the Fifteenth Century', in Heiko A. Oberman (ed.), *Itinerarium Italicum: The Profile of the Italian Renaissance in the Mirror of its European Transformations*, Studies in Medieval and Reformation Thought, 14 (Brill, 1975), 305–67.

Hecht, Jamey. 'Limitations of Textuality in Thomas More's *Confutation of Tyndale's Answer*', *Sixteenth-Century Journal*, 26 (1995), 823–8.

Heffernan, Thomas. *Sacred Biography: Saints and their Biographers in the Middle Ages* (Clarendon Press, 1988).

Hellinga, Lotte, 'Printing', in Hellinga and Trapp (eds.), 3. 65–108.

—— and Trapp, J. B. (eds.). *The Cambridge History of the Book in Britain*, 3. *1400–1557* (Cambridge University Press, 1999).

Henryson, Robert. *The Poems of Robert Henryson*, ed. Denton Fox (Clarendon Press, 1981).

Heresy Trials in the Diocese of Norwich, 1428–1431, ed. Norman P. Tanner, Camden Series, 4th ser. 20 (Royal Historical Society, 1977).

Hexter, J. H. *More's 'Utopia': The Biography of an Idea* (Princeton University Press, 1952).

Heylyn, Peter. *Ecclesia Restaurata: The History of the Reformation of the Church of England*, 3rd edn. (H. Twyford, T. Place and T. Basset, 1674).

Heywood, John. *The Plays of John Heywood*, ed. Richard Axton and Peter Happé (Brewer, 1991).

**Hick Scorner*. See *Two Tudor Interludes*, ed. Lancashire.

Hilton, Walter. *The Scale of Perfection*, trans. John P. H. Clark and Rosemary Dorward (Paulist Press, 1991).

—— **Epistle on the Mixed Life*, in *English Mystics of the Middle Ages*, ed. Barry Windeatt (Cambridge University Press, 1994), 110–36.

Hines, John. *The Fabliau in English* (Longman, 1993).

Hirsch, John C. 'Margery Kempe', in Edwards (ed.), *Middle English Prose: A Critical Guide to Major Authors and Genres*, 109–19.

Hoccleve, Thomas. **The Series*, in *Hoccleve's Works: The Minor Poems*, ed. Frederick J. Furnivall and I. Gollancz, rev. Jerome Mitchell and A. I. Doyle, EETS, ES 61 (1892; rev. edn. Oxford University Press, 1970).

—— **Remonstrance against Oldcastle*, in *Selections from Hoccleve*, ed. M. C. Seymour (Clarendon Press, 1981).

—— **Male Regle*, in *Selections from Hoccleve*, ed. M. C. Seymour (Clarendon Press, 1981).

—— **Thomas Hoccleve: The Regiment of Princes*, ed. Charles R. Blyth (TEAMS, 1999).

—— **Thomas Hoccleve's 'Complaint' and 'Dialogue'*, ed. J. A. Burrow, EETS 313 (Oxford University Press, 1999).

HOGG, JAMES. 'The Brigettine Contribution to Late Medieval English Spirituality', in Hogg (ed.), *Spiritualität Heute und Gestern* (Analecta Cartusiana, 35/3; Institut für Anglistik and Amerikanistik, 1982), 153–74.

The Holy Bible . . . made from the Vulgate by John Wycliffe and his Followers, ed. Josiah Forshall and Frederic Madden, 4 vols. (Oxford University Press, 1850).

HOPKINS, ANDREA. *The Sinful Knights: A Study of Middle English Penitential Romance* (Clarendon Press, 1990).

HOWARD, DONALD R. 'Experience, Language, and Consciousness: *Troilus and Criseyde* 2. 596–931', in Jerome Mandel and Bruce A. Rosenberg, *Medieval Literature and Folklore Studies: Essays in Honour of Francis Lee Utley* (Rutgers University Press, 1970), 173–92.

HOWARD, HENRY. **The Poems of Henry Howard Earl of Surrey*, ed. Frederick Morgan Padelford, rev. edn., University of Washington Publications, Language and Literature, 5 (University of Washington Press, 1928).

—— *The 'Aeneid' of Henry Howard Earl of Surrey*, ed. Florence H. Ridley (University of California Press, 1963).

—— **Henry Howard, Earl of Surrey: Poems*, ed. Emrys Jones (Clarendon Press, 1964).

HUDSON, ANNE. '"No Newe Thyng": The Printing of Medieval Texts in the Early Reformation Period', in Douglas Gray and E. G. Stanley (eds.), *Middle English Studies Presented to Norman Davis* (Clarendon Press, 1983), 157–74.

—— 'John Stow (1525?–1605)', in Ruggiers (ed.), 53–70.

—— *Lollards and their Books* (Hambledon Press, 1985).

—— 'Lollardy: The English Heresy?', in Hudson, *Lollards and their Books*, 141–63.

—— 'The Legacy of *Piers Plowman*', in Alford (ed.), *A Companion to 'Piers Plowman'*, 251–66.

—— *The Premature Reformation: Wycliffite Texts and Lollard History* (Clarendon Press, 1988).

HUIZINGA, JOHAN. 'The Problem of the Renaissance', in Huizinga, *Men and Ideas*, trans. J. S. Holmes and H. van Marle (Eyre and Spottiswoode, 1960), 243–87 (1st pub. in Dutch, 1920).

—— *The Waning of the Middle Ages*, trans. F. Hopman (Penguin, 1972) (1st pub. in Dutch, 1919).

—— *The Autumn of the Middle Ages*, trans. Rodney J. Payton and Ulrich Mammitzsch (University of Chicago Press, 1996) (1st pub. in Dutch, 1919).

HULL, ELEANOR. **The Seven Psalms: A Commentary on the Penitential Psalms . . . by Dame Eleanor Hull*, ed. Alexandra Barratt, EETS 307 (Oxford University Press, 1995).

HUME, ANTHEA. 'English Protestant Books Printed Abroad, 1525–1535: An Annotated Bibliography', in Thomas More, *Confutation of Tyndale's Answer*, 2. 1065–91.

HUME, KATHRYN. 'The Formal Nature of Middle English Romance', *PQ* 53 (1974), 158–80.

HURD, RICHARD. *Hurd's Letters on Chivalry and Romance, with the Third Elizabethan Dialogue*, ed. Edith J. Morley (Frowde, 1911).

HUTCHISON, ANN M. 'Devotional Reading in the Monastery and in the Late Medieval Household', in Michael G. Sargent (ed.), *De Cella in Seculum: Religious and Secular Life and Devotion in Late Medieval England* (Brewer, 1989), 215–27.

INGLEDEW, FRANCIS. 'The Book of Troy and the Genealogical Construction of History: The Case of Geoffrey of Monmouth's *Historia regum Britanniae*', *Speculum*, 69 (1994), 665–704.

The Interlude of Youth. See *Two Tudor Interludes*, ed. Lancashire.

**I playne Piers which cannot flatter* (London, ?1546) (*RSTC* 19903a).

Jack Upland, Friar Daw's Reply and Upland's Rejoinder, ed. P. L. Heyworth (Clarendon Press, 1968).

JACKSON, W. A. 'Wayland's Edition of *The Mirror of Magistrates*,' *Library*, 4th ser. 13 (1932–3), 155–7.

JACKSON, W. J. H. (ed.). *The Interpretation of Medieval Lyric* (Macmillan, 1980).

JACOBUS DE VORAGINE. *The Golden Legend: Readings on the Saints*, trans. William Granger Ryan (Princeton University Press, 1993).

JAEGER, STEPHEN C. *The Origins of Courtliness: Civilizing Trends and the Formation of Courtly Ideals 939–1210* (Pennsylvania University Press, 1985).

JAMES I OF SCOTLAND. **James I of Scotland: The Kingis Quair*, ed. John Norton-Smith (Clarendon Press, 1971).

JAMES, MERVYN. 'Ritual, Drama and the Social Body in the late Medieval English Town', *Past and Present*, 98 (1983), 3–29.

—— 'English Politics and the Concept of Honour 1485–1642', in Mervyn James, *Society, Politics and Culture: Studies in Early Modern England* (Cambridge University Press, 1986), 308–415.

JOHNSTON, ALEXANDRA. 'The Procession and Play of Corpus Christi in York after 1426', *LSE* 7 (1973–4), 55–62.

—— and ROGERSON, MARGARET (eds.). *York*, 2 vols., REED (Manchester University Press, 1979).

JOHNSTON, ARTHUR. *Enchanted Ground, The Study of Medieval Romance in the Eighteenth Century* (Athlone Press, 1964).

JOLLIFFE, P. S. *A Check-List of Middle English Prose Writings of Spiritual Guidance*, Subsidia Mediaevalia, 2 (Pontifical Institute of Medieval Studies, 1974).

JONES, MICHAEL (ed.). *The New Cambridge Medieval History*, 6. *c.1300–c.1415* (Cambridge University Press, 2000).

JORDAN, ROBERT M. *Chaucer and the Shape of Creation: The Aesthetic Possibilities of Inorganic Form* (Harvard University Press, 1967).

JULIAN OF NORWICH. **A Book of Showings to the Anchoress Julian of Norwich*, ed. Edmund Colledge and James Walsh, 2 pts., Studies and Texts, 35 (Pontifical Institute of Medieval Studies, 1978).

JUSTICE, STEVEN. *Writing and Rebellion: England in 1381* (University of California Press, 1994).

KAEUPER, RICHARD W. *War, Justice and Public Order: England and France in the Later Middle Ages* (Clarendon Press, 1988).

**Kalendre of the Newe Legende of Englande*, ed. Manfred Görlach, Middle English Texts, 27 (C. Winter, 1994).

KANE, GEORGE. '*Piers Plowman*': *The Evidence for Authorship* (Athlone Press, 1965).

KEEN, M. H. *England in the Later Middle Ages: A Political History* (Methuen, 1973).

KEISER, GEORGE R. 'The Romances', in Edwards (ed.), *Middle English Prose*, 271–89.

—— 'The Mystics and Early English Printers: The Economics of Devotionalism', in Marion Glasscoe (ed.), *The Medieval Mystical Tradition in England* (Brewer, 1987), 9–26.

KEKEWICH, M. 'Edward IV, William Caxton, and Literary Patronage in Yorkist England', *MLR* 66 (1971), 481–7.

KELLY, HENRY ANSGAR. *Ideas and Forms of Tragedy from Aristotle to the Middle Ages*, Cambridge Studies in Medieval Literature, 18 (Cambridge University Press, 1993).

KEMPE, DOROTHY. 'A Middle English Tale of Troy', *Englische Studien*, 29 (1901), 1–26.

KEMPE, MARGERY. **The Book of Margery Kempe*, ed. Barry Windeatt (Longman, 2000).

KEMPIS, THOMAS À. *The Imitation of Christ*, ed. B. J. H. Biggs, EETS 309 (Oxford University Press, 1997).

KENDALL, RITCHIE D. *The Drama of Dissent: The Radical Poetics of Nonconformity, 1380–1590* (University of North Carolina Press, 1986).

KERBY-FULTON, KATHRYN, and JUSTICE, STEVEN. 'Langlandian Reading Circles and Civil Service in London and Dublin, 1380–1427', *New Medieval Literatures*, 1 (1997), 59–83.

KERRIGAN, WILLIAM, and BRADEN, GORDON. *The Idea of the Renaissance* (Johns Hopkins University Press, 1989).

KING, JOHN N. *English Reformation Literature: The Tudor Origins of the Protestant Tradition* (Princeton University Press, 1982).

KING, PAMELA M. 'Contemporary Cultural Models for the Trial Plays in the York Cycle', in Alan Hindley (ed.), *Drama and Community: People and Plays in Northern Europe* (Brepols, 1999), 200–16.

—— 'Morality Plays', in Beadle (ed.), *Medieval English Theatre*, 240–64.

KIPLING, GORDON. *The Triumph of Honour: The Burgundian Origins of the Elizabethan Renaissance* (Brill, 1977).

—— *Enter the King: Theatre, Liturgy, and Ritual in the Medieval Civic Triumph* (Clarendon Press, 1998).

KLAUSNER, DAVID N. (ed.). *Hereford and Worcestershire*, REED (University of Toronto Press, 1990).

KNIGHTON, HENRY. *Knighton's Chronicle, 1337–1396*, ed. and trans. G. H. Martin (Clarendon Press, 1995).

KNOWLES, DAVID. *The Religious Orders in England*, 3 vols. (Cambridge University Press, 1948–59).

KOLVE, V. A. *The Play called Corpus Christi* (Stanford University Press, 1966).

KRATZMANN, GREGORY. *Anglo-Scottish Literary Relations 1430–1550* (Cambridge University Press, 1980).

KRAY, JILL (ed.). *The Cambridge Companion to Renaissance Humanism* (Cambridge University Press, 1996).

KUCZYNSKI, MICHAEL P. *Prophetic Song: The Psalms as Moral Discourse in Late Medieval England* (University of Pennsylvania Press, 1995).

LANCASHIRE, IAN (ed.). *Dramatic Texts and Records of Britain: A Chronological Topography to 1558* (Cambridge University Press, 1984).

LANDER, J. R. *Government and Community: England 1450–1509* (Edward Arnold, 1980).

LANGLAND, WILLIAM. *The Vision of Pierce Plowman, nowe the seconde time imprinted by Roberte Crowley* (London, 1550).

—— *Piers Plowman: The A-Version*, ed. George Kane (Athlone, 1960).

—— **Piers Plowman by William Langland: An Edition of the C-Text*, ed. Derek Pearsall (Edward Arnold, 1978).

—— *William Langland, Piers Plowman: The Z Version*, ed. A. G. Rigg and Charlotte Brewer (Pontifical Institute of Medieval Studies, 1983).

—— **William Langland, The Vision of Piers Plowman: A Critical Edition of the B-Text*, ed. A. V. C. Schmidt, 2nd edn. (Dent, 1995).

**The Lanterne of Light*, ed. Lilian M. Swinburn, EETS 151 (Kegan Paul, Trench and Trübner, 1917).

LASS, ROGER, (ed.). *The Cambridge History of the English Language*, 3. *1476–1776* (Cambridge University Press, 1999).

The Late Medieval Religious Plays of Bodleian MSS Digby 133 and E Museo 160, ed. Donald C. Baker, John L. Murphy, and Louis B. Hall, EETS 283 (Oxford University Press, 1982).

LATIMER, HUGH. 'Sermon on the Plowers', in *Selected Sermons of Hugh Latimer*, ed. Allan G. Chester (University Press of Virginia, 1968), 28–49.

LATINI, BRUNETTO. **Li Livres dou Tresor*, ed. F. J. Carmody (University of California Press, 1948).

The Laud Troy Book, ed. J. Ernst Wülfing, 2 parts, EETS 121–2 (Kegan Paul, Trench and Trübner, 1902–3).

LAWTON, DAVID. 'The *Destruction of Troy* as Translation from Latin Prose: Aspects of Form and Style', *SN* 52 (1980), 259–70.

—— 'Lollardy and the *Piers Plowman* Tradition', *MLR* 76 (1981), 780–93.

—— (ed.). *Middle English Alliterative Poetry and its Literary Background* (Brewer, 1982).

—— 'Middle English Alliterative Poetry: An Introduction', in Lawton (ed.), *Middle English Alliterative Poetry*, 1–19.

—— 'Dullness and the Fifteenth Century', *ELH* 54 (1987), 761–99.

—— 'Englishing the Bible, 1066–1549', in Wallace (ed.), *Medieval English Literature*, 454–82.

LAWTON, LESLEY. 'The Illustration of Late Medieval Secular Texts, with Special Reference to Lydgate's *Troy Book*', in Pearsall (ed.), *Manuscripts and Readers*, 41–69.

The Lay Folk's Catechism, ed. Thomas Frederick Simmons and Henry Edward Nolloth, EETS 118 (Kegan Paul, Trench and Trübner, 1901).

Leff, Gordon. *The Dissolution of the Medieval Outlook: An Essay in Intellectual and Spiritual Change in the Fourteenth Century* (New York University Press, 1976).

Leland, John. **Naeniae in mortem Thomae Viati equitis incomparabilis* (London, 1542).

—— *'New Year's Gift', printed as part of Bale, *Laboryouse journey*.

—— **Commentarii de scriptoribus britannicis*, 2 vols. (Anthony Hall, 1709).

—— **The Itinerary of John Leland*, ed. Lucy Toulmin Smith, 5 vols. (G. Bell, 1907–10).

—— **Assertio inclytissimi Arthuri*, in Christopher Middleton, *The Famous Historie of Chinon of England*, ed. William Edward Mead, EETS, 165 (Oxford University Press, 1925), 91–150.

Lerer, Seth. *Chaucer and his Readers: Imagining the Author in Late-Medieval England* (Princeton University Press, 1993).

—— '"Representyd now in yowr syght": The Culture of Spectatorship in Late Fifteenth-Century England', in Barbara A. Hannawalt and David Wallace (eds.), *Bodies and Disciplines: Intersections of Literature and History in Fifteenth-Century England*, Medieval Cultures 9 (University of Minnesota Press, 1996), 29–62.

—— *Courtly Letters in the Age of Henry VIII*, Cambridge Studies in Renaissance Literature and Culture, 18 (Cambridge University Press, 1997).

—— 'The Chaucerian Critique of Medieval Theatricality', in James J. Paxson, Lawrence M. Clopper, and Sylvia Tomasch (eds.), *The Peformance of Middle English Culture* (Brewer, 1998), 59–76.

The Letters of Alexander to Dindimus, King of the Brahmins, ed. W. W. Skeat, EETS, ES 31 (Trübner, 1878).

Letters to Cromwell and Others on the Suppression of the Monasteries, ed. G. H. Cook (John Baker, 1965).

Levine, Joseph M. *Humanism and History: Origins of Modern English Historiography* (Cornell University Press, 1987).

Lewis, C. S. *The Allegory of Love* (Oxford University Press, 1936; repr. 1972).

The Libelle of Englyshe Polycye, ed. George Warner (Clarendon Press, 1926).

'The Life of Mary of Oignies', in Carl Horstmann (ed.), 'Prosalegenden: Die Legenden des ms Douce 114', *Anglia*, 8 (1885), 134–84.

The Life of St Anne, in *The Middle English Stanzaic Versions of the Life of St Anne*, ed. Roscoe E. Parker, EETS 174 (Oxford University Press, 1928).

Literae Cantuarienses, ed. J. Brigstocke Sheppard, Rolls Series, 3 vols. (HMSO, 1889), 3. 274–85.

LOADES, D. M. 'The Theory and Practice of Censorship in Sixteenth-Century England', in D. M. Loades, *Politics, Censorship, and the English Reformation* (Pinter, 1991), 96–108.

LOCHRIE, KARMA. *Margery Kempe and the Translations of the Flesh* (University of Pennsylvania Press, 1991).

LOOMIS, LAURA HIBBARD. 'Chaucer and the Breton Lays of the Auchinleck Manuscript', *SP* 38 (1941), 14–33.

LOOMIS, ROGER SHERMAN. 'Chivalric and Dramatic Imitations of Arthurian Romance', in W. R. W. Koehler (ed.), *Medieval Studies in Memory of A. Kingsley Porter*, 2 vols. (Harvard University Press, 1939), 1. 79–97.

—— 'Edward I: Arthurian Enthusiast', *Speculum*, 28 (1953), 114–27.

LOVATT, ROGER. 'The *Imitation of Christ* in Late Medieval England', *Transactions of the Royal Historical Society*, 5th ser. 18 (1958), 97–121.

—— 'Henry Suso and the Medieval Mystical Tradition in England', in Marion Glasscoe (ed.), *The Medieval Mystical Tradition in England* (University of Exeter, 1982), 47–62.

LOVE, NICHOLAS. **Nicholas Love's Mirror of the Blessed Life of Jesus Christ*, ed. Michael G. Sargent, Garland Medieval Texts, 18 (Garland, 1992).

LOVELICH, HENRY. *Merlin*, 3 vols., EETS ES 93, 112; OS 185 (Kegan Paul, Trench and Trübner, 1904, 1913, and 1932).

LUMIANSKY, R. M. and MILLS, DAVID (eds.). *The Chester Mystery Cycle: Essays and Documents* (University of North Carolina Press, 1983).

LUTTRELL, C. A. 'Three North-West Midland Manuscripts', *Neophilologus*, 42 (1958), 38–50.

LYDGATE, JOHN. *Saint Edmund and Saint Fremund*, ed. C. Horstmann, in *Altenglischen Legenden: Neue Folge*, 2 vols. (Heilbron, Leipzig, 1878–81), 2. 376–440.

—— *SS. Albon and Amphabal*, ed. C. Horstmann (Berlin, no publisher listed, 1882).

—— *Isopes Fabules*, ed. P. Sauerstein, 'Lydgate's Aesopübersetzung', *Anglia*, 9 (1886), 1–24.

—— **Lydgate and Burgh's Secrees of Old Philosoffres*, ed. Robert Steele, EETS, ES 66 (Kegan Paul, Trench and Trübner, 1894).

—— *Fabula Duorum Mercatorum*, ed. J. Zupitza (Trübner, 1897).

—— *The Complaint of the Black Knight*, ed. E. Krausser, *Anglia*, 19 (1897), 211–90.

—— *Lydgate's Horse, Goose and Sheep*, ed. M. Degenhart, Münchener Beiträge, 19 (Deichert, 1900).

—— **Lydgate's Troy Book*, ed. Henry Bergen, 4 parts, EETS, ES 97, 103, 106, and 126 (Kegan Paul, Trench and Trübner, 1906, 1908, 1910, and 1935).

—— *Destruction of Thebes*. See Lydgate, *Lydgate's 'Siege of Thebes'*.

—— **Lydgate's 'Siege of Thebes'*, ed. Axel Erdmann and Eilert Ekwall, 2 vols., EETS, ES 108, 125 (Kegan Paul, Trench and Trübner, 1911 and 1930; repr. 1960).

—— **The Minor Poems*, 2 parts, ed. Henry Noble MacCracken, EETS, ES 107, 192 (Oxford University Press, 1911, 1934; repr. 1961).

—— *Dietary*, ed. Max Förster, in 'Kleinere Mittelenglische Texte', *Anglia* 42 (1918), (176–92).

—— **Lydgate's Fall of Princes*, ed. Henry Bergen, 4 vols., EETS, ES 121–4 (Oxford University Press, 1924; repr. 1967).

—— **The Dance of Death*, ed. Florence Warren, EETS, 181 (Oxford University Press, 1931).

—— *Dance Machabré*. See Lydgate, *Dance of Death*.

—— **A Critical Edition of John Lydgate's 'Life of Our Lady'*, ed. Joseph A. Lauritis, Ralph A. Klinefelter, and Vernon F. Gallagher (Duquesne University Press, 1961).

—— **Saint Albon and Saint Amphibalus*, ed. George F. Reinecke, Garland Medieval Texts, 11 (Garland, 1985).

McConica, James Kelsey. *English Humanists and Reformation Politics under Henry VIII and Edward VI* (Clarendon Press, 1965).

MacCulloch, Diarmaid, *Thomas Cranmer: A Life* (New Haven, 1996).

McCusker, Honor. *John Bale, Dramatist and Antiquary* (Bryn Mawr University Press, 1942).

McGovern, John F. 'The Rise of New Economic Attitudes: Economic Humanism, Economic Nationalism, during the Later Middle Ages and the Renaissance 1200–1500', *Traditio*, 26 (1970), 217–54.

McGrath, A. E. *Iustitia Dei: A History of the Christian Doctrine of Justification*, 2 vols. (Cambridge University Press, 1986).

Machan, Tim William. *Textual Criticism and Middle English Texts* (University Press of Virginia, 1994).

—— 'Thomas Berthelette and Gower's *Confessio Amantis*', *SAC* 18 (1996), 143–66.

McHardy, A. K. '*De haeretico comburendo, 1401*', in Margaret Aston and Colin Richmond (eds.), *Lollardy and the Gentry in the Later Middle Ages* (Alan Sutton, 1997), 112–26.

The Macro Plays, ed. Mark Eccles, EETS 262 (Oxford University Press, 1969).

MAIDSTONE [Maydiston], RICHARD. *Concordia: Facta inter Regem Riccardum II et Civitatem Londonie*, ed. Charles Roger Smith, unpublished Ph.D. dissertation, Princeton University, University Microfilms, 1972.

—— **Richard Maidstone's Penitential Psalms*, ed. Valerie Edden, Middle English Texts, 22 (C. Winter, 1990).

MALORY, THOMAS. **Caxton's Malory*, ed. James W. Spisak, 2 vols. (University of California Press, 1983).

—— **The Works of Sir Thomas Malory*, ed. Eugène Vinaver, rev. P. J. C. Field, 3 vols. (Clarendon Press, 1990).

MANN, JILL. *Chaucer and Medieval Estates Satire: The Literature of Social Classes and the 'General Prologue' to the 'Canterbury Tales'* (Cambridge University Press, 1973).

—— '"Taking the Adventure": Malory and the *Suite du Merlin*', in Toshiyuki Takamiya and Derek Brewer (eds.), *Aspects of Malory*, Arthurian Studies, 1 (Brewer, 1981), 71–91.

—— 'Parents and Children in the *Canterbury Tales*', in Boitani and Torti (eds.), *Literature in Fourteenth-Century England*, 165–83.

—— 'Chance and Destiny in *Troilus and Criseyde* and the *Knight's Tale*', in Boitani and Mann (eds.), 75–92.

—— 'Price and Value in *Sir Gawain and the Green Knight*', *Essays in Criticism*, 36 (1986), 298–318.

—— 'The Planetary Gods in Chaucer and Henryson', in Morse and Windeatt (eds.), 91–106.

—— *Geoffrey Chaucer* (Harvester Wheatsheaf, 1991).

—— 'The Power of the Alphabet: A Reassessment of the Relation between the A and the B Versions of *Piers Plowman*', *YLS* 8 (1994), 21–50.

MAROTTI, ARTHUR F. *Manuscript, Print, and the English Renaissance Lyric* (Cornell University Press, 1995).

MATHESON, LISTER M. 'The Middle English *Brut*: A Location List of the Manuscripts and Early Printed Editions', *Analytical and Ennumerative Bibliography*, 3 (1979), 254–66.

MATTHEW OF VENDÔME. *Ars versificatoria*, in *Les Arts Poétiques du xii et du xiii Siècle*, ed. Edmond Faral, Bibliothèque de l'École des Hautes Études, 138 (Champion, 1924).

MATTHEWS, DAVID. *The Making of Middle English, 1765–1910* (University of Minnesota Press, 1999).

MATTHEWS, WILLIAM. *The Tragedy of Arthur: A Study of the Alliterative 'Morte Arthure'* (University of California Press, 1960).

MEALE, CAROL M. 'Caxton, de Worde and the Publication of Romance in Late Medieval England', *Library*, 6th ser. (1992), 283–98.

MEALE, CAROL M. (ed.). *Women and Literature in Britain, 1150–1500* (Cambridge University Press, 1993).

—— '" . . . Alle the bokes that I have of latyn, englisch, and frensch": Laywomen and Their Books in Late Medieval England', in Meale (ed.), *Women and Literature in Britain*, 128–58.

—— (ed.). *Readings in Medieval English Romance* (Brewer, 1994).

—— '"Gode men | Wiues maydenes and alle men": Romance and its Audiences', in Meale (ed.), *Readings in Medieval English Romance*, 209–25.

—— '"The Hoole Book": Editing and the Creation of Meaning in Malory's Text', in Archibald and Edwards (eds.), 3–17.

—— '"oft sithis with grete devotion I thought what I might do pleysyng to god": The Early Ownership and Readership of Love's *Mirror*, with Special Reference to its Female Audience', in Oguro et al. (eds.), 19–46.

MECHTHILD OF HACKEBORN. *The Booke of Ghostlye Grace*, ed. Theresa A. Halligan, Studies and Texts, 46 (Pontifical Institute of Medieval Studies, 1979).

MEDWALL, HENRY. **The Plays of Henry Medwall*, ed. Alan H. Nelson, Tudor Interludes 2 (Brewer, Rowman and Littlefield, 1980).

Melusine, ed. A. K. Donald, EETS, ES 68 (Kegan Paul, Trench and Trübner, 1895).

METHAM, JOHN. *Amoryus and Cleopes*, in *The Works of John Metham*, ed. Hardin Craig, EETS 132 (Kegan Paul, Trench and Trübner, 1916).

The Metrical Life of St Robert of Knaresborough, ed. Joyce Bazire, EETS 228 (Oxford University Press, 1953).

**The Middle English Translation of the 'Rosarium Theologie'*, ed. Christina von Nolcken, Middle English Texts, 10 (C. Winter, 1979).

**The Middle English Versions of Partonope of Blois*, ed. A. Trampe Bödtker, EETS, ES 109 (Kegan Paul, Trench and Trübner, 1912).

MIDDLETON, ANNE. 'The Idea of Public Poetry in the Reign of Richard II', *Speculum*, 53 (1978), 94–114.

—— 'Acts of Vagrancy: The C Version "Autobiography" and the Statute of 1388', in Steven Justice and Kathryn Kerby-Fulton (eds.), *Written Work: Langland, Labor, and Authorship* (University of Pennsylvania Press, 1997), 208–317.

MILLER, HELEN. *Henry VIII and the English Nobility* (Blackwell, 1986).

MILLS, M. 'The Composition and Style of the "Southern" *Octavian*, *Sir Launfal*, and *Libeaus Desconus*', *Medium Aevum*, 31 (1962), 88–109.

MINNIS, A. J. '"Authorial Intention" and the "Literal Sense" in the Exegetical Theories of Richard Fitzralph and John Wyclif', *Proceedings of the Royal Irish Academy*, 75 (1975), 1–31.

—— *Chaucer and Pagan Antiquity*, Chaucer Studies, 8 (Brewer, 1982).
—— (ed.). *Gower's 'Confessio Amantis': Responses and Reassessments* (Brewer, 1983).
—— 'The *Cloud of Unknowing* and Walter Hilton's *Scale of Perfection*', in Edwards (ed.), *Middle English Prose: A Critical Guide to Major Authors and Genres*, 61–81.
—— *Medieval Theory of Authorship: Scholastic Literary Attitudes in the Later Middle Ages* (Scolar Press, 1984).
—— 'From Medieval to Renaissance?: Chaucer's Position on Past Gentility', *Proceedings of the British Academy*, 72 (1986), 205–46.
—— 'Theorizing the Rose: Commentary Tradition in the *Querelle de la Rose*', in Piero Boitani and Anna Torti (eds.), *Poetics: Theory and Practice in Middle English Literature* (Brewer, 1991), 13–36.
—— 'Looking for a Sign: The Quest for Nominalism in Chaucer and Langland', in A. J. Minnis, Charlotte C. Morse, and Thorlac Turville-Petre (eds.), *Essays on Ricardian Literature in Honour of J. A. Burrow* (Oxford, 1997), 142–78.
—— and SCOTT, A. B. (eds.), (with the assistance of David Wallace). *Medieval Literary Theory and Criticism, c.1100–c.1375: The Commentary Tradition* (Clarendon Press, 1988).
—— (with V. J. Scattergood and J. J. Smith). *The Shorter Poems*, Oxford Guides to Chaucer (Oxford University Press, 1995).
**The Mirour of Oure Ladye*, ed. John Henry Blunt, EETS, ES 19 (Kegan Paul, Trench and Trübner, 1873).
MITCHELL. R. J. *John Tiptoft, 1427–1470* (Longman, Green and Co., 1938).
Die Mittelenglische Umdichtung von Boccaccio's 'De claris mulieribus', ed. Gustav Schleich (Mayer and Müller, 1924).
MORAN, JO ANN HOEPPNER. *The Growth of English Schooling, 1340–1548: Learning, Literacy, and Laicization in Pre-Reformation York Diocese* (Princeton University Press, 1985).
MORE, THOMAS. **The Utopia of Sir Thomas More*, ed. J. H. Lupton (Clarendon Press, 1895).
—— **St Thomas More: Selected Letters*, ed. Elizabeth Frances Rogers (Yale University Press, 1961).
—— **The History of King Richard III*, ed. Richard S. Sylvester, in *The Complete Works of St Thomas More*, 2 (Yale University Press, 1963).
—— **Utopia*, ed. Edward Surtz and J. H. Hexter, in *The Complete Works of St Thomas More*, 4 (Yale University Press, 1965).
—— **The Confutation of Tyndale's Answer*, ed. Louis A. Schuster et al., 2 pts., in *The Complete Works of St Thomas More*, 8 (Yale University Press, 1973).

MORE, THOMAS. **Translations of Lucian*, ed. Craig R. Thompson, in *The Complete Works of St Thomas More*, 3/1 (Yale University Press, 1974).

—— **A Dialogue of Comfort against Tribulation*, ed. L. L. Martz and F. Manley, in *The Complete Works of St Thomas More*, 12 (Yale University Press, 1976).

—— **A Dialogue Concerning Heresies*, ed. T. M. C. Lawler, Germain Marc'hadour, and Richard Marius, 2 parts, in *The Complete Works of St Thomas More*, 6 (Yale University Press, 1981).

—— **Latin Poems*, ed. Clarence H. Miller, Leicester Bradner, Charles A. Lynch, and Revilo P. Oliver, in *The Complete Works of St Thomas More*, 3/2 (Yale University Press, 1984).

—— **Life of Pico*, ed. A. S. G. Edwards, in *The Complete Works of St Thomas More*, 1 (Yale University Press, 1997).

MORISON, RICHARD. *A Remedy for Sedition* (London, 1536).

MORSE, RUTH and WINDEATT, BARRY (eds.). *Chaucer Traditions: Studies in Honour of Derek Brewer* (Cambridge University Press, 1990).

**Morte Arthure: A Critical Edition*, ed. Mary Hamel, Garland Medieval Texts, 9 (Garland, 1984).

MUIR, LAURENCE. 'Translations and Paraphrases of the Bible, and Commentaries', in Severs and Hartung (eds.), 2. 381–412 and 534–52.

MULLANEY, STEVEN. *The Place of the Stage: License, Play and Power in Renaissance England* (University of Chicago Press, 1988).

**Mum and the Sothsegger*, in *The Piers Plowman Tradition*, ed. Barr

MURDOCH, BRIAN O. 'The Cornish Medieval Drama', in Beadle (ed.), *Medieval English Theatre*, 211–39.

MUSCATINE, CHARLES. *Chaucer and the French Tradition: A Study in Style and Meaning* (University of California Press, 1957).

MYERS, A. R. 'Parliament, 1422–1509', in Davies and Denton (eds.), 141–84.

**The N-Town Play*, ed. Stephen Spector, 2 vols., EETS, SS 11–12 (Oxford University Press, 1991).

NELSON, ALAN H. *The Medieval English Stage: Corpus Christi Pageants and Plays* (University of Chicago Press, 1974).

NEVANLINNA, SAARA and TAAVITSAINEN, IRMA. *St Katherine of Alexandria: The Late Middle English Prose Legend in Southwell Minster MS 7* (Brewer and Finnish Academy of Science and Letters, 1993).

NICHOLLS, JONATHAN. *The Matter of Courtesy: Medieval Courtesy Books and the Gawain-Poet* (Brewer, 1992).

NICHOLSON, RANALD. *Scotland: The Later Middle Ages* (University of Edinburgh Press, 1974).

NISSÉ, RUTH. 'Reversing Discipline: The *Tretise of Miraclis Pleyinge*,

Lollard Exegesis, and the Failure of Representation', *YLS* 11 (1997), 163–94.

NITZSCHE, JANE CHANCE. *The Genius Figure in Antiquity and the Middle Ages* (Columbia University Press, 1975).

NOLAN, BARBARA. 'Nicholas Love', in Edwards (ed.), *Middle English Prose: A Critical Guide to Major Authors and Genres*, 83–95.

—— *Chaucer and the Tradition of the Roman Antique*, Cambridge Studies in Medieval Literature, 15 (Cambridge University Press, 1992).

—— 'The *Tale of Sir Gareth* and *The Tale of Sir Lancelot*', in Archibald and Edwards (eds.), 153–81.

Non-Cycle Plays and Fragments, ed. Norman Davis, EETS, SS 1 (Oxford University Press, 1970).

North English Legendary, ed. Carl Horstmann, in *Altenglische Legenden: Neue Folge* (Henniger, 1881).

O'DAY, ROSEMARY. *The Debate on the English Reformation* (Methuen, 1986).

OGURO, SHOICHI, BEADLE, RICHARD, and SARGENT, MICHAEL G.(eds.). *Nicholas Love at Waseda* (Brewer, 1997).

OLSON, GLENDING. 'Towards a Poetics of the Late Medieval Court Lyric', in Ebin (ed.), *Vernacular Poetics*, 227–48.

ORME, NICHOLAS. *English Schools in the Middle Ages* (Methuen, 1973).

—— *Education and Society in Medieval and Renaissance England* (Hambledon, 1989).

PACE, RICHARD. *De fructu qui ex doctrina percipitur*, ed. and trans. Frank Manley and Richard S. Sylvester (Renaissance Society of America, 1967).

PAGE, CHRISTOPHER. *Discarding Images: Reflections on Music and Culture in Medieval France* (Clarendon Press, 1993).

PANOFSKY, ERWIN. *Renaissance and Renaissances in Western Art* (1960; Icon, 1972).

PARINS, MARYLYN JACKSON (ed.). *Malory: The Critical Heritage* (Routledge, 1988).

PARKER, HENRY, Lord Morley. **Forty-Six Lives, translated from Boccaccio's 'De Claris Mulieribus' by Henry Parker, Lord Morley*, ed. Herbert G. Wright, EETS, 214 (Oxford University Press, 1943).

—— **Lord Morley's 'Tryumphes of Fraunces Petrarcke'*, ed. D. D. Carnicelli (Harvard University Press, 1971).

PARKES, M. B. 'The Literacy of the Laity', in David Daiches and A. K. Thorlby (eds.), *Literature and Western Civilization: The Mediaeval World* (Aldus Books, 1973), 557–78.

**Partonope of Blois*. See **The Middle English Versions of Partonope of Blois*.

PARTRIDGE, A. C. *English Biblical Translation* (Deutsch, 1973).
PARYS, WILLIAM. *'Life of Saint Cristina', in Carl Horstmann (ed.), *Sammlung Altenglischer Legenden* (Henniger, 1875), 183–90.
Patience, in *The Poems of the Pearl Manuscript*, ed. Andrew and Waldron.
PATTERSON, LEE. *Negotiating the Past: The Historical Understanding of Medieval Literature* (University of Wisconsin Press, 1987).
—— 'Historical Criticism and the Development of Chaucer Studies', in Patterson, *Negotiating the Past*, 3–39.
PATTERSON, LEE. 'Historical Criticism and the Claims of Humanism', in Patterson, *Negotiating the Past*, 41–74.
—— 'Virgil and the Historical Consciousness of the Twelfth Century: The *Roman d'Enéas* and *Erec et Enide*', in Patterson, *Negotiating the Past*, 157–95.
—— 'The Romance of History and the Alliterative *Morte Arthure*', in Patterson, *Negotiating the Past*, 197–230.
—— '"What Man Artow?": Authorial Self-Definition in *The Tale of Sir Thopas* and *The Tale of Melibee*', *SAC* 11 (1989), 117–75.
—— (ed.). *Literary Practice and Social Change in Britain, 1380–1530*, New Historicism, 8 (University of California Press, 1990).
—— 'On the Margin: Postmodernism, Ironic History, and Medieval Studies', *Speculum*, 65 (1990), 87–108.
—— *Chaucer and the Subject of History* (Routledge, 1991).
—— 'Court Politics and the Invention of Literature: The Case of Sir John Clanvowe', in Aers (ed.), *Culture and History 1350–1600*, 7–42.
—— 'Making Identities in Fifteenth Century England: Henry V and John Lydgate', in Cox and Reynolds (eds.), 69–107.
—— 'Perpetual Motion: Alchemy and the Technology of the Self', *SAC* 15 (1993), 25–57.
**Pearl*, in *The Poems of the Pearl Manuscript*, ed. Andrew and Waldron.
PEARSALL, DEREK. 'The Development of Middle English Romance', *MS* 27 (1965), 91–116.
—— *John Lydgate* (Routledge and Kegan Paul, 1970).
—— 'The English Romance in the Fifteenth Century', *Essays and Studies* (1976), 57–83.
—— *Old and Middle English Poetry*, Routledge History of English Poetry, 1 (Routledge and Kegan Paul, 1977).
—— 'The Alliterative Revival: Origins and Social Backgrounds', in Lawton (ed.), *Middle English Alliterative Poetry*, 34–53.
—— (ed.). *Manuscripts and Readers in Fifteenth-Century England: The Literary Implications of Manuscript Study* (Brewer, 1983).
—— *The Canterbury Tales* (Allen and Unwin, 1985).

——'Middle English Romance and its Audiences', in Mary-Jo Arn and Hanneke Wirtjes (eds.), *Historical and Editorial Studies* (Wolters-Noordhoff, 1985), 37–47.

——'Signs of Life in Lydgate's *Danse Macabre*', in James Hogg (ed.), *Zeit, Tod, und Ewigkeit in der Renaissance Literatur*, 3 vols. (Analecta Cartusiana, 117; Institut für Anglistik und Amerikanistik, 1987), 3. 58–71.

——'Chaucer and Lydgate', in Morse and Windeatt (eds.), 39–53.

——'Lydgate as Innovator', *MLQ* 53 (1992), 5–22.

——*The Life of Geoffrey Chaucer: A Critical Biography* (Blackwell, 1992).

——'Hoccleve's *Regement of Princes*: The Poetics of Royal Self-Representation', *Speculum*, 69 (1994), 386–410.

——*John Lydgate (1371–1449): A Bio-Bibliography*, English Literary Studies, 71 (University of Victoria, 1997).

PECOCK, REGINALD. **Repressor of Over Much Blaming of the Clergy*, ed. Churchill Babington, 2 vols., Rolls Series (HMSO, 1860; repr. Kraus, 1966).

PERKINS, NICHOLAS. *Hoccleve's 'Regiment of Princes': Counsel and Constraint* (D. S. Brewer, 2001).

PERSSON, E. P. *Sacra Doctrina: Reason and Revelation in Aquinas*, trans. R. MacKenzie (Blackwell, 1957).

PETRARCH, FRANCIS. *Petrarch's 'Africa'*, trans. Thomas G. Bergin and Alice S. Wilson (Yale University Press, 1977).

**Pierce Plowman's Crede*, in *The Piers Plowman Tradition*, ed. Barr, pp. 63–97.

The Piers Plowman Tradition, ed. Helen Barr (Dent, 1993).

A Pistel of Susan, in *Alliterative Poetry of the Later Middle Ages: An Anthology*, ed. Thorlac Turville-Petre, Routledge Medieval Texts (Routledge, 1989), 120–39.

PLATT, COLIN. *The English Medieval Town* (Granada, 1976).

**The Play of the Sacrament*, in *Non-Cycle Plays and Fragments*, ed. Davis.

The Poems of the Pearl Manuscript, ed. Malcolm Andrew and Ronald Waldron, Exeter Medieval English Texts and Studies, rev. edn. (University of Exeter, 1987).

POTTER, G. R. (ed.). *The New Cambridge Modern History*, 1. *The Renaissance, 1493–1520* (Cambridge University Press, 1957).

PRATT, KAREN (ed.). *Shifts and Transpositions in Medieval Narrative: A Festschrift for Dr Elspeth Kennedy* (Brewer, 1994).

The prayer and complaynte of the plowman (Antwerp, 1530; London, 1531).

The prayer and complaynte of the plowman, ed. Douglas H. Parker (Toronto University Press, 1997).

The Pre-Reformation Records of All Saints', Bristol, pt. I, ed. Clive Burgess, Bristol Record Society, 46 (Alan Sutton, 1995).

The Pricke of Conscience, ed. Richard Morris (A. Asher and the Philological Society, 1863).

The Prickynge of Love, ed. Harold Kane, 2 vols. (Institut für Anglistik und Amerikanistik, Universität Salzburg, 1983).

The Prose Life of Alexander, ed. J. S. Westlake, EETS 143 (Kegan Paul, Trench and Trübner, 1913).

PUTTENHAM, GEORGE. *The Arte of English Poesie*, ed. Gladys Doidge Willcock and Alice Walker (Cambridge University Press, 1936).

PUTTER, AD. *'Sir Gawain and the Green Knight' and French Arthurian Romance* (Clarendon Press, 1995).

—— *An Introduction to the 'Gawain'-Poet* (Longman, 1996).

—— 'Gifts and Commodities in *Sir Amadace*', *RES*, NS 51 (2000), 371–94.

**Pyers Plowman's Exhortation unto the Lordes of the Parlyamenthouse* (London, ?1550) (facs. in The English Experience, 821; Theatre Orbis, 1976) (*RSTC* 19905).

RASTELL, JOHN. *Three Rastell Plays*, ed. Richard Axton, Tudor Interludes 1 (Brewer, Rowman and Littlefield, 1979).

RAYMO, ROBERT R. 'Works of Religious and Philosophical Instruction', in Severs and Hartung (eds.), 7. 2255–2378, and 2467–2582.

RENOIR, ALAIN. 'The Immediate Source of Lydgate's *Siege of Thebes*', *SN* 33 (1961), 86–95.

—— *The Poetry of John Lydgate* (Routledge and Kegan Paul, 1967).

—— and BENSON, C. DAVID. 'John Lydgate', in Severs and Hartung (eds.), 6. 1809–1920, 2071–2175.

REX, RICHARD. *Henry VIII and the English Reformation* (Macmillan, 1993).

REYNOLDS, SUSAN. *Kingdoms and Communities in Western Europe, 900–1300* (Clarendon Press, 1984).

RICE, JOANNE A. (ed.). *Middle English Romance: An Annotated Bibliography 1955–1985*, Garland Reference Library of the Humanities, 545 (Garland, 1987).

**Richard the Redeless*, in *The Piers Plowman Tradition*, ed. Barr.

RIDDY, FELICITY. *Sir Thomas Malory* (Brill, 1987).

—— 'Reading for England: Arthurian Literature and National Consciousness', *Bibliographical Bulletin of the International Arthurian Society*, 43 (1991), 314–32.

——'"Women Talking about the Things of God": A Late Medieval Sub-Culture', in Meale (ed.), *Women and Literature in Britain*, 104–17.

RIGG, A. G. *A History of Anglo-Latin Literature, 1066–1422* (Cambridge University Press, 1992).

RINGLER, WILLIAM A. (ed.). *Bibliography and Index of English Verse: Printed 1476–1558* (Mansell, 1988).

——(ed.). *Bibliography and Index of English Verse in Manuscript, 1501–1558* (Mansell, 1992).

ROBBINS, ROSSELL HOPE. 'The Structure of Longer Middle English Court Poems', in Edward Vasta and Zacharias P. Thumby (eds.), *Chaucerian Problems and Perspectives: Essays Presented to Paul Beichner* (Indiana University Press, 1979), 244–64.

——'The Middle English Court Love Lyric', in W. J. H. Jackson (ed.), 205–30.

——and CUTLER, JOHN L. (eds.). *Supplement to the Index of Middle English Verse* (University of Kentucky Press, 1965).

ROBERTS, BRYNLEY F. 'Writing in Wales', in Wallace (ed.), 182–207.

ROOS, SIR ROBERT (trans.). *Chartier's La Belle Dame Sans Mercy*, in Chaucer, *Complete Works*, ed. Skeat, suppl. vol., pp. 299–326.

**Rosarium Theologie*. See *The Middle English Translation of the 'Rosarium Theologie'*.

ROSS, T. 'Dissolution and the Making of the English Literary Canon: The Catalogues of Leland and Bale', *Renaissance and Reformation*, NS 15 (1991), 57–80.

**Rotuli Parliamentorum*, ed. J. Strachey, 6 vols. (House of Lords, 1783).

ROUSE, R. H. '*Bostonus buriensis* and the Author of the *Catalogus scriptorum ecclesiae*', *Speculum*, 41 (1966), 471–99.

RUGGIERS, PAUL G. (ed.). *Editing Chaucer: The Great Tradition* (Pilgrim Books, 1984).

**St Erkenwald*, in *Alliterative Poetry of the later Middle Ages*, ed. Thorlac Turville-Petre, Routledge Medieval Texts (Routledge, 1989), 105–19.

SALTER, ELIZABETH. *Nicholas Love's 'Mirrour of the Blessed Lyf of Jesu Christ'* Analecta Cartusiana, 10 (Institut für Englische Sprache und Literatur, 1974).

SARGENT, MICHAEL G. 'Minor Devotional Writings', in Edwards (ed.), *Middle English Prose: A Critical Guide to Major Authors and Genres*, 147–63.

——'Contemplative Literature and Bourgeois Piety in Late Medieval England', in Love, *Mirror*, ed. Sargent, pp. lviii-lxxii.

——'Hilton, Walter', in Szarmach, Tavormina and Rosenthal (eds.), 358–9

SAUL, NIGEL. 'Richard II and the Vocabulary of Kingship', *EHR* 110 (1995), 854–77.

SCAGLIONE, ALDO. *Knights at Court: Courtliness, Chivalry and Courtesy from Ottonian Germany to the Italian Renaissance* (University of California Press, 1991).

SCANLON, LARRY. *Narrative, Authority and Power: The Medieval Exemplum and the Chaucerian Tradition*, Cambridge Studies in Medieval Literature, 20 (Cambridge University Press, 1994).

SCANLON, PAUL A. 'A Checklist of Prose Romances in English, 1474–1603', *Library*, 5th ser., 33 (1978), 143–52.

SCARISBRICK, J. J. *Henry VIII* (Eyre and Spottiswoode, 1968).

—— *The Reformation and the English People* (Blackwell, 1984).

SCASE, WENDY. '"Strange and Wonderful Bills": Bill-Casting and Political Discourse in Late Medieval England', *New Medieval Literatures*, 2 (1998), 225–47.

—— *Reginald Pecock*, Authors of the Middle Ages, 8 (Variorum, 1996).

SCATTERGOOD, JOHN. '*The Tale of Gamelyn*: The Noble Robber as Provincial Hero', in Meale (ed.), *Readings in Medieval English Romance*, 159–94.

—— *Reading the Past: Essays on Medieval and Renaissance Literature* (Four Courts, 1996).

—— 'George Ashby's *Prisoner's Reflections* and the Virtue of Patience' in Scattergood, *Reading the Past*, 266–74.

—— 'The Date and Composition of George Ashby's Poems' in Scattergood, *Reading the Past*, 258–65.

SCHIRMER, WALTER F. *Der englische Frühhumanismus* (1931; 2nd edn., Niemeyer, 1963).

—— *John Lydgate: A Study in the Culture of the Fifteenth Century*, trans. Ann E. Keep (Methuen, 1961) (1st pub. in German, 1952).

SCHOECK, R. J. *Erasmus of Europe: The Prince of Humanists, 1501–1536* (Edinburgh University Press, 1993).

SEATON, E. '"The Devonshire Manuscript" and its Medieval Fragments', *RES*, NS 7 (1956), 55–6.

**Secretum Secretorum: Nine English Versions*, ed. M. A. Manzalaoui, EETS 267 (Oxford University Press, 1977).

Secular Lyrics of the XIVth and XVth Centuries, ed. Rossell Hope Robbins, 2nd edn. (Clarendon Press, 1955).

SEEBOHM, FREDERIC. *The Oxford Reformers: John Colet, Erasmus, and Thomas More*, 3rd edn. (Longmans, Green, 1896).

Selections from English Wycliffite Writings, ed. Anne Hudson (Cambridge University Press, 1978).

SELWYN, D. G., 'Thomas Cranmer's Writings: A Bibliographical Survey', in Paul Ayris and David Selwyn (eds.), *Thomas Cranmer: Churchman and Scholar* (Boydell, 1993), 281–302.

SESSIONS, WILLIAM A. *Henry Howard, the Poet Earl of Surrey: A Life* (Oxford University Press, 1999).

SEVERS, J. BURKE. '*The Clerk's Tale*', in *Sources and Analogues*, ed. Bryan and Dempster, 288–331.

—— and HARTUNG, A. E. (gen. eds.), *A Manual of the Writings in Middle English, 1050–1500*, 9 vols., in progress (Connecticut Academy of Arts and Sciences, 1967–).

SEYMOUR, M. C. 'Some Lydgate Manuscripts: *Lives of SS Edmund and Fremund* and *Danse Macabre*', *Edinburgh Bibliographical Society Transactions*, 5/4 (1983–5), 10–24.

—— *John Capgrave*, Authors of the Middle Ages, 11 (Variorum, 1996).

SEZNEC, JEAN. *The Survival of the Pagan Gods*, trans. Barbara F. Sessions (1940; Harper, 1953).

SHEPHERD, GEOFFREY. 'English Versions of the Scriptures before Wyclif', in T. A. Shippey and John Pickles (eds.), *Poets and Prophets: Essays in Medieval Studies by G. T. Shepherd* (Brewer, 1990), 59–83.

The Siege of Jerusalem, ed. E. Kölbing and Mabel Day, EETS 188 (Oxford University Press, 1932).

SIMPSON, JAMES. 'Dante's "Astripetam Aquilam" and the Theme of Poetic Discretion in the *House of Fame*', *Essays and Studies*, NS 39 (1986), 1–18.

—— *Piers Plowman: An Introduction to the B-Text* (Longman, 1990).

—— 'The Constraints of Satire in *Piers Plowman* and *Mum and the Sothsegger*' in Helen Phillips (ed.), *Langland, the Mystics and the Medieval English Religious Tradition: Essays in Honour of S. S. Hussey* (Brewer, 1990), 11–30.

—— 'Madness and Texts: Hoccleve's *Series*', in Julia Boffey and Janet Cowen (eds.), *Chaucer and Fifteenth-Century Poetry*, King's College London Medieval Studies, 5 (King's College London, 1991), 15–29.

—— '"After Craftes Conseil clotheth yow and fede": Langland and London City Politics', in Nicholas Rogers (ed.), *England in the Fourteenth Century* (Paul Watkins, 1993), 109–27.

—— '*Ut Pictura Poesis*: A Critique of Robert Jordan's *Chaucer and the Shape of Creation*', in Boitani and Torti (eds.), *Interpretation*, 167–87.

—— *Sciences and the Self in Medieval Poetry: Alan of Lille's 'Anticlaudianus' and John Gower's 'Confessio Amantis'*, Cambridge Studies in Medieval Literature, 25 (Cambridge University Press, 1995).

—— 'Nobody's Man: Thomas Hoccleve's *Regement of Princes*', in Julia

Boffey and Pamela King (eds.), *London and Europe in the Later Middle Ages* (Queen Mary and Westfield College, 1995), 149–80.

—— 'Desire and the Scriptural Text: Will as Reader in *Piers Plowman*', in Rita Copeland (ed.), *Criticism and Dissent in the Middle Ages* (Cambridge University Press, 1996), 215–43.

—— ' "Dysemol daies and fatal houres": Lydgate's *Destruction of Thebes* and Chaucer's *Knight's Tale*', in Cooper and Mapstone, 15–33.

—— 'Ethics and Interpretation: Reading Wills in Chaucer's *Legend of Good Women*', *SAC* 20 (1998), 73–100.

SIMPSON, JAMES. 'Beast Epic and Fable', in Szarmach, et al. (eds.), 111–12.

—— 'Violence, Narrative and Proper Name: *Sir Degaré*, "The Tale of Sir Gareth of Orkney", and the Anglo-Norman *Folie Tristan d'Oxford*', in Jane Gilbert and Ad Putter (eds.), *The Spirit of Medieval English Popular Romance* (Longman, 1999), 122–141.

—— 'The Sacrifice of Lady Rochford: Henry Parker Lord Morley's Translation of *De claris mulieribus*', in Axton and Carley (eds.), 153–69.

—— 'Chaucer's Contemporaries', in Peter Brown (ed.), *A Companion to Chaucer* (Blackwell, 2000), 114–32.

—— 'The Power of Impropriety: Authorial Naming in *Piers Plowman*', in Kathryn Hewett-Smith (ed.), *William Langland's 'Piers Plowman': A Book of Essays* (Garland, 2001), 145–65.

—— 'The Rule of Medieval Imagination', in Dimmick et al. (eds.), 4–24.

SINGERMAN, JEROME E. *Under Clouds of Poesy: Poetry and Truth in French and English Reworkings of the 'Aeneid', 1160–1513* (Garland, 1986).

**Sir Amadace*, in *Six Middle English Romances*, ed. Maldwyn Mills (Dent, 1973).

**Sir Gawain and the Green Knight*. See *The Poems of the Pearl Manuscript*, ed. Andrew and Waldron.

SKELTON, JOHN. *The Poetical Works of John Skelton*, ed. Alexander Dyce, 2 vols. (Cambridge University Press, 1843).

—— **John Skelton: The Complete English Poems*, ed. John Scattergood (Penguin, 1983).

SKINNER, QUENTIN. *The Foundations of Modern Political Thought*, 2 vols. (Cambridge University Press, 1970).

—— 'The Principles and Practice of Opposition: The Case of Bolingbroke versus Walpole', in N. McKendrick (ed.), *Historical Perspectives: Studies in English Thought and Society in Honour of J. H. Plumb* (Europa, 1974), 93–128.

—— 'Sir Thomas More's *Utopia* and the Language of Renaissance Humanism', in Anthony Pagden (ed.), *The Languages of Political*

Theory in Early Modern Europe (Cambridge University Press, 1987), 123–57.

SMITH, ALAN G. R. *The Emergence of a Nation State: The Commonwealth of England 1529–1660* (Longman, 1984).

SMITH, LESLEY and TAYLOR, JANE H. (eds.). *Women, the Book and the World: Selected Proceedings of the St Hilda's Conference*, 2 vols. (Brewer, 1995).

SOLODOW, JOSEPH B. 'Ovid's *Ars Amatoria*: The Lover as Cultural Ideal', *Wiener Studien*, NS 11 (1977), 106–27.

Sources and Analogues of Chaucer's 'Canterbury Tales', ed. W. F. Bryan and Germaine Dempster (University of Chicago Press, 1941).

SOUTHALL, RAYMOND. 'The Devonshire Manuscript Collection of Early Tudor Poetry, 1532–41', *RES*, NS 15 (1964), 142–50.

SPEARING, A. C. 'Conciseness and the *Testament of Cresseid*', in Spearing, *Criticism and Medieval Poetry*, 2nd edn. (Edward Arnold, 1972), 157–92.

—— *Medieval to Renaissance in English Poetry* (Cambridge University Press, 1985).

—— 'Early Medieval Narrative Style', in A. C. Spearing, *Readings in Medieval Poetry* (Cambridge University Press, 1987), 24–55.

—— 'Marie de France and her Middle English Adapters', *SAC* 12 (1990), 117–56.

—— 'Prison, Writing, Absence: Representing the Subject in the English Poems of Charles d'Orléans', *MLQ* 53 (1992), 83–99.

Speculum Christiani, ed. Gustaf Holmstedt, EETS 182 (Oxford University Press, 1933).

SPENCER, H. LEITH. *English Preaching in the Late Middle Ages* (Clarendon Press, 1993).

STACEY, ROBERT C. 'Jews', in Szarmach, et al. (eds.), 380–1.

STANBURY, SARAH. 'The Vivacity of Images: St Katherine, Knighton's Lollards and the Breaking of Idols', in Dimmick et al. (eds.), 131–50.

A Stanzaic Life of Christ, ed. Frances A. Foster, EETS 166 (Oxford University Press, 1926).

STARKEY, DAVID. 'The Age of the Household: Politics, Society and the Arts c.1350–c.1550', in Stephen Medcalf (ed.), *The Later Middle Ages* (Methuen, 1981), 225–90.

—— 'The Court: Castiglione's Ideal and Tudor Reality', *JWCI* 45 (1982), 232–9.

—— 'Intimacy and Innovation: the Rise of the Privy Chamber, 1485–1547', in David Starkey (ed.), *The English Court: from the Wars of the Roses to the Civil War* (Longman, 1987), 71–118.

STARKEY, DAVID (ed.). *Henry VIII: A European Court in England* (Collins and Brown, 1991).
——'King Henry and King Arthur', *Arthurian Literature*, 16 (1998), 171–96.
——'An Attendant Lord? Henry Parker, Lord Morley', in Axton and Carley (eds.), 1–25.
STARKEY, THOMAS. **A Dialogue between Reginald Pole and Thomas Lupset*, ed. Kathleen M. Burton (Chatto and Windus, 1948).
——*Thomas Starkey: A Dialogue between Pole and Lupset*, ed. T. F. Mayer, Camden Society, 4th ser., 37 (Royal Historical Society, 1989).
STEEVES, HARRISON ROSS. *Learned Societies and English Literary Scholarship* (1913; repr. AMS Press, 1970).
STEVENS, JOHN. *Music and Poetry in the Early Tudor Court* (Cambridge University Press, 1961; repr. 1979).
STEVENS, MARTIN. *Four Middle English Mystery Cycles: Textual, Contextual and Critical Interpretations* (Princeton University Press, 1987).
STOCK, BRIAN. 'The Middle Ages as Subject and Object', *NLH* 5 (1974), 527–47.
STONES, E. L. G. 'The Appeal to History in Anglo-Scottish Relations between 1291 and 1401', pt. 2, *Archives*, 9 (1969), 80–3.
STOW, JOHN. **A Survey of London, Reprinted from the Text of 1603*, ed. Charles Lethbridge Kingsford, 2 vols. (Clarendon Press, 1908; repr. 1971).
STRATHAM, MARGARET. 'The Guildhall, Bury St Edmunds', *Proceedings of the Suffolk Institute of Archaeology*, 31 (1968), 117–57.
STROHM, PAUL. 'Politics and Poetics: Usk and Chaucer in the 1380's', in Patterson (ed.), *Literary Practice and Social Change*, 83–112.
——*Social Chaucer* (Harvard University Press, 1989).
——*Hochon's Arrow: The Social Imagination of Fourteenth-Century Texts* (Princeton University Press, 1992).
——'Saving the Appearances: Chaucer's "Purse" and the Fabrication of the Lancastrian Claim', in Strohm, *Hochon's Arrow*, 75–94.
——'Queens as Intercessors', in Strohm, *Hochon's Arrow*, 95–119.
——*England's Empty Throne: Usurpation and the Language of Legitimation 1399–1422* (Yale University Press, 1996).
STUBBS, WILLIAM. *The Constitutional History of England in its Origin and Development*, 3 vols. (Clarendon Press, 1874–8).
SUMMIT, JENNIFER. 'William Caxton, Margaret Beaufort and the Romance of Female Patronage', in Smith and Taylor (eds.), 2. 151–65.
——*Lost Property: The Woman Writer and English Literary History, 1380–1589* (University of Chicago Press, 2000).

SUNDWALL, MCKAY. 'The *Destruction of Troy*, Chaucer's *Troilus and Criseyde*, and Lydgate's *Troy Book*', *RES* 26 (1975), 313–17.

SZARMACH, PAUL E., TAVORMINA, M. TERESA, AND ROSENTHAL, JOEL T. (eds.). *Medieval England: An Encyclopaedia* (Garland, 1998).

The Tale of Beryn, ed. Frederick J. Furnivall, EETS, ES 105 (Kegan Paul, Trench, Trübner, 1909).

TAYLOR, JANE H. M. 'Translation as Reception: La Danse Macabré', in Pratt (ed.), 181–92.

TAYLOR, JOHN. *English Historical Literature in the Fourteenth Century* (Clarendon Press, 1987).

THOMPSON, JOHN. A. F. 'Wyclif, John', in Szarmach, et al (eds.), 821–2.

——*The Transformation of Medieval England 1370–1529* (Longman, 1983).

THOMPSON, JOHN J. *Robert Thornton and the London Thorton Manuscript*, Manuscript Studies, 2 (Brewer, 1987).

THOMSON, PATRICIA. *Sir Thomas Wyatt and his Background* (Routledge and Kegan Paul, 1964).

——(ed.). *Wyatt: The Critical Heritage* (Routledge and Kegan Paul, 1974).

THORNE, J. R. and UHART, MARIE-CLAIRE. 'Robert Crowley's *Piers Plowman*', *Medium Aevum*, 55 (1986), 248–54.

THORPE, WILLIAM. **The Testimony of William Thorpe*, in *Two Wycliffite Texts*, ed. Anne Hudson, EETS 301 (Oxford University Press, 1993).

TIPTOFT, JOHN. 'Of True Nobility', in R. J. Mitchell, *John Tiptoft, 1427–1470* (Longman, Green and Co., 1938), app. 1.

**Tottel's Miscellany (1557–1587)*, ed. Hyder Edward Rollins, 2 vols. (Harvard University Press, 1928).

TRAPP, J. B. 'Verses by Lydgate at Long Melford', *RES*, NS 6 (1955), 1–11.

——'Thomas More and the Visual Arts', in Sergio Rossi (ed.), *Saggi sul Rinascimento* (Unicopli, 1985), 27–54.

——'Literacy, Books and Readers', in Hellinga and Trapp (eds.), 3. 31–43.

**A Tretise of Miraclis Pleyinge*, ed. Clifford Davidson (Medieval Institute Publications, 1993).

TREVISA, JOHN. *The Middle English Harrowing of Hell and Gospel of Nicodemus*, ed. W. H. Hulme, EETS, ES 100 (Kegan Paul, Trench and Trübner, 1907).

——*Dialogus inter militem et clericum; Richard Fitzralph's Sermon: 'Defensio curatorum' . . . translated by John Trevisa*, ed. A. J. Perry, EETS 167 (Oxford University Press, 1925).

——*On the Properties of Things; John Trevisa's Translation of*

Bartholomeus Anglicus 'De proprietatibus rerum', ed. M. C. Seymour et al. (Clarendon Press, 1975–88).

TREVISA, JOHN. *The Governance of Kings and Princes: John Trevisa's Middle English Translation of the 'De regimine principum' of Aegidius Romanus*, ed. David C. Fowler, Charles F. Briggs, and Paul G. Remley, Garland Medieval Texts, 19 (Garland, 1997).

TRIMPI, WESLEY. *Muses of One Mind: The Literary Analysis of Experience and Its Continuity* (Princeton University Press, 1978).

TRUEMAN, CARL. *Luther's Legacy: Salvation and English Reformers, 1525–1556* (Clarendon Press, 1994).

Tudor Royal Proclamations, ed. P. L. Hughes and J. F. Larkin, I. *The Early Tudors (1485–1553)* (Yale University Press, 1964).

TURVILLE-PETRE, THORLAC. *The Alliterative Revival* (Brewer, 1977)

—— 'The Author of the *Destruction of Troy*', *Medium Aevum*, 57 (1988), 264–9.

**Twenty Six Political and Other Poems*, ed. J. Kail, EETS 124 (Kegan Paul, Trench, Trübner, 1904).

**Two Coventry Corpus Christi Plays*, ed. Hardin Craig, EETS, ES 87 (Oxford University Press, 1902; repr. 1967).

**Two Tudor Interludes: 'The Interlude of Youth'; 'Hick Scorner'*, ed. Ian Lancashire (Manchester University Press, 1980).

TWYCROSS, MEG. 'The Theatricality of Medieval English Plays', in Beadle (ed.), *Medieval English Theatre*, 37–84.

TYNDALE, WILLIAM and FRITH, JOHN. **The Works of the English Reformers: William Tyndale and John Frith*, ed. T. Russell, 4 vols. (Palmer, 1831).

—— *Doctrinal Treatises and Introductions to Different Portions of the Holy Scriptures*, ed. Henry Walter, Parker Society (Cambridge University Press, 1848).

—— **The Parable of the Wicked Mammon*, in Tyndale, *Doctrinal Treatises*, ed. Walter.

—— **The Obedience of a Christian Man*, in Tyndale, *Doctrinal Treatises*, ed. Walter.

—— *An Answer to Thomas More's Dialogue*, ed. Henry Walter, Parker Society (Cambridge University Press, 1850).

—— **The Work of William Tyndale*, ed. G. E. Duffield (Appleford, Berks., 1964).

—— **Tyndale's New Testament*, ed. David Daniell (Yale University Press, 1989).

—— **Tyndale's Old Testament*, ed. David Daniell (Yale University Press, 1992).

—— 'The Preface of Master William Tyndale that he made before the Five

Books of Moses called Genesis' (1530), in *Tyndale's Old Testament*, ed. Daniell, 3–11.

—— FRITH, JOHN, and BARNES, ROBERT. **The Whole Workes of W. Tyndall, Iohn Frith, and Doctour Barnes* (John Day, 1573).

USK, THOMAS. **The Testament of Love*, in Chaucer, *The Complete Works*, ed. W. W. Skeat, suppl. vol.

—— *The Testament of Love*, ed. R. A. Shoaf, TEAMS (Medieval Institute Publications, 1998).

VALE, JULIET. *Edward III and Chivalry: Chivalric Society and its Context 1270–1350* (Brewer, 1982).

VALE, MALCOLM. *War and Chivalry: Warfare and Aristocratic Culture in England, France and Burgundy at the End of the Middle Ages* (Duckworth, 1981).

VAUCHEZ, ANDRÉ. *Sainthood in the Later Middle Ages*, trans. Jean Birrell (Cambridge University Press, 1997 (1st pub. in French, 1988)).

VERGIL, POLYDORE. **Polydore Vergil's English History*, ed. Henry Ellis, 2 vols. (Camden Society, 1st ser, 29, 36; 1844, 1846).

Visitation Articles and Injunctions, ed. Walter Howard Frere and William McClure Kennedy, Alcuin Club Collections, 15, 3 vols. (Longmans, Green, 1910).

VON NOLCKEN, CHRISTINA. 'Julian of Norwich', in Edwards (ed.), *Middle English Prose: A Critical Guide to Major Authors and Genres*, 97–108.

—— '*Piers Plowman*, the Wycliffites, and *Pierce Plowman's Crede*', *YLS* 2 (1988), 71–102.

—— 'A "Certain Sameness" and our Response to It in English Wycliffite Texts', in Richard G. Newhauser and John A. Alford (eds.), *Literature and Religion in the Later Middle Ages: Philological Studies in Honor of Siegfried Wenzel* (Medieval and Renaissance Texts and Studies, 1995), 191–208.

WADE, LAURENCE. 'Life of Thomas Becket', in Carl Horstmann (ed.), 'Thomas Becket, Epische Legende von Laurentius Wade (1497)', *Englische Studien*, 3 (1880), 409–69.

WAGNER, ANTHONY RICHARD. *Heralds and Heraldry in the Middle Ages: An Inquiry into the Growth of the Armorial Functions of Heralds* (Oxford University Press, 1939).

—— *English Genealogy*, 2nd edn. (Clarendon Press, 1972).

WALKER, GREG. *John Skelton and the Politics of the 1520s* (Cambridge University Press, 1988).

—— *The Politics of Performance* (Cambridge University Press, 1998).

WALKER, SIMON. *The Lancastrian Affinity, 1361–1399* (Clarendon Press, 1990).

WALLACE, DAVID. '"Whan she translated was": A Chaucerian Critique of the Petrarchan Academy', in Patterson (ed.), *Literary Practice*, 156–215.

—— *Chaucerian Polity: Absolutist Lineages and Associational Forms in England and Italy* (Stanford University Press, 1997).

—— (ed.). *The Cambridge History of Medieval English Literature* (Cambridge University Press, 1999).

WALLER, GARY F. *English Poetry of the Sixteenth Century* (Longman, 1993).

WALSINGHAM, THOMAS. *Historia Anglicana*, ed. Henry Thomas Riley, 2 vols., Rolls Series (Longman, 1864).

WALTON, JOHN (trans.). **Boethius: De Consolatione Philosophiae, translated by John Walton*, ed. Mark Science, EETS 170 (Oxford University Press, 1927).

**The Wars of Alexander*, ed. Hoyt Duggan and Thorlac Turville-Petre, EETS, SS, 10 (Oxford University Press, 1989).

WARTON, THOMAS. *The History of English Poetry from the Close of the Eleventh to the Commencement of the Eighteenth Centuries*, 3 vols. (Dodsley et. al., 1774–81).

WASWO, RICHARD. 'Our Ancestors, the Trojans', *Exemplaria*, 7 (1995), 269–90.

WATKINS, JOHN. '"Wrestling for this World": Wyatt and the Tudor Canonization of Chaucer', in Theresa M. Krier (ed.), *Refiguring Chaucer in the Renaissance* (University Press of Florida, 1998), 21–39.

WATSON, HENRY (trans.), *Valentine and Orson*, ed. Arthur Dickson, EETS 204 (Oxford University Press, 1937).

WATSON, NICHOLAS. *Richard Rolle and the Invention of Authority* (Cambridge University Press, 1991).

—— 'The Trinitarian Hermeneutic in Julian of Norwich's *Revelation of Love*', in Marion Glasscoe (ed.), *The Medieval Mystical Tradition in England* (Brewer, 1992), 79–100.

—— 'The Composition of Julian of Norwich's *Revelation of Divine Love*', *Speculum*, 68 (1993), 637–83.

—— 'On Outdoing Chaucer: Lydgate's *Troy Book* and Henryson's *Testament of Cresseid* as Competitive Imitations of *Troilus and Criseyde*', in Pratt (ed.), 89–108.

—— 'Censorship and Cultural Change in Late-Medieval England: Vernacular Theology, the Oxford Translation Debate, and Arundel's Constitutions of 1409', *Speculum*, 70 (1995), 822–64.

—— 'The Middle English Mystics', in Wallace (ed.), *Medieval English Literature*, 539–65.

WATTS, JOHN. *Henry VI and the Politics of Kingship* (Cambridge University Press, 1996).

WAWN, ANDREW. 'The Genesis of the *Plowman's Tale*', *YES* 2 (1972), 21–40.

—— 'Chaucer, *The Ploughman's Tale* and Reformation Propaganda: The Testimonies of Thomas Godfray and *I Playne Piers*', *BJRL* 56 (1973), 174–92.

WEBBE, WILLIAM. **A Discourse of English Poetrie* (1586), in *Elizabethan Critical Essays*, ed. G. Gregory Smith, 2 vols. (Clarendon Press, 1904).

WEISS, ROBERTO. *Humanism in England during the Fifteenth Century*, 3rd edn. (Blackwell, 1967).

WESTLAKE, HERBERT F. *The Parish Guilds of Medieval England* (Society for the Propagation of Christian Knowledge, 1919).

WETHERBEE, WINTHROP. *Platonism and Poetry in the Twelfth Century: the Literary Influence of the School of Chartres* (Princeton University Press, 1972).

—— *Chaucer and the Poets: An Essay on 'Troilus and Criseyde'* (Cornell University Press, 1984).

WEVER, R. *An Interlude called Lusty Iuventus*, ed. H. S. Thomas (New York and London, 1982).

WHITE, PAUL WHITFIELD. *Theatre and Reformation: Protestantism, Patronage and Playing in Tudor England* (Cambridge University Press, 1993).

—— 'Reforming Mysteries' End: A New Look at Protestant Intervention in English Provincial Drama', *JMEMS* 29 (1999), 121–47.

WICKHAM, GLYNNE. *Early English Stages, 1300–1660*, 3 vols. (Routledge and Kegan Paul, 1959–81).

—— *The Medieval Theatre*, 3rd edn. (Cambridge University Press, 1987).

WILKINS, DAVID (ed.). *Concilia Magnae Britanniae et Hiberniae*, 4 vols. (1737).

WILKS, MICHAEL. *The Problem of Sovereignty in the Middle Ages* (Cambridge University Press, 1963).

William of Palerne: An Alliterative Romance, ed. G. H. V. Bunt, Mediaevalia Groningana, 6 (Boumas Boekhuis, 1985).

WILSON, THOMAS. *The Arte of Rhetorique, for the use of all suche as are Studious of Eloquence, sette forth in English* (London, 1553).

WINDEATT, BARRY. 'Chaucer and Fifteenth-Century Romance: *Partonope of Blois*', in Morse and Windeatt (eds.), 62–80.

—— *Troilus and Criseyde*. Oxford Guides to Chaucer (Oxford University Press, 1992).

WINSER, LEIGH. '*The Bouge of Courte*: Drama Doubling as Dream', *English Literary Renaissance*, 6 (1976), 3–39.

Winstead, Karen. 'Capgrave's Saint Katherine and the Perils of Gynecocracy', *Viator*, 25 (1994), 361–76.

—— *Virgin Martyrs: Legends of Sainthood in Late Medieval England* (Cornell University Press, 1997).

Wittig, Susan. *Stylistic and Narrative Structures in the Middle English Romances* (University of Texas Press, 1978).

Wogan-Browne, Jocelyn. 'The Apple's Message: Some Post-Conquest Hagiographic Accounts of Textual Transmission', in A. J. Minnis (ed.), *Late Medieval Texts and their Transmission* (Brewer, 1994), 39–53.

—— Evans, Ruth, Taylor, Andrew, and Watson, Nicholas (eds.). *The Idea of the Vernacular: An Anthology of Middle English Literary Theory, 1280–1520* (University of Exeter Press, 1999).

Wood, Anthony. *Athenae Oxonienses*, ed. P. Bliss, 3 vols. (Rivington et al., 1813).

Woods, Marjorie Curry and Copeland, Rita. 'Classroom and Confession', in Wallace (ed.), *Medieval English Literature*, 376–406.

Woolf, Rosemary. *The English Religious Lyric in the Middle Ages* (Clarendon Press, 1968).

Wright, C. E. 'The Dispersal of the Monastic Libraries and the Beginnings of Anglo-Saxon Studies', *Transactions of the Cambridge Bibliographical Society*, 1 (1949–53), 208–37.

—— 'The Dispersal of the Libraries in the Sixteenth Century', in F. Wormald and C. E. Wright (eds.), *The English Library before 1700* (Athlone Press, 1958), 148–75.

Wright, Louis B. *Middle Class Culture in Elizabethan England* (University of North Carolina Press, 1935).

Wright, Sylvia. 'The Author Portraits in the Bedford Psalter Hours: Gower, Chaucer and Hoccleve', *British Library Journal*, 18 (1992), 190–201.

Wriothesley, Charles. *A Chronicle of England during the Reigns of the Tudors*, ed. William Douglas Hamilton, 2 vols, Camden Society, NS 11, 20 (Camden Society, 1875 and 1877).

Wülfing, J. Ernst. 'Das Laud-*Troy Book*', *Englische Studien*, 29 (1901), 374–96.

Wyatt, Thomas. *Plutarch's Quyete of Mynde, Translated by Thomas Wyatt*, (facs. edn., Harvard University Press, 1931).

—— **The Life and Letters of Sir Thomas Wyatt*, ed. Kenneth Muir (University of Liverpool Press, 1963).

—— **Collected Poems of Sir Thomas Wyatt*, ed. Kenneth Muir and Patricia Thomson (University of Liverpool Press, 1969).

—— **Sir Thomas Wyatt: The Complete Poems*, ed. R. A. Rebholz (Penguin, 1978).

WYCLIF, JOHN. *De veritate sacrae scripturae*, ed. Rudolf Buddensieg, 3 vols. (Wyclif Society, 1905–7).

Wynnere and Wastoure, ed. Stephanie Trigg, EETS 297 (Oxford University Press, 1990).

**The York Plays*, ed. Richard Beadle (Edward Arnold, 1982).

YOUNG, KARL. *The Drama of the Medieval Church*, 2 vols. (Clarendon Press, 1933).

Ywain and Gawain, ed. Albert B. Friedman and Norman T. Harrington, EETS 254 (Oxford University Press, 1964).

ZIM, RIVKAH. *English Metrical Psalms: Poetry as Praise and Prayer 1535–1601* (Cambridge University Press, 1987).

Index

Reference is made to persons, topics, and primary texts. Separate works of a given author are listed only in cases where there is substantial discussion of more than one work. Secondary scholarship is listed only when a scholarly work is discussed in the main body of the text. Page numbers marked in bold refer to the relevant pages of the Author Bibliographies.